Basic Statistics for

Business & Economics

McGraw-Hill/Irwin Series
Operations and Decisions Sciences

Business Statistics

Alwan
Statistical Process Analysis
First Edition

Aczel, Sounderpandian
Complete Business Statistics
Fifth Edition

Bowerman, O'Connell, and Hand
Business Statistics in Practice
Third Edition

Bryant and Smith
Practical Data Analysis: Case Studies in Business Statistics
Volumes I and II, Second Edition; Volume III, First Edition

Butler
Business Research Sources
First Edition

Cooper and Schindler
Business Research Methods
Eighth Edition

Delurgio
Forecasting Principles and Applications
First Edition

Doane, Mathieson, and Tracy
Visual Statistics
Second Edition, 2.0

Doane, Mathieson, and Tracy
Visual Statistics: Statistical Process Control
First Edition, 1.0

Gitlow, Oppenheim, and Oppenheim
Quality Management: Tools and Methods for Improvement
Second Edition

Lind, Marchal, and Wathen
Basic Statistics for Business and Economics
Fourth Edition

Lind, Marchal, and Mason
Statistical Techniques in Business and Economics
Eleventh Edition

Merchant, Goffinet, and Koehler
Basic Statistics Using Excel for Office 97
Second Edition

Merchant, Goffinet, and Koehler
Basic Statistics Using Excel for Office 2000
Third Edition

Neter, Kutner, Nachtsheim, and Wasserman
Applied Linear Statistical Models
Fourth Edition

Neter, Kutner, Nachtsheim, and Wasserman
Applied Linear Regression Models
Third Edition

Siegel
Practical Business Statistics
Fifth Edition

Webster
Applied Statistics for Business and Economics: An Essentials Version
Third Edition

Wilson and Keating
Business Forecasting
Fourth Edition

Quantitative Methods and Management Science

Bodily, Carraway, Frey, Pfeifer
Quantitative Business Analysis: Casebook
First Edition

Bodily, Carraway, Frey, Pfeifer
Quantitative Business Analysis: Text and Cases
First Edition

Bonini, Hausman, and Bierman
Quantitative Analysis for Business Decisions
Ninth Edition

Hesse
Managerial Spreadsheet Modeling and Analysis
First Edition

Hillier, Hillier, Lieberman
Introduction to Management Science: A Modeling and Case Studies Approach with Spreadsheets
First Edition

Basic Statistics for Business & Economics

Fourth Edition

Douglas A. Lind
Coastal Carolina University and The University of Toledo

William G. Marchal
The University of Toledo

Samuel A. Wathen
Coastal Carolina University

McGraw-Hill Irwin

Boston Burr Ridge, IL Dubuque, IA Madison, WI New York San Francisco St. Louis
Bangkok Bogotá Caracas Kuala Lumpur Lisbon London Madrid Mexico City
Milan Montreal New Delhi Santiago Seoul Singapore Sydney Taipei Toronto

McGraw-Hill Higher Education

*A Division of The **McGraw-Hill** Companies*

BASIC STATISTICS FOR BUSINESS AND ECONOMICS
Published by McGraw-Hill/Irwin, a business unit of The McGraw-Hill Companies, Inc. 1221 Avenue of the Americas, New York, NY, 10020.

This book is printed on acid-free paper.

domestic 1 2 3 4 5 6 7 8 9 0 DOW/DOW 0 9 8 7 6 5 4 3 2
international 1 2 3 4 5 6 7 8 9 0 DOW/DOW 0 9 8 7 6 5 4 3 2

ISBN 0-07-247104-2 (student edition)
ISBN 0-07-247106-9 (instructor's edition)

Publisher: *Brent Gordon*
Executive editor: *Richard T. Hercher, Jr.*
Developmental editor: *Christina A. Sanders*
Senior marketing manager: *Zina Craft*
Producer, Media technology: *Anthony Sherman*
Project manager: *Anna M. Chan*
Senior production supervisor: *Michael R. McCormick*
Senior designer: *Jennifer McQueen*
Cover image: *© Photodisc, 2002. All rights reserved.*
Photo research coordinator: *Judy Kausal*
Photo researcher: *Mary Reeg*
Supplement producer: *Joyce J. Chappetto*
Senior digital content specialist: *Brian Nacik*
Typeface: *9.5/11 Helvetica Neue 55*
Compositor: *GAC/Indianapolis*
Printer: *R. R. Donnelley*

Library of Congress Cataloging-in-Publication Data

Lind, Douglas A.
Basic statistics for business and economics / Douglas A. Lind, William G. Marchal, Samuel A. Wathen.—4th ed.
p. cm.—(McGraw-Hill/Irwin series Operations and decision sciences)
Includes index.
ISBN 0-07-247104-2 (student ed.: alk. paper)—ISBN 0-07-247106-9 (instructor's ed.: alk. paper)
1. Social sciences—Statistical methods. 2. Economics—Statistical methods. 3. Industrial management—Statistical methods. 4. Commercial statistics. I. Marchal, William G. II. Wathen, Samuel Adam. III. Title. IV. Series.
HA29.L75 2003
519.5—dc21 2002067756

INTERNATIONAL EDITION ISBN 0-07-119850-4

www.mhhe.com

To Jane, my wife and best friend, and to our sons,
Mike, Steve, and Mark

Douglas A. Lind

To Andrea, my heart and the mother of my children:
Rachel Anne (and Eric), Joseph Andrew, Sarah Louise,
Christopher Brophy, and Mary Bridget

William G. Marchal

To students beginning to study statistics

Samuel A. Wathen

Preface

As the name implies, the objective of *Basic Statistics for Business and Economics* is to provide students majoring in economics, finance, marketing, accounting, management, and other fields of business administration, with an introductory survey of the many business applications of descriptive and inferential statistics. While we have focused on business applications, we have also attempted to use examples and problems that are student oriented and that do not require previous business courses.

When Robert Mason wrote the first edition of this series of texts back in 1967, locating relevant data was difficult. That has changed! Today, locating data is not a problem. The number of items you purchase at the grocery store is automatically recorded at the checkout stand. Phone companies keep track of the length of a call, the time it was made, and the number of the person called. Medical devices can automatically monitor and record our heart rate, blood pressure, and temperature. A large amount of business information is recorded and reported almost instantly. CNN, *USA Today,* and Yahoo!, for example, have websites where you can track stock prices with a delay of less than 20 minutes.

Today, skills are needed to deal with all this numerical information. First, we need to be critical consumers of information presented by others. Second, we need to be able to reduce large amounts of data into a meaningful form so that we can make effective interpretations, judgments, and decisions.

All students not only have calculators, but many have their own computers or at least have access to a computer in a campus lab. Statistical software is also widely available, as is electronically stored data. In response to these changes, we include screen captures from Excel and MINITAB within the chapters. This enables the student to actually view the output. The commands necessary to achieve the software results are at the end of the chapter. We have replaced many of the calculation examples with interpretation ones, to aid the student in communicating the statistical results.

While making these changes, we have not moved away from presenting, as best we can, the key concepts, along with supporting examples. The fourth edition of *Basic Statistics for Business and Economics* is the product of many people: students, colleagues, reviewers, and the staff at McGraw-Hill/Irwin. We thank them all. We wish to express our sincere gratitude to the reviewers:

Mary Jo Boehms
Jackson State Community College
Fatteneh Cauley
Purdue University
Ricardo Clemente
Loyola Marymount University
Abdul Fazal
California State University–Stanislaus
Gordon Johnson
California State University–Northridge
Muleka Kikwebati
Hampton University
Duk Lee
Indiana Wesleyan University
Jodey Lingg
City University
Constantine Loucopoulos
Northeastern Illinois University
John Lymberopoulos
University of Colorado–Boulder
James Perry
Owens Community College
Stan Stephenson
Southwest Texas State University

Their suggestions and thorough review of the previous edition and the manuscript for this edition made this a better text.

A special thanks goes to a number of people. Professor Thomas Georginis, of Lewis University, checked the text for accuracy; Professor Walter H. Lange, of The University of Toledo, prepared the Study Guide; Temoleon Rousos checked the study guide for accuracy, and Dr. Samuel Wathen, of Coastal Carolina University, prepared the test bank. Ms. Denise Heban and the text authors prepared the Instructor's Manual, and Ms. Jane Lind the PowerPoint Presentation. We appreciate their efforts on the project.

We also would like to thank the staff at McGraw-Hill/Irwin. This includes Richard T. Hercher, Jr., Executive Editor; Christina Sanders, Development Editor; Zina Craft, Marketing Manager; Anna Chan, Project Manager; and others who we don't know personally, but who we know made valuable contributions.

A Note to the Student

We have tried to make this material "no more difficult than it needs to be." By that we mean we always keep the explanations practical without oversimplifying. We have used examples similar to those you will encounter in the business world or that you encounter in everyday life. When you have completed this book, you will understand how to apply statistical tools to help make business decisions. In addition, you will find that many of the topics and methods you learn can be used in other courses in your business education, and that they are consistent with what you encounter in other quantitative or statistics electives.

There is no doubt that today there is more data available to a business than ever. However, people who can convert data into useful information and interpret it well are in short supply. If you thoughtfully work through this text, you will be well prepared to contribute to the success and development of your company. Remember, as one of the authors read recently in a fortune cookie, "None of the secrets of success will work unless you do."

Learning Aids

We have designed the text to assist you in taking this course without the anxiety often associated with statistics. These learning aids are all intended to help you in your study.

Objectives Each chapter begins with a set of learning objectives. They are designed to provide focus for the chapter and to motivate learning. These objectives indicate what you should be able to do after completing the chapter. We include a photo that ties these chapter objectives to one of the exercises within the chapter.

Introduction At the start of each chapter, we review the important concepts of the previous chapter(s) and describe how they link to what the current chapter will cover.

Definitions Definitions of new terms or terms unique to the study of statistics are set apart from the text and highlighted. This allows easy reference and review.

Formulas Whenever a formula is used for the first time, it is boxed and numbered for easy reference. In addition, a formula card that summarizes the key formulas is bound into the text. This can be removed and carried for quick reference as you do homework or review for exams.

Margin Notes There are more than 200 concise notes in the margin. Each emphasizes the key concept being presented immediately adjacent to it.

Examples/Solutions We include numerous examples with solutions. These are designed to show you immediately, in detail, how the concepts can be applied to business situations.

Statistics in Action Statistics in Action articles are scattered throughout the text, usually about two per chapter. They provide unique and interesting applications and historical insights into statistics.

Self-Reviews Self-reviews are interspersed throughout the chapter and each is closely patterned after the preceding **Example/Solution.** They will help you monitor your progress and provide immediate reinforcement for that particular technique. The answers and methods of solution are located at the end of the chapter.

Exercises We include exercises within the chapter, after the **Self-Reviews,** and at the end of the chapter. The answers and method of solution for all odd-numbered exercises are at the end of the book. For most exercises with more than 20 observations, the data are on the CD-ROM in the text.

Chapter Outline As a summary, each chapter includes a chapter outline. This learning aid provides an opportunity to review material, particularly vocabulary, and to see and review the formulas again.

Web Exercises Almost all chapters have references to the Internet for companies, government organizations, and university data sets. These sites contain interesting and relevant information to enhance the exercises at the end of the chapters.

Computer Data Exercises In most chapters, the last four exercises refer to four large business data sets. A complete listing of the data is available in the back of the text and on the CD-ROM included with the text.

Supplements

The **Student CD,** packaged free with all copies of the text, features self-graded practice quizzes, software tutorials, PowerPoint slides, the data files (in MINITAB, Excel, and ASCII formats) for the end-of-chapter data and for exercises having 20 or more data values. Also included on the CD is an Internet link to the text website and to the websites listed in the Web exercises in the text. **MegaStat for Excel,** by J. B. Orris, software that enhances the power of Excel in statistical analysis and Visual Statistics 2.0, written by Doane, Tracy, and Mathieson, are also included. Visual Statistics is a software program for teaching and learning statistics through interactive experimentation and visualization.

A comprehensive **Study Guide,** written by Professor Walter Lange of The University of Toledo, is organized much like the textbook. Each chapter includes objectives, a brief summary of the chapter, problems and their solution, self-review exercises, and assignment problems.

The Online Learning Center includes online content for assistance and reference. The site provides chapter objectives, a summary, glossary of key terms, solved problems, downloadable data files, practice quizzes, PowerPoint, web links and much more. Visit the text website at http://www.mhhe.com/lindbasics4e.

ALEKS for Business Statistics (Assessment and Learning in Knowledge Spaces) is an artificial intelligence based system that acts much like a human tutor and can provide individualized assessment, practice, and learning. By assessing your knowledge, ALEKS focuses clearly on what you are ready to learn next and helps you master the course content more quickly and clearly. You can visit ALEKS at www.business.aleks.com.

Douglas A. Lind
William G. Marchal
Samuel A. Wathen

Brief Contents

Contents

Chapter

10 Two-Sample Tests of Hypothesis 319

Chapter

11 Analysis of Variance 351

Chapter

12 Linear Regression and Correlation 380

Chapter

13 Multiple Regression and Correlation Analysis 424

Basic Statistics for

Business & Economics

1

What Is Statistics?

The four largest American companies, ranked by sales in 2001 are Exxon Mobil, Wal-Mart Stores, General Motors, and Ford. (See Goal 5 and Statistics in Action box on page 4.)

GOALS

When you have completed this chapter you will be able to:

1. Understand why we study statistics.
2. Explain what is meant by *descriptive statistics* and *inferential statistics.*
3. Distinguish between a *qualitative variable* and a *quantitative variable.*
4. Distinguish between a *discrete variable* and a *continuous variable.*
5. Distinguish among the *nominal, ordinal, interval,* and *ratio* levels of measurement.
6. Define the terms *mutually exclusive* and *exhaustive.*

Introduction

More than 100 years ago H. G. Wells, an English author and historian, noted that "statistical thinking will one day be as necessary for efficient citizenship as the ability to read." He made no mention of business because the Industrial Revolution was just beginning. Were he to comment on statistical thinking today, he would probably say that "statistical thinking is necessary not only for effective citizenship but also for effective decision making in various facets of business."

The late W. Edwards Deming, a noted statistician and quality-control expert, insisted that statistics education should begin before high school. He liked to tell the story of an 11-year-old who devised a quality-control chart to track the on-time performance of his school bus. Deming commented, "He's got a good start in life." We hope that this book will give you a solid foundation in statistics for your future life in marketing, management, accounting, sales, or some other facet of business.

Almost daily we apply statistical concepts in our lives. For example, to start the day you turn on the shower and let it run for a few moments. Then you put your hand in the shower to sample the temperature and decide to add more hot water or more cold water, or you conclude that the temperature is just right and enter the shower. As a second example, suppose you are at the grocery store and wish to buy a frozen pizza. One of the pizza makers has a stand, and they offer a small wedge of their pizza. After sampling the pizza, you decide whether to purchase the pizza or not. In both the shower and pizza examples, you make a decision and select a course of action based on a sample.

Businesses face similar problems. The Kellogg Company must ensure that the mean amount of Raisin Bran in the 25.5-gram box meets label specifications. To do so, they might set a "target" weight somewhat higher than the amount specified on the label. Each box is then weighed after it is filled. The weighing machine reports a distribution of the content weights for each hour as well as the number "kicked-out" for being under the label specification during the hour. The Quality Inspection Department also randomly selects samples from the production line and checks the quality of the product and the weight of the box. If the mean product weight differs significantly from the target weight or the percent of kick-outs is too large, the process is adjusted.

On a national level, a candidate for the office of President of the United States wants to know what percent of the voters in Illinois will support him in the upcoming election. There are several ways he could go about answering this question. He could have his staff call all those people in Illinois who plan to vote in the upcoming election and ask for whom they plan to vote. He could go out on a street in Chicago, stop 10 people who look to be of voting age, and ask them for whom they plan to vote. He could select a random sample of about 2,000 voters from the state, contact these voters, and, based on this cross-section, make an estimate of the percent who will vote for him in the upcoming election. In this text we will show you why the third choice is the best course of action.

Why Study Statistics?

If you look through your university catalog, you will find that statistics is required for many college programs. Why is this so? What are the differences in the statistics courses taught in the Engineering College, Psychology or Sociology Departments in the Liberal Arts College, and that of the College of Business? The biggest difference is the examples used. The course content is basically the same. In the College of

Business we are interested in such things as profits, hours worked, and wages. In the Psychology Department they are interested in test scores, and in Engineering they may be interested in how many units are manufactured on a particular machine. However, all three are interested in what is a typical value and how much variation there is in the data. There may also be a difference in the level of mathematics required. An engineering statistics course usually requires calculus. Statistics courses in colleges of business and education usually teach the course at a more applied level. You should be able to handle the mathematics in this text if you have completed high school algebra.

Examples of why we study statistics

So why is statistics required in so many majors? The first reason is that numerical information is everywhere. Look in the newspapers (*USA Today*), news magazines (*Time, Newsweek, U.S. News and World Report*), business magazines (*Business Week, Forbes*), or general interest magazines (*People*), women's magazines (*Home and Garden*), or sports magazines (*Sports Illustrated, ESPN The Magazine*), and you will be bombarded with numerical information.

Here are some examples:

- The General Electric Company reported revenues of $129,853,000 in 2000, up from $111,630,000 in 1999. The 2000 year end closing price for a share of common stock was $59.94, up from $53.17 at the end of 1999.

- Graduates of the University of Notre Dame Master of Business Administration Program had a mean starting salary of $54,000 and 91 percent were employed within 3 months of graduation.
- There are 26.4 million golfers age 12 and over in the United States. Approximately 6.1 million are avid golfers, that is, they play 25 or more rounds in a year. The typical golfer is male, 40 years old, has a household income of $68,209, and plays 21.3 rounds per year.
- People in the United States drink more coffee than in any other country, an average of 1.75 cups per person per day.

How are we to determine if the conclusions reported are reasonable? Was the sample large enough? How were the sampled units selected? To be an educated consumer of this information, we need to be able to read the charts and graphs and understand the discussion of the numerical information. An understanding of the concepts of basic statistics will be a big help.

The second reason for taking a statistics course is that statistical techniques are used to make decisions that affect our daily lives. That is, they affect our personal welfare. Here are a few examples:

- Insurance companies use statistical analysis to set rates for home, automobile, life, and health insurance. Tables are available that summarize the probability that a 25-year-old woman will survive the next year, the next 5 years, and so on. On the basis of these probabilities, life insurance premiums can be established.
- The Environmental Protection Agency is interested in the water quality of Lake Erie. They periodically take water samples to establish the level of contamination and maintain the level of quality.
- Medical researchers study the cure rates for diseases, based on the use of different drugs and different forms of treatment. For example, what is the effect of treating a certain type of knee injury surgically or with physical therapy? If you take an aspirin each day, does that reduce your risk of a heart attack?

A third reason for taking a statistics course is that the knowledge of statistical methods will help you understand why decisions are made and give you a better understanding of how they affect you.

Statistics in Action

We want to call your attention to a feature we call *Statistics in Action.* Read each one carefully to get an appreciation of the wide application of statistics in management, economics, nursing, law enforcement, sports, and other disciplines. Following is an assortment of statistical information, from surveys published in *USA Today, Forbes, Time,* and other magazines and newspapers.

- *Forbes* publishes annually a list of the richest Americans. According to 2002 data William Gates, founder of Microsoft Corporation, is the richest. His net worth is estimated at $52.8 billion.
- The four largest American companies, ranked by sales in 2001 are Exxon Mobil, Wal-Mart Stores, General Motors, and Ford.
- The typical American earns $1,235,720 and pays $178,364 in taxes in his or her lifetime.

No matter what line of work you select, you will find yourself faced with decisions where an understanding of data analysis is helpful. In order to make an informed decision, you will need to be able to:

1. Determine whether the existing information is adequate or additional information is required.
2. Gather additional information, if it is needed, in such a way that it does not provide misleading results.
3. Summarize the information in a useful and informative manner.
4. Analyze the available information.
5. Draw conclusions and make inferences while assessing the risk of an incorrect conclusion.

The statistical methods presented in the text will provide you with a framework for the decision-making process.

In summary, there are at least three reasons for studying statistics: (1) data are everywhere, (2) statistical techniques are used to make many decisions that affect our lives, and (3) no matter what your future career, you will make decisions that involve data. An understanding of statistical methods will help you make these decisions more effectively.

What Is Meant by Statistics?

How do we define the word *statistics*? We encounter it frequently in our everyday language. It really has two meanings. In the more common usage, statistics refers to numerical information. Examples include the average starting salary of college graduates, the average number of Fords sold per month at Kistler Ford over the last year, the percentage of undergraduates attending Harvard who will attend graduate school, the number of deaths due to alcoholism last year, the change in the Dow Jones Industrial Average from yesterday to today, or the number of home runs hit by the Chicago Cubs during the 2001 season. In these examples statistics are a value or a percentage. Other examples include:

- The typical automobile in the United States travels 11,099 miles per year, the typical bus 9,353 miles per year, and the typical truck 13,942 miles per year. In Canada the corresponding information is 10,371 miles for automobiles, 19,823 miles for busses, and 7,001 miles for trucks.
- The mean time waiting for technical support is 17 minutes.
- The Bureau of the Census projects the population of the United States to be 335,050,000 by the year 2025.
- The mean length of the business cycle since 1945 (measured from peak to peak) is 61 months.

The above are all examples of **statistics.** A collection of numerical information is called **statistics** (plural).

We often present statistical information in a graphical form. A graph is often useful for capturing reader attention and to portray a large amount of information. For example, Chart 1–1 shows Frito-Lay volume and market share for the major snack and potato chip categories in supermarkets in the United States. It requires only a quick glance to discover there were nearly 800 million pounds of potato chips sold and that Frito-Lay sold 64 percent of that total. Also note that Frito-Lay has 82 percent of the corn chip market.

The subject of statistics, as we will explore it in this text, has a much broader meaning than just collecting and publishing numerical information. We define statistics as:

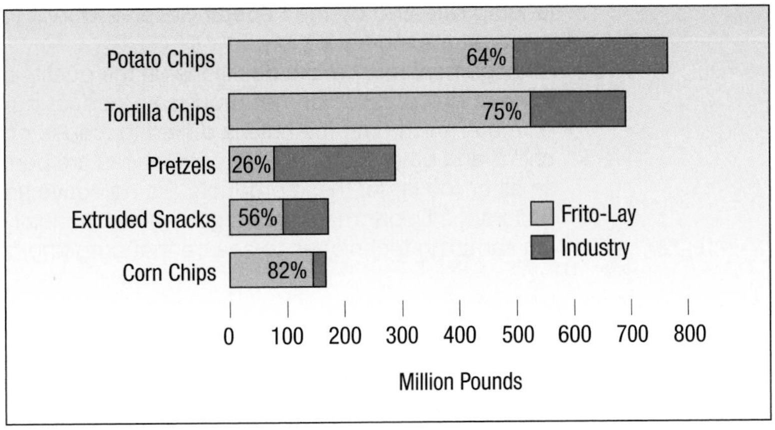

CHART 1–1 Frito-Lay Volume and Share of Major Snack Chip Categories in U.S. Supermarkets

> **STATISTICS** The science of collecting, organizing, presenting, analyzing, and interpreting data to assist in making more effective decisions.

As the definition suggests, the first step in investigating a problem is to collect relevant data. It must be organized in some way and perhaps presented in a chart, such as Chart 1–1. Only after the data have been organized are we then able to analyze and interpret it. Here are some examples of the need for data collection.

- Research analysts for Merrill Lynch evaluate many facets of a particular stock before making a "buy" or "sell" recommendation. They collect the past sales data of the company and estimate future earnings. Other factors, such as the projected worldwide demand for the company's products, the strength of the competition, and the effect of the new union-management contract, are also considered before making a recommendation.

- The marketing department at Lever Brothers, a manufacturer of soap products, has the responsibility of making recommendations regarding the potential profitability of a newly developed group of face soaps having fruit smells, such as grape, orange, and pineapple. Before making a final decision, they will test it in several markets. That is, they may advertise and sell it in Topeka, Kansas, and Tampa, Florida. Based on the test marketing in these two regions, Lever Brothers will make a decision whether to market the soaps in the entire country.
- The United States government is concerned with the present condition of our economy and with predicting future economic trends. The government conducts a large number of surveys to determine consumer confidence and the outlook of management regarding sales and production for the next 12 months. Indexes, such as the Consumer Price Index, are constructed each month to assess inflation. Information on department store sales, housing starts, money turnover, and industrial production are just a few of the hundreds of items used to form the basis of the projections. These evaluations are used by banks to decide their prime

lending rate and by the Federal Reserve Board to decide the level of control to place on the money supply.

- Management must make decisions on the quality of production. For example, automatic drill presses do not produce a perfect hole that is always 1.30 inches in diameter each time the hole is drilled (because of drill wear, vibration of the machine, and other factors). Slight tolerances are permitted, but when the hole is too small or too large, these products are defective and cannot be used. The Quality Assurance Department is charged with continually monitoring production by using sampling techniques to ensure that outgoing production meets standards.

Types of Statistics

Descriptive Statistics

The study of statistics is usually divided into two categories: descriptive statistics and inferential statistics. The definition of statistics given earlier referred to "organizing, presenting, analyzing . . . data." This facet of statistics is usually referred to as **descriptive statistics.**

DESCRIPTIVE STATISTICS Methods of organizing, summarizing, and presenting data in an informative way.

For instance, the United States government reports the population of the United States was 179,323,000 in 1960, 203,302,000 in 1970, 226,542,000 in 1980, 248,709,000 in 1990, and 265,000,000 in 2000. This information is descriptive statistics. It is descriptive statistics if we calculate the percentage growth from one decade to the next. However, it would **not** be descriptive statistics if we used the data to forecast the population of the United States in the year 2010 or the percentage growth from 2000 to 2010. The following are some other examples of descriptive statistics.

- There are a total of 42,796 miles of interstate highways in the United States. The interstate system represents only 1 percent of the nation's total roads but carries more than 20 percent of the traffic. The longest is I-90, which stretches from Boston to Seattle, a distance of 3,081 miles. The shortest is I-878 in New York City, which is 0.70 of a mile in length. Alaska does not have any interstate highways, Texas has the most interstate miles at 3,232, and New York has the most interstate routes with 28.
- According to the Bureau of Labor Statistics, the average hourly earnings of production workers increased 3.85 percent from 1999 to 2000. The increase was from $13.24 per hour in 1999 to $13.75 per hour in 2000. You can review the latest values by going to the Bureau of Labor Statistics website at www.bls.gov and click on "Average Hourly Earnings."
- The Internal Revenue Service reports that the mean time to file Form 1040EZ is 2 hours and 46 minutes. This compares with 7 hours and 34 minutes for Form 1040A, and 10 hours and 53 minutes for Form 1040. The average time to complete a return via the TeleFile system is 37 minutes.

Masses of unorganized data—such as the census of population, the weekly earnings of thousands of computer programmers, and the individual responses of 2,340 registered voters regarding their choice for President of the United States—are of little value as is. However, statistical techniques are available to organize this type of data into a meaningful form. Some data can be organized into a **frequency distribu-**

tion. (The procedure for doing this is covered in Chapter 2.) Various **charts** may be used to describe data; several basic chart forms are also presented in Chapter 2.

Specific measures of central tendency, such as the mean, describe the central value of a group of numerical data. A number of statistical measures are used to describe how closely the data cluster about an average. These measures of central tendency and dispersion are discussed in Chapter 3.

Inferential Statistics

Another facet of statistics is **inferential statistics**—also called **statistical inference** and **inductive statistics.** Our main concern regarding inferential statistics is finding something about a population based on a sample taken from that population. For example, based on a sample survey by the federal government reported in *USA Today,* only 46 percent of high school seniors can solve problems involving fractions, decimals, and percentages. And only 77 percent of high school seniors correctly totaled the cost of soup, a burger, fries, and a cola on a restaurant menu. Since these are inferences about the population (all high school seniors) based on sample data, we refer to them as inferential statistics.

INFERENTIAL STATISTICS The methods used to determine something about a population, based on a sample.

Note the words *population* and *sample* in the definition of inferential statistics. We often make reference to the population living in the United States or the 1 billion population of China. However, in statistics the word *population* has a broader meaning. A *population* may consist of *individuals*—such as all the students enrolled at Utah State University, all the students in Accounting 201, or all the inmates at Attica prison. A population may also consist of *objects,* such as all the XB-70 tires produced at Cooper Tire and Rubber Company in the Findlay, Ohio plant; the accounts receivable at the end of October for Lorrange Plastics, Inc.; or auto claims filed in the first quarter of 2002 at the Northeast Regional Office of State Farm Insurance. The *measurement* of interest might be the scores on the first examination of all students in Accounting 201, the wall weight of the Cooper Tires, the dollar amount of Lorrange Plastics accounts receivable, or the amount of auto insurance claims at State Farm. Thus, a population in the statistical sense does not always refer to people.

POPULATION The entire set of individuals or objects of interest or the measurements obtained from all individuals or objects of interest.

To infer something about a population, we usually take a **sample** from the population.

SAMPLE A portion, or part, of the population of interest.

Reasons for sampling

Why take a sample instead of studying every member of the population? A sample of registered voters is necessary because of the prohibitive cost of contacting millions of voters before an election. Testing wheat for moisture content destroys the wheat, thus making a sample imperative. If the wine tasters tested all the wine, none would be available for sale. It would be physically impossible for a few marine biologists to capture and tag all the seals in the ocean. (These and other reasons for sampling are discussed in Chapter 7.)

As noted, taking a sample to learn something about a population is done extensively in business, agriculture, politics, and government, as cited in the following examples:

- Television networks constantly monitor the popularity of their programs by hiring Nielsen and other organizations to sample the preferences of TV viewers. For example, in a sample of 800 prime-time viewers, 320 or 40 percent indicated they watched *West Wing* last night. These program ratings are used to set advertising rates or to cancel programs.
- A public accounting firm selects a random sample of 100 invoices and checks each invoice for accuracy. There is at least one error on five of the invoices; hence the accounting firm estimates that 5 percent of the population of invoices contain at least one error.
- A random sample of 1,260 accounting graduates from four-year schools showed their mean starting salary was $32,694. We therefore estimate the mean starting salary for all accounting graduates of four-year institutions to be $32,694.

The relationship between a sample and a population is portrayed below. For example, we wish to estimate the mean miles per gallon of SUVs. Six SUVs are selected from the population. The mean MPG of the six is used to estimate MPG for the population.

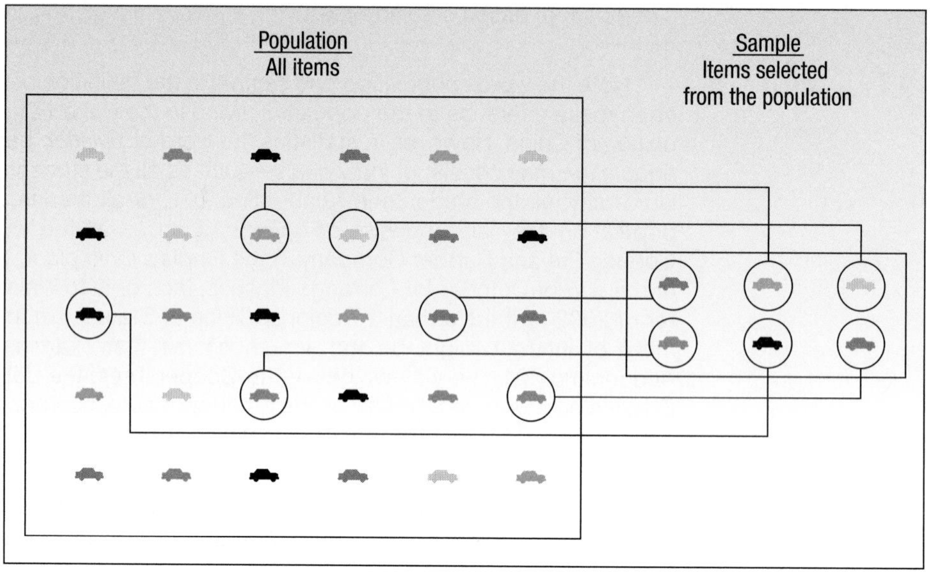

We strongly suggest you do the Self-Review exercises.

Following is a self-review problem. There are a number of them interspersed throughout each chapter. They test your comprehension of the preceding material. The answer and method of solution are given at the end of the chapter. You can find the answer to the following Self-Review on page 20. We recommend that you solve each one and then check your answer.

Self-Review 1–1

The answers are at the end of the chapter.

Chicago-based Market Facts asked a sample of 1,960 consumers to try a newly developed frozen fish dinner by Morton called Fish Delight. Of the 1,960 sampled, 1,176 said they would purchase the dinner if it is marketed.

(a) What would Market Facts report to Morton Foods regarding acceptance of Fish Delight in the population?

(b) Is this an example of descriptive statistics or inferential statistics? Explain.

Types of Variables

Qualitative variable

There are two basic types of variables: (1) qualitative and (2) quantitative (see Chart 1–2). When the characteristic being studied is nonnumeric, it is called a **qualitative variable** or an **attribute.** Examples of qualitative variables are gender, religious affiliation, type of automobile owned, state of birth, and eye color. When the data are qualitative, we are usually interested in how many or what proportion fall in each category. For example, what percent of the population has blue eyes? How many Catholics and how many Protestants are there in the United States? What percent of the total number of cars sold last month were Buicks? Qualitative data are often summarized in charts and bar graphs (Chapter 2).

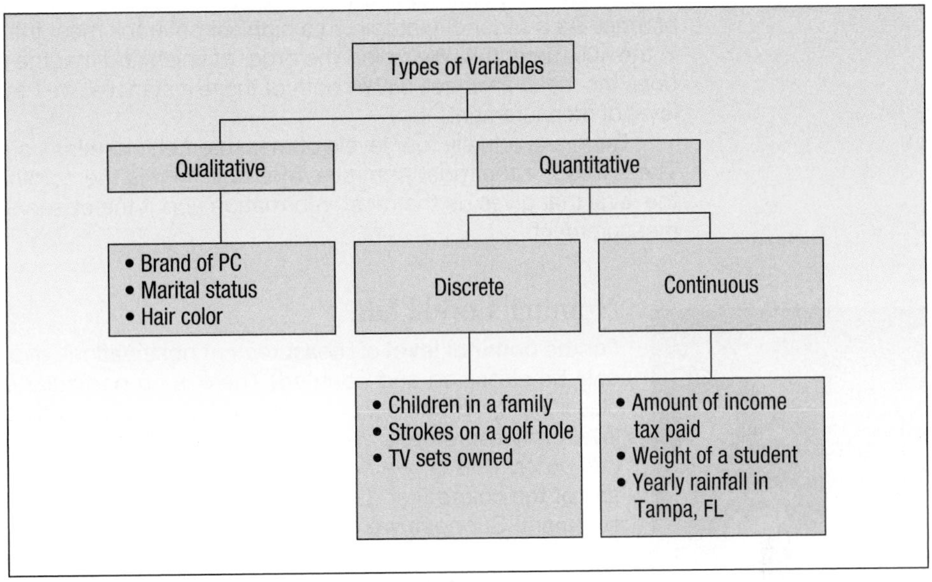

CHART 1–2 Summary of the Types of Variables

Statistics in Action

Where did statistics get its start? In 1662 John Graunt published an article called "Natural and Political Observations Made upon Bills of Mortality." The author's "observations" were the result of his study and analysis of a weekly church publication called "Bill of Mortality," which listed births, christenings, and deaths and their causes. This analysis and interpretation of social and political data are thought to mark the start of statistics.

When the variable studied can be reported numerically, the variable is called a **quantitative variable.** Examples of quantitative variables are the balance in your checking account, the ages of company presidents, the life of a battery (such as 42 months), the speeds of automobiles traveling along Interstate 5 near Seattle, and the number of children in a family.

Quantitative variables are either discrete or continuous. **Discrete variables** can assume only certain values, and there are usually "gaps" between the values. Examples of discrete variables are the number of bedrooms in a house (1, 2, 3, 4, etc.), the number of cars arriving at Exit 25 on I-4 in Florida near Walt Disney World in an hour (326, 421, etc.), and the number of students in each section of a statistics course (25 in section A, 42 in section B, and 18 in section C). We count, for example, the number of cars arriving at Exit 25 on I-4, and we count the number of statistics students in each section. Notice that a home can have 3 or 4 bedrooms, but it cannot have 3.56 bedrooms. Thus, there is a "gap" between possible values. Typically, discrete variables result from counting.

Observations of a **continuous variable** can assume any value within a specific range. Examples of continuous variables are the air pressure in a tire and the weight of a shipment of grain. Other examples are the amount of raisin bran in a box and the duration of flights from Orlando to San Diego. Typically, continuous variables result from measuring something.

Levels of Measurement

Data can be classified according to levels of measurement. The level of measurement of the data often dictates the calculations that can be done to summarize and present the data. It will also determine the statistical tests that should be performed. For example, there are six colors of candies in a bag of M&M's candies. Suppose we assign brown a value of 1, yellow 2, blue 3, orange 4, green 5, and red 6. From a bag of candies, we add the assigned color values and divide by the number of candies and report that the mean color is 3.56. Does this mean that the average color is blue or orange? As a second example, in a high school track meet there are eight competitors in the 400 meter run. We report the order of finish and that the mean finish is 4.5. What does the mean finish tell us? In both of these instances, we have not properly used the level of measurement.

There are actually four levels of measurement: nominal, ordinal, interval, and ratio. The lowest, or the most primitive, measurement is the nominal level. The highest, or the level that gives us the most information about the observation, is the ratio level of measurement.

Nominal Level Data

For the **nominal level** of measurement observations of a qualitative variable can only be classified and counted. There is no particular order to the labels. The classification of the six colors of M&M's candies is an example of the nominal level of measurement. We simply classify the candies by color. There is no natural order. That is, we could report the brown candies first, the orange first, or any of the colors first. Gender is another example of the nominal level of measurement. Suppose we count the number of students entering a football game with a student ID and report how many are men and how many are women. We could report either the men or the women first. For the nominal level the only measurement involved consists of counts. Table 1–1 shows a breakdown of U.S. long distance telephone usage. This is a nominal level variable because we recorded which carrier each customer used. Do not be distracted by the fact that we then summarized the variable by reporting how many times each carrier was used.

TABLE 1–1 Long Distance Telephone Usage by Carrier

Carrier	Number of Calls	Percent
AT&T	108,115,800	75
MCI	20,577,310	14
Sprint	8,238,740	6
Other	7,130,620	5
Total	144,062,470	100

The arrangement of the carriers in Table 1–1 could have been changed. That is, we could have reported MCI first, Sprint second, and so on. This essentially indicates the major feature of the nominal level of measurement: there is no particular order to the categories.

These categories are **mutually exclusive,** meaning, for example, that a particular phone call cannot originate with both AT&T and MCI.

MUTUALLY EXCLUSIVE A property of a set of categories such that an individual or object is included in only one category.

The categories in Table 1–1 are also **exhaustive,** meaning that every member of the population or sample must appear in one of the categories. So if a call did not originate with AT&T, MCI, or Sprint, it is classified as Other.

EXHAUSTIVE A property of a set of categories such that each individual or object must appear in a category.

In order to process data on telephone usage, gender, employment by industry, and so forth, the categories are often numerically coded 1, 2, 3, and so on, with 1 representing AT&T, 2 representing MCI, for example. This facilitates counting by the computer. However, because we have assigned numbers to the various companies, this does not give us license to manipulate the numbers. For example, 1 + 2 does not equal 3, that is, AT&T + MCI does not equal Sprint. To summarize, the nominal level data have the following properties:

1. Data categories are mutually exclusive and exhaustive.
2. Data categories have no logical order.

Ordinal Level Data

The next higher level of data is the **ordinal level.** Table 1–2 lists the student ratings of Professor James Brunner in an Introduction to Finance course. Each student in the class answered the question "Overall how did you rate the instructor in this class?" The variable rating illustrates the use of the ordinal scale of measurement. One classification is "higher" or "better" than the next one. That is, "Superior" is better than "Good," "Good" is better than "Average," and so on. However, we are not able to distinguish the magnitude of the differences between groups. Is the difference between "Superior" and "Good" the same as the difference between "Poor" and "Inferior"? We cannot tell. If we substitute a 5 for "Superior" and a 4 for "Good," we can conclude that the rating of "Superior" is better than the rating of "Good," but we cannot add a ranking of "Superior" and a ranking of "Good," with the result being meaningful. Further we cannot conclude that a rating of "Good" (rating is 4) is necessarily twice as high as a "Poor" (rating is 2). We can only conclude that a rating of "Good" is better than a rating of "Poor." We cannot conclude how much better the rating is.

TABLE 1–2 Rating of a Finance Professor

Rating	Frequency
Superior	6
Good	28
Average	25
Poor	12
Inferior	3

In summary, the properties of ordinal level data are:

1. The data classifications are mutually exclusive and exhaustive.
2. Data classifications are ranked or ordered according to the particular trait they possess.

Interval Level Data

The **interval level** of measurement is the next highest level. It includes all the characteristics of the ordinal level, but in addition, the difference between values is a constant size. An example of the interval level of measurement is temperature. Suppose the high temperatures on three consecutive winter days in Boston are 28, 31, and 20 degrees Fahrenheit. These temperatures can be easily ranked, but we can also determine the difference between temperatures. This is possible because 1 degree Fahrenheit represents a constant unit of measurement. Equal differences between two temperatures are the same, regardless of their position on the scale. That is, the difference between 10 degrees Fahrenheit and 15 degrees is 5, the difference between 50 and 55 degrees is also 5 degrees. It is also important to note that 0 is just a point on the scale. It does not represent the absence of the condition. Zero degrees Fahrenheit does not represent the absence of heat, just that it is cold! In fact 0 degrees Fahrenheit is about −18 degrees on the Celsius scale.

The properties of the interval level data are:

1. Data classifications are mutually exclusive and exhaustive.
2. Data classifications are ordered according to the amount of the characteristic they possess.
3. Equal differences in the characteristic are represented by equal differences in the measurements.

There are few examples of the interval scale of measurement. Temperature, which was just cited, is one example. Others are shoe size and IQ scores.

Ratio Level Data

Practically all quantitative data are the ratio level of measurement. The **ratio level** is the "highest" level of measurement. It has all the characteristics of the interval level, but in addition, the 0 point is meaningful and the ratio between two numbers is meaningful. Examples of the ratio scale of measurement include: wages, units of production, weight, changes in stock prices, distance between branch offices, and height. Money is a good illustration. If you have zero dollars, then you have no money. Weight is another example. If the dial on the scale is at zero, then there is a complete absence of weight. The ratio of two numbers is also meaningful. If Jim earns $30,000 per year selling insurance and Rob earns $60,000 per year selling cars, then Rob earns twice as much as Jim.

The properties of the ratio level data are:

1. Data classifications are mutually exclusive and exhaustive.
2. Data classifications are ordered according to the amount of the characteristics they possess.
3. Equal differences in the characteristic are represented by equal differences in the numbers assigned to the classifications.
4. The zero point is the absence of the characteristic.

Table 1–3 illustrates the use of the ratio scale of measurement. It shows the incomes of four father and son combinations.

TABLE 1–3 Father–Son Income Combinations

Name	Father	Son
Lahey	$80,000	$ 40,000
Nale	90,000	30,000
Rho	60,000	120,000
Steele	75,000	130,000

Observe that the senior Lahey earns twice as much as his son. In the Rho family the son makes twice as much as the father.

Chart 1–3 summarizes the major characteristics of the various levels of measurement.

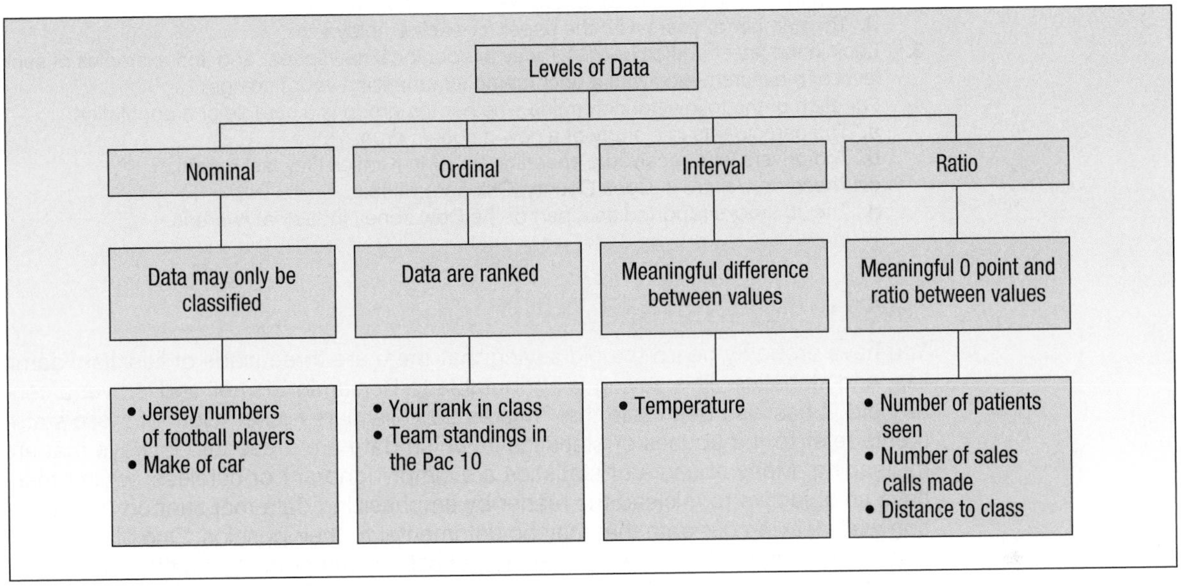

CHART 1–3 Summary of the Characteristics for Levels of Measurement

Self-Review 1–2

What is the level of measurement reflected by the following data?

(a) The age of a sample of 50 adults who listen to the nearly 700 Oldies radio stations in the United States is:

35	29	41	34	44	46	42	42	37	47
30	36	41	39	44	39	43	43	44	40
47	37	41	27	33	33	39	38	43	22
44	39	35	35	41	42	37	42	38	43
35	37	38	43	40	48	42	31	51	34

(b) In a survey of 200 luxury-car owners, 100 were from California, 50 from New York, 30 from Illinois, and 20 from Ohio.

Exercises

The answers to the odd-numbered exercises are at the end of the book.

1. What is the level of measurement for each of the following variables?
   a. Student IQ ratings.
   b. Distance students travel to class.
   c. Student scores on the first statistics test.
   d. A classification of students by state of birth.
   e. A ranking of students by freshman, sophomore, junior, and senior.
   f. Number of hours students study per week.

2. What is the level of measurement for these items related to the newspaper business?
   a. The number of papers sold each Sunday during 2002.
   b. The number of employees in each of the departments, such as editorial, advertising, sports, etc.
   c. A summary of the number of papers sold by county.
   d. The number of years with the paper for each employee.

3. Look in the latest edition of *USA Today* or your local newspaper and find examples of each level of measurement. Write a brief memo summarizing your findings.

4. For each of the following, determine whether the group is a sample or a population.
   a. The participants in a study of a new diabetes drug.
   b. The drivers who received a speeding ticket in Kansas City last month.
   c. Those on welfare in Cook County (Chicago), Illinois.
   d. The 30 stocks reported as a part of the Dow Jones Industrial Average.

Uses and Abuses of Statistics

You have probably heard the old saying that there are three kinds of lies: lies, damn lies, and statistics. This saying is attributable to Benjamin Disraeli and is over a century old. It has also been said that "figures don't lie: liars figure." Both of these statements refer to the abuses of statistics in which data are presented in ways that are misleading. Many abusers of statistics are simply ignorant or careless, while others have an objective to mislead the reader by emphasizing data that support their position while leaving out data that may be detrimental to their position. One of our major goals in this text is to make you a more critical consumer of information. When you see charts or data in a newspaper, in a magazine, or on TV, always ask yourself: What is the person trying to tell me? Does that person have an agenda? Following are several examples of the abuses of statistical analysis.

An average may not be representative of all the data.

The term *average* refers to several different measures of central tendency that we discuss in Chapter 3. To most people, an average is found by adding the values involved and dividing by the number of values. So if a real estate developer tells a client that the average home in a particular subdivision sold for \$150,000, we assume that \$150,000 is a representative selling price for all the homes. But suppose there are only five homes in the subdivision and they sold for \$50,000, \$50,000, \$60,000, \$90,000, and \$500,000. We can correctly claim that the average selling price is \$150,000, but does \$150,000 really seem like a "typical" selling price? Would you like to also know that the same number of homes sold for more than \$60,000 as less than \$60,000? Or that \$50,000 is the selling price that occurred most frequently? So what selling price really is the most "typical"? This example illustrates that a reported average can be misleading, because it can be one of several numbers that could be used to represent the data. There is really no objective set of criteria that states what average should be reported on each occasion. We want to educate you as a consumer of data about how a person or group might report one value that favors their position and exclude other values. We will discuss averages, or measures of location, in Chapter 3.

Charts and graphs can also be used to visually mislead. Suppose school taxes for the Corry Area Exempted School District increased from $100 in 1990 to $200 in the year 2000 (see Chart 1–4). That is, the taxes doubled during the 10-year period. To show this change, the dollar sign on the right is twice as tall as the one on the left. However, it is also twice as wide! Therefore the area of the dollar sign on the right is 4 times (not twice) that on the left.

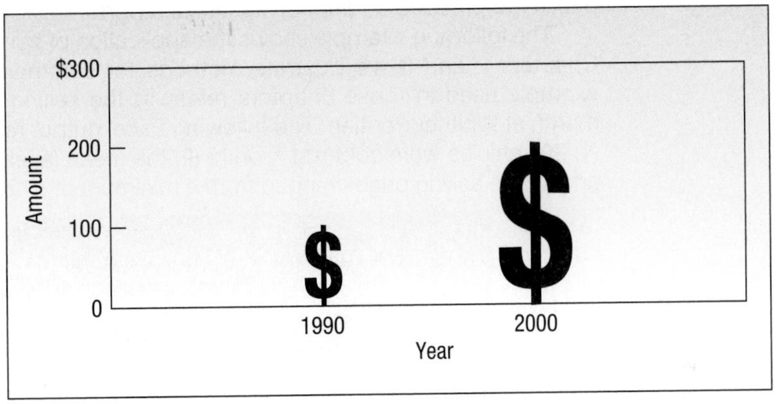

CHART 1–4 School Taxes for 1990 and 2000, Corry Exempted School District

Chart 1–4 is misleading because visually the increase is much larger than it really is. We discuss the construction of tables and charts in Chapter 2.

Study the sampling methods.

Several years ago, a series of TV advertisements reported that "2 out of 3 dentists surveyed indicated they would recommend Brand X toothpaste to their patients." The implication is that 67 percent of all dentists would recommend the product to their patients. The trick is that the manufacturer of the toothpaste could take *many* surveys of 3 dentists and report *only* the survey of 3 dentists that had 2 indicating they would recommend Brand X. Undoubtedly, a survey of more than 3 is needed, and it must be unbiased and representative of the population of all dentists. We discuss sampling methods in Chapter 7.

Another area where there can be a misrepresentation of data is the association between variables. In statistical analysis often we find there is a strong *association* between variables. We find there is a strong association between the number of hours a student studies for an exam and the score he or she receives. Does this mean that studying causes the higher score? No. It means the two variables are related, that is, they tend to act together in a predictable fashion. We study the association between variables in Chapters 12 and 13.

Sometimes numbers themselves can be deceptive. The mean price of homes sold last month in the Tampa, Florida, area is $134,891.58. This sounds like a very precise value and may instill a high degree of confidence in its accuracy. To report that the mean selling price is $135,000 doesn't convey the same precision and accuracy. However, a statistic that is very precise and carries 5 or even 10 decimal places is not necessarily accurate.

There are many other ways that statistical information can be deceiving. Entire books have been written about the subject. The most famous of these is *How to Lie with Statistics* by Darrell Huff. Understanding these practices will make you a better consumer of statistical information and help you defend yourself against those who might wish to mislead.

Computer Applications

Computers are now available to students at most colleges and universities. Spreadsheets, such as Microsoft Excel, and statistical software packages, such as MINITAB, are available in most computer labs. The Microsoft Excel package is bundled with many home computers. In this text we used both Excel and MINITAB for the applications. We also use an Excel add-in called MegaStat. This add-in gives Excel the capability to produce additional statistical reports.

The following example shows the application of computers in statistical analysis. In Chapters 2 and 3 we illustrate methods for summarizing and describing data. An example used in those chapters refers to the selling price of 80 vehicles sold last month at Whitner Pontiac. The following Excel output reveals, among other things, that (1) 80 vehicles were sold last month, (2) the mean (average) selling price was \$20,218, and (3) the selling prices ranged from a minimum of \$12,546 to a maximum of \$32,925.

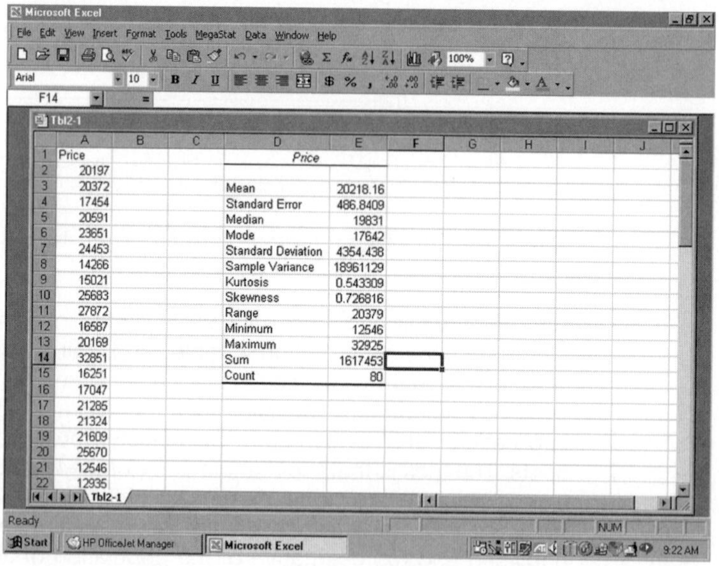

The following output is from the MINITAB system. It contains much of the same information.

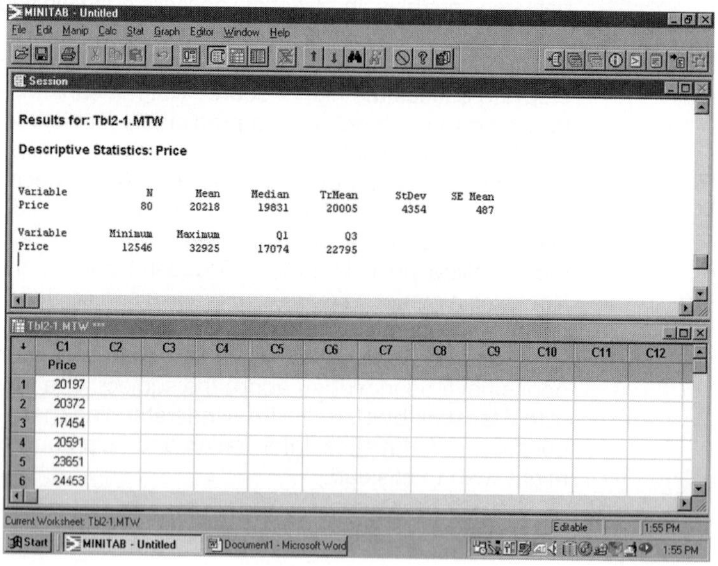

Had we used a calculator to arrive at these measures and others needed to fully analyze the selling prices, hours of calculations would have been required. The likelihood of an error in arithmetic is high when a large number of values are concerned. On the other hand, statistical software packages and spreadsheets can provide accurate information in seconds.

At the option of your instructor, and depending on the operating system available, we urge you to apply a computer package to the exercises in the **Computer Data Exercises** section in each chapter. It will relieve you of the tedious calculations and allow you to concentrate on data analysis.

Chapter Outline

I. Statistics is the science of collecting, organizing, presenting, analyzing, and interpreting data to assist in making more effective decisions.

II. There are two types of statistics.
- **A.** Descriptive statistics are procedures used to organize and summarize data.
- **B.** Inferential statistics involve taking a sample from a population and making estimates about a population based on the sample results.
  1. A population is an entire set of individuals or objects of interest or the measurements obtained from all individuals or objects of interest.
  2. A sample is a part of the population.

III. There are two types of variables.
- **A.** A qualitative variable is nonnumeric.
  1. Usually we are interested in the number or percent of the observations in each category.
  2. Qualitative data are usually summarized in graphs and bar charts.
- **B.** There are two types of quantitative variables and they are usually reported numerically.
  1. Discrete variables can assume only certain values, and there are usually gaps between values.
  2. A continuous variable can assume any value within a specified range.

IV. There are four levels of measurement.
- **A.** With the nominal level, the data are sorted into categories with no particular order to the categories.
  1. The categories are mutually exclusive. An individual or object appears in only one category.
  2. The categories are exhaustive. An individual or object appears in at least one of the categories.
- **B.** The ordinal level of measurement presumes that one classification is ranked higher than another.
- **C.** The interval level of measurement has the ranking characteristic of the ordinal level of measurement plus the characteristic that the distance between values is a constant size.
- **D.** The ratio level of measurement has all the characteristics of the interval level, plus there is a meaningful zero point and the ratio of two values is meaningful.

Chapter Exercises

5. Explain the difference between *qualitative* and *quantitative data.* Give an example of qualitative and quantitative data.

6. Explain the difference between a sample and a population.

7. List the four levels of measurement and give an example (different from those used in the book) of each level of measurement.

8. Define the term *mutually exclusive.*

9. Define the term *exhaustive.*

10. Using data from such publications as the *Statistical Abstract of the United States,* the *World Almanac, Forbes,* or your local newspaper, give examples of the nominal, ordinal, interval, and ratio levels of measurement.

11. A random sample of 300 executives out of 2,500 employed by a large firm showed that 270 would move to another location if it meant a substantial promotion. Based on these findings, write a brief note to management regarding all executives in the firm.
12. A random sample of 500 customers was asked to test a new toothpaste. Of the 500, 400 said it was excellent, 32 thought it was fair, and the remaining customers had no opinion. Based on these sample findings, make an inference about the reaction of all customers to the new toothpaste.
13. Explain the difference between a *discrete* and a *continuous variable.* Give an example of each not included in the text.
14. A survey of U.S. households regarding satisfaction with public school performance revealed the following data, which are portrayed graphically. Note that 1995 = 100. A value of 100 suggests an "average" satisfaction of Americans during the given year. A value of 75 would indicate that consumer satisfaction with school performance for that year is 25 percent below normal. Write an analysis of the level of satisfaction from 1990 to 2001.

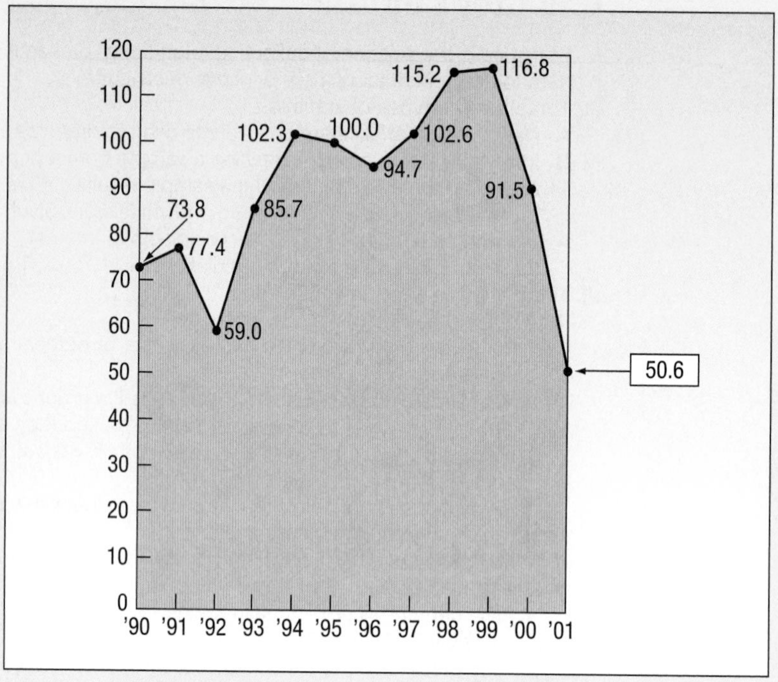

School Performance Survey, 1995 = 100

exercises.com

These exercises use the World Wide Web, a rich and growing source of up-to-date data. Because of the changing nature and the continuous revision of websites, you may well see different menus, and these exact addresses, or URLs, may change. When you visit a page, be prepared to "search" the link.

15. Bill Clegg is a financial consultant for Paine Webber Financial Services. He must recommend to one of his clients whether to purchase stock in Johnson and Johnson, Inc. (a pharmaceutical company) or Pepsico (the parent company of Pepsi and Frito Lay). He checks the Internet for each and finds that 23 brokers have evaluated each stock. Brokers rate a stock a "1" if it is a strong buy and a "5" if it is a strong sell. Go to the following website: http://quote.yahoo.com. To the left of "Get Quotes" type the two stock symbols, which are JNJ and PEP, then click on **Get Quote.** Finally, in the column headed "More Info" click on **Research.** What level is the data? Compare the results. Which stock would you recommend?

Computer Data Exercises

16. Refer to the Real Estate data at the back of the text, which reports information on homes sold in the Venice, Florida, area last year. Consider the following variables: selling price, number of bedrooms, township, and distance from the center of the city.
a. Which of the variables are qualitative and which are quantitative?
b. Determine the level of measurement for each of the variables.

17. Refer to the Baseball 2001 data, which reports information on the 30 Major League Baseball teams for the 2001 season. Consider the following variables: number of wins, team salary, team attendance, whether the team played its home games on a grass or a turf field, and the number of home runs hit.
a. Which of these variables are quantitative and which are qualitative?
b. Determine the level of measurement for each of the variables.

18. Refer to the wage data set, which reports information on annual wages for a sample of 100 workers. Also included are variables relating to industry, years of education, and gender for each worker.
a. Which of the twelve variables are qualitative and which are quantitative?
b. Determine the level of measurement for each variable.

19. Refer to the CIA data, which reports demographic and economic information on 46 countries.
a. Which of the variables are quantitative and which are qualitative?
b. Determine the level of measurement for each of the variables.

Chapter 1 Answers to Self-Review

1–1 **a.** Based on the sample of 1,960 consumers, we estimate that, if it is marketed, 60 percent of all consumers will purchase Fish Delight $(1{,}176/1{,}960) \times 100 = 60$ percent.

b. Inferential statistics, because a sample was used to draw a conclusion about how all consumers in the population would react if Fish Delight were marketed.

1–2 **a.** Age is a ratio scale variable. A 40-year-old is twice as old as someone 20 years old.

b. Nominal scale. We could arrange the states in any order.

2

Describing Data:

Frequency Distributions and Graphic Presentation

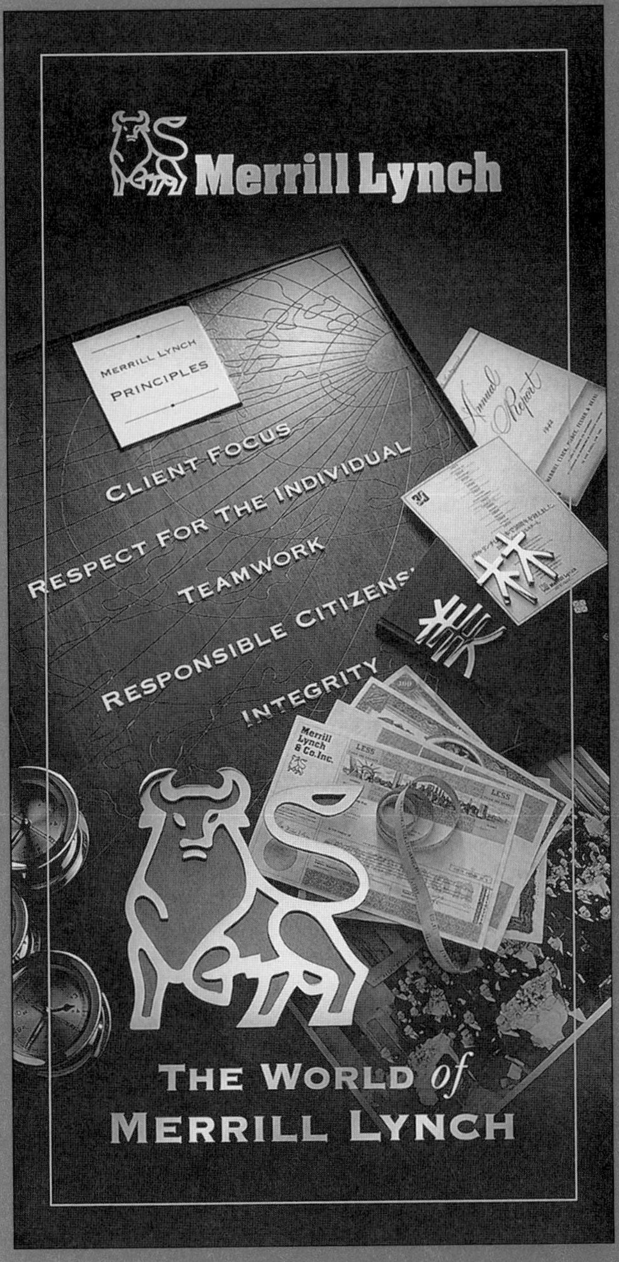

GOALS

When you have completed this chapter, you will be able to:

1 Organize data into a *frequency distribution.*

2 Portray a frequency distribution in a *histogram, frequency polygon,* and *cumulative frequency polygon.*

3 Develop and interpret a *stem-and-leaf display.*

4 Present data using such graphical techniques as *line charts, bar charts,* and *pie charts.*

Merrill Lynch completed a study regarding the size of investment portfolios for a sample of clients in the 40- to 50-year-old age group. Create a histogram and frequency distribution based on the sample. (See Goal 2 and Exercise 43.)

Introduction

Rob Whitner is the owner of Whitner Pontiac in Columbia, South Carolina. Rob's father founded the dealership in 1964, and for more than 30 years they sold exclusively Pontiacs. In the early 1990s Rob's father's health began to fail, and Rob took over more of the day-to-day operation of the dealership. At this same time, the automobile business began to change—dealers began to sell vehicles from several manufacturers—and Rob was faced with some major decisions. The first came when another local dealer, who handled Volvos, Saabs, and Volkswagens, approached Rob about purchasing his dealership. After considerable thought and analysis, Rob purchased that dealership. More recently, the local Chrysler dealership got into difficulty and Rob bought them out. So now, on the same lot, Rob sells the complete line of Pontiacs, the expensive Volvos, Saabs, Volkswagens, and the Chrysler products, including the popular Jeep line.

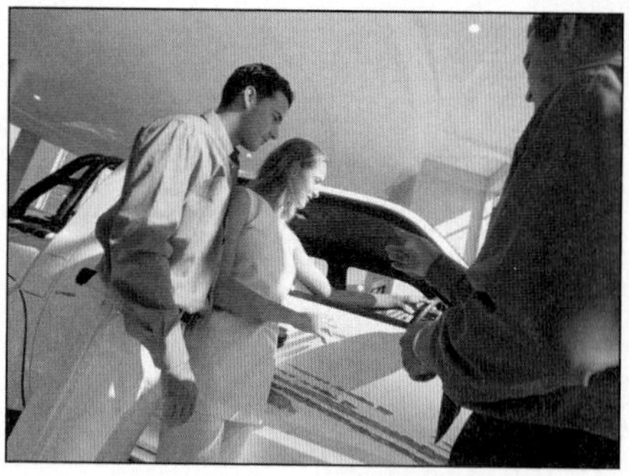

Whitner Pontiac employs 83, including 23 full-time salespeople. Because of the diverse product line, there is considerable variation in the selling price of the vehicles. A top-of-the-line Volvo sells for more than twice that of a Pontiac Grand Am. Rob would like to develop some charts and graphs that he could review monthly to see where the selling prices tend to cluster, to see the variation in the selling prices, and to note any trends. In this chapter we present techniques that will be useful to Rob or someone like him in managing his business.

Constructing a Frequency Distribution

Recall from Chapter 1 that we refer to techniques used to describe a set of data as *descriptive statistics.* To put it another way, we use descriptive statistics to organize data in various ways to point out where the data values tend to concentrate and help distinguish the largest and the smallest values. The first procedure we use to describe a set of data is a **frequency distribution.**

> **FREQUENCY DISTRIBUTION** A grouping of data into mutually exclusive classes showing the number of observations in each.

How do we develop a frequency distribution? The first step is to tally the data into a table that shows the classes and the number of observations in each class. The steps in constructing a frequency distribution are best described using an example. Remember, our goal is to make a table that will quickly reveal the shape of the data.

EXAMPLE

In the Introduction we describe a case where Rob Whitner, owner of Whitner Pontiac, is interested in collecting information on the prices of vehicles sold at his dealership. What is the typical selling price? What is the highest selling price? What is the lowest selling price? Around what value do the selling prices tend to cluster? In order to answer these questions, we need to collect data. According to sales records, Whitner Pontiac sold 80 vehicles last month. The price paid by the customer for each vehicle is shown in Table 2–1. Summarize the prices of the vehicles sold last month. Around what value do the selling prices tend to cluster?

TABLE 2–1 Prices of Vehicles Sold Last Month at Whitner Pontiac

$20,197	$20,372	$17,454	$20,591	$23,651	$24,453	$14,266	$15,021	$25,683	$27,872
16,587	20,169	32,851	16,251	17,047	21,285	21,324	21,609	25,670	12,546 (Lowest)
12,935	16,873	22,251	22,277	25,034	21,533	24,443	16,889	17,004	14,357
17,155	16,688	20,657	23,613	17,895	17,203	20,765	22,783	23,661	29,277
17,642	18,981	21,052	22,799	12,794	15,263	32,925 (Highest)	14,399	14,968	17,356
18,442	18,722	16,331	19,817	16,766	17,633	17,962	19,845	23,285	24,896
26,076	29,492	15,890	18,740	19,374	21,571	22,449	25,337	17,642	20,613
21,220	27,655	19,442	14,891	17,818	23,237	17,445	18,556	18,639	21,296

SOLUTION

We refer to the unorganized information in Table 2–1 as **raw data** or **ungrouped data.** With a little searching, we can find the lowest selling price ($12,546) and the highest selling price ($32,925), but that is about all. It is difficult to determine a typical selling price. It is also difficult to visualize where the selling prices tend to cluster. The raw data are more easily interpreted if organized into a frequency distribution.

The steps for organizing data into a frequency distribution.

Step 1: Decide on the number of classes. The goal is to use just enough groupings or **classes** to reveal the shape of the distribution. Some judgment is needed here. Too many classes or too few classes might not reveal the basic shape of the set of data. In the vehicle selling price problem, for example, three classes would not give much insight into the pattern of the data (see Table 2–2).

TABLE 2–2 An Example of Too Few Classes

Vehicle Selling Price ($)	Number of Vehicles
12,000 up to 21,000	48
21,000 up to 30,000	30
30,000 up to 39,000	2
Total	80

A useful recipe to determine the number of classes is the "2 to the k rule." This guide suggests you select the smallest number (k) for the number of classes such that 2^k (in words, 2 raised to the power of k) is greater than the number of observations (n).

In the Whitner Pontiac example, there were 80 vehicles sold. So $n = 80$. If we try $k = 6$, which means we would use 6 classes, then $2^6 = 64$, somewhat less than 80. Hence, 6 is not enough classes. If we let $k = 7$, then $2^7 = 128$, which is greater than 80. So the recommended number of classes is 7.

Step 2: Determine the class interval or width. Generally the **class interval** or width should be the same for all classes. The classes all taken together must cover at least the distance from the lowest value in the raw data up to the highest value. Expressing these words in a formula:

$$i \geq \frac{H - L}{k}$$

where i is the class interval, H is the highest observed value, L is the lowest observed value, and k is the number of classes.

In the Whitner Pontiac case, the lowest value is $12,546 and the highest value is $32,925. If we need 7 classes, the interval should be at least ($32,925 − $12,546)/7 = $2,911. In practice this interval size is usually rounded up to some convenient number, such as a multiple of 10 or 100. The value of $3,000 might readily be used in this case.

Unequal class intervals present problems in graphically portraying the distribution and in doing some of the computations which we will see in later chapters. Unequal class intervals, however, may be necessary in certain situations to avoid a large number of empty, or almost empty, classes. Such is the case in Table 2–3. The Internal Revenue Service used unequal-sized class intervals to report the adjusted gross income on individual tax returns. Had they used an equal-sized interval of, say, $1,000, more than 1,000 classes would have been required to describe all the incomes. A frequency distribution with 1,000 classes would be difficult to interpret. In this case the distribution is easier to understand in spite of the unequal classes. Note also that the number of income tax returns or "frequencies" is reported in thousands in this particular table. This also makes the information easier to understand.

TABLE 2–3 Adjusted Gross Income for Individuals Filing Income Tax Returns

Adjusted Gross Income	Number of Returns (in thousands)
Under $ 2,000	135
$ 2,000 up to 3,000	3,399
3,000 up to 5,000	8,175
5,000 up to 10,000	19,740
10,000 up to 15,000	15,539
15,000 up to 25,000	14,944
25,000 up to 50,000	4,451
50,000 up to 100,000	699
100,000 up to 500,000	162
500,000 up to 1,000,000	3
$1,000,000 and over	1

Step 3: Set the individual class limits. State clear class limits so you can put each observation into only one category. This means you must avoid overlapping or unclear class limits. For example, classes such as $1,300–$1,400 and $1,400–$1,500 should not be used because it is not clear whether the value $1,400 is in the first or second class. Classes stated as $1,300–$1,400 and $1,500–$1,600 are frequently used, but may also be confusing without the additional common convention of rounding all data at or above $1,450 up to the second class and data below $1,450 down to the first class. In this text we will generally use the format $1,300 up to $1,400 and $1,400 up to $1,500 and so on. With this format it is clear that $1,399 goes into the first class and $1,400 in the second.

Because we round the class interval up to get a convenient class size, we cover a larger than necessary range. For example, 7 classes of width $3,000 in the Whitner Pontiac case result in a range of 7($3,000) = $21,000. The actual range is $20,379, found by $32,925 − $12,546. Comparing that value to $21,000 we have an excess of $621. Because we need to cover only the distance ($H - L$), it is natural to put approxi-

Statistics in Action

In 1788, James Madison, John Jay, and Alexander Hamilton anonymously published a series of essays entitled *The Federalist.* These Federalist papers were an attempt to convince the people of New York that they should ratify the Constitution. In the course of history, the authorship of most of these papers became known, but 12 remained contested. Through the use of statistical analysis, and particularly the study of the frequency of the use of various words, we can now conclude that James Madison is the likely author of the 12 papers. In fact, the statistical evidence that Madison is the author is overwhelming.

mately equal amounts of the excess in each of the two tails. Of course, we should also select convenient class limits. A guideline is to make the lower limit of the first class a multiple of the class interval. Sometimes this is not possible, but the lower limit should at least be rounded. So here are the classes we could use for this data.

$12,000 up to 15,000
15,000 up to 18,000
18,000 up to 21,000
21,000 up to 24,000
24,000 up to 27,000
27,000 up to 30,000
30,000 up to 33,000

Step 4: Tally the vehicle selling prices into the classes. To begin, the selling price of the first vehicle in Table 2–1 is $20,197. It is tallied in the $18,000 up to $21,000 class. The second selling price in the first column of Table 2–1 is $16,587. It is tallied in the $15,000 up to $18,000 class. The other selling prices are tallied in a similar manner. When all the selling prices are tallied, the table would appear as:

Class	Tallies
$12,000 up to $15,000	𝍸 |||
$15,000 up to $18,000	𝍸 𝍸 𝍸 𝍸 |||
$18,000 up to $21,000	𝍸 𝍸 𝍸 ||
$21,000 up to $24,000	𝍸 𝍸 𝍸 |||
$24,000 up to $27,000	𝍸 |||
$27,000 up to $30,000	||||
$30,000 up to $33,000	||

Step 5: Count the number of items in each class. The number of observations in each class is called the **class frequency.** In the $12,000 up to $15,000 class there are 8 observations, and in the $15,000 up to $18,000 class there are 23 observations. Therefore, the class frequency in the first class is 8 and the class frequency in the second class is 23. There is a total of 80 observations or frequencies in the entire set of data.

Often it is useful to express the data in thousands, or some convenient units, rather than the actual data. Table 2–4, for example, reports the vehicle selling prices in thousands of dollars, rather than dollars.

Now that we have organized the data into a frequency distribution, we can summarize the pattern in the selling prices of the vehicles for Rob Whitner. Observe the following:

1. The selling prices ranged from about $12,000 up to about $33,000.
2. The selling prices are concentrated between $15,000 and $24,000. A total of 58, or 72.5 percent, of the vehicles sold within this range.
3. The largest concentration is in the $15,000 up to $18,000 class. The middle of this class is $16,500, so we say that a typical selling price is $16,500.
4. Two of the vehicles sold for $30,000 or more, and 8 sold for less than $15,000.

By presenting this information to Mr. Whitner, we give him a clear picture of the distribution of selling prices for last month.

TABLE 2–4 Frequency Distribution of Selling Prices at Whitner Pontiac Last Month

Selling Prices ($ thousands)	Frequency
12 up to 15	8
15 up to 18	23
18 up to 21	17
21 up to 24	18
24 up to 27	8
27 up to 30	4
30 up to 33	2
Total	80

We admit that arranging the information on selling prices into a frequency distribution does result in the loss of some detailed information. That is, by organizing the data into a frequency distribution, we cannot pinpoint the exact selling price, such as $20,197 or $23,372. Or, we cannot tell that the actual selling price for the least expensive vehicle was $12,546 and for the most expensive $32,925. However, the lower limit of the first class and the upper limit of the largest class convey essentially the same meaning. Rob will make the same judgment if he knows the lowest price is about $12,000 that he will if he knows the exact price is $12,546. The advantages of condensing the data into a more understandable form more than offset this disadvantage.

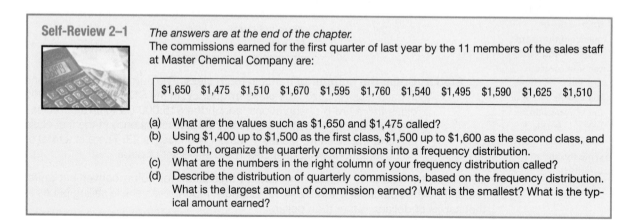

Self-Review 2–1

The answers are at the end of the chapter.
The commissions earned for the first quarter of last year by the 11 members of the sales staff at Master Chemical Company are:

$1,650	$1,475	$1,510	$1,670	$1,595	$1,760	$1,540	$1,495	$1,590	$1,625	$1,510

(a) What are the values such as $1,650 and $1,475 called?
(b) Using $1,400 up to $1,500 as the first class, $1,500 up to $1,600 as the second class, and so forth, organize the quarterly commissions into a frequency distribution.
(c) What are the numbers in the right column of your frequency distribution called?
(d) Describe the distribution of quarterly commissions, based on the frequency distribution. What is the largest amount of commission earned? What is the smallest? What is the typical amount earned?

Class Intervals and Class Midpoints

We will use two other terms frequently: **class midpoint** and **class interval.** The midpoint is halfway between the lower limits of two consecutive classes. It is computed by adding the lower limits of consecutive classes and dividing the result by 2. Referring to Table 2–4, for the first class the lower class limit is $12,000 and the next limit is $15,000. The class midpoint is $13,500, found by ($12,000 + $15,000)/2. The midpoint of $13,500 best represents, or is typical of, the selling price of the vehicles in that class.

To determine the class interval, subtract the lower limit of the class from the lower limit of the next class. The class interval of the vehicle selling price data is $3,000, which we find by subtracting the lower limit of the first class, \$12,000, from the lower limit of the next class; that is, \$15,000 − \$12,000 = \$3,000. You can also determine the class interval by finding the difference between consecutive midpoints. The midpoint of the first class is \$13,500 and the midpoint of the second class is \$16,500. The difference is \$3,000.

A Software Example

As we mentioned in Chapter 1, there are many software packages that perform statistical calculations and output the results. Throughout this text we will show the output from Microsoft Excel; from MegaStat, which is an add-in to Microsoft Excel; and from MINITAB. The commands necessary to generate the outputs are given in the **Computer Commands** section at the end of each chapter.

The following is a frequency distribution, produced by MegaStat, showing the prices of the 80 vehicles sold last month at Whitner Pontiac. The form of the output is somewhat different than the frequency distribution of Table 2–4, but the overall conclusions are the same.

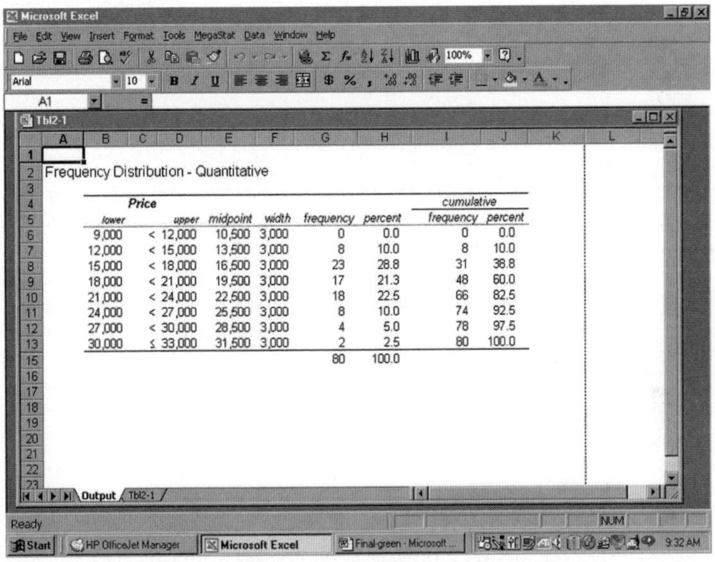

Frequency Distribution - Quantitative

Price						cumulative	
lower	upper	midpoint	width	frequency	percent	frequency	percent
9,000	< 12,000	10,500	3,000	0	0.0	0	0.0
12,000	< 15,000	13,500	3,000	8	10.0	8	10.0
15,000	< 18,000	16,500	3,000	23	28.8	31	38.8
18,000	< 21,000	19,500	3,000	17	21.3	48	60.0
21,000	< 24,000	22,500	3,000	18	22.5	66	82.5
24,000	< 27,000	25,500	3,000	8	10.0	74	92.5
27,000	< 30,000	28,500	3,000	4	5.0	78	97.5
30,000	≤ 33,000	31,500	3,000	2	2.5	80	100.0
				80	100.0		

Self-Review 2–2

Barry Bonds of the San Francisco Giants established a new single season home run record by hitting 73 home runs during the 2001 season. The longest of these home runs traveled 488 feet and the shortest 320 feet. You need to construct a frequency distribution of these home run lengths.

(a) How many classes would you use?
(b) What class interval would you suggest?
(c) What actual classes would you suggest?

Relative Frequency Distribution

A relative frequency distribution converts the frequency to a percent.

It may be desirable to convert class frequencies to **relative class frequencies** to show the fraction of the total number of observations in each class. In our vehicle sales example, we may want to know what percent of the vehicle prices are in the \$18,000 up to \$21,000 class. In another study, we may want to know what percent of the employees are absent between 1 and 3 days per year due to illness.

To convert a frequency distribution to a *relative* frequency distribution, each of the class frequencies is divided by the total number of observations. Using the distribution of vehicle sales again (Table 2–4, where the selling price is reported in thousands of dollars), the relative frequency for the $12,000 up to $15,000 class is 0.10, found by dividing 8 by 80. That is, the price of 10 percent of the vehicles sold at Whitner Pontiac is between $12,000 and $15,000. The relative frequencies for the remaining classes are shown in Table 2–5.

TABLE 2–5 Relative Frequency Distribution of the Prices of Vehicles Sold Last Month at Whitner Pontiac

Selling Price ($ thousands)	Frequency	Relative Frequency	Found by
12 up to 15	8	0.1000 ←	8/80
15 up to 18	23	0.2875	23/80
18 up to 21	17	0.2125	17/80
21 up to 24	18	0.2250	18/80
24 up to 27	8	0.1000	8/80
27 up to 30	4	0.0500	4/80
30 up to 33	2	0.0250	2/80
Total	80	1.0000	

Self-Review 2–3

Refer to Table 2–5, which shows the relative frequency distribution for the vehicles sold last month at Whitner Pontiac.
(a) How many vehicles sold for $15,000 up to $18,000?
(b) What percent of the vehicles sold for a price between $15,000 and $18,000?
(c) What percent of the vehicles sold for $27,000 or more?

Exercises

The answers to the odd-numbered exercises are at the end of the book.

1. A set of data consists of 38 observations. How many classes would you recommend for the frequency distribution?
2. A set of data consists of 45 observations between $0 and $29. What size would you recommend for the class interval?
3. A set of data consists of 230 observations between $235 and $567. What class interval would you recommend?
4. A set of data contains 53 observations. The lowest value is 42 and the largest is 129. The data are to be organized into a frequency distribution.
   a. How many classes would you suggest?
   b. What would you suggest as the lower limit of the first class?
5. The Wachesaw Outpatient Center, designed for same-day minor surgery, opened last month. Following is the number of patients served the first 16 days.

27	27	27	28	27	25	25	28
26	28	26	28	31	30	26	26

The information is to be organized into a frequency distribution.

a. How many classes would you recommend?
b. What class interval would you suggest?
c. What lower limit would you recommend for the first class?
d. Organize the information into a frequency distribution and determine the relative frequency distribution.
e. Comment on the shape of the distribution.

6. The Quick Change Oil Company has a number of outlets in the metropolitan Seattle area. The numbers of oil changes at the Oak Street outlet in the past 20 days are:

65	98	55	62	79	59	51	90	72	56
70	62	66	80	94	79	63	73	71	85

The data are to be organized into a frequency distribution.

a. How many classes would you recommend?
b. What class interval would you suggest?
c. What lower limit would you recommend for the first class?
d. Organize the number of oil changes into a frequency distribution.
e. Comment on the shape of the frequency distribution. Also determine the relative frequency distribution.

7. The manager of the BiLo Supermarket in Mt. Pleasant, Rhode Island, gathered the following information on the number of times a customer visits the store during a month. The responses of 51 customers were:

5	3	3	1	4	4	5	6	4	2	6	6	6	7	1
1	14	1	2	4	4	4	5	6	3	5	3	4	5	6
8	4	7	6	5	9	11	3	12	4	7	6	5	15	1
1	10	8	9	2	12									

a. Starting with 0 as the lower limit of the first class and using a class interval of 3, organize the data into a frequency distribution.
b. Describe the distribution. Where do the data tend to cluster?
c. Convert the distribution to a relative frequency distribution.

8. Moore Travel Agency, a nationwide travel agency, offers special rates on certain Caribbean cruises to senior citizens. The president of Moore Travel wants additional information on the ages of those people taking cruises. A random sample of 40 customers taking a cruise last year revealed these ages.

77	18	63	84	38	54	50	59	54	56	36	26	50	34	44
41	58	58	53	51	62	43	52	53	63	62	62	65	61	52
60	60	45	66	83	71	63	58	61	71					

a. Organize the data into a frequency distribution, using seven classes and 15 as the lower limit of the first class. What class interval did you select?
b. Where do the data tend to cluster?
c. Describe the distribution.
d. Determine the relative frequency distribution.

Graphic Presentation of a Frequency Distribution

Sales managers, stock analysts, hospital administrators, and other busy executives often need a quick picture of the trends in sales, stock prices, or hospital costs. These trends can often be depicted by the use of charts and graphs. Three charts that will help portray a frequency distribution graphically are the histogram, the frequency polygon, and the cumulative frequency polygon.

Histogram

One of the most common ways to portray a frequency distribution is a **histogram.**

HISTOGRAM A graph in which the classes are marked on the horizontal axis and the class frequencies on the vertical axis. The class frequencies are represented by the heights of the bars, and the bars are drawn adjacent to each other.

Thus, a histogram describes a frequency distribution using a series of adjacent rectangles, where the height of each rectangle is proportional to the frequency the class represents. The construction of a histogram is best illustrated by reintroducing the prices of the 80 vehicles sold last month at Whitner Pontiac.

EXAMPLE

Below is the frequency distribution.

Selling Prices ($ thousands)	Frequency
12 up to 15	8
15 up to 18	23
18 up to 21	17
21 up to 24	18
24 up to 27	8
27 up to 30	4
30 up to 33	2
Total	80

Construct a histogram. What conclusions can you reach based on the information presented in the histogram?

SOLUTION

The class frequencies are scaled along the vertical axis (*Y*-axis) and either the class limits or the class midpoints along the horizontal axis. To illustrate the construction of the histogram, the first three classes are shown in Chart 2–1.

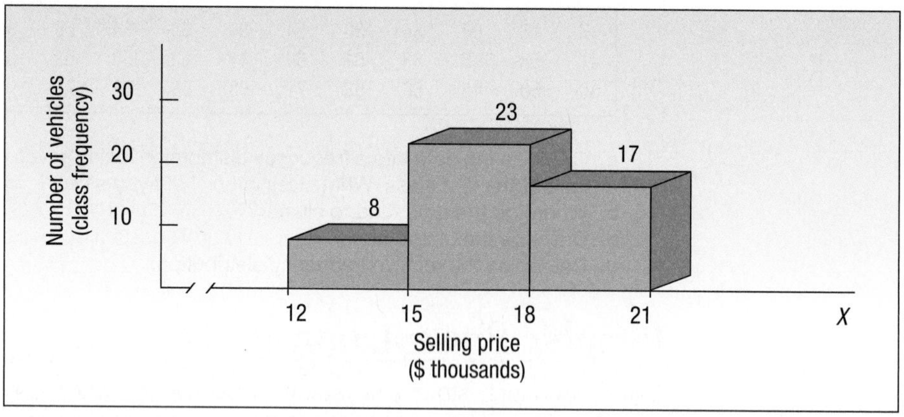

CHART 2–1 Construction of a Histogram

From Chart 2–1 we note that there are eight vehicles in the $12,000 up to $15,000 class. Therefore, the height of the column for that class is 8. There are 23 vehicles in the $15,000 up to $18,000 class, so, logically, the height of that column is 23. The height of the bar represents the number of observations in the class.

This procedure is continued for all classes. The complete histogram is shown in Chart 2–2. Note that there is no space between the bars. This is a feature of the histogram. In bar charts, which are described in a later section, the vertical bars are separated.

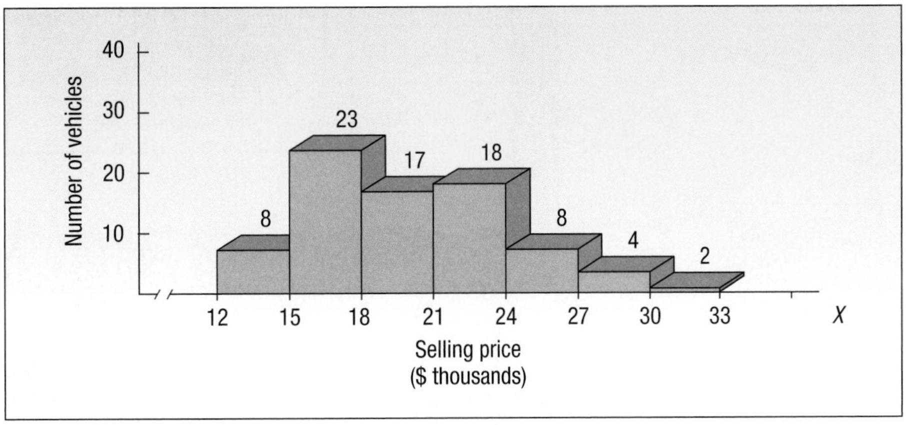

CHART 2–2 Histogram of the Selling Prices of 80 Vehicles at Whitner Pontiac

Based on the histogram in Chart 2–2, we conclude:

1. The lowest selling price is about $12,000, and the highest is about $33,000.
2. The largest class frequency is the $15,000 up to $18,000 class. A total of 23 of the 80 vehicles sold are within this price range.
3. Fifty-eight of the vehicles, or 72.5 percent, had a selling price between $15,000 and $24,000.

Thus, the histogram provides an easily interpreted visual representation of a frequency distribution. We should also point out that we would have reached the same conclusions and the shape of the histogram would have been the same had we used a relative frequency distribution instead of the actual frequencies. That is, if we had used the relative frequencies of Table 2–5, found on page 28, we would have had a histogram of the same shape as Chart 2–2. The only difference is that the vertical axis would have been reported in percent of vehicles instead of the number of vehicles.

We used the Microsoft Excel system to produce the histogram for the Whitner Pontiac vehicle sales data (which is shown on page 32). The commands to create this output are given in the Computer Commands section at the end of the chapter.

Frequency Polygon

In a frequency polygon the class midpoints are connected with a line segment.

A **frequency polygon** is similar to a histogram. It consists of line segments connecting the points formed by the intersections of the class midpoints and the class frequencies. The construction of a frequency polygon is illustrated in Chart 2–3 (on page 33). We use the vehicle prices for the cars sold last month at Whitner Pontiac. The

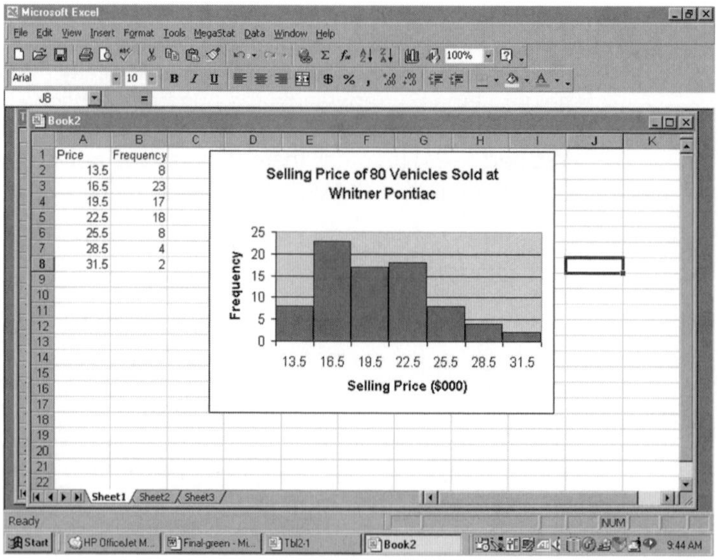

Statistics in Action

Florence Nightingale is known as the founder of the nursing profession. However, she also saved many lives by using statistical analysis. When she encountered an unsanitary condition or an undersupplied hospital, she improved the conditions and then used statistical data to document the improvement. Thus, she was able to convince others of the need for medical reform, particularly in the area of sanitation. She developed original graphs to demonstrate that, during the Crimean War, more soldiers died from unsanitary conditions than were killed in combat.

midpoint of each class is scaled on the *X*-axis and the class frequencies on the *Y*-axis. Recall that the class midpoint is the value at the center of a class and represents the values in that class. The class frequency is the number of observations in a particular class. The vehicle selling prices at Whitner Pontiac are:

Selling Price ($ thousands)	Midpoint	Frequency
12 up to 15	13.5	8
15 up to 18	16.5	23
18 up to 21	19.5	17
21 up to 24	22.5	18
24 up to 27	25.5	8
27 up to 30	28.5	4
30 up to 33	31.5	2
Total		80

As noted previously, the $12,000 up to $15,000 class is represented by the midpoint $13,500. To construct a frequency polygon, move horizontally on the graph to the midpoint, $13.5, and then vertically to 8, the class frequency, and place a dot. The *X* and the *Y* values of this point are called the *coordinates.* The coordinates of the next point are $X = \$16.5$ and $Y = 23$. The process is continued for all classes. Then the points are connected in order. That is, the point representing the lowest class is joined to the one representing the second class and so on.

Note in Chart 2–3 that, to complete the frequency polygon, midpoints of $10.5 and $34.5 are added to the *X*-axis to "anchor" the polygon at zero frequencies. These two values, $10.5 and $34.5, were derived by subtracting the class interval of $3.0 from the lowest midpoint ($13.5) and by adding $3.0 to the highest midpoint ($31.5) in the frequency distribution.

Both the histogram and the frequency polygon allow us to get a quick picture of the main characteristics of the data (highs, lows, points of concentration, etc.).

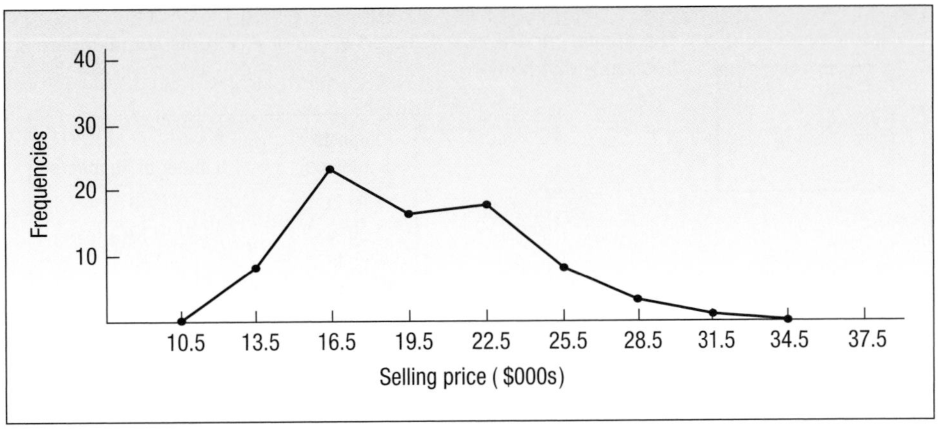

CHART 2–3 Frequency Polygon of the Selling Prices of 80 Vehicles at Whitner Pontiac

Although the two representations are similar in purpose, the histogram has the advantage of depicting each class as a rectangle, with the height of the rectangular bar representing the number in each class. The frequency polygon, in turn, has an advantage over the histogram. It allows us to compare directly two or more frequency distributions. Suppose that Rob Whitner, the owner of Whitner Pontiac, wants to compare the sales last month at his dealership with those at Midtown Cadillac. To do this, two frequency polygons are constructed, one on top of the other, as in Chart 2–4. It is clear from Chart 2–4 that the typical vehicle selling price is higher at the Cadillac dealership.

The total number of frequencies at Whitner Pontiac and at Midtown Cadillac are about the same, so a direct comparison is possible. If the difference in the total number of frequencies is quite large, converting the frequencies to relative frequencies and then plotting the two distributions would allow a clearer comparison.

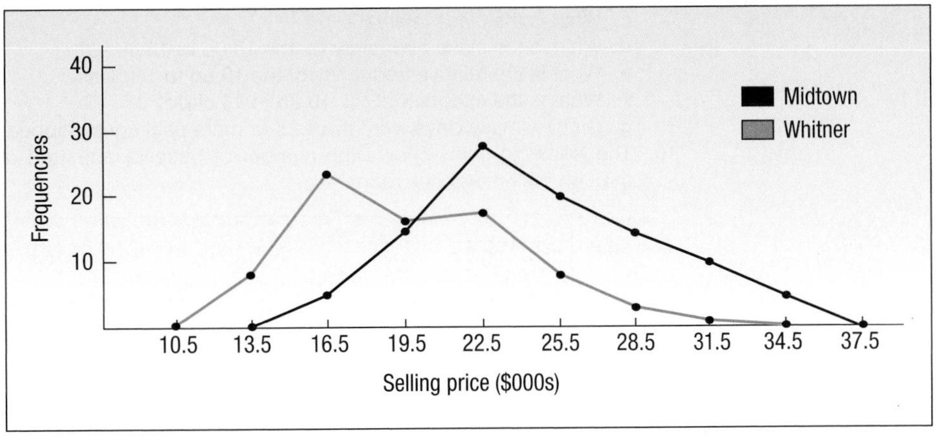

CHART 2–4 Distribution of Vehicle Selling Prices at Whitner Pontiac and Midtown Cadillac

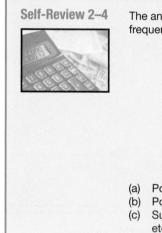

Self-Review 2–4

The annual imports of a selected group of electronic suppliers are shown in the following frequency distribution.

Imports ($ millions)	Number of Suppliers
2 up to 5	6
5 up to 8	13
8 up to 11	20
11 up to 14	10
14 up to 17	1

(a) Portray the imports as a histogram.
(b) Portray the imports as a relative frequency polygon.
(c) Summarize the important facets of the distribution (such as low and high, concentration, etc.)

Exercises

9. Molly's Candle Shop has several retail stores in the coastal areas of North and South Carolina. Many of Molly's customers ask her to ship their purchases. The following chart shows the number of packages shipped per day for the last 100 days.

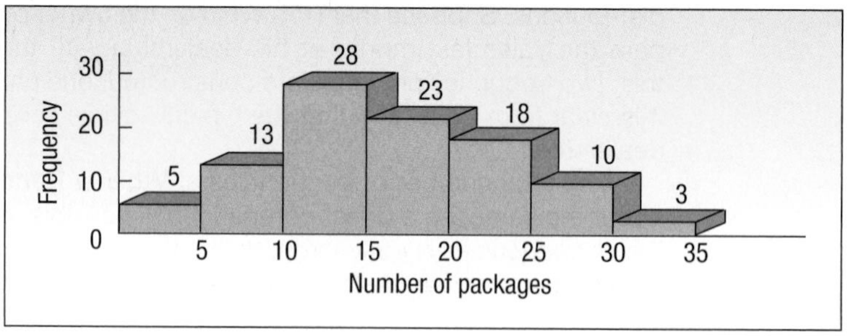

a. What is this chart called?
b. What is the total number of frequencies?
c. What is the class interval?
d. What is the class frequency for the 10 up to 15 class?
e. What is the relative frequency of the 10 up to 15 class?
f. What is the midpoint of the 10 up to 15 class?
g. On how many days were there 25 or more packages shipped?

10. The following chart shows the number of patients admitted daily to Memorial Hospital through the emergency room.

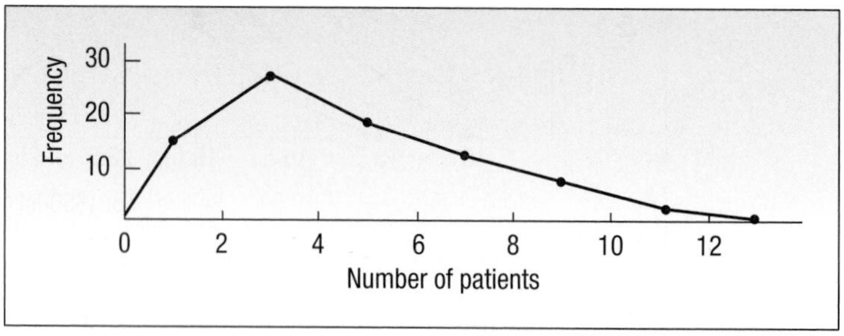

a. What is the midpoint of the 2 up to 4 class?
b. How many days were 2 up to 4 patients admitted?
c. Approximately how many days were studied?
d. What is the class interval?
e. What is this chart called?

11. The following frequency distribution reports the number of frequent flier miles, reported in thousands, for employees of Brumley Statistical Consulting, Inc. during the first quarter of 2002.

Frequent Flier Miles (000)	Number of Employees
0 up to 3	5
3 up to 6	12
6 up to 9	23
9 up to 12	8
12 up to 15	2
Total	50

a. How many employees were studied?
b. What is the midpoint of the first class?
c. Construct a histogram.
d. A frequency polygon is to be drawn. What are the coordinates of the plot for the first class?
e. Construct a frequency polygon.
f. Interpret the frequent flier miles accumulated using the two charts.

12. Ecommerce.com, a large Internet retailer, is studying the lead time (elapsed time between when an order is placed and when it is filled) for a sample of recent orders. The lead times are reported in days.

Lead Time (days)	Frequency
0 up to 5	6
5 up to 10	7
10 up to 15	12
15 up to 20	8
20 up to 25	7
Total	40

a. How many orders were studied?
b. What is the midpoint of the first class?
c. What are the coordinates of the first class for a frequency polygon?
d. Draw a histogram.
e. Draw a frequency polygon.
f. Interpret the lead times using the two charts.

Cumulative Frequency Distributions

Consider once again the distribution of the selling prices of vehicles at Whitner Pontiac. Suppose we were interested in the number of vehicles that sold for less than $18,000, or the value below which 40 percent of the vehicles sold. These numbers can be approximated by developing a **cumulative frequency distribution** and portraying it graphically in a **cumulative frequency polygon.**

EXAMPLE

The frequency distribution of the vehicle selling prices at Whitner Pontiac is repeated from Table 2–4.

Selling Price ($ thousands)	Frequency
12 up to 15	8
15 up to 18	23
18 up to 21	17
21 up to 24	18
24 up to 27	8
27 up to 30	4
30 up to 33	2
Total	80

Construct a cumulative frequency polygon. Fifty percent of the vehicles were sold for less than what amount? Twenty-five of the vehicles were sold for less than what amount?

SOLUTION

As the name implies, a cumulative frequency distribution and a cumulative frequency polygon require *cumulative frequencies*. To construct a cumulative frequency distribution, refer to the preceding table and note that there were eight vehicles sold for less than $15,000. Those 8 vehicles, plus the 23 in the next higher class, for a total of 31, were sold for less than $18,000. The cumulative frequency for the next higher class is 48, found by 8 + 23 + 17. This process is continued for all the classes. All the vehicles were sold for less than $33,000. (See Table 2–6.)

TABLE 2–6 Cumulative Frequency Distribution for Vehicle Selling Price

Selling Price ($ thousands)	Frequency	Cumulative Frequency	Found by
12 up to 15	8	8	
15 up to 18	23	31	8 + 23
18 up to 21	17	48	8 + 23 + 17
21 up to 24	18	66	8 + 23 + 17 + 18
24 up to 27	8	74	
27 up to 30	4	78	
30 up to 33	2	80	
Total	80		

To plot a cumulative frequency distribution, scale the upper limit of each class along the X-axis and the corresponding cumulative frequencies along the Y-axis. To provide additional information, you can label the vertical axis on the left in units and the vertical axis on the right in percent. In the Whitner Pontiac example, the vertical axis on the left is labeled from 0 to 80 and on the right from 0 to 100 percent. The value of 50 percent corresponds to 40 vehicles sold.

To begin the plotting, 8 vehicles sold for less than \$15,000, so the first plot is at $X = 15$ and $Y = 8$. The coordinates for the next plot are $X = 18$ and $Y = 31$. The rest of the points are plotted and then the dots connected to form the chart (see Chart 2–5). To find the selling price below which half the cars sold, we draw a horizontal line from the 50 percent mark on the right-hand vertical axis over to the polygon, then drop down to the X-axis and read the selling price. The value on the X-axis is about 19.5, so we estimate that 50 percent of the vehicles sold for less than \$19,500.

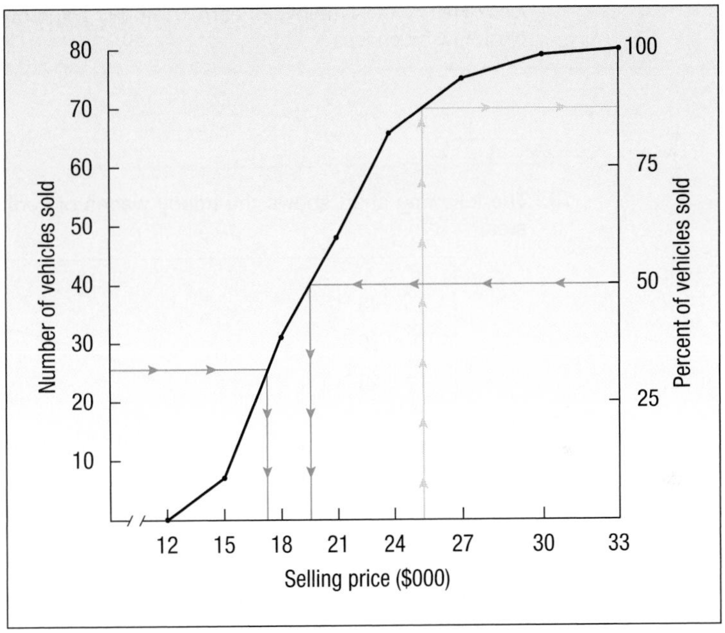

CHART 2–5 Cumulative Frequency Distribution for Vehicle Selling Price

To find the price below which 25 of the vehicles sold, we locate the value of 25 on the left-hand vertical axis. Next, we draw a horizontal line from the value of 25 to the polygon, and then drop down to the X-axis and read the price. It is about 17.5, so we estimate that 25 of the vehicles sold for less than \$17,500. We can also make estimates of the percent of vehicles that sold for less than a particular amount. To explain, suppose we want to estimate the percent of vehicles that sold for less than \$25,500. We begin by locating the value of 25.5 on the X-axis, move vertically to the polygon, and then horizontally to the vertical axis on the right. The value is about 87 percent, so we conclude that 87 percent of the vehicles sold for less than \$25,500.

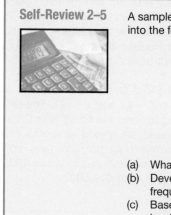

Self-Review 2–5

A sample of the hourly wages of 15 employees at Food City Supermarkets was organized into the following table.

Hourly Wages	Number of Employees
\$ 6 up to \$ 8	3
8 up to 10	7
10 up to 12	4
12 up to 14	1

(a) What is the table called?
(b) Develop a cumulative frequency distribution and portray the distribution in a cumulative frequency polygon.
(c) Based on the cumulative frequency polygon, how many employees earn \$9 an hour or less? Half of the employees earn an hourly wage of how much more? Four employees earn how much less?

Exercises

13. The following chart shows the hourly wages of certified welders in the Atlanta, Georgia, area.

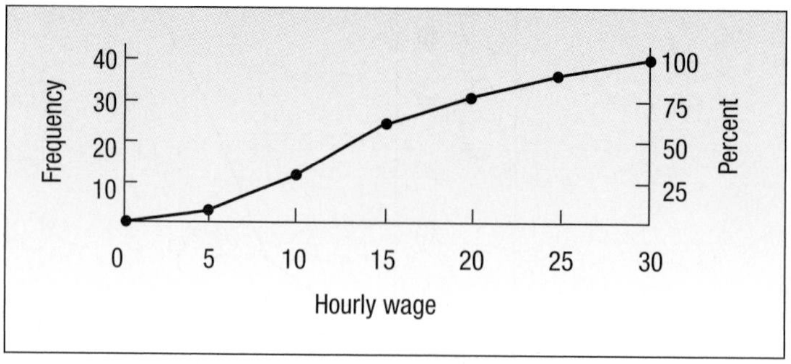

a. How many welders were studied?
b. What is the class interval?
c. About how many welders earn less than \$10.00 per hour?
d. About 75 percent of the welders make less than what amount?
e. Ten of the welders studied made less than what amount?
f. What percent of the welders make less than \$20.00 per hour?

14. The following chart shows the selling price (\$000) of houses sold in the Billings, Montana, area.

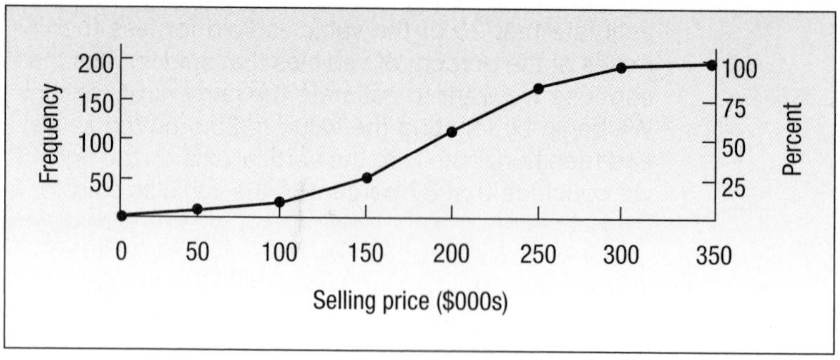

a. How many homes were studied?
b. What is the class interval?
c. One hundred homes sold for less than what amount?
d. About 75 percent of the homes sold for less than what amount?
e. Estimate the number of homes in the $150 up to $200 class.
f. About how many homes sold for less than $225?

15. The frequency distribution representing the number of frequent flier miles accumulated by employees at Brumley Statistical Consulting Company is repeated from Exercise 11.

Frequent Flier Miles (000)	Frequency
0 up to 3	5
3 up to 6	12
6 up to 9	23
9 up to 12	8
12 up to 15	2
Total	50

a. How many employees accumulated less than 3,000 miles?
b. Convert the frequency distribution to a cumulative frequency distribution.
c. Portray the cumulative distribution in the form of a cumulative frequency polygon.
d. Based on the cumulative frequency polygon, about 75 percent of the employees accumulated how many miles or less?

16. The frequency distribution of order lead time at Ecommerce.com from Exercise 12 is repeated below.

Lead Time (days)	Frequency
0 up to 5	6
5 up to 10	7
10 up to 15	12
15 up to 20	8
20 up to 25	7
Total	40

a. How many orders were filled in less than 10 days? In less than 15 days?
b. Convert the frequency distribution to a cumulative frequency distribution.
c. Develop a cumulative frequency polygon.
d. About 60 percent of the orders were filled in less than how many days?

Stem-and-Leaf Displays

In the previous section, we showed how to organize data into a frequency distribution so we could summarize the raw data into a meaningful form. The major advantage to organizing the data into a frequency distribution is that we get a quick visual picture of the shape of the distribution without doing any further calculation. That is, we can see where the data are concentrated and also determine whether there are any extremely large or small values. There are two disadvantages, however, to organizing the data into a frequency distribution: (1) we lose the exact identity of each value and (2) we are not sure how the values within each class are distributed. To explain, the following frequency distribution shows the number of advertising spots purchased by the 45 members of the Greater Buffalo Automobile Dealers Association in the year 2000. We observe that 7 of the 45 dealers purchased between 90 and 99 spots (but less than 100). However, is the number of spots purchased within this class clustered about 90, spread evenly throughout the class, or clustered near 99? We cannot tell.

Number of Spots Purchased	Frequency
80 up to 90	2
90 up to 100	7
100 up to 110	6
110 up to 120	9
120 up to 130	8
130 up to 140	7
140 up to 150	3
150 up to 160	3
Total	45

One technique that is used to display quantitative information in a condensed form is the **stem-and-leaf display.** An advantage of the stem-and-leaf display over a frequency distribution is that we do not lose the identity of each observation. In the above example, we would not know the identity of the values in the 90 up to 100 class. To illustrate the construction of a stem-and-leaf display using the number of advertising spots purchased, suppose the seven observations in the 90 up to 100 class are: 96, 94, 93, 94, 95, 96, and 97. The **stem** value is the leading digit or digits, in this case 9. The **leaves** are the trailing digits. The stem is placed to the left of a vertical line and the leaf values to the right.

The values in the 90 up to 100 class would appear as follows:

```
9 | 6 4 3 4 5 6 7
```

Finally, we sort the values within each stem from smallest to largest. Thus, the second row of the stem-and-leaf display would appear as follows:

```
9 | 3 4 4 5 6 6 7
```

With the stem-and-leaf display, we can quickly observe that there were two dealers who purchased 94 spots and that the number of spots purchased ranged from 93 to 97. A stem-and-leaf display is similar to a frequency distribution with more information, that is, data values instead of tallies.

STEM-AND-LEAF DISPLAY A statistical technique to present a set of data. Each numerical value is divided into two parts. The leading digit(s) becomes the stem and the trailing digit the leaf. The stems are located along the vertical axis, and the leaf values are stacked against each other along the horizontal axis.

The following example will explain the details of developing a stem-and-leaf display.

EXAMPLE

Listed in Table 2–7 is the number of 30-second radio advertising spots purchased by each of the 45 members of the Greater Buffalo Automobile Dealers Association last year. Organize the data into a stem-and-leaf display. Around what values do the number of advertising spots tend to cluster? What is the fewest number of spots purchased by a dealer? The largest number purchased?

TABLE 2–7 Number of Advertising Spots Purchased by Members of the Greater Buffalo Automobile Dealers Association

96	93	88	117	127	95	113	96	108	94	148	156
139	142	94	107	125	155	155	103	112	127	117	120
112	135	132	111	125	104	106	139	134	119	97	89
118	136	125	143	120	103	113	124	138			

SOLUTION

From the data in Table 2–7 we note that the smallest number of spots purchased is 88. So we will make the first stem value 8. The largest number is 156, so we will have the stem values begin at 8 and continue to 15. The first number in Table 2–7 is 96, which will have a stem value of 9 and a leaf value of 6. Moving across the top row, the second value is 93 and the third is 88. After the first 3 data values are considered, your chart is as follows.

Stem	Leaf
8	8
9	6 3
10	
11	
12	
13	
14	
15	

Organizing all the data, the stem-and-leaf chart looks as follows.

Stem	Leaf
8	8 9
9	6 3 5 6 4 4 7
10	8 7 3 4 6 3
11	7 3 2 7 2 1 9 8 3
12	7 5 7 0 5 5 0 4
13	9 5 2 9 4 6 8
14	8 2 3
15	6 5 5

The usual procedure is to sort the leaf values from the smallest to largest. The last line, the row referring to the values in the 150s, would appear as:

15	5 5 6

The final table would appear as follows, where we have sorted all of the leaf values.

Stem	Leaf
8	8 9
9	3 4 4 5 6 6 7
10	3 3 4 6 7 8
11	1 2 2 3 3 7 7 8 9
12	0 0 4 5 5 5 7 7
13	2 4 5 6 8 9 9
14	2 3 8
15	5 5 6

You can draw several conclusions from the stem-and-leaf display. First the lowest number of spots purchased is 88 and the largest is 156. Two dealers purchased less than 90 spots, and three purchased 150 or more. You can observe, for example, that the three dealers who purchased more than 150 spots actually purchased 155, 155, and 156 spots. The concentration of the number of spots is between 110 and 130. There were nine dealers who purchased between 110 and 119 spots and eight who purchased between 120 and 129 spots. We can also tell that within the 120 to 129 group the actual number of spots purchased was spread evenly throughout. That is, two dealers purchased 120 spots, one dealer purchased 124 spots, three dealers purchased 125 spots, and two purchased 127 spots.

MINITAB

We can also generate this information on the MINITAB software system. We have named the variable *Spots.* The MINITAB output is below. You can find the MINITAB commands that will produce this output at the end of the chapter.

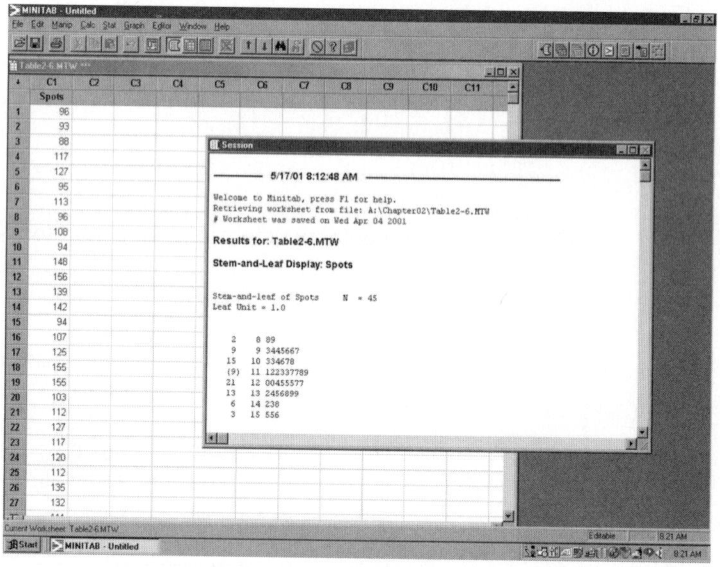

The MINITAB solution provides some additional information regarding cumulative totals. In the column to the left of the stem values are numbers such as 2, 9, 15, and so on. The number 9 indicates that there are 9 observations that have occurred before the value of 100. The number 15 indicates that 15 observations have occurred prior to 110. About halfway down the column the number 9 appears in parentheses. The parentheses indicate that the middle value appears in that row. In this case, we describe the middle value as the value below which half of the observations occur. There are a total of 45 observations, so the middle value, if the data were arranged from smallest to largest, would be the 23rd observation. After the middle row, the values begin to decline. These values represent the "more than" cumulative totals. There are 21 observations of 120 or more, 13 of 130 or more, and so on. The number 9 in parentheses also tells you there are 9 observations in the middle row.

Self-Review 2–6

The price-earnings ratios for 21 stocks in the retail trade category are:

8.3	9.6	9.5	9.1	8.8	11.2	7.7	10.1	9.9	10.8	
10.2	8.0	8.4	8.1	11.6	9.6	8.8	8.0	10.4	9.8	9.2

Organize this information into a stem-and-leaf display.
(a) How many values are less than 9.0?
(b) List the values in the 10.0 up to 11.0 category.
(c) What is the middle value?
(d) What are the largest and the smallest price-earnings ratios?

Exercises

17. The first row of a stem-and-leaf chart appears as follows: 62 | 1 3 3 7 9. Assume whole number values.
  a. What is the "possible range" of the values in this row?
  b. How many data values are in this row?
  c. List the actual values in this row of data.

18. The third row of a stem-and-leaf chart appears as follows: 21 | 0 1 3 5 7 9. Assume whole number values.
  a. What is the "possible range" of the values in this row?
  b. How many data values are in this row?
  c. List the actual values in this row of data.

19. The following stem-and-leaf chart shows the number of units produced per day in a factory.

1	3	8
1	4	
2	5	6
9	6	0133559
(7)	7	0236778
9	8	59
7	9	00156
2	10	36

  a. How many days were studied?
  b. How many observations are in the first class?
  c. What are the smallest value and the largest value?
  d. List the actual values in the fourth row.
  e. List the actual values in the second row.
  f. How many values are less than 70?
  g. How many values are 80 or more?
  h. What is the middle value?
  i. How many values are between 60 and 89, inclusive?

20. The following stem-and-leaf chart reports the number of movies rented per day at Video Connection.

3	12	689
6	13	123
10	14	6889
13	15	589
15	16	35
20	17	24568
23	18	268
(5)	19	13456
22	20	034679
16	21	2239
12	22	789
9	23	00179
4	24	8
3	25	13
1	26	
1	27	0

a. How many days were studied?
b. How many observations are in the last class?
c. What are the largest and the smallest values in the entire set of data?
d. List the actual values in the fourth row.
e. List the actual values in the next to the last row.
f. On how many days were less than 160 movies rented?
g. On how many days were 220 or more movies rented?
h. What is the middle value?
i. On how many days were between 170 and 210 movies rented?

21. A survey of the number of calls received by a sample of Southern Phone Company subscribers last week revealed the following information. Develop a stem-and-leaf chart. How many calls did a typical subscriber receive? What were the largest and the smallest number of calls received?

52	43	30	38	30	42	12	46	39
37	34	46	32	18	41	5		

22. Aloha Banking Co. is studying the number of times their automatic teller, located in Loblaws Supermarket, is used each day. The following is the number of times it was used during each of the last 30 days. Develop a stem-and-leaf chart. Summarize the data on the number of times the automatic teller was used: How many times was the teller used on a typical day? What were the largest and the smallest number of times the teller was used? Around what values did the number of times the teller was used tend to cluster?

83	64	84	76	84	54	75	59	70	61
63	80	84	73	68	52	65	90	52	77
95	36	78	61	59	84	95	47	87	60

Other Graphic Presentations of Data

The histogram, the frequency polygon, and the cumulative frequency polygon all have strong visual appeal. That is, they are designed to capture the attention of the reader. In this section we will examine some other graphical forms, namely the line chart, the bar chart, and the pie chart. These charts are seen extensively in *USA Today, U.S. News and World Report, Business Week,* and other newspapers, magazines, and government reports.

Line Graphs

Charts 2–6 and 2–7 are examples of **line charts.** Line charts are particularly effective for business data because we can show the change in a variable over time. The variable, such as the number of units sold or the total value of sales, is scaled along the vertical axis and time along the horizontal axis. Chart 2–6 shows the Dow Jones Industrial Average and the Nasdaq, the two most widely reported measures of stock market activity. Both measures were down for the day. The Dow closed at 9,863.74, down 21.04 points or 0.21 percent for the day. The Nasdaq was down 12.45 or 0.67 percent for the day.

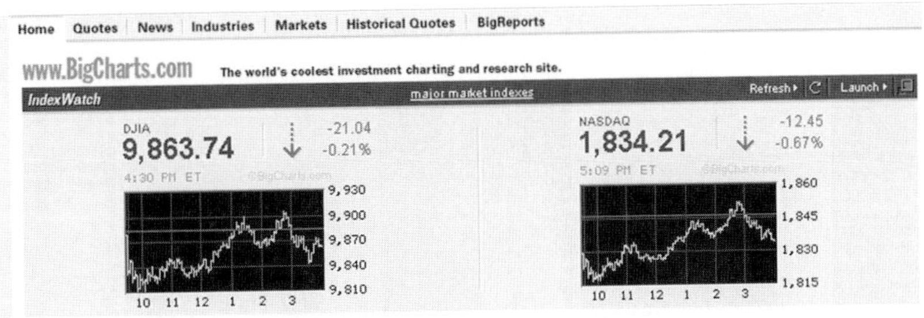

CHART 2–6 Line Chart for the Dow Jones Industrial Average and the Nasdaq

Chart 2–7 is also a line chart. It shows the net operating income of Verizon Communications, Inc. from 1996 to 2000. Net operating income increased from $11,392,000 in 1996 to $16,758,000 in 2000. Verizon was formed in 2000 by the merger of Bell Atlantic Corporation and GTE Corporation. The above information is based on combined company data. Verizon is the largest provider of wireline and wireless communications in the United States and employs more than 260,000 people.

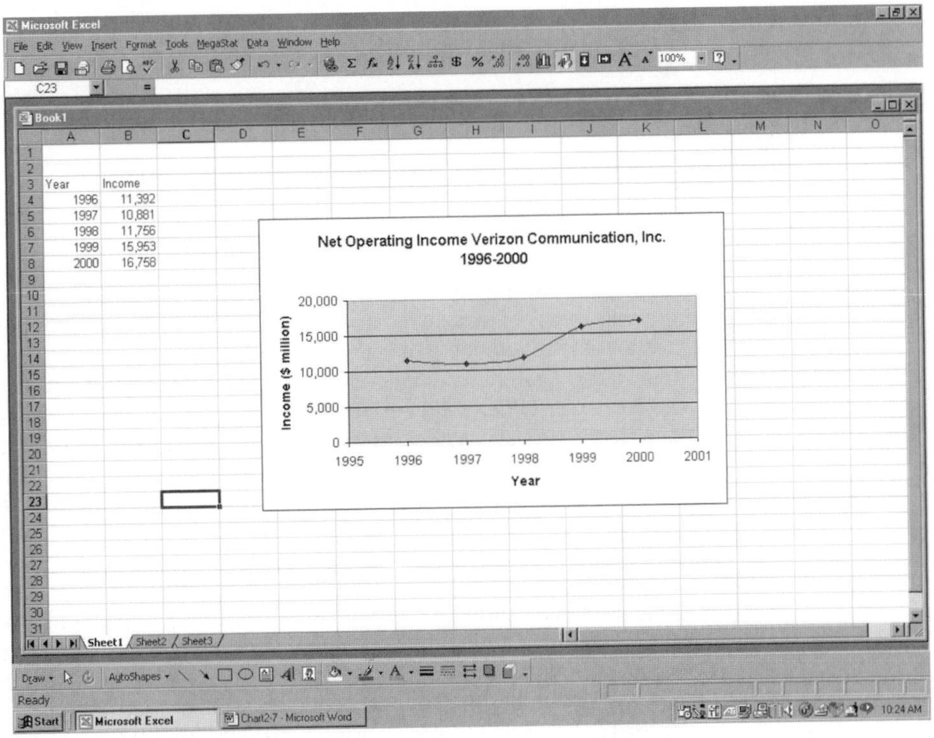

CHART 2–7 Net Operating Income of Verizon Communications, Inc. from 1996 to 2000

Quite often two or more series of data are plotted on the same line chart. Thus, one chart can show the trend of those series. This allows for a comparison of several series over a period of time. Chart 2–8 shows the price of first-class postage (bottom line) and the price of first-class postage adjusted for inflation for the period from 1971 to 2001. The adjusted data is reported in year 2001 dollars. We can quickly see that the actual postage rate has increased, but when this rate is adjusted for inflation there has been little change over the period.

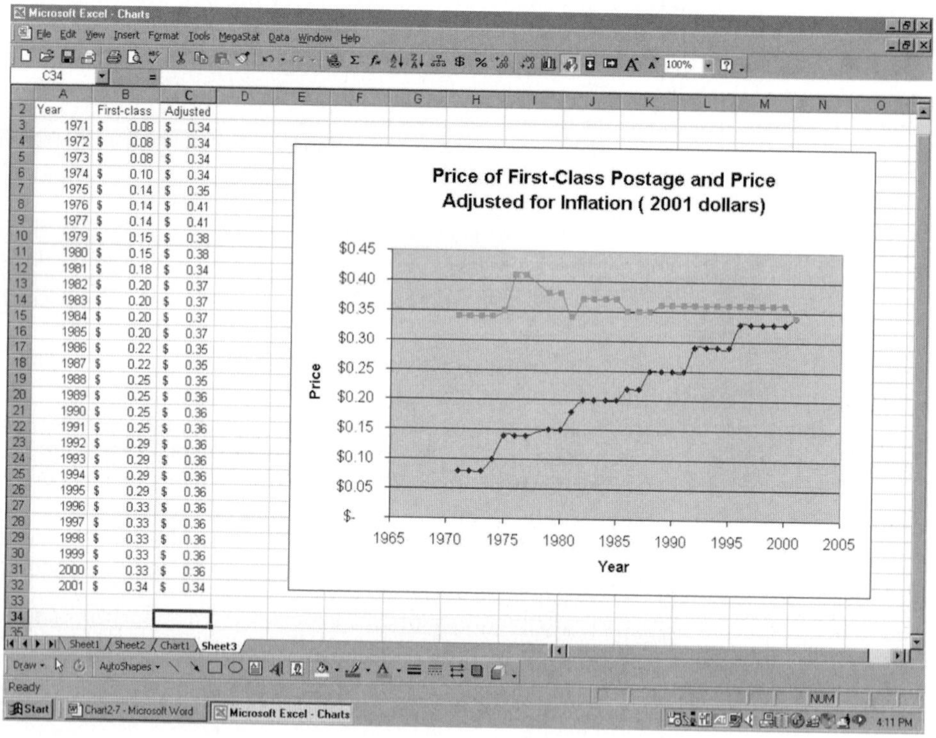

CHART 2–8 Price of First-Class Postage from 1971 to 2001

Bar Charts

A bar chart can be used to depict any of the levels of measurement—nominal, ordinal, interval, or ratio. Recall we discussed the levels of data in Chapter 1. Suppose we wish to show the difference in earnings based on highest level of education. From the Census Bureau Current Population Reports, the average earnings for someone over the age of 18 are $22,895 if a high school diploma is the highest degree earned. With a bachelor's degree the average earnings increase to $40,478, and with a master's/professional degree the amount increases to $73,165. This information is summarized in Chart 2–9. We call this chart a **horizontal bar chart** because the bars are horizontal. With this chart it is easy to see that a person with a bachelor's degree can expect to earn almost twice as much as someone with a high school diploma. The expected earnings of someone with a master's or professional degree is nearly twice that of a bachelor's degree and more than three times that of someone with a high school diploma.

Chart 2–10, a **vertical bar chart,** shows the number of years it took five key technologies, after their introduction, to enter one-quarter of American homes. It took only 7 years for the Internet to reach one-quarter of the homes, but it took the telephone 35 years. The years correspond to the height of the bars.

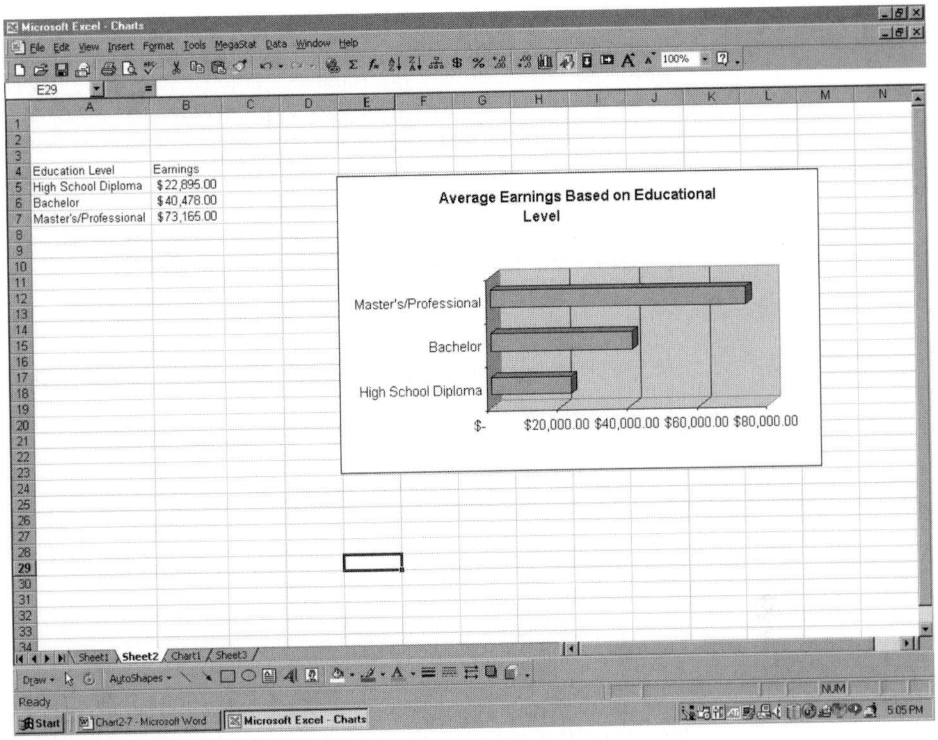

CHART 2–9 Average Earnings Based on Educational Level

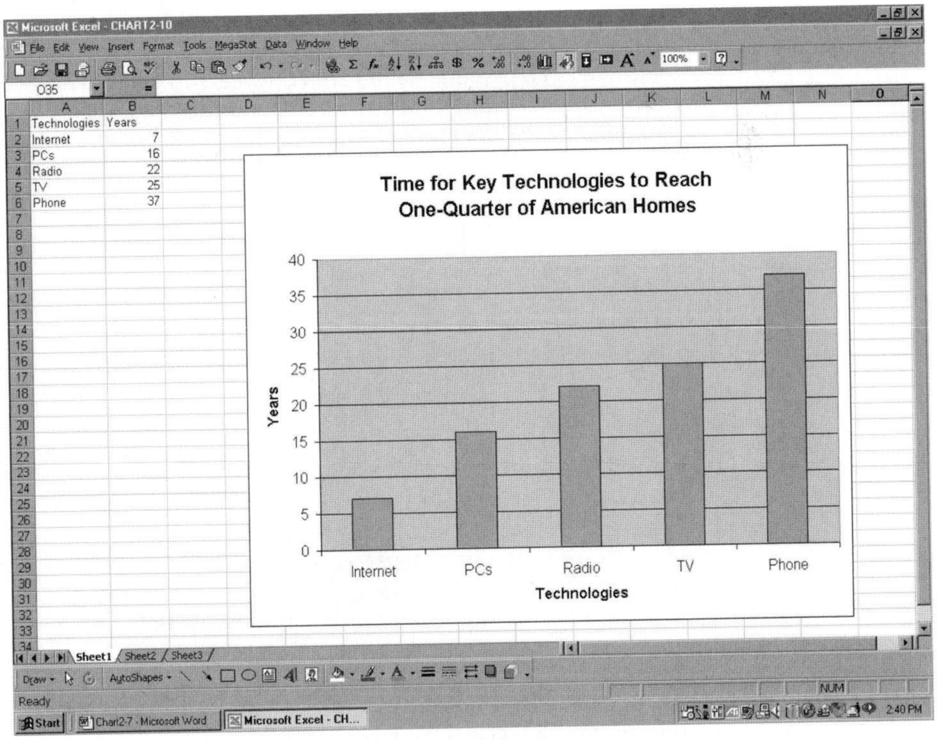

CHART 2–10 Time for Key Technologies to Reach One-Quarter of American Homes

There is space between the bars representing the time for the various technologies. This is one way in which a histogram and a bar chart differ. There is no space between the bars in a histogram (see Chart 2–2), because the vehicle selling price data are ratio scale. The technologies are nominal scale; therefore the bars are separated.

Pie Charts

A **pie chart** is especially useful for depicting nominal level data. We will use the information in Table 2–8, which shows a breakdown of state lottery proceeds since 1964, to explain the details of constructing a pie chart.

TABLE 2–8 State Lottery Proceeds

Use of Profits	Percent Share
Education	56
General fund	23
Cities	10
Senior citizens	9
Other	2
Total	100

The first step is to record the percentages 0, 5, 10, 15, and so on evenly around the circumference of a circle. To plot the 56 percent share for education, draw a line from 0 to the center of the circle and then another line from the center to 56 percent on the circle. The area of this "slice" represents the lottery proceeds that were given to education. Next, add the 56 percent transferred to education to the 23 percent transferred to the general fund; the result is 79 percent. Draw a line from the center of the circle to 79 percent, so the area between 56 percent and 79 percent represents the percent of the lottery proceeds transferred to the general fund of the state. Continuing, add 10, the component given to the cities, which gives us a total of 89 percent.

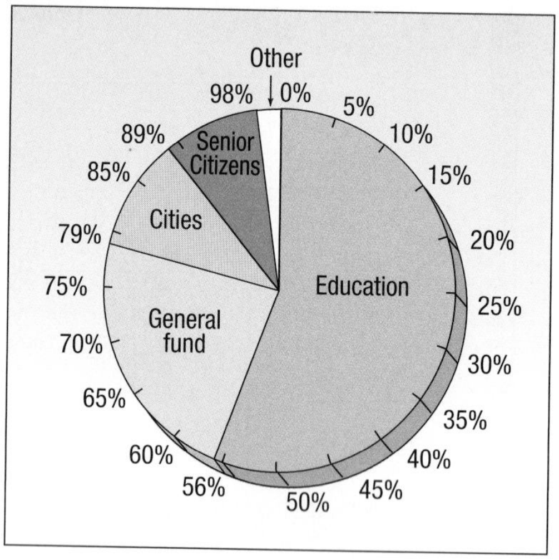

Percent of State Lottery Proceeds

Draw a line from the center out to the value 89, so the area between 79 and 89 represents the share transferred to cities. Continue the same process for the senior citizen programs and "Other." Because the areas of the pie represent the relative shares of each category, we can quickly compare them: The largest percent of the proceeds goes to education; this amount is more than half the total, and it is more than twice the amount given to the next largest category.

The Excel system will develop a pie chart and output the result. Following is an Excel chart showing the percentage of viewers watching each of the major television networks during prime time.

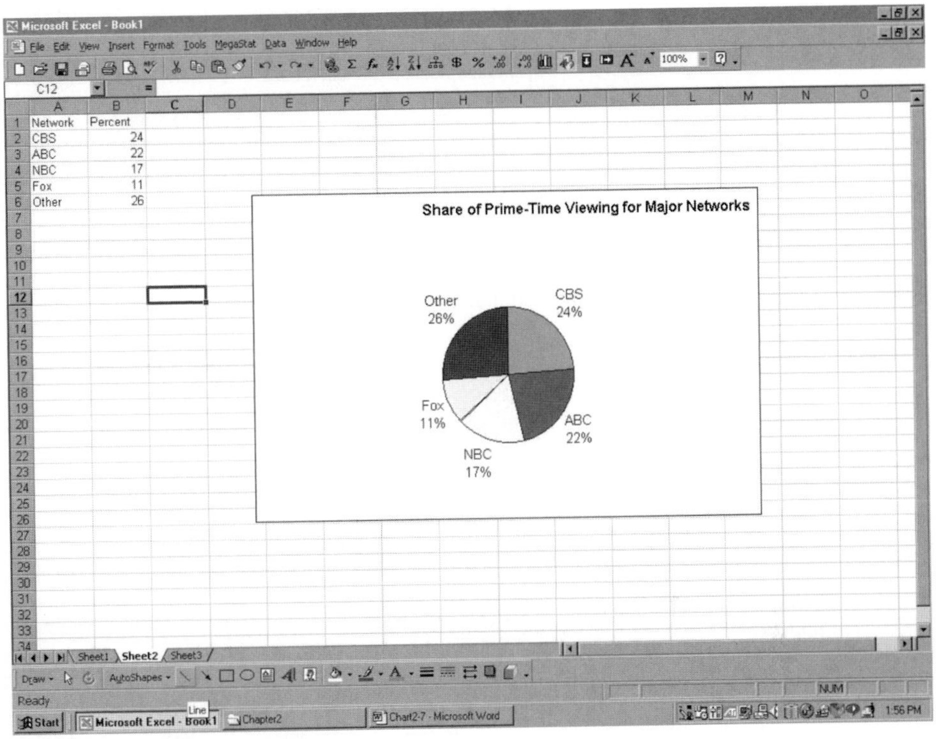

Self-Review 2-7

The Clayton County Commissioners want a chart to show taxpayers attending the forthcoming meeting what happens to their tax dollars. The total amount of taxes collected is \$2 million. Expenditures are: \$440,000 for schools, \$1,160,000 for roads, \$320,000 for administration, and \$80,000 for supplies. A pie chart seems ideal to show the portion of each tax dollar going for schools, roads, administration, and supplies. Convert the dollar amounts to percents of the total and portray the percents in the form of a pie chart.

Exercises

23. A small business consultant is investigating the performance of several companies. The sales in 2001 (in thousands of dollars) for the selected companies were:

Corporation	Fourth-Quarter Sales ($ thousands)
Hoden Building Products	$ 1,645.2
J & R Printing, Inc.	4,757.0
Long Bay Concrete Construction	8,913.0
Mancell Electric and Plumbing	627.1
Maxwell Heating and Air Conditioning	24,612.0
Mizelle Roofing & Sheet Metals	191.9

The consultant wants to include a chart in his report comparing the sales of the six companies. Use a bar chart to compare the fourth quarter sales of these corporations and write a brief report summarizing the bar chart.

24. The Blair Corporation, located in Warren, Pennsylvania, sells fashion apparel for men and women plus a broad range of home products. It services its customers by mail. Listed below are the net sales for Blair from 1995 through 2000. Draw a line chart depicting the net sales over the time period and write a brief report.

Year	Net Sales ($ millions)
1995	500.0
1996	519.2
1997	526.5
1998	550.7
1999	562.9
2000	619.4

25. A headline in a Toledo, Ohio, newspaper reported that crime was on the decline. Listed below are the number of homicides from 1986 to 2001. Draw a line chart to summarize the data and write a brief summary of the homicide rates for the last 16 years.

Year	Homicides	Year	Homicides
1986	21	1994	40
1987	34	1995	35
1988	26	1996	30
1989	42	1997	28
1990	37	1998	25
1991	37	1999	21
1992	44	2000	19
1993	45	2001	23

26. A report prepared for the governor of a western state indicated that 56 percent of the state's tax revenue went to education, 23 percent to the general fund, 10 percent to the counties, 9 percent to senior programs, and the remainder to other social programs. Develop a pie chart to show the breakdown of the budget.

27. The following table, in millions, shows the population of the United States in five-year intervals from 1950 to 2000. Develop a line chart depicting the population growth and write a brief report summarizing your findings.

Year	Population (millions)	Year	Population (millions)
1950	152.3	1980	227.7
1955	165.9	1985	238.5
1960	180.7	1990	249.9
1965	194.3	1995	263.0
1970	205.1	2000	281.4
1975	216.0		

28. Shown below are the military and civilian personnel expenditures for the eight largest military locations in the United States. Develop a bar chart and summarize the results in a brief report.

Location	Amount Spent (millions)	Location	Amount Spent (millions)
St. Louis, MO	$6,087	Norfolk, VA	$3,228
San Diego, CA	4,747	Marietta, GA	2,828
Pico Rivera, CA	3,272	Fort Worth, TX	2,492
Arlington, VA	3,284	Washington, DC	2,347

Chapter Outline

I. A frequency distribution is a grouping of data into mutually exclusive classes showing the number of observations in each class.
- **A.** The steps in constructing a frequency distribution are:
  - **1.** Decide how many classes you wish.
  - **2.** Determine the class interval or width.
  - **3.** Set the individual class limits.
  - **4.** Tally the raw data into the classes.
  - **5.** Count the number of tallies in each class.
- **B.** The class frequency is the number of observations in each class.
- **C.** The class interval is the difference between the limits of two consecutive classes.
- **D.** The class midpoint is halfway between the limits of two consecutive classes.

II. A relative frequency distribution shows the percent of the observations in each class.

III. There are three methods for graphically portraying a frequency distribution.
- **A.** A histogram portrays the number of frequencies in each class in the form of rectangles.
- **B.** A frequency polygon consists of line segments connecting the points formed by the intersections of the class midpoints and the class frequencies.
- **C.** A cumulative frequency polygon shows the number of observations below a certain value.

IV. A stem-and-leaf display is an alternative to a frequency distribution.
- **A.** The leading digit is the stem and the trailing digit the leaf.
- **B.** The advantages of the stem-and-leaf chart over a frequency distribution include:
  - **1.** The identity of each observation is not lost.
  - **2.** The digits themselves give a picture of the distribution.
  - **3.** The cumulative frequencies are also reported.

V. There are many charts used in newspapers and magazines.
- **A.** A line chart is ideal for showing the trend of sales or income over time.
- **B.** Bar charts are similar to line charts and are useful for showing changes in nominal scale data.
- **C.** Pie charts are useful for showing the percent that various components are of the total.

Chapter Exercises

29. A data set consists of 83 observations. How many classes would you recommend for a frequency distribution?

30. A data set consists of 145 observations that range from 56 to 490. What size class interval would you recommend?

31. The following is the number of minutes to commute from home to work for a group of automobile executives.

28	25	48	37	41	19	32	26	16	23	23	29	36
31	26	21	32	25	31	43	35	42	38	33	28	

a. How many classes would you recommend?
b. What class interval would you suggest?
c. What would you recommend as the lower limit of the first class?
d. Organize the data into a frequency distribution.
e. Comment on the shape of the frequency distribution.

32. The following data give the weekly amounts spent on groceries for a sample of households.

$271	$363	$159	$ 76	$227	$337	$295	$319	$250
279	205	279	266	199	177	162	232	303
192	181	321	309	246	278	50	41	335
116	100	151	240	474	297	170	188	320
429	294	570	342	279	235	434	123	325

a. How many classes would you recommend?
b. What class interval would you suggest?
c. What would you recommend as the lower limit of the first class?
d. Organize the data into a frequency distribution.

33. The following stem-and-leaf display shows the number of minutes of daytime TV viewing for a sample of college students.

2	0	05
3	1	0
6	2	137
10	3	0029
13	4	499
24	5	00155667799
30	6	023468
(7)	7	1366789
33	8	01558
28	9	1122379
21	10	022367899
12	11	2457
8	12	4668
4	13	249
1	14	5

a. How many college students were studied?
b. How many observations are in the second class?
c. What are the smallest value and the largest value?
d. List the actual values in the fourth row.
e. How many students watched less than 60 minutes of TV?
f. How many students watched 100 minutes or more of TV?
g. What is the middle value?
h. How many students watched at least 60 minutes but less than 100 minutes?

34. The following stem-and-leaf display reports the number of orders received per day by a mail-order firm.

1	9	1
2	10	2
5	11	235
7	12	69
8	13	2
11	14	135
15	15	1229
22	16	2266778
27	17	01599
(11)	18	00013346799
17	19	03346
12	20	4679
8	21	0177
4	22	45
2	23	17

a. How many days were studied?
b. How many observations are in the fourth class?
c. What are the smallest value and the largest value?
d. List the actual values in the sixth class.
e. How many days did the firm receive less than 140 orders?
f. How many days did the firm receive 200 or more orders?
g. On how many days did the firm receive 180 orders?
h. What is the middle value?

35. The following histogram shows the scores on the first statistics exam.

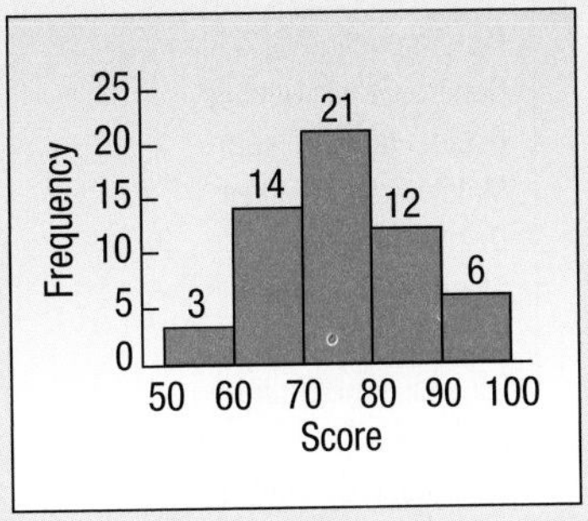

a. How many students took the exam?
b. What is the class interval?
c. What is the class midpoint for the first class?
d. How many students earned a score of less than 70?

36. The following chart summarizes the selling price of homes sold last month in the Sarasota, Florida, area.

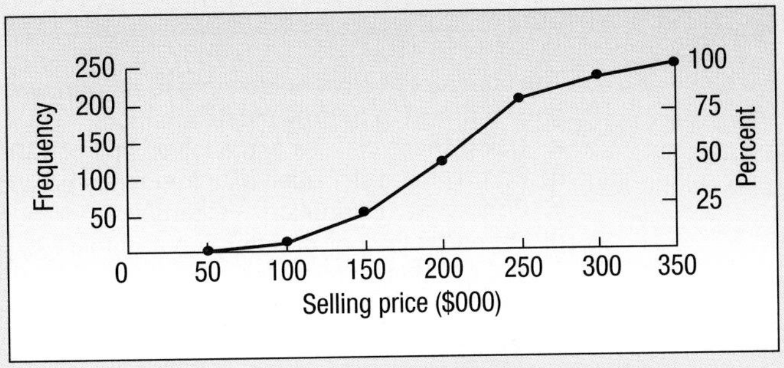

a. What is the chart called?
b. How many homes were sold during the last month?
c. What is the class interval?
d. About 75 percent of the houses sold for less than what amount?
e. One hundred seventy-five of the homes sold for less than what amount?

37. A chain of sport shops catering to beginning skiers, headquartered in Aspen, Colorado, plans to conduct a study of how much a beginning skier spends on his or her initial purchase of equipment and supplies. Based on these figures, they want to explore the possibility of offering combinations, such as a pair of boots and a pair of skis, to induce customers to buy more. A sample of their cash register receipts revealed these initial purchases:

$140	$ 82	$265	$168	$ 90	$114	$172	$230	$142
86	125	235	212	171	149	156	162	118
139	149	132	105	162	126	216	195	127
161	135	172	220	229	129	87	128	126
175	127	149	126	121	118	172	126	

a. Arrive at a suggested class interval. Use five classes, and let the lower limit of the first class be $80.
b. What would be a better class interval?
c. Organize the data into a frequency distribution using a lower limit of $80.
d. Interpret your findings.

38. The numbers of shareholders for a selected group of large companies (in thousands) are:

Company	Number of Shareholders (thousands)	Company	Number of Shareholders (thousands)
Pan American World Airways	144	Northeast Utilities	200
General Public Utilities	177	Standard Oil (Indiana)	173
Occidental Petroleum	266	Home Depot	195
Middle South Utilities	133	Detroit Edison	220
DaimlerChrysler	209	Eastman Kodak	251
Standard Oil of California	264	Dow Chemical	137
Bethlehem Steel	160	Pennsylvania Power	150
Long Island Lighting	143	American Electric Power	262
RCA	246	Ohio Edison	158
Greyhound Corporation	151	Transamerica Corporation	162
Pacific Gas & Electric	239	Columbia Gas System	165
Niagara Mohawk Power	204	International Telephone & Telegraph	223
E. I. du Pont de Nemours	204	Union Electric	158
Westinghouse Electric	195	Virginia Electric and Power	162
Union Carbide	176	Public Service Electric & Gas	225
BankAmerica	175	Consumers Power	161

The numbers of shareholders are to be organized into a frequency distribution and several graphs drawn to portray the distribution.

a. Using seven classes and a lower limit of 130, construct a frequency distribution.
b. Portray the distribution as a frequency polygon.
c. Portray the distribution in a cumulative frequency polygon.
d. Based on the polygon, three out of four (75 percent) of the companies have how many shareholders or less?
e. Write a brief analysis of the number of shareholders based on the frequency distribution and graphs.

39. A recent survey showed that the typical American car owner spends $2,950 per year on operating expenses. Below is a breakdown of the various expenditure items. Draw an appropriate chart to portray the data and summarize your findings in a brief report.

Expenditure Item	Amount
Fuel	$ 603
Interest on car loan	279
Repairs	930
Insurance and license	646
Depreciation	492
Total	$2,950

40. The Midland National Bank selected a sample of 40 student checking accounts. Below are their end-of-the-month balances.

$404	$ 74	$234	$149	$279	$215	$123	$ 55	$ 43	$321
87	234	68	489	57	185	141	758	72	863
703	125	350	440	37	252	27	521	302	127
968	712	503	489	327	608	358	425	303	203

a. Tally the data into a frequency distribution using $100 as a class interval and $0 as the starting point.
b. Draw a cumulative frequency polygon.
c. The bank considers any student with an ending balance of $400 or more a "preferred customer." Estimate the percentage of preferred customers.
d. The bank is also considering a service charge to the lowest 10 percent of the ending balances. What would you recommend as the cutoff point between those who have to pay a service charge and those who do not?

41. The United States Department of Transportation keeps track of the percentage of flights that arrive within 15 minutes of the scheduled time, by airline. Below is the latest information. Construct a stem-and-leaf chart from these data. Summarize your conclusion.

Airline	Percent on Time	Airline	Percent on Time
Pan Am	82.7	American	78.1
America West	82.7	United	76.4
Northwest	81.0	Delta	76.1
USAir	80.1	Continental	76.9
Southwest	79.7	British Airways	80.4
Alaska	79.7	Japan Airlines	81.4

42. A recent study of home technologies reported the number of hours of personal computer usage per week for a sample of 60 persons. Excluded from the study were people who worked out of their home and used the computer as a part of their work.

9.3	5.3	6.3	8.8	6.5	0.6	5.2	6.6	9.3	4.3
6.3	2.1	2.7	0.4	3.7	3.3	1.1	2.7	6.7	6.5
4.3	9.7	7.7	5.2	1.7	8.5	4.2	5.5	5.1	5.6
5.4	4.8	2.1	10.1	1.3	5.6	2.4	2.4	4.7	1.7
2.0	6.7	1.1	6.7	2.2	2.6	9.8	6.4	4.9	5.2
4.5	9.3	7.9	4.6	4.3	4.5	9.2	8.5	6.0	8.1

a. Organize the data into a frequency distribution. How many classes would you suggest? What value would you suggest for a class interval?

b. Draw a histogram. Interpret your result.

43. Merrill Lynch recently completed a study regarding the size of investment portfolios (stocks, bonds, mutual funds, and certificates of deposit) for a sample of clients in the 40 to 50 age group. Listed below is the value of all the investments in $000 for the 70 participants in the study.

$669.9	$ 7.5	$ 77.2	$ 7.5	$125.7	$516.9	$219.9	$645.2
301.9	235.4	716.4	145.3	26.6	187.2	315.5	89.2
136.4	616.9	440.6	408.2	34.4	296.1	185.4	526.3
380.7	3.3	363.2	51.9	52.2	107.5	82.9	63.0
228.6	308.7	126.7	430.3	82.0	227.0	321.1	403.4
39.5	124.3	118.1	23.9	352.8	156.7	276.3	23.5
31.3	301.2	35.7	154.9	174.3	100.6	236.7	171.9
221.1	43.4	212.3	243.3	315.4	5.9	1002.2	171.7
295.7	437.0	87.8	302.1	268.1	899.5		

a. Organize the data into a frequency distribution. How many classes would you suggest? What value would you suggest for a class interval?

b. Draw a histogram. Interpret your result.

44. In its annual report ExxonMobil reported its total worldwide earnings as $5,886 million. Of this total (all reported in millions of dollars), $1,541 were in the United States, $1,757 in Europe, $1,219 in Asia-Pacific, $439 in Canada, and $930 in other parts of the world. Develop a bar chart depicting this information.

45. The American Heart Association reported the following percentage breakdown of expenses. Draw a pie chart depicting the information. Interpret.

Category	Percent
Research	32.3
Public Health Education	23.5
Community Service	12.6
Fund Raising	12.1
Professional and Educational Training	10.9
Management and General	8.6

46. In their 2000 annual report Schering-Plough Corporation reported their income, in millions of dollars, for the years 1996 to 2000 as follows. Develop a line chart depicting the results and comment on your findings.

Year	Income ($ million)
1996	1,213
1997	1,444
1998	1,756
1999	2,110
2000	2,423

47. Annual revenues, by type of tax, for the state of Georgia are as follows. Develop an appropriate chart or graph and write a brief report summarizing the information.

Type of Tax	Amount (000)
Sales	$2,812,473
Income (Individual)	2,732,045
License	185,198
Corporate	525,015
Property	22,647
Death and Gift	37,326
Total	$6,314,704

48. Annual imports from selected Canadian trading partners are listed below. Develop an appropriate chart or graph and write a brief report summarizing the information.

Partner	Annual Imports (million)
Japan	$9,550
United Kingdom	4,556
South Korea	2,441
China	1,182
Australia	618

49. Farming has changed from the early 1900s. In the early 20th century, machinery gradually replaced animal power. For example, in 1910 U.S. farms used 24.2 million horses and mules and only about 1,000 tractors. By 1960, 4.6 million tractors were used and only 3.2 million horses and mules. In 1920 there were over 6 million farms in the United States. Today there are less than 2 million. Listed below is the number of farms, in thousands, for each of the 50 states. Write a paragraph summarizing your findings.

47	1	8	46	76	26	4	3	39	45
4	21	80	63	100	65	91	29	7	15
7	52	87	39	106	25	55	2	3	8
14	38	59	33	76	71	37	51	1	24
35	86	185	13	7	43	36	20	79	9

50. One of the most popular candies in the United States is M&M's, which is produced by the Mars Company. For many years the M&M's plain candies were produced in six colors: red, green, orange, tan, brown, and yellow. Recently, tan was replaced by blue. Did you ever wonder how many candies were in a bag, or how many of each color? Are there about the same number of each color, or are there more of some colors than others? Here is some information for a one-pound bag of M&M's plain candies. It contained a total of 544 candies. There were 135 brown, 156 yellow, 128 red, 22 green, 50 blue, and 53 orange. Develop a chart depicting this information and a brief report summarizing the information.

51. The following graph compares the average selling prices of the Ford Taurus and the Toyota Camry from 1993 to 2000. Write a brief report summarizing the information in the graph. Be sure to include the selling price of the two cars, the change in the selling price, and the direction of the change in the eight-year period.

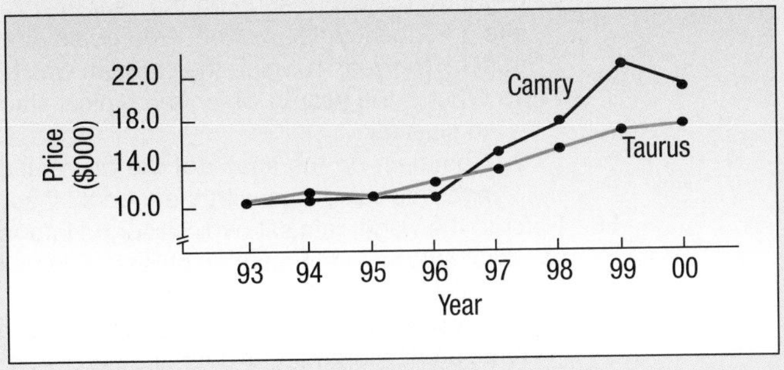

exercises.com

www

52. Monthly and year-to-date truck sales are available at the website: http://www.pickuptruck.com. Go to this site and under **Features** click on **News** to obtain the most recent information. Make a pie chart or a bar chart showing the most recent information. What is the best selling truck? What are the four or five best selling trucks? What is their market share? You may wish to group some of the trucks into a category called "Other" to get a better picture of market share. Comment on your findings.

53. Go to an employment website such as http://www.salary.com. Select **Job Category** and a **Geographic Region.** For example, you might select **Banking** as the job category and

Orlando, Florida, as the location. Make a stem-and-leaf display of the salaries offered for the various jobs. To make valid comparisons convert all wages to a yearly basis (assume 40 hours per week and 50 weeks in a year). Where a range is given for salaries, use the center of the range. Then write a brief summary describing the typical salary and the shape of the distribution.

Computer Data Exercises

54. Refer to the Real Estate data, which reports information on homes sold in the Venice, Florida, area during the last year.
  a. Select an appropriate class interval and organize the selling prices into a frequency distribution.
    1. Around what values do the data tend to cluster?
    2. What is the largest selling price? What is the smallest selling price?
  b. Draw a cumulative frequency distribution based on the frequency distribution developed in part (a).
    1. How many homes sold for less than $200,000?
    2. Estimate the percent of the homes that sold for more than $220,000.
    3. What percent of the homes sold for less than $125,000?
  c. Write a report summarizing the selling prices of the homes.

55. Refer to the Baseball 2001 data, which reports information on the 30 Major League Baseball teams for the 2001 season.
  a. Organize the information on the team salaries into a frequency distribution. Select an appropriate class interval.
    1. What is a typical team salary? What is the range of salaries?
    2. Comment on the shape of the distribution. Does it appear that any of the team salaries are out of line with the others?
  b. Draw a cumulative frequency distribution based on the frequency distribution developed in part (a).
    1. Forty percent of the teams are paying less than what amount in total team salary?
    2. About how many teams have total salaries of less than $50,000,000?
    3. Below what amount do the lowest five teams pay in total salary?
  c. Organize the information on the size of the various stadiums into a frequency distribution.
    1. What is a typical stadium size? Where do the stadium sizes tend to cluster?
    2. Comment on the shape of the distribution. Does it appear that any of the stadium sizes are out of line with the others?
  d. Organize the information on the year in which the 30 major league stadiums were built into a frequency distribution. (You could also create a new variable called AGE by subtracting the year in which the stadium was built from the current year.)
    1. What is the year in which the typical stadium was built? Where do these years tend to cluster?
    2. Comment on the shape of the distribution. Does it appear that any of the stadium ages are out of line with the others? If so, which ones?

56. Refer to the wage data set, which reports information on annual wages for a sample of 100 workers. Also included are variables relating to industry, years of education, and gender for each worker.
  a. Develop a stem-and-leaf chart for the variable annual wage. Are there any outliers? Write a brief summary of your findings.
  b. Develop a stem-and-leaf chart for the variable years of education. Are there any outliers? Write a brief summary of your findings.
  c. Draw a bar chart of the variable occupation. Write a brief report summarizing your findings.

57. Refer to the CIA data, which reports demographic and economic information on 46 countries.
  a. Develop a frequency distribution for the variable GNP per capita. Summarize your findings. What is the shape of the distribution?
  b. Develop a stem-and-leaf chart for the variable referring to the number of cell phones. Summarize your findings.

Computer Commands

1. The MegaStat commands for the frequency distribution on page 27 are:
   a. Open Excel and from the CD provided, select **Go to the Data Sets,** and select the Excel format; go to Chapter 2, and select **Table 2–1.** Click on **MegaStat, Frequency Distribution,** and select **Quantitative.**
   b. In the dialog box, input the range from *A1:A81,* select **Equal width intervals,** use *3,000* as the interval width, *12,000* as the lower boundary of the first interval, select **Histogram,** and then click **OK.**

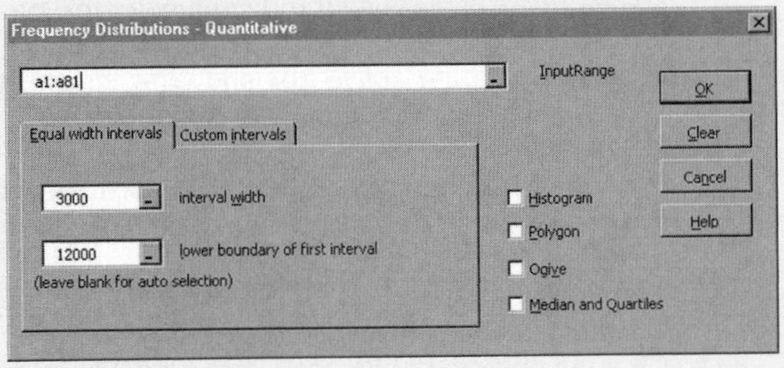

2. The Excel commands for the histogram on page 32 are:
   a. In cell A1 indicate that the column of data is the selling price and in B1 that it is the frequency. In columns A2 to A8 insert the midpoints of the selling prices in $000. In B2 to B8 record the class frequencies.
   b. With your mouse arrow on A1, click and drag to highlight the cells A1:B8.
   c. From the **Tool bar** select **Chart Wizard,** under **Chart type** select **Column,** under **Chart sub-type** select the vertical bars in the upper left corner, and finally click on **Next** in the lower right corner.
   d. At the top select the **Series** tab. Under the Series list box, **Price** is highlighted. Select **Remove.** (We do not want Price to be a part of the values.) At the bottom, in the **Category (X)** axis labels text box, click the icon at the far right. Put your cursor on cell A2, click and drag to cell A8. There will be a running box around cells A2 to A8. Touch the **Enter** key. This identifies the column of **Prices** as the *X*-axis labels. Click on **Next.**
   e. At the top of the dialog box click on **Titles.** Click on the **Chart title** box and key in *Selling Price of 80 Vehicles Sold at Whitner Pontiac.* Tab to the **Category (X)** axis box and key in the label *Selling Price in ($000).* Tab to the **Category (Y)** axis box and key in *Frequency.* At the top select **Legend** and remove the check from the **Show legend** box. Click **Finish.**
   f. To make the chart larger, click on the middle handle of the top line and drag the line to row 1. Make sure the handles show on the chart box. With your right mouse button, click on one of the columns. Select **Format Data Series.** At the top select the **Options** tab. In the **Gap width** text box, click the down arrow until the gap width reads 0, and click **OK.**
3. The MINITAB commands for the stem-and-leaf display on page 42 are:
   a. Import the data from the CD. The file name is Table 2–7. Use the MINITAB format.
   b. Select **Stat, EDA, Stem-and-leaf,** and then hit **Enter.**
   c. Select the variable **Spots,** enter *10* for the **Increment,** and then click **OK.**

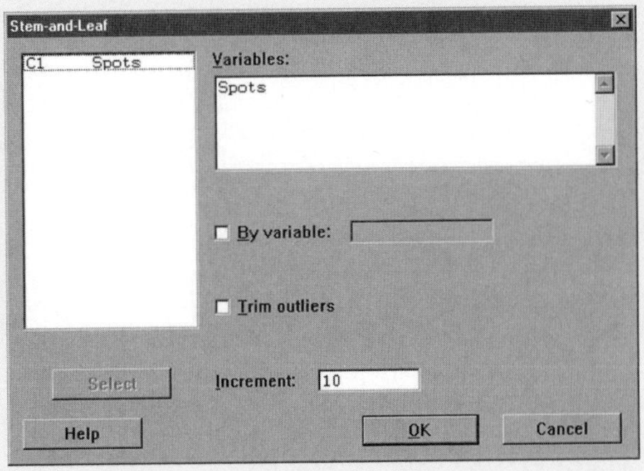

4. Excel commands for the pie chart on page 49 are:
   a. Set cell A1 as the active cell and type the words *Market Share.* In cells A2 through A6 enter the major networks: CBS, ABC, NBC, Fox, and Other.
   b. Set cell B1 as the active cell and type the word *Percent.* In cells B2 through B6 enter the values 24, 22, 26, 17, and 11.
   c. From the **Tool Bar** select the **Chart Wizard.** Select **Pie** as the chart type, select the chart type in the upper left corner, and then click on **Next.**
   d. For the Data Range type *A1:B6,* indicate that the data are in a column, and finally click on **Next.**
   e. Click on the chart title area and type *Share of Prime-Time Viewing for the Major Networks.* Then click **Finish.**

Chapter 2 Answers to Self-Review

2–1 **a.** The raw data.

b.

Commission	Number of Salespeople
$1,400 up to $1,500	2
1,500 up to 1,600	5
1,600 up to 1,700	3
1,700 up to 1,800	1
Total	11

c. Class frequencies.

d. The largest concentration of commissions is $1,500 up to $1,600. The smallest commission is about $1,400 and the largest is about $1,800.

2–2 **a.** $2^6 = 64 < 73 < 128 = 2^7$. So 7 classes are recommended.

b. The interval width should be at least $(488 - 320)/7 = 24$. Class limits of 25 or 30 feet are both reasonable.

c. If we use a class interval of 25 feet and begin with 300 feet, eight classes would be necessary. A class interval of 30 feet beginning with 300 feet is also reasonable. This alternative requires only seven classes.

2–3 **a.** 23

b. 28.75%, found by $(23/80) \times 100$

c. 7.5%, found by $(6/80) \times 100$

2–4 **a.**

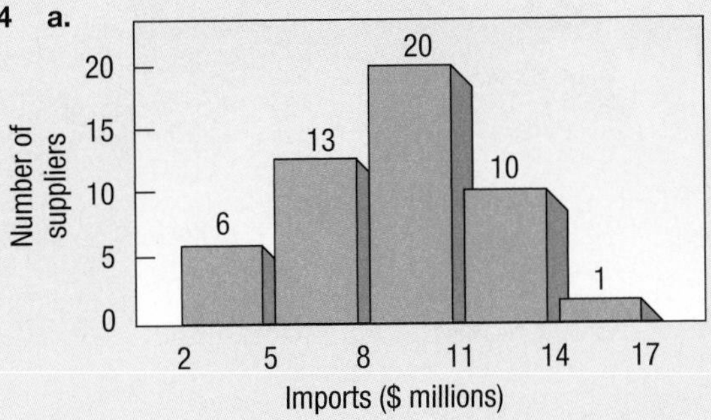

b.

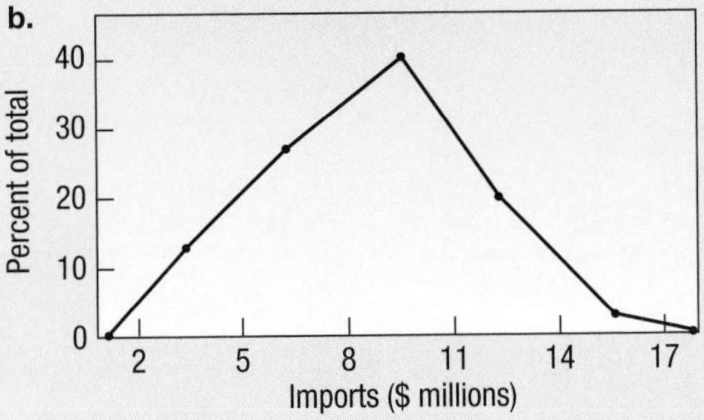

The plots are: (3.5, 12), (6.5, 26), (9.5, 40), (12.5, 20), and (15.5, 2).

c. The smallest annual sales volume of imports by a supplier is about $2 million, the highest about $17 million. The concentration is between $8 million and $11 million.

2–5 **a.** A frequency distribution.

b.

Hourly Wages	Cumulative Number
Less than $6	0
Less than $8	3
Less than $10	10
Less than $12	14
Less than $14	15

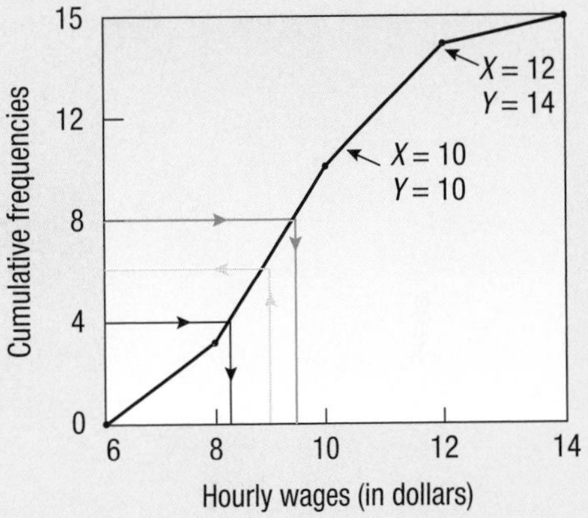

c. About seven employees earn $9.00 or less. About half the employees earn $9.25 or more. About four employees earn $8.25 or less.

2–6

7	7
8	0013488
9	1256689
10	1248
11	26

a. 8

b. 10.1, 10.2, 10.4, 10.8

c. 9.5

d. 7.7, 11.6

2–7

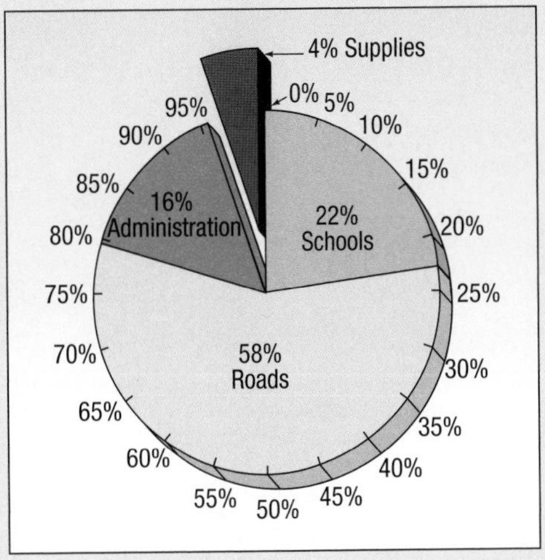

3

Describing Data:

Numerical Measures

GOALS

When you have completed this chapter, you will be able to:

1 **Calculate the *arithmetic mean, median, mode, weighted mean,* and *geometric mean.***

2 **Explain the characteristics, uses, advantages, and disadvantages of each *measure of location.***

3 **Identify the position of the *arithmetic mean, median,* and *mode* for both symmetric and skewed distributions.**

4 **Compute and interpret the *range, mean deviation, variance,* and *standard deviation.***

5 **Explain the characteristics, uses, advantages, and disadvantages of each *measure of dispersion.***

6 **Understand *Chebyshev's theorem* and the *Empirical Rule* as they relate to a set of observations.**

7 **Compute and interpret *quartiles, interquartile range,* and *percentiles.***

8 **Compute and interpret the *coefficient of skewness* and the *coefficient of variation.***

The weights (in pounds) of a sample of five boxes being sent by UPS are: 12, 6, 7, 3, and 10. Compute the standard deviation. (See Goal 4 and Exercise 86.)

Introduction

Chapter 2 began our study of descriptive statistics. To transform a mass of raw data into a meaningful form, we organized it into a frequency distribution and portrayed it graphically in a histogram or a frequency polygon. We also looked at other graphical techniques such as line charts and pie charts.

This chapter is concerned with two numerical ways of describing data, namely, **measures of location** and **measures of dispersion.** Measures of location are often referred to as **averages.** The purpose of a measure of central location is to pinpoint the center of a set of values.

Statistics in Action

Did you ever meet the "average" American man? Well, his name is Robert (that is the nominal level of measurement), he is 31 years old (that is the ratio level), he is 69.5 inches tall (again the ratio level of measurement), weighs 172 pounds, wears a size 9½ shoe, has a 34-inch waist, and wears a size 40 suit. In addition, the average man eats 4 pounds of potato chips, watches 2,567 hours of TV, and eats 26 pounds of bananas each year. Also, he sleeps 7.7 hours per night. Is this really an "average" man or would it be better to refer to him as a "typical" man? Would you expect to find a man with all these characteristics?

You are familiar with the concept of an average. Averages appear daily on TV, in the newspaper, and in news magazines. Here are some examples:

- The average U.S. home changes ownership every 11.8 years.
- The average price of a gallon of gasoline last week in South Carolina was $1.43, according to a study by the American Automobile Association.
- The average cost to drive a private automobile is 55.8 cents per mile in Los Angeles, 49.8 cents per mile in Boston, 49.0 cents per mile in Philadelphia.
- An American receives an average of 568 pieces of mail per year.
- The average starting salary for a business school graduate last year was $36,357. For a graduate with a Liberal Arts major it was $31,599.
- There are 26.4 million golfers over the age of 12 in the United States. Approximately 6.1 million are avid golfers, that is, they play an average of 25 rounds a year. Some additional information on golfers and golfing: the median cost of a round of golf on an 18-hole course at a municipal course in the United States is $30. Today's typical golfer is male, 40 years old, has a household income of $68,209, and plays 21.3 rounds per year.
- In Chicago the mean high temperature is 84 degrees in July and 31 in January. The mean amount of precipitation is 3.80 inches in July and 1.90 inches in January.

If we consider only the central value in a set of data, or if we compare several sets of data using central values, we may draw an erroneous conclusion. In addition to the central values, we should consider the **dispersion**—often called the *variation* or the *spread*—in the data. As an illustration, suppose the average annual income of marketing executives for Internet-related companies is $80,000, and the average income for executives in pharmaceutical firms is also $80,000. If we looked only at the average incomes, we might wrongly conclude that the two salary distributions are identical or nearly identical. A look at the salary ranges indicates that this conclusion is not correct. The salaries for the marketing executives in the Internet firms range from $70,000 to $90,000, but salaries for the marketing executives in pharmaceuticals range from $40,000 to $120,000. Thus, we conclude that although the average salaries are the same for the two industries, there is much more spread or dispersion in salaries for the pharmaceutical executives. To evaluate the dispersion we will consider the range, the mean deviation, the variance, and the standard deviation.

We begin by discussing measures of location. There is not just one measure of location; in fact, there are many. We will consider five: the arithmetic mean, the weighted mean, the median, the mode, and the geometric mean. The arithmetic mean is the most widely used and widely reported measure of central tendency. We study the mean as both a population parameter and a sample statistic.

The Population Mean

Many studies involve all the values in a population. For example, there are 39 exits on I-75 through the state of Kentucky. The mean distance between these state exits is 4.76 miles. This is an example of a population because we have studied *all* the exits. There are 12 sales associates employed at the Reynolds Road outlet of Carpets by Otto. The mean amount of commission they earned last month was $1,345. We consider this a population value because we considered *all* the sales associates. Other examples of a population mean would be: the mean closing price for Johnson and Johnson stock for the last 5 days is $48.75; the mean annual rate of return for the last 10 years for Berger Funds is 8.67 percent; and the mean number of hours of overtime worked last week by the six welders in the welding department of Butts Welding Inc. is 6.45 hours.

For raw data, that is, data that has not been grouped in a frequency distribution or a stem-and-leaf display, the population mean is the sum of all the values in the population divided by the number of values in the population. To find the population mean, we use the following formula.

$$\text{Population mean} = \frac{\text{Sum of all the values in the population}}{\text{Number of values in the population}}$$

Instead of writing out in words the full directions for computing the population mean (or any other measure), it is more convenient to use the shorthand symbols of mathematics. The mean of a population using mathematical symbols is:

POPULATION MEAN $$\mu = \frac{\Sigma X}{N} \qquad [3\text{–}1]$$

where:

μ represents the population mean. It is the Greek lowercase letter "mu."
N is the number of items in the population.
X represents any particular value.
Σ is the Greek capital letter "sigma" and indicates the operation of adding.
ΣX is the sum of the X values.

Any measurable characteristic of a population is called a **parameter.** The mean of a population is a parameter.

PARAMETER A characteristic of a population.

EXAMPLE

There are 12 automobile companies in the United States. Listed below is the number of patents granted by the United States government to each company last year.

Company	Number of Patents Granted	Company	Number of Patents Granted
General Motors	511	Mazda	210
Nissan	385	Chrysler	97
DaimlerChrysler	275	Porsche	50
Toyota	257	Mitsubishi	36
Honda	249	Volvo	23
Ford	234	BMW	13

Is this information a sample or a population? What is the arithmetic mean number of patents granted?

SOLUTION

This is a population because we are considering all the automobile companies obtaining patents. We add the number of patents for each of the 12 companies. The total number of patents for the 12 companies is 2,340. To find the arithmetic mean, we divide this total by 12. So the arithmetic mean is 195, found by 2340/12. Using formula (3–1):

$$\mu = \frac{511 + 385 + \cdots + 13}{12} = \frac{2340}{12} = 195$$

How do we interpret the value of 195? The typical number of patents received by an automobile company is 195. Because we considered all the companies receiving patents, this value is a population parameter.

The Sample Mean

As explained in Chapter 1, we often select a sample from the population to find something about a specific characteristic of the population. The quality assurance department, for example, needs to be assured that the ball bearings being produced have an acceptable outside diameter. It would be very expensive and time consuming to check the outside diameter of all the bearings produced. Therefore, a sample of five bearings is selected and the mean outside diameter of the five bearings is calculated to estimate the mean diameter of all the bearings.

For raw data, that is, ungrouped data, *the mean is the sum of all the sampled values divided by the total number of sampled values.* To find the mean for a sample:

Mean of ungrouped sample data

$$\text{Sample mean} = \frac{\text{Sum of all the values in the sample}}{\text{Number of values in the sample}}$$

The mean of a sample and the mean of a population are computed in the same way, but the shorthand notation used is different. The formula for the mean of a *sample* is:

SAMPLE MEAN $$\overline{X} = \frac{\Sigma X}{n}$$ **[3–2]**

where:

$\overline{X}$ is the sample mean. It is read "X bar."
n is the number in the sample.

The mean of a sample, or any other measure based on sample data, is called a **statistic**. If the mean outside diameter of a sample of five ball bearings is 0.625 inches, this is an example of a statistic.

STATISTIC A characteristic of a sample.

EXAMPLE

The Merrill Lynch Global Fund specializes in long-term obligations of foreign countries. We are interested in the interest rate on these obligations. A random sample of six bonds revealed the following.

Issue	Interest Rate
Australian government bonds	9.50%
Belgian government bonds	7.25
Canadian government bonds	6.50
French government "B-TAN"	4.75
Buoni Poliennali de Tesora (Italian government bonds)	12.00
Bonos del Estado (Spanish government bonds)	8.30

What is the arithmetic mean interest rate on this sample of long-term obligations?

SOLUTION

Using formula (3–2), the sample mean is:

$$\text{Sample mean} = \frac{\text{Sum of all the values in the sample}}{\text{Number of values in the sample}}$$

$$\overline{X} = \frac{\Sigma X}{n} = \frac{9.50\% + 7.25\% + \cdots + 8.30\%}{6} = \frac{48.3\%}{6} = 8.05\%$$

The arithmetic mean interest rate of the sample of long-term obligations is 8.05 percent.

The Properties of the Arithmetic Mean

The arithmetic mean is a widely used measure of central tendency. It has several important properties:

1. Every set of interval- or ratio-level data has a mean. (Recall from Chapter 1 that ratio-level data include such data as ages, incomes, and weights, with the distance between numbers being constant.)
2. All the values are included in computing the mean.
3. A set of data has only one mean. The mean is unique. (Later in the chapter we will discover an average that might appear twice, or more than twice, in a set of data.)
4. The mean is a useful measure for comparing two or more populations. It can, for example, be used to compare the performance of the production employees on the first shift at the Chrysler transmission plant with the performance of those on the second shift.

5. The arithmetic mean is the only measure of central tendency where *the sum of the deviations of each value from the mean will always be zero.* Expressed symbolically:

$$\Sigma(X - \overline{X}) = 0$$

As an example, the mean of 3, 8, and 4 is 5. Then:

$$\begin{aligned}\Sigma(X - \overline{X}) &= (3 - 5) + (8 - 5) + (4 - 5) \\ &= -2 + 3 - 1 \\ &= 0\end{aligned}$$

Mean as a balance point

Thus, we can consider the mean as a balance point for a set of data. To illustrate, we have a long board with the numbers 1, 2, 3, . . . , *n* evenly spaced on it. Suppose three bars of equal weight were placed on the board at numbers 3, 4, and 8, and the balance point was set at 5, the mean of the three numbers. We would find that the board balanced perfectly! The deviations below the mean (−3) are equal to the deviations above the mean (+3). Shown schematically:

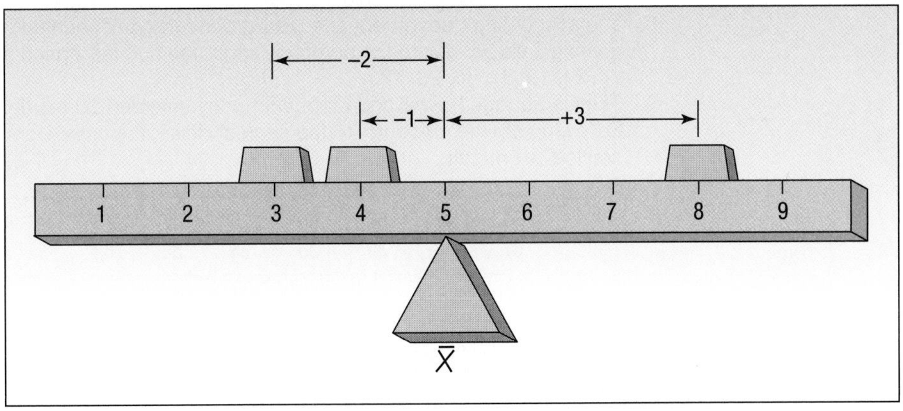

Mean unduly affected by unusually large or small values

The mean does have a major weakness. Recall that the mean uses the value of every item in a sample, or population, in its computation. If one or two of these values are either extremely large or extremely small, the mean might not be an appropriate average to represent the data. For example, suppose the annual incomes of a small group of stockbrokers at Merrill Lynch are \$62,900, \$61,600, \$62,500, \$60,800, and \$1.2 million. The mean income is \$289,560. Obviously, it is not representative of this group, because all but one broker has an income in the \$60,000 to \$63,000 range. One income (\$1.2 million) is unduly affecting the mean.

Self-Review 3–1

1. The annual incomes of a sample of several middle-management employees at Westinghouse are: \$62,900, \$69,100, \$58,300, and \$76,800.
   (a) Give the formula for the sample mean.
   (b) Find the sample mean.
   (c) Is the mean you computed in (b) a statistic or a parameter? Why?
   (d) What is your best estimate of the population mean?
2. All the students in advanced Computer Science 411 are considered the population. Their course grades are 92, 96, 61, 86, 79, and 84.
   (a) Give the formula for the population mean.
   (b) Compute the mean course grade.
   (c) Is the mean you computed in (b) a statistic or a parameter? Why?

Exercises

The answers to the odd-numbered exercises are at the end of the book.

1. Compute the mean of the following population values: 6, 3, 5, 7, 6.
2. Compute the mean of the following population values: 7, 5, 7, 3, 7, 4.
3. **a.** Compute the mean of the following sample values: 5, 9, 4, 10.
   b. Show that $\Sigma(X - \overline{X}) = 0$.
4. **a.** Compute the mean of the following sample values: 1.3, 7.0, 3.6, 4.1, 5.0.
   b. Show that $\Sigma(X - \overline{X}) = 0$.
5. Compute the mean of the following sample values: 16.25, 12.91, 14.58.
6. Compute the mean hourly wage paid to carpenters who earned the following wages: \$15.40, \$20.10, \$18.75, \$22.76, \$30.67, \$18.00.

For Exercises 7–10, (a) compute the arithmetic mean and (b) indicate whether it is a statistic or a parameter.

7. There are 10 salespeople employed by Midtown Ford. The numbers of new cars sold last month by the respective salespeople were: 15, 23, 4, 19, 18, 10, 10, 8, 28, 19.
8. The accounting department at a mail-order company counted the following numbers of incoming calls per day to the company's toll-free number during the first 7 days in May 2001: 14, 24, 19, 31, 36, 26, 17.
9. The Cambridge Power and Light Company selected 20 residential customers at random. Following are the amounts, to the nearest dollar, the customers were charged for electrical service last month:

54	48	58	50	25	47	75	46	60	70
67	68	39	35	56	66	33	62	65	67

10. The Human Relations Director at Mercy Hospital began a study of the overtime hours of the registered nurses. Fifteen RNs were selected at random, and these overtime hours during June were noted:

13	13	12	15	7	15	5	12
6	7	12	10	9	13	12	

The Weighted Mean

The weighted mean is a special case of the arithmetic mean. It occurs when there are several observations of the same value. To explain, suppose the nearby Wendy's Restaurant sold medium, large, and Biggie-sized soft drinks for \$.90, \$1.25, and \$1.50, respectively. Of the last 10 drinks sold, 3 were medium, 4 were large, and 3 were Biggie-sized. To find the mean price of the last 10 drinks sold, we could use formula (3–2).

$$\overline{X} = \frac{\$.90 + \$.90 + \$.90 + \$1.25 + \$1.25 + \$1.25 + \$1.25 + \$1.50 + \$1.50 + \$1.50}{10}$$

$$= \frac{\$12.20}{10} = \$1.22$$

The mean selling price of the last 10 drinks is \$1.22.

An easier way to find the mean selling price is to determine the weighted mean. That is, we multiply each observation by the number of times it happens. We will refer to the weighted mean as $\overline{X}_w$. This is read "X bar sub w."

$$\bar{X}_w = \frac{3(\$0.90) + 4(\$1.25) + 3(\$1.50)}{10} = \frac{\$12.20}{10} = \$1.22$$

In general the weighted mean of a set of numbers designated $X_1, X_2, X_3, \ldots, X_n$ with the corresponding weights $w_1, w_2, w_3, \ldots, w_n$ is computed by:

WEIGHTED MEAN $$\bar{X}_w = \frac{w_1X_1 + w_2X_2 + w_3X_3 + \cdots + w_nX_n}{w_1 + w_2 + w_3 + \cdots + w_n} \quad \textbf{[3–3]}$$

This may be shortened to:

$$\bar{X}_w = \frac{\Sigma(wX)}{\Sigma w}$$

EXAMPLE

The Carter Construction Company pays its hourly employees \$6.50, \$7.50, or \$8.50 per hour. There are 26 hourly employees, 14 are paid at the \$6.50 rate, 10 at the \$7.50 rate, and 2 at the \$8.50 rate. What is the mean hourly rate paid the 26 employees?

SOLUTION

To find the mean hourly rate, we multiply each of the hourly rates by the number of employees earning that rate. Using formula (3–3), the mean hourly rate is

$$\bar{X}_w = \frac{14(\$6.50) + 10(\$7.50) + 2(\$8.50)}{14 + 10 + 2} = \frac{\$183.00}{26} = \$7.038$$

The weighted mean hourly wage is rounded to \$7.04.

Self-Review 3–2

Springers sold 95 Antonelli men's suits for the regular price of \$400. For the spring sale the suits were reduced to \$200 and 126 were sold. At the final clearance, the price was reduced to \$100 and the remaining 79 suits were sold.

(a) What was the weighted mean price of an Antonelli suit?
(b) Springers paid \$200 a suit for the 300 suits. Comment on the store's profit per suit if a salesperson receives a \$25 commission for each one sold.

Exercises

11. In June an investor purchased 300 shares of Oracle stock at \$20 per share. In August she purchased an additional 400 shares at \$25 per share. In November she purchased an additional 400 shares, but the stock declined to \$23 per share. What is the weighted mean price per share?

12. The Bookstall, Inc., is a specialty bookstore concentrating on used books. Paperbacks are \$1.00 each, and hardcover books are \$3.50. Of the 50 books sold last Tuesday morning, 40 were paperback and the rest were hardcover. What was the weighted mean price of a book?

13. The Loris Healthcare System employs 200 persons on the nursing staff. Fifty are nurse's aides, 50 are practical nurses, and 100 are registered nurses. Nurse's aides receive \$8 an hour, practical nurses \$10 an hour, and registered nurses \$14 an hour. What is the weighted mean hourly wage?

14. Andrews and Associates specialize in corporate law. They charge \$100 an hour for researching a case, \$75 an hour for consultations, and \$200 an hour for writing a brief. Last week one of the associates spent 10 hours consulting with her client, 10 hours researching the case, and 20 hours writing the brief. What was the weighted mean hourly charge for her legal services?

The Median

We have stressed that for data containing one or two very large or very small values, the arithmetic mean may not be representative. The center point for such data can be better described using a measure of location called the **median.**

To illustrate the need for a measure of central tendency other than the arithmetic mean, suppose you are seeking to buy a condominium in Palm Aire. Your real estate agent says that the average price of the units currently available is $110,000. Would you still want to look? If you had budgeted your maximum purchase price between $60,000 and $75,000, you might think they are out of your price range. However, checking the individual prices of the units might change your mind. They are $60,000, $65,000, $70,000, $80,000, and a superdeluxe penthouse costs $275,000. The arithmetic mean price is $110,000, as the real estate agent reported, but one price ($275,000) is pulling the arithmetic mean upward, causing it to be an unrepresentative average. It does seem that a price between $65,000 and $75,000 is a more typical or representative average, and it is. In cases such as this, the median provides a more valid measure of location.

MEDIAN The midpoint of the values after they have been ordered from the smallest to the largest, or the largest to the smallest.

The data must be at least ordinal level of measurement. The median price of the units available is $70,000. To determine this, we ordered the prices from low ($60,000) to high ($275,000) and selected the middle value ($70,000).

Prices Ordered from Low to High		Prices Ordered from High to Low
$ 60,000		$275,000
65,000		80,000
70,000	← Median →	70,000
80,000		65,000
275,000		60,000

Median unaffected by extreme values

Note that there are the same number of prices below the median of $70,000 as above it. There are as many values below the median as above. The median is, therefore, unaffected by extremely low or high prices. Had the highest price been $90,000, or $300,000, or even $1 million, the median price would still be $70,000. Likewise, had the lowest price been $20,000 or $50,000, the median price would still be $70,000.

In the previous illustration there is an *odd* number of observations (five). How is the median determined for an *even* number of observations? As before, the observations are ordered. Then we calculate the mean of the two middle observations. Note that for an even number of observations, the median may not be one of the given values.

EXAMPLE

The five-year annualized total returns of the six top-performing stock mutual funds with emphasis on aggressive growth are listed below. What is the median annualized return?

Name of Fund	Annualized Total Return
PBHG Growth	28.5%
Dean Witter Developing Growth	17.2
AIM Aggressive Growth	25.4
Twentieth Century Giftrust	28.6
Robertson Stevens Emerging Growth	22.6
Seligman Frontier A	21.0

SOLUTION

Note that the number of returns is *even* (6). As before, the returns are first ordered from low to high. Then the two middle returns are identified. The arithmetic mean of the two middle observations gives us the median return. Arranging from low to high:

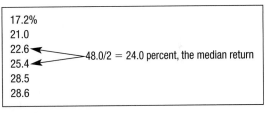

17.2%
21.0
22.6 ←
25.4 ← 48.0/2 = 24.0 percent, the median return
28.5
28.6

Notice that the median is not one of the values. Also, half of the returns are below the median and half are above it.

The major properties of the median are:

1. The median is unique; that is, like the mean, there is only one median for a set of data.
2. It is not affected by extremely large or small values and is therefore a valuable measure of location when such values do occur.
3. It can be computed for ratio-level, interval-level, and ordinal-level data. (Recall from Chapter 1 that ordinal-level data can be ranked from low to high—such as the responses "excellent," "very good," "good," "fair," and "poor" to a question on a marketing survey.) To use a simple illustration, suppose five people rated a new fudge bar. One person thought it was excellent, one rated it very good, one called it good, one rated it fair, and one considered it poor. The median response is "good." Half of the responses are above "good"; the other half are below it.

Median can be determined for all levels of data except nominal

The Mode

The **mode** is another measure of central tendency.

MODE The value of the observation that appears most frequently.

The mode is especially useful in describing nominal and ordinal levels of measurement. As an example of its use for nominal-level data, a company has developed five bath oils. Chart 3–1 shows the results of a marketing survey designed to find which bath oil consumers prefer. The largest number of respondents favored Lamoure, as evidenced by the highest bar. Thus, Lamoure is the mode.

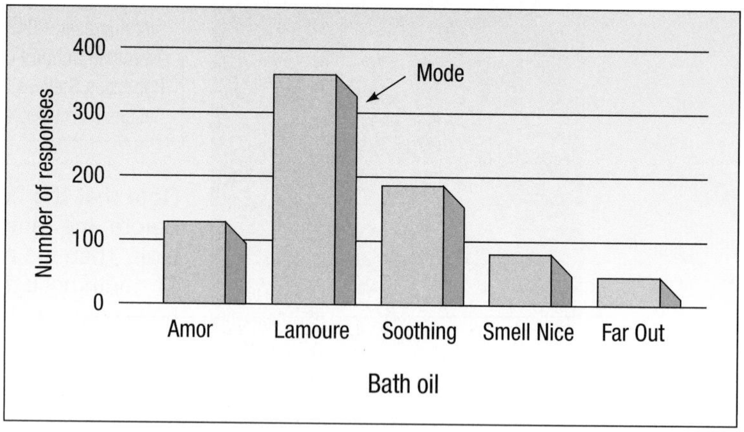

CHART 3–1 Number of Respondents Favoring Various Bath Oils

EXAMPLE

The annual salaries of quality-control managers in selected states are shown below. What is the modal annual salary?

State	Salary	State	Salary	State	Salary
Arizona	$35,000	Illinois	$58,000	Ohio	$50,000
California	49,100	Louisiana	60,000	Tennessee	60,000
Colorado	60,000	Maryland	60,000	Texas	71,400
Florida	60,000	Massachusetts	40,000	West Virginia	60,000
Idaho	40,000	New Jersey	65,000	Wyoming	55,000

SOLUTION

A perusal of the salaries reveals that the annual salary of $60,000 appears more often (six times) than any other salary. The mode is, therefore, $60,000.

In summary, we can determine the mode for all levels of data—nominal, ordinal, interval, and ratio. The mode also has the advantage of not being affected by extremely high or low values.

Disadvantages of the mode

The mode does have a number of disadvantages, however, that cause it to be used less frequently than the mean or median. For many sets of data, there is no mode because no value appears more than once. For example, there is no mode for this set of price data: $19, $21, $23, $20, and $18. Since every value is different, however, it could be argued that every value is the mode. Conversely, for some data sets there is more than one mode. Suppose the ages of a group are 22, 26, 27, 27, 31, 35, and 35. Both the ages 27 and 35 are modes. Thus, this grouping of ages is referred to as *bimodal* (having two modes). One would question the use of two modes to represent the central tendency of this set of age data.

Self-Review 3–3

1. A sample of single persons in Towson, Texas, receiving Social Security payments revealed these monthly benefits: $426, $299, $290, $687, $480, $439, and $565.
   (a) What is the median monthly benefit?
   (b) How many observations are below the median? Above it?
2. The numbers of work stoppages in the automobile industry for selected months are 6, 0, 10, 14, 8, and 0.
   (a) What is the median number of stoppages?
   (b) How many observations are below the median? Above it?
   (c) What is the modal number of work stoppages?

Exercises

15. What would you report as the modal value for a set of observations if there were a total of:
   a. 10 observations and no two values were the same?
   b. 6 observations and they were all the same?
   c. 6 observations and the values were 1, 2, 3, 3, 4, and 4?

For Exercises 16–19, (a) determine the median and (b) the mode.

16. The following is the number of oil changes for the last 7 days at the Jiffy Lube located at the corner of Elm Street and Pennsylvania Ave.

41	15	39	54	31	15	33

17. The following is the percent change in net income from 2000 to 2001 for a sample of 12 construction companies in Denver.

5	1	−10	−6	5	12	7	8	2	5	−1	11

18. The following are the ages of the 10 people in the video arcade at the Southwyck Shopping Mall at 10 A.M. this morning.

12	8	17	6	11	14	8	17	10	8

19. Listed below are several indicators of long-term economic growth in the United States. The projections are through the year 2005.

Economic Indicator	Percent Change	Economic Indicator	Percent Change
Inflation	4.5	Real GNP	2.9
Exports	4.7	Investment (residential)	3.6
Imports	2.3	Investment (nonresidential)	2.1
Real disposable income	2.9	Productivity (total)	1.4
Consumption	2.7	Productivity (manufacturing)	5.2

   a. What is the median percent change?
   b. What is the modal percent change?

20. Listed below are the total automobile sales (in millions) in the United States for the last 14 years. During this period, what was the median number of automobiles sold? What is the mode?

9.0	8.5	8.0	9.1	10.3	11.0	11.5	10.3	10.5	9.8	9.3	8.2	8.2	8.5

Computer Solution

We can use a computer software package to find many measures of central tendency.

EXAMPLE

Table 2–1 on page 23 shows the prices of the 80 vehicles sold last month at Whitner Pontiac. Determine the mean and the median selling price.

SOLUTION

The mean and the median selling prices are reported in the following Excel output. (Remember: The instructions to create the output appear in the **Computer Commands** section at the end of the chapter.) There are 80 vehicles in the study, so the calculations with a calculator would be tedious and prone to error.

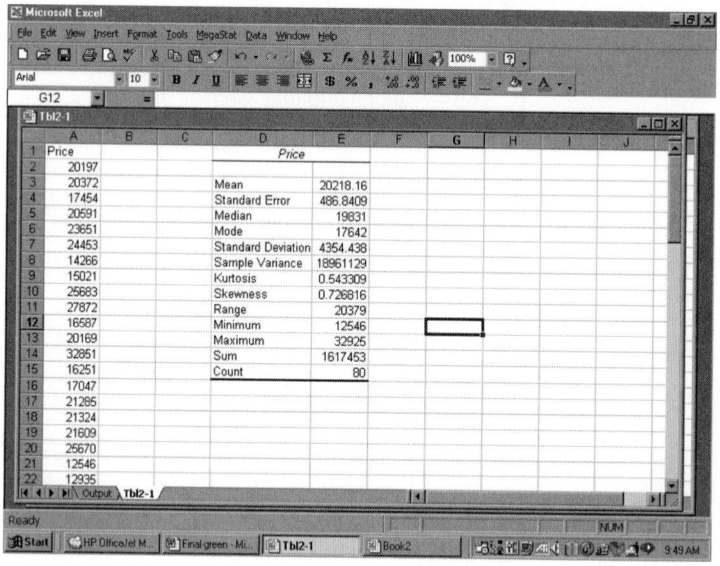

The mean selling price is $20,218 and the median is $19,831. These two values are less than $400 apart. So either value is reasonable. We can also see from the Excel output that there were 80 vehicles sold and their total price is $1,617,453.

What can we conclude? The typical vehicle sold for about $20,000. Mr. Whitner might use this value in his revenue projections. For example, if the dealership could increase the number sold in a month from 80 to 90, this would result in an additional $200,000 of revenue, found by 10 × $20,000.

The Relative Positions of the Mean, Median, and Mode

For a symmetric, mound-shaped distribution, mean, median, and mode are equal.

Refer to the frequency polygon in Chart 3–2. It is a symmetric distribution, which is also mound-shaped. This distribution *has the same shape on either side of the center.* If the polygon were folded in half, the two halves would be identical. For this symmetric distribution, the mode, median, and mean are located at the center and are always equal. They are all equal to 20 years in Chart 3–2. We should point out that there are symmetric distributions that are not mound-shaped.

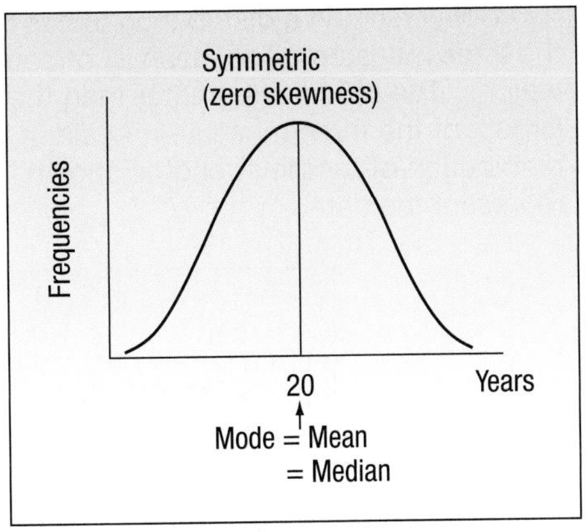

CHART 3–2 A Symmetric Distribution

The number of years corresponding to the highest point of the curve is the *mode* (20 years). Because the frequency curve is symmetrical, the *median* corresponds to the point where the distribution is cut in half (20 years). The total number of frequencies representing many years is offset by the total number representing few years, resulting in an *arithmetic mean* of 20 years. Logically, any of the three measures would be appropriate to represent this distribution.

A skewed distribution is not symmetrical.

If a distribution is nonsymmetrical, or **skewed,** the relationship among the three measures changes. In a **positively skewed distribution,** the arithmetic mean is the largest of the three measures. Why? Because the mean is influenced more than the median or mode by a few extremely high values. The median is generally the next largest measure in a positively skewed frequency distribution. The mode is the smallest of the three measures.

If the distribution is highly skewed, such as the weekly incomes in Chart 3–3, the mean would not be a good measure to use. The median and mode would be more representative.

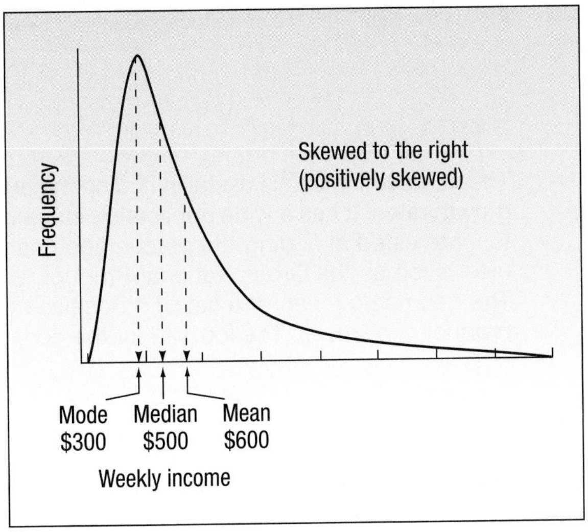

CHART 3–3 A Positively Skewed Distribution

Conversely, in a distribution that is **negatively skewed,** the mean is the lowest of the three measures. The mean is, of course, influenced by a few extremely low observations. The median is greater than the arithmetic mean, and the modal value is the largest of the three measures. Again, if the distribution is highly skewed, such as the distribution of tensile strengths shown in Chart 3–4, the mean should not be used to represent the data.

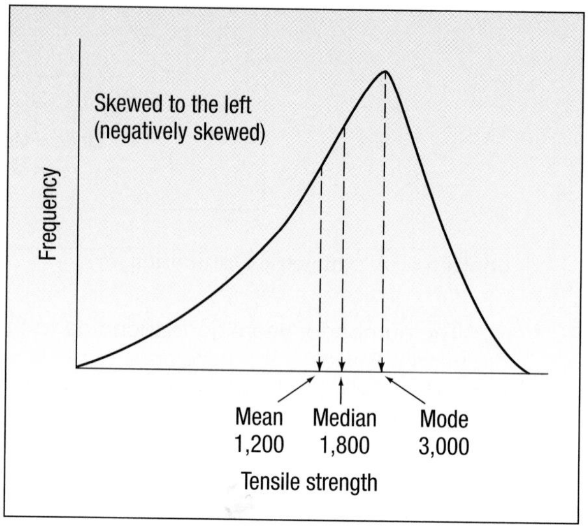

CHART 3–4 A Negatively Skewed Distribution

Self-Review 3–4

The weekly sales from a sample of Hi-Tec electronic supply stores were organized into a frequency distribution. The mean of weekly sales was computed to be \$105,900, the median \$105,000, and the mode \$104,500.

(a) Sketch the sales in the form of a smoothed frequency polygon. Note the location of the mean, median, and mode on the *X*-axis.
(b) Is the distribution symmetrical, positively skewed, or negatively skewed? Explain.

The Geometric Mean

The geometric mean is never greater than the arithmetic mean.

The geometric mean is useful in finding the average of percentages, ratios, indexes, or growth rates. It has a wide application in business and economics because we are often interested in finding the percentage changes in sales, salaries, or economic figures, such as the Gross National Product, which compound or build on each other. The geometric mean of a set of *n* positive numbers is defined as the *n*th root of the product of *n* values. The formula for the geometric mean is written:

GEOMETRIC MEAN

$$GM = \sqrt[n]{(X_1)(X_2)\cdots(X_n)} \qquad \textbf{[3–4]}$$

The geometric mean will always be less than or equal to (never more than) the arithmetic mean. Also all the data values must be positive.

As an example of the geometric mean, suppose you receive a 5 percent increase in salary this year and a 15 percent increase next year. The average percent increase is

9.886, not 10.0. Why is this so? We begin by calculating the geometric mean. Recall, for example, that a 5 percent increase in salary is 105 or 1.05. We will write it as 1.05.

$$GM = \sqrt{(1.05)(1.15)} = 1.09886$$

This can be verified by assuming that your monthly earning was $3,000 to start and you received two increases of 5 percent and 15 percent.

Raise 1 = $3,000 (.05) =	$150.00
Raise 2 = $3,150 (.15) =	472.50
Total	$622.50

Your total salary increase is $622.50. This is equivalent to:

$3,000.00 (.09886) =	$296.58
$3,296.58 (.09886) =	325.90
	$622.48 is about $622.50

The following example shows the geometric mean of several percentages.

EXAMPLE

The return on investment earned by Atkins Construction Company for four successive years was: 30 percent, 20 percent, −40 percent, and 200 percent. What is the geometric mean rate of return on investment?

SOLUTION

The number 1.3 represents the 30 percent return on investment, which is the "original" investment of 1.0 plus the "return" of 0.3. The number 0.6 represents the loss of 40 percent, which is the original investment of 1.0 reduced by 40 percent (−0.4). This calculation assumes the total return each period is reinvested or becomes the base for the next period. In other words, the base for the second period is 1.3 and the base for the third period is (1.3)(1.2) and so forth.

Then the geometric mean rate of return is 29.4 percent, found by

$$GM = \sqrt[n]{(X_1)(X_2) \cdots (X_n)} = \sqrt[4]{(1.3)(1.2)(0.6)(3.0)} = 1.294$$

The geometric mean is the fourth root of 2.808. So, the average rate of return (compound annual growth rate) is 29.4 percent. In other words, if Dunking Construction started with the same capital that Atkins had and earned a return on investment of 29.4 percent per year for four successive years, they would be in exactly the same position.

Notice also that if you compute the arithmetic mean [(30 + 20 − 40 + 200)/4 = 52.5], you would have a much larger number, which would overstate the true rate of return!

A second application of the geometric mean is to find an average percent increase over a period of time. For example, if you earned $30,000 in 1992 and $50,000 in 2002, what is your annual rate of increase over the period? The rate of increase is determined from the following formula.

AVERAGE PERCENT INCREASE OVER TIME

$$GM = \sqrt[n]{\frac{\text{Value at end of period}}{\text{Value at beginning of period}}} - 1 \qquad \textbf{[3–5]}$$

In the above box n is the number of periods. An example will show the details of finding the average annual percent increase.

EXAMPLE

The population of Haarlan, Alaska, in 1992 was 2 persons, by 2002 it was 22. What is the average annual rate of percentage increase during the period?

SOLUTION

There are 10 years between 1992 and 2002 so $n = 10$. The formula (3–5) for the geometric mean as applied to this type of problem is:

$$GM = \sqrt[n]{\frac{\text{Value at end of period}}{\text{Value at beginning of period}}} - 1$$

$$= \sqrt[10]{\frac{22}{2}} - 1 = 1.271 - 1 = 0.271$$

The final value is 0.271. So the annual rate of increase is 27.1 percent. This means that the rate of population growth in Haarlan is 27.1 percent per year.

Self-Review 3–5

1. The annual dividends, in percent, for the last 4 years at Combs Cosmetics are: 4.91, 5.75, 8.12, and 21.60.
   (a) Find the geometric mean dividend.
   (b) Find the arithmetic mean dividend.
   (c) Is the arithmetic mean equal to or greater than the geometric mean?
2. Production of Cablos trucks increased from 23,000 units in 1982 to 120,520 units in 2002. Find the geometric mean annual percent increase.

Exercises

21. Compute the geometric mean of the following percent increases: 8, 12, 14, 26, and 5.

22. Compute the geometric mean of the following percent increases: 2, 8, 6, 4, 10, 6, 8, and 4.

23. Listed below is the percent increase in sales for the MG Corporation over the last 5 years. Determine the geometric mean percent increase in sales over the period.

9.4	13.8	11.7	11.9	14.7

24. In 1998 revenue from gambling was \$651 million. In 2001 the revenue increased to \$2.4 billion. What is the geometric mean annual increase for the period?

25. In 1988 hospitals spent 3.9 billion on computer systems. In 2001 this amount increased to \$14.0 billion. What is the geometric mean annual increase for the period?

26. In 1990 there were 9.19 million cable TV subscribers. By 2000 the number of subscribers increased to 54.87 million. What is the geometric mean annual increase for the period?

27. In 1996 there were 42.0 million pager subscribers. By 2001 the number of subscribers increased to 70.0 million. What is the geometric mean annual increase for the period?

28. The information below shows the cost for a year of college in public and private colleges in 1990 and 2001. What is the geometric mean annual increase for the period for the two types of colleges? Compare the rates of increase.

Type of College	1990	2001
Public	$ 4,975	$ 8,954
Private	12,284	22,608

Why Study Dispersion?

A measure of location, such as the mean or the median, only describes the center of the data. It is valuable from that standpoint, but it does not tell us anything about the spread of the data. For example, if your nature guide told you that the river ahead averaged 3 feet in depth, would you cross it without additional information? Probably not. You would want to know something about the variation in the depth. Is the maximum depth of the river 3.25 feet and the minimum 2.75 feet? If that is the case, you would probably agree to cross. What if you learned the river depth ranged from 0.50 feet to 5.5 feet? Your decision would probably be not to cross. Before making a decision about crossing the river, you want information on both the typical depth and the dispersion in the depth of the river.

A small value for a measure of dispersion indicates that the data are clustered closely, say, around the arithmetic mean. The mean is therefore considered representative of the data. Conversely, a large measure of dispersion indicates that the mean is not reliable. Refer to Chart 3–5. The 100 employees of Hammond Iron Works, Inc., a steel fabricating company, are organized into a histogram based on the number of years of employment with the company. The mean is 4.9 years, but the spread of the data is from 6 months to 16.8 years. The mean of 4.9 years is not very representative of all the employees.

The average is not representative because of the large spread.

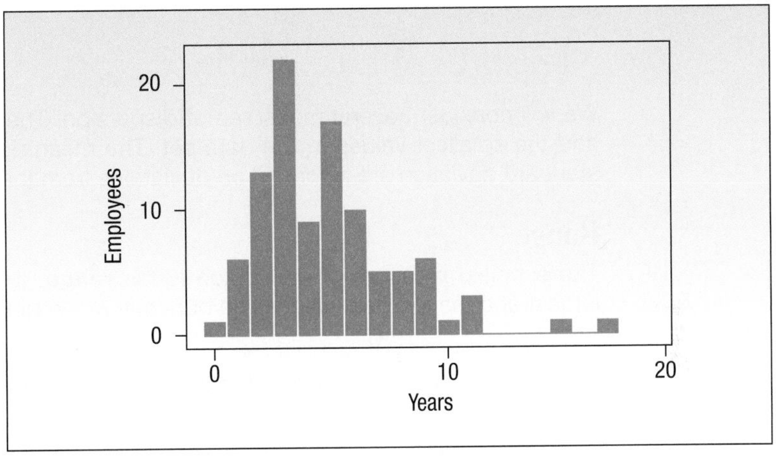

CHART 3–5 Histogram of Years of Employment at Hammond Iron Works, Inc.

A second reason for studying the dispersion in a set of data is to compare the spread in two or more distributions. Suppose, for example, that the new PDM/3 computer is assembled in Baton Rouge and also in Tucson. The arithmetic mean hourly output in both the Baton Rouge plant and the Tucson plant is 50. Based on the two means, one might conclude that the distributions of the hourly outputs are identical. Production records for 9 hours at the two plants, however, reveal that this conclusion is not correct (see Chart 3–6). Baton Rouge production varies from 48 to 52 assemblies per hour. Production at the Tucson plant is more erratic, ranging from 40 to 60 per hour. Therefore, the hourly output for Baton Rouge is clustered near the mean of 50; the hourly output for Tucson is more dispersed.

A measure of dispersion can be used to evaluate the reliability of two or more measures of location.

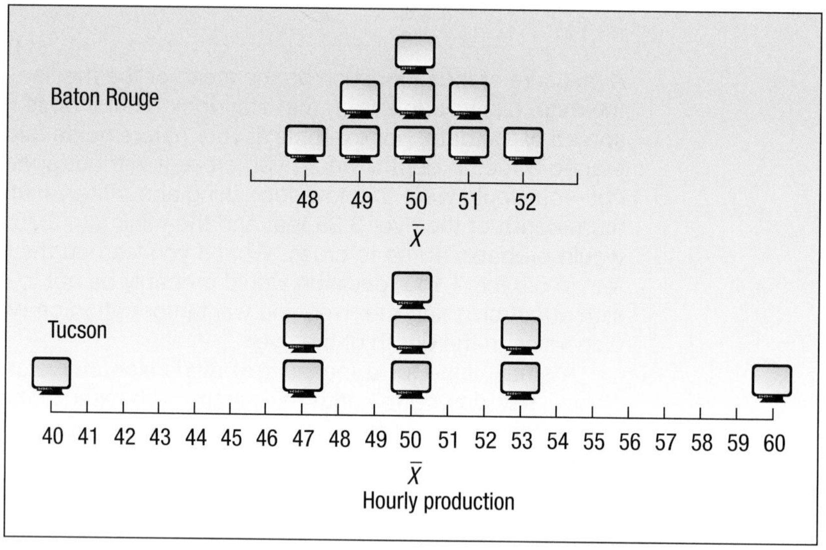

CHART 3–6 Hourly Production of Computers at the Baton Rouge and Tucson Plants

Measures of Dispersion

We will consider several measures of dispersion. The range is based on the largest and the smallest values in the data set. The mean deviation, the variance, and the standard deviation are all based on deviations from the arithmetic mean.

Range

The simplest measure of dispersion is the **range.** It is the difference between the largest and the smallest values in a data set. In the form of an equation:

RANGE Range = Largest value − Smallest value **[3–6]**

The range is widely used in statistical process control (SPC) applications because it is very easy to calculate and understand.

EXAMPLE

Refer to Chart 3–6. Find the range in the number of computers produced per hour for the Baton Rouge and the Tucson plants. Interpret the two ranges.

SOLUTION

The range of the hourly production of computers at the Baton Rouge plant is 4, found by the difference between the largest hourly production of 52 and the smallest of 48. The range in the hourly production for the Tucson plant is 20 computers, found by 60 − 40. We therefore conclude that (1) there is less dispersion in the hourly production in the Baton Rouge plant than in the Tucson plant because the range of 4 computers is less than a range of 20 computers, and (2) the production is clustered more closely around the mean of 50 at the Baton Rouge plant than at the Tucson plant (because a range of 4 is less than a range of 20). Thus, the mean production in the Baton Rouge plant (50 computers) is a more representative measure of location than the mean of 50 computers for the Tucson plant.

Statistics in Action

The United States Postal Service has tried to become more "user friendly" in the last several years. A recent survey showed that customers were interested in more *consistency* in the time it takes to make a delivery. Under the old conditions, a local letter might take only one day to deliver, or it might take several. "Just tell me how many days ahead I need to mail the birthday card to Mom so it gets there on her birthday, not early, not late," was a common complaint. The level of consistency is measured by the standard deviation of the delivery times. A smaller standard deviation indicates more consistency.

Mean Deviation

A serious defect of the range is that it is based on only two values, the highest and the lowest; it does not take into consideration all of the values. The **mean deviation** does. It measures the mean amount by which the values in a population, or sample, vary from their mean. In terms of a definition:

MEAN DEVIATION The arithmetic mean of the absolute values of the deviations from the arithmetic mean.

In terms of a formula, the mean deviation, designated *MD,* is computed for a sample by:

MEAN DEVIATION
$$MD = \frac{\Sigma|X - \overline{X}|}{n} \qquad \textbf{[3–7]}$$

where:

- X is the value of each observation.
- $\overline{X}$ is the arithmetic mean of the values.
- n is the number of observations in the sample.
- $||$ indicates the absolute value.

Why do we ignore the signs of the deviations from the mean? If we didn't, the positive and negative deviations from the mean would exactly offset each other, and the mean deviation would always be zero. Such a measure (zero) would be a useless statistic.

EXAMPLE

The number of patients seen in the emergency room at St. Luke's Memorial Hospital for a sample of 5 days last year were: 103, 97, 101, 106, and 103. Determine the mean deviation and interpret.

SOLUTION

The mean deviation is the mean of the amounts that individual observations differ from the arithmetic mean. To find the mean deviation of a set of data, we begin by finding the arithmetic mean. The mean number of patients is 102, found by (103 + 97 + 101 + 106 + 103) / 5. Next we find the amount by which each observation differs from the mean. Then we sum these differences, ignoring the signs, and divide the sum by the number of observations. The result is the mean amount the observations differ from the mean. A small value for the mean deviation indicates the mean is representative of the data, whereas a large value for the mean deviation indicates dispersion in the data. Below are the details of the calculations using formula (3–7).

Number of Cases	$(X - \bar{X})$	Absolute Deviation
103	(103 − 102) = 1	1
97	(97 − 102) = −5	5
101	(101 − 102) = −1	1
106	(106 − 102) = 4	4
103	(103 − 102) = 1	1
		Total 12

$$MD = \frac{\Sigma|X - \bar{X}|}{n} = \frac{12}{5} = 2.4$$

The mean deviation is 2.4 patients per day. The number of patients deviates, on average, by 2.4 patients from the mean of 102 patients per day.

Advantages of mean deviation

The mean deviation has two advantages. First, it uses all the values in the computation. Recall that the range uses only the highest and the lowest values. Second, it is easy to understand—it is the average amount by which values deviate from the mean. However, its major drawback is the use of absolute values. Generally, absolute values are difficult to work with, so the mean deviation is not used as frequently as other measures of dispersion, such as the standard deviation.

Self-Review 3–6

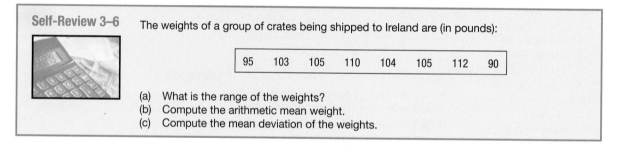

The weights of a group of crates being shipped to Ireland are (in pounds):

95	103	105	110	104	105	112	90

(a) What is the range of the weights?
(b) Compute the arithmetic mean weight.
(c) Compute the mean deviation of the weights.

Exercises

For Exercises 29–34, calculate the (a) range, (b) arithmetic mean, and (c) mean deviation, and (d) interpret the range and the mean deviation.

29. There were five customer service representatives on duty at the Electronic Super Store during last Friday's sale. The numbers of VCRs these representatives sold are: 5, 8, 4, 10, and 3.

30. The Department of Statistics at Western State University offers eight sections of basic statistics. Following are the numbers of students enrolled in these sections: 34, 46, 52, 29, 41, 38, 36, and 28.

31. Dave's Automatic Door installs automatic garage door openers. The following list indicates the number of minutes needed to install a sample of 10 doors: 28, 32, 24, 46, 44, 40, 54, 38, 32, and 42.

32. A sample of eight companies in the aerospace industry was surveyed as to their return on investment last year. The results are (in percent): 10.6, 12.6, 14.8, 18.2, 12.0, 14.8, 12.2, and 15.6.

33. Ten experts rated a newly developed pizza on a scale of 1 to 50. The ratings were: 34, 35, 41, 28, 26, 29, 32, 36, 38, and 40.

34. A sample of the personnel files of eight employees at Acme Carpet Cleaners, Inc. revealed that, during a six-month period, they lost the following numbers of days due to illness: 2, 0, 6, 3, 10, 4, 1, and 2.

Variance and standard deviation are based on squared deviations from the mean.

Variance and Standard Deviation

The **variance** and **standard deviation** are also based on the deviations from the mean. However, instead of using the absolute value of the deviations, the variance, and the standard deviation square the deviations.

> **VARIANCE** The arithmetic mean of the squared deviations from the mean.

Note that the variance is nonnegative, and it is zero only if all observations are the same.

> **STANDARD DEVIATION** The square root of the variance.

Population Variance The formulas for the population variance and the sample variance are slightly different. The population variance is considered first. (Recall that a population is the totality of all observations being studied.) The **population variance** is found by:

POPULATION VARIANCE

$$\sigma^2 = \frac{\Sigma(X - \mu)^2}{N} \qquad \textbf{[3–8]}$$

where:

- σ^2 is the symbol for the population variance (σ is the lowercase Greek letter sigma). It is usually referred to as "sigma squared."
- X is the value of an observation in the population.
- μ is the arithmetic mean of the population.
- N is the number of observations in the population.

EXAMPLE

The ages of all the patients in the isolation ward of Yellowstone Hospital are 38, 26, 13, 41, and 22 years. What is the population variance?

SOLUTION

Age (X)	$X - \mu$	$(X - \mu)^2$
38	+10	100
26	−2	4
13	−15	225
41	+13	169
22	−6	36
140	0*	534

$$\mu = \frac{\Sigma X}{N} = \frac{140}{5} = 28$$

$$\sigma^2 = \frac{\Sigma(X - \mu)^2}{N} = \frac{534}{5} = 106.8$$

*Sum of the deviations from mean must equal zero.

Like the range and the mean deviation, the variance can be used to compare the dispersion in two or more sets of observations. For example, the variance for the ages of the patients in isolation was just computed to be 106.8. If the variance in the ages of the cancer patients in the hospital is 342.9, we conclude that (1) there is less dispersion in the distribution of the ages of patients in isolation than in the age distribution of all cancer patients (because 106.8 is less than 342.9); and (2) the ages of the patients in isolation are clustered more closely about the mean of 28 years than the ages of those in the cancer ward. Thus, the mean age for the patients in isolation is a more representative measure of location than the mean for all cancer patients.

Variance is difficult to interpret because the units are squared.

Population Standard Deviation Both the range and the mean deviation are easy to interpret. The range is the difference between the high and low values of a set of data, and the mean deviation is the mean of the deviations from the mean. However, the variance is difficult to interpret for a single set of observations. The variance of 106.8 for the ages of the patients in isolation is not in terms of years, but rather "years squared."

Standard deviation is in the same units as the data.

There is a way out of this dilemma. By taking the square root of the population variance, we can transform it to the same unit of measurement used for the original data. The square root of 106.8 years-squared is 10.3 years. The square root of the population variance is called the **population standard deviation.**

POPULATION STANDARD DEVIATION

$$\sigma = \sqrt{\frac{\Sigma(X - \mu)^2}{N}} \qquad [3\text{–}9]$$

Self-Review 3-7

The Philadelphia office of Price Waterhouse Coopers LLP hired five accounting trainees this year. Their monthly starting salaries were: $2,536; $2,173; $2,448; $2,121; and $2,622.

(a) Compute the population mean.
(b) Compute the population variance.
(c) Compute the population standard deviation.
(d) The Pittsburgh office hired six trainees. Their mean monthly salary was $2,550, and the standard deviation was $250. Compare the two groups.

Exercises

35. Consider these five values a population: 8, 3, 7, 3, and 4.
 a. Determine the mean of the population.
 b. Determine the variance.

36. Consider these six values a population: 13, 3, 8, 10, 8, and 6.
 a. Determine the mean of the population.
 b. Determine the variance.

37. The annual report of Dennis Industries cited these primary earnings per common share for the past 5 years: $2.68, $1.03, $2.26, $4.30, and $3.58. If we assume these are population values, what is:
 a. The arithmetic mean primary earnings per share of common stock?
 b. The variance?

38. Referring to Exercise 37, the annual report of Dennis Industries also gave these returns on stockholder equity for the same five-year period (in percent): 13.2, 5.0, 10.2, 17.5, and 12.9.
 a. What is the arithmetic mean return?
 b. What is the variance?

39. Plywood, Inc. reported these returns on stockholder equity for the past 5 years: 4.3, 4.9, 7.2, 6.7, and 11.6. Consider these as population values.
 a. Compute the range, the arithmetic mean, the variance, and the standard deviation.
 b. Compare the return on stockholder equity for Plywood, Inc. with that for Dennis Industries cited in Exercise 38.

40. The annual incomes of the five vice presidents of TMV Industries are: $75,000; $78,000; $72,000; $83,000; and $90,000. Consider this a population.
 a. What is the range?
 b. What is the arithmetic mean income?
 c. What is the population variance? The standard deviation?

d. The annual incomes of officers of another firm similar to TMV Industries were also studied. The mean was $79,000 and the standard deviation $8,612. Compare the means and dispersions in the two firms.

Statistics in Action

Larry Walker of the Colorado Rockies and Ichiro Suzuki of the Seattle Mariners tied for the highest batting average at .350 during the 2001 Major League Baseball season. The highest batting average in recent times was by Tony Gwynn, .394 in 1994, but this was during a strike-shortened season. Ted Williams batted .406 in 1941, and nobody has hit over .400 since. The mean batting average has remained constant at about .260 for more than 100 years, but the standard deviation of that average has declined from .049 to .031. This indicates less dispersion in the batting averages today and helps explain the lack of any .400 hitters in recent times.

Sample Variance The formula for the population mean is $\mu = \Sigma X/N$. We just changed the symbols for the sample mean, that is $\overline{X} = \Sigma X/n$. Unfortunately, the conversion from the population variance to the sample variance is not as direct. It requires a change in the denominator. Instead of substituting n (number in the sample) for N (number in the population), the denominator is $n - 1$. Thus the formula for the **sample variance** is:

SAMPLE VARIANCE, DEVIATION FORMULA

$$s^2 = \frac{\Sigma(X - \overline{X})^2}{n - 1} \qquad \textbf{[3–10]}$$

where:

s^2 is the sample variance.
X is the value of each observation in the sample.
$\overline{X}$ is the mean of the sample.
n is the number of observations in the sample.

Why is this change made in the denominator? Although the use of n is logical, it tends to underestimate the population variance, σ^2. The use of $(n - 1)$ in the denominator provides the appropriate correction for this tendency. Because the primary use of sample statistics like s^2 is to estimate population parameters like σ^2, $(n - 1)$ is preferred to n when defining the sample variance. We will also use this convention when computing the sample standard deviation.

An easier way to compute the numerator of the variance is:

$$\Sigma(X - \overline{X})^2 = \Sigma X^2 - \frac{(\Sigma X)^2}{n}$$

The second term is much easier to use, even with a hand calculator, because it avoids all but one subtraction. Hence, we recommend formula (3–11) for calculating a sample variance.

SAMPLE VARIANCE, DIRECT FORMULA

$$s^2 = \frac{\Sigma X^2 - \frac{(\Sigma X)^2}{n}}{n - 1} \qquad \textbf{[3–11]}$$

EXAMPLE

The hourly wages for a sample of part-time employees at Fruit Packers, Inc. are: $12, $20, $16, $18, and $19. What is the sample variance?

SOLUTION

The sample variance is computed using two methods. On the left is the deviation method, using formula (3–10). On the right is the direct method, using formula (3–11).

$$\overline{X} = \frac{\Sigma X}{n} = \frac{\$85}{5} = \$17$$

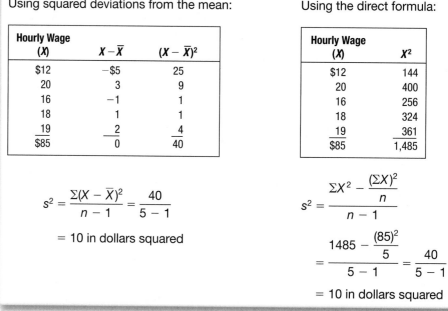

Using squared deviations from the mean:

Hourly Wage (X)	$X - \bar{X}$	$(X - \bar{X})^2$
\$12	−\$5	25
20	3	9
16	−1	1
18	1	1
19	2	4
\$85	0	40

$$s^2 = \frac{\Sigma(X - \bar{X})^2}{n - 1} = \frac{40}{5 - 1}$$

$= 10$ in dollars squared

Using the direct formula:

Hourly Wage (X)	X^2
\$12	144
20	400
16	256
18	324
19	361
\$85	1,485

$$s^2 = \frac{\Sigma X^2 - \frac{(\Sigma X)^2}{n}}{n - 1}$$

$$= \frac{1485 - \frac{(85)^2}{5}}{5 - 1} = \frac{40}{5 - 1}$$

$= 10$ in dollars squared

Sample Standard Deviation The sample standard deviation is used as an estimator of the population standard deviation. As noted previously, the population standard deviation is the square root of the population variance. Likewise, the *sample standard deviation is the square root of the sample variance.* The sample standard deviation is most easily determined by:

STANDARD DEVIATION, DIRECT FORMULA

$$s = \sqrt{\frac{\Sigma X^2 - \frac{(\Sigma X)^2}{n}}{n - 1}} \quad [3\text{–}12]$$

EXAMPLE

The sample variance in the previous example involving hourly wages was computed to be 10. What is the sample standard deviation?

SOLUTION

The sample standard deviation is \$3.16, found by $\sqrt{10}$. Note again that the sample variance is in terms of dollars squared, but taking the square root of 10 gives us \$3.16, which is in the same units (dollars) as the original data.

Self-Review 3–8 The weights of the contents of several small aspirin bottles are (in grams): 4, 2, 5, 4, 5, 2, and 6. What is the sample variance? Compute the sample standard deviation.

Exercises

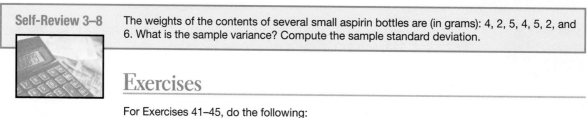

For Exercises 41–45, do the following:

a. Compute the variance using the deviation formula.
b. Compute the variance using the direct formula.
c. Determine the sample standard deviation.

41. Consider these values a sample: 7, 2, 6, 2, and 3.
42. The following five values are a sample: 11, 6, 10, 6, and 7.
43. Dave's Automatic Door, referred to in Exercise 31, installs automatic garage door openers. Based on a sample, following are the times, in minutes, required to install 10 doors: 28, 32, 24, 46, 44, 40, 54, 38, 32, and 42.
44. The sample of eight companies in the aerospace industry, referred to in Exercise 32, was surveyed as to their return on investment last year. The results are: 10.6, 12.6, 14.8, 18.2, 12.0, 14.8, 12.2, and 15.6.
45. Trout, Inc. feeds fingerling trout in special ponds and markets them when they attain a certain weight. A sample of 10 trout were isolated in a pond and fed a special food mixture, designated RT-10. At the end of the experimental period, the weights of the trout were (in grams): 124, 125, 125, 123, 120, 124, 127, 125, 126, and 121.
46. Refer to Exercise 45. Another special mixture, AB-4, was used in another pond. The mean of a sample was computed to be 126.9 grams, and the standard deviation 1.2 grams. Which food results in a more uniform weight?

Interpretation and Uses of the Standard Deviation

The standard deviation is commonly used as a measure to compare the spread in two or more sets of observations. For example, the standard deviation of the biweekly amounts invested in the Dupree Paint Company profit-sharing plan is computed to be \$7.51. Suppose these employees are located in Georgia. If the standard deviation for a group of employees in Texas is \$10.47, and the means are about the same, it indicates that the amounts invested by the Georgia employees are not dispersed as much as those in Texas (because \$7.51 $<$ \$10.47). Since the amounts invested by the Georgia employees are clustered more closely about the mean, the mean for the Georgia employees is a more reliable measure than the mean for the Texas group.

Statistics in Action

An average is a value used to represent all the data. However, often an average does not give the full picture of the set of data. Stockbrokers are often faced with this problem when they are considering two investments, where the mean rate of return is the same. They usually calculate the standard deviation of the rates of return to assess the risk associated with the two investments. The investment with the larger standard deviation is considered to have the greater risk. In this context the standard deviation plays a vital part in making critical decisions regarding the composition of an investor's portfolio.

Chebyshev's Theorem

We have stressed that a small standard deviation for a set of values indicates that these values are located close to the mean. Conversely, a large standard deviation reveals that the observations are widely scattered about the mean. The Russian mathematician P. L. Chebyshev (1821–1894) developed a theorem that allows us to determine the minimum proportion of the values that lie within a specified number of standard deviations of the mean. For example, based on **Chebyshev's theorem,** at least three of four values, or 75 percent, must lie between the mean plus two standard deviations and the mean minus two standard deviations. This relationship applies regardless of the shape of the distribution. Further, at least eight of nine values, or 88.9 percent, will lie between plus three standard deviations and minus three standard deviations of the mean. At least 24 of 25 values, or 96 percent, will lie between plus and minus five standard deviations of the mean.

Chebyshev's theorem states:

CHEBYSHEV'S THEOREM For any set of observations (sample or population), the proportion of the values that lie within k standard deviations of the mean is at least $1 - 1/k^2$, where k is any constant greater than 1.

EXAMPLE

The arithmetic mean biweekly amount contributed by the Dupree Paint employees to the company's profit-sharing plan was \$51.54, and the standard deviation is \$7.51. At least what percent of the contributions lie within plus 3.5 standard deviations and minus 3.5 standard deviations of the mean?

SOLUTION

About 92 percent, found by

$$1 - \frac{1}{k^2} = 1 - \frac{1}{(3.5)^2} = 1 - \frac{1}{12.25} = 0.92$$

The Empirical Rule

Empirical Rule applies only to symmetrical, bell-shaped distributions.

Chebyshev's theorem is concerned with any set of values; that is, the distribution of values can have any shape. However, for a symmetrical, bell-shaped distribution such as the one in Chart 3–7, we can be more precise in explaining the dispersion about the mean. These relationships involving the standard deviation and the mean are the **Empirical Rule,** sometimes called the **Normal Rule.**

EMPIRICAL RULE For a symmetrical, bell-shaped frequency distribution, approximately 68 percent of the observations will lie within plus and minus one standard deviation of the mean; about 95 percent of the observations will lie within plus and minus two standard deviations of the mean; and practically all (99.7 percent) will lie within plus and minus three standard deviations of the mean.

These relationships are portrayed graphically in Chart 3–7 for a bell-shaped distribution with a mean of 100 and a standard deviation of 10.

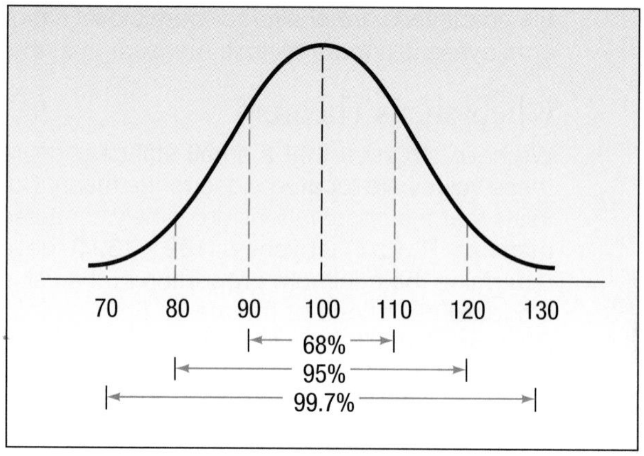

CHART 3–7 A Symmetrical, Bell-Shaped Curve Showing the Relationships between the Standard Deviation and the Observations

It has been noted that if a distribution is symmetrical and bell-shaped, practically all of the observations lie between the mean plus and minus three standard deviations. Thus, if $\overline{X} = 100$ and $s = 10$, practically all the observations lie between $100 + 3(10)$ and $100 - 3(10)$, or 70 and 130. The range is therefore 60, found by $130 - 70$.

Conversely, if we know that the range is 60, we can approximate the standard deviation by dividing the range by 6. For this illustration: range $\div 6 = 60 \div 6 = 10$, the standard deviation.

EXAMPLE

A sample of the monthly amounts spent for food by a senior citizen living alone approximates a symmetrical, bell-shaped distribution. The sample mean is \$150; the standard deviation is \$20. Using the Empirical Rule:

1. About 68 percent of the monthly food expenditures are between what two amounts?
2. About 95 percent of the monthly food expenditures are between what two amounts?
3. Almost all of the monthly expenditures are between what two amounts?

SOLUTION

1. About 68 percent are between \$130 and \$170, found by $\overline{X} \pm 1s = \$150 \pm 1(\$20)$.
2. About 95 percent are between \$110 and \$190, found by $\overline{X} \pm 2s = \$150 \pm 2(\$20)$.
3. Almost all (99.7 percent) are between \$90 and \$210, found by $\overline{X} \pm 3s = \$150 \pm 3(\$20)$.

Self-Review 3–9

The Pitney Pipe Company is one of several domestic manufacturers of PVC pipe. The quality control department sampled 600 10-foot lengths. At a point 1 foot from the end of the pipe they measured the outside diameter. The mean was 14.0 inches and the standard deviation 0.1 inches.

(a) If the shape of the distribution is not known, at least what percent of the observations will be between 13.85 inches and 14.15 inches?
(b) If we assume that the distribution of diameters is symmetrical and bell-shaped, about 95 percent of the observations will be between what two values?

Exercises

47. According to Chebyshev's theorem, at least what percent of any set of observations will be within 1.8 standard deviations of the mean?

48. The mean income of a group of sample observations is \$500; the standard deviation is \$40. According to Chebyshev's theorem, at least what percent of the incomes will lie between \$400 and \$600?

49. The distribution of the weights of a sample of 1,400 cargo containers is somewhat normally distributed. Based on the Empirical Rule, what percent of the weights will lie?

a. Between $\overline{X} - 2s$ and $\overline{X} + 2s$?
b. Between $\overline{X}$ and $\overline{X} + 2s$? Below $\overline{X} - 2s$?

50. The following figure portrays the appearance of a distribution of efficiency ratings for employees of Nale Nail Works, Inc.

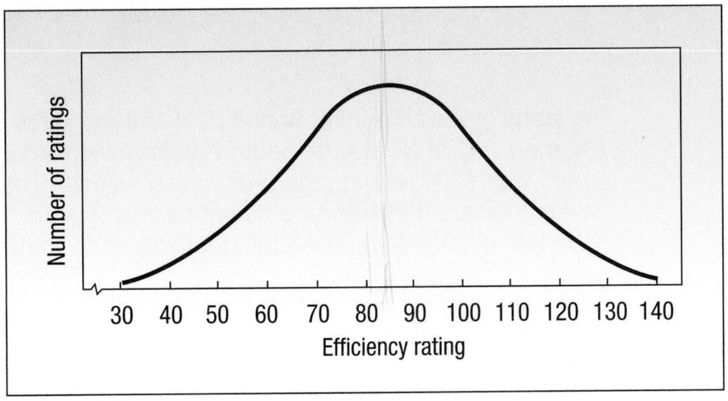

a. Estimate the mean efficiency rating.
b. Estimate the standard deviation to the nearest whole number.
c. About 68 percent of the efficiency ratings are between what two values?
d. About 95 percent of the efficiency ratings are between what two values?

Relative Dispersion

A direct comparison of two or more measures of dispersion—say, the standard deviation for a distribution of annual incomes and the standard deviation of a distribution of absenteeism for this same group of employees—is impossible. Can we say that the standard deviation of $1,200 for the income distribution is greater than the standard deviation of 4.5 days for the distribution of absenteeism? Obviously not, because we cannot directly compare dollars and days absent from work. In order to make a meaningful comparison of the dispersion in incomes and absenteeism, we need to convert each of these measures to a *relative value*—that is, a percent. Karl Pearson (1857–1936), pictured at left, who contributed significantly to the science of statistics, developed a relative measure called the **coefficient of variation** (CV). It is a very useful measure when:

When to use CV

1. The data are in different units (such as dollars and days absent).
2. The data are in the same units, but the means are far apart (such as the incomes of the top executives and the incomes of the unskilled employees).

COEFFICIENT OF VARIATION The ratio of the standard deviation to the arithmetic mean, expressed as a percent.

In terms of a formula for a sample:

COEFFICIENT OF VARIATION $$CV = \frac{s}{\overline{X}}(100) \leftarrow$$ Multiplying by 100 converts the decimal to a percent **[3–13]**

EXAMPLE

A study of the amount of bonus paid and the years of service of employees at Sea Pro Marine, Inc. of Newberry, South Carolina, resulted in these statistics: The mean bonus paid was $200; the standard deviation was 40. The mean number of years of service was 20 years; the standard deviation was 2 years. Compare the relative dispersion in the two distributions using the coefficient of variation.

SOLUTION

The distributions are in different units (dollars and years of service). Therefore, they are converted to coefficients of variation.

For the bonus paid:

$$CV = \frac{s}{\overline{X}}(100) = \frac{\$40}{\$200}(100) = 20 \text{ percent}$$

For years of service:

$$CV = \frac{s}{\overline{X}}(100) = \frac{2}{20}(100) = 10 \text{ percent}$$

Interpreting, there is more dispersion relative to the mean in the distribution of bonus paid compared with the distribution of years of service (because 20 percent > 10 percent).

The same procedure is used when the data are in the same units but the means are far apart. (See the following example.)

EXAMPLE

The variation in the annual incomes of executives at Nash-Rambler Products, Inc. is to be compared with the variation in incomes of unskilled employees. For a sample of executives, $\overline{X} = \$500{,}000$ and $s = \$50{,}000$. For a sample of unskilled employees, $\overline{X} = \$32{,}000$ and $s = \$3{,}200$. We are tempted to say that there is more dispersion in the annual incomes of the executives because \$50,000 > \$3,200. The means are so far apart, however, that we need to convert the statistics to coefficients of variation to make a meaningful comparison of the variations in annual incomes.

SOLUTION

For the executives:

$$CV = \frac{s}{\overline{X}}(100) = \frac{\$50{,}000}{\$500{,}000}(100) = 10 \text{ percent}$$

For the unskilled employees:

$$CV = \frac{s}{\overline{X}}(100) = \frac{\$3{,}200}{\$32{,}000}(100) = 10 \text{ percent}$$

There is no difference in the relative dispersion of the two groups.

Self-Review 3–10

A large group of Air Force inductees was given two experimental tests—a mechanical aptitude test and a finger dexterity test. The arithmetic mean score on the mechanical aptitude test was 200, with a standard deviation of 10. The mean and standard deviation for the finger dexterity test were: $\overline{X} = 30$, $s = 6$. Compare the relative dispersion in the two groups.

Exercises

51. For a sample of students in the College of Business Administration at Mid-Atlantic University, the mean grade point average is 3.10 with a standard deviation of 0.25. Compute the coefficient of variation.

52. United Airlines is studying the weight of luggage for each passenger. For a large group of domestic passengers, the mean is 47 pounds with a standard deviation of 10 pounds. For a large group of overseas passengers, the mean is 78 pounds and the standard deviation is 15 pounds. Compute the relative dispersion of each group. Comment on the difference in relative dispersion.

53. The research analyst for the Sidde Financial stock brokerage firm wants to compare the dispersion in the price-earnings ratios for a group of common stocks with the dispersion of their return on investment. For the price-earnings ratios, the mean is 10.9 and the standard deviation 1.8. The mean return on investment is 25 percent and the standard deviation 5.2 percent.
- **a.** Why should the coefficient of variation be used to compare the dispersion?
- **b.** Compare the relative dispersion for the price-earnings ratios and return on investment.

54. The spread in the annual prices of stocks selling for under \$10 and the spread in prices of those selling for over \$60 are to be compared. The mean price of the stocks selling for under \$10 is \$5.25 and the standard deviation \$1.52. The mean price of those stocks selling for over \$60 is \$92.50 and the standard deviation \$5.28.
- **a.** Why should the coefficient of variation be used to compare the dispersion in the prices?
- **b.** Compute the coefficients of variation. What is your conclusion?

Skewness

In this chapter we have described measures of location of a set of observations by reporting the mean, median, and mode. We have also described measures that show the amount of spread or variation in a set of data, such as the range and the standard deviation.

Another characteristic of a set of data is the shape. There are four shapes commonly observed: symmetric, positively skewed, negatively skewed, and bimodal. In a **symmetric** set of observations the mean and median are equal and the data values are evenly spread around these values. The data values below the mean and median are a mirror image of those above. A set of values is **skewed to the right** or **positively skewed** if there is a single peak and the values extend much further to the right of the peak than to the left of the peak. In this case the mean is larger than the median. In a **negatively skewed** distribution there is a single peak but the observations extend further to the left, in the negative direction, than to the right. In a negatively skewed distribution the mean is smaller than the median. Positively skewed distributions are more common. Salaries often follow this pattern. Think of the salaries of those employed in a small company of about 100 people. The president and a few top executives would have very large salaries relative to the other workers and hence the distribution of salaries would exhibit positive skewness. A **bimodal distribution** will have two or more peaks. This is often the case when the values are from two or more populations. This information is summarized in Chart 3–8.

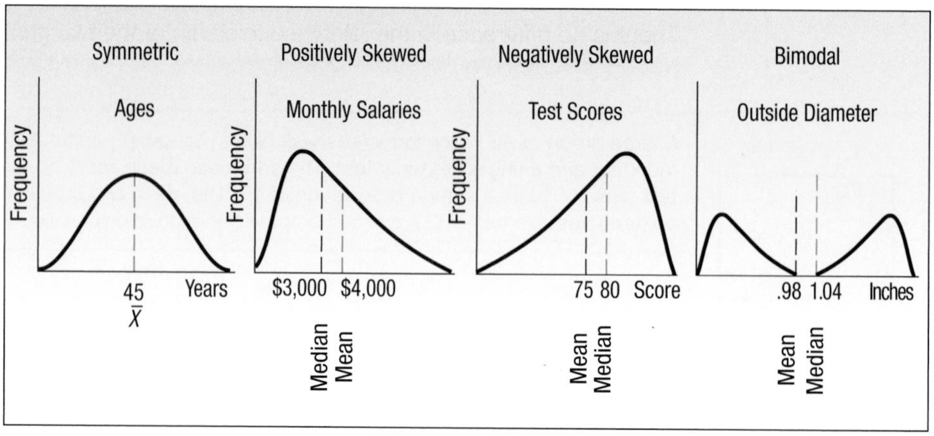

CHART 3–8 Shapes of Frequency Polygons

There are several formulas in the statistical literature used to calculate skewness. The simplest, developed by Professor Karl Pearson, is based on the difference between the mean and the median.

PEARSON'S COEFFICIENT OF SKEWNESS

$$sk = \frac{3(\bar{X} - \text{Median})}{s} \qquad \textbf{[3–14]}$$

Using this relationship the coefficient of skewness can range from −3 up to 3. A value near −3, such as −2.57, indicates considerable negative skewness. A value such as 1.63 indicates moderate positive skewness. A value of 0, which will occur when the mean and median are equal, indicates the distribution is symmetrical and that there is no skewness present.

In this text we present output from the statistical software packages MINITAB and Excel. Both of these software packages compute a value for the coefficient of skewness that is based on the cubed deviations from the mean. The formula is:

SOFTWARE COEFFICIENT OF SKEWNESS

$$sk = \frac{n}{(n-1)(n-2)}\left[\Sigma\left(\frac{X-\bar{X}}{s}\right)^3\right] \quad \textbf{[3–15]}$$

Formula (3–15) offers an insight into skewness. The right-hand side of the formula is the difference between each value and the mean, divided by the standard deviation. That is the portion $(X - \bar{X})/s$ of the formula. This idea is called **standardizing.** We will discuss the idea of standardizing a value in more detail in Chapter 6 when we describe the normal probability distribution. At this point, observe that the result is to report the difference between each value and the mean in units of the standard deviation. If this difference is positive, the particular value is larger than the mean; if it is negative, it is smaller than the mean. When we cube these values, we retain the information on the direction of the difference. Recall that in the formula for the standard deviation [see formula (3–9)] we squared the difference between each value and the mean, so that the result was all positive values.

If the set of data values under consideration is symmetric, when we cube the standardized values and sum over all the values the result would be near zero. If there are several large values, clearly separate from the others, the sum of the cubed differences would be a large positive value. Several values much smaller will result in a negative cubed sum.

An example will illustrate the idea of skewness.

EXAMPLE

Following are the earnings per share for a sample of 15 software companies for the year 2002. The earnings per share are arranged from smallest to largest.

$0.09	$0.13	$0.41	$0.51	$ 1.12	$ 1.20	$ 1.49	$3.18
3.50	6.36	7.83	8.92	10.13	12.99	16.40	

Compute the mean, median, and standard deviation. Find the coefficient of skewness using Pearson's estimate and the software methods. What is your conclusion regarding the shape of the distribution?

SOLUTION

These are sample data, so we use formula (3–2) to determine the mean

$$\bar{X} = \frac{\Sigma X}{n} = \frac{\$74.26}{15} = \$4.95$$

The median is the middle value in a set of data, arranged from smallest to largest. In this case the middle value is $3.18, so the median earnings per share is $3.18.

We use formula (3–12) on page 86 to determine the sample standard deviation.

$$s = \sqrt{\frac{\Sigma X^2 - \frac{(\Sigma X)^2}{n}}{n-1}} = \sqrt{\frac{749.372 - \frac{(74.26)^2}{15}}{15-1}} = 5.22$$

Pearson's coefficient of skewness is 1.017, found by

$$sk = \frac{3(\overline{X} - \text{Median})}{s} = \frac{3(\$4.95 - \$3.18)}{\$5.22} = 1.017$$

This indicates there is moderate positive skewness in the earnings per share data.

We obtain a similar, but not exactly the same, value from the software method. The details of the calculations are shown in Table 3–1. To begin we find the difference between each earnings per share value and the mean and divide this result by the standard deviation. Recall that we referred to this as standardizing. Next, we cube, that is, raise it to the third power, the result of the first step. Finally, we sum the cubed values. The details of the first row, that is, the company with an earnings per share of \$0.09, are:

$$\left(\frac{X - \overline{X}}{s}\right)^3 = \left(\frac{0.09 - 4.95}{5.22}\right)^3 = (-0.9310)^3 = -0.8070$$

When we sum the 15 cubed values, the result is 11.8274. That is, the term $\Sigma[(X - \overline{X})/s]^3 = 11.8274$. To find the coefficient of skewness, we use formula (3–15), with $n = 15$.

$$sk = \frac{n}{(n-1)(n-2)}\Sigma\left(\frac{X - \overline{X}}{s}\right)^3 = \frac{15}{(15-1)(15-2)}(11.8274) = 0.975$$

TABLE 3–1 Calculation of the Coefficient of Skewness

Earnings per Share	$\frac{(X - \overline{X})}{s}$	$\left(\frac{X - \overline{X}}{s}\right)^3$
0.09	−0.9310	−0.8070
0.13	−0.9234	−0.7873
0.41	−0.8697	−0.6579
0.51	−0.8506	−0.6154
1.12	−0.7337	−0.3950
1.20	−0.7184	−0.3708
1.49	−0.6628	−0.2912
3.18	−0.3391	−0.0390
3.50	−0.2778	−0.0214
6.36	0.2701	0.0197
7.83	0.5517	0.1679
8.92	0.7605	0.4399
10.13	0.9923	0.9772
12.99	1.5402	3.6539
16.40	2.1935	10.5537
		11.8274

We conclude that the earnings per share values are somewhat positively skewed. The following chart, from MINITAB, reports the descriptive measures, such as the mean, median, and standard deviation of the earnings per share data. Also included are the coefficient of skewness and a histogram with a bell-shaped curve superimposed.

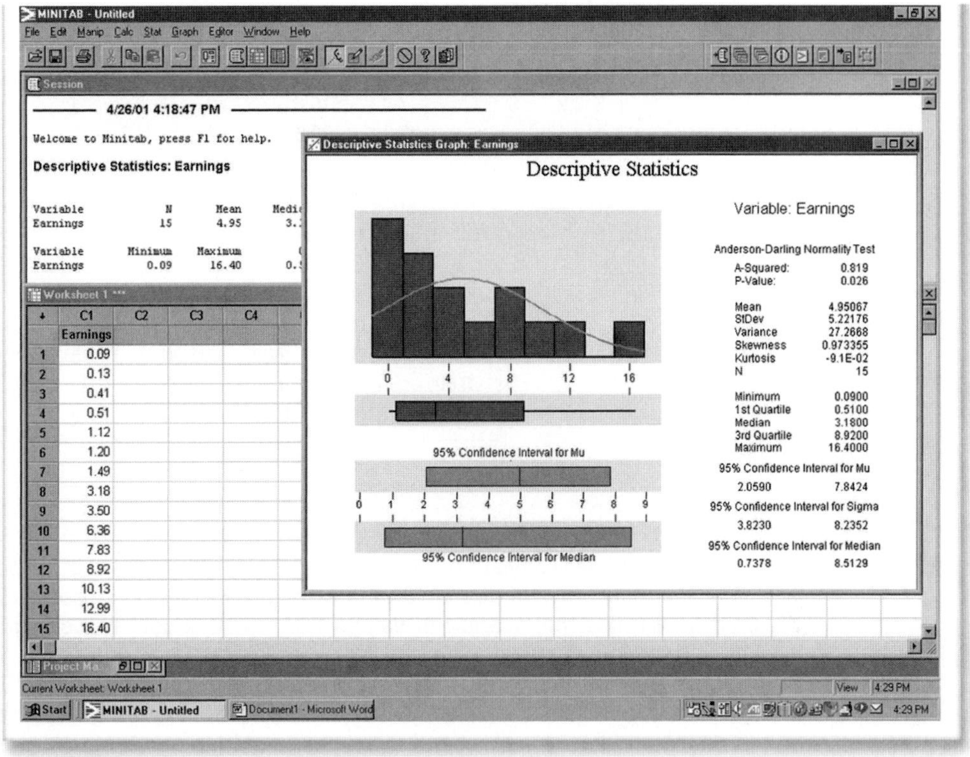

Self-Review 3–11

A sample of five data entry clerks employed in the Horry County Tax Office revised the following number of tax records last hour: 73, 98, 60, 92, and 84.

(a) Find the mean, median, and the standard deviation.
(b) Compute the coefficient of skewness using Pearson's method.
(c) Calculate the coefficient of skewness using the software method.
(d) What is your conclusion regarding the skewness of the data?

Exercises

For Exercises 55–58, do the following:

a. Determine the mean, median, and the standard deviation.
b. Determine the coefficient of skewness using Pearson's method.
c. Determine the coefficient of skewness using the software method.

55. The following values are the starting salaries, in \$000, for a sample of five accounting graduates who accepted positions in public accounting last year.

36.0	26.0	33.0	28.0	31.0

56. Listed below are the salaries, in \$000, for a sample of 15 chief financial officers in the electronics industry.

\$516.0	\$548.0	\$566.0	\$534.0	\$586.0	\$529.0
546.0	523.0	538.0	523.0	551.0	552.0
486.0	558.0	574.0			

57. Listed below are the commissions earned ($000) last year by the sales representatives at the Furniture Patch, Inc.

$ 3.9	$ 5.7	$ 7.3	$10.6	$13.0	$13.6	$15.1	$15.8	$17.1
17.4	17.6	22.3	38.6	43.2	87.7			

58. Listed below are the salaries for the New York Yankees for the year 2000. The salary information is reported in millions of dollars.

$9.86	$9.50	$8.25	$6.25	$6.00	$5.95
5.25	5.00	4.33	4.30	4.25	3.40
3.13	2.02	2.00	1.90	1.85	1.82
0.80	0.38	0.35	0.35	0.20	0.20
0.20	0.20	0.20	0.20	0.20	

Other Measures of Dispersion

The standard deviation is the most widely used measure of dispersion. However, there are other ways of describing the variation or spread in a set of data. One method is to determine the *location* of values that divide a set of observations into equal parts. These measures include *quartiles, deciles,* and *percentiles.*

Quartiles divide a set of observations into four equal parts. To explain further, think of any set of values arranged from smallest to largest. Earlier in this chapter we called the middle value of a set of data arranged from smallest to largest the median. That is, 50 percent of the observations are larger than the median and 50 percent are smaller. The median is a measure of location because it pinpoints the center of the data. In a similar fashion quartiles divide a set of observations into four equal parts. The first quartile, usually labeled Q_1, is the value below which 25 percent of the observations occur, and the third quartile, usually labeled Q_3, is the value below which 75 percent of the observations occur. Logically, Q_2 is the median. The values corresponding to Q_1, Q_2, and Q_3 divide a set of data into four equal parts. Q_1 can be thought of as the "median" of the lower half of the data and Q_3 the "median" of the upper half of the data.

In a similar fashion deciles divide a set of observations into 10 equal parts and percentiles into 100 equal parts. So if you found that your GPA was in the 8th decile at your university, you could conclude that 80 percent of the students had a GPA lower than yours and 20 percent had a higher GPA. A GPA in the 33rd percentile means that 33 percent of the students have a lower GPA and 67 percent have a higher GPA. Percentile scores are frequently used to report results on such national standardized tests as the SAT, ACT, GMAT (used to judge entry into many Master of Business Administration programs), and LSAT (used to judge entry into law school).

Quartiles, Deciles, and Percentiles

To formalize the computational procedure, let L_p refer to the location of a desired percentile. So if we wanted to find the 33rd percentile we would use L_{33} and if we wanted the median, the 50th percentile, then L_{50}. The number of observations is n, so if we want to locate the middle observation, its position is at $(n + 1)/2$, or we could write this as $(n + 1)(P/100)$, where P is the desired percentile.

LOCATION OF A PERCENTILE

$$L_p = (n + 1)\frac{P}{100} \qquad \textbf{[3–16]}$$

An example will help to explain further.

EXAMPLE

Listed below are the commissions earned last month by a sample of 15 brokers at Salomon Smith Barney's Oakland, California, office. Salomon Smith Barney is an investment company with offices located throughout the United States.

\$2,038	\$1,758	\$1,721	\$1,637	\$2,097	\$2,047	\$2,205	\$1,787	\$2,287
1,940	2,311	2,054	2,406	1,471	1,460			

Locate the median, the first quartile, and the third quartile for the commissions earned.

SOLUTION

The first step is to organize the data from the smallest commission to the largest.

\$1,460	\$1,471	\$1,637	\$1,721	\$1,758	\$1,787	\$1,940	\$2,038
2,047	2,054	2,097	2,205	2,287	2,311	2,406	

The median value is the observation in the center. The center value or L_{50} is located at $(n + 1)(50/100)$, where n is the number of observations. In this case that is position number 8, found by $(15 + 1)(50/100)$. The eighth largest commission is \$2,038. So we conclude this is the median and that half the brokers earned commissions more than \$2,038 and half earned less than \$2,038.

Recall the definition of a quartile. Quartiles divide a set of observations into four equal parts. Hence 25 percent of the observations will be less than the first quartile. Seventy-five percent of the observations will be less than the third quartile. To locate the first quartile, we use formula (3–16), where $n = 15$ and $P = 25$:

$$L_{25} = (n + 1)\frac{P}{100} = (15 + 1)\frac{25}{100} = 4$$

and to locate the third quartile, $n = 15$ and $P = 75$:

$$L_{75} = (n + 1)\frac{P}{100} = (15 + 1)\frac{75}{100} = 12$$

Therefore, the first and third quartile values are located at positions 4 and 12. The fourth value in the ordered array is \$1,721 and the twelfth is \$2,205. These are the first and third quartiles, respectively.

In the above example the location formula yielded a whole number result. That is, we wanted to find the first quartile and there were 15 observations, so the location formula indicated we should find the fourth ordered value. What if there were 20 observations in the sample, that is $n = 20$, and we wanted to locate the first quartile? From the location formula (3–16):

$$L_{25} = (n + 1)\frac{P}{100} = (20 + 1)\frac{25}{100} = 5.25$$

We would locate the fifth value in the ordered array and then move .25 of the distance between the fifth and sixth values and report that as the first quartile. Like the median, the quartile does not need to be one of the actual values in the data set.

To explain further, suppose a data set contained the six values: 91, 75, 61, 101, 43, and 104. We want to locate the first quartile. We order the values from smallest to largest: 43, 61, 75, 91, 101, and 104. The first quartile is located at

$$L_{25} = (n + 1)\frac{P}{100} = (6 + 1)\frac{25}{100} = 1.75$$

The position formula tells us that the first quartile is located between the first and the second value and that it is .75 of the distance between the first and the second values. The first value is 43 and the second is 61. So the distance between these two values is 18. To locate the first quartile, we need to move .75 of the distance between the first and second values, so .75(18) = 13.5. To complete the procedure, we add 13.5 to the first value and report that the first quartile is 56.5.

We can extend the idea to include both deciles and percentiles. If we wanted to locate the 23rd percentile in a sample of 80 observations, we would look for the 18.63 position.

$$L_{23} = (n + 1)\frac{P}{100} = (80 + 1)\frac{23}{100} = 18.63$$

To find the value corresponding to the 23rd percentile, we would locate the 18th value and the 19th value and determine the distance between the two values. Next, we would multiply this difference by 0.63 and add the result to the smaller value. The result would be the 23rd percentile.

With a computer software package, it is quite easy to sort the data from smallest to largest and to locate percentiles and deciles. Both MINITAB and Excel output summary statistics. Listed below is the MINITAB output. It includes the first and third quartiles, as well as the mean, median, standard deviation, and coefficient of skewness for the Whitner Pontiac data (see Table 2–1). We conclude that 25 percent of the vehicles sold for less than $17,074 and that 75 percent sold for less than $22,795.

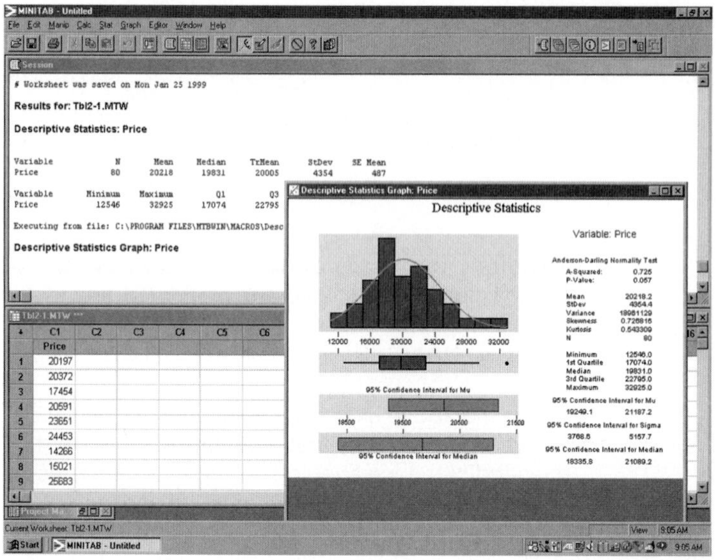

The Excel output on the following page includes the same information regarding the mean, median, standard deviation, and coefficient of skewness. It will also output the quartiles, but the method of calculation is not as precise. To find the quartiles, we multiply the sample size by the desired percentile and report the integer of that value. To explain, in the Whitner Pontiac data there are 80 observations, and we wish to locate the 25th percentile. We multiply 80 by .25; the result is 20.25. Excel will not allow us to enter a fractional value, so we use 20 and request the location of the largest 20 values and the smallest 20 values. The result is a good approximation of the 25th and 75th percentiles.

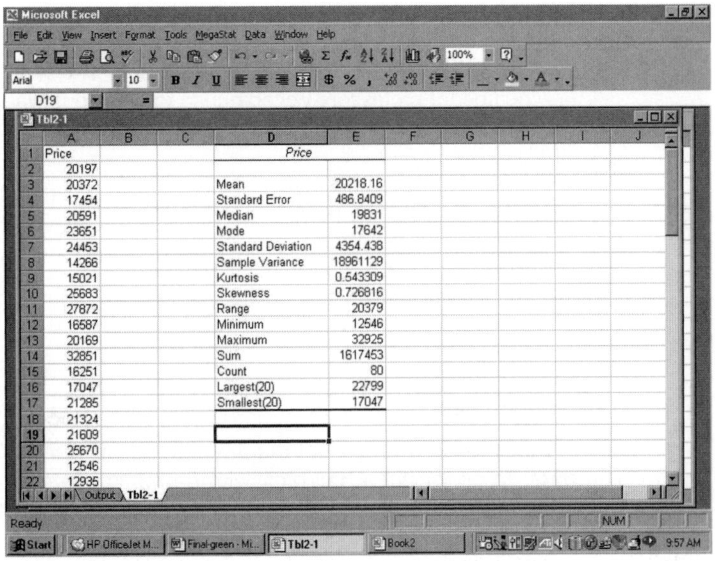

Self-Review 3–12

The quality control department of the Plainsville Peanut Company is responsible for checking the weight of the 8-ounce jar of peanut butter. The weights of a sample of nine jars produced last hour are:

7.69	7.72	7.8	7.86	7.90	7.94	7.97	8.06	8.09

(a) What is the median weight?
(b) Determine the weights corresponding to the first and third quartiles.

Exercises

59. Determine the median and the values corresponding to the first and third quartiles in the following data.

46	47	49	49	51	53	54	54	55	55	59

60. Determine the median and the values corresponding to the first and third quartiles in the following data.

5.24	6.02	6.67	7.30	7.59	7.99	8.03	8.35	8.81	9.45
9.61	10.37	10.39	11.86	12.22	12.71	13.07	13.59	13.89	15.42

61. The Thomas Supply Company, Inc. is a distributor of small electrical motors. As with any business, the length of time customers take to pay their invoices is important. Listed below, arranged from smallest to largest, is the time, in days, for a sample of The Thomas Supply Company, Inc. invoices.

13	13	13	20	26	27	31	34	34	34	35	35	36	37	38
41	41	41	45	47	47	47	50	51	53	54	56	62	67	82

a. Determine the first and third quartiles.
b. Determine the second decile and the eighth decile.
c. Determine the 67th percentile.

62. Kevin Horn is the national sales manager for National Textbooks, Inc. He has a sales staff of 40 who visit college professors all over the United States. Each Saturday morning he requires his sales staff to send him a report. This report includes, among other things, the number of professors visited during the previous week. Listed below, ordered from smallest to largest, are the number of visits last week.

38	40	41	45	48	48	50	50	51	51	52	52	53	54	55	55	55	56	56	57
59	59	59	62	62	62	63	64	65	66	66	67	67	69	69	71	77	78	79	79

a. Determine the median number of calls.
b. Determine the first and third quartiles.
c. Determine the first decile and the ninth decile.
d. Determine the 33rd percentile.

Box Plots

A **box plot** is a graphical display, based on quartiles, that helps us picture a set of data. To construct a box plot, we need only five statistics: the minimum value, Q_1 (the first quartile), the median, Q_3 (the third quartile), and the maximum value. An example will help to explain.

EXAMPLE

Alexander's Pizza offers free delivery of its pizza within 15 miles. Alex, the owner, wants some information on the time it takes for delivery. How long does a typical delivery take? Within what range of times will most deliveries be completed? For a sample of 20 deliveries, he determined the following information:

$$\text{Minimum value} = 13 \text{ minutes}$$
$$Q_1 = 15 \text{ minutes}$$
$$\text{Median} = 18 \text{ minutes}$$
$$Q_3 = 22 \text{ minutes}$$
$$\text{Maximum value} = 30 \text{ minutes}$$

Develop a box plot for the delivery times. What conclusions can you make about the delivery times?

SOLUTION

The first step in drawing a box plot is to create an appropriate scale along the horizontal axis. Next, we draw a box that starts at Q_1 (15 minutes) and ends at Q_3 (22 minutes). Inside the box we place a vertical line to represent the median (18 minutes). Finally, we extend horizontal lines from the box out to the minimum value (13 minutes) and the maximum value (30 minutes). These horizontal lines outside of the box are sometimes called "whiskers" because they look a bit like a cat's whiskers.

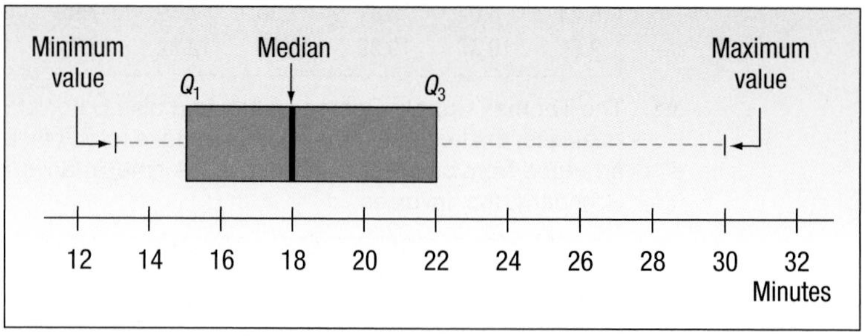

The box plot shows that the middle 50 percent of the deliveries take between 15 minutes and 22 minutes. The distance between the ends of the box, 7 minutes, is the **interquartile range.** The interquartile range is the distance between the first and the third quartile.

The box plot also reveals that the distribution of delivery times is positively skewed. How do we know this? In this case there are actually two pieces of information that suggest that the distribution is positively skewed. First, the dashed line to the right of the box from 22 minutes (Q_3) to the maximum time of 30 minutes is longer than the dashed line from the left of 15 minutes (Q_1) to the minimum value of 13 minutes. To put it another way, the 25 percent of the data larger than the third quartile is more spread out than the 25 percent less than the first quartile. A second indication of positive skewness is that the median is not in the center of the box. The distance from the first quartile to the median is smaller than the distance from the median to the third quartile. We know that the number of delivery times between 15 minutes and 18 minutes is the same as the number of delivery times between 18 minutes and 22 minutes.

EXAMPLE

Refer to the Whitner Pontiac data in Table 2–1. Develop a box plot of the data. What can we conclude about the distribution of the vehicle selling prices?

SOLUTION

The MINITAB statistical software system was used to develop the following chart.

MINITAB

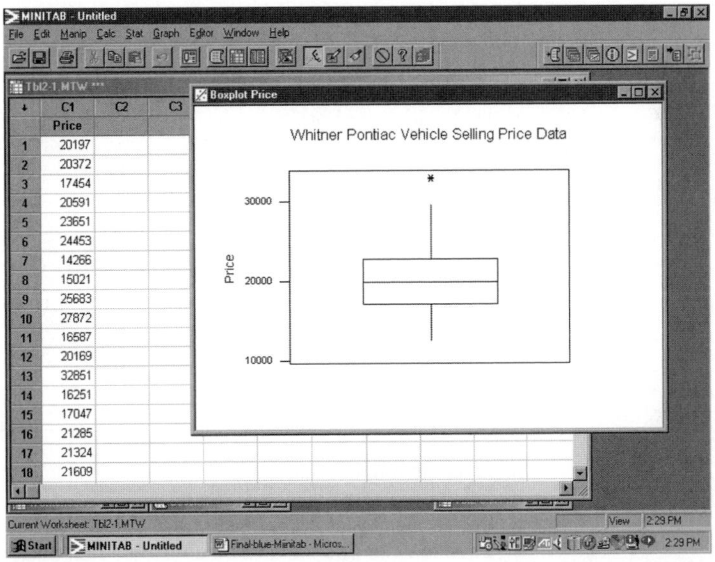

We conclude that the median vehicle selling price is about \$20,000, that about 25 percent of the vehicles sell for less than \$17,000, and that about 25 percent sell for more than \$23,000. About 50 percent of the vehicles sell for between \$17,000 and \$23,000. The distribution is positively skewed because the solid line above \$23,000 is somewhat longer than the line below \$17,000.

There is an asterisk (*) above the \$30,000 selling price. An asterisk indicates an outlier. An **outlier** is a value that is inconsistent with the rest of the data. The standard definition of an outlier is a value that is more than 1.5 times the interquartile range smaller than Q_1 or larger than Q_3. In this example, an outlier would be a value larger than \$32,000, found by

$$\text{Outlier} > Q_3 + 1.5(Q_3 - Q_1) = \$23{,}000 + 1.5(\$23{,}000 - \$17{,}000) = \$32{,}000$$

A value less than \$8,000 is also an outlier.

$$\text{Outlier} < Q_1 - 1.5(Q_3 - Q_1) = \$17{,}000 - 1.5(\$23{,}000 - \$17{,}000) = \$8{,}000$$

The MINITAB box plot indicates that there is only one value larger than \$32,000. However, if you look at the actual data in Table 2–1 on page 23 you will notice that there are actually two values (\$32,851 and \$32,925). The software was not able to graph two data points so close together, so it shows only one asterisk.

Self-Review 3–13 The following box plot is given.

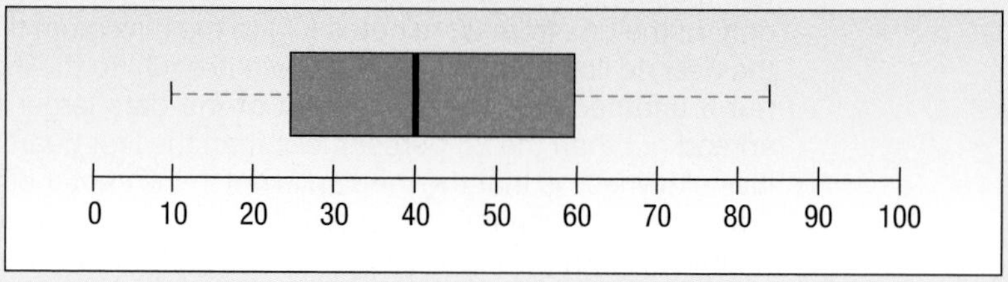

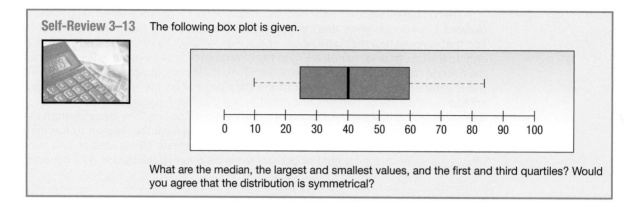

What are the median, the largest and smallest values, and the first and third quartiles? Would you agree that the distribution is symmetrical?

Exercises

63. Refer to the box plot below.

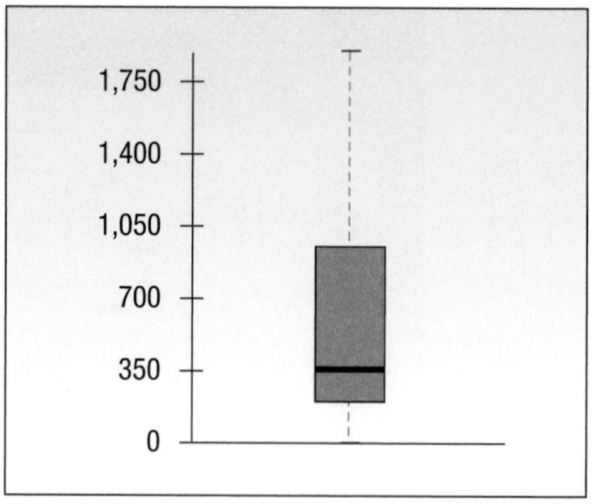

a. Estimate the median.
b. Estimate the first and third quartiles.
c. Determine the interquartile range.
d. Beyond what point is a value considered an outlier?
e. Identify any outliers and estimate their value.
f. Is the distribution symmetrical or positively or negatively skewed?

64. Refer to the following box plot.

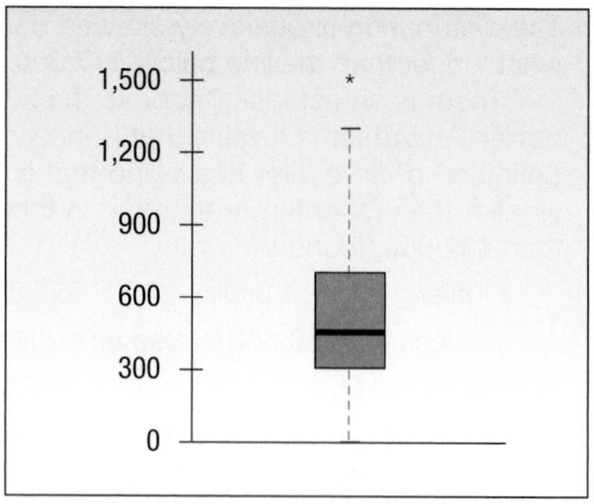

a. Estimate the median.
b. Estimate the first and third quartiles.
c. Determine the interquartile range.
d. Beyond what point is a value considered an outlier?
e. Identify any outliers and estimate their value.
f. Is the distribution symmetrical or positively or negatively skewed?

65. In a study of the gasoline mileage of model year 2002 automobiles, the mean miles per gallon was 27.5 and the median was 26.8. The smallest value in the study was 12.70 miles per gallon, and the largest was 50.20. The first and third quartiles were 17.95 and 35.45 miles per gallon, respectively. Develop a box plot and comment on the distribution. Is it a symmetric distribution?

66. A sample of 28 hospitals in Florida revealed the following daily charges for a semiprivate room. For convenience the data are ordered from smallest to largest. Construct a box plot to represent the data. Comment on the distribution. Be sure to identify the first and third quartiles and the median.

$116	$121	$157	$192	$207	$209	$209
229	232	236	236	239	243	246
260	264	276	281	283	289	296
307	309	312	317	324	341	353

The Mean and Standard Deviation of Grouped Data

In most instances measures of location, such as the mean, and measures of variability, such as the standard deviation, are determined by using the individual values. MINITAB and Excel make it easy to calculate these values, even for large data sets. However, sometimes we are only given the frequency distribution and wish to estimate the mean or standard deviation. In the following discussion we show how we can estimate the mean and standard deviation from data organized into a frequency distribution. We should stress that a mean or a standard deviation from grouped data is an *estimate* of the corresponding actual values.

The Arithmetic Mean

To approximate the arithmetic mean of data organized into a frequency distribution, we begin by assuming the observations in each class are represented by the *midpoint* of the class. The mean of a sample of data organized in a frequency distribution is computed by:

ARITHMETIC MEAN OF GROUPED DATA

$$\overline{X} = \frac{\Sigma fM}{n} \quad \textbf{[3–17]}$$

where:

$\overline{X}$ is the designation for the sample mean.
M is the midpoint of each class.
f is the frequency in each class.
fM is the frequency in each class times the midpoint of the class.
ΣfM is the sum of these products.
n is the total number of frequencies.

EXAMPLE

The computations for the arithmetic mean of data grouped into a frequency distribution will be shown based on the Whitner Pontiac data. Recall in Chapter 2, in Table 2–4 on page 26 we constructed a frequency distribution for the vehicle selling prices. The information is repeated below. Determine the arithmetic mean vehicle selling price.

Selling Price ($ thousands)	Frequency
12 up to 15	8
15 up to 18	23
18 up to 21	17
21 up to 24	18
24 up to 27	8
27 up to 30	4
30 up to 33	2
Total	80

SOLUTION

The mean vehicle selling price can be estimated from data grouped into a frequency distribution. To find the estimated mean, assume the midpoint of each class is representative of the data values in that class. Recall that the midpoint of a class is halfway between the upper and the lower class limits. To find the midpoint of a particular class, we add the upper and the lower class limits and divide by 2. Hence, the midpoint of the first class is \$13.5, found by (\$12 + \$15)/2. We assume that the value of \$13.5 is representative of the eight values in that class. To put it another way, we assume the sum of the eight values in this class is \$108, found by 8(\$13.5). We continue the process of multiplying the class midpoint by the class frequency for each class and then sum these products. The results are summarized in Table 3–2.

TABLE 3–2 Price of 80 New Vehicles Sold Last Month at Whitner Pontiac

Selling Price ($ thousands)	Frequency (f)	Midpoint (M)	fM
12 up to 15	8	\$13.5	\$ 108.0
15 up to 18	23	16.5	379.5
18 up to 21	17	19.5	331.5
21 up to 24	18	22.5	405.0
24 up to 27	8	25.5	204.0
27 up to 30	4	28.5	114.0
30 up to 33	2	31.5	63.0
Total	80		\$1,605.0

Solving for the arithmetic mean using formula (3–17), we get:

$$\overline{X} = \frac{\Sigma fM}{n} = \frac{\$1,605}{80} = \$20.1 \text{ (thousands)}$$

So we conclude that the mean vehicle selling price is about \$20,100.

Standard Deviation

Recall that for *ungrouped* data, one formula for the sample standard deviation is:

$$s = \sqrt{\frac{\Sigma X^2 - \frac{(\Sigma X)^2}{n}}{n - 1}}$$

If the data of interest are in *grouped* form (in a frequency distribution), the sample standard deviation can be approximated by substituting ΣfM^2 for ΣX^2 and ΣfM for ΣX. The formula for the *sample standard deviation* then converts to:

STANDARD DEVIATION, GROUPED DATA

$$s = \sqrt{\frac{\Sigma fM^2 - \frac{(\Sigma fM)^2}{n}}{n - 1}} \quad \textbf{[3–18]}$$

where:

s is the symbol for the sample standard deviation.
M is the midpoint of a class.
f is the class frequency.
n is the total number of sample observations.

EXAMPLE

Refer to the frequency distribution for Whitner Pontiac reported in Table 3-2. Compute the standard deviation of the vehicle selling prices.

SOLUTION

Following the same practice used earlier for computing the mean of data grouped into a frequency distribution, M represents the midpoint of each class.

Selling Price ($ thousands)	Frequency (f)	Midpoint (M)	fM	fM^2
12 up to 15	8	$13.5	$ 108.0	1,458.00
15 up to 18	23	16.5	379.5	6,261.75
18 up to 21	17	19.5	331.5	6,464.25
21 up to 24	18	22.5	405.0	9,112.50
24 up to 27	8	25.5	204.0	5,202.00
27 up to 30	4	28.5	114.0	3,249.00
30 up to 33	2	31.5	63.0	1,984.50
Total	80		$1,605.0	33,732.00

To find the standard deviation:

Step 1: Each class frequency is multiplied by its class midpoint. That is, multiply f times M. Thus, for the first class $8 \times \$13.5 = \$108.0$, for the second class $fM = 23 \times \$16.5 = \$379.5$, and so on.

Step 2: Calculate fM^2. This could be written $fM \times M$. For the first class it would be $\$108.0 \times \$13.5 = \$1{,}458.0$, for the second class it would be $\$379.5 \times \$16.5 = \$6{,}261.75$, and so on.

Step 3: Sum the fM and fM^2 columns. The totals are $1,605 and 33,732, respectively. We have omitted the units involved with the fM^2 column, but it is "dollar squared."

To find the standard deviation we insert these values in formula (3–18).

$$s = \sqrt{\frac{\Sigma fM^2 - \frac{(fM)^2}{n}}{n - 1}} = \sqrt{\frac{33{,}732 - \frac{(1605)^2}{80}}{80 - 1}} = 4.403$$

The mean and standard deviation calculated from data grouped into a frequency distribution are usually close to the values calculated from raw data. The grouping results in some loss of information. For the vehicle selling price problem the mean selling price reported in the Excel output on page 74 is $20,218 and the standard deviation is $4,354. The respective values estimated from data grouped into a frequency distribution are $20,100 and $4,403. The difference in the means is $118 or about 0.58 percent. The standard deviations differ by $49 or 1.1 percent. Based on the percentage difference, the estimates are very close to the actual values.

Self-Review 3–14 The net incomes of a sample of large importers of antiques were organized into the following table:

Net Income ($ millions)	Number of Importers
2 up to 6	1
6 up to 10	4
10 up to 14	10
14 up to 18	3
18 up to 22	2

(a) What is the table called?
(b) Based on the distribution, what is the estimate of the arithmetic mean net income?
(c) Based on the distribution, what is the estimate of the standard deviation?

Exercises

67. When we compute the mean of a frequency distribution, why do we refer to this as an *estimated* mean?

68. Determine the mean and the standard deviation of the following frequency distribution.

Class	Frequency
0 up to 5	2
5 up to 10	7
10 up to 15	12
15 up to 20	6
20 up to 25	3

69. Determine the mean and the standard deviation of the following frequency distribution.

Class	Frequency
20 up to 30	7
30 up to 40	12
40 up to 50	21
50 up to 60	18
60 up to 70	12

70. SCCoast, an Internet provider in the Southeast, developed the following frequency distribution on the age of Internet users. Find the mean and the standard deviation.

Age (years)	Frequency
10 up to 20	3
20 up to 30	7
30 up to 40	18
40 up to 50	20
50 up to 60	12

71. The following frequency distribution reports the amount, in thousands of dollars, owed by a sample of 50 public accounting firms in the Dallas–Ft. Worth area. Find the mean and the standard deviation.

Amount ($ thousands)	Frequency
20 up to 30	1
30 up to 40	15
40 up to 50	22
50 up to 60	8
60 up to 70	4

72. Advertising expenses are a significant component of the cost of goods sold. Listed below is a frequency distribution showing the advertising expenditures for 60 manufacturing companies located in the Southwest. Estimate the mean and the standard deviation of advertising expense.

Advertising Expenditure ($ millions)	Number of Companies
25 up to 35	5
35 up to 45	10
45 up to 55	21
55 up to 65	16
65 up to 75	8
Total	60

Chapter Outline

I. A measure of location is a value used to describe the center of a set of data.

A. The arithmetic mean is the most widely reported measure of location.

1. It is calculated by adding the values of the observations and dividing by the total number of observations.

a. The formula for a population mean of ungrouped or raw data is:

$$\mu = \frac{\Sigma X}{N} \quad \text{[3–1]}$$

b. The formula for the mean of a sample is

$$\overline{X} = \frac{\Sigma X}{n} \quad \text{[3–2]}$$

c. The formula for the sample mean of data in a frequency distribution is

$$\overline{X} = \frac{\Sigma fM}{n} \quad \text{[3–17]}$$

Statistics in Action

Most colleges report the "average class size." This information can be misleading because average class size can be found several ways. If we find the number of students *in each class* at a particular university, the result is the mean number of students per class. If we compiled a list of the class sizes for each student and find the mean class size, we might find the mean to be quite different. One school found the mean number of students in each of their 747 classes to be 40. But when they found the mean from a list of the class sizes of each student it was 147. Why the disparity? Because there are few students in the small classes and a larger number of students in the larger class, which has the effect of increasing the mean class size when it is calculated this way. A school could reduce this mean class size for each student by reducing the number of students in each class. That is, cut out the large freshman lecture classes.

2. The major characteristics of the arithmetic mean are:
   a. At least the interval scale of measurement is required.
   b. All the data values are used in the calculation.
   c. A set of data has only one mean. That is, it is unique.
   d. The sum of the deviations from the mean equals 0.

B. The weighted mean is found by multiplying each observation by its corresponding weight.
1. The formula for determining the weighted mean is:

$$\bar{X}_w = \frac{w_1X_1 + w_2X_2 + w_3X_3 + \cdots + w_nX_n}{w_1 + w_2 + w_3 + \cdots + w_n} \qquad \textbf{[3–3]}$$

2. It is a special case of the arithmetic mean.

C. The median is the value in the middle of a set of ordered data.
1. To find the median, sort the observations from smallest to largest and identify the middle value.
2. The major characteristics of the median are:
   a. At least the ordinal scale of measurement is required.
   b. It is not influenced by extreme values.
   c. Fifty percent of the observations are larger than the median.
   d. It is unique to a set of data.

D. The mode is the value that occurs most often in a set of data.
1. The mode can be found for nominal-level data.
2. A set of data can have more than one mode.

E. The geometric mean is the *n*th root of the product of *n* values.
1. The formula for the geometric mean is:

$$GM = \sqrt[n]{(X_1)(X_2)(X_3)\cdots(X_n)} \qquad \textbf{[3–4]}$$

2. The geometric mean is also used to find the rate of change from one period to another.

$$GM = \sqrt[n]{\frac{\text{Value at end of period}}{\text{Value at beginning of period}}} - 1 \qquad \textbf{[3–5]}$$

3. The geometric mean is always equal to or less than the arithmetic mean.

II. The dispersion is the variation or spread in a set of data.

A. The range is the difference between the largest and the smallest value in a set of data.
1. The formula for the range is:

$$\text{Range} = \text{Highest value} - \text{Lowest value} \qquad \textbf{[3–6]}$$

2. The major characteristics of the range are:
   a. Only two values are used in its calculation.
   b. It is influenced by extreme values.
   c. It is easy to compute and to understand.

B. The mean absolute deviation is the sum of the absolute deviations from the mean divided by the number of observations.
1. The formula for computing the mean absolute deviation is

$$MD = \frac{\Sigma|X - \bar{X}|}{n} \qquad \textbf{[3–7]}$$

2. The major characteristics of the mean absolute deviation are:
   a. It is not unduly influenced by large or small values.
   b. All observations are used in the calculation.
   c. The absolute values are somewhat difficult to work with.

C. The variance is the mean of the squared deviations from the arithmetic mean.
1. The formula for the population variance is:

$$\sigma^2 = \frac{\Sigma(X - \mu)^2}{N} \qquad \textbf{[3–8]}$$

2. The formula for the sample variance is:

$$s^2 = \frac{\Sigma(X - \overline{X})^2}{n - 1} \quad \textbf{[3–10]}$$

3. The major characteristics of the variance are:
   a. All observations are used in the calculation.
   b. It is not unduly influenced by extreme observations.
   c. The units are somewhat difficult to work with; they are the original units squared.

D. The standard deviation is the square root of the variance.
   1. The major characteristics of the standard deviation are:
      a. It is in the same units as the original data.
      b. It is the square root of the average squared distance from the mean.
      c. It cannot be negative.
      d. It is the most widely reported measure of dispersion.
   2. The formula for the sample standard deviation is:

$$s = \sqrt{\frac{\Sigma X^2 - \frac{(\Sigma X)^2}{n}}{n - 1}} \quad \textbf{[3–12]}$$

   3. The formula for the standard deviation of grouped data is:

$$s = \sqrt{\frac{\Sigma fM^2 - \frac{(\Sigma fM)^2}{n}}{n - 1}} \quad \textbf{[3–18]}$$

III. Chebyshev's theorem states that regardless of the shape of the distribution, at least $1 - 1/k^2$ of the observations will be within k standard deviations of the mean, where k is greater than 1.

IV. The coefficient of variation is a measure of relative dispersion.
   A. The formula for the coefficient of variation is:

$$CV = \frac{s}{\overline{X}}(100) \quad \textbf{[3–13]}$$

   B. It reports the variation relative to the mean.
   C. It is useful for comparing distributions with different units.

V. The coefficient of skewness measures the symmetry of a distribution.
   A. In a positively skewed set of data the long tail is to the right.
   B. In a negatively skewed distribution the long tail is to the left.

VI. Measures of location also describe the spread in a set of observations.
   A. A quartile divides a set of observations into four equal parts.
      1. Twenty-five percent of the observations are less than the first quartile, 50 percent are less than the second quartile (the median), and 75 percent are less than the third quartile.
      2. The interquartile range is the difference between the third and the first quartile.
   B. Deciles divide a set of observations into 10 equal parts.
   C. Percentiles divide a set of observations into 100 equal parts.
   D. A box plot is a graphic display of a set of data.
      1. It is drawn enclosing the first and third quartiles.
         a. A line through the inside of the box shows the median.
         b. Dotted line segments from the third quartile to the largest value and from the first quartile to the smallest value show the range of the largest 25 percent of the observations and the smallest 25 percent.
      2. A box plot is based on five statistics: the largest and smallest observation, the first and third quartiles, and the median.

Pronunciation Key

SYMBOL	MEANING	PRONUNCIATION
μ	Population mean	*mu*
Σ	Operation of adding	*sigma*
ΣX	Adding a group of values	*sigma X*
$\overline{X}$	Sample mean	*X bar*
$\overline{X}_w$	Weighted mean	*X bar sub w*
GM	Geometric mean	*G M*
ΣfM	Adding the product of the frequencies and the class midpoints	*sigma f M*
σ^2	Population variance	*sigma squared*
σ	Population standard deviation	*sigma*
ΣfM^2	Sum of the product of the class midpoints squared and the class frequency	*sigma f M squared*
L_p	Location of percentile	*L sub p*
Q_1	First quartile	*Q sub 1*
Q_3	Third quartile	*Q sub 3*

Chapter Exercises

73. The accounting firm of Crawford and Associates has five senior partners. Yesterday the senior partners saw six, four, three, seven, and five clients, respectively.
  a. Compute the mean number and median number of clients seen by a partner.
  b. Is the mean a sample mean or a population mean?
  c. Verify that $\Sigma(X - \mu) = 0$.

74. Owens Orchards sells apples in a large bag by weight. A sample of seven bags contained the following numbers of apples: 23, 19, 26, 17, 21, 24, 22.
  a. Compute the mean number and median number of apples in a bag.
  b. Verify that $\Sigma(X - \overline{X}) = 0$.

75. A sample of households that subscribe to the United Bell Phone Company revealed the following numbers of calls received last week. Determine the mean and the median number of calls received.

52	43	30	38	30	42	12	46	39	37
34	46	32	18	41	5				

76. The Citizens Banking Company is studying the number of times the ATM, located in a Loblaws Supermarket at the foot of Market Street, is used per day. Following are the numbers of times the machine was used over each of the last 30 days. Determine the mean number of times the machine was used per day.

83	64	84	76	84	54	75	59	70	61
63	80	84	73	68	52	65	90	52	77
95	36	78	61	59	84	95	47	87	60

77. Listed below is the number of lampshades produced during the last 50 days at the American Lampshade Company in Rockville, GA. Compute the mean.

348	371	360	369	376	397	368	361	374
410	374	377	335	356	322	344	399	362
384	365	380	349	358	343	432	376	347
385	399	400	359	329	370	398	352	396
366	392	375	379	389	390	386	341	351
354	395	338	390	333				

78. Trudy Green works for the True-Green Lawn Company. Her job is to solicit lawn-care business via the telephone. Listed below are the number of appointments she made in each of the last 25 hours of calling. What is the arithmetic mean number of appointments she made per hour? What is the median number of appointments per hour? Write a brief report summarizing the findings.

9	5	2	6	5	6	4	4	7	2	3	6	3
4	4	7	8	4	4	5	5	4	8	3	3	

79. The Split-A-Rail Fence Company sells three types of fence to homeowners in suburban Seattle, Washington. Grade A costs \$5.00 per running foot to install, Grade B costs \$6.50 per running foot, and Grade C, the premium quality, costs \$8.00 per running foot. Yesterday, Split-A-Rail installed 270 feet of Grade A, 300 feet of Grade B, and 100 feet of Grade C. What was the mean cost per foot of fence installed?

80. Rolland Poust is a sophomore in the College of Business at Scandia Tech. Last semester he took courses in statistics and accounting, 3 hours each, and earned an A in both. He earned a B in a five-hour history course and a B in a two-hour history of jazz course. In addition, he took a one-hour course dealing with the rules of basketball so he could get his license to officiate high school basketball games. He got an A in this course. What was his GPA for the semester? Assume that he receives 4 points for an A, 3 for a B, and so on. What measure of central tendency did you just calculate?

81. The table below shows the percent of the labor force that is unemployed and the size of the labor force for three counties in Northwest Ohio. Jon Elsas is the Regional Director of Economic Development. He must present a report to several companies that are considering locating in Northwest Ohio. What would be an appropriate unemployment rate to show for the entire region?

County	Percent Unemployed	Size of Workforce
Wood	4.5	15,300
Ottawa	3.0	10,400
Lucas	10.2	150,600

82. The American Automobile Association checks the prices of gasoline before many holiday weekends. Listed below are the self-service prices for a sample of 15 retail outlets during the May 2002 Memorial Day weekend in the Detroit, Michigan, area.

1.44	1.42	1.35	1.39	1.49	1.49	1.41	1.46
1.41	1.49	1.45	1.48	1.39	1.46	1.44	

a. What is the arithmetic mean selling price?
b. What is the median selling price?
c. What is the modal selling price?

83. The metropolitan area of Los Angeles–Long Beach, California, is the area expected to show the largest increase in the number of jobs between 1989 and 2010. The number of jobs is expected to increase from 5,164,900 to 6,286,800. What is the geometric mean expected yearly rate of increase?

84. A recent article suggested that if you earn $25,000 a year today and the inflation rate continues at 3 percent per year, you'll need to make $33,598 in 10 years to have the same buying power. You would need to make $44,771 if the inflation rate jumped to 6 percent. Confirm that these statements are accurate by finding the geometric mean rate of increase.

85. The ages of a sample of Canadian tourists flying from Toronto to Hong Kong were: 32, 21, 60, 47, 54, 17, 72, 55, 33, and 41.
a. Compute the range.
b. Compute the mean deviation.
c. Compute the standard deviation.

86. The weights (in pounds) of a sample of five boxes being sent by UPS are: 12, 6, 7, 3, and 10.
a. Compute the range.
b. Compute the mean deviation.
c. Compute the standard deviation.

87. A southern state has seven state universities in its system. The numbers of volumes (in thousands) held in their libraries are 83, 510, 33, 256, 401, 47, and 23.
a. Is this a sample or a population?
b. Compute the standard deviation.
c. Compute the coefficient of variation. Interpret.

88. Health issues are a concern of managers, especially as they evaluate the cost of medical insurance. A recent survey of 150 executives at Elvers Industries, a large insurance and financial firm located in the Southwest, reported the number of pounds by which the executives were overweight. Compute the range and the standard deviation.

Pounds Overweight	Frequency
0 up to 6	14
6 up to 12	42
12 up to 18	58
18 up to 24	28
24 up to 30	8

89. A major airline wanted some information on those enrolled in their "frequent flyer" program. A sample of 48 members resulted in the following number of miles flown last year, to the nearest 1,000 miles, by each participant. Develop a box plot of the data and comment on the information.

22	29	32	38	39	41	42	43	43	43	44	44
45	45	46	46	46	47	50	51	52	54	54	55
56	57	58	59	60	61	61	63	63	64	64	67
69	70	70	70	71	71	72	73	74	76	78	88

90. The National Muffler Company claims they will change your muffler in less than 30 minutes. An investigative reporter for WTOL Channel 11 monitored 30 consecutive muffler changes at the National outlet on Liberty Street. The number of minutes to perform changes is reported below.

44	12	22	31	26	22	30	26	18	28	12
40	17	13	14	17	25	29	15	30	10	28
16	33	24	20	29	34	23	13			

a. Develop a box plot for the time to change a muffler.
b. Does the distribution show any outliers?
c. Summarize your findings in a brief report.

91. The Walter Gogel Company is an industrial supplier of fasteners, tools, and springs. The amounts of their invoices vary widely, from less than $20.00 to over $400.00. During the month of January they sent out 80 invoices. Here is a box plot of these invoices. Write a brief report summarizing the amounts of their invoices. Be sure to include information on the values of the first and third quartile, the median, and whether there is any skewness. If there are any outliers, approximate the value of these invoices.

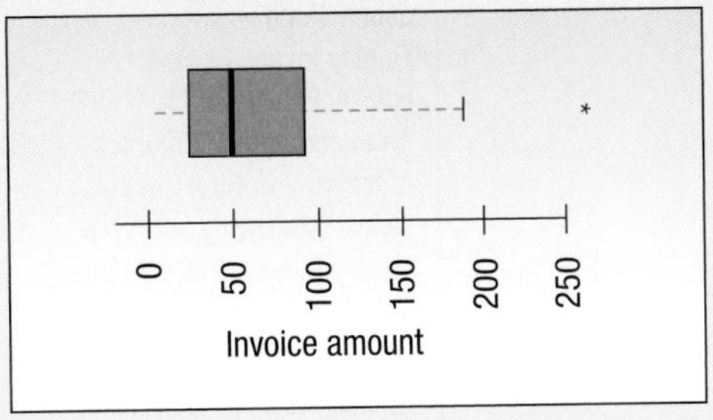

92. The following box plot shows the number of daily newspapers published in each state and the District of Columbia. Write a brief report summarizing the number published. Be sure to include information on the values of the first and third quartiles, the median, and whether there is any skewness. If there are any outliers, estimate their value.

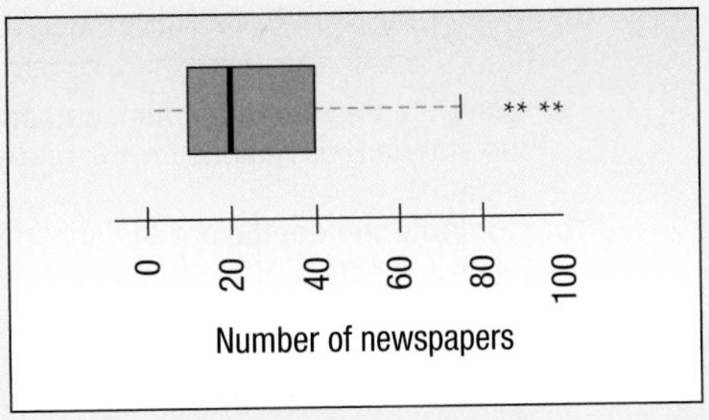

93. The following data are the estimated market values (in $millions) of 50 companies in the auto parts business.

26.8	8.6	6.5	30.6	15.4	18.0	7.6	21.5	11.0	10.2
28.3	15.5	31.4	23.4	4.3	20.2	33.5	7.9	11.2	1.0
11.7	18.5	6.8	22.3	12.9	29.8	1.3	14.1	29.7	18.7
6.7	31.4	30.4	20.6	5.2	37.8	13.4	18.3	27.1	32.7
6.1	0.9	9.6	35.0	17.1	1.9	1.2	16.6	31.1	16.1

a. Determine the mean and the median of the market values.
b. Determine the standard deviation of the market values.
c. Using Chebyshev's theorem, between what values would you expect about 56 percent of the market values to occur?
d. Using the Empirical Rule, about 95 percent of the values would occur between what values?
e. Determine the coefficient of variation.
f. Determine the coefficient of skewness.
g. Estimate the values of Q_1 and Q_3. Draw a box plot.
h. Write a brief report summarizing the results.

94. Listed below are 20 of the largest mutual funds, their assets in millions of dollars, their five-year rate of return, and their one-year rate of return. Assume the data are a sample.

Fund	Assets ($Mil)	Return-5yr	Return-1yr
Vanguard Index Fds: 500	104357	143.5	−4.4
Fidelity Invest: Magellan	101625	118.8	−3.9
American Funds A: ICAA	56614	129.8	3.1
American Funds A: WshA	46780	108.1	−2.4
Janus: Fund	46499	177.5	−2.2
Fidelity Invest: Contra	42437	133.4	1.6
Fidelity Invest: Grolnc	42059	127.7	0.1
American Funds: Growth A	39400	202.8	−6.4
American Century: Ultra	38559	128.2	−5.8
Janus: WorldWide	37780	187.3	2.2
Fidelity Invest: GroCo	34255	202.1	13.2
American Funds A: EupacA	32826	98.0	−2.8
American Funds A: PerA	32308	122.8	−2.0
Janus: Twen	31023	264.3	−12.9
Fidelity Invest: Blue Chip	29708	132.0	−1.2
Vanguard Instl Fds: Instidx	28893	145.0	−4.3
PIMCO Funds Instl: TotRt	28201	41.4	7.7
Putman Funds A: VoyA	24262	144.7	−0.5
Vanguard Funds: Wndsll	24069	105.7	4.6
Vanguard Funds: Prmcp	22742	203.0	10.9

a. Compute the mean, median, and standard deviation for each of the variables. Compare the standard deviations for the one-year and five-year rates of return. Comment on your findings.

b. Compute the coefficient of variation for each of the above variables. Comment on the relative variation of the three variables.

c. Compute the coefficient of skewness for each of the above variables. Comment on the skewness of the three variables.

d. Compute the first and third quartiles for the one-year and five-year rates of return.

e. Draw a box plot for the one-year and five-year rates of return. Comment on the results. Are there any outliers?

95. The Apollo space program lasted from 1967 until 1972 and included 13 missions. The missions lasted from as little as 7 hours to as long as 301 hours. The duration of each flight is listed below.

9	195	241	301	216	260	7	244	192	147
10	295	142							

a. Find the mean, median, and standard deviation of the duration for the Apollo flights.

b. Compute the coefficient of variation and the coefficient of skewness. Comment on your findings.

c. Find the 45th and 82nd percentiles.

d. Draw a box plot and comment on your findings.

96. A recent report in *Woman's World* magazine suggested that the typical family of four with an intermediate budget spends about $96 per week on food. The following frequency distribution was included in the report. Compute the mean and the standard deviation.

Amount Spent	Frequency
$ 80 up to $ 85	6
85 up to 90	12
90 up to 95	23
95 up to 100	35
100 up to 105	24
105 up to 110	10

97. Bidwell Electronics, Inc., recently surveyed a sample of employees to determine how far they lived from corporate headquarters. The results are shown below. Compute the mean and the standard deviation.

Distance (miles)	Frequency	*M*
0 up to 5	4	2.5
5 up to 10	15	7.5
10 up to 15	27	12.5
15 up to 20	18	17.5
20 up to 25	6	22.5

exercises.com

WWW

98. The National Center for Health Statistics maintains a website at: http://www.cdc.gov/nchs. Under the section labeled **Tabulated State Data**, click on **Births**. Go to that page and locate the table "Live Births by Race and Hispanic Origin of Mother: U.S., Each State, Puerto Rico, Virgin Islands, and Guam." Suppose you are interested in birth rates for the 50 states. Develop a box plot of the data. Compute the mean, median, standard deviation, and coefficient of skewness. What can you conclude about the shape of the distribution?

99. There are many financial websites that provide information on stocks by industry. For example, go to http://biz.yahoo.com and select **Stock Research,** under **Analyst Research** select **Sector/Industry**. There are many choices available here such as **Energy**, **Financial**, and **Healthcare**. Select one of these sectors, such as **Healthcare**. Another list of choices is now available; select one such as **Major Drug**. A list of companies in that industry will appear. Select one of the variables available, such as the price to earnings ratio, listed as P/E. This variable is the ratio of the selling price of a share of the company's common stock to the earnings per share of common stock. Download this information into Excel and find the mean, median, and standard deviation. Go back to **Sector/Industry** and choose another **Sector** and **Industry**. You might want to select **Energy** and then **Coal**. A list of companies will appear. Select the same variable as before. Download the information to Excel and find the mean, median, and standard deviation for this Industry. Compare the information on the two sectors. Write a brief report summarizing your findings. Are the means different? Is there more variability in one industry than another?

100. One of the most famous averages, the Dow Jones Industrial Average (DJIA), is not really an average. The following is a listing of the 30 companies whose stock prices make up the DJIA. Also listed is the selling price on November 8, 2001, the change from the previous day's price, the percent change, and the number of shares sold. Compute the mean selling price of the 30 stocks. At the time of this snapshot the DJIA was reported at 9587.52. Compare that value to the mean of the 30 stocks. You may read about the history of the DJIA by going to http://www.djindexes.com and clicking on **About the Dow**. This will explain why it is not really average. There are many sites you can visit to check the current value of the DJIA, http://www.cnnfn.com, http://foxnews.com/news/ features/dow, and http://www.usatoday.com are three of the many sources. To find a list of the actual stocks that make up the average go to http://bloomberg.com. On the toolbar, click on **Markets**, then down the left side of the screen select **Stocks in the Dow**. You should now have available a listing of the current selling price of 30 stocks that comprise the DJIA.

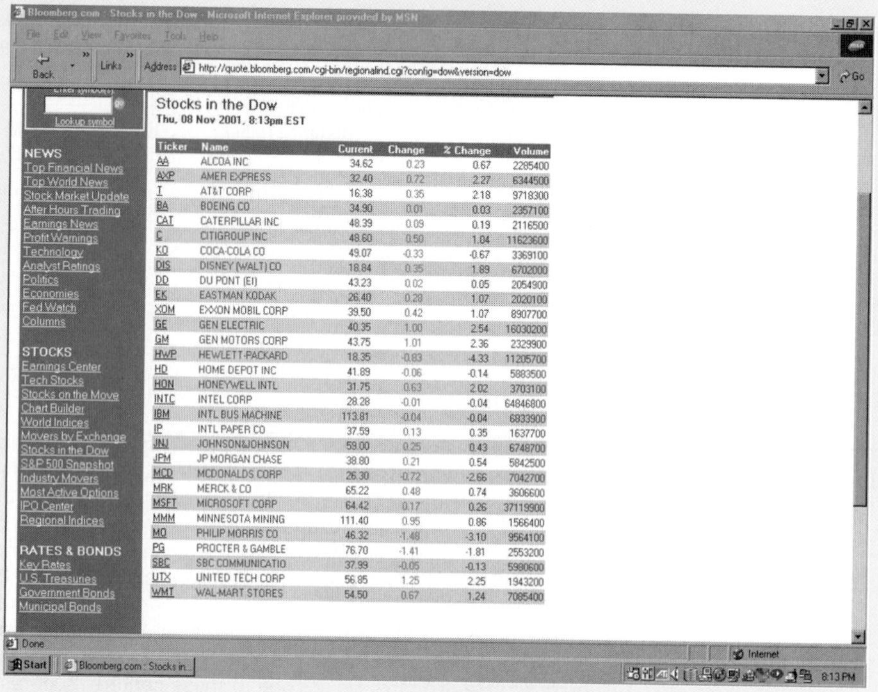

Stocks in the Dow
Thu, 08 Nov 2001, 8:13pm EST

Ticker	Name	Current	Change	% Change	Volume
AA	ALCOA INC	34.62	0.23	0.67	2285400
AXP	AMER EXPRESS	32.40	0.72	2.27	6344500
T	AT&T CORP	16.38	0.35	2.18	9718300
BA	BOEING CO	34.90	0.01	0.03	2357100
CAT	CATERPILLAR INC	48.39	0.09	0.19	2116500
C	CITIGROUP INC	48.60	0.50	1.04	11623600
KO	COCA-COLA CO	49.07	-0.33	-0.67	3369100
DIS	DISNEY (WALT) CO	18.84	0.35	1.89	6702000
DD	DU PONT (EI)	43.23	0.02	0.05	2054900
EK	EASTMAN KODAK	26.40	0.28	1.07	2020100
XOM	EXXON MOBIL CORP	39.50	0.42	1.07	8907700
GE	GEN ELECTRIC	40.35	1.00	2.54	16030200
GM	GEN MOTORS CORP	43.75	1.01	2.36	2329900
HWP	HEWLETT-PACKARD	18.35	-0.83	-4.33	11205700
HD	HOME DEPOT INC	41.89	-0.06	-0.14	5883500
HON	HONEYWELL INTL	31.75	0.63	2.02	3703100
INTC	INTEL CORP	28.28	-0.01	-0.04	64846800
IBM	INTL BUS MACHINE	113.81	-0.04	-0.04	6833900
IP	INTL PAPER CO	37.59	0.13	0.35	1637700
JNJ	JOHNSON&JOHNSON	59.00	0.25	0.43	6748700
JPM	JP MORGAN CHASE	38.80	0.21	0.54	5842500
MCD	MCDONALDS CORP	26.30	-0.72	-2.66	7042700
MRK	MERCK & CO	65.22	0.48	0.74	3606600
MSFT	MICROSOFT CORP	64.42	0.17	0.26	37119900
MMM	MINNESOTA MINING	111.40	0.95	0.86	1566400
MO	PHILIP MORRIS CO	46.32	-1.48	-3.10	9564100
PG	PROCTER & GAMBLE	76.70	-1.41	-1.81	2553200
SBC	SBC COMMUNICATIO	37.99	-0.05	-0.13	5980600
UTX	UNITED TECH CORP	56.85	1.25	2.25	1943200
WMT	WAL-MART STORES	54.50	0.67	1.24	7085400

Computer Data Exercises

101. Refer to the Real Estate data, which reports information on homes sold in the Venice, Florida, area last year.

a. Select the variable selling price.
   1. Find the mean, median, and the standard deviation.
   2. Determine the coefficient of skewness. Is the distribution positively or negatively skewed?
   3. Develop a box plot. Are there any outliers? Estimate the first and third quartiles.
   4. Write a brief summary of the distribution of selling prices.

b. Select the variable referring to the area of the home in square feet.
   1. Find the mean, median, and the standard deviation.
   2. Determine the coefficient of skewness. Is the distribution positively or negatively skewed?
   3. Develop a box plot. Are there any outliers? Estimate the first and third quartiles.
   4. Write a brief summary of the distribution of the area of homes.

102. Refer to the Baseball 2001 data, which reports information on the 30 major league teams for the 2001 baseball season.

a. Select the variable team salary.
   1. Find the mean, median, and the standard deviation.
   2. Determine the coefficient of skewness. Is the distribution positively or negatively skewed?
   3. Develop a box plot. Are there any outliers? Estimate the first and third quartiles.
   4. Write a brief summary of the distribution of team salaries.

b. Select the variable that refers to the year in which the stadium was built. (Hint: Subtract the current year from the year in which the stadium was built to find the stadium age and work with that variable.)
   1. Find the mean, median, and the standard deviation.
   2. Determine the coefficient of skewness. Is the distribution positively or negatively skewed?
   3. Develop a box plot. Are there any outliers? Estimate the first and third quartiles.
   4. Write a brief summary of the distribution of the age of the stadium.

c. Select the variable that refers to the seating capacity of the stadium.
   1. Find the mean, median, and the standard deviation.
   2. Determine the coefficient of skewness. Is the distribution positively or negatively skewed?
   3. Develop a box plot. Are there any outliers? Estimate the first and third quartiles.
   4. Write a brief summary of the distribution of the seating capacity variable.

103. Refer to the CIA data, which reports demographic and economic information on 46 countries.

a. Select the variable Life Expectancy.
   1. Find the mean, median, and the standard deviation.
   2. Determine the coefficient of skewness. Is the distribution positively or negatively skewed?
   3. Develop a box plot. Are there any outliers? Estimate the first and third quartiles.
   4. Write a brief summary of the distribution of life expectancy.

b. Select the variable GDP/cap.
   1. Find the mean, median, and the standard deviation.
   2. Determine the coefficient of skewness. Is the distribution positively or negatively skewed?
   3. Develop a box plot. Are there any outliers? Estimate the first and third quartiles.
   4. Write a brief summary of the distribution GDP/cap.

Computer Commands

1. The Excel Commands for the descriptive statistics on page 73 are:
   a. From the CD retrieve the Whitner data file, which is called **Table 2–1.**
   b. From the menu bar select **Tools** and then **Data Analysis.** Select **Descriptive Statistics** and then click **OK.**
   c. For the **Input Range,** type *A1:A81,* indicate that the data are grouped by column and that the labels are in the first row. Click on **Output Range,** indicate that the output should go in D1 (or any place you wish), click on **Summary statistics,** then click **OK.**
   d. After you get your results, double-check the count in the output to be sure it contains the correct number of items.

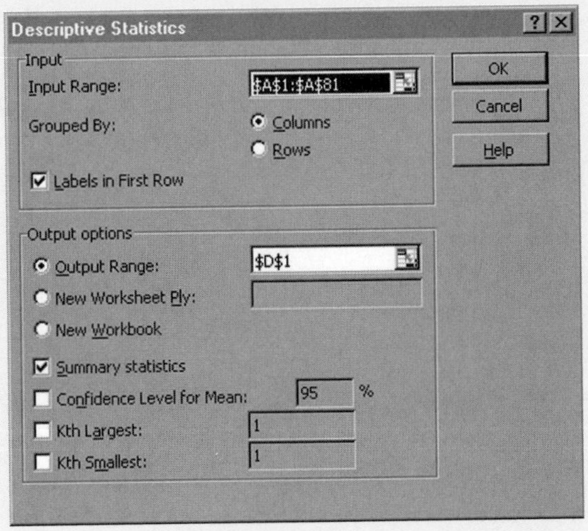

2. The MINITAB commands for the descriptive summary on page 95 are:
   a. Enter the earnings reported in the Example on page 93 in column C1 of the spreadsheet. Name the variable **Earnings**.
   b. Select **Stat**, **Basic Statistics**, and then **Display Descriptive Statistics**. In the dialog box select Earnings as the variable and then click on **Graphs** in the lower right corner. Within this dialog box select **Graphic summary** and click **OK**. Click **OK** in the next dialog box.

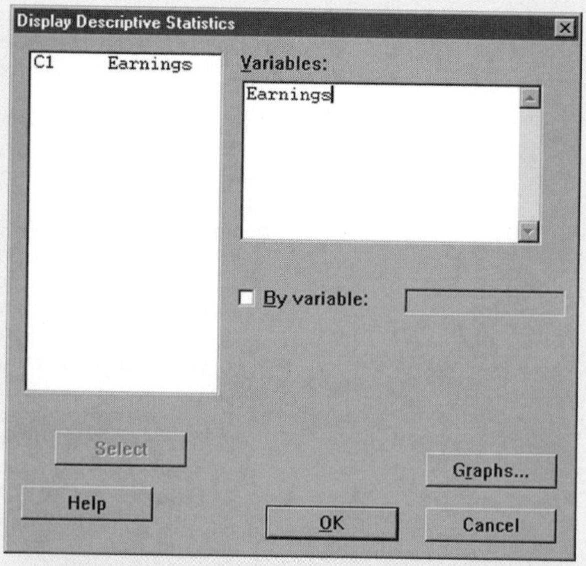

3. The MINITAB Commands for the summary of the Whitner Pontiac data on page 98 are:
   a. Import the data from the CD. The file name is **Table 2–1.**
   b. Use the same commands as in the previous description. The dialog boxes will appear the same.

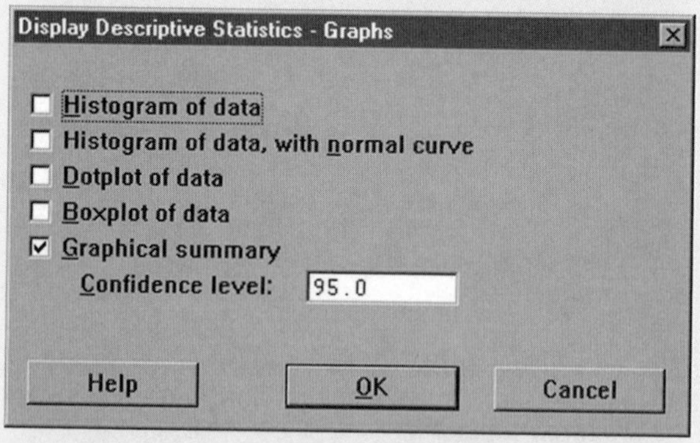

4. The Excel commands for the summary of descriptive statistics on page 99 are:
   a. Import the data from the CD. Select the Excel format. The file is **Table 2–1.**
   b. Select **Tools** and then **Data Analysis** and hit **Enter.**
   c. Select **Descriptive Statistics** and select **OK**.
   d. The **Input Range** is *a1:a81,* select **Grouped by Columns**, click on **Labels in First Row**, **Output Range** is *D1,* click on **Summary Statistics**, and then click **OK**.

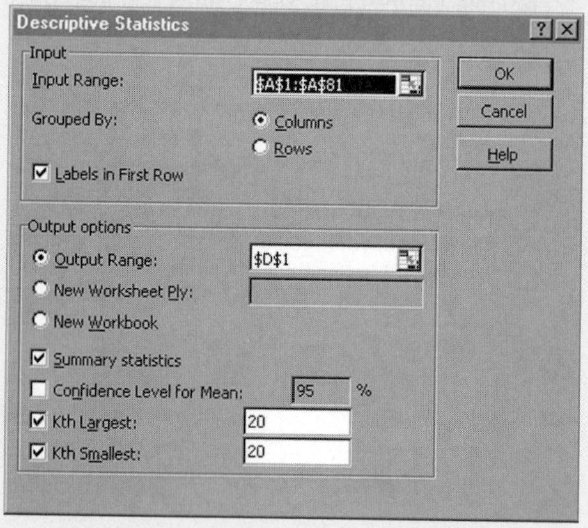

5. The MINITAB commands for the box plot on page 101 are:
   a. Import the data from the CD. The file name is **Table 2–1.**
   b. Select **Graph** and then **Boxplots.** In the dialog box select *Price* as the variable and click **OK.**

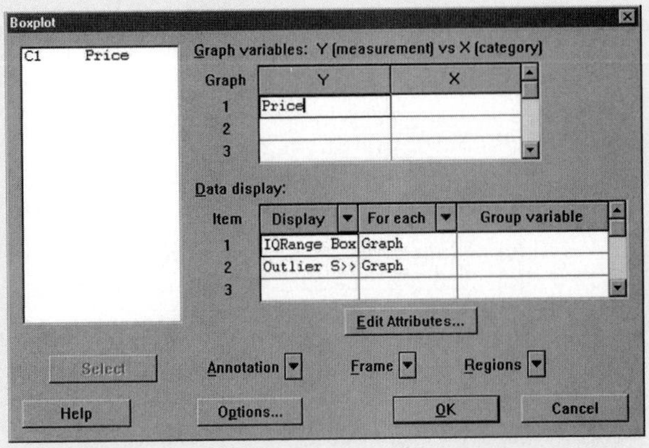

Chapter 3 Answers to Self-Review

3–1 1. (a) $\overline{X} = \frac{\Sigma X}{n}$

(b) $\overline{X} = \frac{\$267{,}100}{4} = \$66{,}775$

(c) Statistic, because it is a sample value.

(d) $66,775. The sample mean is our best estimate of the population mean.

2. (a) $\mu = \frac{\Sigma X}{N}$

(b) $\mu = \frac{498}{6} = 83$

(c) Parameter, because it was computed using all the population values.

3–2 (a) $237, found by:

$$\frac{(95 \times \$400) + (126 \times \$200) + (79 \times \$100)}{95 + 126 + 79} = \$237.00$$

(b) The profit per suit is $12, found by $237 − $200 cost − $25 commission. The total profit for the 300 suits is $3,600, found by 300 × $12.

3–3 1. (a) $439

(b) 3, 3

2. (a) 7, found by (6 + 8)/2 = 7

(b) 3, 3

(c) 0

3–4 (a)

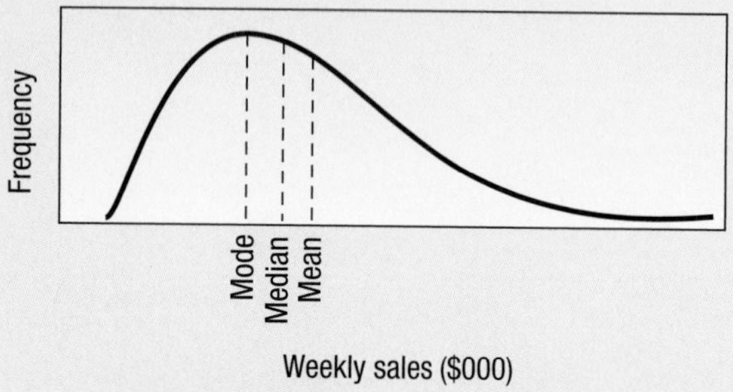

(b) Positively skewed, because the mean is the largest average and the mode is the smallest.

3–5 1. (a) About 8.39 percent, found by $\sqrt[4]{4951.75464}$

(b) About 10.095 percent

(c) Greater than, because 10.095 > 8.39

2. 8.63 percent, found by $\sqrt[20]{\frac{120{,}520}{23{,}000}} - 1 =$ 1.0863 − 1

3–6 (a) 22, found by 112 − 90

(b) $\overline{X} = \frac{824}{8} = 103$

(c)

X	$\lvert X - \overline{X} \rvert$	Absolute Deviation
95	$\lvert -8 \rvert$	8
103	$\lvert 0 \rvert$	0
105	$\lvert +2 \rvert$	2
110	$\lvert +7 \rvert$	7
104	$\lvert +1 \rvert$	1
105	$\lvert +2 \rvert$	2
112	$\lvert +9 \rvert$	9
90	$\lvert -13 \rvert$	13
	Total	42

$$MD = \frac{42}{8} = 5.25 \text{ pounds}$$

3–7 (a) $\mu = \frac{\$11{,}900}{5} = \$2{,}380$

(b) $\sigma^2 = \frac{(2536 - 2380)^2 + \cdots + (2622 - 2380)^2}{5}$

$$= \frac{(156)^2 + (-207)^2 + (68)^2 + (-259)^2 + (242)^2}{5}$$

$$= \frac{197{,}454}{5} = 39{,}490.8$$

(c) $\sigma = \sqrt{39{,}490.8} = 198.72$

(d) There is more variation in the Pittsburgh office because the standard deviation is larger. The mean is also larger in the Pittsburgh office.

3–8 2.33, found by:

$$\overline{X} = \frac{\Sigma X}{n} = \frac{28}{7} = 4$$

X	$X - \overline{X}$	$(X - \overline{X})^2$	X^2
4	0	0	16
2	−2	4	4
5	1	1	25
4	0	0	16
5	1	1	25
2	−2	4	4
6	2	4	36
28	0	14	126

$$s^2 = \frac{\Sigma(X - \overline{X})^2}{n - 1} \quad \text{or} \quad s^2 = \frac{\Sigma X^2 - \frac{(\Sigma X)^2}{n}}{n - 1}$$

$$= \frac{14}{7 - 1} \qquad = \frac{126 - \frac{(28)^2}{7}}{7 - 1}$$

$$= 2.33 \qquad = \frac{126 - 112}{6}$$

$$= 2.33$$

$$s = \sqrt{2.33} = 1.53$$

3–9 **(a)** $k = \frac{14.15 - 14.00}{.10} = 1.5$

$$1 - \frac{1}{(1.5)^2} = 1 - .44 = .56$$

(b) 13.8 and 14.2

3–10 *CV* for mechanical is 5 percent, found by (10/200)(100). For finger dexterity, *CV* is 20 percent, found by (6/30)(100). Thus, relative dispersion in finger dexterity scores is greater than relative dispersion in mechanical, because 20 percent > 5 percent.

3–11 **(a)** $\overline{X} = \frac{407}{5} = 81.4$, Median = 84

$$s = \sqrt{\frac{34{,}053 - \frac{(407)^2}{5}}{5 - 1}} = 15.19$$

(b) $sk = \frac{3(81.4 - 84.0)}{15.19} = -0.51$

(c)

X	$\frac{X - \overline{X}}{s}$	$\left[\frac{(X - \overline{X})}{s}\right]^3$
73	−0.5530	−0.1691
98	1.0928	1.3051
60	−1.4088	−2.7962
92	0.6978	0.3398
84	0.1712	0.0050
		−1.3154

$$sk = \frac{5}{(4)(3)}[-1.3154]$$

$$= -0.5481$$

(d) The distribution is somewhat negatively skewed.

3–12 **(a)** 7.90

(b) $Q_1 = 7.76$, $Q_2 = 8.015$

3–13 The smallest value is 10 and the largest 85; the first quartile is 25 and the third 60. About 50 percent of the values are between 25 and 60. The median value is 40. The distribution is somewhat positively skewed.

3–14 **a.** Frequency distribution.

b.

f	M	fM	fM^2
1	4	4	16
4	8	32	256
10	12	120	1,440
3	16	48	768
2	20	40	800
20		244	3,280

$$\overline{X} = \frac{\Sigma fM}{M} = \frac{\$244}{20} = \$12.20$$

c. $s = \sqrt{\frac{3280 - \frac{(244)^2}{20}}{20 - 1}} = \$3.99$

4

A Survey of Probability Concepts

GOALS

When you have completed this chapter you will be able to:

1. Define *probability.*
2. Describe the *classical, empirical,* and *subjective* approaches to probability.
3. Understand the terms *experiment, event, outcome, permutations,* and *combinations.*
4. Define the terms *conditional probability* and *joint probability.*
5. Calculate probabilities using the *rules of addition* and *rules of multiplication.*
6. Use a tree diagram to organize and compute probabilities.

A study found that 60 percent of the tourists to China visited historical sites in or near Beijing. Forty percent visited sites in Xian, 30 percent of the tourists went to both Beijing and Xian. What is the probability that a tourist visited at least one of these locations? (See Goal 5 and Exercise 66.)

Introduction

The emphasis in Chapters 2 and 3 is on descriptive statistics. In Chapter 2 we organize the prices of 80 vehicles sold last month at Whitner Pontiac into a frequency distribution. This frequency distribution shows the lowest and the highest selling prices and where the largest concentration of data occur. In Chapter 3 we use measures of location and dispersion to locate a typical selling price and to examine the spread in the data. We describe the spread in the selling prices with such measures of dispersion as the range and the standard deviation.

Descriptive statistics is concerned with summarizing data collected from past events. For example, we described the vehicle selling prices last month at Whitner Pontiac. We now turn to the second facet of statistics, namely, *computing the chance that something will occur in the future.* This facet of statistics is called **statistical inference** or **inferential statistics.**

Seldom does a decision maker have complete information from which to make a decision. For example:

- Toys and Things, a toy and puzzle manufacturer, recently developed a new game based on sports trivia. They want to know whether sports buffs will purchase the game. "Slam Dunk" and "Home Run" are two of the names under consideration. One way to minimize the risk of making a wrong decision is to hire a market research firm to take a sample of, say, 2,000 consumers from the population and ask each respondent for a reaction to the new game and its proposed titles.
- The quality assurance department of a Bethlehem Steel mill must assure management that the quarter-inch wire being produced has an acceptable tensile strength. Obviously, not all the wire produced can be tested for tensile strength because testing requires the wire to be stretched until it breaks—thus destroying it. So a random sample of 10 pieces is selected and tested. Based on the test results, all the wire produced is deemed to be either satisfactory or unsatisfactory.

- Other questions involving uncertainty are: Should the daytime drama *Days of Our Lives* be discontinued immediately? Will a newly developed mint-flavored cereal be profitable if marketed? Will Charles Linden be elected to county auditor in Batavia County?

Statistical inference deals with conclusions about a population based on a sample taken from that population. (The populations for the preceding illustrations are: all consumers who like sports trivia games, all the quarter-inch steel wire produced, all television viewers who watch soaps, all who purchase breakfast cereal, and so on.)

Because there is uncertainty in decision making, it is important that all the known risks involved be scientifically evaluated. Helpful in this evaluation is *probability theory,* which has often been referred to as the science of uncertainty. The use of probability theory allows the decision maker with only limited information to analyze the risks and minimize the gamble inherent, for example, in marketing a new product or accepting an incoming shipment possibly containing defective parts.

Because probability concepts are so important in the field of statistical inference (to be discussed starting with Chapter 7), this chapter introduces the basic language of probability, including such terms as *experiment, event, subjective probability,* and *addition* and *multiplication rules.*

What Is a Probability?

No doubt you are familiar with terms such as *probability, chance,* and *likelihood.* They are often used interchangeably. The weather forecaster announces that there is a 70 percent chance of rain for Super Bowl Sunday. Based on a survey of consumers who tested a newly developed pickle with a banana taste, the probability is .03 that, if marketed, it will be a financial success. (This means that the chance of the banana-flavor pickle being accepted by the public is rather remote.) What is a probability? In general, it is a number that describes the chance that something will happen.

PROBABILITY A value between zero and one, inclusive, describing the relative possibility (chance or likelihood) an event will occur.

A probability is frequently expressed as a decimal, such as .70, .27, or .50. However, it may be given as a fraction such as 7/10, 27/100, or 1/2. It can assume any number from 0 to 1, inclusive. If a company has only five sales regions, and each region's name or number is written on a slip of paper and the slips put in a hat, the probability of selecting one of the five regions is 1. The probability of selecting from the hat a slip of paper that reads "Pittsburgh Steelers" is 0. Thus, the probability of 1 represents something that is certain to happen, and the probability of 0 represents something that cannot happen.

The closer a probability is to 0, the more improbable it is the event will happen. The closer the probability is to 1, the more sure we are it will happen. The relationship is shown in the following diagram along with a few of our personal beliefs. You might, however, select a different probability for Slo Poke's chances to win the Kentucky Derby or for an increase in federal taxes.

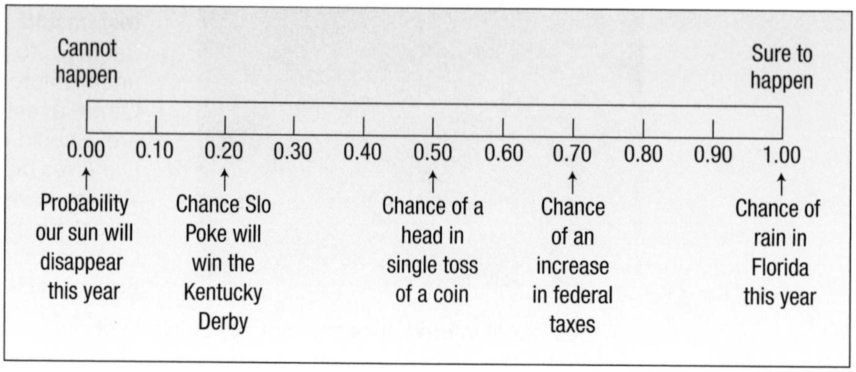

Three key words are used in the study of probability: **experiment, outcome,** and **event.** These terms are used in our everyday language, but in statistics they have specific meanings.

EXPERIMENT A process that leads to the occurrence of one and only one of several possible observations.

This definition is more general than the one used in the physical sciences, where we picture someone manipulating test tubes or microscopes. In reference to probability, an experiment has two or more possible results, and it is uncertain which will occur.

> **OUTCOME** A particular result of an experiment.

For example, the tossing of a coin is an experiment. You may observe the toss of the coin, but you are unsure whether it will come up "heads" or "tails." Similarly, asking 500 college students whether they would purchase a new Dell computer system at a particular price is an experiment. If the coin is tossed, one particular outcome is a "head." The alternative outcome is a "tail." In the computer purchasing experiment, one possible outcome is that 273 students indicate they would purchase the computer. Another outcome is that 317 students would purchase the computer. Still another outcome is that 423 students indicate that they would purchase it. When one or more of the experiment's outcomes are observed, we call this an event.

> **EVENT** A collection of one or more outcomes of an experiment.

Examples to clarify the definitions of the terms *experiment, outcome,* and *event* are on the next several pages.

In the die-rolling experiment there are six possible outcomes, but there are many possible events. When counting the number of members of the board of directors for Fortune 500 companies over 60 years of age, the number of possible outcomes can be anywhere from zero to the total number of members. There are an even larger number of possible events in this experiment.

Experiment	Roll a die	Count the number of members of the board of directors for Fortune 500 companies who are over 60 years of age
All possible outcomes	Observe a 1 Observe a 2 Observe a 3 Observe a 4 Observe a 5 Observe a 6	None are over 60 One is over 60 Two are over 60 ... 29 are over 60 ... ... 48 are over 60
Some possible events	Observe an even number Observe a number greater than 4 Observe a number 3 or less	More than 13 are over 60 Fewer than 20 are over 60

Self-Review 4–1

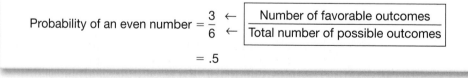

Video Games, Inc. recently developed a new video game. Its market potential is to be tested by 80 veteran game players.

(a) What is the experiment?
(b) What is one possible outcome?
(c) Suppose 65 players tried the new game and said they liked it. Is 65 a probability?
(d) The probability that the new game will be a success is computed to be −1.0. Comment.
(e) Specify one possible event.

Approaches to Probability

Two approaches to probability will be discussed, namely, the *objective* and the *subjective* viewpoints. **Objective probability** is subdivided into (1) *classical probability* and (2) *empirical probability.*

Classical Probability

Classical probability is based on the assumption that the outcomes of an experiment are *equally likely.* Using the classical viewpoint, the probability of an event happening is computed by dividing the number of favorable outcomes by the number of possible outcomes:

DEFINITION OF CLASSICAL PROBABILITY

$$\text{Probability of an event} = \frac{\text{Number of favorable outcomes}}{\text{Total number of possible outcomes}} \quad \textbf{[4–1]}$$

EXAMPLE

Consider an experiment of rolling a six-sided die. What is the probability of the event "an even number of spots appear face up"?

SOLUTION

The possible outcomes are:

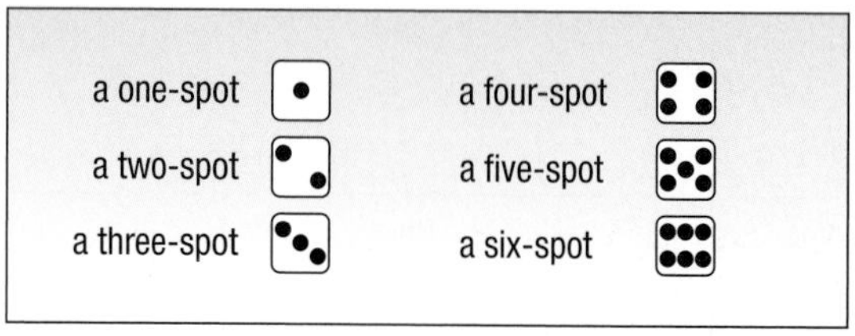

There are three "favorable" outcomes (a two, a four, and a six) in the collection of six equally likely possible outcomes. Therefore:

$$\text{Probability of an even number} = \frac{3}{6} \begin{array}{l} \leftarrow \text{Number of favorable outcomes} \\ \leftarrow \text{Total number of possible outcomes} \end{array}$$

$$= .5$$

We use the mutually exclusive concept in the study of frequency distributions. We create classes so that a particular observation is included in only one of the classes and there is no overlap between the classes. We use the same concept in the study of probability. Only one of several events can occur at one time.

MUTUALLY EXCLUSIVE The occurrence of one event means that none of the other events can occur at the same time.

The variable "gender" presents two mutually exclusive outcomes, male and female. An employee selected at random is either male or female but cannot be both. A manufactured part is acceptable or unacceptable. The part cannot be both acceptable and unacceptable at the same time. In a sample of manufactured parts, the event of selecting an unacceptable part and the event of selecting an acceptable part are mutually exclusive.

If an experiment has a set of events that includes every possible outcome, such as the events "an even number" and "an odd number" in the die-tossing experiment, then the set of events is **collectively exhaustive.** For the die-tossing experiment, every outcome will be either even or odd. So the set is collectively exhaustive.

COLLECTIVELY EXHAUSTIVE At least one of the events must occur when an experiment is conducted.

If the set of events is collectively exhaustive and the events are mutually exclusive, the sum of the probabilities equals 1.

Historically, the classical approach to probability was developed and applied in the 17th and 18th centuries to games of chance, such as cards and dice. It is unnecessary to do an experiment to determine the probability of an event occurring using the classical approach. We can logically arrive at the probability of getting a tail on the toss of one coin or three heads on the toss of three coins. We do not need to conduct an experiment to determine the probability that your income tax return will be audited if there are 2 million returns mailed to your district office and 2,400 are to be audited. Assuming that each return has an equal chance of being audited, your probability is .0012—found by 2,400 divided by 2 million. Obviously, the chance of your return being audited is rather remote.

Empirical Concept

Another way to define probability is based on **relative frequencies.** The probability of an event happening is determined by observing what fraction of the time similar events happened in the past. In terms of a formula:

$$\text{Probability of event happening} = \frac{\text{Number of times event occurred in past}}{\text{Total number of observations}}$$

EXAMPLE

A study of 750 business administration graduates of the University of Toledo revealed 450 of the 750 were *not* employed in their major area of study in college. For illustration, a person who majored in accounting is now the marketing manager of an e-commerce firm. What is the probability that a particular business graduate will be employed in an area other than his or her college major?

SOLUTION

To simplify, letters or numbers may be used. P stands for probability, and in this case $P(A)$ stands for the probability a graduate is not employed in his or her major area of college study.

$$\text{Probability of event happening} = \frac{\text{Number of times event occurred in past}}{\text{Total number of observations}}$$

$$P(A) = \frac{450}{750} = .60$$

Because 450 out of 750, or 60 percent, are in a different field of employment from their major in college, we can use this as an estimate of the probability. In other words, based on past experience, the probability is .60 that a new business graduate will be employed in a field other than his or her college major.

Subjective Probability

If there is little or no past experience on which to base a probability, it may be arrived at subjectively. Essentially, this means evaluating the available opinions and other information and then estimating or assigning the probability. This probability is aptly called a **subjective probability.**

SUBJECTIVE CONCEPT OF PROBABILITY The likelihood (probability) of a particular event happening that is assigned by an individual based on whatever information is available.

Illustrations of subjective probability are:

1. Estimating the likelihood the New England Patriots will play in the Super Bowl next year.
2. Estimating the probability General Motors Corp. will lose its number 1 ranking in total units sold to Ford Motor Co. or DaimlerChrysler within 2 years.
3. Estimating the likelihood you will earn an *A* in this course.

The types of probability are summarized in Chart 4–1. A probability statement always constitutes an estimate of an unknown value that will govern an event that has not yet occurred. There is, of course, a considerable latitude in the degree of uncertainty that surrounds this estimate, based primarily on the knowledge possessed by the individual concerning the underlying process. The individual possesses a great deal of knowledge about the toss of a die and can state that the probability that a one-spot will appear face up on the toss of a true die is one-sixth. But we know very little concerning the acceptance in the marketplace of a new and untested product. For example, even though a market research director tests a newly developed product in 40 retail stores and states that there is a 70 percent chance that the product will have sales of more than 1 million units, she still has little knowledge of how consumers will react when it is marketed nationally. In both cases (the case of the person rolling a die and the testing of a new product) the individual is assigning a probability value to an event of interest, and a difference exists only in the predictor's confidence in the precision of the estimate. However, regardless of the viewpoint, the same laws of probability (presented in the following sections) will be applied.

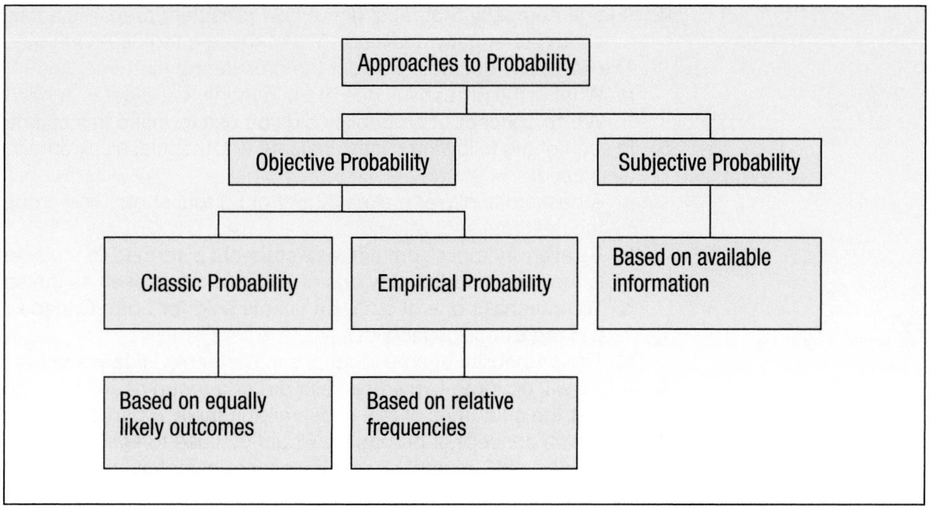

CHART 4–1 Summary of Approaches to Probability

Self-Review 4–2

1. One card will be randomly selected from a standard 52-card deck. What is the probability the card will be a queen? Which approach to probability did you use to answer this question?
2. The National Center for Health Statistics reports that of 883 deaths, 24 resulted from an automobile accident, 182 from cancer, and 333 from heart disease. What is the probability that a particular death is due to an automobile accident? Which approach to probability did you use to answer this question?
3. What is the probability that the Dow Jones Industrial Average will exceed 12,000? Which approach to probability did you use to answer this question?

Exercises

1. Some people are in favor of reducing Social Security benefits in order to achieve a balanced budget and others are against it. Two persons are selected and their opinions are recorded. List the possible outcomes.

2. A quality control inspector selects a part to be tested. The part is then declared acceptable, repairable, or scrapped. Then another part is tested. List the possible outcomes of this experiment regarding two parts.

3. A survey of 34 students at the Wall College of Business showed the following majors:

Accounting	10
Finance	5
Info. Systems	3
Management	6
Marketing	10

Suppose you select a student and observe his or her major.

a. What is the probability he or she is a management major?

b. Which concept of probability did you use to make this estimate?

4. A large company that must hire a new president prepares a final list of five candidates, all of whom are equally qualified. Two of these candidates are members of a minority group. The company decides to select the president by lottery.
   a. What is the probability one of the minority candidates is hired?
   b. Which concept of probability did you use to make this estimate?
5. In each of the following cases, indicate whether classical, empirical, or subjective probability is used.
   a. A basketball player makes 30 out of 50 foul shots. The probability is .6 that she makes the next foul shot attempted.
   b. A seven-member committee of students is formed to study environmental issues. What is the likelihood that any one of the seven is chosen as the spokesperson?
   c. You purchase one of 5 million tickets sold for Lotto Canada. What is the likelihood you win the $1 million jackpot?
   d. The probability of an earthquake in northern California in the next 10 years is .80.
6. A firm will promote two employees out of a group of six men and three women.
   a. List the outcomes of this experiment if there is particular concern about gender equity.
   b. Which concept of probability would you use to estimate these probabilities?
7. A sample of 40 minority executives were selected to test a questionnaire. One question about environmental issues required a yes or no answer.
   a. What is the experiment?
   b. List one possible event.
   c. Ten of the 40 executives responded "yes." Based on these sample responses, what is the probability an executive responded "yes"?
   d. What concept of probability does this illustrate?
   e. Are each of the possible outcomes equally likely and mutually exclusive?
8. A sample of 2000 licensed drivers revealed the following number of violations.

Number of Violations	Number of Drivers
0	1,910
1	46
2	18
3	12
4	9
5 or more	5
Total	2,000

   a. What is the experiment?
   b. List one possible event.
   c. What is the probability that a particular driver had exactly two violations?
   d. What concept of probability does this illustrate?
9. Bank of America customers select their own three-digit personal identification number (PIN) for use at ATMs.
   a. Think of this as an experiment and list four possible outcomes.
   b. What is the probability Mr. Jones and Mrs. Smith select the same PIN?
   c. Which concept of probability did you use to answer the question above?
10. An investor buys 100 shares of AT&T stock and records its price change daily.
   a. List several possible events for this experiment.
   b. Estimate the probability for each event you described in a.
   c. Which concept of probability did you use in b.?

Some Rules of Probability

Now that we have defined probability and described the different approaches to probability, we turn our attention to combining events by applying rules of addition and multiplication.

Rules of Addition

Mutually exclusive events cannot both happen.

Special Rule of Addition To apply the **special rule of addition,** the events must be mutually exclusive. Recall that *mutually exclusive* means that when one event occurs, none of the other events can occur at the same time. An illustration of mutually exclusive events in the die-tossing experiment is the events "a number 4 or larger" and "a number 2 or smaller." If the outcome is in the first group {4, 5, and 6}, then it cannot also be in the second group {1 and 2}. And a product coming off the assembly line cannot be defective and satisfactory at the same time.

If two events A and B are mutually exclusive, the special rule of addition states that the probability of one *or* the other event's occurring equals the sum of their probabilities. This rule is expressed in the following formula:

SPECIAL RULE OF ADDITION $$P(A \text{ or } B) = P(A) + P(B) \qquad \textbf{[4–2]}$$

For three mutually exclusive events designated A, B, and C, the rule is written:

$$P(A \text{ or } B \text{ or } C) = P(A) + P(B) + P(C)$$

An example will help to show the details.

EXAMPLE

An automatic Shaw machine fills plastic bags with a mixture of beans, broccoli, and other vegetables. Most of the bags contain the correct weight, but because of the variation in the size of the beans and other vegetables, a package might be underweight or overweight. A check of 4,000 packages filled in the past month revealed:

Weight	Event	Number of Packages	Probability of Occurrence	
Underweight	*A*	100	.025	← $\frac{100}{4,000}$
Satisfactory	*B*	3,600	.900	
Overweight	*C*	300	.075	
		4,000	1.000	

What is the probability that a particular package will be either underweight or overweight?

SOLUTION

The outcome "underweight" is the event A. The outcome "overweight" is the event C. Applying the special rule of addition:

$$P(A \text{ or } C) = P(A) + P(C) = .025 + .075 = .10$$

Note that the events are mutually exclusive, meaning that a package of mixed vegetables cannot be underweight, satisfactory, and overweight at the same time. They are also collectively exhaustive; that is, a selected package must be either underweight, satisfactory, or overweight.

English logician J. Venn (1835–1888) developed a diagram to portray graphically the outcome of an experiment. The *mutually exclusive* concept and various other rules for combining probabilities can be illustrated using this device. To construct a Venn

A Venn diagram is a useful tool to depict addition or multiplication rules.

diagram, a space is first enclosed representing the total of all possible outcomes. This space is usually in the form of a rectangle. An event is then represented by a circular area which is drawn inside the rectangle proportional to the probability of the event. The following Venn diagram represents the *mutually exclusive* concept. There is no overlapping of events, meaning that the events are mutually exclusive.

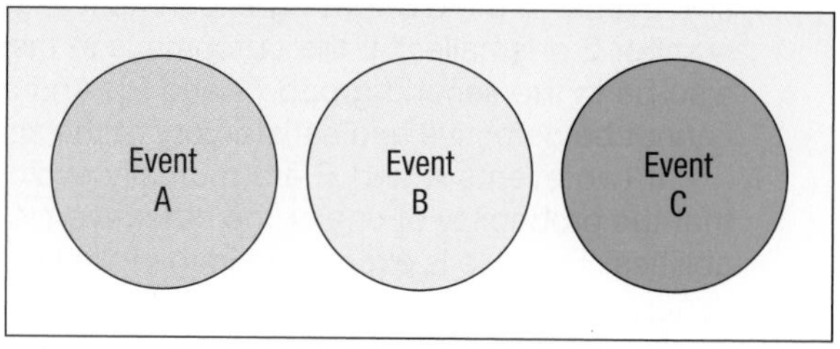

The probability that a bag of mixed vegetables selected is underweight, $P(A)$, plus the probability that it is not an underweight bag, written $P(\sim A)$ and read "not *A*," must logically equal 1. This is written:

$$P(A) + P(\sim A) = 1$$

This can be revised to read:

COMPLEMENT RULE	$P(A) = 1 - P(\sim A)$	**[4–3]**

This is the **complement rule.** Notice that the events A and $\sim A$ are mutually exclusive and collectively exhaustive.

The complement rule is used to determine the probability of an event occurring by subtracting the probability of the event *not* occurring from 1. A Venn diagram illustrating the complement rule might appear as:

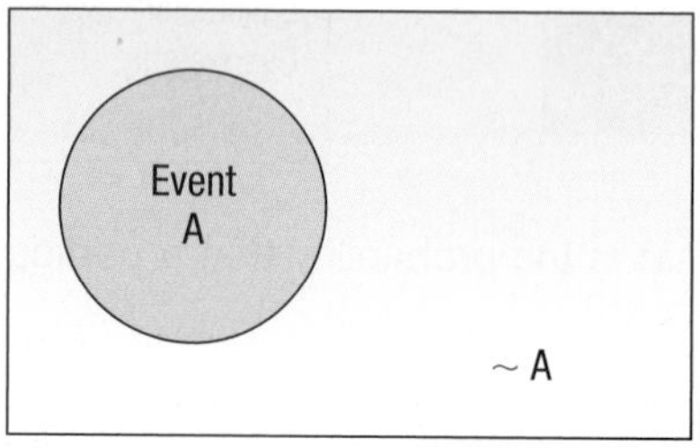

EXAMPLE

Recall the probability a bag of mixed vegetables is underweight is .025 and the probability of an overweight bag is .075. Use the complement rule to show the probability of a satisfactory bag is .900. Show the solution using a Venn diagram.

SOLUTION

The probability the bag is unsatisfactory equals the probability the bag is overweight plus the probability it is underweight. That is, $P(A \text{ or } C) = P(A) + P(C) = .025 + .075 = .100$. The bag is satisfactory if it is not underweight or overweight, so $P(B) = 1 - [P(A) + P(C)] = 1 - [.025 + .075] = 0.900$. The Venn diagram portraying this situation is:

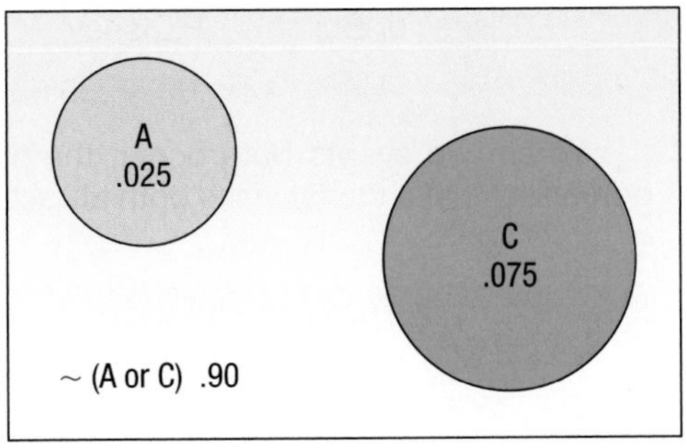

The complement rule is important in the study of probability. Often it is easier to calculate the probability of an event happening by determining the probability of it not happening and subtracting the result from 1.

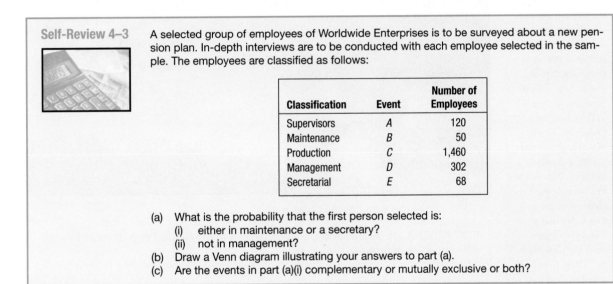

Self-Review 4–3

A selected group of employees of Worldwide Enterprises is to be surveyed about a new pension plan. In-depth interviews are to be conducted with each employee selected in the sample. The employees are classified as follows:

Classification	Event	Number of Employees
Supervisors	*A*	120
Maintenance	*B*	50
Production	*C*	1,460
Management	*D*	302
Secretarial	*E*	68

(a) What is the probability that the first person selected is:
  (i) either in maintenance or a secretary?
  (ii) not in management?
(b) Draw a Venn diagram illustrating your answers to part (a).
(c) Are the events in part (a)(i) complementary or mutually exclusive or both?

The General Rule of Addition The outcomes of an experiment may not be mutually exclusive. Suppose, for illustration, that the Florida Tourist Commission selected a sample of 200 tourists who visited the state during the year. The survey revealed that 120 tourists went to Disney World and 100 went to Busch Gardens near Tampa. What is the probability that a person selected visited either Disney World or Busch Gardens? If the special rule of addition is used, the probability of selecting a tourist who went to Disney World is .60, found by 120/200. Similarly, the probability of a tourist going to Busch Gardens is .50. The sum of these probabilities is 1.10. We know, however, that this probability cannot be greater than 1. The explanation is that many tourists visited both attractions and are being counted twice! A check of the survey responses revealed that 60 out of 200 sampled did, in fact, visit both attractions.

To answer our question, "What is the probability a selected person visited either Disney World or Busch Gardens?" (1) add the probability that a tourist visited Disney World and the probability he/she visited Busch Gardens, and (2) subtract the probability of visiting both. Thus:

$$P(\text{Disney or Busch}) = P(\text{Disney}) + P(\text{Busch}) - P(\text{both Disney and Busch})$$
$$= .60 + .50 - .30 = .80$$

When two events both occur, the probability is called a **joint probability.** The probability that a tourist visits both attractions (.30) is an example of a joint probability.

Statistics in Action

If you wish to get some attention at the next gathering you attend, announce that you believe that at least two people present were born on the same date—that is, the same day of the year but not necessarily the same year. If there are 30 people in the room, the probability of a duplicate is .706. If there are 60 people in the room, the probability is .994 that at least two people share the same birthday. With as few as 23 people the chances are even, that is .50, that at least two people share the same birthday. Hint: To compute this, find the probability everyone was born on a different day and use the complement rule.

JOINT PROBABILITY A probability that measures the likelihood two or more events will happen concurrently.

In summary, the general rule of addition refers to events that are not mutually exclusive. This rule for two events designated A and B is written:

GENERAL RULE OF ADDITION $$P(A \text{ or } B) = P(A) + P(B) - P(A \text{ and } B) \quad \textbf{[4–4]}$$

For the expression $P(A \text{ or } B)$, the word *or* suggests that A may occur or B may occur. This also includes the possibility that A and B may occur. This use of *or* is sometimes called an **inclusive.** You could also write $P(A \text{ or } B \text{ or both})$ to emphasize that the union of the events includes the intersection of A and B.

EXAMPLE

What is the probability that a card chosen at random from a standard deck of cards will be either a king or a heart?

SOLUTION

We may be inclined to add the probability of a king and the probability of a heart. But this creates a problem. If we do that, the king of hearts is counted with the kings and also with the hearts. So, if we simply add the probability of a king (there are 4 in a deck of 52 cards) to the probability of a heart (there are 13 in a deck of 52 cards) and report that 17 out of 52 cards meet the requirement, we have counted the king of hearts twice. We need to subtract 1 card from the 17 so the king of hearts is counted only once. Thus, there are 16 cards that are either hearts or kings. So the probability is 16/52 = .3077.

Card	Probability	Explanation
King	$P(A) = 4/52$	4 kings in a deck of 52 cards
Heart	$P(B) = 13/52$	13 hearts in a deck of 52 cards
King of hearts	$P(A \text{ and } B) = 1/52$	1 king of hearts in a deck of 52 cards

Using formula (4–4):

$$P(A \text{ or } B) = P(A) + P(B) - P(A \text{ and } B)$$
$$= 4/52 + 13/52 - 1/52$$
$$= 16/52, \text{ or } .3077$$

A Venn diagram portrays these outcomes, which are not mutually exclusive.

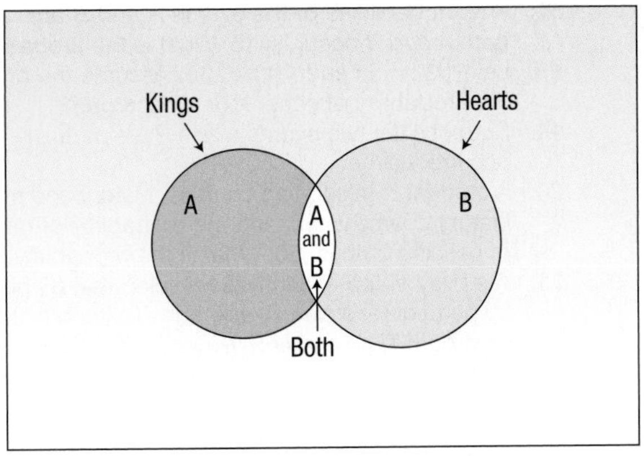

Self-Review 4–4

Routine physical examinations are conducted annually as part of a health service program for General Concrete, Inc. employees. It was discovered that 8 percent of the employees need corrective shoes, 15 percent need major dental work, and 3 percent need both corrective shoes and major dental work.

(a) What is the probability that an employee selected at random will need either corrective shoes or major dental work?
(b) Show this situation in the form of a Venn diagram.

Exercises

11. The events *A* and *B* are mutually exclusive. Suppose $P(A) = .30$ and $P(B) = .20$. What is the probability of either *A* or *B* occurring? What is the probability that neither *A* nor *B* will happen?

12. The events *X* and *Y* are mutually exclusive. Suppose $P(X) = .05$ and $P(Y) = .02$. What is the probability of either *X* or *Y* occurring? What is the probability that neither *X* nor *Y* will happen?

13. A study of 200 grocery chains revealed these incomes after taxes:

Income after Taxes	Number of Firms
Under $1 million	102
$1 million to $20 million	61
$20 million or more	37

a. What is the probability a particular chain has under $1 million in income after taxes?
b. What is the probability a grocery chain selected at random has either an income between $1 million and $20 million, or an income of $20 million or more? What rule of probability was applied?

14. The chair of the board of directors says, "There is a 50 percent chance this company will earn a profit, a 30 percent chance it will break even, and a 20 percent chance it will lose money next quarter."
a. Use an addition rule to find the probability they will not lose money next quarter.
b. Use the complement rule to find the probability they will not lose money next quarter.

15. Suppose the probability you will get a grade of *A* in this class is .25 and the probability you will get a *B* is .50. What is the probability your grade will be above a *C*?

16. Two coins are tossed. If *A* is the event "two heads" and *B* is the event "two tails," are *A* and *B* mutually exclusive? Are they complements?

17. The probabilities of the events *A* and *B* are .20 and .30, respectively. The probability that both *A* and *B* occur is .15. What is the probability of either *A* or *B* occurring?

18. Let $P(X) = .55$ and $P(Y) = .35$. Assume the probability that they both occur is .20. What is the probability of either *X* or *Y* occurring?

19. Suppose the two events *A* and *B* are mutually exclusive. What is the probability of their joint occurrence?

20. A student is taking two courses, history and math. The probability the student will pass the history course is .60, and the probability of passing the math course is .70. The probability of passing both is .50. What is the probability of passing at least one?

21. A survey of top executives revealed that 35 percent of them regularly read *Time* magazine, 20 percent read *Newsweek,* and 40 percent read *U.S. News and World Report.* Ten percent read both *Time* and *U.S. News and World Report.*
a. What is the probability that a particular top executive reads either *Time* or *U.S. News and World Report* regularly?
b. What is the probability .10 called?
c. Are the events mutually exclusive? Explain.

22. A study by the National Park Service revealed that 50 percent of vacationers going to the Rocky Mountain region visit Yellowstone Park, 40 percent visit the Tetons, and 35 percent visit both.
a. What is the probability a vacationer will visit at least one of these attractions?
b. What is the probability .35 called?
c. Are the events mutually exclusive? Explain.

Rules of Multiplication

Special Rule of Multiplication

The special rule of multiplication requires that two events *A* and *B* be **independent.** Two events are independent if the occurrence of one does not alter the probability of the other. So if the events *A* and *B* are independent, the occurrence of *A* does not alter the probability of *B*.

> **INDEPENDENT** The occurrence of one event has no effect on the probability of the occurrence of another event.

For two independent events *A* and *B*, the probability that *A* and *B* will both occur is found by multiplying the two probabilities. This is the **special rule of multiplication** and is written symbolically as:

SPECIAL RULE OF MULTIPLICATION	$P(A \text{ and } B) = P(A)P(B)$	[4–5]

This rule for combining probabilities presumes that a second event is *not* affected by the first event. To illustrate what is meant by independence of events, suppose two coins are tossed. The outcome of one coin (head or tail) is unaffected by the outcome of the other coin (head or tail). To put it another way, two events are independent if the outcome of the second event does not depend on the outcome of the first event.

For three independent events A, B, and C, the special rule of multiplication used to determine the probability that all three events will occur is:

$$P(A \text{ and } B \text{ and } C) = P(A)P(B)P(C)$$

EXAMPLE

A survey by the American Automobile Association (AAA) revealed 60 percent of its members made airline reservations last year. Two members are selected at random. What is the probability both made airline reservations last year?

SOLUTION

The probability the first member made an airline reservation last year is .60, written $P(R_1) = .60$, where R_1 refers to the fact that the first member made a reservation. The probability that the second member selected made a reservation is also .60, so $P(R_2) = .60$. Since the number of AAA members is very large, you may assume that R_1 and R_2 are independent. Consequently, using formula (4–5), the probability they both make a reservation is .36, found by:

$$P(R_1 \text{ and } R_2) = P(R_1)P(R_2) = (.60)(.60) = .36$$

All possible outcomes can be shown as follows. R means a reservation is made, and NR means no reservation was made.

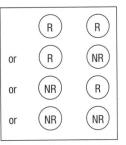

	R	R
or	R	NR
or	NR	R
or	NR	NR

Self-Review 4–5

From long experience, Teton Tire knows the probability is .80 that their XB-70 will last 60,000 miles before it becomes bald or fails. An adjustment is made on any tire that does not last 60,000 miles. You purchase four XB-70s. What is the probability all four tires will last at least 60,000 miles?

If two events are not independent, they are referred to as **dependent.** To illustrate dependency, suppose there are 10 rolls of film in a box, and it is known that 3 are defective. A roll of film is selected from the box. The probability of selecting a defective roll is 3/10, and the probability of selecting a good roll is 7/10. Then a second roll is selected from the box without the first one being returned to the box. The probability this second roll is defective *depends* on whether the first roll selected was defective or good. The probability that the second roll is defective is:

2/9, if the first roll was defective. (Only two defective rolls remain in the box containing nine rolls.)
3/9, if the first roll selected was good. (All three defective rolls are still in the box containing nine rolls.)

The fraction 2/9 (or 3/9) is aptly called a **conditional probability** because its value is conditional on (dependent on) whether a defective or a good roll of film is chosen in the first selection from the box.

CONDITIONAL PROBABILITY The probability of a particular event occurring, given that another event has occurred.

General Rule of Multiplication We use the **general rule of multiplication** to find the *joint probability* that two events will occur, such as selecting 2 defective rolls from the box of 10 rolls, one after the other. In general, the rule states that for two events *A* and *B*, the joint probability that both events will happen is found by multiplying the probability event *A* will happen by the conditional probability of event *B* occurring. Symbolically, the joint probability $P(A \text{ and } B)$ is found by:

GENERAL RULE OF MULTIPLICATION $$P(A \text{ and } B) = P(A)P(B \mid A) \qquad \textbf{[4–6]}$$

where $P(B \mid A)$ stands for the probability B will occur *given that A has already occurred.* The vertical line means "given that."

EXAMPLE

To illustrate the formula, let's use the problem with 10 rolls of film in a box, 3 of which are defective. Two rolls are to be selected, one after the other. What is the probability of selecting a defective roll followed by another defective roll?

SOLUTION

The first roll of film selected from the box being found defective is event D_1, $P(D_1) = 3/10$ because 3 out of the 10 are defective. The second roll selected being found defective is event D_2. Therefore, $P(D_2 \mid D_1) = 2/9$, because after the first selection was found to be defective, only 2 defective rolls of film remained in the box containing 9 rolls. Determining the probability of two defectives [see formula (4–6)]:

$$P(D_1 \text{ and } D_2) = P(D_1)P(D_2 \mid D_1) = \left(\frac{3}{10}\right)\left(\frac{2}{9}\right) = \frac{6}{90}, \text{ or about .07}$$

Incidentally, it is assumed that this experiment was conducted *without replacement*—that is, the first defective roll of film was not thrown back in the box before the next roll was selected. It should also be noted that the general rule of multiplication can be extended to more than two events. For three events, *A*, *B*, and *C*, the formula would be:

$$P(A \text{ and } B \text{ and } C) = P(A)P(B \mid A)P(C \mid A \text{ and } B)$$

For illustration, the probability the first three rolls chosen from the box will all be defective is .00833, found by:

$$P(D_1 \text{ and } D_2 \text{ and } D_3) = P(D_1)P(D_2 \mid D_1)P(D_3 \mid D_1 \text{ and } D_2)$$
$$= \left(\frac{3}{10}\right)\left(\frac{2}{9}\right)\left(\frac{1}{8}\right) = \frac{6}{720} = .00833$$

Self-Review 4–6

The board of directors of Tarbell Industries consists of eight men and four women. A four-member search committee is to be chosen at random to conduct a nationwide search for a new company president.

(a) What is the probability all four members of the search committee will be women?
(b) What is the probability all four members will be men?
(c) Does the sum of the probabilities for the events described in parts (a) and (b) equal 1? Explain.

Statistics in Action

In 2000 George W. Bush won the Presidency by the slimmest of margins. Many election stories resulted, some involving voting irregularities, others raising interesting election questions. In a local Michigan election there was a tie between two candidates for an elected position. To break the tie the candidates drew a slip of paper from a box that contained two slips of paper, one marked "Winner" and the other unmarked. To determine which candidate drew first, election officials flipped a coin. The winner of the coin flip also drew the winning slip of paper. But was the coin flip really necessary? No, because the two events are independent. Winning the coin flip did not alter the probability of either candidate drawing the winning slip of paper.

Contingency Tables

Often we tally the results of a survey into a two-way table and use these results of this tally to determine various probabilities. We refer to this two-way table as a contingency table.

CONTINGENCY TABLE A table used to classify sample observations according to two or more identifiable characteristics.

A contingency table is a cross tabulation that simultaneously summarizes two variables of interest and their relationship. Below are several examples.

- A survey of 150 adults classified each as to gender and the number of movies attended last month. Each respondent is classified according to two criteria—the number of movies attended and gender.

	Gender		
Movies Attended	**Men**	**Women**	**Total**
0	20	40	60
1	40	30	70
2 or more	10	10	20
Total	70	80	150

- The American Coffee Producers Association reports the following information on age and the amount of coffee consumed in a month.

	Coffee Consumption			
Age (Years)	**Low**	**Moderate**	**High**	**Total**
Under 30	36	32	24	92
30 up to 40	18	30	27	75
40 up to 50	10	24	20	54
50 and over	26	24	29	79
Total	90	110	100	300

According to this table each of the 300 respondents is classified according to two criteria: (1) their age and (2) the amount of coffee consumed.

The following example shows how the rules of addition and multiplication are used when we employ contingency tables.

EXAMPLE

A survey of executives dealt with their loyalty to the company. One of the questions was, "If you were given an offer by another company equal to or slightly better than your present position, would you remain with the company or take the other position?" The responses of the 200 executives in the survey were cross-classified with their length of service with the company. (See Table 4–1.)

TABLE 4–1 Loyalty of Executives and Length of Service with Company

	Length of Service				
Loyalty	Less than 1 Year B_1	1–5 Years B_2	6–10 Years B_3	More than 10 Years B_4	Total
Would remain, A_1	10	30	5	75	120
Would not remain, $\sim A$	25	15	10	30	80
	35	45	15	105	200

What is the probability of randomly selecting an executive who is loyal to the company (would remain) and who has more than 10 years of service? What is the probability of selecting an executive that would remain *or* has less than 1 year of service?

SOLUTION

Note that two events occur at the same time—the executive would remain with the company, and he or she has more than 10 years of service.

1. Event A_1 happens if a randomly selected executive will remain with the company despite an equal or slightly better offer from another company. To find the probability that event A_1 will happen, refer to Table 4–1. Note there are 120 executives out of the 200 in the survey who would remain with the company, so $P(A_1) = 120/200$, or .60.
2. Event B_4 happens if a randomly selected executive has more than 10 years of service with the company. Thus, $P(B_4 \mid A_1)$ is the conditional probability that an executive with more than 10 years of service would remain with the company despite an equal or slightly better offer from another company. Referring to the contingency table, Table 4–1, 75 of the 120 executives who would remain have more than 10 years of service, so $P(B_4 \mid A_1) = 75/120$.

Solving for the probability that an executive randomly selected will be one who would remain with the company and who has more than 10 years of service with the company, using the general rule of multiplication in formula (4–6):

$$P(A_1 \text{ and } B_4) = P(A_1)P(B_4 \mid A_1) = \left(\frac{120}{200}\right)\left(\frac{75}{120}\right) = \frac{9{,}000}{24{,}000} = .375$$

To find the probability of selecting an executive who would remain with the company *or* has less than 1 year of experience we use the general rule of addition, formula (4–4).

1. Event A_1 refers to executives that would remain with the company. So $P(A_1) = 120/200 = .60$.
2. Event B_1 refers to executives that have been with the company less than 1 year. The probability of B_1 is $P(B_1) = 35/200 = .175$.
3. The events A_1 and B_1 are not mutually exclusive. That is, an executive can both be willing to remain with the company and have less than 1 year of experience. We

write this probability, which is called the joint probability, as $P(A_1 \text{ and } B_1)$. There are 10 executives who would both stay with the company and have less than 1 year of service, so $P(A_1 \text{ and } B_1) = 10/200 = .05$. These 10 people are in both groups, those who would remain with the company and those with less than 1 year with the company. They are actually being counted twice, so we need to subtract out this value.

4. We insert these values in formula (4–4) and the result is as follows.

$$P(A_1 \text{ or } B_1) = P(A_1) + P(B_1) - P(A_1 \text{ and } B_1)$$
$$= .60 + .175 - .05 = .725$$

So the likelihood that a selected executive would either remain with the company or has been with the company less than 1 year is .725. The following chart summarizes the results and emphasizes the need to remove the 10 executives who would remain with the company and have less than 1 year of service.

	Length of Service				
Loyalty	Less than 1 Year B_1	1–5 Years B_2	6–10 Years B_3	More than 10 Years B_4	Total
Would remain, A_1	10	30	5	75	120
Would not remain, ~A	25	15	10	30	80
Total	35	45	15	105	200

Self-Review 4–7

Refer to Table 4-1 to find the following probabilities.

(a) What is the probability of selecting an executive with more than 10 years of service?
(b) What is the probability of selecting an executive who would not remain with the company, given that he or she has more than 10 years of service?
(c) What is the probability of selecting an executive with more than 10 years of service or one who would not remain with the company?

Tree Diagrams

The **tree diagram** is a graph that is helpful in organizing calculations that involve several stages. Each segment in the tree is one stage of the problem. The branches of a tree diagram are weighted by probabilities. We will use the data in Table 4–1 to show the construction of a tree diagram.

Steps in constructing a tree diagram

1. To construct a tree diagram, we begin by drawing a heavy dot on the left to represent the root of the tree (see Chart 4–2).
2. For this problem, two main branches go out from the root, the upper one representing "would remain" and the lower one "would not remain." Their probabilities are written on the branches, namely, 120/200 and 80/200. These probabilities could also be denoted $P(A)$ and $P(\sim A)$.
3. Four branches "grow" out of each of the two main branches. These branches represent the length of service—less than 1 year, 1–5 years, 6–10 years, and more than 10 years. The conditional probabilities for the upper branch of the tree, 10/120, 30/120, 5/120, and so on are written on the appropriate branches. These are $P(B_1 \mid A_1)$, $P(B_2 \mid A_1)$, $P(B_3 \mid A_1)$, and $P(B_4 \mid A_1)$, where B_1 refers to less than 1

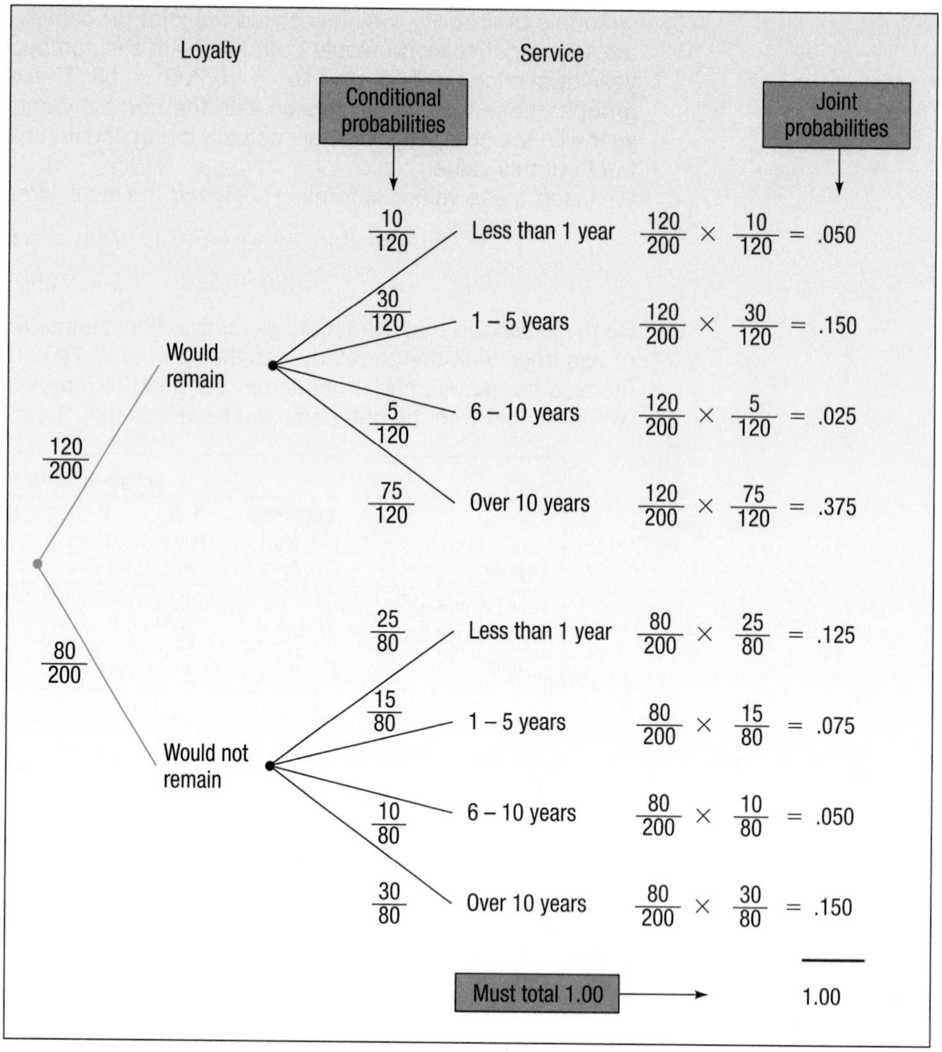

CHART 4–2 Tree Diagram Showing Loyalty and Length of Service

year of service, B_2 1 to 5 years, B_3 6 to 10 years, and B_4 more than 10 years. Next, write the conditional probabilities for the lower branch.

4. Finally, joint probabilities, that the events A_1 and B_i, or the events $\sim A$ and B_i will occur together, are shown on the right side. For example, the joint probability of randomly selecting an executive who would remain with the company and who has less than 1 year of service, using formula (4–6), is:

$$P(A_1 \text{ and } B_1) = P(A_1)P(B_1 \mid A_1) = \left(\frac{120}{200}\right)\left(\frac{10}{120}\right) = .05$$

Because the joint probabilities represent all possible selections (would remain, 6–10 years service; would not remain, more than 10 years of service; etc.), they must sum to 1.00 (see Chart 4–2).

Self-Review 4–8

A random sample of the employees of the Hardware Manufacturing Company was chosen to determine their retirement plans after age 65. Those selected in the sample were divided into management and production. The results were:

	Plans after Age 65		
Employee	**Retire**	**Not Retire**	**Total**
Management	5	15	20
Production	30	50	80
			100

(a) What is the table called?
(b) Draw a tree diagram, and determine the joint probabilities.
(c) Do the joint probabilities total 1.00? Why?

Exercises

23. Suppose $P(A) = .40$ and $P(B \mid A) = .30$. What is the joint probability of A and B?

24. Suppose $P(X_1) = .75$ and $P(Y_2 \mid X_1) = .40$. What is the joint probability of X_1 and Y_2?

25. A local bank reports that 80 percent of its customers maintain a checking account, 60 percent have a savings account, and 50 percent have both. If a customer is chosen at random, what is the probability the customer has either a checking or a savings account? What is the probability the customer does not have either a checking or a savings account?

26. All Seasons Plumbing has two service trucks which frequently break down. If the probability the first truck is available is .75, the probability the second truck is available is .50, and the probability that both trucks are available is .30, what is the probability neither truck is available?

27. Refer to the following table.

	First Event			
Second Event	A_1	A_2	A_3	**Total**
B_1	2	1	3	6
B_2	1	2	1	4
Total	3	3	4	10

a. Determine $P(A_1)$.
b. Determine $P(B_1 \mid A_2)$.
c. Determine $P(B_2 \text{ and } A_3)$.

28. Three defective electric toothbrushes were accidentally shipped to a drugstore by Cleanbrush Products along with 17 nondefective ones.
a. What is the probability the first two electric toothbrushes sold will be returned to the drugstore because they are defective?
b. What is the probability the first two electric toothbrushes sold will not be defective?

29. Each salesperson at Stiles-Compton is rated either below average, average, or above average with respect to sales ability. Each salesperson is also rated with respect to his or her potential for advancement—either fair, good, or excellent. These traits for the 500 salespeople were cross-classified into the following table.

	Potential for Advancement		
Sales Ability	**Fair**	**Good**	**Excellent**
Below average	16	12	22
Average	45	60	45
Above average	93	72	135

a. What is this table called?
b. What is the probability a salesperson selected at random will have above average sales ability and excellent potential for advancement?
c. Construct a tree diagram showing all the probabilities, conditional probabilities, and joint probabilities.

30. An investor owns three common stocks. Each stock, independently of the other, has equally likely chances of (1) increasing in value, (2) decreasing in value, or (3) remaining the same value. List the possible outcomes of this experiment. Estimate the probability at least two of the stocks increase in value.
31. The board of directors of a small company consists of five people. Three of those are "strong leaders." If they buy an idea, the entire board will agree. The other "weak" members have no influence. Three salesmen are scheduled, one after the other, to make sales presentations to a board member of the salesman's choice. The salesmen are convincing but do not know who the "strong leaders" are. However, they will know who the previous salesmen spoke to. The first salesman to find a strong leader will win the account. Do the three salesmen have the same chance of winning the account? If not, find their respective probabilities of winning.
32. If you ask three strangers on campus, what is the probability: (a) All were born on Wednesday? (b) All were born on different days of the week? (c) None were born on Saturday?

Statistics in Action

A recent study by the National Collegiate Athletic Association (NCAA) reported that of 150,000 senior boys playing on their high school basketball team, 64 would make a professional team. To put it another way, the odds of a high school senior basketball player making a professional team are 1 in 2,344. From the same study:

1. The odds of a high school senior playing some college basketball are about 1 in 40.
2. The odds of a high school senior playing college basketball as a senior in college are about 1 in 60.
3. If you play as a senior in college, the odds of making a professional team are about 1 in 37.5.

Principles of Counting

If the number of possible outcomes in an experiment is small, it is relatively easy to count them. There are six possible outcomes, for example, resulting from the roll of a die, namely:

If, however, there are a large number of possible outcomes, such as the number of boys and girls for families with 10 children, it would be tedious to count all the possibilities. They could have all boys, one boy and nine girls, two boys and eight girls, and so on. To facilitate counting, three counting formulas will be examined: the **multiplication formula** (not to be confused with the multiplication *rule* described earlier in the chapter), the **permutation formula,** and the **combination formula.**

The Multiplication Formula

MULTIPLICATION FORMULA If there are m ways of doing one thing and n ways of doing another thing, there are $m \times n$ ways of doing both.

In terms of a formula:

MULTIPLICATION FORMULA Total number of arrangements $= (m)(n)$ **[4–7]**

This can be extended to more than two events. For three events m, n, and o:

$$\text{Total number of arrangements} = (m)(n)(o)$$

EXAMPLE

An automobile dealer wants to advertise that for $29,999 you can buy a convertible, a two-door, or a four-door model with your choice of either wire wheel covers or solid wheel covers. How many different arrangements of models and wheel covers can the dealer offer?

SOLUTION

Of course the dealer could determine the total number of arrangements by picturing and counting them. There are six.

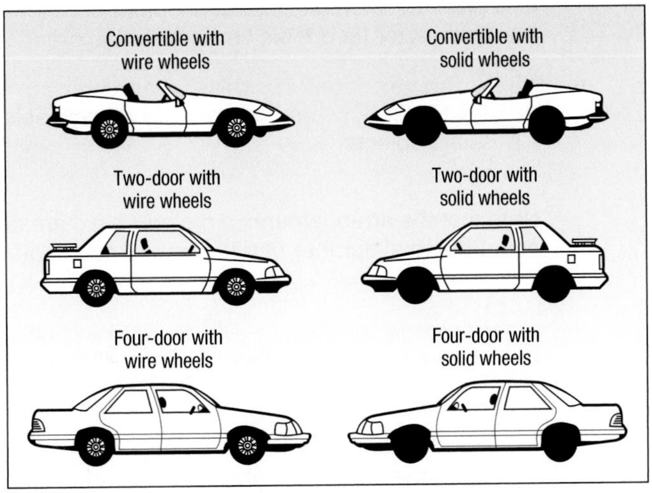

We can employ the multiplication formula as a check (where m is the number of models and n the wheel cover type). Using formula (4–7):

$$\text{Total possible arrangements} = (m)(n) = (3)(2) = 6$$

It was not difficult to count all the possible model and wheel cover combinations in this example. Suppose, however, that the dealer decided to offer eight models and six types of wheel covers. It would be tedious to picture and count all the possible alternatives. Instead, the multiplication formula can be used. In this case, there are $(m)(n) = (8)(6) = 48$ possible arrangements.

Note in the preceding applications of the multiplication formula that there were *two or more groupings from which you made selections.* The automobile dealer, for example, offered a choice of models and a choice of wheel covers. If a home builder offered you four different exterior styles of a home to choose from and three interior floor plans, the multiplication formula would be used to find how many different arrangements were possible.

Self-Review 4–9

1. Stiffin Lamps has developed five lamp bases and four lamp shades that can be used together. How many different arrangements of base and shade can be offered?
2. Pioneer manufactures three models of stereo receivers, two cassette decks, four speakers, and three CD carousels. When the four types of components are sold together, they form a "system." How many different systems can the electronics firm offer?

The Permutation Formula

As noted, the multiplication formula is applied to find the number of possible arrangements for two or more groups. The **permutation formula** is applied to find the possible number of arrangements when there is only *one* group of objects. As illustrations of this type of problem:

- Three electronic parts are to be assembled into a plug-in unit for a television set. The parts can be assembled in any order. The question involving counting is: In how many different ways can the three parts be assembled?
- A machine operator must make four safety checks before starting his machine. It does not matter in which order the checks are made. In how many different ways can the operator make the checks?

One order for the first illustration might be: the transistor first, the LEDs second, and the synthesizer third. This arrangement is called a **permutation.**

> **PERMUTATION** Any arrangement of r objects selected from a single group of n possible objects.

Note that the arrangements $a\ b\ c$ and $b\ a\ c$ are different permutations. The formula to count the total number of different permutations is:

PERMUTATION FORMULA
$$_nP_r = \frac{n!}{(n - r)!} \qquad [4\text{–}8]$$

where:

n is the total number of objects.
r is the number of objects selected.

Before we solve the two problems illustrated, note that permutations and combinations (to be discussed shortly) use a notation called *n factorial.* It is written $n!$ and means the product of $n(n - 1)(n - 2)(n - 3) \cdots (1)$. For instance, $5! = 5 \cdot 4 \cdot 3 \cdot 2 \cdot 1 = 120$.

As shown below, numbers can be canceled when the same numbers are included in the numerator and denominator.

$$\frac{6!3!}{4!} = \frac{6 \cdot 5 \cdot \cancel{4} \cdot \cancel{3} \cdot \cancel{2} \cdot \cancel{1}(3 \cdot 2 \cdot 1)}{\cancel{4} \cdot \cancel{3} \cdot \cancel{2} \cdot \cancel{1}} = 180$$

By definition, zero factorial, written 0!, is 1. That is, $0! = 1$.

EXAMPLE

Referring to the group of three electronic parts that are to be assembled in any order, in how many different ways can they be assembled?

SOLUTION

$n = 3$ because there are three electronic parts to be assembled. $r = 3$ because all three are to be inserted in the plug-in unit. Solving using formula (4–8):

$$_nP_r = \frac{n!}{(n - r)!} = \frac{3!}{(3 - 3)!} = \frac{3!}{0!} = \frac{3!}{1} = 6$$

A check can be made as to the number of permutations arrived at using the permutation formula. To check, we merely determine how many "spaces" have to be filled and the possibilities for each "space." In the problem involving three electronic parts, there are three locations in the plug-in unit for the three parts. There are three possibilities for the first place, two for the second (one has been used up), and one for the third, as follows:

$$(3)(2)(1) = 6 \text{ permutations}$$

The six ways in which the three electronic parts, lettered A, B, C, can be arranged are:

ABC	*BAC*	*CAB*	*ACB*	*BCA*	*CBA*

In the previous example we selected and arranged all the objects, that is $n = r$. In many cases, only some objects are selected and arranged from the n possible objects. We explain the details of this application in the following example.

EXAMPLE

The Betts Machine Shop, Inc., has eight screw machines but only three spaces available in the production area for the machines. In how many different ways can the eight machines be arranged in the three spaces available?

SOLUTION

There are eight possibilities for the first available space in the production area, seven for the second space (one has been used up), and six for the third space. Thus:

$$(8)(7)(6) = 336,$$

that is, there are a total of 336 different possible arrangements. This could also be found using formula (4–8). If $n = 8$ machines, and $r = 3$ spaces available, the formula leads to

$$_{n}P_{r} = \frac{n!}{(n-r)!} = \frac{8!}{(8-3)!} = \frac{8!}{5!} = \frac{(8)(7)(6)5!}{5!} = 336$$

The Combination Formula

If the order of the selected objects is *not* important, any selection is called a **combination.** The formula to count the number of r object combinations from a set of n objects is:

COMBINATION FORMULA $$_{n}C_{r} = \frac{n!}{r!(n-r)!} \quad \textbf{[4–9]}$$

For example, if executives Able, Baker, and Chauncy are to be chosen as a committee to negotiate a merger, there is only one possible combination of these three; the committee of Able, Baker, and Chauncy is the same as the committee of Baker, Chauncy, and Able. Using the combination formula:

$$_{n}C_{r} = \frac{n!}{r!(n-r)!} = \frac{3 \cdot 2 \cdot 1}{3 \cdot 2 \cdot 1(1)} = 1$$

EXAMPLE

The marketing department has been given the assignment of designing color codes for the 42 different lines of compact discs sold by Goody Records. Three colors are to be used on each CD, but a combination of three colors used for one CD cannot be rearranged and used to identify a different CD. This means that if green, yellow, and violet were used to identify one line, then yellow, green, and violet (or any other combination of these three colors) cannot be used to identify another line. Would seven colors taken three at a time be adequate to color code the 42 lines?

SOLUTION

Using formula (4–9), there are 35 combinations, found by

$$_{7}C_{3} = \frac{n!}{r!(n-r)!} = \frac{7!}{3!(7-3)!} = \frac{7!}{3!4!} = 35$$

The seven colors taken three at a time (i.e., three colors to a line) would not be adequate to color code the 42 different lines because they would provide only 35 combinations. Eight colors taken three at a time would give 56 different combinations. This would be more than adequate to color code the 42 different lines.

When the number of permutations or combinations is large, the calculations are tedious. Computer software and handheld calculators have "functions" to compute these numbers. The Excel output for the location of the eight screw machines in the production area of Betts Machine Shop, Inc. is shown below. There are a total of 336 arrangements.

EXCEL

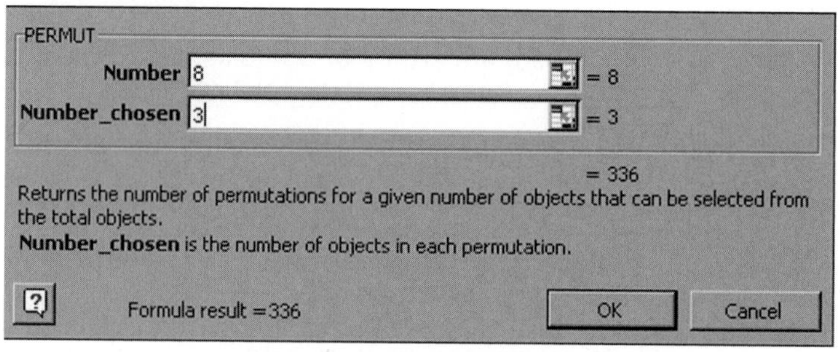
PERMUT
Number 8 = 8
Number_chosen 3 = 3
= 336
Returns the number of permutations for a given number of objects that can be selected from the total objects.
Number_chosen is the number of objects in each permutation.
Formula result =336
OK
Cancel

Below is the output for the color codes at Goody Records, Inc. Three colors are chosen from among seven possible. The number of combinations possible is 35.

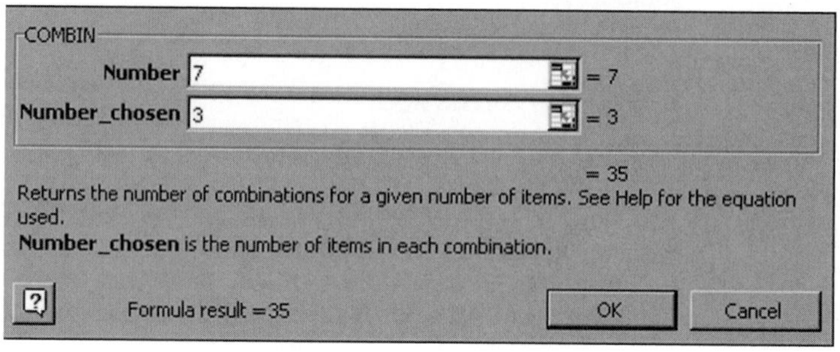
COMBIN
Number 7 = 7
Number_chosen 3 = 3
= 35
Returns the number of combinations for a given number of items. See Help for the equation used.
Number_chosen is the number of items in each combination.
Formula result =35
OK
Cancel

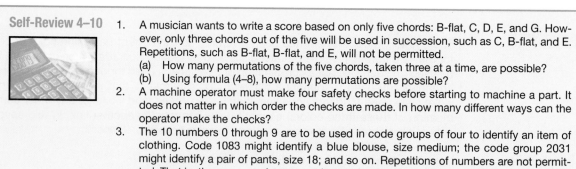

Self-Review 4–10

1. A musician wants to write a score based on only five chords: B-flat, C, D, E, and G. However, only three chords out of the five will be used in succession, such as C, B-flat, and E. Repetitions, such as B-flat, B-flat, and E, will not be permitted.
   (a) How many permutations of the five chords, taken three at a time, are possible?
   (b) Using formula (4–8), how many permutations are possible?
2. A machine operator must make four safety checks before starting to machine a part. It does not matter in which order the checks are made. In how many different ways can the operator make the checks?
3. The 10 numbers 0 through 9 are to be used in code groups of four to identify an item of clothing. Code 1083 might identify a blue blouse, size medium; the code group 2031 might identify a pair of pants, size 18; and so on. Repetitions of numbers are not permitted. That is, the same number cannot be used twice (or more) in a total sequence. For example, 2256, 2562, or 5559 would not be permitted. How many different code groups can be designed?

4. In the above example involving Goody Records, we said that eight colors taken three at a time would give 56 different combinations.
   (a) Use formula (4–9) to show this is true.
   (b) As an alternative plan for color coding the 42 different lines, it has been suggested that only two colors be placed on a disc. Would 10 colors be adequate to color code the 42 different lines? (Again, a combination of two colors could be used only once—that is, if pink and blue were coded for one line, blue and pink could not be used to identify a different line.)

Exercises

33. Solve the following:
  a. 40!/35!
  b. ${}_7P_4$
  c. ${}_5C_2$

34. Solve the following:
  a. 20!/17!
  b. ${}_9P_3$
  c. ${}_7C_2$

35. A pollster randomly selected 4 of 10 available people. How many different groups of 4 are possible?

36. A telephone number consists of seven digits, the first three representing the exchange. How many different telephone numbers are possible within the 537 exchange?

37. An overnight express company must include five cities on its route. How many different routes are possible, assuming that it does not matter in which order the cities are included in the routing?

38. A representative of the Environmental Protection Agency (EPA) wants to select samples from 10 landfills. The director has 15 landfills from which she can collect samples. How many different samples are possible?

39. A national pollster has developed 15 questions designed to rate the performance of the President of the United States. The pollster will select 10 of these questions. How many different arrangements are there for the order of the 10 selected questions?

40. A company is creating three new divisions and seven managers are eligible to be appointed head of a division. How many different ways could the three new heads be appointed?

Chapter Outline

I. A probability is a value between 0 and 1 inclusive that represents the likelihood a particular event will happen.
  A. An experiment is the observation of some activity or the act of taking some measurement.
  B. An outcome is a particular result of an experiment.
  C. An event is the collection of one or more outcomes of an experiment.

II. There are three definitions of probability.
  A. The classical definition applies when there are *n* equally likely outcomes to an experiment.
  B. The empirical definition occurs when the number of times an event happens is divided by the number of observations.
  C. A subjective probability is based on whatever information is available.

III. Two events are mutually exclusive if by virtue of one event happening the other cannot happen.

IV. Events are independent if the occurrence of one event does not affect the occurrence of another event.

Statistics in Action

Many states, such as Ohio, Michigan, California, and Florida, have lotteries in which a player buys a single ticket, often for only a dollar, and may win a large sum of money. In some states the amount of money to be won exceeds $20 million. In order to win, the player must match all six numbers randomly drawn from a pool of 49 numbers. The odds of winning such a lottery are 1 in 13,983,816. The odds of obtaining 23 heads in a row while flipping a coin are 1 in 8,388,608. To put it another way, you have a better chance of flipping a coin 23 times and getting all heads than you do of winning the lottery.

V. The rules of addition refer to the union of events.

- **A.** The special rule of addition is used when events are mutually exclusive.

$$P(A \text{ or } B) = P(A) + P(B) \qquad \textbf{[4–2]}$$

- **B.** The general rule of addition is

$$P(A \text{ or } B) = P(A) + P(B) - P(A \text{ and } B) \qquad \textbf{[4–4]}$$

- **C.** The complement rule is used to determine the probability of an event happening by subtracting the probability of the event not happening from 1.

$$P(A) = 1 - P(\sim A) \qquad \textbf{[4–3]}$$

VI. The rules of multiplication refer to the product of events.

- **A.** The special rule of multiplication refers to events that are independent.

$$P(A \text{ and } B) = P(A)P(B) \qquad \textbf{[4–5]}$$

- **B.** The general rule of multiplication refers to events that are not independent.

$$P(A \text{ and } B) = P(A)P(B \mid A) \qquad \textbf{[4–6]}$$

- **C.** A joint probability is the likelihood that two or more events will happen at the same time.
- **D.** A conditional probability is the likelihood that an event will happen, given that another event has already happened.

VII. There are three counting rules that are useful in determining the number of outcomes in an experiment.

- **A.** The multiplication rule states that if there are *m* ways one event can happen and *n* ways another event can happen, then there are *mn* ways the two events can happen.

$$\text{Number of arrangements} = (m)(n) \qquad \textbf{[4–7]}$$

- **B.** A permutation is an arrangement in which the order of the objects selected from a specific pool of objects is important.

$$_nP_r = \frac{n!}{(n-r)!} \qquad \textbf{[4–8]}$$

- **C.** A combination is an arrangement where the order of the objects selected from a specific pool of objects is not important.

$$_nC_r = \frac{n!}{r!(n-r)!} \qquad \textbf{[4–9]}$$

Pronunciation Key

SYMBOL	MEANING	PRONUNCIATION
$P(A)$	Probability of *A*	*P* of *A*
$P(\sim A)$	Probability of not *A*	*P* of not *A*
$P(A \text{ and } B)$	Probability of *A* and *B*	*P* of *A* and *B*
$P(A \text{ or } B)$	Probability of *A* or *B*	*P* of *A* or *B*
$P(A \mid B)$	Probability of *A* given *B* has happened	*P* of *A* given *B*
$_nP_r$	Permutation of *n* items selected *r* at a time	*Pnr*
$_nC_r$	Combination of *n* items selected *r* at a time	*Cnr*

Chapter Exercises

41. The marketing research department at Vernors plans to survey teenagers about a newly developed soft drink. Each will be asked to compare it with his or her favorite soft drink.

- **a.** What is the experiment?
- **b.** What is one possible event?

42. The number of times a particular event occurred in the past is divided by the number of occurrences. What is this approach to probability called?

43. The probability that the cause and the cure for all cancers will be discovered before the year 2010 is .20. What viewpoint of probability does this statement illustrate?

44. Berdine's Chicken Factory has several stores in the Hilton Head, South Carolina, area. When interviewing applicants for server positions, the owner would like to include information on the amount of tip a server can expect to earn per check (or bill). A study of 500 recent checks indicated the server earned the following tip.

Amount of Tip	Number
\$ 0 up to \$ 5	200
5 up to 10	100
10 up to 20	75
20 up to 50	75
50 or more	50
Total	500

a. What is the probability of a tip of \$50 or more?
b. Are the categories "\$0 up to \$5," "\$5 up to \$10," and so on considered mutually exclusive?
c. If the probabilities associated with each outcome were totaled, what would that total be?
d. What is the probability of a tip of up to \$10?
e. What is the probability of a tip of less than \$50?

45. Define each of these items:
a. Conditional probability.
b. Event.
c. Joint probability.

46. The first card selected from a standard 52-card deck was a king.
a. If it is returned to the deck, what is the probability that a king will be drawn on the second selection?
b. If the king is not replaced, what is the probability that a king will be drawn on the second selection?
c. What is the probability that a king will be selected on the first draw from the deck and another king on the second draw (assuming that the first king was not replaced)?

47. Armco, a manufacturer of traffic light systems, found that under accelerated-life tests, 95 percent of the newly developed systems lasted 3 years before failing to change signals properly.
a. If a city purchased four of these systems, what is the probability all four systems would operate properly for at least 3 years?
b. Which rule of probability does this illustrate?
c. Using letters to represent the four systems, write an equation to show how you arrived at the answer to part a.

48. Refer to the following picture.

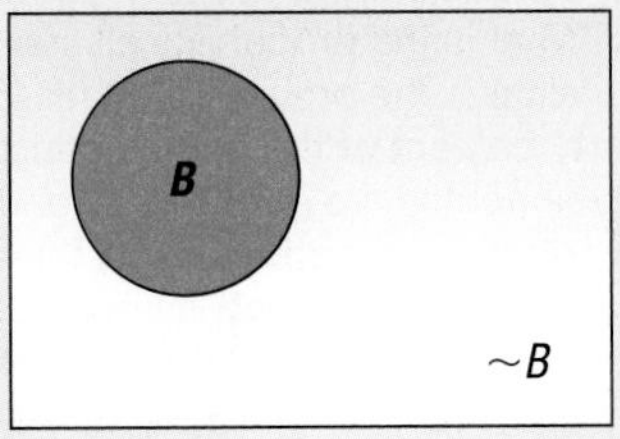

a. What is the picture called?
b. What rule of probability is illustrated?
c. *B* represents the event of choosing a family that receives welfare payments. What does $P(B) + P(\sim B)$ equal?

49. In a management trainee program at Claremont Enterprises, 80 percent of the trainees are female and 20 percent male. Ninety percent of the females attended college, and 78 percent of the males attended college.

a. A management trainee is selected at random. What is the probability that the person selected is a female who did not attend college?

b. Construct a tree diagram showing all the probabilities, conditional probabilities, and joint probabilities.

c. Do the joint probabilities total 1.00? Why?

50. Assume the likelihood that any flight on American Airlines arrives within 15 minutes of the scheduled time is .90. We select four flights from yesterday for study.

a. What is the likelihood all four of the selected flights arrived within 15 minutes of the scheduled time?

b. What is the likelihood that none of the selected flights arrived within 15 minutes of the scheduled time?

c. What is the likelihood at least one of the selected flights did not arrive within 15 minutes of the scheduled time?

51. There are 100 employees at Kiddie Carts International. Fifty-seven of the employees are production workers, 40 are supervisors, 2 are secretaries, and the remaining employee is the president. Suppose an employee is selected:

a. What is the probability the selected employee is a production worker?

b. What is the probability the selected employee is either a production worker or a supervisor?

c. Refer to part b. Are these events mutually exclusive?

d. What is the probability the selected employee is neither a production worker nor a supervisor?

52. Larry Walker of the Colorado Rockies and Ichiro Suzuki of the Seattle Mariners tied for the highest batting average in the 2001 Major League Baseball season. Each had an average of .350. So assume the probability of their getting a hit is .350 for each time either batted. In a particular game assume either batted three times.

a. This is an example of what type of probability?

b. What is the probability of getting three hits in a particular game?

c. What is the probability of not getting any hits in a game?

d. What is the probability of getting at least one hit?

53. The probability that a bomber hits its target on any particular mission is .80. Four bombers are sent after the same target. What is the probability:

a. They all hit the target?

b. None hit the target?

c. At least one hits the target?

54. Ninety students will graduate from Lima Shawnee High School this spring. Of the 90 students, 50 are planning to attend college. Two students are to be picked at random to carry flags at the graduation.

a. What is the probability both of the selected students plan to attend college?

b. What is the probability one of the two selected students plans to attend college?

55. Brooks Insurance, Inc. wishes to offer life insurance to men age 60 via the Internet. Mortality tables indicate the likelihood of a 60-year-old man surviving another year is .98. If the policy is offered to five men age 60:

a. What is the probability all five men survive the year?

b. What is the probability at least one does not survive?

56. Forty percent of the homes constructed in the Quail Creek area include a security system. Three homes are selected at random:

a. What is the probability all three of the selected homes have a security system?

b. What is the probability none of the three selected homes have a security system?

c. What is the probability at least one of the selected homes has a security system?

d. Did you assume the events to be dependent or independent?

57. Refer to Exercise 56, but assume there are ten homes in the Quail Creek area and four of them have a security system. Three homes are selected at random:

a. What is the probability all three of the selected homes have a security system?

b. What is the probability none of the three selected homes have a security system?

c. What is the probability at least one of the selected homes has a security system?

d. Did you assume the events to be dependent or independent?

58. A juggler has a bag containing three green balls, two yellow balls, one red ball, and four blues. The juggler picks a ball at random. Then, without replacing it, he chooses a second ball. What is the probability the juggler first draws a yellow ball followed by a blue ball?

59. The board of directors of Saner Automatic Door Company consists of 12 members, 3 of whom are women. A new policy and procedures manual is to be written for the company. A committee of 3 is randomly selected from the board to do the writing.

a. What is the probability that all members of the committee are men?

b. What is the probability that at least 1 member of the committee is a woman?

60. A survey of undergraduate students in the School of Business at Northern University revealed the following regarding the gender and majors of the students:

	Major			
Gender	**Accounting**	**Management**	**Finance**	**Total**
Male	100	150	50	300
Female	100	50	50	200
Total	200	200	100	500

a. What is the probability of selecting a female student?

b. What is the probability of selecting a finance or accounting major?

c. What is the probability of selecting a female or an accounting major? Which rule of addition did you apply?

d. What is the probability of selecting an accounting major, given that the person selected is a male?

e. Suppose two students are selected randomly to attend a lunch with the president of the university. What is the probability that both of those selected are accounting majors?

61. The Wood County sheriff classifies crimes by age (in years) of the criminal and whether the crime is violent or nonviolent. As shown below, a total of 150 crimes were reported by the sheriff last year.

	Age (in years)			
Type of Crime	**Under 20**	**20 to 40**	**Over 40**	**Total**
Violent	27	41	14	82
Nonviolent	12	34	22	68
Total	39	75	36	150

a. What is the probability of selecting a case to analyze and finding it involved a violent crime?

b. What is the probability of selecting a case to analyze and finding the crime was committed by someone less than 40 years old?

c. What is the probability of selecting a case that involved a violent crime or an offender less than 20 years old? Which rule of addition did you apply?

d. Given that a violent crime is selected for analysis, what is the probability the crime was committed by a person under 20 years old?

e. Two crimes are selected for review by Judge Tybo. What is the probability that both are violent crimes?

62. Mr. and Mrs. Wilhelms are both retired and living in a retirement community in Arizona. Suppose the probability that a retired man will live another 10 years is .60. The probability that a retired woman will live another 10 years is .70.

a. What is the probability that both Mr. and Mrs. Wilhelms will be alive 10 years from now?

b. What is the probability that in 10 years Mr. Wilhelms is not living and Mrs. Wilhelms is living?

c. What is the probability that in 10 years at least one is living?

63. With each purchase of a large pizza at Tony's Pizza, the customer receives a coupon that can be scratched to see if a prize will be awarded. The odds of winning a free soft drink are 1 in 10, and the odds of winning a free large pizza are 1 in 50. You plan to eat lunch tomorrow at Tony's. What is the probability:

a. That you will win either a large pizza or a soft drink?

b. That you will not win a prize?
c. That you will not win a prize on three consecutive visits to Tony's?
d. That you will win at least one prize on one of your next three visits to Tony's?

64. For the daily lottery game in Illinois, participants select three numbers between 0 and 9. A number cannot be selected more than once, so a winning ticket could be, say, 307. Purchasing one ticket allows you to select one set of numbers. The winning numbers are announced on TV each night.
a. How many different outcomes (three-digit numbers) are possible?
b. If you purchase a ticket for the game tonight, what is the likelihood you will win?
c. Suppose you purchase three tickets for tonight's drawing and select a different number for each ticket. What is the probability that you will not win with any of the tickets?

65. Several years ago Wendy's Hamburgers advertised that there are 256 different ways to order your hamburger. You may choose to have, or omit, any combination of the following on your hamburger: mustard, ketchup, onion, pickle, tomato, relish, mayonnaise, and lettuce. Is the advertisement correct? Show how you arrive at your answer.

66. It was found that 60 percent of the tourists to China visited the Forbidden City, the Temple of Heaven, the Great Wall, and other historical sites in or near Beijing. Forty percent visited Xi'an with its magnificent terracotta soldiers, horses, and chariots, which lay buried for over 2,000 years. Thirty percent of the tourists went to both Beijing and Xi'an. What is the probability that a tourist visited at least one of these places?

67. A new chewing gum has been developed that is helpful to those who want to stop smoking. If 60 percent of those people chewing the gum are successful in stopping smoking, what is the probability that in a group of four smokers using the gum at least one quits smoking?

68. Reynolds Construction Company has agreed not to erect all "look-alike" homes in a new subdivision. Five exterior designs are offered to potential home buyers. The builder has standardized three interior plans that can be incorporated in any of the five exteriors. How many different ways can the exterior and interior plans be offered to potential home buyers?

69. A new sports car model has defective brakes 15 percent of the time and a defective steering mechanism 5 percent of the time. Let's assume (and hope) that these problems occur independently. If one or the other of these problems is present, the car is called a "lemon." If both of these problems are present, the car is a "hazard." Your instructor purchased one of these cars yesterday. What is the probability it is:
a. A lemon?
b. A hazard?

70. The state of Maryland has license plates with three numbers followed by three letters. How many different license plates are possible?

71. There are four people being considered for the position of chief executive officer of Dalton Enterprises. Three of the applicants are over 60 years of age. Two are female, of which only one is over 60.
a. What is the probability that a candidate is over 60 and female?
b. Given that the candidate is male, what is the probability he is less than 60?
c. Given that the person is over 60, what is the probability the person is female?

72. Tim Bleckie is the owner of Bleckie Investment and Real Estate Company. The company recently purchased four tracts of land in Holly Farms Estates and six tracts in Newburg Woods. The tracts are all equally desirable and sell for about the same amount.
a. What is the probability that the next two tracts sold will be in Newburg Woods?
b. What is the probability that of the next four sold at least one will be in Holly Farms?
c. Are these events independent or dependent?

73. A computer password consists of four characters. The characters can be one of the 26 letters of the alphabet. Each character may be used more than once. How many different passwords are possible?

74. A case of 24 cans contains 1 can that is contaminated. Three cans are to be chosen randomly for testing.
a. How many different combinations of 3 cans could be selected?
b. What is the probability that the contaminated can is selected for testing?

75. A puzzle in the newspaper presents a matching problem. The names of 10 U.S. presidents are listed in one column, and their vice presidents are listed in random order in the second column. The puzzle asks the reader to match each president with his vice president. If you make the matches randomly, how many matches are possible? What is the probability all 10 of your matches are correct?

76. The following diagram represents a system of two components, *A* and *B*, which are in series. (Being in series means that for the system to operate, both components *A* and *B* must work.) Suppose the system works if *either A* or *B* works. What is the probability the system works under these conditions? The probability *A* works is .90 and the probability *B* functions is also .90.

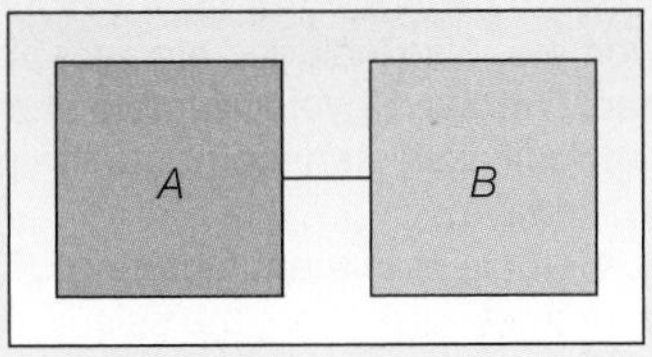

exercises.com

77. During the 1970s the game show *Let's Make a Deal* had a long run on TV. In the show a contestant was given a choice of three doors, behind one of which was a prize. The other two doors contained a gag gift of some type. After the contestant selected a door, the host of the show then revealed to them one of the doors from among the two not selected. The host asked the contestant if they wished to switch doors to one of those not chosen. Should the contestant switch? Are the odds of winning increased by switching doors?

Go to the following website, which is administered by the Department of Statistics at the University of South Carolina, and try your strategy: http://www.stat.sc.edu/~west/applets/LetsMakeaDeal.html; Go to the following website and read about the odds for the game: http://www.stat.sc.edu/~west/javahtml/LetsMakeaDeal.html. Was your strategy correct?

Computer Data Exercises

78. Refer to the Real Estate data, which reports information on homes sold in the Venice, Florida, area during the last year.

a. Sort the data into a table that shows the number of homes that have a pool versus the number that don't have a pool in each of the five townships. If a home is selected at random, compute the following probabilities.

(1) The home is in Township 1 or has a pool.
(2) Given that it is in Township 3, that it has a pool.
(3) Has a pool and is in Township 3.

b. Sort the data into a table that shows the number of homes that have a garage versus those that don't have a garage in each of the five townships. If a home is selected at random, compute the following probabilities:

(1) The home has a garage.
(2) Given that it is in Township 5, that it does not have a garage.
(3) The home has a garage and is in Township 3.
(4) Does not have a garage or is in Township 2.

79. Refer to the Baseball 2001 data, which reports information on the 30 Major League Baseball teams for the 2001 season. Set up a variable that divides the teams into two groups, those that had a winning season and those that did not. That is, create a variable to count the teams that won 81 games or more, and those that won 80 or less. Next create a new variable for attendance, using three categories: attendance less than 2.0 million, attendance of 2.0 million up to 3.0 million, and attendance of 3.0 million or more.

a. Create a table that shows the number of teams with a winning season versus those with a losing season by the three categories of attendance. If a team is selected at random, compute the following probabilities:

(1) Having a winning season.
(2) Having a winning season or attendance of more than 3.0 million.
(3) Given attendance of more than 3.0 million, having a winning season.
(4) Having a losing season and drawing less than 2.0 million.

b. Create a table that shows the number of teams that play on artificial surfaces and natural surfaces by winning and losing records. If a team is selected at random, compute the following probabilities:

(1) Selecting a team with a home field that has a natural surface.

(2) Is the likelihood of selecting a team with a winning record larger for teams with natural or artificial surfaces?

(3) Having a winning record or playing on an artificial surface.

80. Refer to the wage data set, which reports information on annual wages for a sample of 100 workers. Also included are variables relating to industry, years of education, and gender for each worker. Develop a table showing the industry of employment by gender. A worker is randomly selected; compute the probability the person selected is:

a. Female.

b. Female or in manufacturing.

c. Female given that the selected person is in manufacturing.

d. Female and in manufacturing.

Computer Commands

1. The Excel commands to determine the number of permutations shown on page 148 are:

a. Click on **Insert** on the toolbar, then select the f_x **function** and click **OK**.

b. In the **Paste Function** box select **Statistical** and in the **Function name** column scroll down to **PERMUT** and click **OK**.

c. In the PERMUT box after **Number** enter 8 and in the **Number_chosen** box enter 3. The correct answer of 336 appears twice in the box.

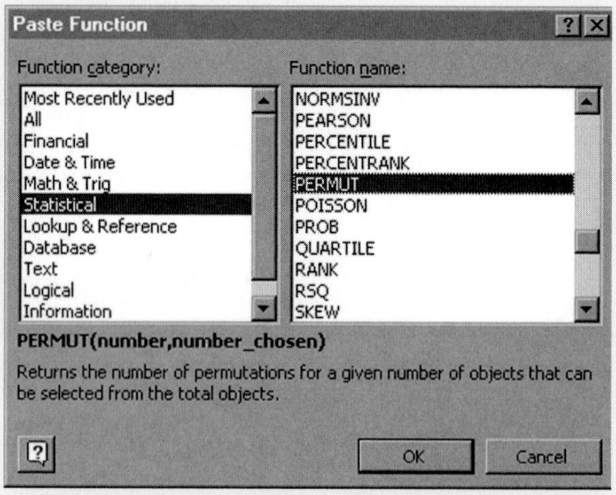

2. The Excel commands to determine the number of combinations shown on page 148 are:

a. Click on **Insert** on the toolbar, then select the f_x **function** and click **OK**.

b. In the **Paste Function** box select **Math & Trig** and in the Function name column scroll down to **COMBIN** and click **OK**.

c. In the **COMBIN** box after **Number** enter 7 and in the **Number_chosen** box enter 3. The correct answer 35 appears twice in the box.

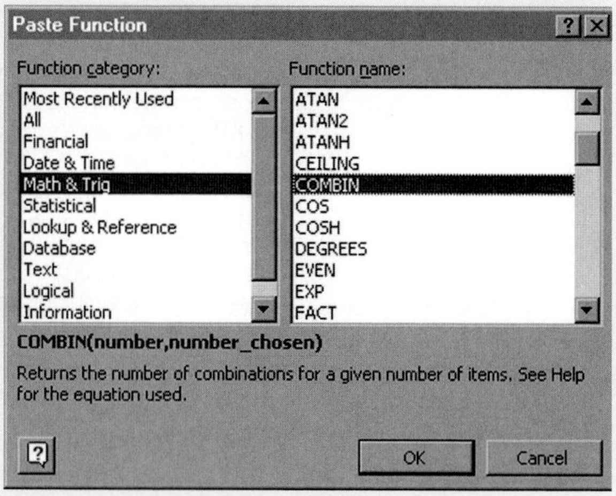

Chapter 4 Answers to Self-Review

4–1 **(a)** Testing of the new computer game.
(b) Seventy-three players liked the game.
(c) No. Probability cannot be greater than 1. The probability that the game, if put on the market, will be successful is 65/80, or .8125.
(d) Cannot be less than 0. Perhaps a mistake in arithmetic.
(e) More than half of the persons testing the game liked it. (Of course, other answers are possible.)

4–2 **1.** $\frac{\text{4 queens in deck}}{\text{52 cards total}} = \frac{4}{52} = .0769$
Classical.
2. $\frac{24}{883} = .027$ Empirical.
3. The author's view when writing the text of the chance that the DJIA will climb to 12,000 is .25. You may be more optimistic or less optimistic.
Subjective.

4–3 **(a)** **(i)** $\frac{(50 + 68)}{2{,}000} = .059$
(ii) $1 - \frac{302}{2{,}000} = .849$
(b)

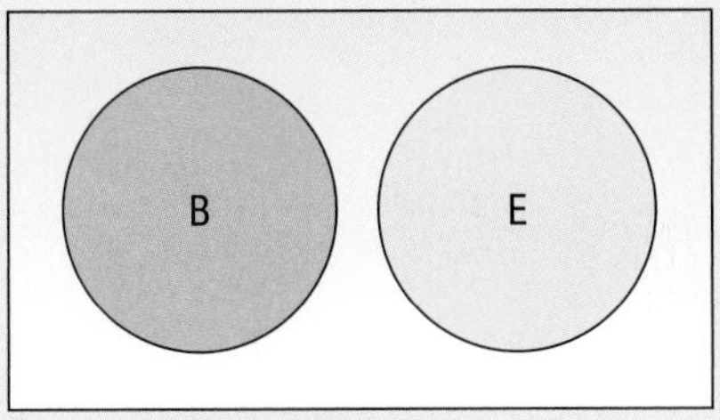

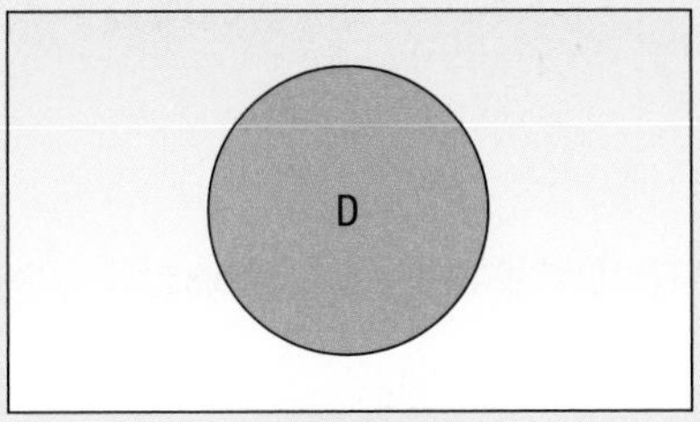

(c) They are not complementary, but are mutually exclusive.

4–4 **(a)** Need for corrective shoes is event A. Need for major dental work is event B.

$$P(A \text{ or } B) = P(A) + P(B) - P(A \text{ and } B)$$
$$= .08 + .15 - .03$$
$$= .20$$

(b) One possibility is:

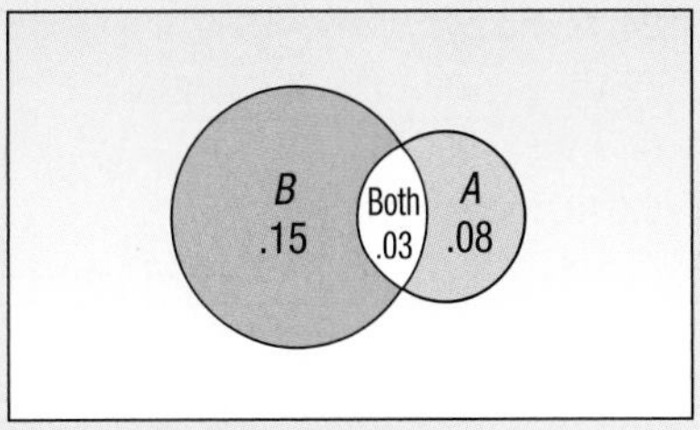

4–5 $(.80)(.80)(.80)(.80) = .4096$.

4–6 **(a)** .002, found by:
$$\left(\frac{4}{12}\right)\left(\frac{3}{11}\right)\left(\frac{2}{10}\right)\left(\frac{1}{9}\right) = \frac{24}{11{,}880} = .002$$
(b) .14, found by:
$$\left(\frac{8}{12}\right)\left(\frac{7}{11}\right)\left(\frac{6}{10}\right)\left(\frac{5}{9}\right) = \frac{1{,}680}{11{,}880} = .1414$$
(c) No, because there are other possibilities, such as three women and one man.

4–7 **a.** $P(B_4) = \frac{105}{200} = .525$
b. $P(A_2 \mid B_4) = \frac{30}{105} = .286$
c. $P(A_2 \text{ or } B_4) = \frac{80}{200} + \frac{105}{200} - \frac{30}{200} = \frac{155}{200} = .775$

4–8 **(a)** Contingency table.
(b)

Employee		Plans		Joint
Management	$\frac{20}{100}$	Retire	$\frac{5}{20}$	$\left(\frac{20}{100}\right)\left(\frac{5}{20}\right) = \frac{100}{2{,}000} = .05$
		Not retire	$\frac{15}{20}$	$\left(\frac{20}{100}\right)\left(\frac{15}{20}\right) = \frac{300}{2{,}000} = .15$
Production	$\frac{80}{100}$	Retire	$\frac{30}{80}$	$\left(\frac{80}{100}\right)\left(\frac{30}{80}\right) = \frac{2{,}400}{8{,}000} = .30$
		Not retire	$\frac{50}{80}$	$\left(\frac{80}{100}\right)\left(\frac{50}{80}\right) = \frac{4{,}000}{8{,}000} = .50$

(c) Yes, all possibilities are included.

4–9 **1.** There are 20, found by (5)(4)
2. There are 72, found by (3)(2)(4)(3)

4–10 **1.** **(a)** 60, found by (5)(4)(3).

(b) 60, found by:

$$\frac{5!}{(5-3)!} = \frac{5 \cdot 4 \cdot 3 \cdot \cancel{2 \cdot 1}}{\cancel{2 \cdot 1}}$$

2. 24, found by:

$$\frac{4!}{(4-4)!} = \frac{4!}{0!} = \frac{4!}{1} = \frac{4 \cdot 3 \cdot 2 \cdot 1}{1}$$

3. 5,040, found by:

$$\frac{10!}{(10-4)!} = \frac{10 \cdot 9 \cdot 8 \cdot 7 \cdot \cancel{6 \cdot 5 \cdot 4 \cdot 3 \cdot 2 \cdot 1}}{\cancel{6 \cdot 5 \cdot 4 \cdot 3 \cdot 2 \cdot 1}}$$

4. **(a)** 56 is correct, found by:

$${}_8C_3 = \frac{n!}{r!(n-r)!} = \frac{8!}{3!(8-3)!} = 56$$

(b) Yes. There are 45 combinations, found by:

$${}_{10}C_2 = \frac{n!}{r!(n-r)!} = \frac{10!}{2!(10-2)!} = 45$$

Discrete Probability Distributions

5

An American Society of Investors survey found 30 percent of individual investors have used a discount broker. In a random sample of nine individuals, what is the probability that exactly two of the sampled individuals have used a discount broker? (See Goal 4 and Exercise 11.)

GOALS

When you have completed this chapter, you will be able to:

1 Define the terms *probability distribution* and *random variable.*

2 Distinguish between discrete and continuous probability distributions.

3 Calculate the mean, variance, and standard deviation of a discrete probability distribution.

4 Describe the characteristics of and compute probabilities using the binomial probability distribution.

5 Describe the characteristics of and compute probabilities using the hypergeometric probability distribution.

6 Describe the characteristics of and compute probabilities using the Poisson probability distribution.

Introduction

Chapters 2 and 3 are devoted to descriptive statistics. We describe raw data by organizing them into a frequency distribution and portraying the distribution in charts. Also, we compute a measure of location—such as the arithmetic mean, median, or mode—to locate a typical value near the center of the distribution. The range and the standard deviation are used to describe the spread in the data. These chapters focus on describing *something that has already happened.*

Starting with Chapter 4, the emphasis changes—we begin examining *something that would probably happen.* We note that this facet of statistics is called *statistical inference.* The objective is to make inferences (statements) about a population based on a number of observations, called a sample, selected from the population. In Chapter 4, we state that a probability is a value between 0 and 1 inclusive, and we examine how probabilities can be combined using rules of addition and multiplication.

This chapter will begin the study of **probability distributions.** A probability distribution gives the entire range of values that can occur based on an experiment. A probability distribution is similar to a relative frequency distribution. However, instead of describing the past, it describes how likely some future event is. For example, a drug manufacturer may claim a treatment will cause weight loss for 80 percent of the population. A consumer protection agency may test the treatment on a sample of six people. If the manufacturer's claim is true, it is *almost impossible* to have an outcome where no one in the sample loses weight and it is *most likely* that five out of the six do lose weight.

The mean, variance, and standard deviation for probability distributions as well as three frequently occurring families of probability distributions (the binomial, hypergeometric, and Poisson) are also presented in this chapter.

What Is a Probability Distribution?

A probability distribution shows the possible outcomes of an experiment and the probability of each of these outcomes.

PROBABILITY DISTRIBUTION A listing of all the outcomes of an experiment and the probability associated with each outcome.

How can we generate a probability distribution?

EXAMPLE

Suppose we are interested in the number of heads showing face up on three tosses of a coin. This is the experiment. The possible results are: zero heads, one head, two heads, and three heads. What is the probability distribution for the number of heads?

SOLUTION

There are eight possible outcomes. A tail might appear face up on the first toss, another tail on the second toss, and another tail on the third toss of the coin. Or we might get a tail, tail, and head, in that order. Listed below are the possible results.

Possible Result	Coin Toss First	Second	Third	Number of Heads
1	T	T	T	0
2	T	T	H	1
3	T	H	T	1
4	T	H	H	2

Possible Result	Coin Toss First	Second	Third	Number of Heads
5	H	T	T	1
6	H	T	H	2
7	H	H	T	2
8	H	H	H	3

Note that the outcome "zero heads" occurred only once, "one head" occurred three times, "two heads" occurred three times, and the outcome "three heads" occurred only once. That is, "zero heads" happened one out of eight times. Thus, the probability of zero heads is one eighth, the probability of one head is three eighths, and so on. The probability distribution is shown in Table 5–1. Note that, since one of these outcomes must happen because they are mutually exclusive and collectively exhaustive, the total of the probabilities of all possible events is 1.000. This is always true. The same information is shown in Chart 5–1.

TABLE 5–1 Probability Distribution for the Events of Zero, One, Two, and Three Heads Showing Face Up on Three Tosses of a Coin

Number of Heads, x	Probability of Outcome, $P(x)$
0	$\frac{1}{8} = .125$
1	$\frac{3}{8} = .375$
2	$\frac{3}{8} = .375$
3	$\frac{1}{8} = .125$
Total	$\frac{8}{8} = 1.000$

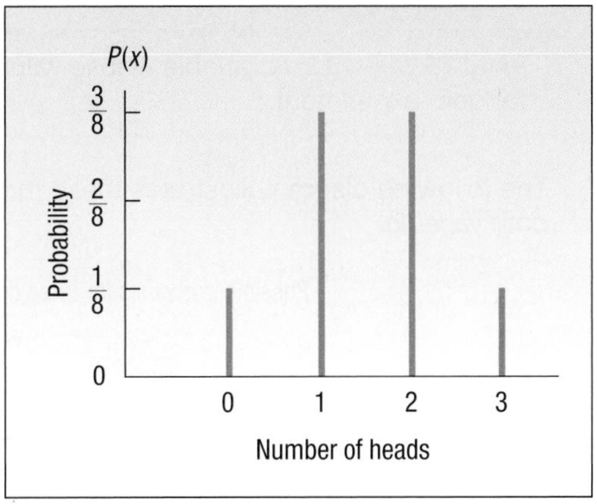

CHART 5–1 Graphical Presentation of the Number of Heads Resulting from Three Tosses of a Coin and the Corresponding Probability

Characteristics of a probability distribution

Before continuing, we should note two important characteristics of a probability distribution.

1. The probability of a particular value is between 0 and 1, inclusive. (The probabilities of x, written $P(x)$ in the coin tossing example, were .125, .375, etc.)
2. The sum of the probabilities of all mutually exclusive values is 1.000. (Referring to Table 5–1, .125 + .375 + .375 + .125 = 1.000.)

Self-Review 5-1

The possible outcomes of an experiment involving the roll of a six-sided die are: a one-spot, a two-spot, a three-spot, a four-spot, a five-spot, and a six-spot.

(a) Develop a probability distribution for the number of possible spots.
(b) Portray the probability distribution graphically.
(c) What is the sum of the probabilities?

Random Variables

In any experiment of chance, the outcomes occur randomly. So it is often called a *random variable.* For example, rolling a single die is an experiment: any one of six possible outcomes can occur. Some experiments result in outcomes that are quantitative (such as dollars, weight, or number of children), and others result in qualitative outcomes (such as color or religious preference). A few examples will further illustrate what is meant by a **random variable.**

- If we count the number of employees absent from the day shift on Monday, the number might be 0, 1, 2, 3, ... The number absent is the random variable.
- If we weigh a steel ingot, it might be 24,928 pounds, or 2,497 pounds, or 2,506 pounds, and so on. The weight is the random variable.
- Suppose three customers enter a restaurant. The number of these customers who purchase a dessert item after their meal could be 0, 1, 2, or 3. The number purchasing a dessert item is a random variable.
- Other random variables might be: the number of defective light bulbs produced during the week, the heights of the members of the girls' basketball team, and the daily number of drivers charged with driving under the influence of alcohol in Texas.

RANDOM VARIABLE A variable whose value is determined by the outcome of a random experiment.

The following diagram illustrates these three related terms: *outcome, event,* and *random variable.*

Possible *outcomes* for three coin tosses

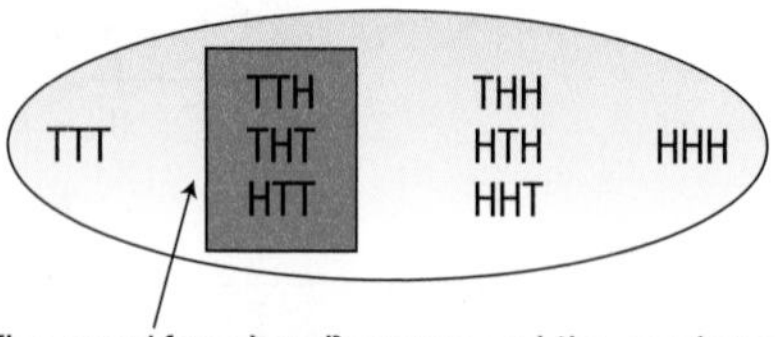

The *event* {one head} occurs and the *random variable* $x = 1$.

A random variable may be either *discrete* or *continuous.*

Discrete Random Variable

A discrete random variable can assume only a certain number of separated values. If there are 100 employees, then the count of the number of workers absent on Monday can only be 0, 1, 2, 3, . . . , 100. A discrete random variable is usually the result of counting something. By way of definition:

DISCRETE RANDOM VARIABLE A variable that can assume only certain clearly separated values.

A discrete variable can, in some cases, assume fractional or decimal values. These values must be separated, that is, have distance between them. As an example, the scores awarded by judges for technical competence and artistic form in figure skating are decimal values, such as 7.2, 8.9, and 9.7. Such values are discrete because there is distance between scores of, say, 8.3 and 8.4. A score cannot be 8.34 or 8.347, for example.

Continuous Random Variable

On the other hand, if the random variable is continuous, then the distribution is a continuous probability distribution. If we measure something such as the width of a room, the height of a person, or the pressure in an automobile tire, the variable is a *continuous random variable.* It can assume one of an infinitely large number of values, within certain limitations. As examples:

- The times of commercial flights between Atlanta and Los Angeles are 4.67 hours, 5.13 hours, and so on. The random variable is hours.
- Tire pressures, measured in pounds per square inch (psi), for a sample of new Chevy Blazers are 32 psi, 31 psi, 33 psi, and so on. The random variable is the tire pressure.

Logically, if we organize a set of possible values of a discrete random variable in a probability distribution, the distribution is a **discrete probability distribution.**

The tools used, as well as the probability interpretations, are different for discrete and continuous random variables. This chapter is limited to discrete probability distributions. The next chapter will address an important example of continuous probability distributions.

The Mean, Variance, and Standard Deviation of a Probability Distribution

In Chapter 3 we discussed measures of location and variation for a frequency distribution. The mean reports the central location of the data, and the variance describes the spread in the data. In a similar fashion, a probability distribution is summarized by its mean and variance. We identify the mean of a probability distribution by the lower-case Greek letter mu (μ) and the standard deviation by the lower-case Greek letter sigma (σ).

Mean

The mean is a typical value used to represent a probability distribution. It also is the long-run average value of the random variable. The mean of a probability distribution is also referred to as its **expected value.** It is a weighted average where the possible values are weighted by their corresponding probabilities of occurrence.

The mean of a discrete probability distribution is computed by the formula:

MEAN OF A PROBABILITY DISTRIBUTION	$\mu = \Sigma[xP(x)]$	**[5–1]**

where $P(x)$ is the probability of taking on a particular value x. In other words, to find the mean, multiply each x value by its probability of occurrence, and then add these products.

Variance and Standard Deviation

As noted, the mean is a typical value used to summarize a discrete probability distribution. However, it does not describe the amount of spread (variation) in a distribution. The variance does this. The formula for the variance of a probability distribution is:

VARIANCE OF A PROBABILITY DISTRIBUTION	$\sigma^2 = \Sigma[(x - \mu)^2 P(x)]$	**[5–2]**

The computational steps are:

1. Subtract the mean from each value, and square this difference.
2. Multiply each squared difference by its probability.
3. Sum the resulting products to arrive at the variance.

The standard deviation, σ, is found by taking the square root of σ^2; that is, $\sigma = \sqrt{\sigma^2}$.

EXAMPLE

John Ragsdale sells new cars for Pelican Ford. John usually sells the largest number of cars on Saturday. He has the following probability distribution for the number of cars he expects to sell on a particular Saturday.

Number of Cars Sold, x	Probability, $P(x)$
0	.1
1	.2
2	.3
3	.3
4	.1
Total	1.0

1. What type of distribution is this?
2. On a typical Saturday, how many cars does John expect to sell?
3. What is the variance of the distribution?

SOLUTION

1. This is a discrete probability distribution. Note that John expects to sell only within a certain range of cars; he does not expect to sell 5 cars or 50 cars. Further, he cannot sell half a car. He can sell only 0, 1, 2, 3, or 4 cars. Also, the outcomes are mutually exclusive—he cannot sell a total of both 3 and 4 cars on the same Saturday.
2. The mean number of cars sold is computed by weighting the number of cars sold by the probability of selling that number and totaling the products using formula (5–1):

$$\mu = \Sigma[xP(x)]$$
$$= 0(.1) + 1(.2) + 2(.3) + 3(.3) + 4(.1)$$
$$= 2.1$$

These calculations are summarized in the following table.

Number of Cars Sold, x	Probability, $P(x)$	$x \cdot P(x)$
0	.1	0.0
1	.2	0.2
2	.3	0.6
3	.3	0.9
4	.1	0.4
Total	1.00	$\mu = 2.1$

How do we interpret a mean of 2.1? This value indicates that, over a large number of Saturdays, John Ragsdale expects to sell a mean of 2.1 cars a day. (Of course, it is not possible for him to sell *exactly* 2.1 cars on any particular Saturday.) Thus, the mean is sometimes called the expected value.

3. Again, a table is useful for systemizing the computations for the variance, which is 1.290.

Number of Cars Sold, x	Probability, $P(x)$	$(x - \mu)$	$(x - \mu)^2$	$(x - \mu)^2P(x)$
0	.1	0 − 2.1	4.41	0.441
1	.2	1 − 2.1	1.21	0.242
2	.3	2 − 2.1	0.01	0.003
3	.3	3 − 2.1	0.81	0.243
4	.1	4 − 2.1	3.61	0.361
				$\sigma^2 = 1.290$

Recall that the standard deviation, σ, is the square root of the variance. In this example, $\sqrt{\sigma^2} = \sqrt{1.290} = 1.136$ cars. How do we interpret a standard deviation of 1.136 cars? If salesperson Rita Kirsch also sold a mean of 2.1 cars on Saturdays, and the standard deviation in her sales was 1.91 cars, we would conclude that there is more variability in the Saturday sales of Ms. Kirsch than in those of Mr. Ragsdale (because $1.91 > 1.136$).

Self-Review 5-2

The Pizza Palace offers three sizes of cola—small, medium, and large—to go with its pizza. The colas are sold for $0.80, $0.90, and $1.20, respectively. Thirty percent of the orders are for small, 50 percent are for medium, and 20 percent are for the large sizes. Organize the size of the colas and the probability of a sale into a probability distribution.

(a) Is this a discrete probability distribution? Indicate why or why not.
(b) Compute the mean amount charged for a cola.
(c) What is the variance in the amount charged for a cola? The standard deviation?

Exercises

1. Compute the mean and variance of the following discrete probability distribution.

x	*P*(*x*)
0	.20
1	.40
2	.30
3	.10

2. Compute the mean and variance of the following discrete probability distribution.

x	*P*(*x*)
2	.50
8	.30
10	.20

3. Dan Woodward is the owner and manager of Dan's Truck Stop. Dan offers free refills on all coffee orders. He gathered the following information on coffee refills. Compute the mean, variance, and standard deviation for the distribution of number of refills.

Refills	Percent
0	30
1	40
2	20
3	10

4. The director of admissions at Kinzua University in Nova Scotia estimated the distribution of student admissions for the fall semester based on past experience. What is the expected number of admissions for the fall semester? Compute the variance and the standard deviation.

Admissions	Probability
1,000	.60
1,200	.30
1,500	.10

5. The following table lists the probability distribution for cash prizes in a lottery conducted at Lawson's Department Store.

Prize ($)	Probability
0	.45
10	.30
100	.20
500	.05

If you buy a single ticket, what is the probability that you win:
a. Exactly $100? **b.** At least $10? **c.** No more than $100?
d. Compute the mean, variance, and standard deviation of this distribution.

6. You are asked to match three songs with the performers who made those songs famous. If you guess, the probability distribution for the number of correct matches is:

Probability	.333	.500	0	.167
Number correct	0	1	2	3

What is the probability you get:
a. Exactly one correct? **b.** At least one correct? **c.** Exactly two correct?
d. Compute the mean, variance, and standard deviation of this distribution.

Binomial Probability Distribution

The **binomial probability distribution** is a widely occurring discrete probability distribution. One characteristic of a binomial distribution is that there are only two possible outcomes on a particular trial of an experiment. For example, the statement in a true/false question is either true or false. The outcomes are *mutually exclusive,* meaning that the answer to a true/false question cannot be both true and false at the same time. As other examples, a product is classified as either acceptable or not acceptable by the quality control department, a worker is classified as employed or unemployed, and a sales call results in the customer either purchasing the product or not purchasing the product. Frequently, we classify the two possible outcomes as "success" and "failure." However, this classification does *not* imply that one outcome is good and the other is bad.

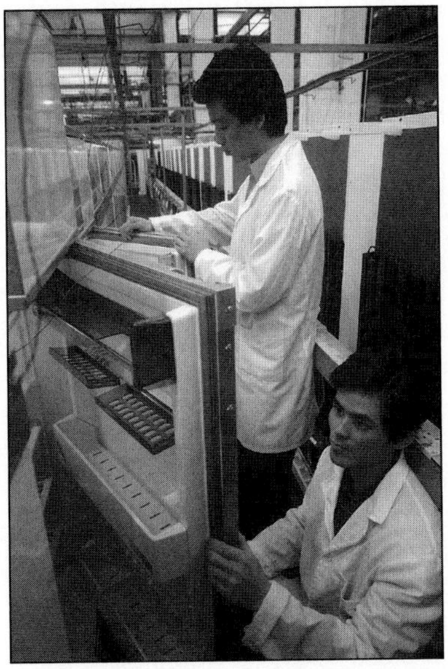

Another characteristic of the binomial distribution is that the random variable is the result of counts. That is, we count the number of successes in the total number of trials. We flip a fair coin five times and count the number of times a head appears; we select 10 workers and count the number who are over 50 years of age, or we select 20 boxes of Kellogg's Raisin Bran and count the number that weigh more than the amount indicated on the package.

Another characteristic of a binomial distribution is that the probability of a success remains the same from one trial to another. Two examples are:

- The probability you will guess the first question of a true/false test correctly (a success) is one half. This is the first "trial." The probability that you will guess correctly on the second question (the second trial) is also one half, the probability of success on the third trial is one half, and so on.
- If past experience revealed the swing bridge over the Waterway in Socastee was raised one out of every twenty times you approach it, then the probability is one-twentieth that it will be raised (a "success") the next time you approach it, one-twentieth the following time, and so on.

The final characteristic of a binomial probability distribution is that each trial is *independent* of any other trial. This means that there is no pattern with respect to the outcomes. As an example, the answers to a true/false test are not arranged T, T, T, F, F, F, T, T, T, and so forth.

In summary, a binomial distribution has these characteristics:

A binomial distribution has these characteristics.

BINOMIAL PROBABILITY DISTRIBUTION

1. An outcome on each trial of an experiment is classified into one of two mutually exclusive categories—a success or a failure.
2. The random variable is the number of successes in a fixed number of trials.
3. The probability of a success stays the same for each trial. So does the probability of a failure.
4. The trials are independent, meaning that the outcome of one trial does not affect the outcome of any other trial.

How Is a Binomial Probability Distribution Computed?

To construct a particular binomial probability distribution, we use (1) the number of trials and (2) the probability of success on each trial. For example, if an examination at the conclusion of a management seminar consists of 20 multiple-choice questions, the number of trials is 20. If each question has five choices and only one choice is correct, the probability of success for a person with no knowledge of the subject on each trial is .20. Thus, the probability is .20 that a person with no knowledge of the subject matter will guess the answer to a question correctly. So the conditions of the binomial distribution just noted are met.

The binomial probability distribution is computed by the formula:

BINOMIAL PROBABILITY DISTRIBUTION $P(x) = {}_nC_x\,\pi^x(1-\pi)^{n-x}$ **[5–3]**

where:

- C denotes a combination.
- n is the number of trials.
- x is the number of successes.
- π is the probability of a success on each trial.

We use the Greek letter π (pi) to denote a binomial population parameter. Do not confuse it with the mathematical constant 3.1416.

EXAMPLE

There are five flights daily from Pittsburgh, Pennsylvania, via Allegheny Airlines into the Bradford (Pennsylvania) Regional Airport. Suppose the probability that any flight arrives late is .20, found by 1/5. What is the probability that none of the flights are late today? What is the probability that exactly one of the flights is late today?

SOLUTION

We can use formula (5–3). The probability that a particular flight is late is .20, so let $\pi = .20$. There are five flights, so $n = 5$, and x refers to the number of successes. In this case a "success" is a plane that arrives late. Because there are no late arrivals $x = 0$.

$$P(0) = {}_nC_x(\pi)^x(1-\pi)^{n-x}$$
$$= {}_5C_0(.20)^0(1-.20)^{5-0} = (1)(1)(.3277) = .3277$$

The probability that exactly one of the five flights will arrive late today is .4096 found by

$$P(1) = {}_nC_x(\pi)^x(1 - \pi)^{n-x}$$
$$= {}_5C_1(.20)^1(1 - .20)^{5-1} = (5)(.20)(.4096) = .4096$$

The entire probability distribution is shown in Table 5–2.

TABLE 5–2 Binomial Probability Distribution for $n = 5$, $\pi = .20$

Number of Late Flights	Probability
0	.3277
1	.4096
2	.2048
3	.0512
4	.0064
5	.0003
Total	1.0000

The random variable in Table 5–2 is plotted in Chart 5–2. Note that the distribution of late arriving flights is positively skewed.

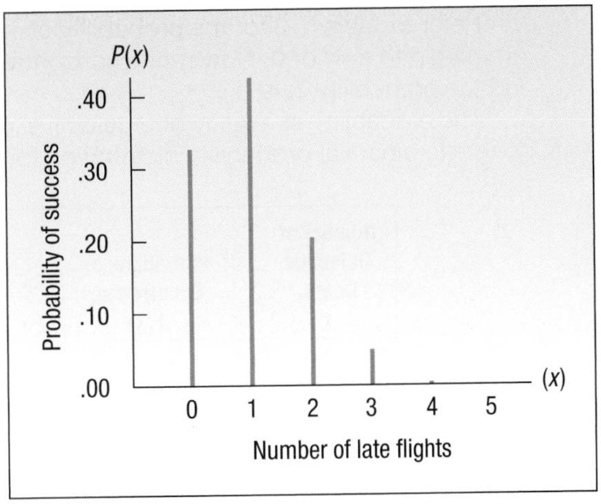

CHART 5–2 Binomial Probability Distribution for $n = 5$, $\pi = .20$

Binomial Probability Tables

Binomial table: Quick way of determining a probability

A binomial probability distribution, as has been shown, can be expressed by a formula. However, except for problems involving small n (say, $n = 3$ or 4), the calculations are rather tedious. As an aid, an extensive table has been developed that gives the probabilities of 0, 1, 2, 3, . . . , n successes for various values of n and π. This table is in Appendix A, and a small portion of the table for the following example is shown in Table 5–3.

TABLE 5–3 Binomial Probabilities for $n = 6$ and Selected Values of π

	$n = 6$ Probability										
x	.05	.1	.2	.3	.4	.5	.6	.7	.8	.9	.95
0	.735	.531	.262	.118	.047	.016	.004	.001	.000	.000	.000
1	.232	.354	.393	.303	.187	.094	.037	.010	.002	.000	.000
2	.031	.098	.246	.324	.311	.234	.138	.060	.015	.001	.000
3	.002	.015	.082	.185	.276	.313	.276	.185	.082	.015	.002
4	.000	.001	.015	.060	.138	.234	.311	.324	.246	.098	.031
5	.000	.000	.002	.010	.037	.094	.187	.303	.393	.354	.232
6	.000	.000	.000	.001	.004	.016	.047	.118	.262	.531	.735

EXAMPLE

Five percent of the worm gears produced by an automatic, high-speed milling machine are defective. What is the probability that out of six gears selected at random none will be defective? Exactly one? Exactly two? Exactly three? Exactly four? Exactly five? Exactly six out of six?

SOLUTION

The binomial conditions are met: (a) There is a constant probability of success (.05), (b) there is a fixed number of trials (6), (c) the trials are independent, and (d) there are only two possible outcomes (a particular gear is either defective or acceptable).

Refer to Table 5–3 for the probability of exactly zero defective gears. Go down the left margin to an *x* of 0. Now move horizontally to the column headed by a π of .05 to find the probability. It is .735.

The probability of exactly one defective in a sample of six worm gears is .232. The complete binomial probability distribution for $n = 6$ and $\pi = .05$ is:

Number of Defective Gears, *x*	Probability of Occurrence, *P*(*x*)	Number of Defective Gears, *x*	Probability of Occurrence, *P*(*x*)
0	.735	4	.000
1	.232	5	.000
2	.031	6	.000
3	.002		

Of course, there is a slight chance of getting exactly five defective gears out of six random selections. It is .00000178, found by inserting the appropriate values in formula (5–3) for the binomial probability distribution.

$$P(5) = {}_6C_5(.05)^5(.95)^1 = (6)(.05)^5(.95) = .00000178$$

For six out of the six, the exact probability is .000000016. Thus, the probability is very small that five or six defective gears will be selected in a sample of six.

Statistics in Action

According to the Annals of Internal Medicine, a blood test on a normal person has a 5 percent chance of being read as abnormal by a laboratory computer. If this is true, and your physician submits a profile of 12 independent tests on you, the chance that your tests all appear normal to the computer is only 54 percent.

The MegaStat software system will also compute the binomial distribution. Here is the output from the previous example. Note that MegaStat uses *p* instead of the Greek letter π and also shows a cumulative probability.

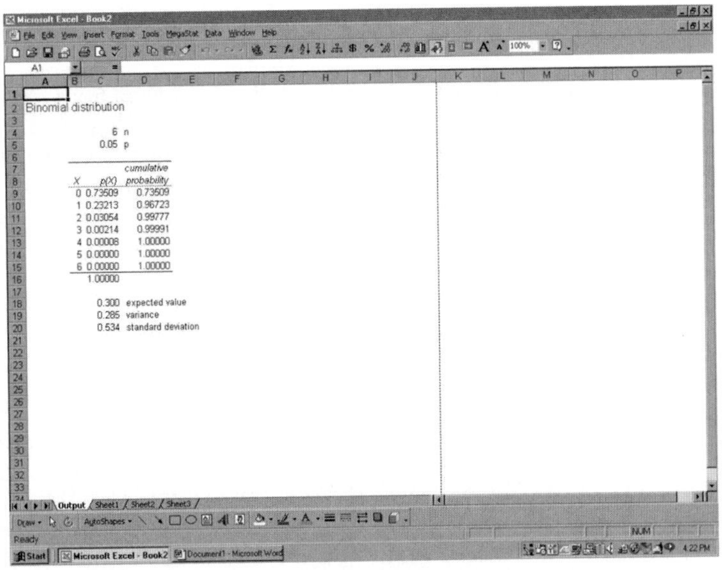

Self-Review 5-3

Eighty percent of State Teacher Retirement System of Ohio benefit recipients have their monthly checks sent directly to their bank by electronic funds transfer. This is also called direct deposit. Suppose we select a random sample of seven recipients.

(a) Does this situation fit the assumptions of the binomial distribution?
(b) What is the probability that all seven recipients use direct deposit?
(c) Use formula (5–3) to determine the exact probability that four of the seven sampled recipients use direct deposit.
(d) Use Appendix A to verify your answers to parts (b) and (c).

Appendix A is limited. It gives probabilities only for n values from 1 through 20 and 25 and π values of .05, .10, .20, . . . , .90, .95. A computer can generate the probabilities for a specified number of successes, given an n and π. The Excel output below shows the probability distribution when $n = 40$ and $\pi = .09$.

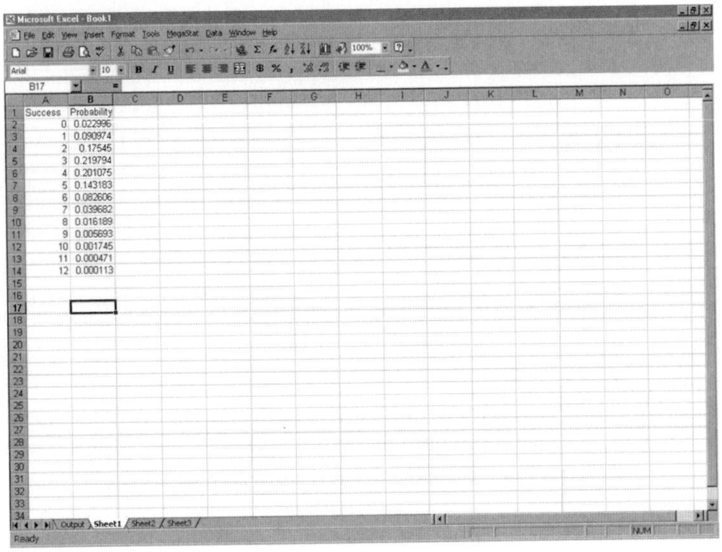

Several additional points should be made regarding the binomial probability distribution.

1. If n remains the same but π increases from .05 to .95, the shape of the distribution changes. Look at Table 5–4 and Chart 5–3. The probabilities for a π of .05 are positively skewed. As π approaches .50, the distribution becomes symmetrical. As π goes beyond .50 and moves toward .95, the probability distribution becomes negatively skewed. Table 5–4 highlights probabilities for $n = 10$ and π of .05, .10, .20, .50, and .70. The graphs of these probability distributions are shown in Chart 5–3.

TABLE 5–4 Probability of 0, 1, 2, . . . Successes for a π of .05, .10, .20, .50, and .70 and an n of 10

x	.05	.1	.2	.3	.4	.5	.6	.7	.8	.9	.95
0	.599	.349	.107	.028	.006	.001	.000	.000	.000	.000	.000
1	.315	.387	.268	.121	.040	.010	.002	.000	.000	.000	.000
2	.075	.194	.302	.233	.121	.044	.011	.001	.000	.000	.000
3	.010	.057	.201	.267	.215	.117	.042	.009	.001	.000	.000
4	.001	.011	.088	.200	.251	.205	.111	.037	.006	.000	.000
5	.000	.001	.026	.103	.201	.246	.201	.103	.026	.001	.000
6	.000	.000	.006	.037	.111	.205	.251	.200	.088	.011	.001
7	.000	.000	.001	.009	.042	.117	.215	.267	.201	.057	.010
8	.000	.000	.000	.001	.011	.044	.121	.233	.302	.194	.075
9	.000	.000	.000	.000	.002	.010	.040	.121	.268	.387	.315
10	.000	.000	.000	.000	.000	.001	.006	.028	.107	.349	.599

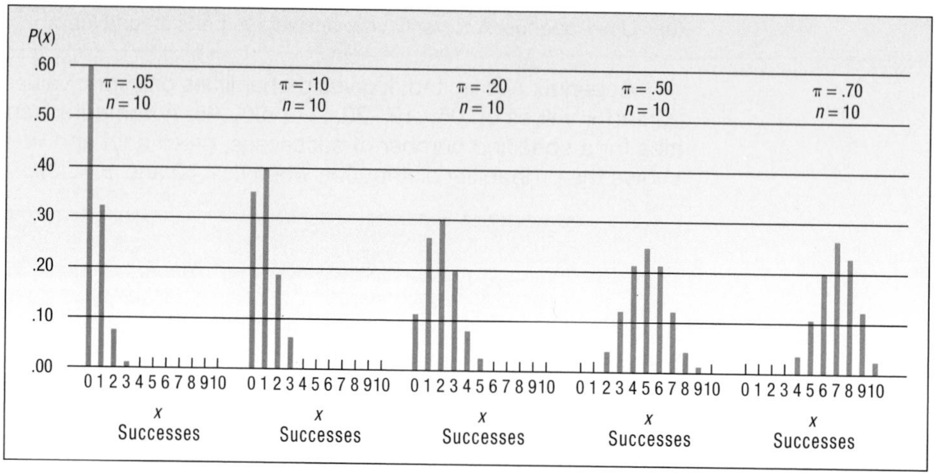

CHART 5–3 Graphing the Binomial Probability Distribution for a π of .05, .10, .20, .50, and .70 and an n of 10

2. If π, the probability of success, remains the same but n becomes larger, the shape of the binomial distribution becomes more symmetrical. Chart 5–4 shows a situation where π remains constant at .10 but n increases from 7 to 40.

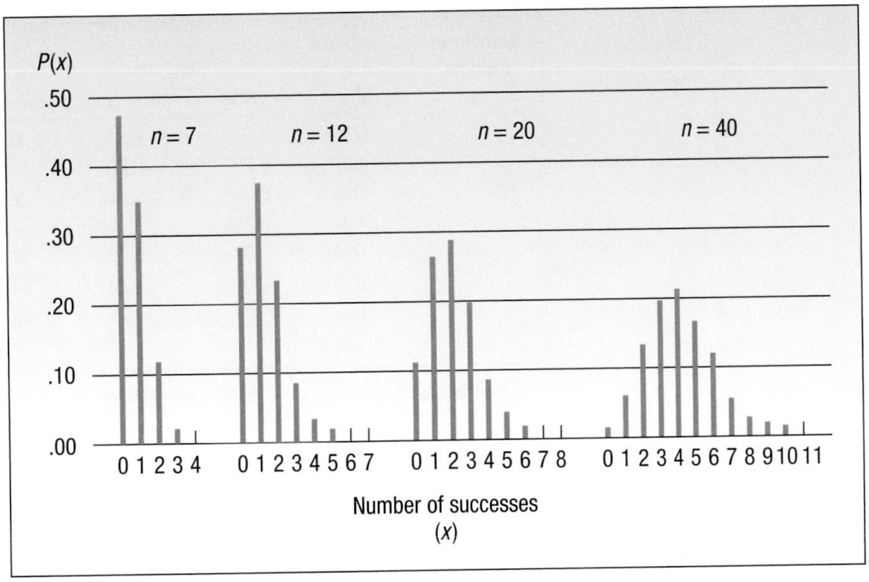

CHART 5–4 Chart Representing the Binomial Probability Distribution for a π of .10 and an n of 7, 12, 20, and 40

3. The mean (μ) and the variance (σ^2) of a binomial distribution can be computed in a "shortcut" fashion by:

MEAN OF A BINOMIAL DISTRIBUTION	$\mu = n\pi$	**[5–4]**

VARIANCE OF A BINOMIAL DISTRIBUTION	$\sigma^2 = n\pi(1 - \pi)$	**[5–5]**

For the example on page 170 regarding defective worm gears, recall that $\pi = .05$ and $n = 6$. Hence:

$$\mu = n\pi = 6(.05) = .30$$

$$\sigma^2 = n\pi(1 - \pi) = 6(.05)(1 - .05) = .285$$

The mean of .30 and the variance of .285 can be verified from formulas (5–1) and (5–2). The probability distribution from Table 5–3 and detailed calculations are shown below.

Number of Defects, x	$P(x)$	$xP(x)$	$x - \mu$	$(x - \mu)^2$	$(x - \mu)^2 P(x)$
0	.735	0	−0.30	0.09	0.06615
1	.232	0.232	0.70	0.49	0.11368
2	.031	0.062	1.70	2.89	0.08959
3	.002	0.006	2.70	7.29	0.01458
4	.000	0	3.70	13.69	0
5	.000	0	4.70	22.09	0
6	.000	0	5.70	32.49	0
		0.30			0.284*

*The slight discrepancy between .285 and .284 is due to rounding.

Exercises

7. In a binomial situation $n = 4$ and $\pi = .25$. Determine the probabilities of the following events using the binomial formula.
   a. $x = 2$
   b. $x = 3$
8. In a binomial situation $n = 5$ and $\pi = .40$. Determine the probabilities of the following events using the binomial formula.
   a. $x = 1$
   b. $x = 2$
9. Assume a binomial distribution where $n = 3$ and $\pi = .60$.
   a. Refer to Appendix A, and list the probabilities for values of x from 0 to 3.
   b. Determine the mean and standard deviation of the distribution from the general definitions given in formulas (5–1) and (5–2).
10. Assume a binomial distribution where $n = 5$ and $\pi = .30$.
    a. Refer to Appendix A, and list the probabilities for values of x from 0 to 5.
    b. Determine the mean and standard deviation of the distribution from the general definitions given in formulas (5–1) and (5–2).
11. An American Society of Investors survey found 30 percent of individual investors have used a discount broker. In a random sample of nine individuals, what is the probability:
    a. Exactly two of the sampled individuals have used a discount broker?
    b. Exactly four of them have used a discount broker?
    c. None of them have used a discount broker?
12. The United States Postal Service reports 95 percent of first class mail within the same city is delivered within 2 days of the time of mailing. Six letters are randomly sent to different locations.
    a. What is the probability that all six arrive within 2 days?
    b. What is the probability that exactly five arrive within 2 days?
    c. Find the mean number of letters that will arrive within 2 days.
    d. Compute the variance and standard deviation of the number that will arrive within 2 days.
13. The industry standards suggest that 10 percent of new vehicles require warranty service within the first year. Jones Nissan in Sumter, South Carolina, sold 12 Nissans yesterday.
    a. What is the probability that none of these vehicles requires warranty service?
    b. What is the probability exactly one of these vehicles requires warranty service?
    c. Determine the probability that exactly two of these vehicles require warranty service.
    d. Compute the mean and standard deviation of this probability distribution.
14. A telemarketer makes six phone calls per hour and is able to make a sale on 30 percent of these contacts. During the next 2 hours, find:
    a. The probability of making exactly four sales.
    b. The probability of making no sales.
    c. The probability of making exactly two sales.
    d. The mean number of sales in the two-hour period.

15. A recent survey by the American Accounting Association revealed 23 percent of students graduating with a major in accounting select public accounting. Suppose we select a sample of 15 recent graduates.

a. What is the probability two select public accounting?

b. What is the probability five select public accounting?

c. How many graduates would you expect to select public accounting?

16. Suppose 60 percent of all people prefer Coke to Pepsi. We select 18 people for further study.

a. How many would you expect to prefer Coke?

b. What is the probability 10 of those surveyed will prefer Coke?

c. What is the probability 15 prefer Coke?

Cumulative Probability Distributions

We may wish to know the probability of correctly guessing the answers to 6 *or more* true/false questions out of 10. Or we may be interested in the probability of *selecting less than two* defectives at random from production during the previous hour. In these cases we need cumulative frequency distributions similar to the ones developed in Chapter 2. The following example will illustrate.

EXAMPLE

A recent study by the American Highway Patrolman's Association revealed that 60 percent of American drivers use their seat belts. A sample of 10 drivers on the Florida Turnpike is selected.

1. What is the probability that exactly seven are wearing seat belts?
2. What is the probability that seven or fewer of the drivers are wearing seat belts?

SOLUTION

This situation meets the binomial requirements, namely:

- A particular driver either is wearing a seat belt or is not. There are only two possible outcomes.
- The probability of "success" (wearing a seat belt) is the same from driver to driver: 60 percent.
- The trials are independent. If the fourth driver selected in the sample is wearing a seat belt, for example, it has no effect on whether the fifth driver selected is wearing a seat belt.
- There is a fixed number of trials—10 in this case, because 10 drivers are checked.

1. To find the likelihood of *exactly* seven drivers, we use Appendix A. Locate the page for $n = 10$. Next find the column for $\pi = .60$ and the row for $x = 7$. The value is .215. Thus, the probability of finding 7 out of 10 drivers in the sample wearing their seat belts is .215. This is often written as follows:

$$P(x = 7 \mid n = 10 \text{ and } \pi = .60) = .215$$

   where x refers to the number of successes, n the number of trials, and π the probability of a success. The bar "|" means "given that."
2. To find the probability that seven or fewer of the drivers will be wearing seat belts, we apply the special rule of addition, formula (4–2), from Chapter 4. Because the events are mutually exclusive, we determine the probability that of the 10 drivers stopped, none was wearing a seat belt, 1 was wearing a seat belt, 2 were wearing a seat belt, and so on up to 7 drivers. The probabilities of the eight possible outcomes are then totaled. From Appendix A, $n = 10$, and $\pi = .60$.

$$P(x \le 7 \mid n = 10 \text{ and } \pi = .60) = P(x = 0) + P(x = 1) + P(x = 2) + P(x = 3) + P(x = 4) + P(x = 5) + P(x = 6) + P(x = 7)$$

$$= .000 + .002 + .011 + .042 + .111 + .201 + .251 + .215$$

$$= .833$$

So the probability of stopping 10 cars at random and finding seven or fewer of the drivers wearing their seat belts is .833.

This value may also be determined, with less computation, using the complement rule. First, find $P(x > 7)$ given that $n = 10$ and $\pi = .60$. This probability is .167, found by $P(x = 8) + P(x = 9) + P(x = 10) = .121 + .040 + .006$. The probability that $x \le 7$ is equal to $1 - P(x > 7)$, so $P(x \le 7) = 1 - .167 = .833$, the same as computed above.

Self-Review 5-4

A survey of college students revealed 60 percent earn at least part of their college expenses from part-time jobs. Suppose we select a random sample of 4 students. Determine the probability that:

(a) Exactly two earn some of their expenses.
(b) Two or fewer earn some of their expenses.
(c) More than two earn some of their expenses.

Exercises

17. In a binomial distribution $n = 8$ and $\pi = .30$. Find the probabilities of the following events.
   a. $x = 2$.
   b. $x \le 2$ (the probability that x is equal to or less than 2).
   c. $x \ge 3$ (the probability that x is equal to or greater than 3).

18. In a binomial distribution $n = 12$ and $\pi = .60$. Find the following probabilities.
   a. $x = 5$.
   b. $x \le 5$.
   c. $x \ge 6$.

19. In a recent study 90 percent of the homes in the United States were found to have color TVs. In a sample of nine homes, what is the probability that:
   a. All nine have color TVs?
   b. Less than five have color TVs?
   c. More than five have color TVs?
   d. At least seven homes have color TVs?

20. A manufacturer of window frames knows from long experience that 5 percent of the production will have some type of minor defect that will require an adjustment. What is the probability that in a sample of 20 window frames:
   a. None will need adjustment?
   b. At least one will need adjustment?
   c. More than two will need adjustment?

21. The speed with which utility companies can resolve problems is very important. GTC, the Georgetown Telephone Company, reports they can resolve customer problems the same day they are reported in 70 percent of the cases. Suppose the 15 cases reported today are representative of all complaints.
   a. How many of the problems would you expect to be resolved today? What is the standard deviation?
   b. What is the probability 10 of the problems can be resolved today?
   c. What is the probability 10 or 11 of the problems can be resolved today?
   d. What is the probability more than 10 of the problems can be resolved today?

The mean number of successes, μ, can be determined by $n\pi$, where n is the total number of trials and π the probability of success.

MEAN OF A POISSON DISTRIBUTION	$\mu = n\pi$	**[5–8]**

The variance of the Poisson is also equal to its mean. If, for example, the probability that a check cashed by a bank will bounce is .0003, and 10,000 checks are cashed, the mean and the variance for the number of bad checks is 3.0, found by $\mu = n\pi = 10{,}000(.0003) = 3.0$.

Recall that for a binomial distribution there is a fixed number of trials. For example, for a four-question multiple-choice test there can only be zero, one, two, three, or four successes (correct answers). The random variable, x, for a Poisson distribution, however, can assume an *infinite number of values*—that is, 0, 1, 2, 3, 4, 5, ... However, *the probabilities become very small after the first few occurrences* (successes).

To illustrate the Poisson probability computation, assume baggage is rarely lost by Northwest Airlines. Most flights do not experience any mishandled bags; some have one bag lost; a few have two bags lost; rarely a flight will have three lost bags; and so on. Suppose a random sample of 1,000 flights shows a total of 300 bags were lost. Thus, the arithmetic mean number of lost bags per flight is 0.3, found by 300/1,000. If the number of lost bags per flight follows a Poisson distribution with $\mu = 0.3$, we can compute the various probabilities by the formula:

$$P(x) = \frac{\mu^x e^{-\mu}}{x!}$$

For example, the probability of not losing any bags is:

$$P(0) = \frac{(0.3)^0(e^{-0.3})}{0!} = 0.7408$$

In other words, 74 percent of the flights will have no lost baggage. The probability of exactly one lost bag is:

5! = 5×4×3×2×1

$$P(1) = \frac{(0.3)^1(e^{-0.3})}{1!} = 0.2222$$

Thus, we would expect to find exactly one lost bag on 22 percent of the flights. In addition, on 96 percent of the flights there are no bags or only one bag lost.

Poisson probabilities can also be found in the table in Appendix C.

EXAMPLE

Recall from the previous illustration that the number of lost bags follows a Poisson distribution with a mean of 0.3. Use Appendix C to find the probability that no bags will be lost on a particular flight. What is the probability exactly one bag will be lost on a particular flight? When should the supervisor become suspicious that a flight is having too many lost bags?

SOLUTION

Part of Appendix C is repeated as Table 5–7. To find the probability of no lost bags, locate the column headed "0.3" and read down that column to the row labeled "0." The probability is .7408. That is the probability of no lost bags. The probability of one lost bag is .2222, which is in the next row of the table, in the same column. The probability of two lost bags is .0333, in the row below; for three lost bags it is .0033; and for four lost bags it is .0003. Thus, a supervisor should not be surprised to find one lost bag but should expect to see more than one lost bag infrequently.

TABLE 5–7 Poisson Table for Various Values of μ (from Appendix C)

	μ								
x	**0.1**	**0.2**	**0.3**	**0.4**	**0.5**	**0.6**	**0.7**	**0.8**	**0.9**
0	0.9048	0.8187	0.7408	0.6703	0.6065	0.5488	0.4966	0.4493	0.4066
1	0.0905	0.1637	0.2222	0.2681	0.3033	0.3293	0.3476	0.3595	0.3659
2	0.0045	0.0164	0.0333	0.0536	0.0758	0.0988	0.1217	0.1438	0.1647
3	0.0002	0.0011	0.0033	0.0072	0.0126	0.0198	0.0284	0.0383	0.0494
4	0.0000	0.0001	0.0003	0.0007	0.0016	0.0030	0.0050	0.0077	0.0111
5	0.0000	0.0000	0.0000	0.0001	0.0002	0.0004	0.0007	0.0012	0.0020
6	0.0000	0.0000	0.0000	0.0000	0.0000	0.0000	0.0001	0.0002	0.0003
7	0.0000	0.0000	0.0000	0.0000	0.0000	0.0000	0.0000	0.0000	0.0000

These probabilities can also be found using the MINITAB system. The commands necessary are reported at the end of the chapter. The output appears below. A graph of the distribution of the number of lost bags is shown in Chart 5–5.

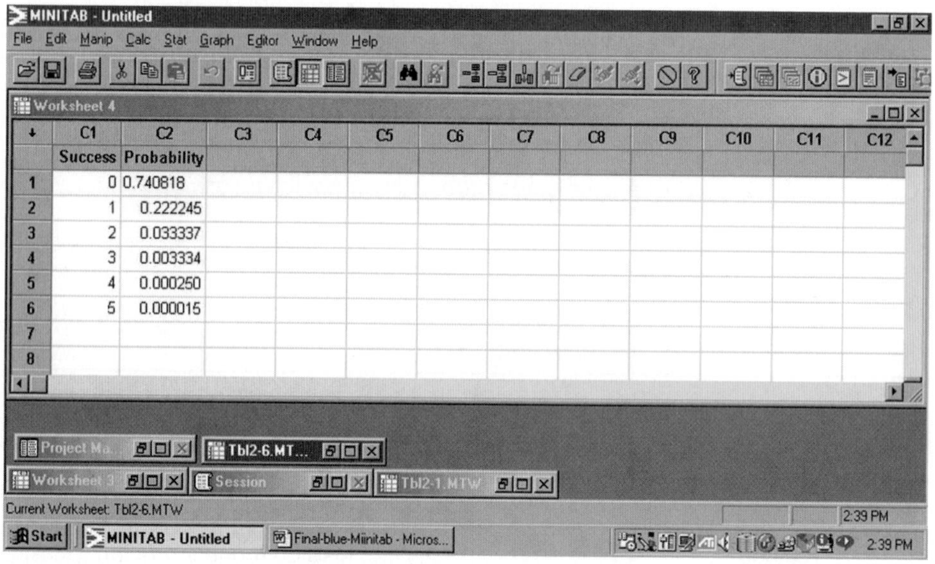

CHART 5–5 Poisson Probability Distribution for $\mu = 0.3$

The Poisson probability distribution is always positively skewed and has no specific upper limit. The Poisson distribution for the lost bags illustration, where $\mu = 0.3$ is highly skewed. As μ becomes larger, the Poisson distribution becomes more symmetrical. For example, Chart 5–6 shows the distributions of the number of transmission services, muffler replacements, and oil changes per day at Avellino's Auto Shop. They follow Poisson distributions with means of 0.7, 2.0, and 6.0, respectively. Observe that the distributions are more symmetrical as μ increases.

Only μ needed to construct Poisson

In summary, the Poisson distribution is actually a family of discrete distributions. All that is needed to construct a Poisson probability distribution is the mean number of defects, errors, and so on—designated as μ.

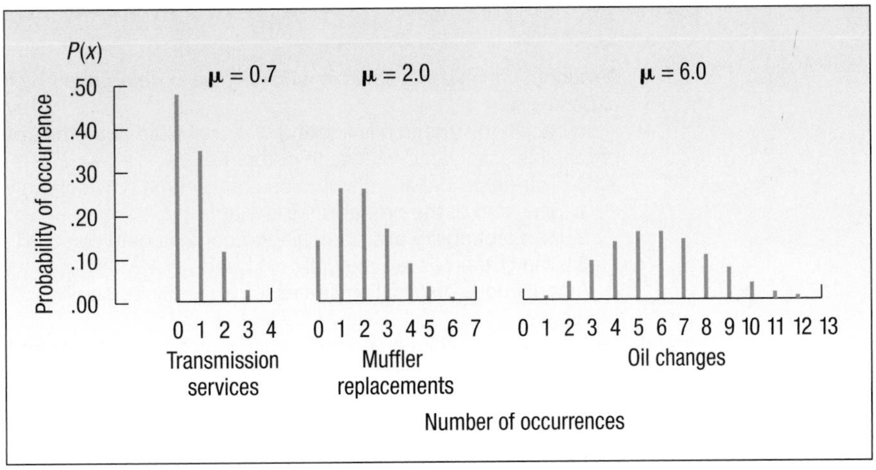

CHART 5–6 Poisson Probability Distributions for Means of 0.7, 2.0, and 6.0

Self-Review 5-6

From actuary tables the Washington Insurance Company determined the likelihood that a man age 25 will die within the next year is .0002. If Washington Insurance sells 4,000 policies to 25-year-old men this year, what is the probability they will pay on exactly one policy?

Exercises

29. In a Poisson distribution $\mu = 0.4$.
   a. What is the probability that $x = 0$?
   b. What is the probability that $x > 0$?

30. In a Poisson distribution $\mu = 4$.
   a. What is the probability that $x = 2$?
   b. What is the probability that $x \leq 2$?
   c. What is the probability that $x > 2$?

31. Ms. Bergen is a loan officer at Coast Bank and Trust. Based on her years of experience, she estimates that the probability is .025 that an applicant will not be able to repay his or her installment loan. Last month she made 40 loans.
   a. What is the probability that three loans will be defaulted?
   b. What is the probability that at least three loans will be defaulted?

32. Automobiles arrive at the Elkhart exit of the Indiana Toll Road at the rate of two per minute. The distribution of arrivals approximates a Poisson distribution.
   a. What is the probability that no automobiles arrive in a particular minute?
   b. What is the probability that at least one automobile arrives during a particular minute?

33. It is estimated that 0.5 percent of the callers to the billing department of the U.S. West Telephone Company will receive a busy signal. What is the probability that of today's 1,200 callers at least 5 received a busy signal?

34. Textbook authors and publishers work very hard to minimize the number of errors in a text. However, some errors are unavoidable. Ms. Christina Sanders, statistics editor, reports that the mean number of errors per chapter is 0.8. What is the probability that there are less than two errors in a particular chapter?

Chapter Outline

I. A random variable is a variable whose value is determined by the outcome of a random experiment.

II. A probability distribution is a listing of all possible outcomes of an experiment and the probability associated with each outcome.

A. A discrete probability distribution can assume only certain values. The main features are:

1. The sum of the probabilities is 1.00.

2. The probability of a particular outcome is between 0.00 and 1.00.

3. The outcomes are mutually exclusive.

B. A continuous distribution can assume an infinite number of values within a specific range.

III. The mean and variance of a probability distribution are computed as follows.

A. The mean is equal to:

$$\mu = \Sigma[xP(x)] \quad \textbf{[5–1]}$$

B. The variance is equal to:

$$\sigma^2 = \Sigma[(x - \mu)^2 P(x)] \quad \textbf{[5–2]}$$

IV. The binomial distribution has the following characteristics.

A. Each outcome is classified into one of two mutually exclusive categories.

B. The probability of a success remains the same from trial to trial.

C. Each trial is independent.

D. The distribution results from a count of the number of successes in a fixed number of trials.

E. A binomial probability is determined as follows:

$$P(x) = {}_nC_x \, \pi^x (1 - \pi)^{n-x} \quad \textbf{[5–3]}$$

F. The mean is computed as:

$$\mu = n\pi \quad \textbf{[5–4]}$$

G. The variance is

$$\sigma^2 = n\pi(1 - \pi) \quad \textbf{[5–5]}$$

V. The hypergeometric distribution has the following characteristics.

A. There are only two possible outcomes.

B. The probability of a success is not the same on each trial.

C. The distribution results from a count of the number of successes in a fixed number of trials.

D. A hypergeometric probability is computed from the following equation.

$$P(x) = \frac{({}_SC_x)({}_{N-S}C_{n-x})}{({}_NC_n)} \quad \textbf{[5–6]}$$

VI. The Poisson distribution has the following characteristics.

A. It describes the number of times some event occurs during a specified interval.

B. The probability of a "success" is proportional to the length of the interval.

C. Nonoverlapping intervals are independent.

D. It is a limiting form of the binomial distribution when n is large and π is small.

E. A Poisson probability is determined from the following equation:

$$P(x) = \frac{\mu^x e^{-\mu}}{x!} \quad \textbf{[5–7]}$$

F. The mean and the variance of a Poisson distribution are the same and are equal to $n\pi$.

Chapter Exercises

35. What is the difference between a random variable and a probability distribution?

36. What is the difference between a discrete and a continuous random variable? For each of the following indicate whether the random variable is a discrete or continuous random variable.

a. The length of time to get a haircut.
b. The number of cars a jogger passes each morning while running.
c. The number of hits for a team in a high school girls' softball game.
d. The number of patients treated at the South Strand Medical Center between 6 and 10 P.M. each night.
e. The number of miles your car traveled on the last fill up.
f. The number of customers at the Oak Street Wendy's who used the drive-through facility.
g. The distance between Gainesville, Florida, and all Florida cities of at least 50,000.

37. What are the requirements for the binomial distribution?

38. Under what conditions will the binomial and the Poisson distributions give roughly the same results?

39. Samson Apartments has a large number of units available to rent each month. A concern of management is the number of vacant apartments each month. A recent study revealed the percent of the time that a given number of apartments are vacant. Compute the mean and standard deviation of the number of vacant apartments.

Number of Vacant Units	Probability
0	.10
1	.20
2	.30
3	.40

40. An investment will be worth $1,000, $2,000, or $5,000 at the end of the year. The probabilities of these values are .25, .60, and .15, respectively. Determine the mean and variance of the worth of the investment.

41. The personnel manager of the Cumberland Pig Iron Company is studying the number of on-the-job accidents over a period of 1 month. He developed the following probability distribution. Compute the mean, variance, and standard deviation of the number of accidents in a month.

Number of Accidents	Probability
0	.40
1	.20
2	.20
3	.10
4	.10

42. Thirty percent of the population in a southwestern community are Spanish-speaking Americans. A Spanish-speaking person is accused of killing a non-Spanish-speaking American. Of the first 12 potential jurors, only 2 are Spanish-speaking Americans, and 10 are not. The defendant's lawyer challenges the jury selection, claiming bias against her client. The government lawyer disagrees, saying that the probability of this particular jury composition is common. What do you think?

43. An auditor for Health Maintenance Services of Georgia reports 40 percent of the policyholders 55 years or older submit a claim during the year. Fifteen policyholders are randomly selected for company records.

a. How many of the policyholders would you expect to have filed a claim within the last year?
b. What is the probability that 10 of the selected policyholders submitted a claim last year?
c. What is the probability that 10 or more of the selected policyholders submitted a claim last year?
d. What is the probability that more than 10 of the selected policyholders submitted a claim last year?

44. Tire and Auto Supply is considering a 2-for-1 stock split. Before the transaction is finalized, at least two thirds of the 1,200 company stockholders must approve the proposal. To evaluate the likelihood the proposal will be approved, the director of finance selected a sample of 18 stockholders. He contacted each and found 14 approved of the proposed split. What is the likelihood of this event, assuming two thirds of the stockholders approve?

45. A Federal study reported that 7.5 percent of the U.S. workforce has a drug problem. A drug enforcement official for the State of Indiana wished to investigate this statement. In his sample of 20 employed workers:
a. How many would you expect to have a drug problem? What is the standard deviation?
b. What is the likelihood that *none* of the workers sampled has a drug problem?
c. What is the likelihood *at least one* has a drug problem?

46. The Bank of Hawaii reports that 7 percent of its credit card holders will default at some time in their life. The Hilo branch just mailed out 12 new cards today.
a. How many of these new cardholders would you expect to default? What is the standard deviation?
b. What is the likelihood that *none* of the cardholders will default?
c. What is the likelihood *at least one* will default?

47. Recent statistics suggest that 15 percent of those who visit a retail site on the World Wide Web make a purchase. A retailer wished to verify this claim. To do so, she selected a sample of 16 "hits" to her site and found that 4 had actually made a purchase.
a. What is the likelihood of exactly four purchases?
b. How many purchases should she expect?
c. What is the likelihood that four or more "hits" result in a purchase?

48. Acceptance sampling is used to monitor the quality of incoming raw materials. Suppose a purchaser of electronic components allows 1 percent of the components to be defective. To ensure the quality of incoming parts, they normally sample 20 parts and allow 1 defect.
a. What is the likelihood of accepting a lot that is 1 percent defective?
b. If the quality of the incoming lot was actually 2 percent, what is the likelihood of accepting it?
c. If the quality of the incoming lot was actually 5 percent, what is the likelihood of accepting it?

49. Colgate-Palmolive, Inc. recently developed a new toothpaste flavored by honey. They tested a group of 10 people. Six of the group said they liked the new flavor, and the remaining four indicated they definitely did not. Four of the ten are selected to participate in an in-depth interview. What is the probability that of those selected for the in-depth interview two liked the new flavor and two did not?

50. Dr. Richmond, a psychologist, is studying the daytime television viewing habits of college students. She believes 45 percent of college students watch soap operas during the afternoon. To further investigate, she selects a sample of 10.
a. Develop a probability distribution for the number of students in the sample who watch soap operas.
b. Find the mean and the standard deviation of this distribution.
c. What is the probability of finding exactly four who watch soap operas?
d. What is the probability less than half of the students selected watch soap operas?

51. A recent study conducted by Penn, Shone, and Borland, on behalf of LastMinute.com, revealed that 52 percent of business travelers plan their trips less than 2 weeks before departure. The study is to be replicated in the tri-state area with a sample of 12 frequent business travelers.
a. Develop a probability distribution for the number of travelers who plan their trips within 2 weeks of departure.
b. Find the mean and the standard deviation of this distribution.

c. What is the probability exactly 5 of the 12 selected business travelers plan their trips within 2 weeks of departure?
d. What is the probability 5 or fewer of the 12 selected business travelers plan their trips within 2 weeks of departure?

52. The law firm of Hagel and Hagel is located in downtown Cincinnati. There are 10 partners in the firm; 7 live in Ohio and 3 in northern Kentucky. Ms. Wendy Hagel, the managing partner, wants to appoint a committee of three partners to look into moving the firm to northern Kentucky. If the committee is selected at random from the 10 partners, what is the probability that:
a. One member of the committee lives in northern Kentucky and the others live in Ohio?
b. At least one member of the committee lives in northern Kentucky?

53. The position of chief of police in the city of Corry, Pennsylvania, is vacant. A search committee of Corry residents is charged with the responsibility of recommending a new chief to the city council. There are 12 applicants, 4 of which are either female or members of a minority. The search committee decides to interview all 12 of the applicants. To begin, they randomly select four applicants to be interviewed on the first day, and none of the four is female or a member of a minority. The local newspaper, the Corry *Press,* suggests discrimination in an editorial. What is the likelihood of this occurrence?

54. Suppose 1.5 percent of the antennas on new Nokia cell phones are defective. For a random sample of 200 antennas, find the probability that:
a. None of the antennas is defective.
b. Three or more of the antennas are defective.

55. A study of the checkout lines at the Safeway Supermarket in the South Strand area revealed that between 4 and 7 P.M. on weekdays there is an average of four customers waiting in line. What is the probability that you visit Safeway today during this period and find:
a. No customers are waiting?
b. Four customers are waiting?
c. Four or fewer are waiting?
d. Four or more are waiting?

56. An internal study at Lahey Electronics, a large software development company, revealed the mean time for an internal e-mail message to arrive at its destination was 2 seconds. Further, the distribution of the arrival times followed the Poisson distribution.
a. What is the probability a message takes exactly 1 second to arrive at its destination?
b. What is the probability it takes more than 4 seconds to arrive at its destination?
c. What is the probability it takes virtually no time, i.e., "zero" seconds?

57. Recent crime reports indicate that 3.1 motor vehicle thefts occur each minute in the United States. Assume that the distribution of thefts per minute can be approximated by the Poisson probability distribution.
a. Calculate the probability exactly *four* thefts occur in a minute.
b. What is the probability there are *no* thefts in a minute?
c. What is the probability there is *at least one* theft in a minute?

58. New Process, Inc., a large mail-order supplier of women's fashions, advertises same-day service on every order. Recently the movement of orders has not gone as planned, and there were a large number of complaints. Bud Owens, director of customer service, has completely redone the method of order handling. The goal is to have fewer than five unfilled orders on hand at the end of 95 percent of the working days. Frequent checks of the unfilled orders at the end of the day revealed that the distribution of the unfilled orders follows a Poisson distribution with a mean of two orders.
a. Has New Process, Inc. lived up to its internal goal? Cite evidence.
b. Draw a histogram representing the Poisson probability distribution of unfilled orders.

59. On January 29, 1986, the space shuttle *Challenger* exploded 46,000 feet above the Atlantic Ocean, resulting in the death of all seven astronauts. A 1985 study published by the National Aeronautics and Space Administration (NASA) suggested that the probability of such a catastrophic occurrence was 1 in 60,000. A similar report by the Air Force set the likelihood of a catastrophe at 1 in 35. The *Challenger* flight was the 25th mission in the shuttle program. Use the Poisson distribution to compare the probabilities of at least one disaster in a sample of 25 missions using both estimates of the probability of occurrence.

60. According to the "January theory," if the stock market is up for the month of January, it will be up for the year. If it is down in January, it will be down for the year. According to an article in *The Wall Street Journal,* this theory held for 29 out of the last 34 years. Suppose there is no truth to this theory. What is the probability this could occur by chance? (You will probably need a software package such as Excel or MINITAB.)
61. During the second round of the 1989 U.S. Open golf tournament, four golfers scored a hole in one on the sixth hole. The odds of a professional golfer making a hole in one are estimated to be 3,708 to 1, so the probability is 1/3,708. There were 155 golfers participating in the second round that day. Estimate the probability that four golfers would score a hole in one on the sixth hole.

Computer Data Exercises

62. Refer to the Real Estate data, which reports information on homes sold in the Venice, Florida, area last year.
    a. Create a probability distribution for the number of bedrooms. Compute the mean and the standard deviation of this distribution.
    b. Create a probability distribution for the number of bathrooms. Compute the mean and the standard deviation of this distribution.
63. Refer to the Baseball 2001 data, which contains information on the 2001 Major League Baseball season. There are 30 teams in the major leagues, and 5 of them have home fields with artificial playing surfaces. As part of the negotiations with the players' union, a study regarding injuries on grass versus artificial surfaces will be conducted. Five teams will be selected to participate in the study, and the teams will be selected at random. What is the likelihood that two of the five teams selected for study play their home games on artificial surfaces?

Computer Commands

1. The Excel MegaStat commands to create the binomial probability distribution on page 171 are:
    a. Select the **MegaStat** option on the toolbar, click on **Probability,** and **Discrete Probability Distributions.**
    b. In the dialog box select **Binomial,** the number of trials is *6,* the probability of a success is *.05.* If you wish to see a graph, click on **display graph.**

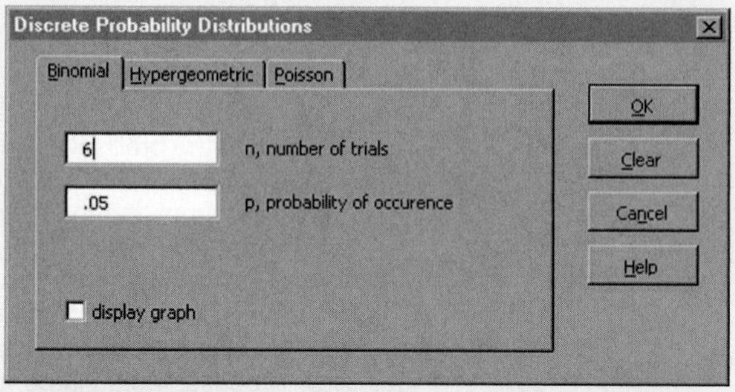

2. The Excel commands necessary to determine the binomial probability distribution on page 171 are:
    a. On a blank Excel worksheet write the word *Success* in cell A1 and the word *Probability* in B1. In cells A2 through A14 write the integers *0* to *12.* Enter *B2* as the active cell.
    b. From the toolbar select **Insert** and **Function Wizard.**
    c. In the first dialog box select **Statistical** in the function category and **BINOMDIST** in the function name category, then click **OK.**
    d. In the second dialog box enter the four items necessary to compute a binomial probability. Make cell B2 the active cell.
        1. Enter *0* for the number of successes.
        2. Enter *40* for the number of trials.

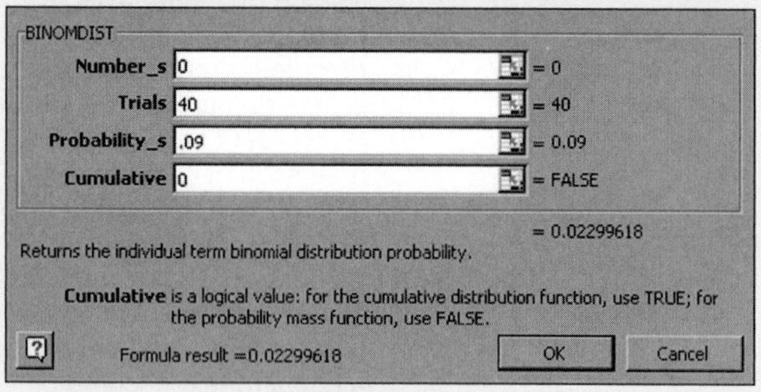

3. Enter *.09* for the probability of a success.
4. Enter the word *false* or the number *0* for the individual probabilities.
5. Excel will compute the probability of 0 successes in 40 trials, with a .09 probability of success. The result, .02299618, is stored in cell B2.

e. To find the complete probability distribution, go to the formula bar and replace the *0* to the right of the open parentheses with *A2:A14.*

f. Move the mouse to the lower right corner of cell B2 and highlight the B column to cell B14. The probability of a success for the various values of the random variable will appear.

3. The Excel commands necessary to determine the hypergeometric distribution on page 179 are:

a. On a blank Excel worksheet write the word *Members* in cell A1 and the word *Probability* in B1. In cells A2 to A7 write the integers 0 to 5. Enter *B2* as the active cell.

b. From the toolbar choose **Insert** and **Function**.

c. In the first dialog box select **Statistical** and **HYPGEOMDIST**, and then click **OK**.

d. In the second dialog box enter the four items necessary to compute a hypergeometric probability.
1. Enter *0* for the number of successes.
2. Enter *5* for the number of trials.
3. Enter *40* for the number of successes in the population.
4. Enter *50* for the size of the population.
5. Excel will compute the probability of 0 successes in 5 trials (.000118937) and store that result in cell B2.

e. To find the complete probability distribution, go to the formula bar and replace the 0 to the right of the open parentheses with *A2:A7.*

f. Move the mouse to the lower right corner of cell B2 and highlight the B column to cell B7. The probability of a success for the various outcomes will appear.

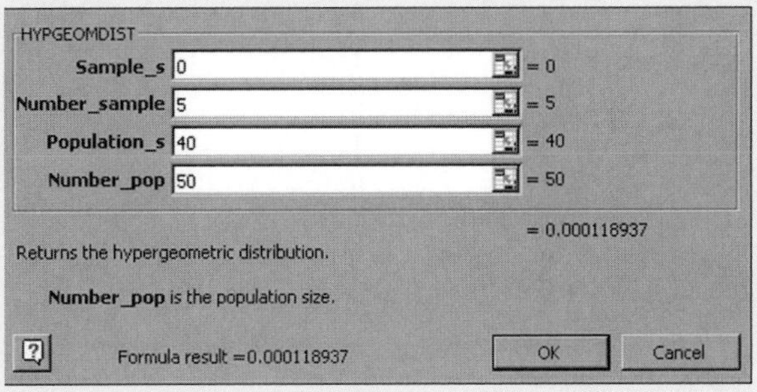

4. The MINITAB commands to generate the Poisson distribution on page 182 are:

a. Label column C1 as *Successes* and C2 as *Probability.* Enter the integers 0 though 5 in the first column.

b. Select **Calc**, then **Probability Distributions,** and **Poisson.**

c. In the dialog box click on **Probability,** set the mean equal to *.3,* and select *C1* as the Input column. Designate *C2* as Optional storage, and then click **OK.**

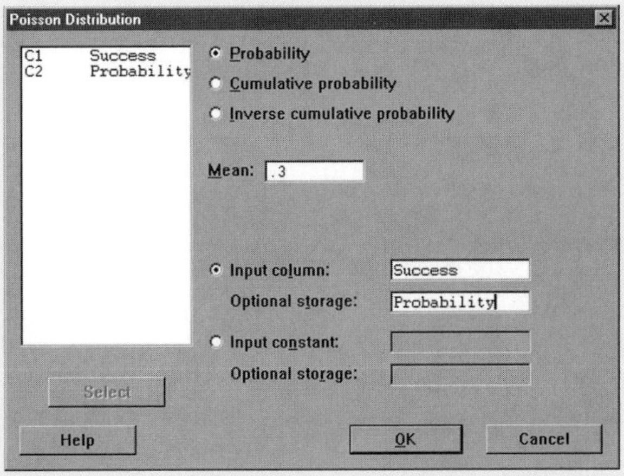

Chapter 5 Answers to Self-Review

5–1 **(a)**

Number of Spots	Probability
1	$\frac{1}{6}$
2	$\frac{1}{6}$
3	$\frac{1}{6}$
4	$\frac{1}{6}$
5	$\frac{1}{6}$
6	$\frac{1}{6}$
Total	$\frac{6}{6} = 1.00$

(b)

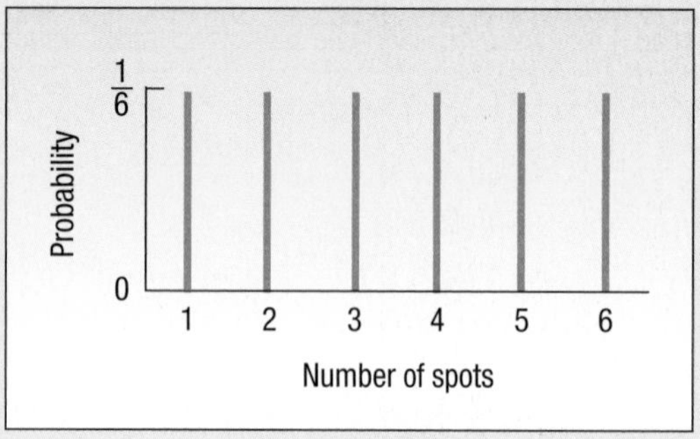

(c) $\frac{6}{6}$, or 1.

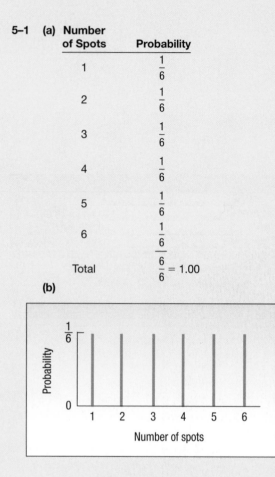

5–2 **(a)** It is discrete, because the values .80, .90, and 1.20 are clearly separated from each other, the sum of the probabilities is 1.00, and the outcomes are mutually exclusive.

(b)

x	$P(x)$	$xP(x)$
\$ .80	.30	0.24
.90	.50	0.45
1.20	.20	0.24
		0.93

The mean is 93 cents.

(c)

x	$P(x)$	$(x - \mu)$	$(x - \mu)^2 P(x)$
\$0.80	.30	−0.13	.00507
0.90	.50	−0.03	.00045
1.20	.20	0.27	.01458
			.02010

The variance is .02010, and the standard deviation is 14 cents.

5–3 **(a)** It is reasonable because: each retiree either uses direct deposit or does not, the retirees are independent, the probability of using direct deposit is 80 percent for all, and we count the number using the service out of 7.

(b) $P(7) = (.80)^7 = .2097$

(c) $P(4) = {}_7C_4(.80)^4(.20)^3 = (35)(.4096)(.008) = .1147$

(d) Answers are in agreement.

5–4 $n = 4, \pi = .60$

(a) $P(x = 2) = .346$

(b) $P(x \leq 2) = .526$

(c) $P(x > 2) = 1 - .526 = .474$

5–5 $$P(3) = \frac{{}_8C_3\,{}_4C_2}{{}_{12}C_5} = \frac{\left(\frac{8!}{3!5!}\right)\left(\frac{4!}{2!2!}\right)}{\frac{12!}{5!7!}}$$

$$= \frac{(56)(6)}{792} = .424$$

5–6 $\mu = 4{,}000(.0002) = 0.8$

$$P(1) = \frac{0.8^1 e^{-0.8}}{1!} = .3595$$

6

The Normal Probability Distribution

GOALS

When you have completed this chapter, you will be able to:

1 List the characteristics of the normal probability distribution.

2 Define and calculate *z* values.

3 Determine the probability that an observation is between two points on a normal distribution using the standard normal distribution.

4 Determine the probability that an observation is above (or below) a point on a normal distribution using the standard normal distribution.

5 Compare two or more observations that are on different probability distributions.

6 Use the normal probability distribution to approximate the binomial probability distribution.

If 95 percent of the international flights in U.S. airports are cleared in 45 minutes, we can assume 5 percent take longer to clear. Assuming that the distribution is approximately normal and the standard deviation of the time to clear an international flight is 5 minutes, what is the mean time to clear a flight? (This refers to Goal 4 and Exercise 45.)

Introduction

Chapter 5 deals with three families of *discrete* probability distributions: the binomial distribution, the hypergeometric distribution, and the Poisson distribution. Recall that these distributions are based on discrete random variables, which can assume only clearly separated values. For example, the number of correct answers on a 10-question examination can only be 0, 1, 2, 3, . . . , 10. There cannot be a negative number of correct answers, such as −7, nor can there be 7¼ or 15 correct answers.

We continue our study of probability distributions in this chapter by examining a very important *continuous* probability distribution, namely, the **normal probability distribution.** As we described in Chapter 5, a continuous random variable is one that can assume an *infinite* number of possible values within a specified range. It usually results from measuring something, such as the weight of an individual. A continuous random variable implies that the weights (in pounds) of 169.7267, 203.8143, 188.6512, and 240.0567 for four men are all possible results of the experiment.

When a continuous random variable follows a normal probability distribution, we can make statements about the likelihood of various outcomes. For example, suppose the life of an Energizer C size battery follows a normal distribution with a mean of 45 hours and a standard deviation of 10 hours when used in a particular toy. We can determine the likelihood the battery will last more than 50 hours, between 35 and 62 hours, or less than 39 hours.

In this chapter we describe the characteristics of a normal probability distribution. Then we show how to determine the probability of specific outcomes using the **standard normal distribution.** Finally we use the normal distribution to estimate binomial probabilities.

The Family of Normal Probability Distributions

The normal probability distribution and its accompanying normal curve have the following characteristics:

1. The normal curve is **bell-shaped** and has a single peak at the center of the distribution. The arithmetic mean, median, and mode of the distribution are equal and located at the peak. Thus, half the area under the curve is above this center point, and the other half is below it.
2. The normal probability distribution is **symmetrical** about its mean. If we cut the normal curve vertically at this central value, the two halves will be mirror images.
3. The normal curve falls off smoothly in either direction from the central value. It is **asymptotic,** meaning that the curve gets closer and closer to the X-axis but never actually touches it. That is, the "tails" of the curve extend indefinitely in both directions.

never hits '0'

These characteristics are shown graphically in Chart 6–1.

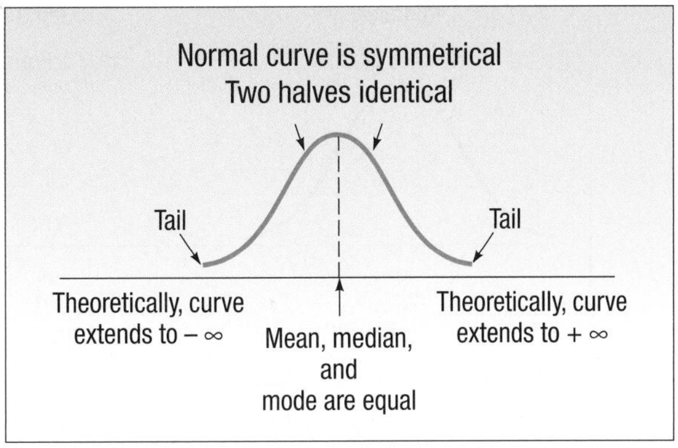

CHART 6–1 Characteristics of a Normal Distribution

For example, in Chart 6–2 the probability distributions of length of employee service in three different plants can be compared. There is not just one normal probability distribution, but rather a "family" of them. In the Camden plant, the mean is 20 years and the standard deviation is 3.1 years. There is another normal probability distribution for the length of service in the Dunkirk plant, where $\mu = 20$ years and $\sigma = 3.9$ years. In the Elmira plant, $\mu = 20$ years and $\sigma = 5.0$. Note that the means are the same but the standard deviations are different.

Equal means, unequal standard deviations

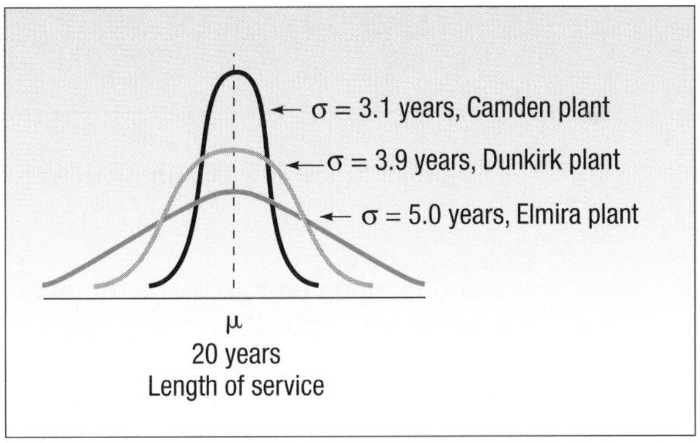

CHART 6–2 Normal Probability Distributions with Equal Means but Different Standard Deviations

Chart 6–3 shows the distribution of box weights of three different cereals. The weights are normally distributed with different means but identical standard deviations.

Finally, Chart 6–4 shows three normal distributions having different means and standard deviations. They show the distribution of tensile strengths, measured in pounds per square inch (psi), for three types of cables.

In Chapter 5, recall that discrete probability distributions show the specific likelihood a discrete value will occur. For example, on page 168, the binomial distribution is used to calculate the probability that none of five flights arriving at the Bradford Pennsylvania Regional Airport would be late.

Unequal means, equal standard deviations

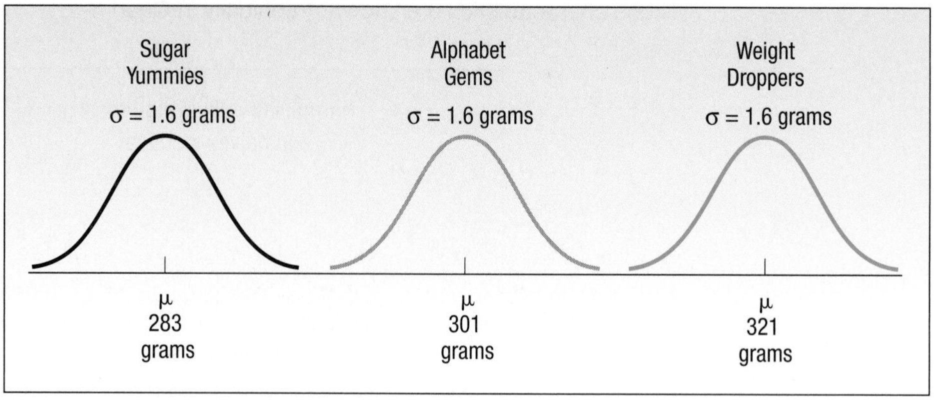

CHART 6–3 Normal Probability Distributions Having Different Means but Equal Standard Deviations

Unequal means, unequal standard deviations

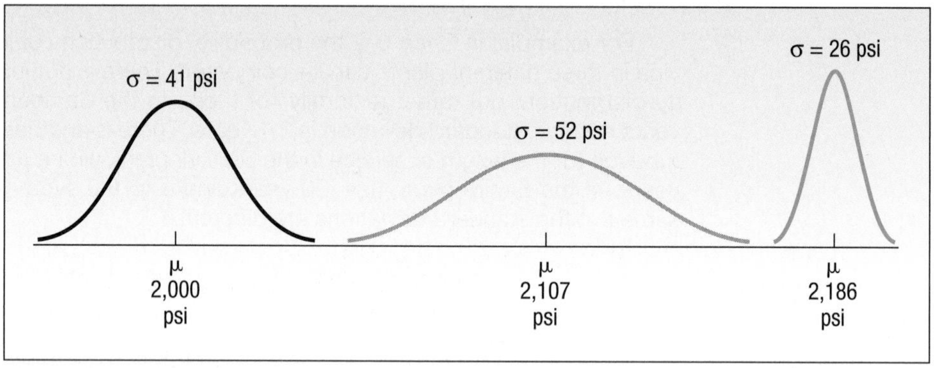

CHART 6–4 Normal Probability Distributions with Different Means and Standard Deviations

With a continuous probability distribution, areas below the curve define probabilities. The total area under the normal curve is 1.0. This accounts for all possible outcomes. Since a normal probability distribution is symmetric, the area under the curve to the left of the mean is 0.5, and the area under the curve to the right of the mean is 0.5. Apply this to the distribution of Sugar Yummies in Chart 6–3. It is normally distributed with a mean of 283 grams. Therefore, the probability of filling a box with more than 283 grams is 0.5 and the probability of filling a box with less than 283 grams is 0.5. We can also determine the probability that a box weighs between 280 and 286 grams. However, to determine this probability we need to know about the standard normal probability distribution.

The Standard Normal Distribution

The number of normal distributions is unlimited, each having a different mean (μ), standard deviation (σ), or both. While it is possible to provide probability tables for discrete distributions such as the binomial and the Poisson, providing tables for the infinite number of normal distributions is impossible. Fortunately, one member of the family can be used to determine the probabilities for all normal distributions. It is called the **standard normal distribution**, and it is unique because it has a mean of 0 and a standard deviation of 1.

Any normal distribution can be converted into a *standard normal distribution* by subtracting the mean from each observation and dividing this difference by the standard deviation. The results are called ***z* values**. They are also referred to as ***z* scores**, the ***z* statistic**, the **standard normal deviate**, or just the **normal deviate**.

> ***z* VALUE** The signed distance between a selected value, designated *X,* and the mean, μ, divided by the standard deviation, σ.

So, a *z* value is the distance from the mean, measured in units of the standard deviation.
In terms of a formula:

STANDARD NORMAL VALUE

$$z = \frac{X - \mu}{\sigma} \qquad \textbf{[6–1]}$$

where:

- X is the value of any particular observation or measurement.
- μ is the mean of the distribution.
- σ is the standard deviation of the distribution.

As noted in the above definition, a *z* value expresses the distance or difference between a particular value of *X* and the arithmetic mean in units of the standard deviation. Once the normally distributed observations are standardized, the *z* values are normally distributed with a mean of 0 and a standard deviation of 1. The table in Appendix D (also on the inside back cover) lists the probabilities for the standard normal probability distribution.

To explain, suppose we wish to compute the probability that boxes of Sugar Yummies weigh between 283 and 285.4 grams. From Chart 6–3, we know that the box weight of Sugar Yummies follows the normal distribution with a mean of 283 grams and a standard deviation of 1.6 grams. We want to know the probability or area under the curve between the mean, 283 grams, and 285.4 grams. We can also express this problem using probability notation, similar to the style used in the previous chapter: $P(283 < \text{weight} < 285.4)$. To find the probability, it is necessary to convert both 283 grams and 285.4 grams to *z* values using formula (6–1). The *z* value corresponding to 283 is 0, found by $(238 - 283)/1.6$. The *z* value corresponding to 284.5 is 1.50 found by $(284.5 - 283)/1.6$. Next we go to the table in Appendix D. A portion of the table is repeated as Table 6–1. Go down the column of the table headed by the letter *z* to 1.5. Then move horizontally to the right and read the probability under the column headed 0.00. It is 0.4332. This means the area under the curve between 0.00 and 1.50 is 0.4332. This is the probability that a randomly selected box of Sugar Yummies will weigh between 283 and 285.4 grams.

TABLE 6–1 Areas under the Normal Curve

z	0.00	0.01	0.02	0.03	0.04	0.05	. . .
1.3	0.4032	0.4049	0.4066	0.4082	0.4099	0.4115	
1.4	0.4192	0.4207	0.4222	0.4236	0.4251	0.4265	
1.5	0.4332	0.4345	0.4357	0.4370	0.4382	0.4394	
1.6	0.4452	0.4463	0.4474	0.4484	0.4495	0.4505	
1.7	0.4554	0.4564	0.4573	0.4582	0.4591	0.4599	
1.8	0.4641	0.4649	0.4656	0.4664	0.4671	0.4678	
1.9	0.4713	0.4719	0.4726	0.4732	0.4738	0.4744	
⋮							

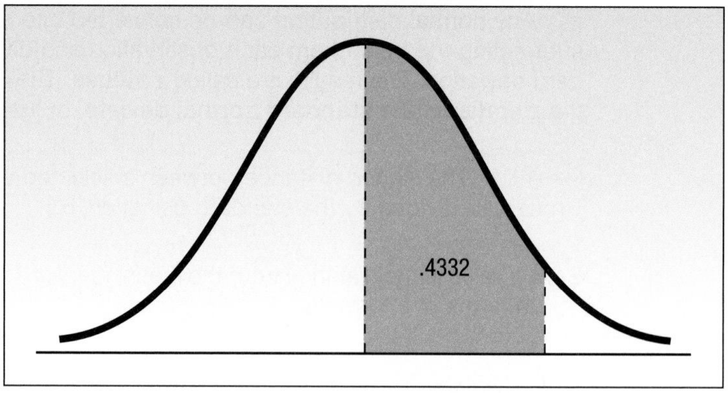

Applications of the Standard Normal Distribution

What is the area under the curve between the mean and X for the following z values? Check your answers against those given. Not all the values are available in Table 6–1. You will need to use Appendix D or the table located on the inside back cover of the text.

Computed z Value	Area under Curve
2.84	.4977
1.00	.3413
0.49	.1879

Now we will compute the z value given the population mean, μ, the population standard deviation, σ, and a selected X.

EXAMPLE

The weekly incomes of shift foremen in the glass industry are normally distributed with a mean of $1,000 and a standard deviation of $100. What is the z value for the income X of a foreman who earns $1,100 per week? For a foreman who earns $900 per week?

SOLUTION

Using formula (6–1), the z values for the two X values ($1,100 and $900) are:

For $X = \$1,100$:

$$z = \frac{X - \mu}{\sigma} = \frac{\$1,100 - \$1,000}{\$100} = 1.00$$

For $X = \$900$:

$$z = \frac{X - \mu}{\sigma} = \frac{\$900 - \$1,000}{\$100} = -1.00$$

The z of 1.00 indicates that a weekly income of $1,100 is one standard deviation above the mean, and a z of -1.00 shows that a $900 income is one standard deviation below the mean. Note that both incomes ($1,100 and $900) are the same distance ($100) from the mean.

Self-Review 6-1

Using the information in the preceding example ($\mu = \$1,000$, $\sigma = \$100$), convert:

(a) The weekly income of $1,225 to a z value.
(b) The weekly income of $775 to a z value.

Statistics in Action

An individual's skills depend on a combination of many hereditary and environmental factors, each having about the same amount of weight or influence on the skills. Thus, much like a binomial distribution with a large number of trials, many skills and attributes follow the normal distribution. For example, scores on the Scholastic Aptitude Test (SAT) are normally distributed with a mean of 1,000 and a standard deviation of 140.

The Empirical Rule

Before examining various applications of the standard normal probability distribution, we will consider three areas under the normal curve that will be used extensively in the following chapters. They are also called the Empirical Rule in Chapter 3.

1. About 68 percent of the area under the normal curve is within one standard deviation of the mean. This can be written as $\mu \pm 1\sigma$.
2. About 95 percent of the area under the normal curve is within two standard deviations of the mean, written $\mu \pm 2\sigma$.
3. Practically all of the area under the normal curve is within three standard deviations of the mean, written $\mu \pm 3\sigma$.

This information is summarized in the following graph.

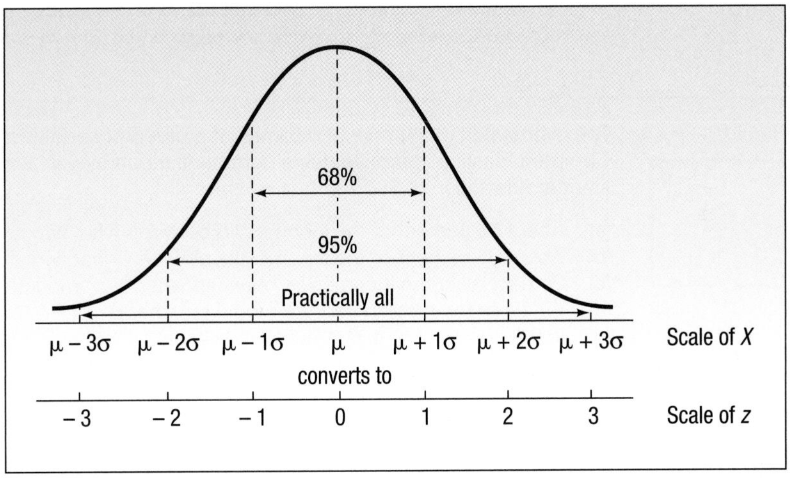

Transforming measurements to standard normal deviates changes the scale. The conversions are also shown in the graph. For example, $\mu + 1\sigma$ is converted to a z value of $+1.00$. Likewise, $\mu - 2\sigma$ is transformed to a z value of -2.00. Note that the center of the z distribution is zero, indicating no deviation from the mean, μ.

EXAMPLE

As part of their quality assurance program, the Autolite Battery Company conducts tests on battery life. For a particular D cell alkaline battery, the mean life is 19 hours. The useful life of the battery follows a normal distribution with a standard deviation of 1.2 hours. Answer the following questions.

1. About 68 percent of the batteries failed between what two values?
2. About 95 percent of the batteries failed between what two values?
3. Virtually all of the batteries failed between what two values?

SOLUTION

We can use the results of the Empirical Rule to answer these questions.

1. About 68 percent of the batteries will fail between 17.8 and 20.2 hours, found by $19.0 \pm 1(1.2)$ hours.
2. About 95 percent of the batteries will fail between 16.6 and 21.4 hours, found by $19.0 \pm 2(1.2)$ hours.
3. Virtually all failed between 15.4 and 22.6 hours, found by $19.0 \pm 3(1.2)$ hours.

This information is summarized on the following chart.

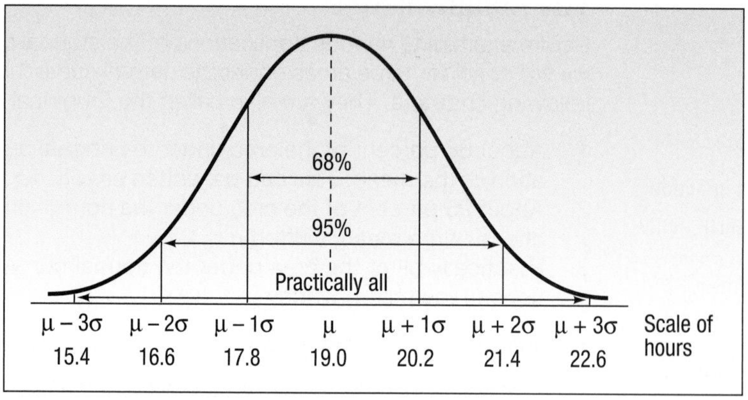

Self-Review 6-2

The distribution of the annual incomes of a group of middle-management employees at Compton Plastics approximates a normal distribution with a mean of $37,200 and a standard deviation of $800.

(a) About 68 percent of the incomes lie between what two amounts?
(b) About 95 percent of the incomes lie between what two amounts?
(c) Virtually all of the incomes lie between what two amounts?
(d) What are the median and the modal incomes?
(e) Is the distribution of incomes symmetrical?

Exercises

1. Explain what is meant by this statement: "There is not just one normal probability distribution but a 'family' of them."
2. List the major characteristics of a normal probability distribution.
3. The mean of a normal probability distribution is 500; the standard deviation is 10.
   a. About 68 percent of the observations lie between what two values?
   b. About 95 percent of the observations lie between what two values?
   c. Practically all of the observations lie between what two values?
4. The mean of a normal probability distribution is 60; the standard deviation is 5.
   a. About what percent of the observations lie between 55 and 65?
   b. About what percent of the observations lie between 50 and 70?
   c. About what percent of the observations lie between 45 and 75?
5. The Kamp family has twins, Rob and Rachel. Both Rob and Rachel graduated from college 2 years ago, and each is now earning $50,000 per year. Rachel works in the retail industry, where the mean salary for executives with less than 5 years' experience is $35,000 with a standard deviation of $8,000. Rob is an engineer. The mean salary for engineers with less than 5 years' experience is $60,000 with a standard deviation of $5,000. Compute the z values for both Rob and Rachel and comment on your findings.
6. A recent article in the Myrtle Beach *Sun Times* reported that the mean labor cost to repair a color TV is $90 with a standard deviation of $22. Monte's TV Sales and Service completed repairs on two sets this morning. The labor cost for the first was $75 and it was $100 for the second. Compute z values for each and comment on your findings.

Finding Areas under the Normal Curve

The first application of the standard normal distribution involves finding the area in a normal distribution between the mean and a selected value, which we identify as *X*. The following example will illustrate the details.

EXAMPLE

Recall in an earlier example (see page 196) we reported that the mean weekly income of a shift foreman in the glass industry is normally distributed with a mean of $1,000 and a standard deviation of $100. That is, μ = $1,000 and σ = $100. What is the likelihood of selecting a foreman whose weekly income is between $1,000 and $1,100? We write this question in probability notation as: *P*($1,000 < weekly income < $1,100).

SOLUTION

We have already converted $1,100 to a *z* value of 1.00 using formula (6–1). To repeat:

$$z = \frac{X - \mu}{\sigma} = \frac{\$1{,}100 - \$1{,}000}{\$100} = 1.00$$

The probability associated with a *z* of 1.00 is available in Appendix D. A portion of Appendix D follows. To locate the probability, go down the left column to 1.0, and then move horizontally to the column headed .00. The value is .3413.

z	.00	.01	.02
⋮	⋮	⋮	⋮
0.7	.2580	.2611	.2642
0.8	.2881	.2910	.2939
0.9	.3159	.3186	.3212
1.0	.3413	.3438	.3461
1.1	.3643	.3665	.3686
⋮	⋮	⋮	⋮

The area under the normal curve between $1,000 and $1,100 is .3413. We could also say 34.13 percent of the shift foremen in the glass industry earn between $1,000 and $1,100 weekly, or the likelihood of selecting a foreman and finding his or her income is between $1,000 and $1,100 is .3413.

This information is summarized in the following chart.

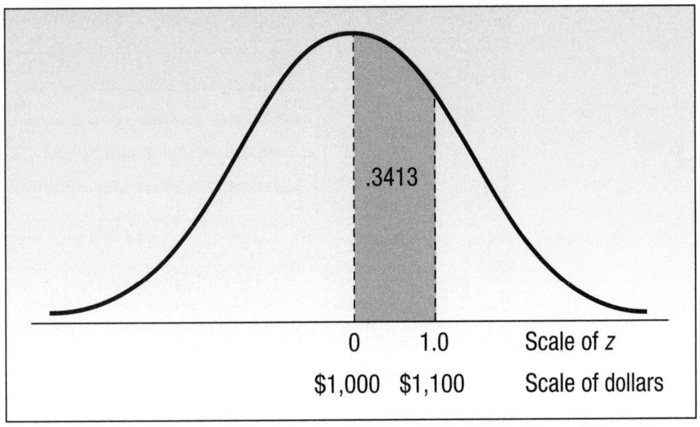

Statistics in Action

Many processes, such as filling soda bottles and canning fruit, are normally distributed. Manufacturers must guard against both over- and underfilling. If they put too much in the can or bottle, they are giving away their product. If they put too little in, the customer may feel cheated and the government may question the label description. "Control Charts," with limits drawn three standard deviations above and below the mean, are routinely used to monitor this type of production process.

In the example just completed, we are interested in the probability between the mean and a given value. Let's change the question. Instead of wanting to know the probability of selecting a foreman at random who earned between \$1,000 and \$1,100, suppose we wanted the probability of selecting a foreman who earned less than \$1,100. In probability notation we write this statement as *P*(weekly income < \$1,100). The method of solution is the same. We find the probability of selecting a foreman who earns between \$1,000, the mean, and \$1,100. This probability is .3413. Next, recall that half the area, or probability, is above the mean and half is below. So the probability of selecting a foreman earning less than \$1,000 is .5000. Finally, we add the two probabilities, so .3413 + .5000 = .8413. About 84 percent of the foremen in the glass industry earn less than \$1,100 per month. See the following diagram.

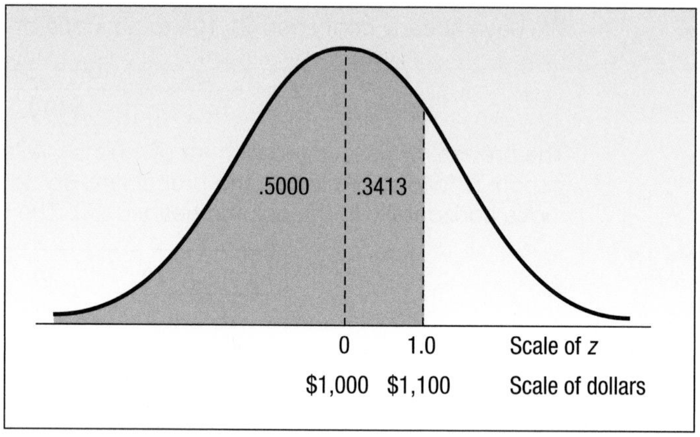

Excel will calculate this probability. The necessary commands are in the **Computer Commands** section at the end of the chapter. The answer is .8413, the same as we calculated.

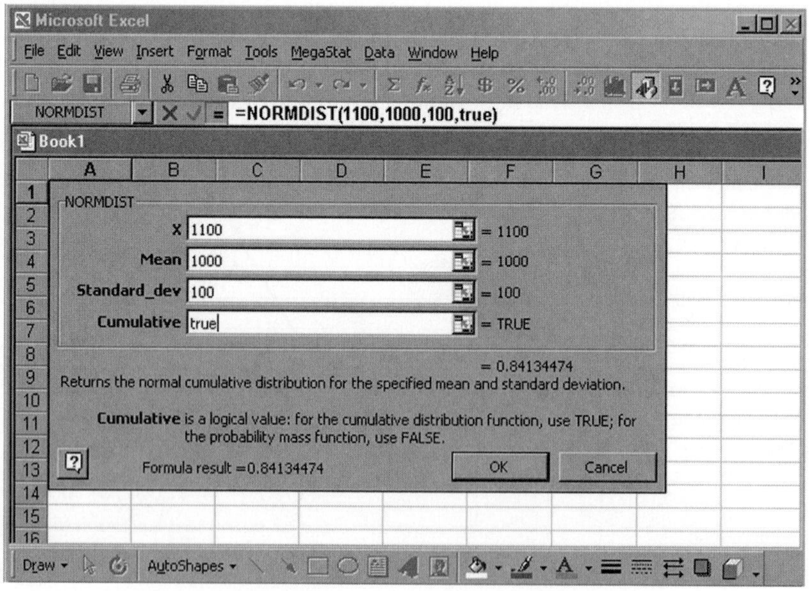

EXAMPLE

Refer to the information regarding the weekly income of shift foremen in the glass industry. The distribution of weekly incomes follows the normal distribution, with a mean of $1,000 and a standard deviation of $100. What is the probability of selecting a shift foreman in the glass industry whose income is:

1. Between $790 and $1,000?
2. Less than $790?

SOLUTION

We begin by finding the z value corresponding to a weekly income of $790. From formula (6–1):

$$z = \frac{X - \mu}{\sigma} = \frac{\$790 - \$1{,}000}{\$100} = -2.10$$

See Appendix D. Move down the left margin to the row 2.1 and across that row to the column headed 0.00. The value is .4821. So the area under the standard normal curve corresponding to a z value of 2.10 is .4821. However, because the normal distribution is symmetric, the area between 0 and a negative z is the same as that between 0 and z. The likelihood of finding a foreman earning between $790 and $1,000 is .4821. In probability notation we write $P(\$790 < \text{weekly income} < \$1000) = .4821$.

z	0.00	0.01	0.02
⋮	⋮	⋮	⋮
2.0	.4772	.4778	.4783
2.1	.4821	.4826	.4830
2.2	.4861	.4864	.4868
2.3	.4893	.4896	.4898
⋮	⋮	⋮	⋮

The mean divides the normal curve into two identical halves. The area under the half to the left of the mean is .5000, and the area to the right is also .5000. Because the area under the curve between $790 and $1,000 is .4821, the area below $790 is .0179, found by .5000 − .4821. In probability notation we write $P(\text{weekly income} < \$790) = .0179$.

This means that 48.21 percent of the foremen have weekly incomes between $790 and $1,000. Further, we can anticipate that 1.79 percent earn less than $790 per week. This information is summarized in the following diagram.

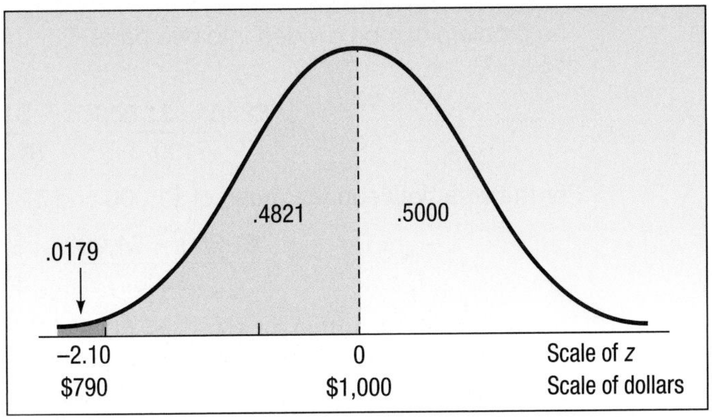

Self-Review 6-3

The employees of Cartwright Manufacturing are awarded efficiency ratings. The distribution of the ratings follows a normal distribution. The mean is 400, the standard deviation 50.

(a) What is the area under the normal curve between 400 and 482? Write this area in probability notation.
(b) What is the area under the normal curve for ratings greater than 482? Write this area in probability notation.
(c) Show the facets of this problem in a chart.

Exercises

7. A normal population has a mean of 20.0 and a standard deviation of 4.0.
   a. Compute the z value associated with 25.0.
   b. What proportion of the population is between 20.0 and 25.0?
   c. What proportion of the population is less than 18.0?

8. A normal population has a mean of 12.2 and a standard deviation of 2.5.
   a. Compute the z value associated with 14.3.
   b. What proportion of the population is between 12.2 and 14.3?
   c. What proportion of the population is less than 10.0?

9. A recent study of the hourly wages of maintenance crews for major airlines showed that the mean hourly salary was $16.50, with a standard deviation of $3.50. If we select a crew member at random, what is the probability the crew member earns:
   a. Between $16.50 and $20.00 per hour?
   b. More than $20.00 per hour?
   c. Less than $15.00 per hour?

10. The mean of a normal distribution is 400 pounds. The standard deviation is 10 pounds.
   a. What is the area between 415 pounds and the mean of 400 pounds?
   b. What is the area between the mean and 395 pounds?
   c. What is the probability of selecting a value at random and discovering that it has a value of less than 395 pounds?

A second application of the normal distribution involves combining two areas, or probabilities. One of the areas is to the right of the mean and the other to the left.

EXAMPLE

Recall the distribution of weekly incomes of shift foremen in the glass industry. The weekly incomes follow the normal distribution, with a mean of $1,000 and a standard deviation of $100. What is the area under this normal curve between $840 and $1,200?

SOLUTION

The problem can be divided into two parts. For the area between $840 and the mean of $1,000:

$$z = \frac{\$840 - \$1,000}{\$100} = \frac{-\$160}{\$100} = -1.60$$

For the area between the mean of $1,000 and $1,200:

$$z = \frac{\$1,200 - \$1,000}{\$100} = \frac{\$200}{\$100} = 2.00$$

The area under the curve for a z of -1.60 is .4452 (from Appendix D). The area under the curve for a z of 2.00 is .4772. Adding the two areas: $.4452 + .4772 = .9224$. Thus, the probability of selecting an income between $840 and $1,200 is .9224. In probability notation we write $P(\$480 < \text{weekly income} < \$1,200) = .4452 + .4772 = .9224$. To summarize, 92.24 percent of the foremen have weekly incomes between $840 and $1,200. This is shown in a diagram:

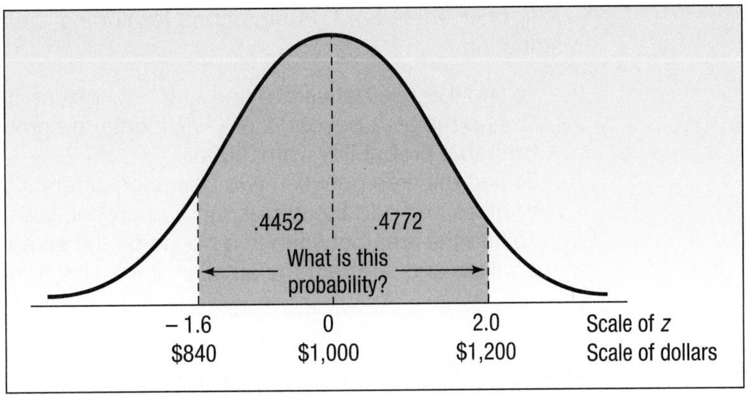

Another application of the normal distribution involves determining area between values on the *same* side of the mean.

EXAMPLE

Returning to the weekly income distribution of shift foremen in the glass industry ($\mu = \$1{,}000$, $\sigma = \$100$), what is the area under the normal curve between \$1,150 and \$1,250?

SOLUTION

The situation is again separated into two parts, and formula (6–1) is used. First, we find the *z* value associated with a weekly salary of \$1,250:

$$z = \frac{\$1{,}250 - \$1{,}000}{\$100} = 2.50$$

Next we find the *z* value for a weekly salary of \$1,150:

$$z = \frac{\$1{,}150 - \$1{,}000}{\$100} = 1.50$$

From Appendix D the area associated with a *z* value of 2.50 is .4938. So the probability of a weekly salary between \$1,000 and \$1,250 is .4938. Similarly, the area associated with a *z* value of 1.50 is .4332, so the probability of a weekly salary between \$1,000 and \$1,150 is .4332. The probability of a weekly salary between \$1,150 and \$1,250 is found by subtracting the area associated with a *z* value of 1.50 (.4332) from that associated with a *z* of 2.50 (.4938). Thus, the probability of a weekly salary between \$1,150 and \$1,250 is .0606. In probability notation we write $P(\$1{,}150 \leq \text{weekly income} \leq \$1{,}250) = .4938 - .4332 = .0606$.

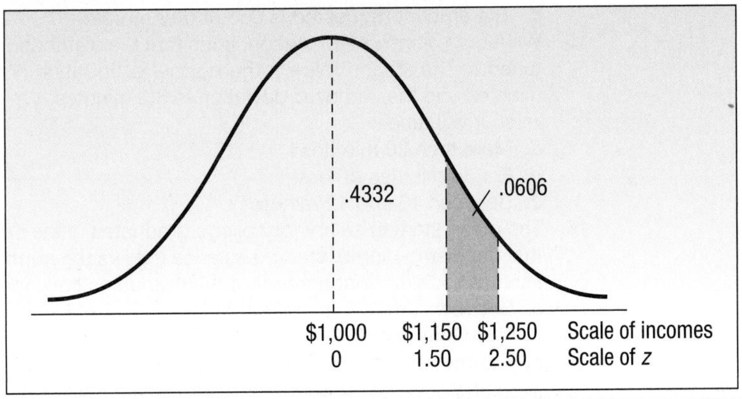

In brief, there are four situations for finding the area under the standard normal distribution.

1. To find the area between 0 and z (or $-z$), look up the probability directly in the table.
2. To find the area beyond z or ($-z$), locate the probability of z in the table and subtract that probability from .5000.
3. To find the area between two points on different sides of the mean, determine the z values and add the corresponding probabilities.
4. To find the area between two points on the same side of the mean, determine the z values and subtract the smaller probability from the larger.

Self-Review 6–4

Refer to the previous example, where the distribution of weekly incomes follows the normal distribution with a mean of $1,000 and the standard deviation is $100.

(a) What percent of the shift foremen earn a weekly income between $750 and $1,225? Draw a normal curve and shade the desired area on your diagram.
(b) What percent of the shift foremen earn a weekly income between $1,100 and $1,225? Draw a normal curve and shade the desired area on your diagram.

Exercises

11. A normal distribution has a mean of 50 and a standard deviation of 4.
- **a.** Compute the probability of a value between 44.0 and 55.0.
- **b.** Compute the probability of a value greater than 55.0.
- **c.** Compute the probability of a value between 52.0 and 55.0.

12. A normal population has a mean of 80.0 and a standard deviation of 14.0.
- **a.** Compute the probability of a value between 75.0 and 90.0.
- **b.** Compute the probability of a value 75.0 or less.
- **c.** Compute the probability of a value between 55.0 and 70.0.

13. A cola-dispensing machine is set to dispense on average 7.00 ounces of cola per cup. The standard deviation is 0.10 ounces. The distribution amounts dispensed follows a normal distribution.
- **a.** What is the probability that the machine will dispense between 7.10 and 7.25 ounces of cola?
- **b.** What is the probability that the machine will dispense 7.25 ounces of cola or more?
- **c.** What is the probability that the machine will dispense between 6.80 and 7.25 ounces of cola?

14. The amounts of money requested on home loan applications at Down River Federal Savings follow the normal distribution, with a mean of $70,000 and a standard deviation of $20,000. A loan application is received this morning. What is the probability:
- **a.** The amount requested is $80,000 or more?
- **b.** The amount requested is between $65,000 and $80,000?
- **c.** The amount requested is $65,000 or more?

15. WNAE, an all-news AM station, finds that the distribution of the lengths of time listeners are tuned to the station follows the normal distribution. The mean of the distribution is 15.0 minutes and the standard deviation is 3.5 minutes. What is the probability that a particular listener will tune in:
- **a.** More than 20 minutes?
- **b.** For 20 minutes or less?
- **c.** Between 10 and 12 minutes?

16. The mean starting salary for college graduates in the spring of 2002 was $31,280. Assume that the distribution of starting salaries follows the normal distribution with a standard deviation of $3,300. What percent of the graduates have starting salaries:
- **a.** Between $30,000 and $35,000?
- **b.** More than $40,000?
- **c.** Between $35,000 and $40,000?

Previous examples require finding the percent of the observations located between two observations or the percent of the observations above, or below, a particular observation X. A further application of the normal distribution involves finding the value of the observation X when the percent above or below the observation is given.

EXAMPLE

The Layton Tire and Rubber Company wishes to set a minimum mileage guarantee on its new MX100 tire. Tests reveal the mean mileage is 67,900 with a standard deviation of 2,050 miles and that the distribution of miles follows the normal distribution. They want to set the minimum guaranteed mileage so that no more than 4 percent of the tires will have to be replaced. What minimum guaranteed mileage should Layton announce?

SOLUTION

The facets of this case are shown in the following diagram, where X represents the minimum guaranteed mileage.

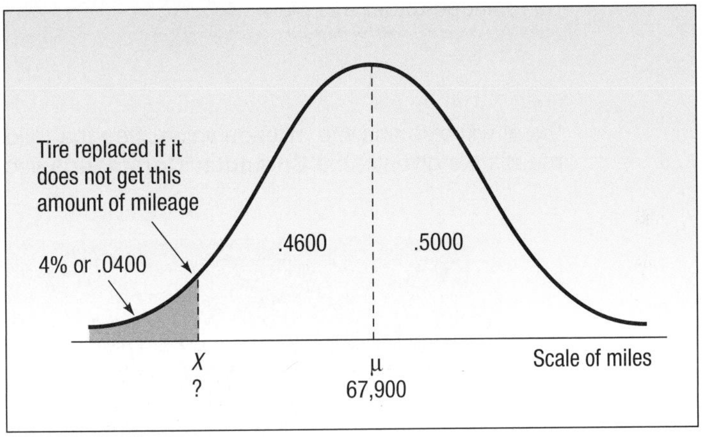

Inserting these values in formula (6–1) for z:

$$z = \frac{X - \mu}{\sigma} = \frac{X - 67{,}900}{2{,}050}$$

Notice that there are two unknowns, z and X. To find X, we first find z, and then solve for X. Notice the area under the normal curve to the left of μ is .5000. The area between μ and X is .4600, found by .5000 − .0400. Now refer to Appendix D. Search the body of the table for the area closest to .4600. The closest area is .4599. Move to the margins from this value and read the z value of 1.75. Because the value is to the left of the mean, it is actually −1.75. These steps are illustrated in Table 6–2.

TABLE 6–2 Selected Areas under the Normal Curve

z	.03	.04	.05	.06
.				
.				
.				
1.5	.4370	.4382	.4394	.4406
1.6	.4484	.4495	.4505	.4515
1.7	.4582	.4591	.4599	.4608
1.8	.4664	.4671	.4678	.4686

Knowing that the distance between μ and X is -1.75σ or $z = -1.75$, we can now solve for X (the minimum guaranteed mileage):

$$z = \frac{X - 67{,}900}{2{,}050}$$

$$-1.75 = \frac{X - 67{,}900}{2{,}050}$$

$$-1.75(2{,}050) = X - 67{,}900$$

$$X = 67{,}900 - 1.75(2{,}050) = 64{,}312$$

So Layton can advertise that it will replace for free any tire that wears out before it reaches 64,312 miles, and the company will know that only 4 percent of the tires will be replaced under this plan.

Excel will also find the mileage value. See the following output. The necessary commands are given in the **Computer Commands** section at the end of the chapter.

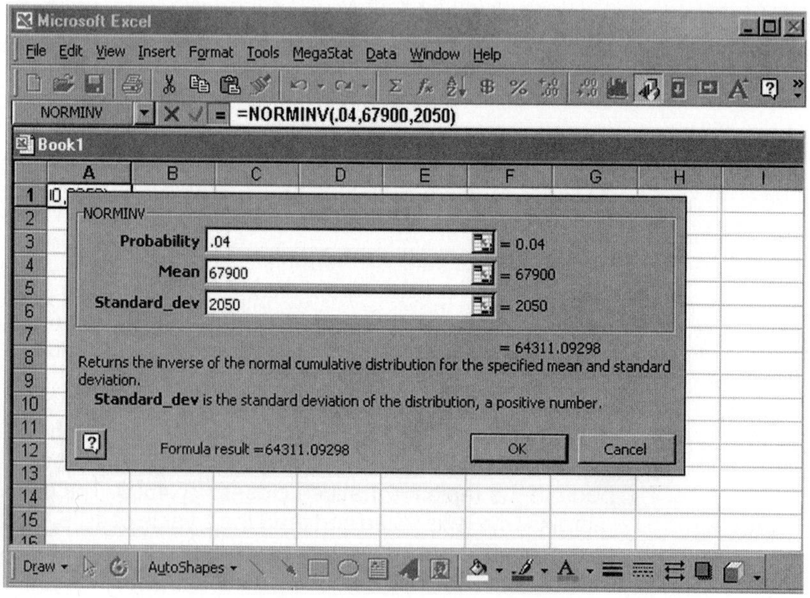

Self-Review 6–5

An analysis of the final test scores for Introduction to Business reveals the scores follow the normal distribution. The mean of the distribution is 75 and the standard deviation is 8. The professor wants to award an A to students whose score is in the highest 10 percent. What is the dividing point for those students who earn an A and those earning a B?

Exercises

17. A normal distribution has a mean of 50 and a standard deviation of 4. Determine the value below which 95 percent of the observations will occur.

18. A normal distribution has a mean of 80 and a standard deviation of 14. Determine the value above which 80 percent of the values will occur.

19. The amounts dispensed by a cola machine follow the normal distribution with a mean of 7 ounces and a standard deviation of 0.10 ounces per cup. How much cola is dispensed in the largest 1 percent of the cups?

20. Refer to Exercise 14, where the amount requested for home loans followed the normal distribution with a mean of $70,000 and a standard deviation of $20,000.

- **a.** How much is requested on the largest 3 percent of the loans?
- **b.** How much is requested on the smallest 10 percent of the loans?

21. Assume that the mean hourly cost to operate a commercial airplane follows the normal distribution with a mean $2,100 per hour and a standard deviation of $250. What is the operating cost for the lowest 3 percent of the airplanes?

22. The monthly sales of mufflers in the Richmond, Virginia, area follow the normal distribution with a mean of 1,200 and a standard deviation of 225. The manufacturer would like to establish inventory levels such that there is only a 5 percent chance of running out of stock. Where should the manufacturer set the inventory levels?

The Normal Approximation to the Binomial

Chapter 5 describes the binomial probability distribution, which is a discrete distribution. The table of binomial probabilities in Appendix A goes successively from an n of 1 to an n of 20, and then to $n = 25$. If a problem involved taking a sample of 60, generating a binomial distribution for that large a number would be very time consuming. A more efficient approach is to apply the *normal approximation to the binomial.*

Using the normal distribution (a continuous distribution) as a substitute for a binomial distribution (a discrete distribution) for large values of n seems reasonable because, as n increases, a binomial distribution gets closer and closer to a normal distribution. Chart 6–5 depicts the change in the shape of a binomial distribution with $\pi = .50$ from an n of 1, to an n of 3, to an n of 20. Notice how the case where $n = 20$ approximates the shape of the normal distribution. That is, compare the case where $n = 20$ to the normal curve in Chart 6–1 on page 193.

When to use the normal approximation

When can we use the normal approximation to the binomial? The normal probability distribution is a good approximation to the binomial probability distribution when $n\pi$ and $n(1 - \pi)$ are both at least 5. However, before we apply the normal approximation, we must make sure that our distribution of interest is in fact a binomial distribution. Recall from Chapter 5 that four criteria must be met:

1. There are only two mutually exclusive outcomes to an experiment: a "success" and a "failure."
2. The distribution results from counting the number of successes in a fixed number of trials.

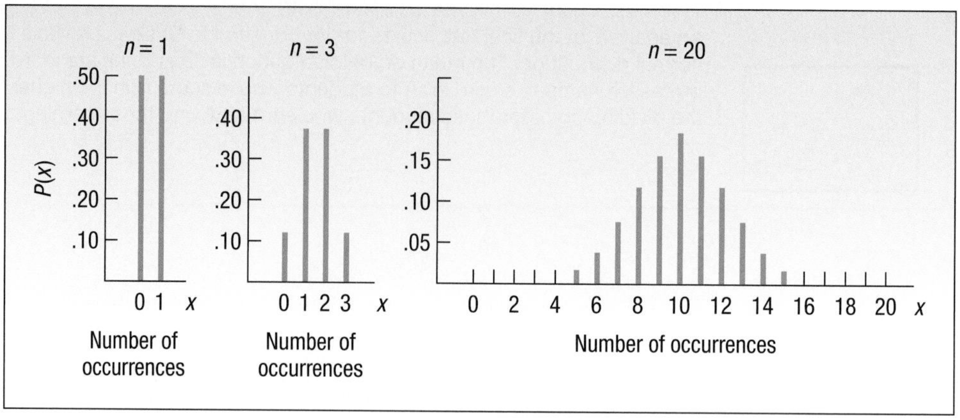

CHART 6–5 Binomial Distributions for an n of 1, 3, and 20, Where $\pi = .50$

3. Each trial is independent.
4. The probability, π, remains the same from trial to trial.

Continuity Correction Factor

To show the application of the normal approximation to the binomial and the need for a correction factor, suppose the management of the Santoni Pizza Restaurant found that 70 percent of their new customers return for another meal. For a week in which 80 new (first-time) customers dined at Santoni's, what is the probability that 60 or more will return for another meal?

Notice the binomial conditions are met: (1) There are only two possible outcomes—a customer either returns for another meal or does not return. (2) We can count the number of successes, meaning, for example, that 57 of the 80 customers return. (3) The trials are independent, meaning that if the 34th person returns for a second meal, that does not affect whether the 58th person returns. (4) The probability of a customer returning remains at .70 for all 80 customers.

Therefore, we could use the binomial formula (5–3) described on page 168.

$$P(x) = {}_nC_x\,(\pi)^x\,(1 - \pi)^{n-x}$$

To find the probability 60 or more customers return for another pizza, we need to first find the probability exactly 60 customers return. That is:

$$P(x = 60) = {}_{80}C_{60}\,(.70)^{60}\,(1 - .70)^{20} = .063$$

Next we find the probability that exactly 61 customers return. It is:

$$P(x = 61) = {}_{80}C_{61}\,(.70)^{61}\,(1 - .70)^{19} = .048$$

We continue this process until we have the probability all 80 customers return. Finally, we add the probabilities from 60 to 80. Solving the above problem in this manner is tedious. We can also use a computer software package such as MINITAB or Excel to find the various probabilities. Listed on the next page are the binomial probabilities for $n = 80$, $\pi = .70$, and x, the number of customers returning, ranging from 43 to 68. The probability of any number of customers less than 43 or more than 68 returning is less than .001.

Number Returning	Probability	Number Returning	Probability
43	0.001	56	0.097
44	0.002	57	0.095
45	0.003	58	0.088
46	0.006	59	0.077
47	0.009	60	0.063
48	0.015	61	0.048
49	0.023	62	0.034
50	0.033	63	0.023
51	0.045	64	0.014
52	0.059	65	0.008
53	0.072	66	0.004
54	0.084	67	0.002
55	0.093	68	0.001

We can find the probability of 60 or more returning by summing $0.063 + 0.048 + \cdots + 0.001$, which is 0.197. However, a look at the plot below shows the similarity of this distribution to a normal distribution. All we need do is "smooth out" the discrete probabilities into a continuous distribution. Furthermore, working with a normal distribution will involve far fewer calculations than working with the binomial.

The trick is to let the discrete probability for 56 customers be represented by an area under the continuous curve between 55.5 and 56.5. Then let the probability for 57 customers be represented by an area between 56.5 and 57.5 and so on. This is just the opposite of rounding off the numbers to a whole number.

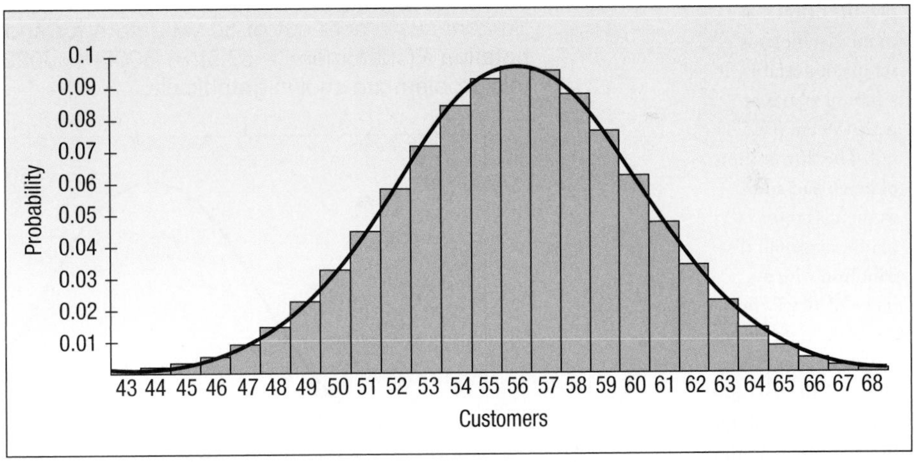

Because we use the normal distribution to determine the binomial probability of 60 or more successes, we must subtract, in this case, .5 from 60. The value .5 is called the **continuity correction factor.** This small adjustment must be made because a continuous distribution (the normal distribution) is being used to approximate a discrete distribution (the binomial distribution). Subtracting, $60 - .5 = 59.5$.

CONTINUITY CORRECTION FACTOR The value .5 subtracted or added, depending on the question, to a selected value when a discrete probability distribution is approximated by a continuous probability distribution.

Statistics in Action

The heights of adults approximate a normal distribution, but those individuals who are very tall can cause design problems. For example, Shaquille O'Neal, a professional basketball player with the Los Angeles Lakers, is 7′2″ tall. The height of the standard doorway is 6′8″, so Shaquille and most other NBA players duck to get into most rooms.

As another example, the driver's seat in most vehicles is set to comfortably fit a person who is at least 159 cm (62.5″) tall. The distribution of heights of adult women is approximately a normal distribution with a mean of 161.5 cm and a standard deviation of 6.3 cm. Thus about 35 percent of adult women will not fit comfortably in the driver's seat.

How to Apply the Correction Factor

Only four cases may arise. These cases are:

1. For the probability *at least* X occur, use the area *above* $(X - .5)$.
2. For the probability that *more than* X occur, use the area *above* $(X + .5)$.
3. For the probability that X *or fewer* occur, use the area *below* $(X + .5)$.
4. For the probability that *fewer than* X occur, use the area *below* $(X - .5)$.

To use the normal distribution to approximate the probability that 60 or more first-time Santoni customers out of 80 will return, follow the procedure shown below.

Step 1. Find the z corresponding to an X of 59.5 using formula (6–1), and formulas (5–4) and (5–5) for the mean and the variance of a binomial distribution:

$$\mu = n\pi = 80(.70) = 56$$

$$\sigma^2 = n\pi(1 - \pi) = 80(.70)(1 - .70) = 16.8$$

$$\sigma = \sqrt{16.8} = 4.10$$

$$z = \frac{X - \mu}{\sigma} = \frac{59.5 - 56}{4.10} = 0.85$$

Step 2. Determine the area under the normal curve between a μ of 56 and an X of 59.5. From step 1, we know that the z value corresponding to 59.5 is 0.85. So we go to Appendix D and read down the left margin to 0.8, and then we go horizontally to the area under the column headed by .05. That area is .3023.

Step 3. Calculate the area beyond 59.5 by subtracting .3023 from .5000 (.5000 − .3023 = .1977). Thus, .1977 is the probability that 60 or more first-time Santoni customers out of 80 will return for another meal. In probability notation $P(\text{customers} > 59.5) = .5000 - .3023 = .1977$. The facets of this problem are shown graphically:

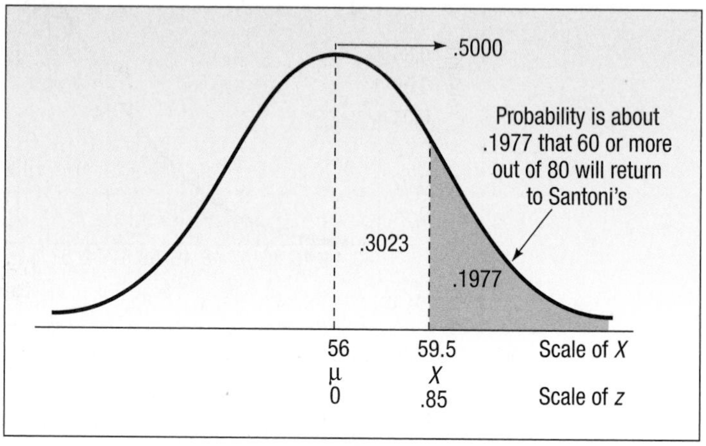

No doubt you will agree that using the normal approximation to the binomial is a more efficient method of estimating the probability of 60 or more first-time customers returning. The result compares favorably with that computed on page 209, using the binomial distribution. The probability using the binomial distribution is .197, whereas the probability using the normal approximation is .1977.

Self-Review 6-6

A study by Great Southern Home Insurance revealed that none of the stolen goods were recovered by the homeowners in 80 percent of reported thefts.

(a) During a period in which 200 thefts occurred, what is the probability that no stolen goods were recovered in 170 or more of the robberies?
(b) During a period in which 200 thefts occurred, what is the probability that no stolen goods were recovered in 150 or more robberies?

Exercises

23. Assume a binomial probability distribution with $n = 50$ and $\pi = .25$. Compute the following:
   a. The mean and standard deviation of the random variable.
   b. The probability that X is 15 or more.
   c. The probability that X is 10 or less.

24. Assume a binomial probability distribution with $n = 40$ and $\pi = .55$. Compute the following:
   a. The mean and standard deviation of the random variable.
   b. The probability that X is 25 or greater.
   c. The probability that X is 15 or less.
   d. The probability that X is between 15 and 25 inclusive.

25. Dottie's Tax Service specializes in federal tax returns for professional clients, such as physicians, dentists, accountants, and lawyers. A recent audit by the IRS of the returns she prepared indicated that an error was made on 5 percent of the returns she prepared last year. Assuming this rate continues into this year and she prepares 60 returns, what is the probability that she makes errors on:
   a. More than six returns?
   b. At least six returns?
   c. Exactly six returns?

26. Shorty's Muffler advertises they can install a new muffler in 30 minutes or less. However, the work standards department at corporate headquarters recently conducted a study and found that 20 percent of the mufflers were not installed in 30 minutes or less. The Maumee branch installed 50 mufflers last month. If the corporate report is correct:
   a. How many of the installations at the Maumee branch would you expect to take more than 30 minutes?
   b. What is the likelihood that fewer than eight installations took more than 30 minutes?
   c. What is the likelihood that eight or fewer installations took more than 30 minutes?
   d. What is the likelihood that exactly 8 of the 50 installations took more than 30 minutes?

27. A study conducted by the nationally known Taurus Health Club revealed that 30 percent of its new members are significantly overweight. A membership drive in a metropolitan area resulted in 500 new members.
   a. It has been suggested that the normal approximation to the binomial be used to determine the probability that 175 or more of the new members are significantly overweight. Does this problem qualify as a binomial problem? Explain.
   b. What is the probability that 175 or more of the new members are significantly overweight?
   c. What is the probability that 140 or more new members are significantly overweight?

28. Research on new juvenile delinquents revealed that 38 percent of them committed another crime.
   a. What is the probability that of the last 100 new juvenile delinquents put on probation, 30 or more will commit another crime?
   b. What is the probability that 40 or fewer of the delinquents will commit another crime?
   c. What is the probability that between 30 and 40 of the delinquents will commit another crime?

Chapter Outline

I. The normal distribution is a continuous probability distribution with the following characteristics.
  A. It is bell-shaped and the mean, median, and mode are equal.
  B. It is symmetrical.
  C. It is asymptotic, meaning the curve approaches but never touches the X-axis.
  D. It is completely described by the mean and standard deviation.
  E. There is a family of normal distributions. Each time the mean or standard deviation changes, a new distribution is created.
  F. The area under a normal curve expresses the probability of an outcome.

II. The standard normal distribution is a particular normal distribution.
  A. It has a mean of 0 and a standard deviation of 1.
  B. Any normal distribution can be converted to the standard normal distribution by the following formula.

$$z = \frac{X - \mu}{\sigma} \qquad \textbf{[6–1]}$$

  C. By standardizing a normal distribution, we can report the distance from the mean in units of the standard deviation.

III. The normal distribution can approximate a binomial distribution under certain conditions.
  A. $n\pi$ and $n(1 - \pi)$ must both be at least 5.
    1. n is the number of observations.
    2. π is the probability of a success.
  B. The four conditions for a binomial distribution are:
    1. There are only two possible outcomes.
    2. π remains the same from trial to trial.
    3. The trials are independent.
    4. The distribution results from a count of the number of successes in a fixed number of trials.
  C. The mean and variance of a binomial distribution are computed as follows:

$$\mu = n\pi$$

$$\sigma^2 = n\pi(1 - \pi)$$

  D. The continuity correction factor of .5 is used to extend the continuous value of X one-half unit in either direction. This correction compensates for estimating a discrete distribution by a continuous distribution.

Chapter Exercises

29. The net sales and the number of employees for aluminum fabricators with similar characteristics are organized into frequency distributions. Both are normally distributed. For the net sales, the mean is $180 million and the standard deviation is $25 million. For the number of employees, the mean is 1,500 and the standard deviation is 120. Clarion Fabricators had sales of $170 million and 1,850 employees.
  a. Convert Clarion's sales and number of employees to z values.
  b. Locate the two z values.
  c. Compare Clarion's sales and number of employees with those of the other fabricators.

30. The accounting department at Weston Materials, Inc., a national manufacturer of unattached garages, reports that it takes two construction workers a mean of 32 hours and a standard deviation of 2 hours to erect the Red Barn model. Assume the assembly times follow the normal distribution.
  a. Determine the z values for 29 and 34 hours. What percent of the garages take between 32 hours and 34 hours to erect?
  b. What percent of the garages take between 29 hours and 34 hours to erect?
  c. What percent of the garages take 28.7 hours or less to erect?
  d. Of the garages, 5 percent take how many hours or more to erect?

31. A recent report in *USA Today* indicated a typical family of four spends $490 per month on food. Assume the distribution of food expenditures for a family of four follows the normal distribution, with a mean of $490 and a standard deviation of $90.
- **a.** What percent of the families spend more than $30 but less than $490 per month on food?
- **b.** What percent of the families spend less than $430 per month on food?
- **c.** What percent spend between $430 and $600 per month on food?
- **d.** What percent spend between $500 and $600 per month on food?

32. A study of long distance phone calls made from the corporate offices of a large company reveals the calls follow the normal distribution. The mean length of time per call was 4.2 minutes and the standard deviation was 0.60 minutes.
- **a.** What fraction of the calls last between 4.2 and 5 minutes?
- **b.** What fraction of the calls last more than 5 minutes?
- **c.** What fraction of the calls last between 5 and 6 minutes?
- **d.** What fraction of the calls last between 4 and 6 minutes?
- **e.** As part of her report to the president the Director of Communications would like to report the length of the longest (in duration) 4 percent of the calls. What is this time?

33. Shaver Manufacturing, Inc. offers dental insurance to its employees. A recent study by the Human Resource Director shows the annual cost per employee per year followed the normal distribution, with a mean of $1,280 and a standard deviation of $420 per year.
- **a.** What fraction of the employees cost more than $1,500 per year for dental expenses?
- **b.** What fraction of the employees cost between $1,500 and $2,000 per year?
- **c.** Estimate the percent that did not have any dental expense.
- **d.** What was the cost for the 10 percent of employees that incurred the highest dental expense?

34. The annual commissions earned by sales representatives of Machine Products Inc., a manufacturer of light machinery, follow the normal distribution. The mean yearly amount earned is $40,000 and the standard deviation is $5,000.
- **a.** What percent of the sales representatives earn more than $42,000 per year?
- **b.** What percent of the sales representatives earn between $32,000 and $42,000?
- **c.** What percent of the sales representatives earn between $32,000 and $35,000?
- **d.** The sales manager wants to award the sales representatives who earn the largest commissions a bonus of $1,000. He can award a bonus to 20 percent of the representatives. What is the cutoff point between those who earn a bonus and those who do not?

35. The weights of cans of Monarch pears follow the normal distribution with a mean of 1,000 grams and a standard deviation of 50 grams. Calculate the percentage of the cans that weigh:
- **a.** Less than 860 grams.
- **b.** Between 1,055 and 1,100 grams.
- **c.** Between 860 and 1,055 grams.

36. The number of passengers on the *Queen Elizabeth II* during one-week cruises in the Caribbean follows the normal distribution. The mean number of passengers per cruise is 1,820 and the standard deviation is 120.
- **a.** What percent of the cruises will have between 1,820 and 1,970 passengers?
- **b.** What percent of the cruises will have 1,970 passengers or more?
- **c.** What percent of the cruises will have 1,600 or fewer passengers?
- **d.** How many passengers are on the cruises with the fewest 25 percent of passengers?

37. Management at Gordon Electronics is considering adopting a bonus system to increase production. One suggestion is to pay a bonus on the highest 5 percent of production based on past experience. Past records indicate weekly production follows the normal distribution. The mean of this distribution is 4,000 units per week and the standard deviation is 60 units per week. If the bonus is paid on the upper 5 percent of production, the bonus will be paid on how many units or more?

38. Fast Service Truck Lines uses the Ford Super 1310 exclusively. Management made a study of the maintenance costs and determined the number of miles traveled during the year followed the normal distribution. The mean of the distribution was 60,000 miles and the standard deviation 2,000 miles.
- **a.** What percent of the Ford Super 1310s logged 65,200 miles or more?
- **b.** What percent of the trucks logged more than 57,060 but less than 58,280 miles?
- **c.** What percent of the Fords traveled 62,000 miles or less during the year?

d. Is it reasonable to conclude that any of the trucks were driven more than 70,000 miles? Explain.

39. A large retailer offers a "no hassle" returns policy. The number of items returned per day follows the normal distribution. The mean number of customer returns is 10.3 per day and the standard deviation is 2.25 per day.

a. In what percent of the days are there 8 or fewer customers returning items?

b. In what percent of the days are between 12 and 14 customers returning items?

c. Is there any chance of a day with no returns?

40. A recent study shows that 20 percent of all employees steal from their company each year. If a company employs 50 people, what is the probability that:

a. Fewer than 5 employees steal?

b. More than 5 employees steal?

c. Exactly 5 employees steal?

d. More than 5 but fewer than 15 employees steal?

41. The Myrtle Beach *Sun Times* reported that 64 percent of American men over the age of 18 consider nutrition a top priority in their lives. Suppose we select a sample of 60 men. What is the likelihood that:

a. 32 or more consider nutrition important?

b. 44 or more consider nutrition important?

c. More than 32 but fewer than 43 consider nutrition important?

d. Exactly 44 consider diet important?

42. It is estimated that 10 percent of those taking the quantitative methods portion of the CPA examination fail that section. Sixty students are taking the exam this Saturday.

a. How many would you expect to fail? What is the standard deviation?

b. What is the probability that exactly two students will fail?

c. What is the probability at least two students will fail?

43. The Georgetown, South Carolina, Traffic Division reported 40 percent of the high-speed chases involving automobiles result in a minor or major accident. During a month in which 50 high-speed chases occur, what is the probability that 25 or more will result in a minor or major accident?

44. Cruise ships of the Royal Viking line report that 80 percent of their rooms are occupied during September. For a cruise ship having 800 rooms, what is the probability that 665 or more are occupied in September?

45. The goal at U.S. airports handling international flights is to clear these flights within 45 minutes. Let's interpret this to mean that 95 percent of the flights are cleared in 45 minutes, so 5 percent of the flights take longer to clear. Let's also assume that the distribution is approximately normal.

a. If the standard deviation of the time to clear an international flight is 5 minutes, what is the mean time to clear a flight?

b. Suppose the standard deviation is 10 minutes, not the 5 minutes suggested in part a. What is the new mean?

c. A customer has 30 minutes from the time her flight landed to catch her limousine. Assuming a standard deviation of 10 minutes, what is the likelihood that she will be cleared in time?

46. An Air Force study indicates that the probability of a disaster such as the January 28, 1986, explosion of the space shuttle *Challenger* was 1 in 35. The *Challenger* flight was the 25th mission.

a. How many disasters would you expect in the first 25 flights?

b. Evaluate the normal approximation to estimate the probability of at least one disaster in 25 missions. Is this a good approximation? Tell why or why not.

47. The registrar at Elmwood University studied the grade point averages (GPAs) of students over many years. Assume the GPA distribution follows a normal distribution with a mean of 3.10 and a standard deviation of 0.30.

a. What is the probability that a randomly selected Elmwood student has a GPA between 2.00 and 3.00?

b. What percent of the students are on probation, that is, have a GPA less than 2.00?

c. The student population at EU is 10,000. How many students are on the dean's list, that is, have GPAs of 3.70 or higher?

d. To qualify for a Bell scholarship, a student must be in the top 10 percent. What GPA must a student attain to qualify for a Bell scholarship?

48. Jon Molnar will graduate from Carolina Forest High School this year. He took the American College Test (ACT) for college admission and received a score of 30. The high school principal informed him that only 2 percent of the students taking the exam receive a higher score. The mean score for all students taking the exam is 18.3. Jon's friends Karrie and George also took the test but were not given any information by the principal other than their scores. Karrie scored 25 and George 18. Based on this information, what were Karrie's and George's percentile ranks? Assume that the distribution of scores follows the normal distribution.

49. The weights of canned hams processed at the Henline Ham Company follow the normal distribution, with a mean of 9.20 pounds and a standard deviation of 0.25 pounds. The label weight is given as 9.00 pounds.

a. What proportion of the hams actually weigh less than the amount claimed on the label?

b. The owner, Glen Henline, is considering two proposals to reduce the proportion of hams below label weight. He can increase the mean weight to 9.25 and leave the standard deviation the same, or he can leave the mean weight at 9.20 and reduce the standard deviation from 0.25 pounds to 0.15. Which change would you recommend?

50. The Cincinnati *Enquirer* reported that the mean number of hours worked per week by those employed full time is 43.9. The article further indicated that about one third of those employed full time work less than 40 hours per week.

a. Given this information and assuming that number of hours worked follows the normal distribution, what is the standard deviation of the number of hours worked?

b. The article also indicated that 20 percent of those working full time work more than 49 hours per week. Determine the standard deviation with this information. Are the two estimates of the standard deviation similar? What would you conclude?

51. Most four-year automobile leases allow up to 60,000 miles. If the lessee goes beyond this amount, a penalty of 10 cents per mile is added to the lease cost. Suppose the distribution of miles driven on four-year leases follows the normal distribution. The mean is 52,000 miles and the standard deviation is 5,000 miles.

a. What percent of the leases will yield a penalty because of excess mileage?

b. If the automobile company wanted to change the terms of the lease so that 25 percent of the leases went over the limit, where should the new upper limit be set?

c. One definition of a low-mileage car is one that is 4 years old and has been driven less than 45,000 miles. What percent of the cars returned are considered low-mileage?

52. The price of shares of Bank of Florida at the end of trading each day for the last year followed the normal distribution. Assume there were 240 trading days in the year. The mean price was $42.00 per share and the standard deviation was $2.25 per share.

a. What percent of the days was the price over $45.00? How many days would you estimate?

b. What percent of the days was the price between $38.00 and $40.00?

c. What was the stock's price on the *highest* 15 days of the year?

53. The annual sales of romance novels follow the normal distribution. However, the mean and the standard deviation are unknown. Forty percent of the time sales are more than 470,000, and 10 percent of the time sales are more than 500,000. What are the mean and the standard deviation?

54. In establishing warranties on TV sets, the manufacturer wants to set the limits so that few will need repair at manufacturer expense. On the other hand, the warranty period must be long enough to make the purchase attractive to the buyer. For a new TV the mean number of months until repairs are needed is 36.84 with a standard deviation of 3.34 months. Where should the warranty limits be set so that only 10 percent of the TVs need repairs at the manufacturer's expense?

55. DeKorte Tele-Marketing Inc. is considering purchasing a machine that randomly selects and automatically dials telephone numbers. DeKorte Tele-Marketing makes most of its calls during the evening, so calls to business phones are wasted. The manufacturer of the machine claims that their programming reduces the calling to business phones to 15 percent of all calls. To test this claim the Director of Purchasing at DeKorte programmed the machine to select a sample of 150 phone numbers. What is the likelihood that more than 30 of the phone numbers selected are that of a business, assuming the manufacturer's claim is correct?

Computer Data Exercises

56. Refer to the Real Estate data set, which reports information on homes sold in the Venice, Florida, area during the last year.

a. The mean selling price (in $ thousands) of the homes was computed earlier to be $221.10, with a standard deviation of $47.11. Use the normal distribution to estimate the percent of homes selling for more than $280.0. Compare this to the actual results. Does the normal distribution yield a good approximation of the actual results?

b. The mean distance from the center of the city is 14.629 miles with a standard deviation of 4.874 miles. Use the normal distribution to estimate the number of homes 18 or more miles but less than 22 miles from the center of the city. Compare this to the actual results. Does the normal distribution yield a good approximation of the actual results?

57. Refer to the Baseball 2001 data set, which reports information on the 30 Major League Baseball teams for the 2001 season.

a. The mean attendance per team for the season was 2.42 (in millions) with a standard deviation of 0.72 (in millions). Use the normal distribution to estimate the number of teams with attendance of more than 3.5 million. Compare that estimate with the actual number. Comment on the accuracy of your estimate.

b. The mean team salary was $65.49 million with a standard deviation of $24.87 million. Use the normal distribution to estimate the number of teams with a team salary of more than $50 million. Compare that estimate with the actual number. Comment on the accuracy of the estimate.

58. Refer to the CIA data, which reports demographic and economic information on 46 countries.

a. The mean of the GDP/capita variable is 16.58 with a standard deviation of 9.27. Use the normal distribution to estimate the percentage of countries with exports above 24. Compare this estimate with the actual proportion. Does the normal distribution appear accurate in this case? Explain.

b. The mean of the Exports is 116.3 with a standard deviation of 157.4. Use the normal distribution to estimate the percentage of countries with Exports above 170. Compare this estimate with the actual proportion. Does the normal distribution appear accurate in this case? Explain.

Computer Commands

1. The Excel commands necessary to produce the output on page 200 are:
   a. Select **Insert** and **Function**, then from the box select **Statistical** and **NORMDIST** and click *OK*.
   b. In the dialog box put *1100* in the box for X, *1000* for the **Mean**, *100* for the **Standard_dev**, *True* in the **Cumulative** box, and click **OK.**
   c. The result will appear in the dialog box. If you click OK, the answer appears in your spreadsheet.

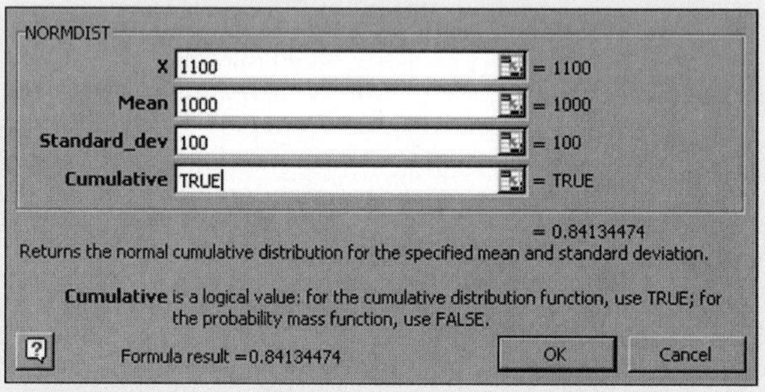
NORMDIST
X 1100 = 1100
Mean 1000 = 1000
Standard_dev 100 = 100
Cumulative TRUE = TRUE
= 0.84134474
Returns the normal cumulative distribution for the specified mean and standard deviation.
Cumulative is a logical value: for the cumulative distribution function, use TRUE; for the probability mass function, use FALSE.
Formula result =0.84134474
OK
Cancel

2. The Excel Commands necessary to produce the output on page 206 are:
   a. Select **Insert** and **Function,** then from the box select **Statistical** and **NORMINV** and click **OK.**
   b. In the dialog box, set the **Probability** to 0.04, the **Mean** to 67,900 and the **Standard_dev** to 2,050.
   c. The results will appear in the dialog box. Note that the answer is different from page 206 because of rounding error. If you click **OK,** the answer also appears in your spreadsheet.
   d. Try entering a Probability of 0.04, a Mean of zero, and a Standard_dev of one. The *z* value will be computed.

Chapter 6 Answers to Self-Review

6–1 **(a)** 2.25, found by:

$$z = \frac{\$1{,}225 - \$1{,}000}{\$100} = \frac{\$225}{\$100} = 2.25$$

(b) −2.25, found by:

$$z = \frac{\$775 - \$1{,}000}{\$100} = \frac{-\$225}{\$100} = -2.25$$

6–2 **(a)** \$36,400 and \$38,000, found by \$37,200 ± 1(\$800).

(b) \$35,600 and \$38,800, found by \$37,200 ± 2(\$800).

(c) \$34,800 and \$39,600, found by \$37,200 ± 3(\$800).

(d) \$37,200. Mean, median, and mode are equal for a normal distribution.

(e) Yes, a normal distribution is symmetrical.

6–3 **(a)** Computing z:

$$z = \frac{482 - 400}{50} = +1.64$$

Referring to Appendix D, the area is .4495.
$P(400 < \text{rating} < 482) = .4495$

(b) .0505, found by .5000 − .4495
$P(\text{rating} > 482) = .5000 - .4495 = .0505$

(c)

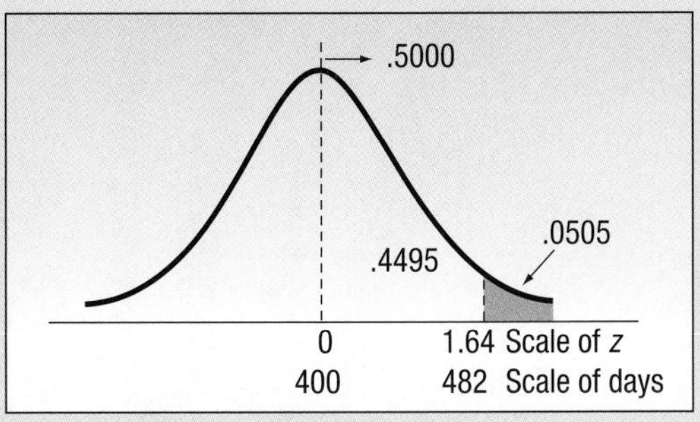

6–4 **(a)** 98.16%, found by 0.4938 + 0.4878.

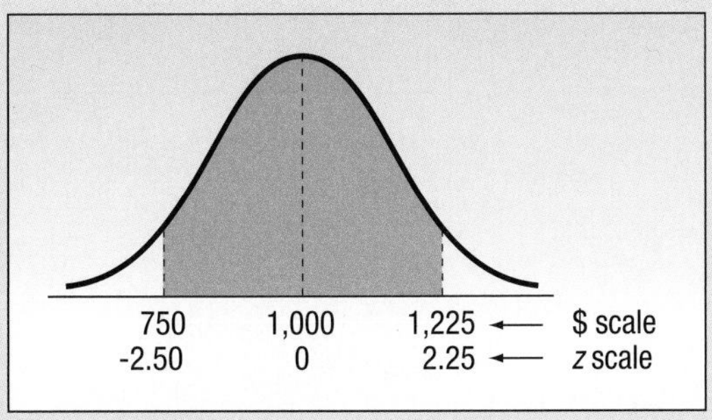

(b) 14.65%, found by 0.4878 − 0.3413.

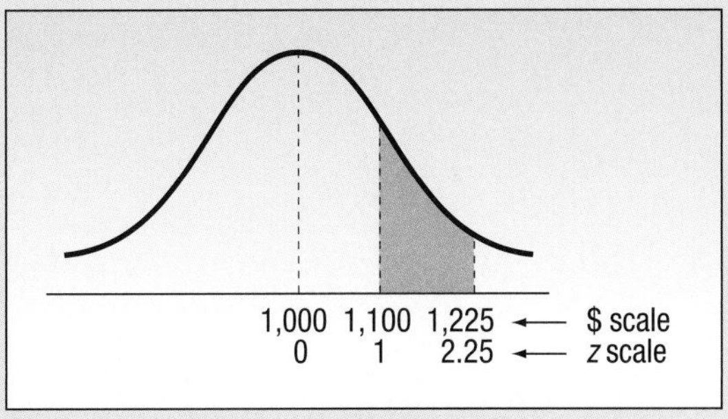

6–5 85.24 (instructor would no doubt make it 85). The closest area to .4000 is .3997; z is 1.28. Then:

$$1.28 = \frac{X - 75}{8}$$

$$10.24 = X - 75$$

$$X = 85.24$$

6–6 **(a)** .0465, found by $\mu = n\pi = 200(.80) = 160$, and $\sigma^2 = n\pi(1 - \pi) = 200(.80)(1 - .80) = 32$. Then,

$$\sigma = \sqrt{32} = 5.66$$

$$z = \frac{169.5 - 160}{5.66} = 1.68$$

Area from Appendix D is .4535. Subtracting from .5000 gives .0465.

(b) .9686, found by .4686 + .5000. First calculate z:

$$z = \frac{149.5 - 160}{5.66} = -1.86$$

Area from Appendix D is .4686.

7

Sampling Methods and the Central Limit Theorem

GOALS

When you have completed this chapter you will be able to:

1. Explain why a sample is often the only feasible way to learn something about a population.
2. Describe methods to select a sample.
3. Define and construct a sampling distribution of the sample mean.
4. Explain the *central limit theorem.*
5. Use the central limit theorem to find probabilities of selecting possible sample means from a specified population.

Plastic Products is concerned about the inside diameter of the plastic PVC pipe it produces. About 720 pipes are produced per machine during a two-hour period. How would you go about taking a sample from the two-hour production period? (See Goal 2 and Exercise 22.)

Introduction

Chapters 1 through 3 emphasize techniques to describe data. To illustrate these techniques, we organize the prices for the 80 vehicles sold last month at Whitner Pontiac into a frequency distribution and compute various measures of location and dispersion. Such measures as the mean and the standard deviation describe the typical selling price and the spread in the selling prices. In these chapters the emphasis is on describing the condition of the data. That is, we describe something that has already happened.

Chapter 4 starts to lay the foundation for statistical inference with the study of probability. Recall that in statistical inference our goal is to determine something about a *population* based only on the *sample.* The population is the entire group of individuals or objects under consideration, and the sample is a part or subset of that population. Chapter 5 extends the probability concepts by describing three discrete probability distributions: the binomial, the hypergeometric, and the Poisson. Chapter 6 describes the normal probability distribution, a widely applicable continuous probability distribution. Probability distributions encompass all possible outcomes of an experiment and the probability associated with each outcome. We use probability distributions to evaluate something that might occur in the future.

This chapter begins our study of sampling. A sample is a tool to infer something about a population. We begin this chapter by discussing methods of selecting a sample from a population. Next, we construct a distribution of the sample mean to understand how the sample means tend to cluster around the population mean. Finally, we show that for any population the shape of this sampling distribution tends to follow the normal probability distribution.

Sampling Methods

In Chapter 1, we said the purpose of inferential statistics is to find something about a population based on a sample. A sample is a portion or part of the population of interest. In many cases, sampling is more effective than studying the entire population. In this section, we show major reasons for sampling, and then several methods for selecting a sample.

Reasons to Sample

When studying characteristics of a population, there are many practical reasons why we prefer to select portions or samples of a population to observe and measure. Some of the reasons for sampling are:

Reasons for sampling

1. **To contact the whole population would often be time consuming.** A candidate for a national office may wish to determine her chances for election. A sample poll using the regular staff and field interviews of a professional polling firm would take only 1 or 2 days. By using the same staff and interviewers and working 7 days a week, it would take nearly 200 years to contact all the voting population! Even if a large staff of interviewers could be assembled, the benefit of contacting all of the voters would probably not be worth the time. If the candidate were extremely popular, the sample poll might indicate that she would most certainly receive between 79 percent and 81 percent of the popular vote. The additional time needed to find that she might receive exactly 80 percent of the popular vote does not seem justified.
2. **The cost of studying all the items in a population is often prohibitive.** Public opinion polls and consumer testing organizations, such as Gallup Polls and

Marketing Facts, usually contact fewer than 2,000 of the nearly 60 million families in the United States. One consumer panel-type organization charges about $40,000 to mail samples and tabulate responses in order to test a product (such as breakfast cereal, cat food, or perfume). The same product test using all 60 million families would cost about $1 billion.

3. **The adequacy of sample results.** Even if funds were available, it is doubtful the additional accuracy of a 100 percent sample—that is, studying the entire population—is essential in most problems. For example, the federal government uses a sample of grocery stores scattered throughout the United States to determine the monthly index of food prices. The prices of bread, beans, milk, and other major food items are included in the index. It is unlikely that the inclusion of all grocery stores in the United States would significantly affect the index, since the prices of milk, bread, and other major foods usually do not vary by more than a few cents from one chain store to another.
4. **The destructive nature of certain tests.** If the wine tasters at the Sutter Home Winery in California drank all the wine to evaluate the vintage, they would consume the entire crop, and none would be available for sale. In the area of industrial production, steel plates, wires, and similar products must have a certain minimum tensile strength. To ensure that the product meets the minimum standard, the Quality Assurance Department selects a sample from the current production. Each piece is stretched until it breaks, and the breaking point (usually measured in pounds per square inch) recorded. Obviously, if all the wire or all the plates were tested for tensile strength, none would be available for sale or use. For the same reason, only a sample of photographic film is selected and tested by Kodak to determine the quality of all the film produced, and only a few seeds are tested for germination by Burpee prior to the planting season.
5. **The physical impossibility of checking all items in the population.** The populations of fish, birds, snakes, mosquitoes, and the like are large and are constantly moving, being born, and dying. Instead of even attempting to count all the ducks in Canada or all the fish in Lake Erie, we make estimates using various techniques—such as counting all the ducks on a pond picked at random, making creel checks, or setting nets at predetermined places in the lake.

When selecting a sample, researchers or analysts must be very careful that the sample is a fair representation of the population. In other words, the sample must be unbiased. In Chapter 1, an example of abusing statistics was the intentional selection of dentists to report that "2 out of 3 dentists surveyed indicated they would recommend Brand X toothpaste to their patients." Clearly, people can select a sample that supports their own biases. The ethical side of statistics always requires unbiased sampling and objective reporting of results. Next, several sampling methods show how to select a fair and unbiased sample from a population.

Simple Random Sampling

The most widely used type of sampling is a **simple random sample.**

SIMPLE RANDOM SAMPLE A sample selected so that each item or person in the population has the same chance of being included.

A table of random numbers is an efficient way to select members of the sample

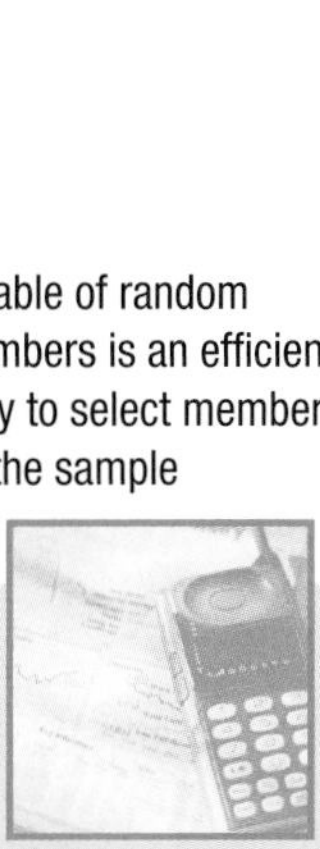

Statistics in Action

Is discrimination taking a bite out of your paycheck? Before you answer, consider a recent article in *Personnel Journal.* These findings indicate that attractive men and women earn about 5 percent more than average lookers, who in turn earn about 5 percent more than their plain counterparts. This is true for both men and women. It is also true for a wide range of occupations, from construction workers to auto repair to telemarketing, occupations for which it would seem that looks would not matter.

To illustrate simple random sampling and selection, suppose a population consists of 845 employees of Nitra Industries. A sample of 52 employees is to be selected from that population. One way of ensuring that every employee in the population has the same chance of being chosen is to first write the name of each one on a small slip of paper and deposit all of the slips in a box. After they have been thoroughly mixed, the first selection is made by drawing a slip out of the box without looking at it. This process is repeated until the sample size of 52 is chosen.

A more convenient method of selecting a random sample is to use the identification number of each employee and a **table of random numbers** such as the one in Appendix E. As the name implies, these numbers have been generated by a random process (in this case, by a computer). For each digit of a number, the probability of 0, 1, 2, . . . , 9 is the same. Thus, the probability that employee number 011 will be selected is the same as for employee 722 or employee 382. By using random numbers to select employees, bias is eliminated from the selection process.

A portion of a table of random numbers is shown in the following illustration. To select a sample of employees, you must first choose a starting point in the table. Any starting point will do. Suppose the time is 3:04. You might look at the third column and then move down to the fourth set of numbers. The number is 03759. Since there are only 845 employees, we will use the first three digits of a five-digit random number. Thus, 037 is the number of the first employee to be a member of the sample. Another way of selecting the starting point is to close your eyes and point at a number in the table. To continue selecting employees, you could move in any direction. Suppose you move right. The first three digits of the number to the right of 03759 are 447—the number of the employee selected to be the second member of the sample. The next three-digit number to the right is 961. You skip 961 because there are only 845 employees. You continue to the right and select employee 784, then 189, and so on.

50525	57454	28455	68226	34656	38884	39018
72507	53380	53827	42486	54465	71819	91199
34986	74297	00144	38676	89967	98869	39744
68851	27305	03759	44723	96108	78489	18910
06738	62879	03910	17350	49169	03850	18910
11448	10734	05837	24397	10420	16712	94496
		Starting point	Second employee		Third employee	Fourth employee

Self-Review 7–1

The following class roster lists the students enrolling in an introductory course in business statistics. Three students are to be randomly selected and asked various questions regarding course content and method of instruction.

(a) The numbers 00 through 45 are handwritten on slips of paper and placed in a bowl. The three numbers selected are 31, 7, and 25. Which students would be included in the sample?
(b) Now use the table of random digits, Appendix E, to select your own sample.
(c) What would you do if you encountered the number 59 in the table of random digits?

CSPM 264 01 BUSINESS & ECONOMIC STAT

8:00 AM 9:40 AM MW ST 118 LIND D

RANDOM NUMBER	NAME	CLASS RANK	RANDOM NUMBER	NAME	CLASS RANK
00	ANDERSON, RAYMOND	SO	23	MEDLEY, CHERYL ANN	SO
01	ANGER, CHERYL RENEE	SO	24	MITCHELL, GREG R	FR
02	BALL, CLAIRE JEANETTE	FR	25	MOLTER, KRISTI MARIE	SO
03	BERRY, CHRISTOPHER G	FR	26	MULCAHY, STEPHEN ROBERT	SO
04	BOBAK, JAMES PATRICK	SO	27	NICHOLAS, ROBERT CHARLES	JR
05	BRIGHT, M. STARR	JR	28	NICKENS, VIRGINIA	SO
06	CHONTOS, PAUL JOSEPH	SO	29	PENNYWITT, SEAN PATRICK	SO
07	DETLEY, BRIAN HANS	JR	30	POTEAU, KRIS E	JR
08	DUDAS, VIOLA	SO	31	PRICE, MARY LYNETTE	SO
09	DULBS, RICHARD ZALFA	JR	32	RISTAS, JAMES	SR
10	EDINGER, SUSAN KEE	SR	33	SAGER, ANNE MARIE	SO
11	FINK, FRANK JAMES	SR	34	SMILLIE, HEATHER MICHELLE	SO
12	FRANCIS, JAMES P	JR	35	SNYDER, LEISHA KAY	SR
13	GAGHEN, PAMELA LYNN	JR	36	STAHL, MARIA TASHERY	SO
14	GOULD, ROBYN KAY	SO	37	ST. JOHN, AMY J	SO
15	GROSENBACHER, SCOTT ALAN	SO	38	STURDEVANT, RICHARD K	SO
16	HEETFIELD, DIANE MARIE	SO	39	SWETYE, LYNN MICHELE	SO
17	KABAT, JAMES DAVID	JR	40	WALASINSKI, MICHAEL	SO
18	KEMP, LISA ADRIANE	FR	41	WALKER, DIANE ELAINE	SO
19	KILLION, MICHELLE A	SO	42	WARNOCK, JENNIFER MARY	SO
20	KOPERSKI, MARY ELLEN	SO	43	WILLIAMS, WENDY A	SO
21	KOPP, BRIDGETTE ANN	SO	44	YAP, HOCK BAN	SO
22	LEHMANN, KRISTINA MARIE	JR	45	YODER, ARLAN JAY	JR

Systematic Random Sampling

The simple random sampling procedure may be awkward in some research situations. For example, suppose the sales division of Computer Printers Unlimited needs to quickly estimate the mean dollar revenue per sale during the past month. They find that 2,000 sales invoices were recorded and stored in file drawers, and decide to select 100 invoices to estimate the mean dollar revenue. Simple random sampling requires the numbering of each invoice before using the random number table to select the 100 invoices. The numbering process would be a very time consuming task. Instead, **systematic random sampling** can be used.

SYSTEMATIC RANDOM SAMPLE A random starting point is selected, and then every *k*th member of the population is selected.

First, *k* is calculated as the population size divided by the sample size. For Computer Printers Unlimited, we would select every 20th (2000/100) invoice from the file drawers; in so doing the numbering process is avoided. If *k* is not a whole number, then round down.

Random sampling is based on the random selection of the first invoice. For example, a number from a random number table between 1 and *k*, or 20, would be selected. Say, the random number was 18. Then, starting with the 18th invoice, every 20th invoice (18, 38, 58, etc.) would be selected as the sample.

Before using systematic random sampling, we should carefully observe the physical order of the population. When the physical order is related to the population characteristic, then systematic random sampling should not be used. For example, if the invoices in the example were filed in order of increasing sales, systematic random sampling would not guarantee a random sample. Other sampling methods should be used.

Stratified Random Sampling

When a population can be clearly divided into groups based on some characteristic, then **stratified random sampling** can be used to guarantee that each group is represented in the sample. The groups are also called **strata.** For example, college students can be grouped as full time or part time, male or female, or traditional or nontraditional. Once the strata are defined, we can apply simple random sampling within each group or strata to collect the sample.

> **STRATIFIED RANDOM SAMPLE** A population is divided into subgroups, called strata, and a sample is randomly selected from each stratum.

For instance, we might study the advertising expenditures for the 352 largest companies in the United States. Suppose the objective of the study is to determine whether firms with high returns on equity (a measure of profitability) spent more of each sales dollar on advertising than firms with a low return or deficit. To make sure that the sample is a fair representation of the 352 companies, the companies are grouped on percent return on equity. Table 7–1 shows the strata and the relative frequencies. If simple random sampling was used, observe that firms in the 3rd and 4th strata have a high chance of selection (probability of 0.87) while firms in the other strata have a low chance of selection (probability of 0.13). We might not select any firms in stratum 1 or 5 *simply by chance.* However, stratified random sampling will guarantee that at least one firm in strata 1 and 5 are represented in the sample. Let's say that 50 firms are selected for intensive study. Then one (0.02 × 50) firm from stratum 1 would be randomly selected, 5 (0.10 × 50) firms from stratum 2 would be randomly selected, and so on. In this case, the number of firms sampled from each stratum is proportional to the stratum's relative frequency in the population. Stratified sampling has the advantage, in some cases, of more accurately reflecting the characteristics of the population than does simple random or systematic random sampling.

TABLE 7–1 Number Selected for a Proportional Stratified Random Sample

Stratum	Profitability (return on equity)	Number of Firms	Relative Frequency	Number Sampled
1	30 percent and over	8	0.02	1*
2	20 up to 30 percent	35	0.10	5*
3	10 up to 20 percent	189	0.54	27
4	0 up to 10 percent	115	0.33	16
5	Deficit	5	0.01	1
Total		352	1.00	50

*0.02 of 50 = 1, 0.10 of 50 = 5, etc.

Cluster Sampling

Another common type of sampling is **cluster sampling.** It is often employed to reduce the cost of sampling a population scattered over a large geographic area.

> **CLUSTER SAMPLING** A population is divided into clusters using naturally occurring geographic or other boundaries. Then, clusters are randomly selected and a sample is collected by randomly selecting from each cluster.

Suppose you want to determine the views of residents in a state about state and federal environmental protection policies. Selecting a random sample of residents in the state and personally contacting each one would be time consuming and very expensive. Instead, you could employ cluster sampling by subdividing the state into small units—either counties or regions. These are often called *primary units.*

Suppose you divided the state into 12 primary units, then selected at random four regions—2, 7, 4, and 12—and concentrated your efforts in these primary units. You could take a random sample of the residents in each of these regions and interview them. (Note that this is a combination of cluster sampling and simple random sampling.)

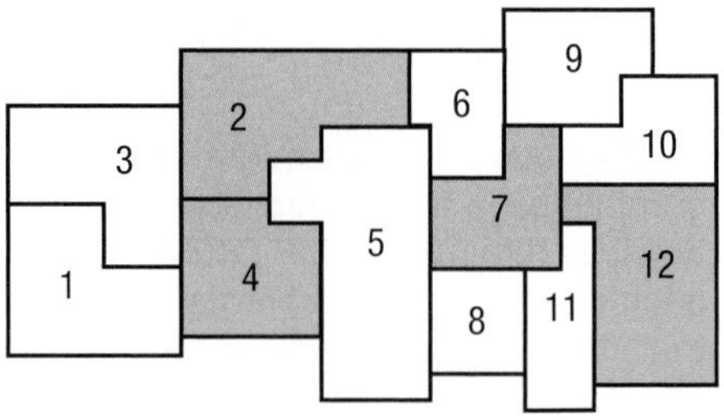

Many other sampling methods

The discussion of sampling methods in the preceding sections did not include all the sampling methods available to a researcher. Should you become involved in a major research project in marketing, finance, accounting, or other areas, you would need to consult books devoted solely to sample theory and sample design.

Self-Review 7–2

Refer to Self-Review 7–1 (page 221) and the class roster on page 222. Suppose a sample is to consist of every ninth student enrolled in the class. Initially, the fourth student on the list was selected at random. That student is numbered 03. Remembering that the random numbers start with 00, which students will be chosen to be members of the sample?

Exercises

1. The following is a list of Marco's Pizza stores in Lucas County. Also noted is whether the store is corporate-owned (C) or manager-owned (M). A sample of four locations is to be selected and inspected for customer convenience, safety, cleanliness, and other features.

ID No.	Address	Type	ID No.	Address	Type
00	2607 Starr Av	C	12	2040 Ottawa River Rd	C
01	309 W Alexis Rd	C	13	2116 N Reynolds Rd	C
02	2652 W Central Av	C	14	3678 Rugby Dr	C
03	630 Dixie Hwy	M	15	1419 South Av	C
04	3510 Dorr St	C	16	1234 W Sylvania Av	C
05	5055 Glendale Av	C	17	4624 Woodville Rd	M
06	3382 Lagrange St	M	18	5155 S Main	M
07	2525 W Laskey Rd	C	19	106 E Airport Hwy	C
08	303 Louisiana Av	C	20	6725 W Central	M
09	149 Main St	C	21	4252 Monroe	C
10	835 S McCord Rd	M	22	2036 Woodville Rd	C
11	3501 Monroe St	M	23	1316 Michigan Av	M

a. The random numbers selected are 08, 18, 11, 54, 02, 41, and 54. Which stores are selected?
b. Use the table of random numbers to select your own sample of locations.
c. A sample is to consist of every seventh location. The number 03 is the starting point. Which locations will be included in the sample?
d. Suppose a sample is to consist of three locations, of which two are corporate-owned and one is manager-owned. Select a sample accordingly.

2. The following is a list of hospitals in the Cincinnati (Ohio) and Northern Kentucky Region. Also included is whether the hospital is a general medical/surgical hospital (M/S) or a specialty hospital (S).

ID Number	Name	Address	Type	ID Number	Name	Address	Type
00	Bethesda North	10500 Montgomery Cincinnati, Ohio 45242	M/S	15	Providence Hospital	2446 Kipling Avenue Cincinnati, Ohio 45239	M/S
01	Ft. Hamilton-Hughes	630 Eaton Avenue Hamilton, Ohio 45013	M/S	16	St. Francis-St. George Hospital	3131 Queen City Avenue Cincinnati, Ohio 45238	M/S
02	Jewish Hospital-Kenwood	4700 East Galbraith Rd. Cincinnati, Ohio 45236	M/S	17	St. Elizabeth Medical Center, North Unit	401 E. 20th Street Covington, Kentucky 41014	M/S
03	Mercy Hospital-Fairfield	3000 Mack Road Fairfield, Ohio 45014	M/S	18	St. Elizabeth Medical Center, South Unit	One Medical Village Edgewood, Kentucky 41017	M/S
04	Mercy Hospital-Hamilton	100 Riverfront Plaza Hamilton, Ohio 45011	M/S	19	St. Luke's Hospital West	7380 Turfway Dr. Florence, Kentucky 41075	M/S
05	Middletown Regional	105 McKnight Drive Middletown, Ohio 45044	M/S	20	St. Luke's Hospital East	85 North Grand Avenue Ft. Thomas, Kentucky 41042	M/S
06	Clermont Mercy Hospital	3000 Hospital Dr. Batavia, Ohio 45103	M/S	21	Care Unit Hospital Cinti.	3156 Glenmore Avenue Cincinnati, Ohio 45211	S
07	Mercy Hospital-Anderson	7500 State Road Cincinnati, Ohio 45255	M/S	22	Emerson Behavioral Science	2446 Kipling Avenue Cincinnati, Ohio 45239	S
08	Bethesda Oak Hospital	619 Oak Street Cincinnati, Ohio 45206	M/S	23	Pauline Warfield Lewis Center for Psychiatric Treat.	1101 Summit Rd. Cincinnati, Ohio 45237	S
09	Children's Hospital Medical Center	3333 Burnet Avenue Cincinnati, Ohio 45229	M/S	24	Children's Psychiatric No. Kentucky	502 Farrell Drive Covington, Kentucky 41011	S
10	Christ Hospital	2139 Auburn Avenue Cincinnati, Ohio 45219	M/S	25	Drake Center Rehab—Long Term	151 W. Galbraith Road Cincinnati, Ohio 45216	S
11	Deaconess Hospital	311 Straight Street Cincinnati, Ohio 45219	M/S	26	No. Kentucky Rehab Hospital—Short Term	201 Medical Village Edgewood, Kentucky	S
12	Good Samaritan Hospital	375 Dixmyth Avenue Cincinnati, Ohio 45220	M/S	27	Shriners Burns Institute	3229 Burnet Avenue Cincinnati, Ohio 45229	S
13	Jewish Hospital	3200 Burnet Avenue Cincinnati, Ohio 45229	M/S	28	VA Medical Center	3200 Vine Cincinnati, Ohio 45220	S
14	University Hospital	234 Goodman Street Cincinnati, Ohio 45267	M/S				

a. A sample of five hospitals is to be randomly selected. The random numbers are 09, 16, 00, 49, 54, 12, and 04. Which hospitals are included in the sample?
b. Use a table of random numbers to develop your own sample of five hospitals.
c. A sample is to consist of every fifth location. We select 02 as the starting point. Which hospitals will be included in the sample?
d. A sample is to consist of four medical and surgical hospitals and one specialty hospital. Select an appropriate sample.

3. Listed below are the 35 members of the Metro Toledo Automobile Dealers Association.

ID Number	Dealer	ID Number	Dealer	ID Number	Dealer
00	Dave White Acura	12	Spurgeon Chevrolet Motor Sales, Inc.	24	Lexus of Toledo
01	Autofair Nissan	13	Dunn Chevrolet	25	Mathews Ford Oregon, Inc.
02	Autofair Toyota-Suzuki	14	Don Scott Chevrolet-Pontiac-Geo, Inc.	26	Northtowne Chevrolet-GEO
03	George Ball's Buick GMC Truck	15	Dave White Chevrolet Co.	27	Quality Ford Sales, Inc.
04	Yark Automotive Group	16	Dick Wilson Pontiac	28	Rouen Chrysler Jeep Eagle
05	Bob Schmidt Chevrolet	17	Doyle Pontiac Buick	29	Saturn of Toledo
06	Bowling Green Lincoln Mercury Jeep Eagle	18	Franklin Park Lincoln Mercury	30	Ed Schmidt Pontiac Jeep Eagle
07	Brondes Ford	19	Genoa Motors	31	Southside Lincoln Mercury
08	Brown Honda	20	Great Lakes Ford Nissan	32	Valiton Chrysler
09	Brown Mazda	21	Grogan Towne Chrysler	33	Vin Divers
10	Charlie's Dodge	22	Hatfield Motor Sales	34	Whitman Ford
11	Thayer Chevrolet Geo Toyota	23	Kistler Ford, Inc.		

a. We want to select a random sample of five dealers. The random numbers are: 05, 20, 59, 21, 31, 28, 49, 38, 66, 08, 29, and 02. Which dealers would be included in the sample?
b. Use the table of random numbers to select your own sample of five dealers.
c. A sample is to consist of every seventh dealer. The number 04 is selected as the starting point. Which dealers are included in the sample?

4. Listed below are the 27 Nationwide Insurance agents in the Toledo, Ohio, metropolitan area.

ID Number	Agent	ID Number	Agent	ID Number	Agent
00	**Bly Scott** 3332 W Laskey Rd	09	**Harris Ev** 2026 Albon Rd	18	**Priest Harvey** 5113 N Summit St
01	**Coyle Mike** 5432 W Central Av	10	**Heini Bernie** 7110 W Central	19	**Riker Craig** 2621 N Reynolds Rd
02	**Denker Brett** 7445 Airport Hwy	11	**Hinckley Dave**	20	**Schwab Dave** 572 W Dussel Dr
03	**Denker Rollie** 7445 Airport Hwy		14 N Holland Sylvania Rd	21	**Seibert John H** 201 S Main
04	**Farley Ron** 1837 W Alexis Rd	12	**Joehlin Bob** 3358 Navarre Av	22	**Smithers Bob** 229 Superior St
05	**George Mark** 7247 W Central Av	13	**Keisser David** 3030 W Sylvania Av	23	**Smithers Jerry** 229 Superior St
06	**Gibellato Carlo** 6616 Monroe St	14	**Keisser Keith** 5902 Sylvania Av	24	**Wright Steve** 105 S Third St
	3521 Navarre Av	15	**Lawrence Grant** 342 W Dussel Dr	25	**Wood Tom** 112 Louisiana Av
07	**Glemser Cathy** 5602 Woodville Rd	16	**Miller Ken** 2427 Woodville Rd	26	**Yoder Scott** 6 Willoughby Av
08	**Green Mike** 4149 Holland Sylvania Rd	17	**O'Donnell Jim** 7247 W Central Av		

a. We want to select a random sample of four agents. The random numbers are: 02, 59, 51, 25, 14, 29, 77, 69, and 18. Which dealers would be included in the sample?
b. Use the table of random numbers to select your own sample of four agents.
c. A sample is to consist of every fifth dealer. The number 02 is selected as the starting point. Which agents will be included in the sample?

Sampling "Error"

The previous section discussed sampling methods that can be used to select a sample that is a fair or unbiased representation of the population. In each method, it is important to note that the selection of every possible sample of a specified size from a population has a known chance or probability. This is another way to describe an unbiased sampling method.

Samples are used to estimate population characteristics. For example, the mean of a sample is used to estimate the population mean. However, since the sample is a part or portion of the population, it is unlikely that the sample mean would be *exactly equal* to the population mean. Similarly, it is unlikely that the sample standard deviation would be *exactly equal* to the population standard deviation. We can therefore expect a difference between a *sample statistic* and its corresponding *population parameter.* This difference is called **sampling error.**

SAMPLING ERROR The difference between a sample statistic and its corresponding population parameter.

Suppose a population of five production employees had efficiency ratings of 97, 103, 96, 99, and 105. Further suppose that a sample of two ratings—97 and 105—is selected to estimate the population mean rating. The mean of that sample would be 101, found by (97 + 105)/2. Another sample of two is selected: 103 and 96, with a sample mean of 99.5. The mean of all the ratings (the population mean) is 100, found by: (97 + 103 + 96 + 99 + 105)/5 = 500/5 = 100. The sampling error for the first sample is 1.0, determined by $\overline{X} - \mu = 101 - 100$. The second sample has a sampling error of -0.5. Each of these differences, 1.0 and -0.5, is the error made in estimating the population mean based on a sample mean, and these sampling errors are due to chance.

In this example, each of the 10 possible samples of size 2 (see page 147 formula 4–9 for the combination rule) has an equal chance of selection. Each sample may have a different sample mean and a different sampling error. The value of the sampling error is based on the random selection of a sample. Therefore, sampling errors are random and occur by chance.

Now that we have discovered the possibility of a sampling error when sample results are used to estimate a population parameter, how can we make an accurate prediction about the possible success of a newly developed toothpaste or other product, based only on sample results? How can the quality-assurance department in a mass-production firm release a shipment of microchips based only on a sample of 10 chips? How can Gallup or Harris polls make an accurate prediction about a presidential race based on a sample of 2,000 registered voters out of a voting population of nearly 90 million? To answer these questions, we first develop a *sampling distribution of the sample mean.*

Sampling Distribution of the Sample Mean

Sample means vary from sample to sample.

The efficiency rating example showed the means for samples of a specified size vary from sample to sample. The mean efficiency rating of the first sample of two employees was 101, and the second sample mean was 99.5. A third sample would probably result in a different mean. The population mean was 100. If we organized the means of all possible samples of 2 ratings into a probability distribution, we would obtain the **sampling distribution of the sample mean.**

SAMPLING DISTRIBUTION OF THE SAMPLE MEAN A probability distribution of all possible sample means of a given sample size.

The following example illustrates the construction of a sampling distribution of the sample mean.

EXAMPLE

Tartus Industries has seven production employees (considered the population). The hourly earnings of each employee are given in Table 7–2.

TABLE 7–2 Hourly Earnings of the Production Employees of Tartus Industries

Employee	Hourly Earnings
Joe	\$7
Sam	7
Sue	8
Bob	8
Jan	7
Art	8
Ted	9

1. What is the population mean?
2. What is the sampling distribution of the sample mean for samples of size 2?
3. What is the mean of the sampling distribution?
4. What observations can be made about the population and the sampling distribution?

SOLUTION

1. The population mean is \$7.71, found by:

$$\mu = \frac{\$7 + \$7 + \$8 + \$8 + \$7 + \$8 + \$9}{7}$$

We identify the population mean with the Greek letter μ. Our policy, stated in Chapters 1 and 3, is to identify population parameters with Greek letters.

2. To arrive at the sampling distribution of the sample mean, all possible samples of 2 were selected without replacement from the population, and their means were computed. There are 21 possible samples, found by using formula 4–9 on page 147.

$${}_NC_n = \frac{N!}{n!(N-n)!} = \frac{7!}{2!(7-2)!} = 21$$

where $N = 7$ is the number of items in the population and $n = 2$ is the number of items in the sample.

The 21 distinct sample means from all possible samples of 2 that can be drawn from the population are shown in Table 7–3. This probability distribution is the sampling distribution of the sample mean and is summarized in Table 7–4.

TABLE 7–3 Sample Means for All Possible Samples of 2 Employees

Sample	Employees	Hourly Earnings	Sum	Mean	Sample	Employees	Hourly Earnings	Sum	Mean
1	Joe, Sam	\$7, \$7	\$14	\$7.00	12	Sue, Bob	\$8, \$8	\$16	\$8.00
2	Joe, Sue	7, 8	15	7.50	13	Sue, Jan	8, 7	15	7.50
3	Joe, Bob	7, 8	15	7.50	14	Sue, Art	8, 8	16	8.00
4	Joe, Jan	7, 7	14	7.00	15	Sue, Ted	8, 9	17	8.50
5	Joe, Art	7, 8	15	7.50	16	Bob, Jan	8, 7	15	7.50
6	Joe, Ted	7, 9	16	8.00	17	Bob, Art	8, 8	16	8.00
7	Sam, Sue	7, 8	15	7.50	18	Bob, Ted	8, 9	17	8.50
8	Sam, Bob	7, 8	15	7.50	19	Jan, Art	7, 8	15	7.50
9	Sam, Jan	7, 7	14	7.00	20	Jan, Ted	7, 9	16	8.00
10	Sam, Art	7, 8	15	7.50	21	Art, Ted	8, 9	17	8.50
11	Sam, Ted	7, 9	16	8.00					

TABLE 7–4 Sampling Distribution of the Sample Mean for n = 2

Sample Mean	Number of Means	Probability
$7.00	3	.1429
7.50	9	.4285
8.00	6	.2857
8.50	3	.1429
	21	1.0000

Population mean is equal to the mean of the sample means

3. The mean of the sampling distribution of the sample mean is obtained by summing the various sample means and dividing the sum by the number of samples. The mean of all the sample means is usually written $\mu_{\bar{X}}$. The μ reminds us that it is a population value because we have considered all possible samples. The subscript $\bar{X}$ indicates that it is the sampling distribution of the sample mean.

$$\mu_{\bar{X}} = \frac{\text{Sum of all sample means}}{\text{Total number of samples}} = \frac{\$7.00 + \$7.50 + \cdots + \$8.50}{21}$$

$$= \frac{\$162}{21} = \$7.71$$

4. Refer to Chart 7–1, which shows both the population distribution and the distribution of the sample mean. These observations can be made:

   a. The mean of the distribution of the sample mean ($7.71) is equal to the mean of the population: $\mu = \mu_{\bar{X}}$.
   b. The spread in the distribution of the sample mean is less than the spread in the population values. The sample mean ranges from $7.00 to $8.50, while the population values vary from $7.00 up to $9.00. In fact, the standard deviation of the distribution of the sample mean is equal to the population standard deviation divided by the square root of the sample size. So the formula for the standard deviation of the distribution of the sample mean is $\sigma/\sqrt{n}$. Notice, as we increase the size of the sample, $\sigma/\sqrt{n}$ becomes smaller so the spread of the distribution becomes narrower.
   c. The shape of the sampling distribution of the sample mean and the shape of the frequency distribution of the population values are different. The distribution of the sample mean tends to be more bell-shaped and to approximate the normal probability distribution.

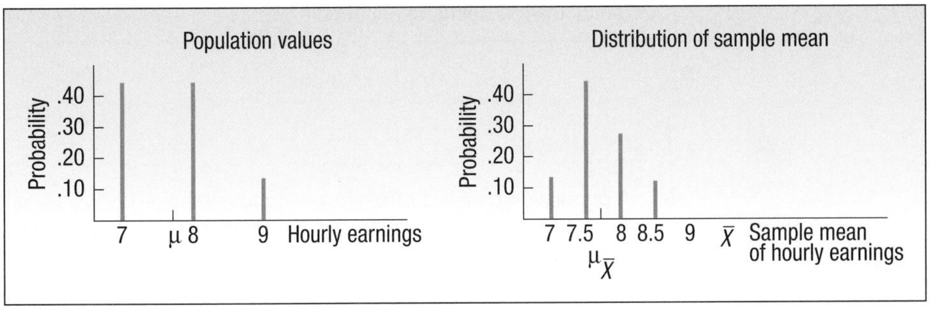

CHART 7–1 Distributions of Population Values and Sample Means

In summary, we took all possible random samples from a population and for each sample calculated a sample statistic (the mean amount earned). This example illustrates important relationships between the population distribution and the sampling distribution of the sample mean. First, the mean of the sample means is exactly equal to the population mean. Second, the dispersion of the sampling distribution of sample means is narrower than the population distribution. Third, the sampling distribution of sample means tends to become bell-shaped and to approximate the normal probability distribution. Given a bell-shaped or normal probability distribution, we will be able to apply concepts from Chapter 6 to determine the probability of selecting a sample with a specified sample mean. In the next section, we will show the importance of sample size as it relates to the sampling distribution of sample means.

Self-Review 7–3

The lengths of service of all the executives employed by Standard Chemicals are:

Name	Years
Mr. Snow	20
Ms. Tolson	22
Mr. Kraft	26
Ms. Irwin	24
Mr. Jones	28

(a) Using the combination formula, how many samples of size 2 are possible?
(b) List all possible samples of 2 executives from the population and compute their means.
(c) Organize the means into a sampling distribution.
(d) Compare the population mean and the mean of the sample means.
(e) Compare the dispersion in the population with that in the distribution of the sample mean.
(f) A chart portraying the population values follows. Is the distribution of population values normally distributed (bell-shaped)?

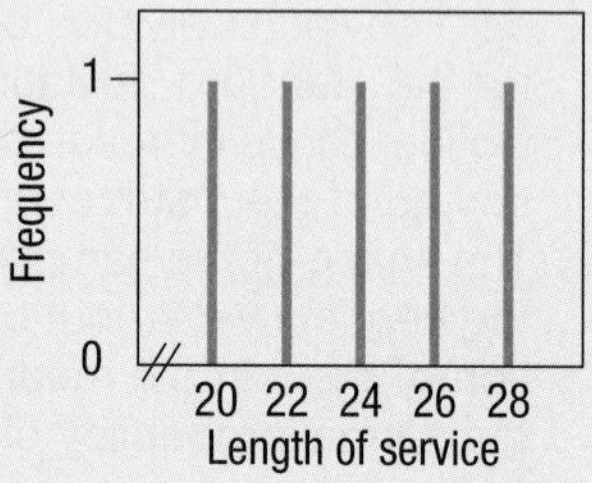

(g) Is the distribution of the sample mean computed in part (c) starting to show some tendency toward being bell-shaped?

Exercises

5. A population consists of the following four values: 12, 12, 14, and 16.
  a. List all samples of size 2, and compute the mean of each sample.
  b. Compute the mean of the distribution of the sample mean and the population mean. Compare the two values.
  c. Compare the dispersion in the population with that of the sample mean.

6. A population consists of the following five values: 2, 2, 4, 4, and 8.
   a. List all samples of size 2, and compute the mean of each sample.
   b. Compute the mean of the distribution of the sample mean and the population mean. Compare the two values.
   c. Compare the dispersion in the population with that of the sample means.

7. A population consists of the following five values: 12, 12, 14, 15, and 20.
   a. List all samples of size 3, and compute the mean of each sample.
   b. Compute the mean of the distribution of the sample mean and the population mean. Compare the two values.
   c. Compare the dispersion in the population with that of the sample means.

8. A population consists of the following five values: 0, 0, 1, 3, 6.
   a. List all samples of size 3, and compute the mean of each sample.
   b. Compute the mean of the distribution of the sample mean and the population mean. Compare the two values.
   c. Compare the dispersion in the population with that of the sample means.

9. In the law firm Tybo and Associates, there are six partners. Listed below is the number of cases each associate actually tried in court last month.

Associate	Number of Cases
Ruud	3
Austin	6
Sass	3
Palmer	3
Wilhelms	0
Schueller	1

   a. How many different samples of 3 are possible?
   b. List all possible samples of size 3, and compute the mean number of cases in each sample.
   c. Compare the mean of the distribution of the sample mean to the population mean.
   d. On a chart similar to Chart 7–1, compare the dispersion in the population with that of the sample means.

10. There are five sales representatives at Mid-Motors Ford. The five representatives and the number of cars they sold last week are:

Sales Representative	Cars Sold
Peter Hankish	8
Connie Stallter	6
Ron Eaton	4
Ted Barnes	10
Peggy Harmon	6

   a. How many different samples of size 2 are possible?
   b. List all possible samples of size 2, and compute the mean of each sample.
   c. Compare the mean of the sampling distribution of the sample mean with that of the population.
   d. On a chart similar to Chart 7–1, compare the dispersion in the sample mean with that of the population.

The Central Limit Theorem

In this section, we examine the **central limit theorem.** Its application to the sampling distribution of the sample mean, introduced in the previous section, allows us to use the normal probability distribution to create confidence intervals for the population mean (described in Chapter 8) and perform tests of hypothesis (described in Chapter 9). The central limit theorem states that, for large random samples, the shape of the sampling distribution of the sample mean is close to a normal probability distribution. The approximation is more accurate for large samples than for small samples. This is one of the most useful conclusions in statistics. We can make statements about the distribution of the sample mean with absolutely no information about the shape of the original distribution from which the sample is taken. In other words, the central limit theorem is true for all distributions.

A formal statement of the central limit theorem follows.

> **CENTRAL LIMIT THEOREM** If all samples of a specified size are selected from any population, the sampling distribution of the sample mean is approximately a normal distribution. This approximation improves with larger samples.

If the population follows a normal probability distribution, then for any sample size the sampling distribution of the sample mean will also be normal. If the population distribution is symmetrical (but not normal), you will see the normal shape of the distribution of the sample mean emerge with samples as small as 10. On the other hand, if you start with a distribution that is skewed or has thick tails, it may require samples of 30 or more to observe the normality feature. This concept is summarized in Chart 7–2. Observe the convergence to a normal distribution regardless of the shape of the population distribution. Most statisticians consider a sample of 30 or more to be large enough for the central limit theorem to be employed.

The idea that the distribution of the sample means from a population that is not normal will converge to normality is also illustrated in Charts 7–3, 7–4, and 7–5. We will discuss this example in more detail shortly, but Chart 7–3 is a graph of a discrete probability distribution that is positively skewed. There are many possible samples of 5 that might be selected from this population. Suppose we randomly select 25 samples of 5 each and compute the mean of each sample. These results are shown in Chart 7–4. Notice that the shape of the distribution of the sample mean has changed from the original population even though we selected only 25 of the many possible samples. To put it another way, we selected 25 random samples of 5 each from a population that is positively skewed and found the distribution of the sample mean has changed from the shape of the population. As we take larger samples, that is, $n = 20$ instead of $n = 5$, we will find the distribution of the sample mean will approach the normal distribution. Chart 7–5 shows the results of 25 random samples of 20 observations each from the same population. Observe the clear trend toward the normal probability distribution. This is the point of the central limit theorem. The following example will underscore this condition.

EXAMPLE

Ed Spence began his sprocket business 20 years ago. The business has grown over the years and now employs 40 people. Spence Sprockets, Inc. faces some major decisions regarding health care for these employees. Before making a final decision on what health care plan to purchase, Ed decides to form a committee of five representative employees. The committee will be asked to study the health care issue carefully and make a recommendation as to what plan best fits the employees' needs. Ed feels the views of newer employees toward health care may differ from those of more experienced employees. If Ed randomly selects this committee, what can he expect in terms of the mean years with Spence Sprockets for those on the committee? How does the shape of the distribution of years of experience of all employees (the popu-

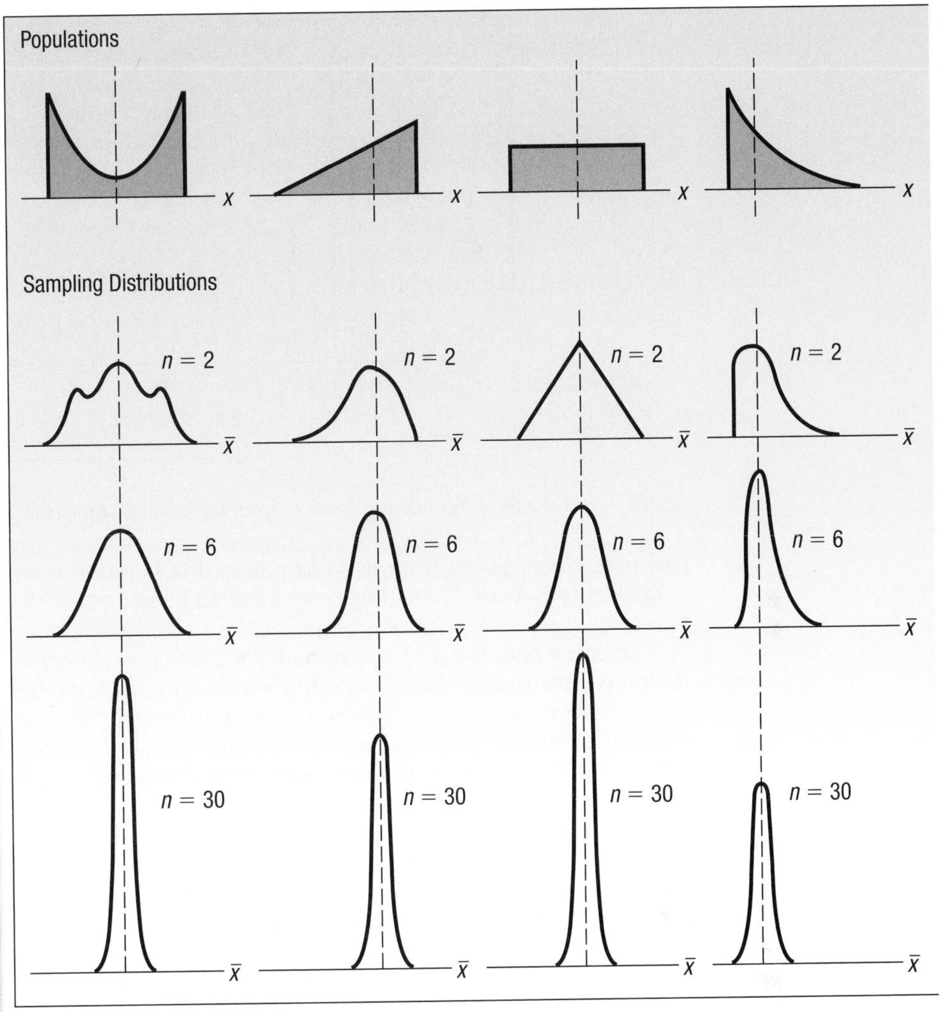

CHART 7–2 Results of the Central Limit Theorem for Several Populations

lation) compare with the shape of the sampling distribution of the mean? The lengths of service (rounded to the nearest year) of the 40 employees currently on the Spence Sprockets, Inc. payroll are as follows.

11	4	18	2	1	2	0	2	2	4
3	4	1	2	2	3	3	19	8	3
7	1	0	2	7	0	4	5	1	14
16	8	9	1	1	2	5	10	2	3

SOLUTION

Chart 7–3 shows the distribution of the years of experience for the population of 40 current employees. This distribution of lengths of service is positively skewed because there are a few employees who have worked at Spence Sprockets for a longer period of time. Specifically, six employees have been with the company 10 years or more.

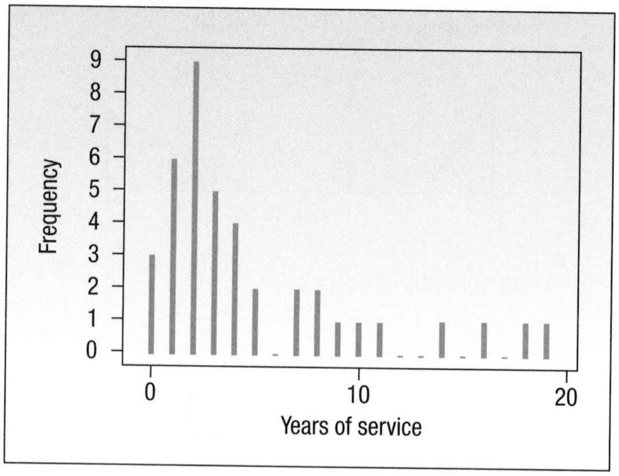

CHART 7–3 Length of Service for Spence Sprockets, Inc. Employees

However, because the business has grown, the number of employees has increased in the last few years. Of the 40 employees, 18 have been with the company two years or less.

Let's consider the first of Ed Spence's problems. He would like to form a committee of five employees to look into the health care question and suggest what type of health care coverage would be most appropriate for the majority of workers. How should he select the committee? If he selects the committee randomly, what might he expect in terms of mean length of service for those on the committee?

To begin, Ed writes the length of service for each of the 40 employees on pieces of paper and puts them into an old baseball hat. Next, he shuffles the pieces of paper around and randomly selects five slips of paper. The lengths of service for these five employees are 1, 9, 0, 19, and 14 years. Thus, the mean length of service for these five sampled employees is 8.60 years. How does that compare with the population mean? At this point Ed does not know the population mean, but the number of employees in the population is only 40, so he decides to calculate the mean length of service for *all* his employees. It is 4.8 years, found by adding the lengths of service for *all* the employees and dividing the total by 40.

$$\mu = \frac{11 + 4 + 18 + \cdots + 2 + 3}{40} = 4.80$$

The difference between the sample mean ($\bar{X}$) and the population mean (μ) is called **sampling error.** In other words, the difference of 3.80 years between the population mean of 4.80 and the sample mean of 8.60 is the sampling error. It is due to chance. Thus, if Ed selected these five employees to constitute the committee, their mean length of service would be larger than the population mean.

What would happen if Ed put the five pieces of paper back into the baseball hat and selected another sample? Would you expect the mean of this second sample to be exactly the same as the previous one? Suppose he selects another sample of five employees and finds the lengths of service in this sample to be 7, 4, 4, 1, and 3. This sample mean is 3.80 years. The result of selecting 25 samples of five employees each is shown in Table 7–5 and Chart 7–4. There are actually 658,008 possible samples of 5 from the population of 40 employees, found by the combination formula (4–9) for 40 things taken 5 at a time. Notice the difference in the shape of the population and the distribution of these sample means. The population of the lengths of service for

TABLE 7–5 Twenty-five Random Samples of Five Employees

Sample I.D.	Sample Data					Sample Mean
A	1	9	0	19	14	8.6
B	7	4	4	1	3	3.8
C	8	19	8	2	1	7.6
D	4	18	2	0	11	7.0
E	4	2	4	7	18	7.0
F	1	2	0	3	2	1.6
G	2	3	2	0	2	1.8
H	11	2	9	2	4	5.6
I	9	0	4	2	7	4.4
J	1	1	1	11	1	3.0
K	2	0	0	10	2	2.8
L	0	2	3	2	16	4.6
M	2	3	1	1	1	1.6
N	3	7	3	4	3	4.0
O	1	2	3	1	4	2.2
P	19	0	1	3	8	6.2
Q	5	1	7	14	9	7.2
R	5	4	2	3	4	3.6
S	14	5	2	2	5	5.6
T	2	1	1	4	7	3.0
U	3	7	1	2	1	2.8
V	0	1	5	1	2	1.8
W	0	3	19	4	2	5.6
X	4	2	3	4	0	2.6
Y	1	1	2	3	2	1.8

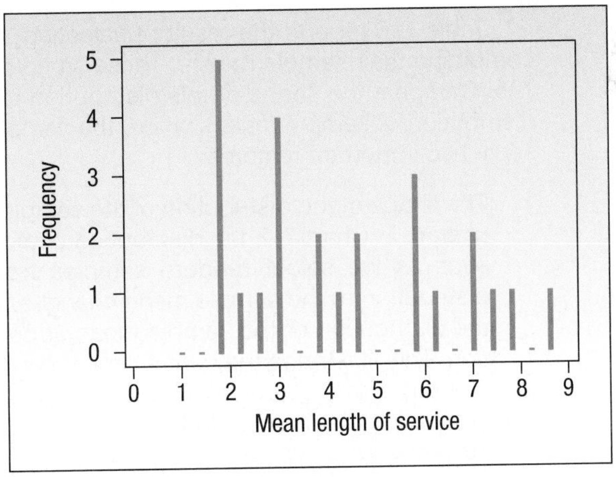

CHART 7–4 Histogram of Mean Lengths of Service for 25 Samples of Five Employees

employees (Chart 7–3) is positively skewed, but the distribution of these 25 sample means does not reflect the same positive skew. There is also a difference in the range of the sample means versus the range of the population. The population ranged from 0 to 19 years, whereas the sample means range from 1.6 to 8.6 years.

TABLE 7–6 Random Samples and Sample Means of 25 Samples of 20 Spence Sprocket, Inc. Employees

Sample I.D.	Sample Data (Length of Service)																				Sample Mean
A	3	8	3	0	2	1	2	3	11	5	1	3	4	2	7	1	1	2	4	16	3.95
B	2	3	8	2	1	5	2	0	3	1	0	7	1	4	3	11	4	4	3	1	3.25
C	14	5	0	3	2	14	11	9	2	2	1	2	19	1	0	1	4	2	19	8	5.95
D	9	2	1	1	4	10	0	8	4	3	2	1	0	8	1	14	5	10	1	3	4.35
E	18	1	2	2	4	3	2	8	2	1	0	19	4	19	0	1	4	0	3	14	5.35
F	10	4	4	18	3	3	1	0	0	2	2	4	7	10	2	0	3	4	2	1	4.00
G	5	7	11	8	11	18	1	1	16	2	2	16	2	3	2	16	2	2	2	4	6.55
H	3	0	2	0	5	4	5	3	8	3	2	5	1	1	2	9	8	3	16	5	4.25
I	0	0	18	2	1	7	4	1	3	0	3	2	11	7	2	8	5	1	2	3	4.00
J	2	7	2	4	1	3	3	2	5	10	0	1	1	2	9	3	2	19	3	2	4.05
K	7	4	5	3	3	0	18	2	0	4	2	7	2	7	4	2	10	1	1	2	4.20
L	0	3	10	5	9	2	1	4	1	2	1	8	18	1	4	3	3	2	0	4	4.05
M	4	1	2	1	7	3	9	14	8	19	4	4	1	2	0	3	1	2	1	2	4.40
N	3	16	1	2	4	4	4	2	1	5	2	3	5	3	4	7	16	1	11	1	4.75
O	2	19	2	0	2	2	16	2	3	11	9	2	8	0	8	2	7	3	2	2	5.10
P	2	18	16	5	2	2	19	0	1	2	11	4	2	2	1	4	2	0	4	3	5.00
Q	3	2	3	11	10	1	1	5	19	16	7	10	3	1	1	1	2	2	3	1	5.10
R	2	3	1	2	7	4	3	19	9	2	2	1	1	2	2	2	1	8	0	2	3.65
S	2	14	19	1	19	2	8	4	2	2	14	2	8	16	4	7	2	9	0	7	7.10
T	0	1	3	3	2	2	3	1	1	0	3	2	3	5	2	10	14	4	2	0	3.05
U	1	0	1	2	16	1	1	2	5	1	4	1	2	2	2	2	2	8	9	3	3.25
V	1	9	4	4	2	8	7	1	14	18	1	5	10	11	19	0	3	7	2	11	6.85
W	8	1	9	19	3	19	0	5	2	1	5	3	3	4	1	5	3	1	8	7	5.35
X	4	2	0	3	1	16	1	11	3	3	2	18	2	0	1	5	0	7	2	5	4.30
Y	1	2	1	2	0	2	7	2	4	8	19	2	5	3	3	0	19	2	1	18	5.05

Table 7–6 reports the result of selecting 25 samples of 20 employees each and computing their sample means. These sample means are shown graphically in Chart 7–5. Compare the shape of this distribution to the population (Chart 7–3) and to the distribution of sample means where the sample is $n = 5$ (Chart 7–4). You should observe two important features:

1. The shape of the distribution of the sample mean is different from that of the population. In Chart 7–3 the distribution of all employees is positively skewed. However, as we select random samples from this population, the shape of the distribution of the sample mean changes. As we increase the size of the sample, the distribution of the sample mean approaches the normal probability distribution. This illustrates the central limit theorem.
2. There is less dispersion in the sampling distribution of sample mean than in the population distribution. In the population the lengths of service ranged from 0 to 19 years. When we selected samples of 5, the sample means ranged from 1.6 to 8.6 years, and when we selected samples of 20, the means ranged from 3.05 to 7.10 years.

We can also compare the mean of the sample means to the population mean. The mean of the 25 samples reported in Table 7–6 is 4.676 years.

$$\mu_{\bar{X}} = \frac{3.95 + 3.25 + \cdots + 4.30 + 5.05}{25} = 4.676$$

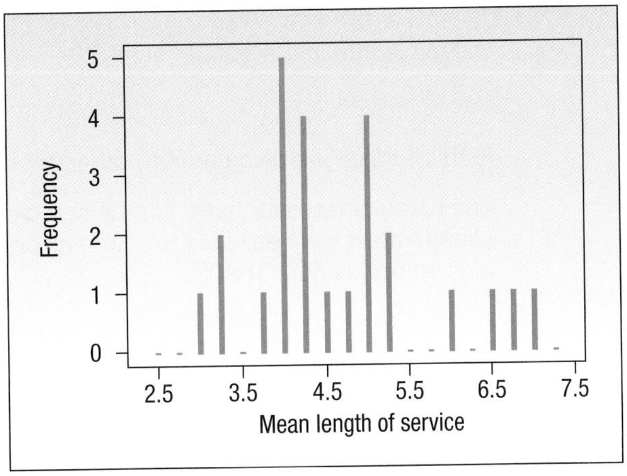

CHART 7–5 Histogram of Mean Lengths of Service for 25 Samples of 20 Employees

We use the symbol $\mu_{\bar{X}}$ to identify the mean of the distribution of the sample mean. The subscript reminds us that the distribution is of the sample mean. It is read "mu sub X bar." We observe that the mean of the sample means, 4.676 years, is very close to the population mean of 4.80.

What should we conclude from this example? The central limit theorem indicates that, regardless of the shape of the population distribution, the sampling distribution of the sample mean will move toward the normal probability distribution. The larger the number of observations in each sample, the stronger the convergence. The Spence Sprockets, Inc. example shows how the central limit theorem works. We began with a positively skewed population (Chart 7–3). Next, we selected 25 random samples of 5 observations, computed the mean of each sample, and finally organized these 25 sample means into a graph (Chart 7–4). We observe a change in the shape of the sampling distribution of sample mean from that of the population. The movement is from a positively skewed distribution to a distribution that has the shape of the normal probability distribution.

To further illustrate the effects of the central limit theorem, we increased the number of observations in each sample from 5 to 20. We selected 25 samples of 20 observations each and calculated the mean of each sample. Finally, we organized these sample means into a graph (Chart 7–5). The shape of the histogram in Chart 7–5 is clearly moving toward the normal probability distribution.

The central limit theorem itself (reread the definition on page 232) does not say anything about the dispersion of the sampling distribution of sample mean or about the comparison of the mean of the sampling distribution of sample mean to the mean of the population. However, in our Example we did observe that there was less dispersion in the distribution of the sample mean than in the population distribution by noting the difference in the range in the population and the range of the sample means. We observe that the mean of the sample means is close to the mean of the population. It can be demonstrated that the mean of the sampling distribution is the population mean and if the standard deviation in the population is σ, the standard deviation of the sample means is $\sigma/\sqrt{n}$, where n is the number of observations in each sample. We refer to $\sigma/\sqrt{n}$ as the **standard error of the mean.** Its longer name is actually the *standard deviation of the sampling distribution of the sample mean.*

STANDARD ERROR OF THE MEAN	$\sigma_{\bar{X}} = \frac{\sigma}{\sqrt{n}}$	[7–1]

In this section we also came to other important conclusions.

1. The mean of the distribution of the sample mean will be *exactly* equal to the population mean if we are able to select all possible samples of a particular size from a given population. That is:

$$\mu = \mu_{\bar{X}}$$

   Even if we do not select all samples, we can expect the mean of the distribution of the sample mean to be close to the population mean.
2. There will be less dispersion in the sampling distribution of the sample mean than in the population. If the standard deviation of the population is σ, the standard deviation of the distribution of the sample mean is $\sigma/\sqrt{n}$. Note that when we increase the size of the sample the standard error of the mean decreases.

Self-Review 7–4

Refer to the Spence Sprockets, Inc. data on page 233. Select 10 random samples of 5 employees each. Use the methods described earlier in the chapter and the Table of Random Numbers (Appendix E) to find the employees to include in the sample. Compute the mean of each sample and plot the sample means on a chart similar to Chart 7–3.

Exercises

11. Appendix E is a table of random numbers. Hence, each digit from 0 to 9 has the same likelihood of occurrence.

a. Draw a graph showing the population distribution. What is the population mean?

b. Below are the first 10 rows of five digits from Appendix E. Assume that these are 10 random samples of five values each. Determine the mean of each sample and plot the means on a chart similar to Chart 7–3. Compare the mean of the sampling distribution of the sample mean with the population mean.

0	2	7	1	1
9	4	8	7	3
5	4	9	2	1
7	7	6	4	0
6	1	5	4	5
1	7	1	4	7
1	3	7	4	8
8	7	4	5	5
0	8	9	9	9
7	8	8	0	4

12. The Scrapper Elevator Company has 20 sales representatives who sell their product throughout the United States and Canada. The number of units sold by each representative is listed below. Assume these sales figures to be the population values.

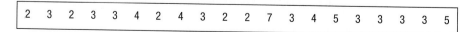

2	3	2	3	3	4	2	4	3	2	2	7	3	4	5	3	3	3	3	5

a. Draw a graph showing the population distribution.
b. Compute the mean of the population.
c. Select five random samples of 5 each. Compute the mean of each sample. Use the methods described in this chapter and Appendix E to determine the items to be included in the sample.
d. Compare the mean of the sampling distribution of the sample mean to the population mean. Would you expect the two values to be about the same?
e. Draw a histogram of the sample means. Do you notice a difference in the shape of the distribution of sample means compared to the population distribution?

Using the Sampling Distribution of the Sample Mean

The previous discussion is important because most business decisions are made on the basis of sampling results. Here are some examples.

1. The Arm and Hammer Company wants to ensure that each container of their laundry detergent actually contains 100 fluid ounces, as indicated on the label. Historical summaries from the filling process indicate the mean amount per container is 100 fluid ounces and the standard deviation is 2 fluid ounces. The quality technician in her 10 A.M. check of 40 containers finds the mean amount per container is 99.8 fluid ounces. Should the technician shut down the filling operation or is the sampling error reasonably small?
2. The A. C. Nielsen Company provides information to companies advertising on television. Prior research indicates that adult Americans watch an average of 6.0 hours per day of television. The standard deviation is 1.5 hours. For a sample of 50 adults in the Greater Boston area, would it be likely that we could randomly select a sample and find that they watch an average of 6.5 hours of television per day?
3. The Haughton Elevator Company wishes to develop specifications for the number of people who can ride in a new oversized elevator. Suppose the mean weight for an adult is 160 pounds and the standard deviation is 15 pounds. However, the distribution of weights does not follow the normal probability distribution. It is positively skewed. What is the likelihood that for a sample of 30 adults their mean weight is 170 pounds or more?

The sampling distribution will follow the normal under these conditions.

In each of these situations we have a population about which we have some information. We take a sample from that population and wish to conclude whether the sampling error, that is, the difference between the population parameter and the sample statistic, is due to chance.

Using ideas discussed in the previous section, we can compute the probability that a sample mean will fall within a certain range. We know that the sampling distribution of the sample mean will follow the normal probability distribution under two conditions:

1. When the samples are taken from populations known to follow the normal distribution. In this case the size of the sample is not a factor.
2. When the shape of the population distribution is not known or the shape is known to be nonnormal, but our sample contains at least 30 observations.

We can use formula 6–1, from Chapter 6, to convert any normal distribution to the standard normal distribution. We also refer to this as a z value. Then we can use the standard normal table, Appendix D, to find the probability of selecting an observation that would fall within a specific range. The formula for finding a z value is:

$$z = \frac{X - \mu}{\sigma}$$

In this formula X is the observed value of the *random variable,* μ is the population mean, and σ the population standard deviation.

However, most business decisions refer to a sample—not just one observation. So we are interested in the distribution of $\overline{X}$, the sample mean, instead of X, the value of one observation. That is the first change we make in formula 6–1. The second is that we use the standard error of the mean of n observations instead of the population standard deviation. That is, we use $\sigma/\sqrt{n}$ in the denominator rather than σ. Therefore, to find the likelihood of a sample mean with a specified range, we first use the following formula to find the corresponding z value. Then we use Appendix D to locate the probability.

FINDING THE *z* VALUE OF $\overline{X}$ WHEN THE POPULATION STANDARD DEVIATION IS KNOWN

$$z = \frac{\overline{X} - \mu}{\sigma/\sqrt{n}} \quad \textbf{[7–2]}$$

The following example will show the application.

EXAMPLE

The Quality Assurance Department for Cola, Inc. maintains records regarding the amount of cola in their "Jumbo" bottle. The actual amount of cola in each bottle is critical, but varies a small amount from one bottle to the next. Cola, Inc. does not wish to underfill the bottles, because they will have a problem with truth in labeling. On the other hand, they cannot overfill each bottle, because they would be giving cola away, hence reducing their profits. Their records indicate that the amount of cola follows the normal probability distribution. The mean amount per bottle is 31.2 ounces and the population standard deviation is 0.4 ounces. At 8 A.M. today the quality technician randomly selected 16 bottles from the filling line. The mean amount of cola contained in the bottles is 31.38 ounces. Is this an unlikely result? Is it likely the process is putting too much soda in the bottles? To put it another way, is the sampling error of 0.18 ounces unusual?

SOLUTION

We can use the results of the previous section to find the likelihood that we could select a sample of 16 (n) bottles from a normal population with a mean of 31.2 (μ) ounces and a population standard deviation of 0.4 (σ) ounces and find the sample mean to be 31.38 ($\overline{X}$). We use formula 7–2 to find the value of z.

$$z = \frac{\overline{X} - \mu}{\sigma/\sqrt{n}} = \frac{31.38 - 31.20}{0.4/\sqrt{16}} = 1.80$$

The numerator of this equation, $\overline{X} - \mu = 31.38 - 31.20 = .18$, is the sampling error. The denominator, $\sigma/\sqrt{n} = 0.40/\sqrt{16} = 0.1$, is the standard error of the sampling distribution of the sample mean. So the z values express the sampling error in standard units, in other words, the standard error.

Next, we compute the likelihood of a z value greater than 1.80. In Appendix D locate the probability corresponding to a z value of 1.80. It is .4641. The likelihood of a z value greater than 1.80 is .0359, found by $.5000 - .4641$.

What do we conclude? It is unlikely, less than a 4 percent chance, we could select a sample of 16 observations from a normal population with a mean of 31.2 ounces and a population standard deviation of 0.4 ounces and find the sample mean equal to or greater than 31.38 ounces. The process is putting too much cola in the bottles. The quality technician should see the production supervisor about reducing the amount of soda in each bottle. This information is summarized in Chart 7–6.

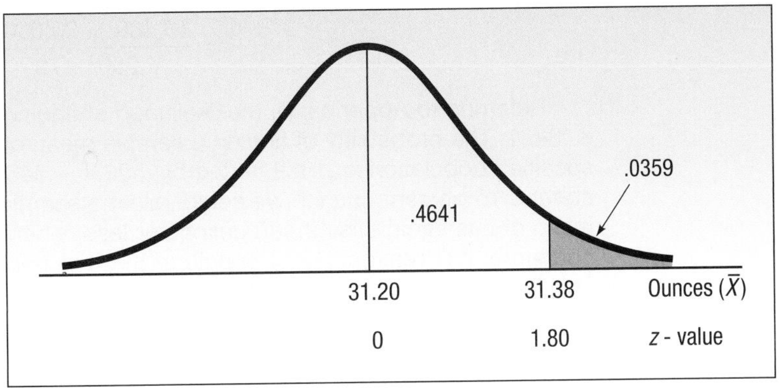

CHART 7–6 Sampling Distribution of the Mean Amount of Cola in a Jumbo Bottle

Self-Review 7–5 Refer to the Cola, Inc. information. Compute the probability that a sample of 16 Jumbo bottles would have a mean of 31.08 ounces or more.

There are many sampling situations in business for which we wish to make a statement about the population, but we do not have much knowledge about the population. Here the power of the central limit theorem helps. We know that, for any shape of the population distribution, if we select a sufficiently large sample, the sampling distribution of the sample mean will follow the normal distribution. Statistical theory has shown that samples of at least 30 are sufficiently large to allow us to assume that the sampling distribution follows the normal distribution.

Often we do not know the value of the population standard deviation, σ. Again, if the sample is at least 30, we estimate the population standard deviation with the sample standard deviation. When we use s to replace σ, the new formula for finding the value of z is:

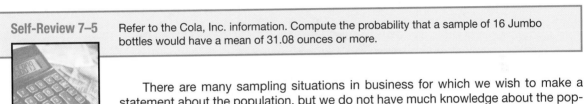

FINDING THE z VALUE OF $\overline{X}$ WHEN THE POPULATION STANDARD DEVIATION IS UNKNOWN

$$z = \frac{\overline{X} - \mu}{s/\sqrt{n}} \qquad \textbf{[7–3]}$$

EXAMPLE

The Metropolitan New York Gas Station Dealers' Association estimates that the mean number of gallons of gasoline sold per day at a gas station is 20,000. The shape of this distribution is unknown. A sample of 70 dealers yesterday revealed the mean number of gallons sold was 19,480. The standard deviation of the sample of 70 dealers was 4,250 gallons. Is the assertion that the population mean is 20,000 gallons reasonable? What is the likelihood of finding a sample with the given statistics from the proposed population? What assumptions do you need to make?

SOLUTION

We are unsure of the shape of the population of gallons sold. However, the sample is sufficiently large to allow us to assume that the sampling distribution of the sample mean follows the normal distribution. The central limit theorem provides the necessary statistical theory. Again, because of the size of the sample, we can substitute the sample standard deviation for the population standard deviation. Formula 7–3 is appropriate for finding the z value.

$$z = \frac{\overline{X} - \mu}{s/\sqrt{n}} = \frac{19{,}480 - 20{,}000}{4{,}250/\sqrt{70}} = -1.02$$

Referring to Appendix D, the likelihood of finding a z value between 0 and -1.02 is .3461. The probability of finding a sample mean of 19,480 gallons or less from the specified population is .1539, found by $.5000 - .3461$. To put it another way, there is about a 15 percent chance we could select a sample of 70 gas stations and find the mean of this sample is 19,480 gallons or less, when the population mean is 20,000. Therefore, it is reasonable to conclude that the population mean is 20,000 gallons. This information is summarized in Chart 7–7.

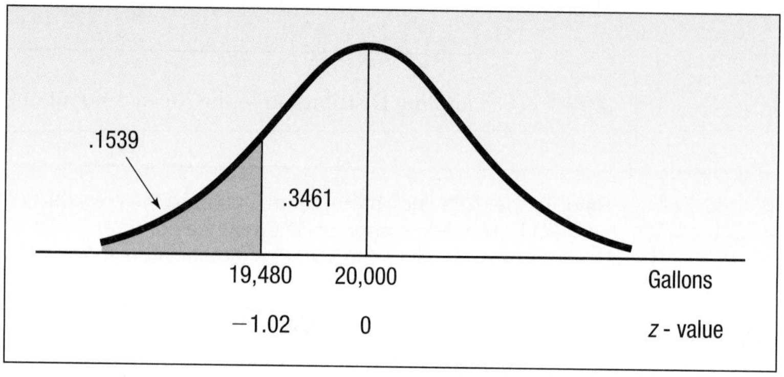

CHART 7–7 Sampling Distribution for the Sample Mean of the Number of Gallons Sold per Day

Self-Review 7–6

The mean annual salary for purchasing agents in the Atlanta, Georgia, region is \$61,000. What is the likelihood that we could select a sample of 50 purchasing agents with a mean salary of \$61,500 or more? The standard deviation of the sample is \$2,000 per year.

Exercises

13. A normal population has a mean of 60 and a standard deviation of 12. You select a random sample of 9. Compute the probability the sample mean is:
- **a.** Greater than 63.
- **b.** Less than 56.
- **c.** Between 56 and 63.

14. A population of unknown shape has a mean of 75. You select a sample of 40. The standard deviation of the sample is 5. Compute the probability the sample mean is:
- **a.** Less than 74.
- **b.** Between 74 and 76.
- **c.** Between 76 and 77.
- **d.** Greater than 77.

15. The mean rent for a one-bedroom apartment in Southern California is \$1,200 per month. The distribution of the monthly costs does not follow the normal distribution. In fact, it is positively skewed. What is the probability of selecting a sample of 50 one-bedroom apartments and finding the mean to be at least \$950 per month? The standard deviation of the sample is \$250.

16. According to an IRS study, it takes an average of 330 minutes for taxpayers to prepare, copy, and mail a 1040 tax form. A consumer watchdog agency selects a random sample of 40 taxpayers and finds the standard deviation of the time to prepare, copy, and mail form 1040 is 80 minutes.

a. What assumption or assumptions do you need to make about the shape of the population?
b. What is the standard error of the mean in this example?
c. What is the likelihood the sample mean is greater than 320 minutes?
d. What is the likelihood the sample mean is between 320 and 350 minutes?
e. What is the likelihood the sample mean is greater than 350 minutes?

Chapter Outline

I. There are many reasons for sampling a population.
  A. The results of a sample may adequately estimate the value of the population parameter, thus saving time and money.
  B. It may be too time consuming to contact all members of the population.
  C. It may be impossible to check or locate all the members of the population.
  D. The cost of studying all the items in the population may be prohibitive.
  E. Often testing destroys the sampled item and it cannot be returned to the population.
II. In an unbiased sample all members of the population have a chance of being selected for the sample. There are several probability sampling methods.
  A. In a simple random sample all members of the population have the same chance of being selected for the sample.
  B. In a systematic sample a random starting point is selected, and then every *k*th item thereafter is selected for the sample.
  C. In a stratified sample the population is divided into several groups, called strata, and then a random sample is selected from each stratum.
  D. In cluster sampling the population is divided into primary units, then samples are drawn from the primary units.
III. The sampling error is the difference between a population parameter and a sample statistic.
IV. The sampling distribution of the sample mean is a probability distribution of all possible sample means of a given size from a population.
  A. For a given sample size, the mean of all possible sample means selected from a population is equal to the population mean.
  B. There is less variation in the distribution of the sample mean than in the population distribution.
    1. The standard error of the mean measures the variation in the sampling distribution of the sample mean.
      a. If we know the population standard deviation, the standard error is

$$\sigma_{\overline{X}} = \frac{\sigma}{\sqrt{n}} \qquad \textbf{[7–1]}$$

      b. If we do not know the population standard deviation, the standard error is estimated by

$$s_{\overline{X}} = \frac{s}{\sqrt{n}}$$

  C. If the population follows the normal distribution, the sampling distribution of the sample mean will also follow the normal distribution for samples of any size.
    1. Assume the population standard deviation is known.
    2. To determine the probability that a sample mean falls in a particular region, use the following formula.

$$z = \frac{\overline{X} - \mu}{\sigma/\sqrt{n}} \qquad \textbf{[7–2]}$$

  D. If the population is not normally distributed but the sample is of at least 30 observations, the sampling distribution of the sample mean is approximately normal.
    1. Assume the population standard deviation is not known.
    2. To determine the probability that a sample mean falls in a particular region, use the normal distribution and the following standardizing formula:

$$z = \frac{\overline{X} - \mu}{s/\sqrt{n}} \qquad \textbf{[7–3]}$$

Pronunciation Key

Symbol	Meaning	Pronunciation
$\mu_{\bar{X}}$	Mean of the sampling distribution of the sample mean	*mu sub X bar*
$\sigma_{\bar{X}}$	Population standard error of the sample mean	*sigma sub X bar*
$s_{\bar{X}}$	Estimate of the standard error of the sample mean	*s sub X bar*

Chapter Exercises

17. The retail stores located in the North Towne Square Mall are:

00	Elder-Beerman	09	Lion Store	18	County Seat
01	Montgomery Ward	10	Bootleggers	19	Kid Mart
02	Deb Shop	11	Formal Man	20	Lerner
03	Frederick's of Hollywood	12	Leather Ltd.	21	Coach House Gifts
04	Petries	13	B Dalton Bookseller	22	Spence Gifts
05	Easy Dreams	14	Pat's Hallmark	23	CPI Photo Finish
06	Summit Stationers	15	Things Remembered	24	Regis Hairstylists
07	E. B. Brown Opticians	16	Pearle Vision Express		
08	Kay-Bee Toy & Hobby	17	Dollar Tree		

a. If the following random numbers are selected, which retail stores should be contacted for a survey? 11, 65, 86, 62, 06, 10, 12, 77, and 04

b. Select a random sample of four retail stores. Use Appendix E.

c. A systematic sampling procedure is to be used. The first store is to be contacted and then every third store. Which stores will be contacted?

18. Medical Mutual Insurance is investigating the cost of a routine office visit to family-practice physicians in the Rochester, New York, area. The following is a list of family-practice physicians in the region. Physicians are to be randomly selected and contacted regarding their charges. The 39 physicians have been coded from 00 to 38. Also noted is whether they are in practice by themselves (S), have a partner (P), or are in a group practice (G).

Number	Physician	Type of Practice	Number	Physician	Type of Practice
00	R. E. Scherbarth, M.D.	S	20	Gregory Yost, M.D.	P
01	Crystal R. Goveia, M.D.	P	21	J. Christian Zona, M.D.	P
02	Mark D. Hillard, M.D.	P	22	Larry Johnson, M.D.	P
03	Jeanine S. Huttner, M.D.	P	23	Sanford Kimmel, M.D.	P
04	Francis Aona, M.D.	P	24	Harry Mayhew, M.D.	S
05	Janet Arrowsmith, M.D.	P	25	Leroy Rodgers, M.D.	S
06	David DeFrance, M.D.	S	26	Thomas Tafelski, M.D.	S
07	Judith Furlong, M.D.	S	27	Mark Zilkoski, M.D.	G
08	Leslie Jackson, M.D.	G	28	Ken Bertka, M.D.	G
09	Paul Langenkamp, M.D.	S	29	Mark DeMichiei, M.D.	G
10	Philip Lepkowski, M.D.	S	30	John Eggert, M.D.	P
11	Wendy Martin, M.D.	S	31	Jeanne Fiorito, M.D.	P
12	Denny Mauricio, M.D.	P	32	Michael Fitzpatrick, M.D.	P
13	Hasmukh Parmar, M.D.	P	33	Charles Holt, D.O.	P
14	Ricardo Pena, M.D.	P	34	Richard Koby, M.D.	P
15	David Reames, M.D.	P	35	John Meier, M.D.	P
16	Ronald Reynolds, M.D.	G	36	Douglas Smucker, M.D.	S
17	Mark Steinmetz, M.D.	G	37	David Weldy, M.D.	P
18	Geza Torok, M.D.	S	38	Cheryl Zaborowski, M.D.	P
19	Mark Young, M.D.	P			

a. The random numbers obtained from Appendix E are: 31, 94, 43, 36, 03, 24, 17, and 09. Which physicians should be contacted?
b. Select a random sample of four physicians using the random numbers of Appendix E.
c. A sample is to consist of every fifth physician. The number 04 is selected as the starting point. Which physicians will be contacted?
d. A sample is to consist of two physicians in solo practice (S), two in partnership (P), and one in group practice (G). Select a sample accordingly. Explain your procedure.

19. What is sampling error? Could the value of the sampling error be zero? If it were zero, what would this mean?

20. List the reasons for sampling. Give an example of each reason for sampling.

21. The commercial banks in the Southwest are to be surveyed. Some of them are very large, with assets of more than $500 million; others are medium-sized, with assets between $100 million and $500 million; and the remaining banks have assets of less than $100 million. Explain how you would select a sample of these banks.

22. Plastic Products is concerned about the inside diameter of the plastic PVC pipe it produces. A machine extrudes the pipe, which is then cut into 10-foot lengths. About 720 pipes are produced per machine during a two-hour period. How would you go about taking a sample from the two-hour production period?

23. A study of motel facilities in Rock Hill, South Carolina showed there are 25 facilities. The city's convention and visitors bureau is studying the number of rooms at each facility. The results are as follows:

90	72	75	60	75	72	84	72	88	74	105	115	68	74	80	64	104	82	48	58	60	80	48	58	100

a. Using a table of random numbers (Appendix E), select a random sample of five motels from this population.
b. Obtain a systematic sample by selecting a random starting point among the first five motels and then select every fifth motel.
c. Suppose the last five motels are "cut-rate" motels. Describe how you would select a random sample of three regular motels and two cut-rate motels.

24. As a part of their customer-service program, United Airlines randomly selected ten passengers from today's 9 A.M. Chicago–Tampa flight. Each sampled passenger is to be interviewed in depth regarding airport facilities, service, food, and so on. To identify the sample, each passenger was given a number as they boarded the aircraft. The numbers started with 001 and ended with 250.
a. Select 10 usable numbers at random using Appendix E.
b. The sample of 10 could have been chosen using a systematic sample. Choose the first number using Appendix E, and then list the numbers to be interviewed.
c. Evaluate the two methods by giving the advantages and possible disadvantages.
d. In what other way could a random sample be selected from the 250 passengers?

25. Suppose your statistics instructor gave six examinations during the semester. You received the following grades (percent correct): 79, 64, 84, 82, 92, and 77. Instead of averaging the six scores, the instructor indicated he would randomly select two grades and report that grade to the student records office.
a. How many different samples of two test grades are possible?
b. List all possible samples of size two and compute the mean of each.
c. Compute the mean of the sample means and compare it to the population mean.
d. If you were a student, would you like this arrangement? Would the result be different from dropping the lowest score? Write a brief report.

26. At the downtown office of First National Bank there are five tellers. Last week the tellers made the following number of errors each: 2, 3, 5, 3, and 5.
a. How many different samples of 2 tellers are possible?
b. List all possible samples of size 2 and compute the mean of each.
c. Compute the mean of the sample means and compare it to the population mean.

27. The quality control department employs five technicians during the day shift. Listed below is the number of times each technician instructed the production foreman to shut down the manufacturing process last week.

Technician	Shutdowns
Taylor	4
Hurley	3
Fowler	5
Rousche	3
Telatko	2

a. How many different samples of two technicians are possible from this population?
b. List all possible samples of two observations each and compute the mean of each sample.
c. Compare the mean of the sample means with the population mean.
d. Compare the shape of the population distribution with the shape of the distribution of the sample means.

28. The Appliance Center has six sales representatives at their North Jacksonville outlet. Listed below is the number of refrigerators sold by each last month.

Sales Representative	Number Sold
Zina Craft	54
Woon Junge	50
Ernie DeBrul	52
Jan Niles	48
Molly Camp	50
Rachel Myak	52

a. How many samples of size two are possible?
b. Select all possible samples of two and compute the mean number sold.
c. Organize the sample means into a frequency distribution.
d. What is the mean of the population? What is the mean of the sample means?
e. What is the shape of the population distribution?
f. What is the shape of the distribution of the sample mean?

29. The Sony Corporation produces an AM/FM Walkman that requires two AA batteries. The mean life of these batteries in this product is 35.0 hours. The distribution of the battery lives closely follows the normal probability distribution with a standard deviation of 5.5 hours. As a part of their testing program Sony tests samples of 25 batteries.
a. What can you say about the shape of the distribution of sample mean?
b. What is the standard error of the distribution of the sample mean?
c. What fraction of the samples will have a mean useful life of more than 36 hours?
d. What fraction of the sample will have a mean useful life greater than 34.5 hours?
e. What fraction of the sample will have a mean useful life between 34.5 and 36.0 hours?

30. CRA CDs, Inc. wants the mean lengths of the "cuts" on a CD to be 135 seconds (2 minutes and 15 seconds). This will allow the disk jockeys to have plenty of time for commercials within each 10-minute segment. Assume the distribution of the length of the cuts follows the normal distribution with a standard deviation of 8 seconds. Suppose we select a sample of 16 cuts from various CDs sold by CRA CDs, Inc.
a. What can we say about the shape of the distribution of the sample mean?
b. What is the standard error of the mean?
c. What percent of the sample means will be greater than 140 minutes?
d. What percent of the sample means will be greater than 128 minutes?
e. What percent of the sample means will be greater than 128 but less than 140 minutes?

31. Recent studies indicate that the typical 50-year-old woman spends $350 per year for personal-care products. The distribution of the amounts spent is positively skewed. We select a random sample of 40 women. The mean amount spent for those sampled is $335, and the standard deviation of the sample is $45. What is the likelihood of finding a sample mean this large or larger from the specified population?

32. Information from the American Institute of Insurance indicates the mean amount of life insurance per household in the United States is $110,000. This distribution is positively skewed. The standard deviation of the population is not known.
    a. A random sample of 50 households revealed a mean of $112,000 and a standard deviation of $40,000. What is the standard error of the mean?
    b. Suppose that you selected 50 samples of households. What is the expected shape of the distribution of the sample mean?
    c. What is the likelihood of selecting a sample with a mean of at least $112,000?
    d. What is the likelihood of selecting a sample with a mean of more than $100,000?
    e. Find the likelihood of selecting a sample with a mean of more than $100,000 but less than $112,000.
33. The mean age at which men in the United States marry for the first time is 24.8 years. The shape and the standard deviation of the population are both unknown. For a random sample of 60 men, what is the likelihood that the age at which they were married for the first time is less than 25.1 years? Assume that the standard deviation of the sample is 2.5 years.
34. A recent study by the Greater Los Angeles Taxi Drivers Association showed that the mean fare charged for service from Hermosa Beach to the Los Angeles International Airport is $18.00 and the standard deviation is $3.50. We select a sample of 15 fares.
    a. What is the likelihood that the sample mean is between $17.00 and $20.00?
    b. What must you assume to make the above calculation?
35. The Crossett Trucking Company claims that the mean weight of their delivery trucks when they are fully loaded is 6,000 pounds and the standard deviation is 150 pounds. Assume that the population follows the normal distribution. Forty trucks are randomly selected and weighed. Within what limits will 95 percent of the sample means occur?
36. The mean amount purchased by each customer at Churchill's Grocery Store is $23.50. The population is positively skewed and the standard deviation is not known. For a sample of 50 customers, answer the following questions.
    a. If the standard deviation of the sample is $5.00, what is the likelihood the sample mean is at least $25.00?
    b. Again, assume the sample standard deviation is $5.00. What is the likelihood the sample mean is greater than $22.50 but less than $25.00?
    c. Again, assume the sample standard deviation is $5.00. Within what limits will 90 percent of the sample means occur?
37. The mean SAT score for Division I student-athletes is 947 with a standard deviation of 205. If you select a random sample of 60 of these students, what is the probability the mean is below 900?
38. Suppose we roll a fair die two times.
    a. How many different samples are there?
    b. List each of the possible samples and compute the mean.
    c. On a chart similar to Chart 7–1, compare the distribution of sample means with the distribution of the population.
    d. Compute the mean and the standard deviation of each distribution and compare them.
39. The following table lists the most recent data available on per capita personal income (in dollars) for each of the 50 states.
    a. You wish to select a sample of eight from this list. The selected random numbers are 45, 15, 81, 09, 39, 43, 90, 26, 06, 45, 01, and 42. Which states are included in the sample?
    b. You wish to use a systematic sample of every sixth item and the digit 02 is chosen as the starting point. Which states are included?
    c. A sample of one state from each region is to be selected. Describe how you would perform the sampling process in detail. That is, show the random numbers you selected and the corresponding states that are included in your sample.

Number	State	Income	Number	State	Income	Number	State	Income
	New England			**Plains**			**Southwest**	
01	Connecticut	$39,300	17	Iowa	25,615	36	Arizona	25,189
02	Maine	24,603	18	Kansas	26,824	37	New Mexico	21,853
03	Massachusetts	35,551	19	Minnesota	30,793	38	Oklahoma	22,953
04	New Hampshire	31,114	20	Missouri	26,376	39	Texas	26,858
05	Rhode Island	29,377	21	Nebraska	27,049		**Rocky Mountain**	
06	Vermont	25,889	22	North Dakota	23,313	40	Colorado	31,546
	Mideast		23	South Dakota	25,045	41	Idaho	22,835
07	Delaware	30,778		**Southeast**		42	Montana	22,019
08	Maryland	32,465	24	Alabama	22,987	43	Utah	23,288
09	New Jersey	35,551	25	Arkansas	22,244	44	Wyoming	26,396
10	New York	33,890	26	Florida	27,780		**Far West**	
11	Pennsylvania	28,605	27	Georgia	27,340	45	Alaska	28,577
	Great Lakes		28	Kentucky	23,237	46	California	29,910
12	Illinois	31,145	29	Louisiana	22,847	47	Hawaii	27,544
13	Indiana	26,143	30	Mississippi	20,688	48	Nevada	31,022
14	Michigan	28,113	31	North Carolina	26,003	49	Oregon	27,023
15	Ohio	27,152	32	South Carolina	23,545	50	Washington	30,392
16	Wisconsin	27,390	33	Tennessee	25,574			
			34	Virginia	29,789			
			35	West Virginia	20,921			

exercises.com

WWW

40. You need to find the "typical" or mean annual dividend per share for large banks. You decide to sample six banks listed in the Standard and Poors 500. These banks and their trading symbol follow.

Bank	Symbol	Bank	Symbol
AmSouth Bancorporation	ASO	National City Corp.	NCC
Bank of America Corp.	BAC	Northern Trust Corp.	NTRS
Bank of New York	BK	PNC Financial Services Group	PNC
Bank One Corp.	ONE	Regions Financial Corp.	RGBK
BB&T Corporation	BBT	SouthTrust Corp.	SOTR
Charter One Financial	CF	SunTrust Banks	STI
Comerica Inc.	CMA	Synovus Financial	SNV
Fifth Third Bancorp	FITB	Union Planters	UPC
FleetBoston Financial Corp.	FBF	U.S. Bancorp	USB
Golden West Financial	GDW	Wachovia Corp.	WB
Huntington Bancshares	HBAN	Washington Mutual, Inc.	WM
KeyCorp	KEY	Wells Fargo & Co. (New)	WFC
Mellon Financial Corp.	MEL	Zions Bancorp	ZION

a. After numbering the banks from 01 to 26, which banks would be included in a sample if the random numbers were 14, 08, 24, 25, 05, 44, 02, and 22? Go to the following website: http://www.quicken.com. Enter the trading symbol for each of the sampled banks and record the Annual Dividend per share (Annual div/shr). Determine the mean annual dividend per share for the sample of banks.

b. Which banks are selected if you use a systematic sample of every fourth bank starting with the random number 03?

41. There are several websites that will output the 30 stocks that make up the Dow Jones Industrial Average (DJIA). One site is www.dbc.com/dbcfiles/dowt.html. Compute the mean of the 30 stocks.

a. Use a random number table, such as Appendix E, to select a random sample of five companies that make up the DJIA. Compute the sample mean. Compare the sample mean to the population mean. What did you find? What did you expect to find?

b. You should not expect to find that the mean of these 30 stocks is the same as the current DJIA. Go to the Dow Jones website at www.dj.com and read the reasons.

Computer Data Exercises

42. Refer to the Real Estate data, which reports information on the homes sold in the Venice, Florida, area last year.

a. Compute the mean and the standard deviation of the distribution of the selling prices for the homes. Assume this to be the population. Develop a histogram of the data. Would it seem reasonable from this histogram to conclude that the population of selling prices follows the normal distribution?

b. Let's assume a normal population. Select a sample of 10 homes. Compute the mean and the standard deviation of the sample. Determine the likelihood of finding a sample mean this large or larger from the population.

43. Refer to the CIA data, which reports demographic and economic information on 46 countries. Select a random sample of 10 countries. For this sample calculate the mean GDP/capita. Repeat this sampling and calculation process five more times. Then find the mean and standard deviation of your six sample means.

a. How do this mean and standard deviation compare with the mean and standard deviation of the original "population" of 46 countries?

b. Make a histogram of the six means and discuss whether the distribution is normal.

c. Suppose the population distribution is normal. For the first sample mean you computed, determine the likelihood of finding a sample mean this large or larger from the population.

Chapter 7 Answers to Self-Review

7–1 **(a)** Students selected are Price, Detley, and Molter.
(b) Answers will vary.
(c) Skip it and move to the next random number.

7–2 The students selected are Berry, Francis, Kopp, Poteau, and Swetye.

7–3 **(a)** 10, found by:

$$_5C_2 = \frac{5!}{2!(5-2)!}$$

(b)

	Service	Sample Mean
Snow, Tolson	20, 22	21
Snow, Kraft	20, 26	23
Snow, Irwin	20, 24	22
Snow, Jones	20, 28	24
Tolson, Kraft	22, 26	24
Tolson, Irwin	22, 24	23
Tolson, Jones	22, 28	25
Kraft, Irwin	26, 24	25
Kraft, Jones	26, 28	27
Irwin, Jones	24, 28	26

(c)

Mean	Number	Probability
21	1	.10
22	1	.10
23	2	.20
24	2	.20
25	2	.20
26	1	.10
27	1	.10
	10	1.00

(d) Identical: population mean, μ, is 24, and mean of sample means, $\mu_{\bar{X}}$, is also 24.
(e) Sample means range from 21 to 27. Population values go from 20 to 28.
(f) Nonnormal.
(g) Yes.

7–4 The answers will vary. Here is one solution.

	Sample Number 1	2	3	4	5	6	7	8	9	10
	8	2	2	19	3	4	0	4	1	2
	19	1	14	9	2	5	8	2	14	4
	8	3	4	2	4	4	1	14	4	1
	0	3	2	3	1	2	16	1	2	3
	2	1	7	2	19	18	18	16	3	7
Total	37	10	29	35	29	33	43	37	24	17
$\bar{X}$	7.4	2	5.8	7.0	5.8	6.6	8.6	7.4	4.8	3.4

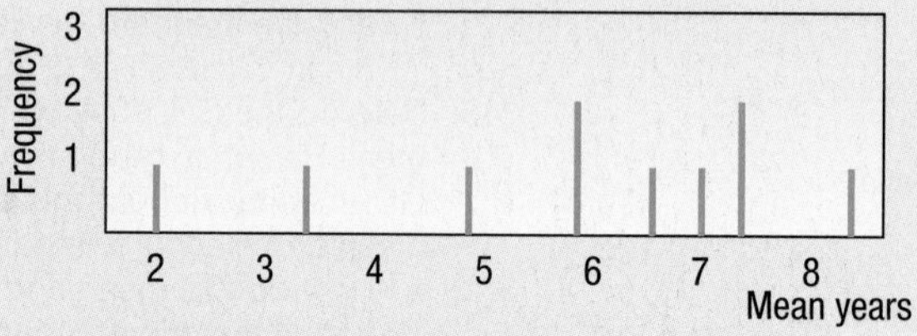

7–5 $z = \frac{31.08 - 31.20}{0.4/\sqrt{16}} = -1.20$

The probability that z is greater than -1.20 is $.5000 + .3849 = .8849$.

7–6 $z = \frac{\$61{,}500 - \$61{,}000}{\$2{,}000/\sqrt{50}} = 1.77$

The probability that z is greater than 1.77 is $.5000 - .4616 = .0394$.

8

Estimation and Confidence Intervals

GOALS

When you have completed this chapter you will be able to:

1. **Define a *point estimate.***
2. **Define *level of confidence.***
3. **Construct a confidence interval for the population mean when the population standard deviation is known.**
4. **Construct a confidence interval for a population mean when the population standard deviation is unknown.**
5. **Construct a confidence interval for a population proportion.**
6. **Determine the sample size for attribute and variable sampling.**

The American Restaurant Association collected information on the number of meals eaten outside the home per week by young married couples. A survey of 60 couples showed the sample mean number of meals eaten outside the home was 2.76 meals per week, with a standard deviation of 0.75 meals per week. Construct a 97% confidence interval for the population mean. (See Goal 3 and Exercise 36.)

Introduction

The previous chapter introduces sampling. We stress that frequently it is not feasible to inspect the entire population. The reasons include: it may be too time consuming to examine the entire population, testing may destroy the product, the cost to examine the entire population is too large, or the results of a sample may be adequate. We introduce several methods of sampling. Simple random sampling is the most widely used method. With this type of sampling, each member of the population has the same chance of being selected to be a part of the sample.

Chapter 7 assumes information about the population, such as the mean, the standard deviation, or the shape of the population. In most business situations, such information is not available. In fact, the purpose of sampling may be to estimate some of these values. So, for example, you select a sample from a population and use the mean of the sample to estimate the mean of the population.

This chapter considers several important aspects of sampling. We begin by studying point estimates. A point estimate is a particular value used to estimate a population value. For example, select a sample of 50 junior executives and ask the number of hours they worked last week. Compute the mean of this sample of 50 and use the value of the sample mean as a point estimate of the unknown population mean. However, a point estimate is a single value. A more informative estimate is to present a range of values in which we expect the population parameter to occur. Such a range of values is called a confidence interval.

Frequently in business we need to determine the size of a sample. How many voters should a polling organization contact to forecast the election outcome? How many products do we need to examine to ensure our quality level? This chapter also develops a strategy for determining the size of the sample.

Point Estimates and Confidence Intervals

Known σ or a Large Sample

In the previous chapter, the data on the length of service of Spence Sprockets employees, presented in the example on page 232, is a population because we present the length of service for all 40 employees. In that case we can easily compute the population mean. We have all the data and the population is not too large. In most situations, however, the population is large or it is difficult to identify all members of the population, so we need to rely on sample information. In other words, we do not know the population parameter and we therefore want to estimate the value from a sample statistic. Consider the following business situations.

1. Tourism is a major source of income for many Caribbean countries, such as Barbados. Suppose the Bureau of Tourism for Barbados wants an estimate of the mean amount spent by tourists visiting the country. It would not be feasible to contact each tourist. So 500 tourists are randomly selected as they depart the country and asked in detail about their spending while visiting the island. The mean amount spent by the sample of 500 tourists is an estimate of the unknown population parameter. That is, we let $\overline{X}$, the sample mean, serve as an estimate of μ, the population mean.
2. Centex Home Builders, Inc. builds quality homes in the southeastern region of the United States. One of the major concerns of new buyers is the date on which the home will be completed. In recent times Centex has been telling customers, "Your home will be completed 45 working days from the date we begin installing drywall." The customer relations department at Centex wishes to compare this

pledge with recent experience. A sample of 50 homes completed this year revealed the mean number of working days from the start of drywall to the completion of the home was 46.7 days. Is it reasonable to conclude that the population mean is still 45 days and that the difference between the sample mean (46.7 days) and the proposed population mean is sampling error?

3. Recent medical studies indicate that exercise is an important part of a person's overall health. The director of human resources at OCF, a large glass manufacturer, wants an estimate of the number of hours per week employees spend exercising. A sample of 70 employees reveals the mean number of hours of exercise last week is 3.3. The sample mean of 3.3 hours is an estimate of the unknown population mean, the mean hours of exercise for all employees.

A point estimate is a single statistic used to estimate a population parameter. Suppose Best Buy, Inc. wants to estimate the mean age of buyers of stereo equipment. They select a random sample of 50 recent purchasers, determine the age of each purchaser, and compute the mean age of the buyers in the sample. The mean of this sample is a point estimate of the mean of the population.

POINT ESTIMATE The statistic, computed from sample information, which is used to estimate the population parameter.

The sample mean, $\overline{X}$, is a point estimate of the population mean, μ; *p,* a sample proportion, is a point estimate of π, the population proportion; and *s,* the sample standard deviation, is a point estimate of σ, the population standard deviation.

A point estimate, however, tells only part of the story. While we expect the point estimate to be close to the population parameter, we would like to measure how close it really is. A confidence interval serves this purpose.

CONFIDENCE INTERVAL An interval that estimates a population parameter within a range of possible values at a specified probability. The specified probability is called the *level of confidence.*

For example, we estimate the mean yearly income for construction workers in the New York–New Jersey area is \$65,000. The range of this estimate might be from \$61,000 to \$69,000. We can describe how confident we are that the population parameter is in the interval by making a probability statement. We might say, for instance, that we are 90 percent sure that the mean yearly income of construction workers in the New York–New Jersey area is between \$61,000 and \$69,000.

The information developed about the shape of a sampling distribution of the sample mean, that is, the sampling distribution of $\overline{X}$, allows us to locate an interval that has a specified probability of containing the population mean, μ. For reasonably large samples, the results of the central limit theorem allow us to state the following:

1. Ninety-five percent of the sample means selected from a population will be within 1.96 standard deviations of the population mean μ.
2. Ninety-nine percent of the sample means will lie within 2.58 standard deviations of the population mean.

The standard deviation discussed here is the standard deviation of the sampling distribution of the sample mean. It is usually called the "standard error." Intervals computed in this fashion are called the **95 percent confidence interval** and the

99 percent confidence interval. How are the values of 1.96 and 2.58 obtained? The *95 percent* and *99 percent* refer to the percent of the time that similarly constructed intervals would include the parameter being estimated. The *95 percent,* for example, refers to the middle 95 percent of the observations. Therefore, the remaining 5 percent are equally divided between the two tails.

See the following diagram.

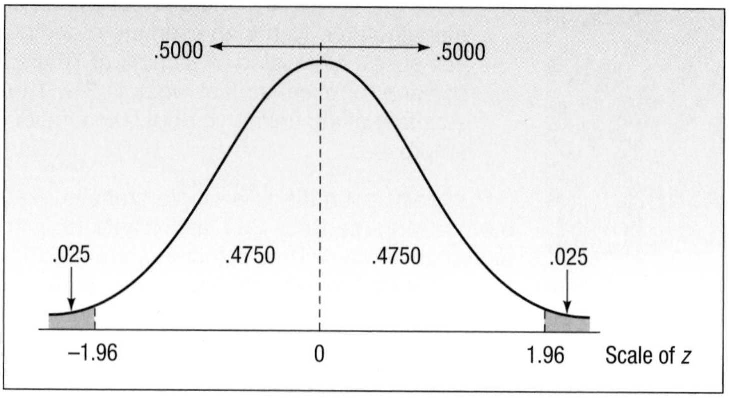

The central limit theorem, discussed in the previous chapter, states that the sampling distribution of the sample means is approximately normal when the sample contains at least 30 observations. Therefore, we can use Appendix D to find the appropriate z values. Locate .4750 in the body of the table. Read the corresponding row and column values. The value is 1.96. Thus, the probability of finding a z value between 0 and 1.96 is .4750. Likewise, the probability of being in the interval between -1.96 and 0 is also .4750. When we combine these two, the probability of being in the interval -1.96 to 1.96 is .9500. On the next page is a portion of Appendix D. The z value for the 90 percent level of confidence is determined in a similar manner. It is 1.65. For a 99 percent level of confidence the z value is 2.58.

How do you compute a 95 percent confidence interval? Assume your research involves the annual starting salary of business school graduates. You compute the sample mean to be $27,000 and the standard deviation (that is, the "standard error") of the sample mean to be $200. Assume your sample contains at least 30 observations. The 95 percent confidence interval is between $26,608 and $27,392, found by $27,000 ± 1.96($200). If 100 samples of the same size were selected from the population of interest and the corresponding 100 confidence intervals determined, you expect to find the population mean in 95 of the 100 confidence intervals.

In the above example, the standard error of the sampling distribution of the sample mean was $200. This is, of course, the standard error of the sample means, discussed in the previous chapter. See formula 7–1 for the case when the population standard deviation is available. In most applied situations, the population standard deviation is not available, so we use the sample estimate of the population standard deviation as follows:

$$s_{\overline{X}} = \frac{s}{\sqrt{n}}$$

The size of the standard error is affected by two values. The first is the standard deviation. If the standard deviation is large, then the standard error will also be large. However, the standard error is also affected by the sample size. As the sample size is increased, the standard error decreases, indicating that there is less variability in the sampling distribution of the sample mean. This conclusion is logical, because an estimate made with a large sample should be more precise than one made from a small sample.

z	0.00	0.01	0.02	0.03	0.04	0.05	0.06	0.07	0.08	0.09
0.0	0.0000	0.0040	0.0080	0.0120	0.0160	0.0199	0.0239	0.0279	0.0319	0.0359
0.1	0.0398	0.0438	0.0478	0.0517	0.0557	0.0596	0.0636	0.0675	0.0714	0.0753
0.2	0.0793	0.0832	0.0871	0.0910	0.0948	0.0987	0.1026	0.1064	0.1103	0.1141
0.3	0.1179	0.1217	0.1255	0.1293	0.1331	0.1368	0.1406	0.1443	0.1480	0.1517
0.4	0.1554	0.1591	0.1628	0.1664	0.1700	0.1736	0.1772	0.1808	0.1844	0.1879
0.5	0.1915	0.1950	0.1985	0.2019	0.2054	0.2088	0.2123	0.2157	0.2190	0.2224
0.6	0.2257	0.2291	0.2324	0.2357	0.2389	0.2422	0.2454	0.2486	0.2517	0.2549
0.7	0.2580	0.2611	0.2642	0.2673	0.2704	0.2734	0.2764	0.2794	0.2823	0.2852
0.8	02881	0.2910	0.2939	0.2967	0.2995	0.3023	0.3051	0.3078	0.3106	0.3133
0.9	0.3159	0.3186	0.3212	0.3238	0.3264	0.3289	0.3315	0.3340	0.3365	0.3389
1.0	0.3413	0.3438	0.3461	0.3485	0.3508	0.3531	0.3554	0.3577	0.3599	0.3621
1.1	0.3643	0.3665	0.3686	0.3708	0.3729	0.3749	0.3770	0.3790	0.3810	0.3830
1.2	0.3849	0.3869	0.3888	0.3907	0.3925	0.3944	0.3962	0.3980	0.3997	0.4015
1.3	0.4032	0.4049	0.4066	0.4082	0.4099	0.4115	0.4131	0.4147	0.4162	0.4177
1.4	0.4192	0.4207	0.4222	0.4236	0.4251	0.4265	0.4279	0.4292	0.4306	0.4319
1.5	0.4332	0.4345	0.4357	0.4370	0.4382	0.4394	0.4406	0.4418	0.4429	0.4441
1.6	0.4452	0.4463	0.4474	0.4484	0.4495	0.4505	0.4515	0.4525	0.4535	0.4545
1.7	0.4554	0.4564	0.4573	0.4582	0.4591	0.4599	0.4608	0.4616	0.4625	0.4633
1.8	0.4641	0.4649	0.4656	0.4664	0.4671	0.4678	0.4686	0.4693	0.4699	0.4706
1.9	0.4713	0.4719	0.4726	0.4732	0.4738	0.4744	0.4750	0.4756	0.4761	0.4767
2.0	0.4772	0.4778	0.4783	0.4788	0.4793	0.4798	0.4803	0.4808	0.4812	0.4817
2.1	0.4821	0.4826	0.4830	0.4834	0.4838	0.4842	0.4846	0.4850	0.4854	0.4857
2.2	0.4861	0.4864	0.4868	0.4871	0.4875	0.4878	0.4881	0.4884	0.4887	0.4890
2.3	0.4893	0.4896	0.4898	0.4901	0.4904	0.4906	0.4909	0.4911	0.4913	0.4916
2.4	0.4918	0.4920	0.4922	0.4925	0.4927	0.4929	0.4931	0.4932	0.4934	0.4936

As we state in Chapter 7, when the sample size, *n,* is at least 30, it is generally agreed that the central limit theorem will ensure that the sample mean follows the normal distribution. This is an important consideration. If the sample mean is normally distributed, we can use the standard normal distribution, that is, *z*, in our calculations.

The 95 percent confidence interval is computed as follows, when the number of observations in the sample is at least 30.

$$\overline{X} \pm 1.96 \frac{s}{\sqrt{n}}$$

Similarly, the 99 percent confidence interval is computed as follows. Again we assume that the sample size is at least 30.

$$\overline{X} \pm 2.58 \frac{s}{\sqrt{n}}$$

As we discussed earlier, the values 1.96 and 2.58 are the *z* values corresponding to the middle 95 percent and the middle 99 percent of the observations, respectively.

We can use other levels of confidence. For those cases the value of *z* changes accordingly. In general, a confidence interval for the population mean is computed by:

CONFIDENCE INTERVAL FOR THE POPULATION MEAN ($n \geq 30$)

$$\overline{X} \pm z \frac{s}{\sqrt{n}} \qquad \textbf{[8–1]}$$

where z depends on the level of confidence. Thus, for a 92 percent level of confidence, the value of z in formula 8–1 is 1.75. The value of z is from Appendix D. This table is based on half the normal distribution, so .9200/2 = .4600. The closest value in the body of the table is .4599 and the corresponding z value is 1.75.

Frequently, we also use the 90 percent level of confidence. In this case, we want the area between 0 and z to be .4500, found by .9000/2. To find the z value for this level of confidence, move down the left column of Appendix D to 1.6 and then over to the columns headed 0.04 and 0.05. The area corresponding to a z value of 1.64 is .4495, and for 1.65 it is .4505. To be conservative, we use 1.65. Try looking up the following levels of confidence and check your answers with the corresponding z values given on the right.

Confidence Level	Nearest Probability	z Value
80 percent	.3997	1.28
94 percent	.4699	1.88
96 percent	.4798	2.05

The following example shows the details for calculating a confidence interval and interpreting the result.

EXAMPLE

The American Management Association wishes to have information on the mean income of middle managers in the retail industry. A random sample of 256 managers reveals a sample mean of $45,420. The standard deviation of this sample is $2,050. The association would like answers to the following questions:

1. What is the population mean?
2. What is a reasonable range of values for the population mean?
3. What do these results mean?

SOLUTION

Generally, distributions of salary and income are positively skewed, because a few individuals earn considerably more than others, thus skewing the distribution in the positive direction. Fortunately, the central limit theorem stipulates that if we select a large sample the distribution of the sample means will follow the normal distribution, regardless of the shape of the population. So, in this instance, with a sample of 256 middle managers (remember, at least 30 is usually large enough), we can be assured that the sampling distribution will follow the normal distribution.

Another issue is that the population standard deviation is not known. Again, it is sound practice to use the sample standard deviation when we have a large sample. Now to answer the questions posed in the example.

1. **What is the population mean?** In this case, we do not know. We do know the sample mean is $45,420. Hence, our best estimate of the unknown population value is the corresponding sample statistic. Thus the sample mean of $45,420 is a *point estimate* of the unknown population mean.
2. **What is a reasonable range of values for the population mean?** The Association decides to use the 95 percent level of confidence. To determine the corresponding confidence interval we use formula 8–1.

$$\overline{X} \pm z\frac{s}{\sqrt{n}} = \$45{,}420 \pm 1.96\frac{\$2{,}050}{\sqrt{256}} = \$45{,}420 \pm \$251$$

The usual practice is to round these endpoints to \$45,169 and \$45,671. These endpoints are called the *confidence limits*. The degree of confidence or the *level of confidence* is 95 percent and the confidence interval is from \$45,169 to \$45,671.

3. **What do these results mean?** Suppose we select many samples of 256 managers, perhaps several hundred. For each sample, we compute the mean and the standard deviation and then construct a 95 percent confidence interval, such as we did in the previous section. We could expect about 95 percent of these confidence intervals to contain the *population* mean. About 5 percent of the intervals would not contain the population mean annual income, which is μ. However, a particular confidence interval either contains the population parameter or it does not. The following diagram shows the results of selecting different samples from the population of middle managers in the retail industry, computing the mean and standard deviation of each, and then, using formula 8–1, determining a 95 percent confidence interval for the population mean. Note that not all intervals include the population mean. Both the endpoints of the fifth sample are less than the population mean. We attribute this to sampling error, and it is the risk we assume when we select the level of confidence.

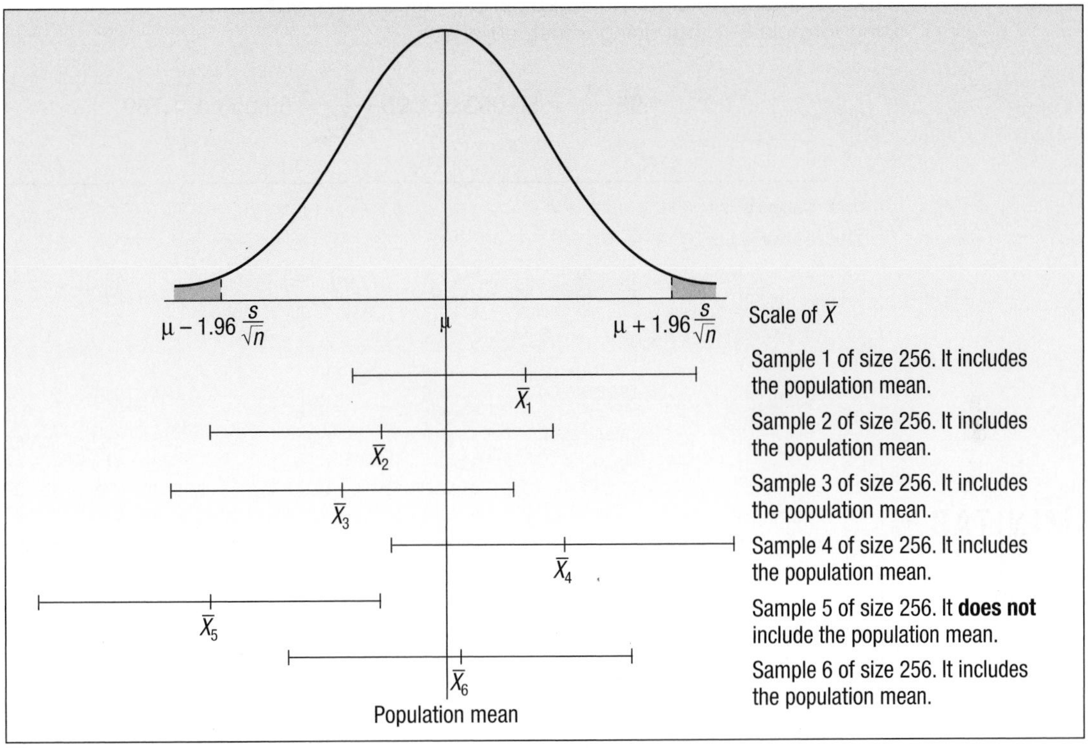
$\mu - 1.96 \frac{s}{\sqrt{n}}$
μ
$\mu + 1.96 \frac{s}{\sqrt{n}}$
Scale of $\bar{X}$
$\bar{X}_1$
$\bar{X}_2$
$\bar{X}_3$
$\bar{X}_4$
$\bar{X}_5$
$\bar{X}_6$
Population mean
Sample 1 of size 256. It includes the population mean.
Sample 2 of size 256. It includes the population mean.
Sample 3 of size 256. It includes the population mean.
Sample 4 of size 256. It includes the population mean.
Sample 5 of size 256. It **does not** include the population mean.
Sample 6 of size 256. It includes the population mean.

A Computer Simulation

With the aid of a computer, we can randomly select samples from a population, quickly compute the confidence interval, and show how confidence intervals usually, but not always, include the population parameter. The following Example will help to explain.

EXAMPLE

From many years in the automobile leasing business, Town Bank knows the mean distance driven on a four-year lease is 50,000 miles and the standard deviation is 5,000. Suppose, using the MINITAB statistical software system, we want to find what proportion of the 95 percent confidence intervals will include the population mean. To make the calculations easier to understand, we'll conduct the study in thousands of miles, instead of miles. We select 60 random samples of size 30 from a population with a mean of 50 and a standard deviation of 5.

SOLUTION

The results of 60 random samples of 30 are in the table below. Of the 60 confidence intervals with a 95 percent confidence level, 2, or 3.33 percent, did not include the population mean of 50. The intervals (C3 and C59) that do *not* include the population mean are highlighted. The value of 3.33 percent is close to the estimate that 5 percent of the intervals will not include the population mean, and the 58 of 60, or 96.67 percent, is close to 95 percent.

To explain the first confidence interval in more detail: MINITAB began by selecting a random sample of 30 observations from a population with a mean of 50 and a standard deviation of 5. The mean of these 30 observations is 50.053. The endpoints of the confidence interval are 48.264 and 51.842. These endpoints are determined by using formula 8–1, but using σ instead of s.

$$\bar{X} \pm 1.96 \frac{\sigma}{\sqrt{n}} = 50.053 \pm 1.96 \frac{5}{\sqrt{30}} = 50.053 \pm 1.789$$

One-Sample Z:

The assumed sigma = 5

Variable	N	Mean	StDev	SE Mean	95.0% CI
C1	30	50.053	5.002	0.913	(48.264, 51.842)
C2	30	49.025	4.450	0.913	(47.236, 50.815)
C3	30	52.023	5.918	0.913	(50.234, 53.812)
C4	30	50.056	3.364	0.913	(48.267, 51.845)
C5	30	49.737	4.784	0.913	(47.948, 51.526)
C6	30	51.074	5.495	0.913	(49.285, 52.863)
C7	30	50.040	5.930	0.913	(48.251, 51.829)
C8	30	48.910	3.645	0.913	(47.121, 50.699)
C9	30	51.033	4.918	0.913	(49.244, 52.822)
C10	30	50.692	4.571	0.913	(48.903, 52.482)
C11	30	49.853	4.525	0.913	(48.064, 51.642)
C12	30	50.286	3.422	0.913	(48.497, 52.076)
C13	30	50.257	4.317	0.913	(48.468, 52.046)
C14	30	49.605	4.994	0.913	(47.816, 51.394)
C15	30	51.474	5.497	0.913	(49.685, 53.264)
C16	30	48.930	5.317	0.913	(47.141, 50.719)
C17	30	49.870	4.847	0.913	(48.081, 51.659)
C18	30	50.739	6.224	0.913	(48.950, 52.528)
C19	30	50.979	5.520	0.913	(49.190, 52.768)
C20	30	48.848	4.130	0.913	(47.059, 50.638)
C21	30	49.481	4.056	0.913	(47.692, 51.270)
C22	30	49.183	5.409	0.913	(47.394, 50.973)
C23	30	50.084	4.522	0.913	(48.294, 51.873)
C24	30	50.866	5.142	0.913	(49.077, 52.655)
C25	30	48.768	5.582	0.913	(46.979, 50.557)
C26	30	50.904	6.052	0.913	(49.115, 52.694)
C27	30	49.481	5.535	0.913	(47.691, 51.270)
C28	30	50.949	5.916	0.913	(49.160, 52.739)
C29	30	49.106	4.641	0.913	(47.317, 50.895)
C30	30	49.994	5.853	0.913	(48.205, 51.784)

Variable	N	Mean	StDev	SE Mean	95.0% CI
C31	30	49.601	5.064	0.913	(47.811, 51.390)
C32	30	51.494	5.597	0.913	(49.705, 53.284)
C33	30	50.460	4.393	0.913	(48.671, 52.249)
C34	30	50.378	4.075	0.913	(48.589, 52.167)
C35	30	49.808	4.155	0.913	(48.019, 51.597)
C36	30	49.934	5.012	0.913	(48.145, 51.723)
C37	30	50.017	4.082	0.913	(48.228, 51.806)
C38	30	50.074	3.631	0.913	(48.285, 51.863)
C39	30	48.656	4.833	0.913	(46.867, 50.445)
C40	30	50.568	3.855	0.913	(48.779, 52.357)
C41	30	50.916	3.775	0.913	(49.127, 52.705)
C42	30	49.104	4.321	0.913	(47.315, 50.893)
C43	30	50.308	5.467	0.913	(48.519, 52.097)
C44	30	49.034	4.405	0.913	(47.245, 50.823)
C45	30	50.399	4.729	0.913	(48.610, 52.188)
C46	30	49.634	3.996	0.913	(47.845, 51.424)
C47	30	50.479	4.881	0.913	(48.689, 52.268)
C48	30	50.529	5.173	0.913	(48.740, 52.318)
C49	30	51.577	5.822	0.913	(49.787, 53.366)
C50	30	50.403	4.893	0.913	(48.614, 52.192)
C51	30	49.717	5.218	0.913	(47.927, 51.506)
C52	30	49.796	5.327	0.913	(48.007, 51.585)
C53	30	50.549	4.680	0.913	(48.760, 52.338)
C54	30	50.200	5.840	0.913	(48.410, 51.989)
C55	30	49.138	5.074	0.913	(47.349, 50.928)
C56	30	49.667	3.843	0.913	(47.878, 51.456)
C57	30	49.603	5.614	0.913	(47.814, 51.392)
C58	30	49.441	5.702	0.913	(47.652, 51.230)
C59	30	47.873	4.685	0.913	(46.084, 49.662)
C60	30	51.087	5.162	0.913	(49.297, 52.876)

Self-Review 8–1

The mean daily sales are $2,000 for a sample of 40 days at a fast-food restaurant. The standard deviation of the sample is $300.

(a) What is the estimated mean daily sales of the population? What is this estimate called?
(b) What is the 99 percent confidence interval?
(c) Interpret your findings.

Exercises

1. A sample of 49 observations is taken from a normal population. The sample mean is 55, and the sample standard deviation is 10. Determine the 99 percent confidence interval for the population mean.
2. A sample of 81 observations is taken from a normal population. The sample mean is 40, and the sample standard deviation is 5. Determine the 95 percent confidence interval for the population mean.
3. A sample of 10 observations is selected from a normal population for which the population standard deviation is known to be 5. The sample mean is 20.
   - **a.** Determine the standard error of the mean.
   - **b.** Explain why we can use formula 8–1 to determine the 95 percent confidence interval even though the sample is less than 30.
   - **c.** Determine the 95 percent confidence interval for the population mean.
4. Suppose you want an 85 percent confidence level. What value would you use to multiply the standard error of the mean?

5. A research firm conducted a survey to determine the mean amount steady smokers spend on cigarettes during a week. A sample of 49 steady smokers revealed that $\overline{X} = \$20$ and $s = \$5$.

a. What is the point estimate of the population mean? Explain what it indicates.

b. Using the 95 percent level of confidence, determine the confidence interval for μ. Explain what it indicates.

6. Refer to the previous exercise. Suppose that 64 smokers (instead of 49) were sampled. Assume the sample mean and the sample standard deviation remained the same (\$20 and \$5, respectively).

a. What is the 95 percent confidence interval estimate of μ?

b. Explain why this confidence interval is narrower than the one determined in the previous exercise.

7. Bob Nale is the owner of Nale's Texaco GasTown. Bob would like to estimate the mean number of gallons of gasoline sold to his customers. From his records, he selects a random sample of 60 sales and finds the mean number of gallons sold is 8.60 and the standard deviation is 2.30 gallons.

a. What is the point estimate of the population mean?

b. Develop a 99 percent confidence interval for the population mean.

c. Interpret the meaning of part b.

8. Dr. Patton is a Professor of English. Recently he counted the number of misspelled words in a group of student essays. For his class of 40 students, the mean number of misspelled words was 6.05 and the standard deviation 2.44 per essay. Construct a 95 percent confidence interval for the mean number of misspelled words in the population of students.

Unknown *s* and a Small Sample

In the previous section we used the standard normal distribution to express the level of confidence. We assumed either:

1. The population followed the normal distribution and the sample standard deviation was known, or
2. The shape of the population was not known, but the number of observations in the sample was at least 30.

What do we do if the sample is less than 30 and we do not know the population standard deviation? This situation is not covered by the results of the central limit theorem but exists in many cases. Often we can reason that the population is normal or reasonably close to a normal distribution. Under these conditions, the correct statistical procedure is to replace the standard normal distribution with the *t* distribution. The *t* distribution is a continuous distribution with many similarities to the standard normal distribution. William Gosset, an English brewmaster, was the first to study the *t* distribution. He did his work in the early 1900s. The brewery that employed Gosset preferred its employees to use pen names when publishing papers. For this reason Gosset's work was published under the pen name "Student." Hence, you will frequently see this distribution referred to as Student's *t*.

Gosset was concerned with the behavior of the following term:

$$t = \frac{\overline{X} - \mu}{s/\sqrt{n}}$$

when s is a point estimate of σ. He was especially worried about the discrepancy between s and σ when s was calculated from a very small sample. The *t* distribution and the standard normal distribution are shown graphically in Chart 8–1. Note that the *t* distribution is flatter, more spread out, than the standard normal distribution. This is because the standard deviation of the *t* distribution is larger than that of the standard normal distribution.

Statistics in Action

William Gosset was born in England in 1876 and died there in 1937. He worked for many years at Arthur Guinness & Sons Brewery. In fact, in his later years he was in charge of Guinness Brewery in London. Guinness preferred their employees to use pen names when publishing papers, so in 1908, when Gosset wrote "The Probable Error of a Mean," he used the name "Student." In this paper he first described the properties of the t distribution.

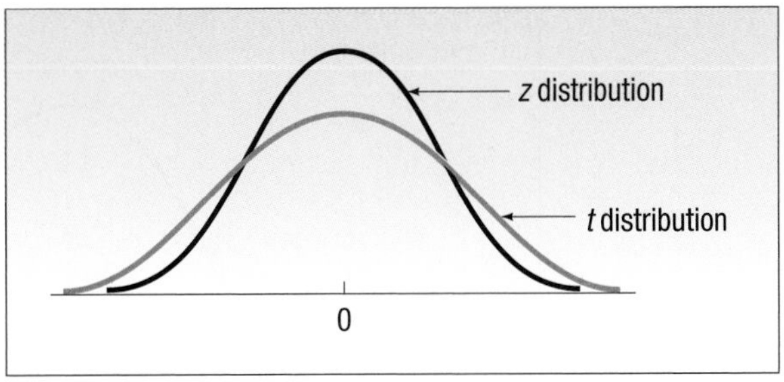

CHART 8–1 The Standard Normal Distribution and Student's t Distribution

The following characteristics of the t distribution are based on the assumption that the population of interest is normal, or nearly normal.

1. It is, like the z distribution, a continuous distribution.
2. It is, like the z distribution, bell-shaped and symmetrical.
3. There is not one t distribution, but rather a "family" of t distributions. All t distributions have a mean of 0, but their standard deviations differ according to the sample size, n. There is a t distribution for a sample size of 20, another for a sample size of 22, and so on. The standard deviation for a t distribution with 5 observations is larger than for a t distribution with 20 observations.
4. The t distribution is more spread out and flatter at the center than is the standard normal distribution (see Chart 8–1). As the sample size increases, however, the t distribution approaches the standard normal distribution, because the errors in using s to estimate σ decrease with larger samples.

Because Student's t distribution has a greater spread than the z distribution, the value of t for a given level of confidence is larger in magnitude than the corresponding z values. Chart 8–2 shows the values of z and of t for a 95 percent level of confidence when the sample size is $n = 5$. How we obtained the actual value of t will be explained shortly. For now, observe that for the same level of confidence the t distribution is flatter or more spread out than the standard normal distribution.

To develop a confidence interval for the population mean using the t distribution, we adjust formula 8–1 as follows.

CONFIDENCE INTERVAL FOR THE POPULATION MEAN, σ UNKNOWN

$$\overline{X} \pm t\frac{s}{\sqrt{n}} \qquad \textbf{[8–2]}$$

To put it another way, to develop a confidence interval for the population mean with an unknown population standard deviation we:

1. Assume the sample is from a normal population.
2. Estimate the population standard deviation (σ) with the sample standard deviation (s).
3. Use the t distribution rather than the z distribution.

We should be clear at this point. We usually employ the standard normal distribution when the sample size is at least 30. We should, strictly speaking, make the decision whether to use z or t based on whether σ is known or not. When σ is known, we use z; when it is not, we use t. The rule of using z when the sample is 30 or more is based on the fact that the t distribution approaches the normal distribution as the sample

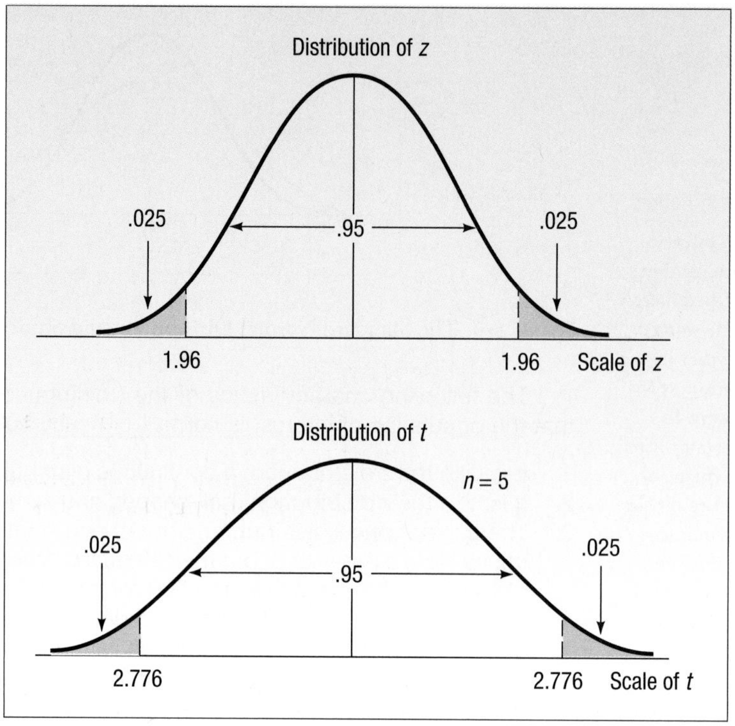

CHART 8–2 Values of z and t for the 95 Percent Level of Confidence

size increases. When the sample reaches 30, there is little difference between the z and t values, so we ignore the difference and use z. We will show this when we discuss the details of the t distribution and how to find values in a t distribution. Chart 8–3 summarizes the decision-making process.

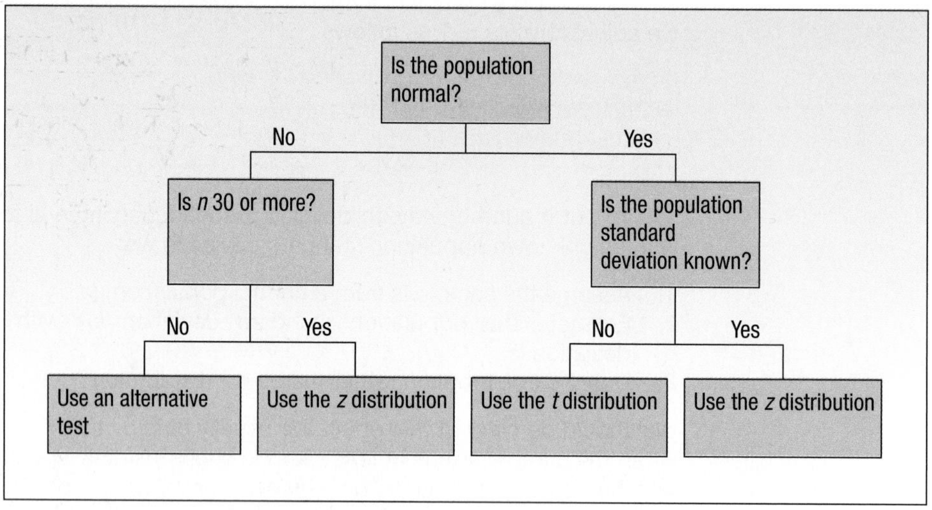

CHART 8–3 Determining When to Use the z Distribution or the t Distribution

The following example will illustrate a confidence interval for a population mean when the population standard deviation is unknown and how to find the appropriate value of t in a table.

EXAMPLE

A tire manufacturer wishes to investigate the tread life of its tires. A sample of 10 tires driven 50,000 miles revealed a sample mean of 0.32 inch of tread remaining with a standard deviation of 0.09 inch. Construct a 95 percent confidence interval for the population mean. Would it be reasonable for the manufacturer to conclude that after 50,000 miles the population mean amount of tread remaining is 0.30 inches?

SOLUTION

To begin, we assume the population distribution is normal. In this case, we don't have a lot of evidence, but the assumption is probably reasonable. We do not know the population standard deviation, but we know the sample standard deviation, which is .09 inches. To use the central limit theorem, we need a large sample, that is, a sample of 30 or more. In this instance there are only 10 observations in the sample. Hence, we cannot use the results of the central limit theorem. That is, formula 8–1 is not applicable. We use formula 8–2:

$$\overline{X} \pm t\frac{s}{\sqrt{n}}$$

From the information given, $\overline{X} = 0.32$, $s = 0.09$, and $n = 10$. To find the value of t we use Appendix F, a portion of which is reproduced below as Chart 8–4. Appendix F is also reproduced on the back inside cover of the text. The first step for locating t is to move across the row identified for "Confidence Intervals" to the level of confidence requested. In this case we want the 95 percent level of confidence, so we move to the row headed "95%." The column on the left margin is identified as "*df.*" This refers to the number of degrees of freedom. The number of degrees of freedom is the number

	Confidence Intervals				
	80%	90%	95%	98%	99%
	Level of Significance for One-Tailed Test				
df	0.100	0.050	0.025	0.010	0.005
	Level of Significance for Two-Tailed Test				
	0.20	0.10	0.05	0.02	0.01
1	3.078	6.314	12.706	31.821	63.657
2	1.886	2.920	4.303	6.965	9.925
3	1.638	2.353	3.182	4.541	5.841
4	1.533	2.132	2.776	3.747	4.604
5	1.476	2.015	2.571	3.365	4.032
6	1.440	1.943	2.447	3.143	3.707
7	1.415	1.895	2.365	2.998	3.499
8	1.397	1.860	2.306	2.896	3.355
9	1.383	1.833	2.262	2.821	3.250
10	1.372	1.812	2.228	2.764	3.169

CHART 8–4 A Portion of the t Distribution

of observations in the sample minus the number of samples, written $n - 1$.[1] In this case it is $10 - 1 = 9$. The value of t is 2.262.

To determine the confidence interval we substitute the values in formula 8–2.

$$\overline{X} \pm t\frac{s}{\sqrt{n}} = 0.32 \pm 2.262\frac{0.09}{\sqrt{10}} = 0.32 \pm .064$$

The endpoints of the confidence interval are 0.256 and 0.384. How do we interpret this result? It is reasonable to conclude that the population mean is in this interval. The manufacturer can be reasonably sure (95 percent confident) that the mean remaining tread depth is between 0.256 and 0.384 inches. Because the value of 0.30 is in this interval, it is possible that the mean of the population is 0.30.

[1]In brief summary, because sample statistics are being used, it is necessary to determine the number of variables that are *free to vary.* To illustrate: assume that the mean of four numbers is known to be 5. The four numbers are 7, 4, 1, and 8. The deviations of these numbers from the mean must total 0. The deviations of +2, −1, −4, and +3 do total 0. If the deviations of +2, −1, and −4 are known, then the value of +3 is fixed (restricted) in order to satisfy the condition that the sum of the deviations must equal 0. Thus, 1 degree of freedom is lost in a sampling problem involving the standard deviation of the sample because one number (the arithmetic mean) is known.

Here is another example to clarify the use of confidence intervals. Suppose an article in your local newspaper reported that the mean time to sell a residential property in the area is 60 days. You select a random sample of 20 homes sold in the last year and find the mean selling time is 65 days. Based on the sample data, you develop a 95 percent confidence interval for the population mean. You find that the endpoints of the confidence interval are 62 days and 68 days. How do you interpret this result? Because the confidence level is 95 percent, you can be reasonably confident the population mean is within this range. The value proposed for the population mean, that is, 60 days, is not included in the interval. It is not likely that the population mean is 60 days. The evidence indicates the statement in the local newspaper is not correct. To put it another way, it is unlikely that you could select the sample you did from a population with a mean selling time of 60 days.

The following Example will show additional details for determining and interpreting a confidence interval.

EXAMPLE

The manager of the Inlet Square Mall, just north of Ft. Meyers, Florida, wants to estimate the mean amount spent per shopping visit by customers. A sample of 20 customers reveals the following amounts spent.

$48.16	$42.22	$46.82	$51.45	$23.78	$41.86	$54.86
37.92	52.64	48.59	50.82	46.94	61.83	61.69
49.17	61.46	51.35	52.68	58.84	43.88	

What is the best point estimate of the population mean? Determine a 95 percent confidence interval. Interpret the result. Would it be reasonable to conclude that the population mean is $50? What about $60?

SOLUTION

The mall manager assumes that the population of the amounts spent follows the normal distribution. This is a reasonable assumption in this case. Additionally, the confidence interval technique is quite powerful and tends to commit any errors on the conservative side if the population is not normal. However, we should not make the normality assumption when the population is severely skewed or when the distribution has "thick tails."

The population standard deviation is not known and the size of the sample is less than 30. Hence, it is appropriate to use the t distribution and formula 8–2 to find the confidence interval. We use the MINITAB system to find the mean and standard deviation of this sample. The results are shown below.

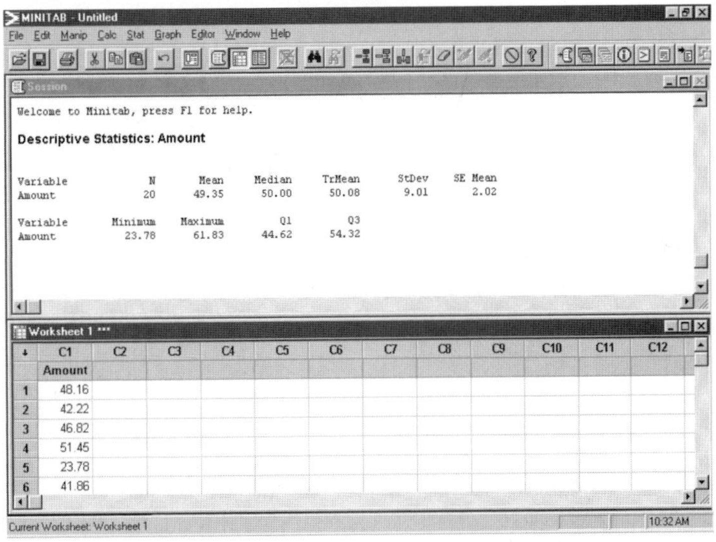

The mall manager does not know the population mean. The sample mean is the best estimate of that value. From the above MINITAB output, the mean is \$49.35, which is the best estimate, the *point estimate*, of the unknown population mean.

We use formula 8–2 to find the confidence interval. The value of t is available from Appendix F. There are $n - 1 = 20 - 1 = 19$ degrees of freedom. We move across the row with 19 degrees of freedom to the column for the 95 percent confidence level. The value at this intersection is 2.093. We substitute these values into formula 8–2 to find the confidence interval.

$$\overline{X} \pm t\frac{s}{\sqrt{n}} = \$49.35 \pm 2.093\frac{\$9.01}{\sqrt{20}} = \$49.35 \pm \$4.22$$

The endpoints of the confidence interval are \$45.13 and \$53.57. It is reasonable (with a 95 percent confidence level) to conclude that the population mean is in that interval. Following is another output from the MINITAB system. The confidence interval is reported on the right-hand side.

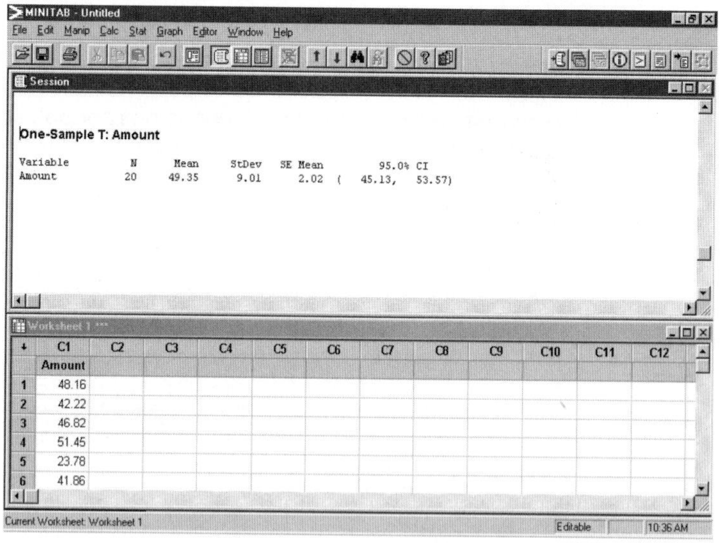

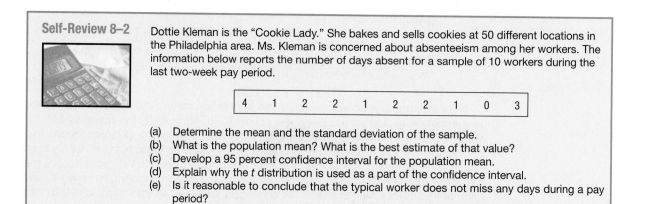

The manager of Inlet Square wondered whether the population mean could have been \$50 or \$60. The value of \$50 is within the confidence interval. It is reasonable that the population mean could be \$50. The value of \$60 is not in the confidence interval. Hence, we conclude that the population mean is unlikely to be \$60.

Self-Review 8–2

Dottie Kleman is the "Cookie Lady." She bakes and sells cookies at 50 different locations in the Philadelphia area. Ms. Kleman is concerned about absenteeism among her workers. The information below reports the number of days absent for a sample of 10 workers during the last two-week pay period.

4	1	2	2	1	2	2	1	0	3

(a) Determine the mean and the standard deviation of the sample.
(b) What is the population mean? What is the best estimate of that value?
(c) Develop a 95 percent confidence interval for the population mean.
(d) Explain why the *t* distribution is used as a part of the confidence interval.
(e) Is it reasonable to conclude that the typical worker does not miss any days during a pay period?

Exercises

9. Use Appendix F to locate the value of *t* under the following conditions.
  a. The sample size is 12 and the level of confidence is 95 percent.
  b. The sample size is 20 and the level of confidence is 90 percent.
  c. The sample size is 8 and the level of confidence is 99 percent.

10. Use Appendix F to locate the value of *t* under the following conditions.
  a. The sample size is 15 and the level of confidence is 95 percent.
  b. The sample size is 24 and the level of confidence is 98 percent.
  c. The sample size is 12 and the level of confidence is 90 percent.

11. The owner of Britten's Egg Farm wants to estimate the mean number of eggs laid per chicken. A sample of 20 chickens shows they laid an average of 20 eggs per month with a standard deviation of 2 eggs per month.

a. What is the value of the population mean? What is the best estimate of this value?
b. Explain why we need to use the *t* distribution. What assumption do you need to make?
c. For a 95 percent confidence interval, what is the value of *t*?
d. Develop the 95 percent confidence interval for the population mean.
e. Would it be reasonable to conclude that the population mean is 21 eggs? What about 25 eggs?

12. The American Sugar Producers Association wants to estimate the mean yearly sugar consumption. A sample of 16 people reveals the mean yearly consumption to be 60 pounds with a standard deviation of 20 pounds. Assume a normal population.
a. What is the value of the population mean? What is the best estimate of this value?
b. Explain why we need to use the *t* distribution. What assumption do you need to make?
c. For a 90 percent confidence interval, what is the value of *t*?
d. Develop the 90 percent confidence interval for the population mean.
e. Would it be reasonable to conclude that the population mean is 63 pounds?

13. Merrill Lynch Securities and Health Care Retirement, Inc. are two large employers in downtown Toledo, Ohio. They are considering jointly offering child care for their employees. As a part of the feasibility study, they wish to estimate the mean weekly child-care cost of their employees. A sample of 10 employees who use child care reveals the following amounts spent last week.

$107	$92	$97	$95	$105	$101	$91	$99	$95	$104

Develop a 90 percent confidence interval for the population mean. Interpret the result.

14. The Greater Pittsburgh Area Chamber of Commerce wants to estimate the mean time workers who are employed in the downtown area spend getting to work. A sample of 15 workers reveals the following number of minutes traveled.

29	38	38	33	38	21	45	34
40	37	37	42	30	29	35	

Develop a 98 percent confidence interval for the population mean. Interpret the result.

A Confidence Interval for a Proportion

The material presented so far in this chapter uses the ratio scale of measurement. That is, we use such variables as incomes, weights, distances, and ages. We now want to consider situations such as the following:

- The career services director at Southern Technical Institute reports that 80 percent of its graduates enter the job market in a position related to their field of study.
- A company representative claims that 45 percent of Burger King sales are made at the drive-through window.
- A survey of homes in the Chicago area indicated that 85 percent of the new construction had central air conditioning.
- A recent survey of married men between the ages of 35 and 50 found that 63 percent felt that both partners should earn a living.

These examples illustrate the nominal scale of measurement. In the nominal scale an observation is classified into one of two or more mutually exclusive groups. For example, a graduate of Southern Tech either entered the job market in a position related to his or her field of study or not. A particular Burger King customer either made a purchase at the drive-through window or did not make a purchase at the drive-through window. There are only two possibilities, and the outcome must be classified into one of the two groups.

Statistics In Action

Many survey results reported in newspapers, in news magazines, and on TV use confidence intervals. For example, a recent survey of 800 TV viewers in Charlotte, North Carolina, found 44 percent watched the evening news on the local NBC affiliate. The article went on to indicate the margin of error was 3.4 percent. The margin of error is actually the amount that is added and subtracted from the point estimate to find the endpoints of a confidence interval. Using formula 8–6 and the 95 percent level of confidence:

$$z\sqrt{\frac{p(1-p)}{n}}$$

$$= 1.96\sqrt{\frac{.44(1-44)}{800}}$$

$$= 0.034$$

PROPORTION The fraction, ratio, or percent indicating the part of the sample or the population having a particular trait of interest.

As an example of a proportion, a recent survey indicated that 92 out of 100 people favored the continued use of daylight savings time in the summer. The sample proportion is 92/100, or .92, or 92 percent. If we let p represent the sample proportion, X the number of successes, and n the number of items sampled, we can determine a sample proportion as follows.

SAMPLE PROPORTION

$$p = \frac{X}{n} \quad \textbf{[8–3]}$$

The population proportion is identified by π. Therefore, π refers to the percent of successes in the population. Recall from Chapter 5 that π is the proportion of successes in a binomial distribution. This continues our policy of using Greek letters to identify population parameters and Roman letters to identify sample statistics.

To develop a confidence interval for a proportion, we need to meet the following assumptions.

1. The binomial conditions, discussed in Chapter 5, have been met. Briefly, these conditions are:
   a. The sample data is the result of counts.
   b. There are only two possible outcomes. (We usually label one of the outcomes a "success" and the other a "failure.")
   c. The probability of a success remains the same from one trial to the next.
   d. The trials are independent. This means the outcome on one trial does not affect the outcome of another.
2. The values $n\pi$ and $n(1 - \pi)$ should both be greater than or equal to 5. This condition allows us to use the normal approximation to the binomial and employ the standard normal distribution, that is, z, as a part of the confidence interval.

Developing a point estimate for a population proportion and a confidence interval for a population proportion is similar to doing so for a mean. To illustrate, John Gail is running for Congress from the third district of Nebraska. From a random sample of 100 voters in the district, 60 indicate they plan to vote for him in the upcoming election. The sample proportion is .60, but the population proportion is unknown. That is, we do not know what proportion of voters in the *population* will vote for Mr. Gail. The sample value, .60, is the best estimate we have of the unknown population parameter. So we let p, which is .60, be an estimate of π, which is not known.

To develop a confidence interval for a population proportion, we change formula 8–1 slightly:

CONFIDENCE INTERVAL FOR A POPULATION PROPORTION

$$p \pm z\sigma_p \quad \textbf{[8–4]}$$

The term σ_p is the "standard error" of the proportion. It measures the variability in the sampling distribution of the sample proportion.

STANDARD ERROR OF THE SAMPLE PROPORTION

$$\sigma_p = \sqrt{\frac{p(1-p)}{n}} \qquad [8\text{–}5]$$

We can then construct a confidence interval for a population proportion from the following formula.

CONFIDENCE INTERVAL FOR A POPULATION PROPORTION

$$p \pm z\sqrt{\frac{p(1-p)}{n}} \qquad [8\text{–}6]$$

EXAMPLE

The union representing the Bottle Blowers of America (BBA) is considering a proposal to merge with the Teamsters Union. According to BBA union bylaws, at least three-fourths of the union membership must approve any merger. A random sample of 2,000 current BBA members reveals 1,600 plan to vote for the merger proposal. What is the estimate of the population proportion? Develop a 95 percent confidence interval for the population proportion. Basing your decision on this sample information, can you conclude that the necessary proportion of BBA members favors the merger?

SOLUTION

First, calculate the sample proportion from formula 8–3. It is .8, found by

$$p = \frac{X}{n} = \frac{1{,}600}{2{,}000} = .8$$

Thus, we estimate that 80 percent of the population favor the merger proposal. We determine the 95 percent confidence interval using formula 8–6. The z value corresponding to the 95 percent level of confidence is 1.96.

$$p \pm z\sqrt{\frac{p(1-p)}{n}} = .8 \pm 1.96\sqrt{\frac{.8(1-.8)}{2000}} = .8 \pm .018$$

The endpoints of the confidence interval are .782 and .818. The lower endpoint is greater than .75. Hence, we conclude that the merger proposal will pass because the interval estimate includes values greater than 75% of the union membership.

Self-Review 8–3

A market survey was conducted to estimate the proportion of homemakers who would recognize the brand name of a cleanser based on the shape and the color of the container. Of the 1,400 homemakers sampled, 420 were able to identify the brand by name.

(a) Estimate the value of the population proportion.
(b) Compute the standard error of the proportion.
(c) Develop a 99 percent confidence interval for the population proportion.
(d) Interpret your findings.

Exercises

15. The owner of the West End Kwick Fill Gas Station wished to determine the proportion of customers who use his pay-at-the-pump feature. This feature allows customers to use a credit card at the pump and never enter the station. He surveys 100 customers and finds that 80 paid at the pump.
a. Estimate the value of the population proportion.
b. Compute the standard error of the proportion.
c. Develop a 95 percent confidence interval for the population proportion.
d. Interpret your findings.

16. Ms. Maria Wilson is considering running for mayor of the town of Bear Gulch, Montana. Before completing the petitions, she decides to conduct a survey of voters in Bear Gulch. A sample of 400 voters reveals that 300 would support her in the November election.
a. Estimate the value of the population proportion.
b. Compute the standard error of the proportion.
c. Develop a 99 percent confidence interval for the population proportion.
d. Interpret your findings.

17. The Fox TV network is considering replacing one of its prime-time crime investigation shows with a new family-oriented comedy show. Before a final decision is made, network executives commission a sample of 400 viewers. After viewing the comedy, 250 indicated they would watch the new show and suggested it replace the crime investigation show.
a. Estimate the value of the population proportion.
b. Compute the standard error of the proportion.
c. Develop a 99 percent confidence interval for the population proportion.
d. Interpret your findings.

18. Schadek Silkscreen Printing, Inc. purchases plastic cups on which to print logos for sporting events, proms, birthdays, and other special occasions. Zack Schadek, the owner, received a large shipment this morning. To ensure the quality of the shipment, he selected a random sample of 300 cups. He found 15 to be defective.
a. What is the estimated proportion defective in the population?
b. Develop a 95 percent confidence interval for the proportion defective.
c. Zack has an agreement with his supplier that he is to return lots that are 10 percent or more defective. Should he return this lot? Explain your decision.

Finite-Population Correction Factor

The populations we have sampled so far have been very large or infinite. What if the sampled population is not very large? We need to make some adjustments in the way we compute the standard error of the sample means and the standard error of the sample proportions.

A population that has a fixed upper bound is *finite.* For example, there are 21,376 students enrolled at Eastern Illinois University, there are 40 employees at Spence Sprockets, DaimlerChrysler assembled 917 Jeep Wranglers at the Alexis Avenue plant yesterday, or there were 65 surgical patients at St. Rose Memorial Hospital in Sarasota yesterday. A finite population can be rather small; it could be all the students registered for this class. It can also be very large, such as all senior citizens living in Florida.

For a finite population, where the total number of objects is N and the size of the sample is n, the following adjustment is made to the standard errors of the sample means and proportions:

STANDARD ERROR OF THE SAMPLE MEAN, USING A CORRECTION FACTOR

$$\sigma_{\bar{X}} = \frac{\sigma}{\sqrt{n}}\sqrt{\frac{N-n}{N-1}} \qquad \textbf{[8–7]}$$

STANDARD ERROR OF THE SAMPLE PROPORTION, USING A CORRECTION FACTOR

$$\sigma_p = \sqrt{\frac{p(1-p)}{n}}\sqrt{\frac{N-n}{N-1}} \qquad \textbf{[8–8]}$$

This adjustment is called the **finite-population correction factor**. Why is it necessary to apply a factor, and what is its effect? Logically, if the sample is a substantial percentage of the population, the estimate is more precise. Note the effect of the term $(N - n)/(N - 1)$. Suppose the population is 1,000 and the sample is 100. Then this ratio is (1,000 − 100)/(1,000 − 1), or 900/999. Taking the square root gives the correction factor, .9492. Multiplying this correction factor by the standard error *reduces* the standard error by about 5 percent (1 − .9492 = .0508). This reduction in the size of the standard error yields a smaller range of values in estimating the population mean or the population proportion. If the sample is 200, the correction factor is .8949, meaning that the standard error has been reduced by more than 10 percent. Table 8–1 shows the effects of various sample sizes. Note that when the sample is less than about 5 percent of the population, the impact of the correction factor is quite small. The usual rule is if the ratio of n/N is less than .05, the correction factor is ignored. When sampling a relatively large proportion of a finite population, the correction factor allows for a narrower confidence interval, and therefore, a more precise estimate of the population mean.

TABLE 8–1 Finite-Population Correction Factor for Selected Sample When the Population Is 1,000

Sample Size	Fraction of Population	Correction Factor
10	.010	.9955
25	.025	.9879
50	.050	.9752
100	.100	.9492
200	.200	.8949
500	.500	.7075

EXAMPLE

There are 250 families in Scandia, Pennsylvania. A poll of 40 families reveals the mean annual church contribution is $450 with a standard deviation of $75. Construct a 90 percent confidence interval for the mean annual contribution.

SOLUTION

First, note that the population is finite. That is, there is a limit to the number of people in Scandia. Second, note that the sample constitutes more than 5 percent of the population; that is, $n/N = 40/250 = .16$. Hence, we use the finite-population correction factor. The 90 percent confidence interval is constructed as follows, using formula 8–7.

$$\bar{X} \pm z\frac{s}{\sqrt{n}}\left(\sqrt{\frac{N-n}{N-1}}\right) = \$450 \pm 1.65\,\frac{\$75}{\sqrt{40}}\left(\sqrt{\frac{250-40}{250-1}}\right) = \$450 \pm \$19.57(\sqrt{.8434})$$

$$= \$450 \pm \$17.97$$

The endpoints of the confidence interval are $432.03 and $467.97. It is likely, given the confidence level is 90 percent, that the population mean falls within this interval.

Self-Review 8-4

The same study of church contributions in Scandia revealed that 15 of the 40 families sampled attend church regularly. Construct the 95 percent confidence interval for the proportion of families attending church regularly. Should the finite-population correction factor be used? Why or why not?

Exercises

19. Thirty-six items are randomly selected from a population of 300 items. The sample mean is 35 and the sample standard deviation 5. Develop a 95 percent confidence interval for the population mean.

20. Forty-nine items are randomly selected from a population of 500 items. The sample mean is 40 and the sample standard deviation 9. Develop a 99 percent confidence interval for the population mean.

21. The attendance at the Durham Bulls minor league baseball game last night was 400. A random sample of 50 of those in attendance revealed that the mean number of soft drinks consumed per person was 1.86 with a standard deviation of 0.50. Develop a 99 percent confidence interval for the mean number of soft drinks consumed per person.

22. There are 300 welders employed at the Maine Shipyards Corporation. A sample of 30 welders revealed that 18 graduated from a registered welding course. Construct the 95 percent confidence interval for the proportion of all welders who graduated from a registered welding course.

Choosing an Appropriate Sample Size

A concern that usually arises when designing a statistical study is "How many items should be in the sample?" If a sample is too large, money is wasted collecting the data. Similarly, if the sample is too small, the resulting conclusions will be uncertain. The necessary sample size depends on three factors:

1. The level of confidence desired.
2. The margin of error the researcher will tolerate.
3. The variability in the population being studied.

The first factor is the *level of confidence*. Those conducting the study select the level of confidence. The 95 percent and the 99 percent levels of confidence are the most common, but any value between 0 and 100 percent is possible. The 95 percent level of confidence corresponds to a z value of 1.96, and a 99 percent level of confidence corresponds to a z value of 2.58. The higher the level of confidence selected, the larger the size of the corresponding sample.

The second factor is the *allowable error*. The maximum allowable error, designated as E, is the amount that is added and subtracted to the sample mean (or sample proportion) to determine the endpoints of the confidence interval. It is the amount of error those conducting the study are willing to tolerate. It is also one-half the width of the corresponding confidence interval. A small allowable error will require a large sample. A large allowable error will permit a smaller sample.

The third factor in determining the size of a sample is the *population standard deviation*. If the population is widely dispersed, a large sample is required. On the other hand, if the population is concentrated (homogeneous), the required sample size will be smaller. However, it may be necessary to use an estimate for the population standard deviation. Here are three suggestions for finding that estimate.

1. **Use a comparable study.** Use this approach when there is an estimate of the dispersion available from another study. Suppose we want to estimate the number of hours worked per week by refuse workers. Information from certain state or federal agencies who regularly sample the workforce might be useful to provide an estimate of the standard deviation. If a standard deviation observed in a previous study is thought to be reliable, it can be used in the current study to help provide an approximate sample size.
2. **Use a range-based approach.** To use this approach we need to know or have an estimate of the largest and smallest values in the population. Recall from Chapter

3, where we described the Empirical Rule, that virtually all the observations could be expected to be within plus or minus 3 standard deviations of the mean, assuming that the distribution was approximately normal. Thus, the distance between the largest and the smallest values is six standard deviations, or 6*s*. We could estimate the standard deviation as one-sixth of the range. For example, the director of operations at University Bank wants an estimate of the number of checks written per month by college students. She believes that the distribution is approximately normal, the minimum number of checks written is 2 per month, and the most is 50 per month. The range of the number of checks written per month is 48, found by 50 − 2. The estimate of the standard deviation then would be 8 checks per month, 48/6.

3. **Conduct a pilot study**. This is the most common method. Suppose we want an estimate of the number of hours per week worked by students enrolled in the College of Business at the University of Texas. To test the validity of our questionnaire, we use it on a small sample of students. From this small sample we compute the standard deviation of the number of hours worked and use this value to determine the appropriate sample size.

We can express the interaction among these three factors and the sample size in the following formula.

$$E = z\frac{s}{\sqrt{n}}$$

Solving this equation for *n* yields the following result.

SAMPLE SIZE FOR ESTIMATING THE POPULATION MEAN	$n = \left(\frac{zs}{E}\right)^2$	**[8–9]**

where:

- n is the size of the sample.
- z is the standard normal value corresponding to the desired level of confidence.
- s is an estimate of the population standard deviation.
- E is the maximum allowable error.

The result of this calculation is not always a whole number. When the outcome is not a whole number, the usual practice is to round up *any* fractional result. For example, 201.22 would be rounded up to 202.

EXAMPLE

A student in public administration wants to determine the mean amount members of city councils in large cities earn per month as remuneration for being a council member. The error in estimating the mean is to be less than $100 with a 95 percent level of confidence. The student found a report by the Department of Labor that estimated the standard deviation to be $1,000. What is the required sample size?

SOLUTION

The maximum allowable error, *E*, is $100. The value of *z* for a 95 percent level of confidence is 1.96, and the estimate of the standard deviation is $1,000. Substituting these values into formula 8–9, the required sample size is:

$$n = \left(\frac{zs}{E}\right)^2 = \left(\frac{(1.96)(\$1{,}000)}{\$100}\right)^2 = 384.16$$

The computed value of 384.16 is rounded up to 385. A sample of 385 is required to meet the specifications. If the student wants to increase the level of confidence, for example to 99 percent, this will require a larger sample. The z value corresponding to the 99 percent level of confidence is 2.58.

$$n = \left(\frac{zs}{E}\right)^2 = \left(\frac{(2.58)(\$1{,}000)}{\$100}\right)^2 = 665.64$$

We recommend a sample of 666. Observe how much the change in the confidence level changed the size of the sample. An increase from the 95 percent to the 99 percent level of confidence resulted in an increase of 281 observations. This could greatly increase the cost of the study, both in terms of time and money. Hence, the level of confidence should be considered carefully.

The procedure just described can be adapted to determine the sample size for a proportion. Again, three items need to be specified:

1. The desired level of confidence.
2. The margin of error in the population proportion.
3. An estimate of the population proportion.

The formula to determine the sample size of a proportion is:

SAMPLE SIZE FOR THE POPULATION PROPORTION

$$n = p(1 - p)\left(\frac{z}{E}\right)^2 \quad \textbf{[8–10]}$$

If an estimate of π is available from a pilot study or some other source, it can be used. Otherwise, .50 is used because the term $p(1 - p)$ can never be larger than when $p = .50$. For example, if $p = .30$, then $p(1 - p) = .3(1 - .3) = .21$, but when $p = .50$, $p(1 - p) = .5(1 - .5) = .25$

EXAMPLE

The study in the previous example also estimates the proportion of cities that have private refuse collectors. The student wants the estimate to be within .10 of the population proportion, the desired level of confidence is 90 percent, and no estimate is available for the population proportion. What is the required sample size?

SOLUTION

The estimate of the population proportion is to be within .10, so $E = .10$. The desired level of confidence is .90, which corresponds to a z value of 1.65. Because no estimate of the population proportion is available, we use .50. The suggested number of observations is

$$n = (.5)(1 - .5)\left(\frac{1.65}{.10}\right)^2 = 68.0625$$

The student needs a random sample of 69 cities.

Self-Review 8–5

Will you assist the college registrar in determining how many transcripts to study? The registrar wants to estimate the arithmetic mean grade point average (GPA) of all graduating seniors during the past 10 years. GPAs range between 2.0 and 4.0. The mean GPA is to be estimated within plus or minus .05 of the population mean. The standard deviation is estimated to be 0.279. Use the 99 percent level of confidence.

Exercises

23. A population is estimated to have a standard deviation of 10. We want to estimate the population mean within 2, with a 95 percent level of confidence. How large a sample is required?

24. We want to estimate the population mean within 5, with a 99 percent level of confidence. The population standard deviation is estimated to be 15. How large a sample is required?

25. The estimate of the population proportion is to be within plus or minus .05, with a 95 percent level of confidence. The best estimate of the population proportion is .15. How large a sample is required?

26. The estimate of the population proportion is to be within plus or minus .10, with a 99 percent level of confidence. The best estimate of the population proportion is .45. How large a sample is required?

27. A survey is being planned to determine the mean amount of time corporation executives watch television. A pilot survey indicated that the mean time per week is 12 hours, with a standard deviation of 3 hours. It is desired to estimate the mean viewing time within one-quarter hour. The 95 percent level of confidence is to be used. How many executives should be surveyed?

28. A processor of carrots cuts the green top off each carrot, washes the carrots, and inserts six to a package. Twenty packages are inserted in a box for shipment. To test the weight of the boxes, a few were checked. The mean weight was 20.4 pounds, the standard deviation 0.5 pounds. How many boxes must the processor sample to be 95 percent confident that the sample mean does not differ from the population mean by more than 0.2 pounds?

29. Suppose the President wants an estimate of the proportion of the population who support his current policy toward gun control. The President wants the estimate to be within .04 of the true proportion. Assume a 95 percent level of confidence. The President's political advisors estimated the proportion supporting the current policy to be .60.

   a. How large a sample is required?

   b. How large a sample would be necessary if no estimate were available for the proportion that support current policy?

30. Past surveys reveal that 30 percent of tourists going to Las Vegas to gamble during a weekend spend more than $1,000. Management wants to update this percentage.

   a. The new study is to use the 90 percent confidence level. The estimate is to be within 1 percent of the population proportion. What is the necessary sample size?

   b. Management said that the sample size determined above is too large. What can be done to reduce the sample? Based on your suggestion recalculate the sample size.

Chapter Outline

I. A point estimate is a single value (statistic) used to estimate a population value (parameter).

II. A confidence interval is a range of values within which the population parameter is expected to occur.

   A. The factors that determine the width of a confidence interval for a mean are:

      1. The number of observations in the sample, *n*.

      2. The variability in the population, usually estimated by the sample standard deviation, *s*.

      3. The level of confidence.

         a. When the population standard deviation is known or the sample is 30 or more, we construct a confidence interval for a mean using the following formula:

$$\overline{X} \pm z\frac{s}{\sqrt{n}} \qquad \textbf{[8–1]}$$

         b. When the population standard deviation is unknown or the sample is less than 30, we construct a confidence interval for a population mean of a normal population using the following formula:

$$\bar{X} \pm t\frac{s}{\sqrt{n}} \qquad \textbf{[8–2]}$$

III. The major characteristics of the *t* distribution are:
- **A.** It is a continuous distribution.
- **B.** It is mound-shaped and symmetrical.
- **C.** It is flatter, or more spread out, than the standard normal distribution.
- **D.** There is a family of *t* distributions, depending on the number of degrees of freedom.

IV. A proportion is a ratio, fraction, or percent that indicates the part of the sample or population that has the particular characteristic.
- **A.** A sample proportion is found by *X*, the number of successes, divided by *n*, the number of observations.
- **B.** The standard error of the sample proportion reports the variability in the distribution of sample proportions. It is found by

$$\sigma_p = \sqrt{\frac{p(1-p)}{n}} \qquad \textbf{[8–5]}$$

- **C.** We construct a confidence interval for a population proportion from the following formula.

$$p \pm z\sqrt{\frac{p(1-p)}{n}} \qquad \textbf{[8–6]}$$

V. We can determine the sample size for estimating population means and proportions.
- **A.** There are three factors that determine the sample size when we wish to estimate the population mean.
  1. The desired level of confidence, which is usually expressed by *z*.
  2. The maximum allowable error, *E*.
  3. The variation in the population, expressed by *s*.
  4. The formula to determine the sample size for the mean is

$$n = \left(\frac{zs}{E}\right)^2 \qquad \textbf{[8–9]}$$

- **B.** There are three factors that determine the sample size when we wish to estimate a population proportion.
  1. The desired level of confidence, which is usually expressed by *z*.
  2. The maximum allowable error, *E*.
  3. An estimate of the population proportion. If no estimate is available, use .50.
  4. The formula to determine the sample size for a proportion is

$$n = p(1-p)\left(\frac{z}{E}\right)^2 \qquad \textbf{[8–10]}$$

Pronunciation Key

SYMBOL	MEANING	PRONUNCIATION
$\sigma_{\bar{X}}$	Standard error of the sample means	*sigma sub X bar*
σ_p	Standard error of the sample proportion	*sigma sub p*

Chapter Exercises

31. A random sample of 85 group leaders, supervisors, and similar personnel at General Motors revealed that, on the average, they spent 6.5 years on the job before being promoted. The standard deviation of the sample was 1.7 years. Construct a 95 percent confidence interval.

32. The Iowa state meat inspector has been given the assignment of estimating the mean net weight of packages of ground chuck labeled "3 pounds." Of course, he realizes that the weights cannot be precisely 3 pounds. A sample of 36 packages reveals the mean weight to be 3.01 pounds, with a standard deviation of 0.03 pounds.
  a. What is the estimated population mean?
  b. Determine a 95 percent confidence interval for the population mean.

33. A recent study of 50 self-service gasoline stations in the Greater Cincinnati–North Kentucky metropolitan area revealed that the mean price of unleaded gas was $1.179 per gallon. The sample standard deviation was $0.03 per gallon.
  a. Determine a 99 percent confidence interval for the population mean price.
  b. Would it be reasonable to conclude that the population mean was $1.20? Why or why not?

34. A recent survey of 50 unemployed male executives showed that it took an average of 26 weeks for them to find another position. The standard deviation of the sample was 6.2 weeks. Construct a 95 percent confidence interval for the population mean. Is it reasonable that the population mean is 28 weeks? Justify your answer.

35. The Badik Construction Company limits its business to constructing decks. The mean time to construct one of their standard decks is 8 hours for a two-person construction crew. The information is based on a sample of 40 decks recently constructed. The standard deviation of the sample was 3 hours.
  a. Determine a 90 percent confidence interval for the population mean.
  b. Would it be reasonable to conclude that the population mean is actually 9 hours? Justify your answer.

36. The American Restaurant Association collected information on the number of meals eaten outside the home per week by young married couples. A survey of 60 couples showed the sample mean number of meals eaten outside the home was 2.76 meals per week, with a standard deviation of 0.75 meals per week. Construct a 97 percent confidence interval for the population mean.

37. The National Collegiate Athletic Association (NCAA) reported that the mean number of hours spent per week on coaching and recruiting by college football assistant coaches during the season is 70. A random sample of 50 assistant coaches showed the sample mean to be 68.6 hours, with a standard deviation of 8.2 hours.
  a. Using the sample data, construct a 99 percent confidence interval for the population mean.
  b. Does the 99 percent confidence interval include the value suggested by the NCAA? Interpret this result.
  c. Suppose you decided to switch from a 99 to a 95 percent confidence interval. Without performing any calculations, will the interval increase, decrease, or stay the same? Which of the values in the formula will change?

38. The Human Relations Department of Electronics, Inc. would like to include a dental plan as part of the benefits package. The question is: How much does a typical employee and his or her family spend per year on dental expenses? A sample of 45 employees reveals the mean amount spent last year was $1,820, with a standard deviation of $660.
  a. Construct a 95 percent confidence interval for the population mean.
  b. The information from part (a) was given to the president of Electronics, Inc. He indicated he could afford $1,700 of dental expenses per employee. Is it possible that the population mean could be $1,700? Justify your answer.

39. A student conducted a study and reported that the 95 percent confidence interval for the mean ranged from 46 to 54. He was sure that the mean of the sample was 50, that the standard deviation of the sample was 16, and that the sample was at least 30, but could not remember the exact number. Can you help him out?

40. A recent study by the American Automobile Dealers Association revealed the mean amount of profit per car sold for a sample of 20 dealers was $290, with a standard deviation of $125. Develop a 95 percent confidence interval for the population mean.

41. A study of 25 graduates of four-year colleges by the American Banker's Association revealed the mean amount owed by a student was $14,381. The standard deviation of the sample was $1,892. Construct a 90 percent confidence interval for the population mean. Is it reasonable to conclude that the mean of the population is actually $15,000? Tell why or why not.

42. An important factor in selling a residential property is the number of people who look through the home. A sample of 15 homes recently sold in the Buffalo, New York, area revealed the mean number looking through each home was 24 and the standard deviation of the sample was 5 people. Develop a 98 percent confidence interval for the population mean.

43. The Warren County Telephone Company claims in its annual report that "the typical customer spends \$60 per month on local and long distance service." A sample of 12 subscribers revealed the following amounts spent last month.

\$64	\$66	\$64	\$66	\$59	\$62	\$67	\$61	\$64	\$58	\$54	\$66

a. What is the point estimate of the population mean?
b. Develop a 90 percent confidence interval for the population mean.
c. Is the company's claim that the "typical customer" spends \$60 per month reasonable? Justify your answer.

44. The manufacturer of a new line of ink jet printers would like to include as part of their advertising the number of pages a user can expect from a print cartridge. A sample of 10 cartridges revealed the following number of pages printed.

2698	2028	2474	2395	2372	2475	1927	3006	2334	2379

a. What is the point estimate of the population mean?
b. Develop a 95 percent confidence interval for the population mean.

45. Dr. Susan Benner is an industrial psychologist. She is currently studying stress among executives of Internet companies. She has developed a questionnaire that she believes measures stress. A score above 80 indicates stress at a dangerous level. A random sample of 15 executives revealed the following stress level scores.

94	78	83	90	78	99	97	90	97	90	93	94	100	75	84

a. Find the mean stress level for this sample. What is the point estimate of the population mean?
b. Construct a 95 percent confidence level for the population mean.
c. Is it reasonable to conclude that Internet executives have a mean stress level in the dangerous level, according to Dr. Benner's test?

46. Furniture Land South surveyed 600 consumers and found that 414 were enthusiastic about a new home dècor they plan to show in their store in High Point, North Carolina. Construct the 99 percent confidence interval for the population proportion.

47. There are 20,000 eligible voters in York County, South Carolina. A random sample of 500 York County voters revealed 350 plan to vote to return Louella Miller to the state senate. Construct a 99 percent confidence interval for the proportion of voters in the county who plan to vote for Ms. Miller. From this sample information, can you confirm she will be reelected?

48. In a poll to estimate presidential popularity, each person in a random sample of 1,000 voters was asked to agree with one of the following statements:

1. The President is doing a good job.
2. The President is doing a poor job.
3. I have no opinion.

A total of 560 respondents selected the first statement, indicating they thought the President was doing a good job.

a. Construct a 95 percent confidence interval for the proportion of respondents who feel the President is doing a good job.
b. Based on your interval in part (a), is it reasonable to conclude that a majority (more than half) of the population believes the President is doing a good job?

49. Police Chief Aaron Ard of River City reports 500 traffic citations were issued last month. A sample of 35 of these citations showed the mean amount of the fine was \$54, with a standard deviation of \$4.50. Construct a 95 percent confidence interval for the mean amount of a citation in River City.

50. The First National Bank of Wilson has 650 checking account customers. A recent sample of 50 of these customers showed 26 to have a Visa card with the bank. Construct the 99 percent confidence interval for the proportion of checking account customers who have a Visa card with the bank.

51. It is estimated that 60 percent of U.S. households now subscribe to cable TV. You would like to verify this statement for your class in mass communications. If you want your estimate to be within 5 percentage points, with a 95 percent level of confidence, how large of a sample is required?
52. You need to estimate the mean number of travel days per year for outside salespeople. The mean of a small pilot study was 150 days, with a standard deviation of 14 days. If you must estimate the population mean within 2 days, how many outside salespeople should you sample? Use the 90 percent confidence level.
53. You are to conduct a sample survey to determine the mean family income in a rural area of central Florida. The question is, how many families should be sampled? In a pilot sample of 10 families, the standard deviation of the sample was $500. The sponsor of the survey wants you to use the 95 percent confidence level. The estimate is to be within $100. How many families should be interviewed?
54. You plan to conduct a survey to find what proportion of the workforce has two or more jobs. You decide on the 95 percent confidence level and state that the estimated proportion must be within 2 percent of the population proportion. A pilot survey reveals that 5 of the 50 sampled hold two or more jobs. How many in the workforce should be interviewed to meet your requirements?
55. The proportion of public accountants who have changed companies within the last three years is to be estimated within 3 percent. The 95 percent level of confidence is to be used. A study conducted several years ago revealed that the percent of public accountants changing companies within 3 years was 21.
   a. To update this study, the files of how many public accountants should be studied?
   b. How many public accountants should be contacted if no previous estimates of the population proportion are available?
56. The Hunington National Bank, like most other large banks, found that using automatic teller machines (ATMs) reduces the cost of routine bank transactions. Hunington installed an ATM in the corporate offices of the Fun Toy Company. The ATM is for the exclusive use of Fun's 605 employees. After several months of operation, a sample of 100 employees revealed the following use of the ATM machine by Fun employees in a month.

Number of Times ATM Used	Frequency
0	25
1	30
2	20
3	10
4	10
5	5

   a. What is the estimate of the proportion of employees who do not use the ATM in a month?
   b. Develop a 95 percent confidence interval for this estimate. Can Hunington be sure that at least 40 percent of the employees of Fun Toy Company will use the ATM?
   c. How many transactions does the average Fun employee make per month?
   d. Develop a 95 percent confidence interval for the mean number of transactions per month.
   e. Is it possible that the population mean is 0? Explain.
57. In a recent Zogby poll of 1,000 adults nationwide, 613 said they believe other forms of life exist elsewhere in the universe. Construct the 99 percent confidence interval for the population proportion of those believing life exists elsewhere in the universe. Does your result imply that a majority of Americans believe life exists outside of Earth?
58. As part of an annual review of its accounts, a discount brokerage selects a random sample of 36 customers. Their accounts are reviewed for total account valuation, which showed a mean of $32,000, with a sample standard deviation of $8,200. What is a 90 percent confidence interval for the mean account valuation of the population of customers?

59. A sample of 352 subscribers to *Wired* magazine shows the mean time spent using the Internet is 13.4 hours per week, with a sample standard deviation of 6.8 hours. Find the 95 percent confidence interval for the mean time *Wired* subscribers spend on the Internet.
60. The Tennessee Tourism Institute (TTI) plans to sample information center visitors entering the state to learn the fraction of visitors who plan to camp in the state. Current estimates are that 35 percent of visitors are campers. How large a sample would you take to estimate at a 95 percent confidence level the population proportion with an allowable error of 2 percent?

exercises.com

WWW

61. Hoover is an excellent source of business information. It includes daily summaries as well as information about various industries and specific companies. Go to the site at *www.hoovers.com.* Click on **Companies and Industries.** Then, click on **Industries** in the next menu, then go to **Sector** and select an **Industry Sector,** such as chemicals or retail. Then, select an industry within the sector. For example, **Chemicals—Diversified** is an industry within the Chemicals sector. This should give you a list of companies. Use a table of random numbers, such as Appendix E, to randomly select 5 to 10 companies in the list. Click on **Capsule,** and then the **Financials** tab to get information about the selected companies. One suggestion is to find the earnings per share. Compute the mean of each sample, and then develop a confidence interval for the mean earnings per share. Because the sample is a large part of the population, you will want to include the correction factor. Interpret the result.
62. The online edition of the *Information Please Almanac* is a valuable source of business information. Go to the Website at *www.infoplease.com.* Click on **Business.** Then in the **Almanac Section,** click on **Taxes,** then click on **State Taxes on Individuals**. The result is a listing of the 50 states and the District of Columbia. Use a table of random numbers to randomly select 5 to 10 states. Compute the mean state tax rate on individuals. Develop a confidence interval for the mean amount. Because the sample is a large part of the population, you will want to include the correction factor. Interpret your result. You might, as an additional exercise, download all the information and use Excel or MINITAB to compute the population mean. Compare that value with the results of your confidence interval.

Computer Data Exercises

63. Refer to the Real Estate data, which reports information on the homes sold in Venice, Florida, last year.
    a. Develop a 95 percent confidence interval for the mean selling price of the homes.
    b. Develop a 95 percent confidence interval for the mean distance the home is from the center of the city.
    c. Develop a 95 percent confidence interval for the proportion of homes with an attached garage.
64. Refer to the Baseball 2001 data, which reports information on the 30 Major League Baseball teams for the 2001 season.
    a. Develop a 95 percent confidence interval for the mean number of home runs per team.
    b. Develop a 95 percent confidence interval for the mean number of errors committed by each team.
    c. Develop a 95 percent confidence interval for the mean number of stolen bases for each team.
65. Refer to the wage data, which reports information on annual wages for a sample of 100 workers. Also included are variables relating to industry, years of education, and gender for each worker.
    a. Develop a 95 percent confidence interval for the mean wage of the workers. Is it reasonable to conclude that the population mean is $35,000?
    b. Develop a 95 percent confidence interval for the mean years of education. Is it reasonable that the population mean is 13 years?
    c. Develop a 95 percent confidence interval for the mean age of the workers. Could the mean age be 40 years?

66. Refer to the CIA data, which reports demographic and economic information on 46 countries.

a. Develop a 90 percent confidence interval for the mean percent of the population over 65 years.

b. Develop a 90 percent confidence interval for the mean GDA per capita.

c. Develop a 90 percent confidence interval for the mean imports.

Computer Commands

1. The MINITAB commands to generate the 60 columns of 30 random numbers used in the Example/Solution on page 258 are:

a. Select **Calc**, **Random Data**, and then click on **Normal**.

b. From the dialog box click on **Generate** and type *30* for the number of rows of data, **Store** in *C1-C60,* the **Mean** is *50,* the **Standard Deviation** is *5.0,* and finally click **OK.**

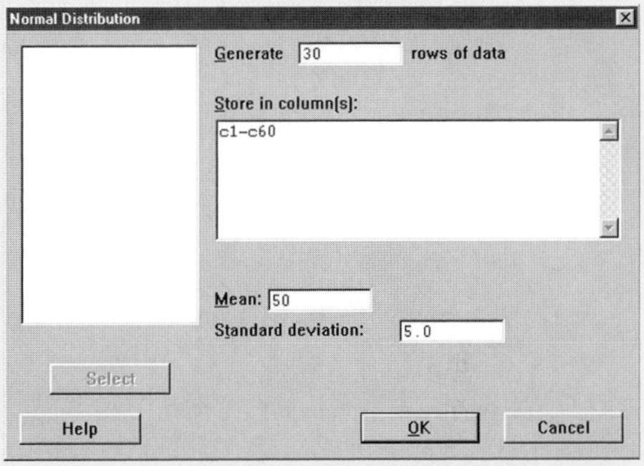

2. The MINITAB commands to create 60 confidence intervals on page 258 follow.

a. Select **Stat**, **Basic Statistics**, and then click on **1-Sample-z**.

b. In the dialog box indicate that the **Variables** are *C1-C60* and that **Sigma** is *5.0.* Next click on **Options** in the lower right corner, in the next dialog box indicate that the **Confidence level** is *95.0,* and then click **OK**. Click **OK** in the main dialog box.

3. The MINITAB commands to create the descriptive statistics on page 265 are the same as those used on page 118 in Chapter 3. Enter the data in the first column and label this column *Amount*. On the Toolbar select **Stat**, **Basic Statistics**, and **Display Basic Statistics**. In the dialog box select *Amount* as the **Variable** and click **OK**.

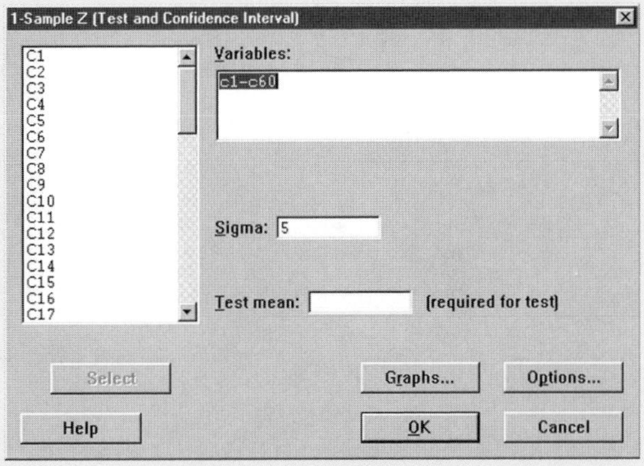

4. The MINITAB commands to create the confidence interval for the amount spent at the Inlet Square Mall on page 266 are:

a. Enter the 20 amounts spent in column c1 and name the variable *Amounts*, or locate the data on the student data disk. It is named "Shopping" and is found in the folder for Chapter 8.

b. On the Toolbar select **Stat**, **Basic Statistics**, and click on **1-Sample t**.

c. Select *Amount* as the **Variable** and click **OK**.

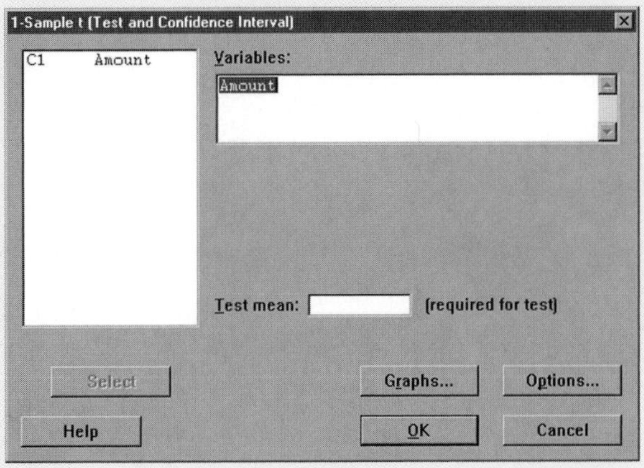

Chapter 8 Answers to Self-Review

8–1 **(a)** \$2,000. This is called the point estimate.

(b) $\$2{,}000 \pm 2.58 \dfrac{\$300}{\sqrt{40}} = \$2{,}000 \pm 122$

(c) The endpoints of the confidence interval are \$1,878 and \$2,122. About 99 percent of the intervals similarly constructed would include the population mean.

8–2 **(a)** $\overline{X} = \dfrac{18}{10} = 1.8 \quad s = \sqrt{\dfrac{44 - \dfrac{(18)^2}{10}}{10 - 1}} = 1.1353$

(b) The population mean is not known. The best estimate is the sample mean, 1.8 days.

(c) $1.80 \pm 2.262 \dfrac{1.1353}{\sqrt{10}} = 1.80 \pm 0.81$

(d) t is used because the standard deviation of a normal population is unknown and the sample contains less than 30 observations.

(e) The value of 0 is not in the interval. It is unreasonable to conclude that the mean number of days of work missed is 0 per employee.

8–3 **(a)** $p = \dfrac{420}{1400} = .30$

(b) $\sigma_p = \sqrt{\dfrac{.30(1 - .30)}{1400}} = .0122$

(c) $.30 \pm 2.58(.0122) = .30 \pm .03$

(d) The interval is between .27 and .33. About 99 percent of the similarly constructed intervals would include the population mean.

8–4 $.375 \pm 1.96\sqrt{\dfrac{.375(1 - .375)}{40}}\sqrt{\dfrac{250 - 40}{250 - 1}} = .375 \pm$
$1.96(.0765)(.9184) = .375 \pm .138$

The correction factor should be applied because $40/240 > .05$.

8–5 $n = \left(\dfrac{2.58(.279)}{.05}\right)^2 = 207.26$

The sample should be rounded to 208.

9

One-Sample Tests of a Hypothesis

GOALS

When you have completed this chapter you will be able to:

1 Define a *hypothesis* and *hypothesis testing.*

2 Describe the five-step hypothesis-testing procedure.

3 Distinguish between a one-tailed and a two-tailed test of hypothesis.

4 Conduct a test of hypothesis about a population mean.

5 Conduct a test of hypothesis about a population proportion.

Dole Pineapple, Inc. is concerned that the 16-ounce can of sliced pineapples is being overfilled. A random sample of 50 cans found that the arithmetic mean weight was 16.05 ounces, with a sample standard deviation of 0.03 ounces. At the 5 percent level of significance, can we conclude that the mean weight is greater than 16 ounces? (See Goal 4 and Exercise 28.)

Introduction

Chapter 7 began our study of statistical inference. We described how we could select a random sample and from this sample estimate the value of a population parameter. For example, we selected a sample of 5 employees at Spence Sprockets, found the number of years of service for each sampled employee, computed the mean years of service, and used the sample mean to estimate the mean years of service for all employees. In other words, we estimated a population parameter from a sample statistic.

Chapter 8 continued the study of statistical inference by developing a confidence interval. A confidence interval is a range of values within which we expect the population parameter to occur. In this chapter, rather than develop a range of values within which we expect the population parameter to occur, we develop a procedure to test the validity of a statement about a population parameter. Some examples of statements we can test are:

- The mean speed of automobiles passing milepost 150 on the West Virginia Turnpike is 68 miles per hour.

- The mean number of miles driven by those leasing a Chevy Blazer for three years is 32,000 miles.
- The mean time an American family lives in a particular single-family dwelling is 11.8 years.
- The mean starting salary for graduates of four-year business schools is $2,200 per month.
- Thirty-five percent of retirees in the upper Midwest sell their home and move to a warm climate within 1 year of their retirement.
- Eighty percent of those who play the state lotteries regularly never win more than $100 in any one play.

This chapter and several of the following chapters describe statistical hypothesis testing. We begin by defining what we mean by a statistical hypothesis and statistical hypothesis testing. Next, we outline the steps in statistical hypothesis testing. Then we conduct tests of hypothesis for means and proportions.

What Is a Hypothesis?

A hypothesis is a statement about a population parameter.

A hypothesis is a statement about a population parameter. Data and probability calculations are then used to check the reasonableness of the statement. To begin we need to define the word *hypothesis.* In the United States legal system, a person is innocent until proven guilty. A jury hypothesizes that a person charged with a crime is innocent and subjects this hypothesis to verification by reviewing the evidence and hearing testimony before reaching a verdict. In a similar sense, a patient goes to his or her physician and reports various symptoms. Based on the symptoms, the physician will order certain diagnostic tests, then based on the symptoms and the test results, determine the treatment to be followed.

In statistical analysis we make a claim, that is, state a hypothesis, then follow up with tests to verify the assertion or to determine that it is untrue. We define a statistical hypothesis as follows.

> **HYPOTHESIS** A statement about a population parameter developed for the purpose of testing.

In most cases the population is so large that it is not feasible to study all the items, objects, or persons in the population. For example, it would not be possible to contact every accountant in the United States to find his or her monthly income. Likewise, the quality assurance department cannot check the breaking strength of each ampul produced to determine whether it is between 5 and 20 psi.

As noted in Chapter 7, an alternative to measuring or interviewing the entire population is to take a sample from the population. We can, therefore, test a statement to determine whether the sample does or does not support the statement concerning the population.

What Is Hypothesis Testing?

The terms *hypothesis testing, significance testing,* and *testing a hypothesis* are used interchangeably. Hypothesis testing starts with a statement, or assumption, about a population parameter—such as the population mean. As noted, this statement is referred to as a *hypothesis.* A hypothesis might be that the mean monthly commission of salespeople in retail computer stores, such as Computerland, is $2,000. We cannot contact all these salespeople to ascertain that the mean is in fact $2,000. The cost of locating and interviewing every computer salesperson in the United States would be exorbitant. To test the validity of the assumption ($\mu = \$2{,}000$), we select a sample from the population of all computer salespeople, calculate sample statistics, and using specific decision rules accept or reject the hypothesis. A sample mean of $1,000 for the computer salespeople would certainly cause rejection of the hypothesis. However, suppose the sample mean is $1,995. Is that close enough to $2,000 for us to accept the assumption that the population mean is $2,000? Can we attribute the difference of $5 between the two means to sampling error, or is that difference statistically significant?

> **HYPOTHESIS TESTING** A procedure based on sample evidence and probability theory to determine whether the hypothesis is a reasonable statement.

Five-Step Procedure for Testing a Hypothesis

A systematic procedure

There is a five-step procedure that systematizes hypothesis testing; when we get to step 5, we are ready to reject or not reject the hypothesis. However, hypothesis testing using sample statistics does not provide proof that something is true, in the manner in which a mathematician "proves" a statement. It does provide a kind of "proof

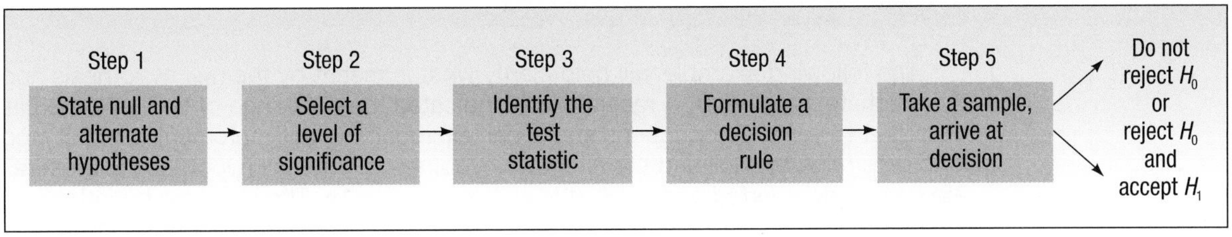

beyond a reasonable doubt," in the manner of the court system. Hence, there are specific rules of evidence, or procedures, that are followed. The steps are shown in the diagram at the bottom of the previous page. We will discuss in detail each of the steps.

Step 1: State the Null Hypothesis (H_0) and the Alternate Hypothesis (H_1)

The first step is to state the hypothesis being tested. It is called the **null hypothesis,** designated H_0, and read "*H sub zero*." The capital letter *H* stands for hypothesis, and the subscript zero implies "no difference." There is usually a "not" or a "no" term in the null hypothesis, meaning that there is "no change." For example, the null hypothesis is that the mean number of miles driven on the steel belted tire is not different from 60,000. The null hypothesis would be written H_0: $\mu = 60{,}000$ miles. Generally speaking, the null hypothesis is developed for the purpose of testing. We either reject or fail to reject the null hypothesis. The null hypothesis is a statement that is not rejected unless our sample data provide convincing evidence that it is false.

We should emphasize that if the null hypothesis is not rejected based on the sample data, we cannot say that the null hypothesis is true. To put it another way, failing to reject the null hypothesis does not prove that H_0 is true, it means we have *failed to disprove H_0*. To prove without any doubt the null hypothesis is true, the population parameter would have to be known. To actually determine it, we would have to test, survey, or count every item in the population. This is usually not feasible. The alternative is to take a sample from the population.

State the null hypothesis and the alternative hypothesis.

It should also be noted that we often begin the null hypothesis by stating, "There is no *significant* difference between . . . ," or "The mean impact strength of the glass is not *significantly* different from . . . ." When we select a sample from a population, the sample statistic is usually numerically different from the hypothesized population parameter. As an illustration, suppose the hypothesized impact strength of a glass plate is 70 psi, and the mean impact strength of a sample of 12 glass plates is 69.5 psi. We must make a decision about the difference of 0.5 psi. Is it a true difference, that is, a significant difference, or is the difference between the sample statistic (69.5) and the hypothesized population parameter (70.0) due to chance (sampling)? As noted, to answer this question we conduct a test of significance, commonly referred to as a test of hypothesis. To define what is meant by a null hypothesis:

NULL HYPOTHESIS A statement about the value of a population parameter.

The **alternate hypothesis** describes what you will conclude if you reject the null hypothesis. It is written H_1 and is read "*H sub one.*" It is also referred to as the research hypothesis. The alternate hypothesis is accepted if the sample data provide us with enough statistical evidence that the null hypothesis is false.

ALTERNATE HYPOTHESIS A statement that is accepted if the sample data provide enough evidence that the null hypothesis is false.

The following example will help clarify what is meant by the null hypothesis and the alternate hypothesis. A recent article indicated the mean age of U.S. commercial aircraft is 15 years. To conduct a statistical test regarding this statement, the first step is to determine the null and the alternate hypotheses. The null hypothesis represents the current or reported condition. It is written H_0: $\mu = 15$. The alternate hypothesis is that the statement is not true, that is, H_1: $\mu \neq 15$. It is important to remember that no matter how the problem is stated, *the null hypothesis will always contain the equal sign.* The equal sign (=) will never appear in the alternate hypothesis. Why? Because the null hypothesis is the statement being tested, and we need a specific value to include in our calculations. We turn to the alternate hypothesis only if we prove the null hypothesis to be untrue.

Step 2: Select a Level of Significance

Select a level of significance or risk.

After setting up the null hypothesis and alternate hypothesis, the next step is to state the level of significance.

LEVEL OF SIGNIFICANCE The probability of rejecting the null hypothesis when it is true.

The level of significance is designated α, the Greek letter alpha. It is also sometimes called the level of risk. This may be a more appropriate term because it is the risk you take of rejecting the null hypothesis when it is really true.

There is no one level of significance that is applied to all tests. A decision is made to use the .05 level (often stated as the 5 percent level), the .01 level, the .10 level, or any other level between 0 and 1. Remember α is a probability. Traditionally, the .05 level is selected for consumer research projects, .01 for quality assurance, and .10 for political polling. You, the researcher, must decide on the level of significance *before* formulating a decision rule and collecting sample data.

To illustrate how it is possible to reject a true hypothesis, suppose a firm manufacturing personal computers uses a large number of printed circuit boards. The contract specifies that the computer manufacturer's quality-assurance department will sample all incoming shipments of circuit boards. If more than 6 percent of the boards sampled are defective, the shipment will be rejected. The null hypothesis is that the incoming shipment of boards contains 6 percent or less substandard boards. The alternate hypothesis is that more than 6 percent of the boards are defective.

A sample of 50 circuit boards received July 21 from Allied Electronics revealed that 4 boards, or 8 percent, were defective. The shipment was rejected because it exceeded the maximum of 6 percent substandard printed circuit boards. If the shipment was actually substandard, then the decision to return the boards to the supplier was correct. However, suppose the 4 substandard printed circuit boards selected in the sample of 50 were the only substandard boards in the shipment of 4,000 boards. Then only 1⁄10 of 1 percent were defective (4/4,000 = .001). In that case, less than 6 percent of the entire shipment was substandard and rejecting the shipment was an error. In terms of hypothesis testing, we rejected the null hypothesis that the shipment was not substandard when we should have accepted the null hypothesis. By rejecting a true null hypothesis, we commit a Type I error. The probability of committing a Type I error is α.

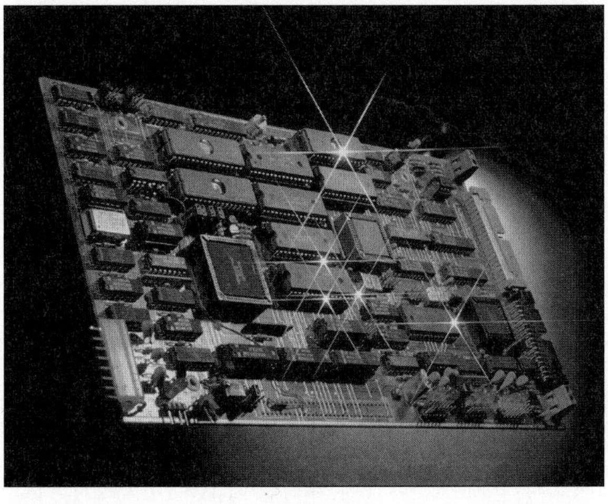

TYPE I ERROR Rejecting the null hypothesis, H_0, when it is true.

The probability of committing another type of error, called a Type II error, is designated by the Greek letter beta (β).

TYPE II ERROR Accepting the null hypothesis when it is false.

The firm manufacturing personal computers would commit a Type II error if, unknown to the manufacturer, an incoming shipment of printed circuit boards from Allied Electronics contained 15 percent defective boards, yet the shipment was accepted. How could this happen? Suppose 2 of the 50 boards in the sample (4 percent) tested were defective, and 48 of the 50 were good boards. According to the stated procedure, because the sample contained less than 6 percent defective boards, the shipment was accepted. It could be that *by chance* the 48 good boards selected in the sample were the only acceptable ones in the entire shipment of thousands of boards!

In retrospect, the researcher cannot study every item or individual in the population. Thus, there is a possibility of two types of error—a Type I error, wherein the null hypothesis is rejected when it should have been accepted, and a Type II error, wherein the null hypothesis is accepted when it should have been rejected. Recall alpha is also the level of significance and is determined in advance when you plan the hypothesis test.

In summary, the probability of these two possible errors are *alpha,* α, and *beta,* β. Alpha (α) is the probability of making a Type I error, and beta (β) is the probability of making a Type II error. The following table summarizes the decisions the researcher could make and the possible consequences.

Null Hypothesis	Researcher: Accepts H_0	Researcher: Rejects H_0
H_0 is true	Correct decision	Type I error
H_0 is false	Type II error	Correct decision

Step 3: Select the Test Statistic

There are many test statistics. In this chapter we use both z and t as the test statistic. In other chapters we will use such test statistics as F and χ^2, called chi-square.

TEST STATISTIC A value, determined from sample information, used to determine whether to reject the null hypothesis.

In hypothesis testing for the mean (μ) when σ is known or the sample size is large, the test statistic z is computed by:

z TEST STATISTIC

$$z = \frac{\overline{X} - \mu}{\sigma/\sqrt{n}} \qquad \textbf{[9–1]}$$

The z value is based on the sampling distribution of $\overline{X}$, which is normally distributed when the sample is reasonably large with a mean ($\mu_{\overline{X}}$) equal to μ, and a standard deviation $\sigma_{\overline{X}}$, which is equal to $\sigma/\sqrt{n}$. We can thus determine whether the difference between $\overline{X}$ and μ is statistically significant by finding the number of standard deviations $\overline{X}$ is from μ using formula 9–1.

Step 4: Formulate the Decision Rule

The decision rule states the conditions when H_0 is rejected.

A decision rule is a statement of the specific conditions under which the null hypothesis is rejected and the conditions under which it is not rejected. The region of rejection defines the location of all the values that are so large or so small that the probability of their occurrence under a true null hypothesis is small. To avoid potential bias, the decision rule, like the significance level, is formulated before selecting the sample.

Chart 9–1 portrays the rejection region for a test of significance that will be conducted later in the chapter.

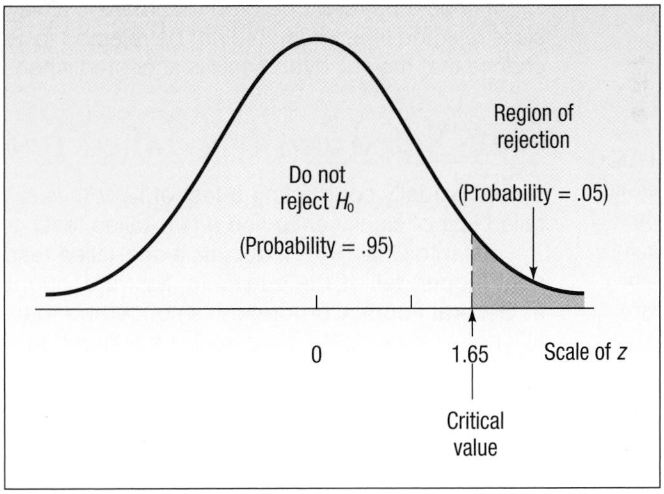

CHART 9–1 Sampling Distribution of the Statistic z, a Right-Tailed Test, .05 Level of Significance

Note in the chart that:

1. The area where the null hypothesis is not rejected is to the left of 1.65. We will explain how to get the 1.65 value shortly.
2. The area of rejection is to the right of 1.65.
3. A one-tailed test is being applied. (This will also be explained later.)
4. The .05 level of significance was chosen.
5. The sampling distribution of the statistic z is normally distributed.
6. The value 1.65 separates the regions where the null hypothesis is rejected and where it is not rejected.
7. The value 1.65 is the **critical value.**

CRITICAL VALUE The dividing point between the region where the null hypothesis is rejected and the region where it is not rejected.

Statistics in Action

During World War II, allied military planners needed estimates of the number of German tanks. The information provided by traditional spying methods was not reliable, but statistical methods proved to be valuable. For example, espionage and reconnaissance led analysts to estimate that 1,550 tanks were produced during June of 1941. However, using the serial numbers of captured tanks and statistical analysis, military planners estimated 244. The actual number produced, as determined from German production records, was 271. The estimate using statistical analysis turned out to be much more accurate. A similar type of analysis was used to estimate the number of Iraqi tanks destroyed during Desert Storm.

Step 5: Make a Decision

The fifth and final step in hypothesis testing is computing the test statistic, comparing it to the critical value, and making a decision to reject or not to reject the null hypothesis. Referring to Chart 9–1, if, based on sample information, *z,* the test statistic, is computed to be 2.34, the null hypothesis is rejected at the .05 level of significance. The decision to reject H_0 was made because 2.34 lies in the region of rejection, that is, beyond the critical value of 1.65. We would reject the null hypothesis, reasoning that it is highly improbable that a computed *z* value this large is due to sampling variation (chance).

Had the computed value been 1.65 or less, say 0.71, the null hypothesis would not be rejected. It would be reasoned that such a small computed value could be attributed to chance, that is, sampling variation. As noted, only one of two decisions is possible in hypothesis testing—either accept or reject the null hypothesis. Instead of "accepting" the null hypothesis, H_0, some researchers prefer to phrase the decision as: "Do not reject H_0," "We fail to reject H_0," or "The sample results do not allow us to reject H_0."

It should be reemphasized that there is always a possibility that the null hypothesis is rejected when it should not be rejected (a Type I error). Also, there is a definable chance that the null hypothesis is accepted when it should be rejected (a Type II error).

One-Tailed and Two-Tailed Tests of Significance

Before actually conducting a test of hypothesis, we will differentiate between a one-tailed test of significance and a two-tailed test.

Refer to Chart 9–1. It depicts a one-tailed test. The region of rejection is only in the right (upper) tail of the curve. To illustrate, suppose that the packaging department at General Foods Corporation is concerned that some boxes of Grape Nuts are significantly overweight. The cereal is packaged in 453-gram boxes, so the null hypothesis is H_0: $\mu \leq 453$. This is read, "the population mean (μ) is equal to or less than 453." The alternate hypothesis is, therefore, H_1: $\mu > 453$. This is read, "μ is greater than 453." Note that the inequality sign in the alternate hypothesis $>$ points to the region of rejection in the upper tail. See Chart 9–1. Also note the null hypothesis includes the equal sign. That is, H_0: $\mu \leq 453$. The equality condition always appears in H_0, never in H_1.

Chart 9–2 portrays a situation where the rejection region is in the left (lower) tail of the normal distribution. As an illustration, consider the problem of automobile manufacturers, large automobile leasing companies, and other organizations that purchase large quantities of tires. They want the tires to average, say, 60,000 miles of wear under normal usage. They will, therefore, reject a shipment of tires if tests reveal that the mean life of the tires is significantly below 60,000 miles. They gladly accept a shipment if the mean life is greater than 60,000 miles! They are not concerned with this possibility, however. They are concerned only if they have sample evidence to conclude that the tires will average less than 60,000 miles of useful life. Thus, the test is set up to satisfy the concern of the automobile manufacturers that *the mean life of the tires is less than 60,000 miles.* The null and alternate hypotheses in this case are written H_0: $\mu \geq 60{,}000$ and H_1: $\mu < 60{,}000$.

Test is one-tailed if H_1 states $\mu >$ or $\mu <$.

One way to determine the location of the rejection region is to look at the direction of the inequality sign in the alternate hypothesis (either $<$ or $>$). In this problem it is pointing to the left, and the rejection region is therefore in the left tail.

If H_1 states a direction, test is one-tailed.

In summary, a test is *one-tailed* when the alternate hypothesis, H_1, states a direction, such as:

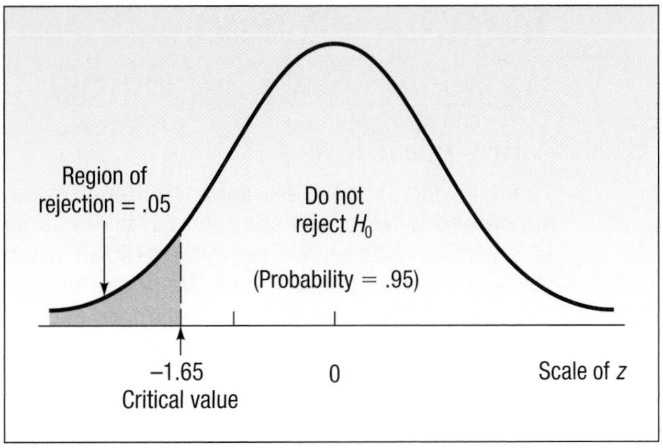

CHART 9–2 Sampling Distribution for the Statistic z, Left-Tailed Test, .05 Level of Significance

H_0: The mean income of female stockbrokers is \$85,000 per year.
H_1: The mean income of female stockbrokers is *greater* than \$85,000 per year.

If no direction is specified in the alternate hypothesis, we use a *two-tailed* test. Changing the previous problem to illustrate:

H_0: The mean income of female stockbrokers is \$85,000 per year.
H_1: The mean income of female stockbrokers is *not equal to* \$85,000 per year.

If the null hypothesis is rejected and H_1 accepted in the two-tailed case, the mean income could be significantly greater than \$85,000 per year, or it could be significantly less than \$85,000 per year. To accommodate these two possibilities, the 5 percent area of rejection is divided equally into the two tails of the sampling distribution (2.5 percent each). Chart 9–3 shows the two probabilities and the critical values. Note that the total probability in the standard normal distribution is 1.0000, found by .9500 + .0250 + .0250.

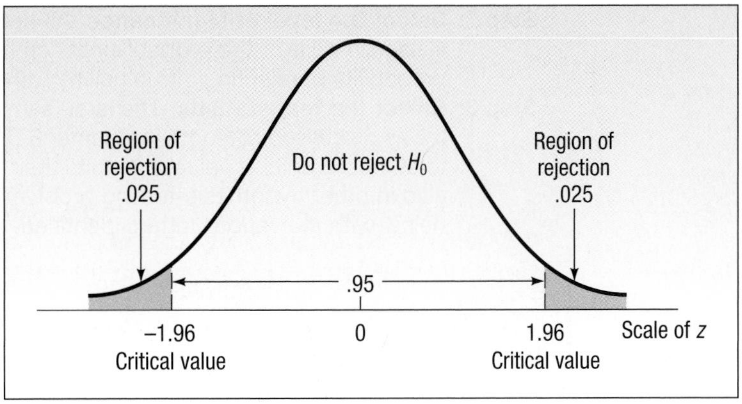

CHART 9–3 Regions of Nonrejection and Rejection for a Two-Tailed Test, .05 Level of Significance

Testing for a Population Mean with a Known Population Standard Deviation

A Two-Tailed Test

The following example expands the idea of hypothesis testing. In this case, we are *not* concerned whether the sample results are larger or smaller than the proposed population mean. Rather, we are interested in whether it is *different from* the proposed value for the population mean. We begin, as we did in the previous chapter, with a situation in which we have historical information about the population and in fact know its standard deviation.

EXAMPLE

The Jamestown Steel Company manufactures and assembles desks and other office equipment at several plants in western New York State. The weekly production of the Model A325 desk at the Fredonia Plant is normally distributed, with a mean of 200 and a standard deviation of 16 desks. Recently, due to market expansion, new production methods have been introduced and new employees hired. The vice president of manufacturing would like to investigate whether there has been a change in the weekly production of the Model A325 desk. To put it another way, is the mean number of desks produced at the Fredonia Plant different from 200 at the .01 significance level?

SOLUTION

We use the statistical hypothesis testing procedure to investigate whether the production rate has changed from 200 per week.

Step 1: State the null hypothesis and the alternate hypothesis. The null hypothesis is "The population mean is 200." The alternate hypothesis is "The mean is different from 200" or "The mean is not 200." These two hypotheses are written:

H_0: $\mu = 200$
H_1: $\mu \neq 200$

This is a *two-tailed test* because the alternate hypothesis does not state a direction. In other words, it does not state whether the mean production is greater than 200 or less than 200. The vice president only wants to find out whether the production rate is different from 200.

Step 2: Select the level of significance. As noted, the .01 level of significance is used. This is α, the probability of committing a Type I error, and it is the probability of rejecting a true null hypothesis using sample data.

Step 3: Select the test statistic. The large sample test statistic for a mean is z. It was discussed at length in Chapter 6. Transforming the production data to standard units (z values) permits their use not only in this problem but also in other hypothesis-testing problems. Formula 9–1 for z is repeated below with the various letters identified.

Formula for the test statistic

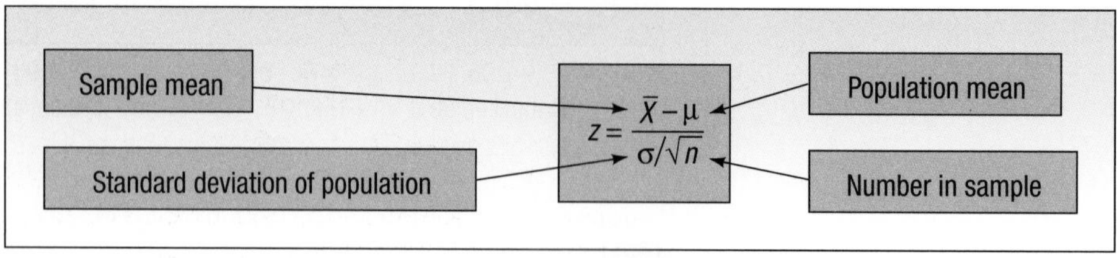

Step 4: Formulate the decision rule. The decision rule is formulated by finding the critical values of *z* from Appendix D. Since this is a two-tailed test, half of .01, or .005, is in each tail. The area where H_0 is not rejected, located between the two tails, is therefore .99. Appendix D is based on half of the area under the curve, or .5000. Then, .5000 − .005 is .4950, so .4950 is the area between 0 and the critical value. Locate .4950 in the body of the table. The value nearest to .4950 is .4951. Then read the critical value in the row and column corresponding to .4951. It is 2.58. For your convenience Appendix D, Areas under the Normal Curve, is repeated in the inside back cover.

All the facets of this problem are shown in the diagram in Chart 9–4.

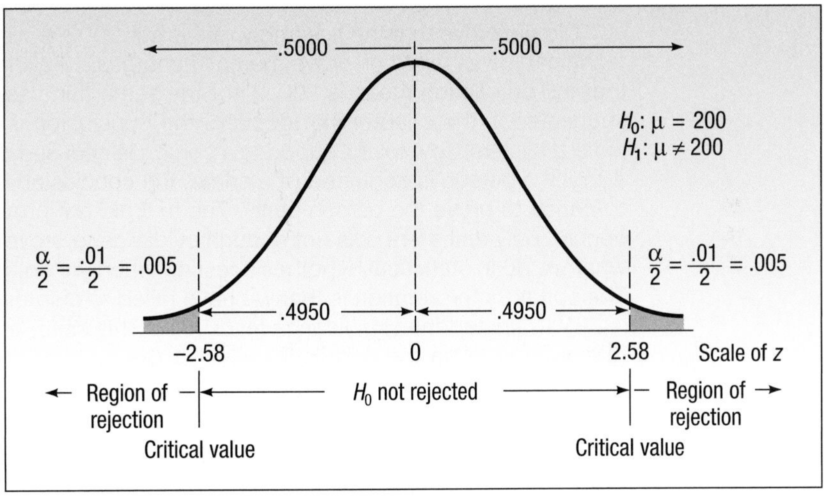

CHART 9–4 Decision Rule for the .01 Significance Level

The decision rule is, therefore: Reject the null hypothesis and accept the alternate hypothesis (which states that the population mean is not 200) if the computed value of *z* is not between −2.58 and +2.58. Do not reject the null hypothesis if *z* falls between −2.58 and +2.58.

Step 5: Make a decision. Take a sample from the population (weekly production), compute *z*, apply the decision rule, and arrive at a decision to reject H_0 or not to reject H_0. The mean number of desks produced last year (50 weeks, because the plant was shut down 2 weeks for vacation) is 203.5. The standard deviation of the population is 16 desks per week. Computing the *z* value from formula 9–1:

$$z = \frac{\overline{X} - \mu}{\sigma/\sqrt{n}} = \frac{203.5 - 200}{16/\sqrt{50}} = 1.55$$

The computed value of 1.55 does not fall in the rejection region. Therefore, H_0 is not rejected. We conclude that the population mean is *not* different from 200. So we would report to the vice president of manufacturing that the sample evidence does not show that the production rate at the Fredonia Plant has changed from 200 per week. The difference of 3.5 units between the historical weekly production rate and that last year can reasonably be attributed to chance. This information is summarized in the following chart.

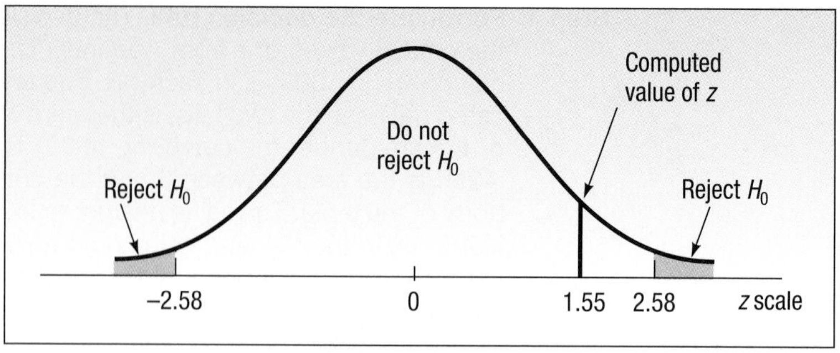

Did we prove that the assembly rate is still 200 per week? Not really. What we did, technically, was *fail to disprove the null hypothesis.* Failing to disprove the hypothesis that the population mean is 200 is not the same thing as proving it to be true. As we suggested in the chapter introduction, the conclusion is analogous to the American judicial system. To explain, suppose a person is accused of a crime but is acquitted by a jury. If a person is acquitted of a crime, the conclusion is that there was not enough evidence to prove the person guilty. The trial did not prove that the individual was innocent, only that there was not enough evidence to prove the defendant guilty. That is what we do in statistical hypothesis testing when we do not reject the null hypothesis. The correct interpretation is that we have failed to disprove the null hypothesis.

We selected the significance level, .01 in this case, before setting up the decision rule and sampling the population. This is the appropriate strategy. The significance level should be set by the investigator, but it should be determined *before* gathering the sample evidence and not changed based on the sample evidence.

How does the hypothesis testing procedure just described compare with that of confidence intervals discussed in the previous chapter? When we conducted the test of hypothesis regarding the production of desks we changed the units from desks per week to a z value. Then we compared the computed value of the test statistic (1.55) to that of the critical values (−2.58 and 2.58). Because the computed value was in the region where the null hypothesis was not rejected, we concluded that the population mean could be 200. To use the confidence interval approach, on the other hand, we would develop a confidence interval, based on formula 8–1. See page 255. The interval would be from 197.66 to 209.34, found by $203.5 \pm 2.58(16/\sqrt{50})$. Note that the hypothesized population parameter, 200, is within this interval. Hence, we would conclude that the population mean could reasonably be 200.

In general, H_0 is rejected if the confidence interval does not include the hypothesized value. If the confidence interval includes the hypothesized value, then H_0 is not rejected. So the "do not reject region" for a test of hypothesis is equivalent to the proposed population value occurring in the confidence interval. The primary difference lies in whether the interval is centered around the sample statistic, such as $\overline{X}$, or around 0, as in the test of hypothesis.

Self-Review 9–1

The mean annual turnover rate of the 200-count bottle of Bayer Aspirin is 6.0 with a standard deviation of 0.50. (This indicates that the stock of Bayer Aspirin turns over on the pharmacy shelves an average of 6 times per year.) It is suspected that the mean turnover has changed and is not 6.0. Use the .05 significance level.

(a) State the null hypothesis and the alternate hypothesis.
(b) What is the probability of a Type I error?
(c) Give the formula for the test statistic.
(d) State the decision rule.
(e) A random sample of 64 bottles of the 200-count size Bayer Aspirin showed a mean of 5.84. Shall we reject the hypothesis that the population mean is 6.0? Interpret the result.

A One-Tailed Test

In the previous example, we emphasized that we were only concerned with reporting to the vice president whether there had been a change in the mean number of desks assembled at the Fredonia Plant. We were not concerned with whether the change was an increase or a decrease in the production.

To illustrate a one-tailed test, let's change the problem. Suppose the vice president wants to know whether there has been an *increase* in the number of units assembled. To put it another way, can we conclude, because of the improved production methods, that the mean number of desks assembled in the last 50 weeks was more than 200? Look at the difference in the way the problem is formulated. In the first case we wanted to know whether there was a *difference* in the mean number assembled, but now we want to know whether there has been an *increase*. Because we are investigating different questions, we will set our hypotheses differently. The biggest difference occurs in the alternate hypothesis. Before, we stated the alternate hypothesis as "different from"; now we want to state it as "greater than." In symbols:

A two-tailed test:	A one-tailed test:
H_0: $\mu = 200$	H_0: $\mu \leq 200$
H_1: $\mu \neq 200$	H_1: $\mu > 200$

The critical values for a one-tailed test are different from a two-tailed test at the same significance level. In the previous example, we split the significance level in half and put half in the lower tail and half in the upper tail. In a one-tailed test we put all the rejection region in one tail. See Chart 9–5.

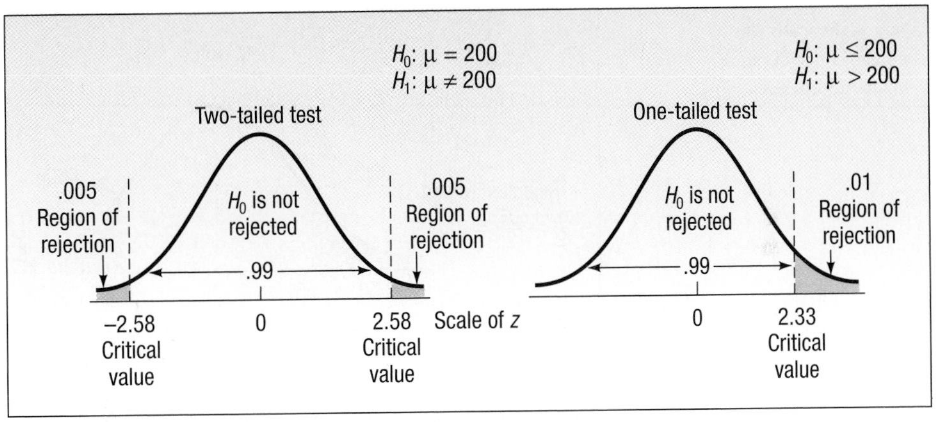

CHART 9–5 Rejection Regions for Two-Tailed and One-Tailed Tests, $\alpha = .01$

For the one-tailed test, the critical value is 2.33, found by: (1) subtracting .01 from .5000 and (2) finding the z value corresponding to .4900.

p-Value in Hypothesis Testing

In testing a hypothesis, we compared the test statistic to a critical value. A decision is made to either reject the null hypothesis or not to reject it. So, for example, if the critical value is 1.96 and the computed value of the test statistic is 2.19, the decision is to reject the null hypothesis.

In recent years, spurred by the availability of computer software, additional information is often reported on the strength of the rejection or acceptance. That is, how confident are we in rejecting the null hypothesis? This approach reports the probability

Statistics in Action

There is a difference between *statistically significant* and *practically significant.* To explain, suppose we develop a new diet pill and test it on 100,000 people. We conclude that the typical person taking the pill for two years lost one pound. Do you think many people would be interested in taking the pill to lose one pound? The results of using the new pill were statistically significant but not practically significant.

(assuming that the null hypothesis is true) of getting a value of the test statistic at least as extreme as the value actually obtained. This process compares the probability, called the ***p*-value,** with the significance level. If the *p*-value is smaller than the significance level, H_0 is rejected. If it is larger than the significance level, H_0 is not rejected.

***p*-VALUE** The probability of observing a sample value as extreme as, or more extreme than, the value observed, when the null hypothesis is true.

Determining the *p*-value not only results in a decision regarding H_0, but it gives us additional insight into the strength of the decision. A very small *p*-value, such as .0001, indicates that there is little likelihood the H_0 is true. On the other hand, a *p*-value of .2033 means that H_0 is not rejected, and there is little likelihood that it is false.

How do we find the *p*-value? To illustrate we use the example in which we tested the null hypothesis that the mean number of desks produced per week at Fredonia was 200. We did not reject the null hypothesis, because the value of 1.55 fell in the region between −2.58 and 2.58. We agreed not to reject the null hypothesis if the computed value of z fell in this region. The probability of finding a z value of 1.55 or more is .0606, found by .5000 − .4394. In other words, the probability of obtaining an $\bar{X}$ greater than 203.5 if $\mu = 200$ is .0606. To compute the *p*-value, we need to be concerned with the region less than −1.55 as well as the values greater than 1.55 (because the rejection region is in both tails). The *p*-value is .1212, found by 2(.0606). The *p*-value of .1212 is greater than the significance level of .01 decided upon initially, so H_0 is not rejected. The details are shown in the following graph.

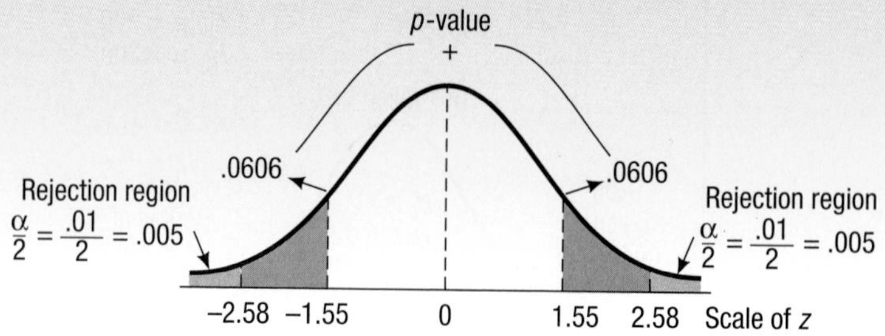

A *p*-value is a way to express the likelihood that H_0 is not true. But how do we interpret a *p*-value? We have already said that if the *p*-value is less than the significance level, then we reject H_0; if it is greater than the significance level, then we do not reject H_0. Also, if the *p*-value is very large, then it is likely that H_0 is true. If the *p*-value is small, then it is likely that H_0 is not true. The following box will help to interpret *p*-values.

INTERPRETING THE WEIGHT OF EVIDENCE AGAINST H_0

If the *p*-value is less than

(a) .10, we have *some evidence* that H_0 is not true.

(b) .05, we have *strong evidence* that H_0 is not true.

(c) .01, we have *very strong evidence* that H_0 is not true.

(d) .001, we have *extremely strong evidence* that H_0 is not true.

Testing for a Population Mean: Large Sample, Population Standard Deviation Unknown

In the preceding example, we knew σ, the population standard deviation. In most cases, however, the population standard deviation is unknown. Thus, σ must be based on prior studies or estimated by the sample standard deviation, s. The population standard deviation in the following example is not known, so the sample standard deviation is used to estimate σ. As long as the sample size, n, is greater than 30, s can be substituted for σ, as illustrated in the following formula:

z STATISTIC, σ UNKNOWN

$$z = \frac{\overline{X} - \mu}{s/\sqrt{n}} \qquad [9\text{–}2]$$

EXAMPLE

The Thompson's Discount Appliance Store issues its own credit card. The credit manager wants to find whether the mean monthly unpaid balance is more than \$400. The level of significance is set at .05. A random check of 172 unpaid balances revealed the sample mean is \$407 and the standard deviation of the sample is \$38. Should the credit manager conclude the population mean is greater than \$400, or is it reasonable that the difference of \$7 (\$407 − \$400 = \$7) is due to chance?

SOLUTION

The null and alternate hypotheses are:

H_0: $\mu \leq \$400$
H_1: $\mu > \$400$

Because the alternate hypothesis states a direction, we use a one-tailed test. The critical value of z is 1.65. The computed value of z is 2.42, found by using formula 9–2:

$$z = \frac{\overline{X} - \mu}{s/\sqrt{n}} = \frac{\$407 - \$400}{\$38/\sqrt{172}} = \frac{\$7}{\$2.8975} = 2.42$$

The decision rule is portrayed in the following chart.

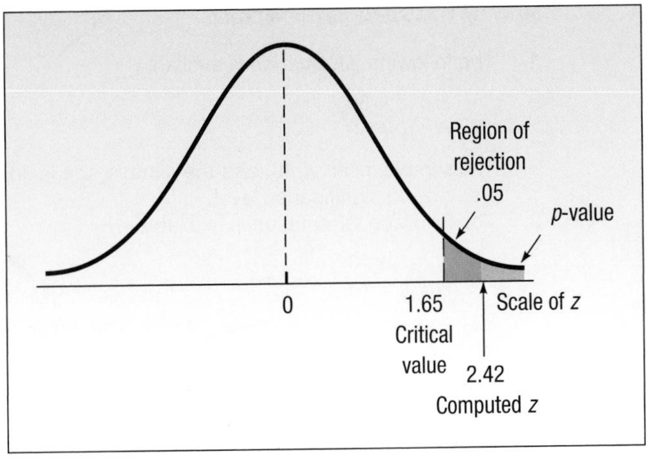

Because the computed value of the test statistic (2.42) is larger than the critical value (1.65), the null hypothesis is rejected. The credit manager can conclude the mean unpaid balance is greater than \$400.

The *p*-value provides additional insight into the decision. Recall the *p*-value is the probability of finding a test statistic as large as or larger than that obtained, when the null hypothesis is true. So we find the probability of a *z* value greater than 2.42. From Appendix D the probability of a *z* value between 0 and 2.42 is .4922. We want to determine the likelihood of a value *greater than* 2.42, so $.5000 - .4922 = .0078$. The *p*-value is .0078. It is unlikely, therefore, that the null hypothesis is true.

Self-Review 9–2

Refer to Self-Review 9–1.

(a) Suppose the hypothesis-testing situation was changed to a one-tailed test. How would the null hypothesis be written symbolically if it read, "The population mean is equal to or greater than 6.0"?
(b) How would the alternate hypothesis be written symbolically if it read, "The population mean is less than 6.0"?
(c) Show the decision rule graphically. Show the rejection region and indicate the critical value.

Exercises

For Exercises 1–4 answer the questions: (a) Is this a one- or two-tailed test? (b) What is the decision rule? (c) What is the value of the test statistic? (d) What is your decision regarding H_0? (e) What is the *p*-value? Interpret it.

1. The following information is available.

$$H_0: \mu = 50$$
$$H_1: \mu \neq 50$$

The sample mean is 49, and the sample size is 36. The population standard deviation is 5. Use the .05 significance level.

2. The following information is available.

$$H_0: \mu \leq 10$$
$$H_1: \mu > 10$$

The sample mean is 12 for a sample of 36. The population standard deviation is 3. Use the .02 significance level.

3. A sample of 36 observations is selected from a normal population. The sample mean is 21, and the sample standard deviation is 5. Conduct the following test of hypothesis using the .05 significance level.

$$H_0: \mu \leq 20$$
$$H_1: \mu > 20$$

4. A sample of 64 observations is selected from a normal population. The sample mean is 215, and the sample standard deviation is 15. Conduct the following test of hypothesis using the .03 significance level.

$$H_0: \mu \geq 220$$
$$H_1: \mu < 220$$

For Exercises 5–8: (a) State the null hypothesis and the alternate hypothesis. (b) State the decision rule. (c) Compute the value of the test statistic. (d) What is your decision regarding H_0? (e) What is the p-value? Interpret it.

5. The manufacturer of the X-15 steel-belted radial truck tire claims that the mean mileage the tire can be driven before the tread wears out is 60,000 miles. The standard deviation of the mileage is 5,000 miles. The Crosset Truck Company bought 48 tires and found that the mean mileage for their trucks is 59,500 miles. Is Crosset's experience different from that claimed by the manufacturer at the .05 significance level?
6. The MacBurger restaurant chain claims that the waiting time of customers for service is normally distributed, with a mean of 3 minutes and a standard deviation of 1 minute. The quality-assurance department found in a sample of 50 customers at the Warren Road MacBurger that the mean waiting time was 2.75 minutes. At the .05 significance level, can we conclude that the mean waiting time is less than 3 minutes?
7. A recent national survey found that high school students watched an average (mean) of 6.8 videos per month. A random sample of 36 college students revealed that the mean number of videos watched last month was 6.2, with a standard deviation of 0.5. At the .05 significance level, can we conclude that college students watch fewer videos a month than high school students?
8. At the time she was hired as a server at the Grumney Family Restaurant, Beth Brigden was told, "You can average more than $20 a day in tips." Over the first 35 days she was employed at the restaurant, the mean daily amount of her tips was $24.85, with a standard deviation of $3.24. At the .01 significance level, can Ms. Brigden conclude that she is earning an average of more than $20 in tips?

Tests Concerning Proportions

In the previous chapter we discussed confidence intervals for proportions. We can also conduct a test of hypothesis for a proportion. Recall that a proportion is the ratio of the number of successes to the number of observations. We let X refer to the number of successes and n the number of observations, so the proportion of success in a fixed number of trials is X/n. Thus, the formula for computing a sample proportion, p, is $p = X/n$. Consider the following potential hypothesis-testing situations.

- Historically, General Motors reports that 70 percent of leased vehicles are returned with less than 36,000 miles. A recent sample of 200 vehicles returned at the end of their lease showed 158 had less than 36,000 miles. Has the proportion increased?
- The American Association of Retired Persons (AARP) reports that 60 percent of retired persons under the age of 65 would return to work on a full-time basis if a suitable job were available. A sample of 500 retirees under 65 revealed 315 would return to work. Can we conclude that more than 60 percent would return to work?
- Able Moving and Storage, Inc. advises its clients for long distance residential moves that their household goods will be delivered in 3 to 5 days from the time they are picked up. Able's records show that they are successful 90 percent of the time with this claim. A recent audit revealed they were successful 190 times out of 200. Can they conclude that their success rate has increased?

Some assumptions must be made and conditions met before testing a population proportion. To test a hypothesis about a population proportion, a random sample is chosen from the population. It is assumed that the binomial assumptions discussed in Chapter 5 are met: (1) the sample data collected are the result of counts; (2) the outcome of an experiment is classified into one of two mutually exclusive categories—a "success" or a "failure"; (3) the probability of a success is the same for each trial; and (4) the trials are independent, meaning the outcome of one trial does not affect the outcome of any other trial. The test we will conduct shortly is appropriate when both $n\pi$ and $n(1 - \pi)$ are at least 5. n is the sample size, and π is the population proportion. It uses the fact that a binomial distribution can be approximated by the normal distribution.

$n\pi$ and $n(1 - \pi)$ must be at least 5.

EXAMPLE

Prior elections in a state indicate it is necessary for a candidate for governor to receive at least 80 percent of the vote in the northern section of the state to be elected. The incumbent governor is interested in assessing his chances of returning to office and plans to conduct a survey of 2,000 registered voters in the northern section of the state.

Using the hypothesis-testing procedure, assess the governor's chances of reelection.

SOLUTION

The following test of hypothesis can be conducted because both $n\pi$ and $n(1 - \pi)$ exceed 5. In this case, $n = 2{,}000$ and $\pi = .80$ (π is the proportion of the vote in the northern part of the state, or 80 percent, needed to be elected). Thus, $n\pi = 2{,}000(.80) = 1{,}600$ and $n(1 - \pi) = 2{,}000(1 - .80) = 400$. Both 1,600 and 400 are greater than 5.

Step 1: State the null hypothesis and the alternate hypothesis. The null hypothesis, H_0, is that the population proportion π is .80 or larger. The alternate hypothesis, H_1, is that the proportion is less than .80. From a practical standpoint, the incumbent governor is concerned only when the proportion is less than .80. If it is equal to or greater than .80, he will have no problem; that is, the sample data would indicate he will probably be reelected. These hypotheses are written symbolically as:

H_0: $\pi \geq .80$
H_1: $\pi < .80$

H_1 states a direction. Thus, as noted previously, the test is one-tailed with the inequality sign pointing to the tail of the distribution containing the region of rejection.

Step 2: Select the level of significance. The level of significance is .05. This is the likelihood that a true hypothesis will be rejected.

Step 3: Select the test statistic. z is the appropriate statistic, found by:

TEST OF HYPOTHESIS, ONE PROPORTION $$z = \frac{p - \pi}{\sigma_p} \quad \textbf{[9–3]}$$

where:

- π is the hypothesized population proportion parameter.
- p is the sample proportion.
- n is the sample size.
- σ_p is the standard error of the population proportion. It is computed by $\sqrt{\pi(1 - \pi)/n}$, so the formula for z becomes:

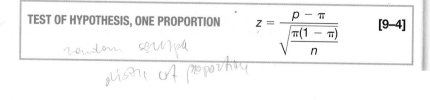

TEST OF HYPOTHESIS, ONE PROPORTION $$z = \frac{p - \pi}{\sqrt{\dfrac{\pi(1 - \pi)}{n}}} \quad \textbf{[9–4]}$$

Finding the critical value

Step 4: State the decision rule. The critical value or values of z form the dividing point or points between the regions where H_0 is rejected and where it is not rejected. Since the alternate hypothesis states a direction, this is a one-tailed test. The sign of the inequality points to the left, so only the left half of the curve is used. See Chart 9–6. The significance level was given as .05 in step 2. This probability is in the left tail and determines the region of rejection. The area between zero and the critical value is .4500, found by .5000 − .0500. Referring to Appendix D and searching for .4500, we find the critical value of z is 1.65. The decision rule is, therefore: Reject the null hypothesis and accept the alternate hypothesis if the computed value of z falls to the left of −1.65; otherwise do not reject H_0.

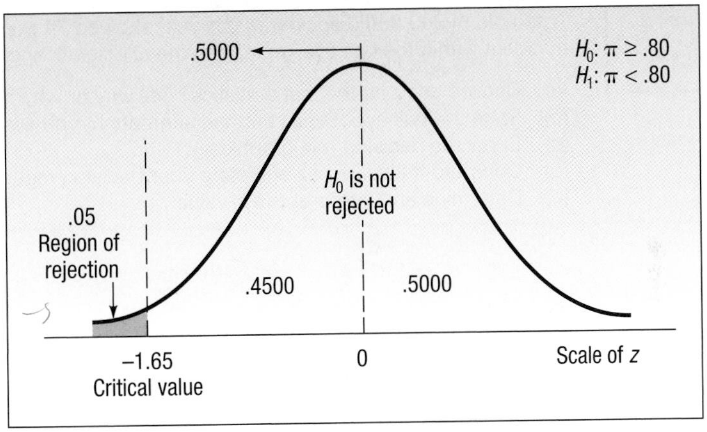

CHART 9–6 Rejection Region for the .05 Level of Significance, One-Tailed Test

Step 5: Make a decision. Select a sample and make a decision about H_0. A sample survey of 2,000 potential voters in the northern part of the state revealed that 1,550 planned to vote for the incumbent governor. Is the sample proportion of .775 (found by 1,550/2,000) close enough to .80 to conclude that the difference is due to chance? In this case:

- p is .775, the proportion in the sample who plan to vote for the governor.
- n is 2,000, the number of voters surveyed.
- π is .80, the hypothesized population proportion.
- z is a normally distributed test statistic when the hypothesis is true and the other assumptions are true.

Using formula 9–4 and computing z:

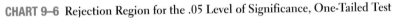

$$z = \frac{p - \pi}{\sqrt{\dfrac{\pi(1-\pi)}{n}}} = \frac{\dfrac{1{,}550}{2{,}000} - .80}{\sqrt{\dfrac{.80(1-.80)}{2{,}000}}} = \frac{.775 - .80}{\sqrt{.00008}} = -2.80$$

The computed value of z (−2.80) is in the rejection region, so the null hypothesis is rejected at the .05 level. The difference of 2.5 percentage points between the sample percent (77.5 percent) and the hypothesized population percent in the northern part of the state necessary to carry the state (80 percent) is statistically significant. It is probably not due to sampling variation. To put it another way, the evidence at this point does not support the claim that the incumbent governor will return to the governor's mansion for another 4 years.

The p-value is the probability of finding a z value less than -2.80. From Appendix D, the probability of a z value between 0 and -2.80 is .4974. So the p-value is .0026, found by $.5000 - .4974$. The governor cannot be confident of reelection!

Self-Review 9–3

A recent insurance industry report indicated that 40 percent of those persons involved in minor traffic accidents this year have been involved in a least one other traffic accident in the last five years. An advisory group decided to investigate this claim, believing it was too large. A sample of 200 traffic accidents this year showed 74 persons were also involved in another accident within the last five years. Use the .01 significance level.

(a) Can we use z as the test statistics? Tell why or why not.
(b) State the null hypothesis and the alternate hypothesis.
(c) Show the decision rule graphically.
(d) Compute the value of z and state your decision regarding the null hypothesis.
(e) Determine and interpret the p-value.

Exercises

9. The following hypotheses are given.

$$H_0: \pi \leq .70$$
$$H_1: \pi > .70$$

A sample of 100 observations revealed that $p = .75$. At the .05 significance level, can the null hypothesis be rejected?

a. State the decision rule.
b. Compute the value of the test statistic.
c. What is your decision regarding the null hypothesis?

10. The following hypotheses are given.

$$H_0: \pi = .40$$
$$H_1: \pi \neq .40$$

A sample of 120 observations revealed that $p = .30$. At the .05 significance level, can the null hypothesis be rejected?

a. State the decision rule.
b. Compute the value of the test statistic.
c. What is your decision regarding the null hypothesis?

Note: It is recommended that you use the five-step hypothesis-testing procedure in solving the following problems.

11. The National Safety Council reported that 52 percent of American turnpike drivers are men. A sample of 300 cars traveling southbound on the New Jersey Turnpike yesterday revealed that 170 were driven by men. At the .01 significance level, can we conclude that a larger proportion of men were driving on the New Jersey Turnpike than the national statistics indicate?

12. A recent article in *USA Today* reported that a job awaits only one in three new college graduates. The major reasons given were an overabundance of college graduates and a weak economy. A survey of 200 recent graduates from your school revealed that 80 students had jobs. At the .02 significance level, can we conclude that a larger proportion of students at your school have jobs?

13. Chicken Delight claims that 90 percent of its orders are delivered within 10 minutes of the time the order is placed. A sample of 100 orders revealed that 82 were delivered within the promised time. At the .10 significance level, can we conclude that less than 90 percent of the orders are delivered in less than 10 minutes?

14. Research at the University of Toledo indicates that 50 percent of the students change their major area of study after their first year in a program. A random sample of 100 students in the College of Business revealed that 48 had changed their major area of study after their first year of the program. Has there been a significant decrease in the proportion of students who change their major after the first year in this program? Test at the .05 level of significance.

Testing for a Population Mean: Small Sample, Population Standard Deviation Unknown

We are able to use the standard normal distribution, that is z, under two conditions:

1. The population is known to follow a normal distribution and the population standard deviation is known, or
2. The shape of the population is not known, but the number of observations in the sample is at least 30.

What do we do when the sample is less than 30 and the population standard deviation is not known? We encountered this same situation when constructing confidence intervals in the previous chapter. See pages 260–261 in Chapter 8. We summarized this problem in Chart 8–3 on page 262. Under these conditions the correct statistical procedure is to replace the standard normal distribution with the t distribution. To review, the major characteristics of the t distribution are:

1. It is a continuous distribution.
2. It is bell-shaped and symmetrical.
3. There is a family of t distributions. Each time the degrees of freedom change, a new distribution is created.
4. As the number of degrees of freedom increases, the shape of the t distribution approaches that of the standard normal distribution.
5. The t distribution is flatter, or more spread out, than the standard normal distribution.

To conduct a test of hypothesis using the t distribution, we use the following formula:

TEST STATISTIC FOR MEAN OF A SMALL SAMPLE

$$t = \frac{\bar{X} - \mu}{s/\sqrt{n}} \quad \textbf{[9–5]}$$

with $n - 1$ degrees of freedom, where:

$\bar{X}$ is the mean of the sample.
μ is the hypothesized population mean.
s is the standard deviation of the sample.
n is the number of observations in the sample.

The following example shows the details.

EXAMPLE

The McFarland Insurance Company Claims Department reports that the mean cost to process a claim is \$60. An industry comparison showed this amount to be larger than most other insurance companies, so they instituted cost-cutting measures. To evaluate the effect of the cost-cutting measures, McFarland selected a random sample of 26 recent claims. The mean cost per claim was \$57 and the standard deviation was \$10. Can they conclude that the cost-cutting measures were effective? Or should they conclude that the difference between the sample mean (\$57) and the population mean (\$60) is due to chance? Use the .01 significance level.

SOLUTION

We will use the five-step hypothesis testing procedure.

Step 1: State the Null Hypothesis and the Alternate Hypothesis The null hypothesis is that the population mean is at least \$60. The alternate hypothesis is that the population mean is less than \$60. We can express the null and alternate hypotheses as follows:

$$H_0: \mu \geq \$60$$
$$H_1: \mu < \$60$$

The test is *one*-tailed because we want to determine if there has been a *reduction* in the cost. The inequality in the alternate hypothesis points to the region of rejection in the left tail of the distribution.

Step 2: Select the Level of Significance We decide on the .01 significance level.

Step 3: Select the Test Statistic The test statistic is the t distribution. Why? First, it is reasonable to assume that the distribution of the cost per claim follows the normal distribution. However, we do not know the population standard deviation. Thus, we must substitute the sample standard deviation for the population standard deviation. When the sample is large, we can make the substitution because of the Central Limit Theorem and still use the standard normal distribution. We usually define large as 30 or more. In this case there are fewer than 30 observations in the sample, so we cannot use the standard normal distribution. Instead, we use t. The value of the test statistic is computed using formula 9–5:

$$t = \frac{\overline{X} - \mu}{s/\sqrt{n}}$$

Step 4: Formulate the Decision Rule The critical values of t are given in Appendix F, a portion of which is shown in Table 9–1. Appendix F is also repeated in the back inside cover of the text. The far left column of the table is labeled "Degrees of Freedom, *df*." The number of degrees of freedom is the total number of observations in the sample minus the number of samples, written $n - 1$. In this case the number of observations in the sample is 26, so there are $26 - 1 = 25$ degrees of freedom. To find the critical value, first locate the row with the appropriate degrees of freedom. This row is shaded in Table 9–1. Next, determine whether the test is one-tailed or two-tailed. In this case, we have a one-tailed test, so find the portion of the table that is labeled "one-tailed." Locate the column with the selected significance level. In this example, the significance level is .01. Move down the column labeled "0.01" until it intersects the row with 25 degrees of freedom. The value is 2.485. Because this is a one-tailed test and the rejection region is in the left tail, the critical value is negative. The decision rule is to reject H_0 if the value of t is less than -2.485.

TABLE 9–1 A Portion of the *t* Distribution Table

	Confidence Intervals					
	80%	90%	95%	98%	99%	99.9%
	Level of Significance for One-Tailed Test					
df	0.100	0.050	0.025	0.010	0.005	0.0005
	Level of Significance for Two-Tailed Test					
	0.20	0.10	0.05	0.02	0.01	0.001
⋮	⋮	⋮	⋮	⋮	⋮	⋮
21	1.323	1.721	2.080	2.518	2.831	3.819
22	1.321	1.717	2.074	2.508	2.819	3.792
23	1.319	1.714	2.069	2.500	2.807	3.768
24	1.318	1.711	2.064	2.492	2.797	3.745
25	1.316	1.708	2.060	2.485	2.787	3.725
26	1.315	1.706	2.056	2.479	2.779	3.707
27	1.314	1.703	2.052	2.473	2.771	3.690
28	1.313	1.701	2.048	2.467	2.763	3.674
29	1.311	1.699	2.045	2.462	2.756	3.659
30	1.310	1.697	2.042	2.457	2.750	3.646

Step 5: Make a Decision In this problem:

$\overline{X}$ = \$57, the sample mean.
μ = \$60, the hypothesized population mean.
s = \$10, the sample standard deviation.
n = 26, the number of observations in the sample.

The value of t is -1.530, found by:

$$t = \frac{\overline{X} - \mu}{s/\sqrt{n}} = \frac{\$57 - \$60}{\$10/\sqrt{26}} = -1.530$$

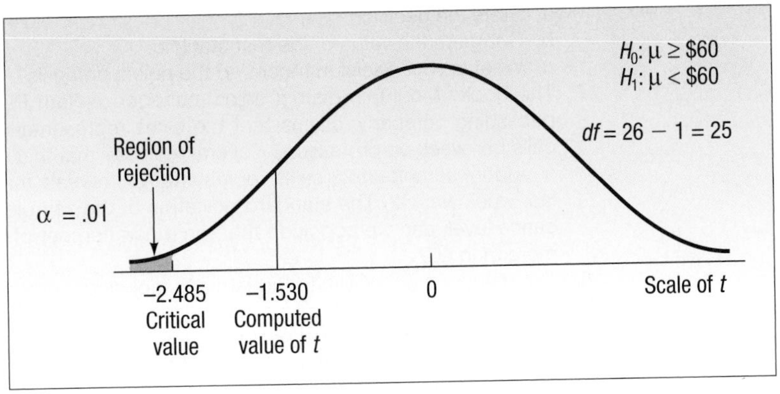

CHART 9–7 Rejection Region, *t* Distribution, .01 Significance Level

Because −1.530 lies in the region to the right of the critical value of −2.485, the null hypothesis is not rejected at the .01 significance level. There is not a statistically significant difference between $\overline{X}$ and μ. This indicates that the cost-cutting measures have not reduced the mean cost per claim to less than \$60. The difference of \$3 between the sample mean and the population mean could be due to chance. The computed value of t is shown in Chart 9–7. It is in the region where the null hypothesis is not rejected.

Self-Review 9–4

The mean life of a battery used in a digital clock is 305 days. The lives of the batteries follow the normal distribution. The battery was recently modified to last longer. A sample of 20 of the modified batteries had a mean life of 311 days with a standard deviation of 12 days. Did the modification increase the mean life of the battery?

(a) State the null hypothesis and the alternate hypothesis.
(b) Show the decision rule graphically. Use the .05 significance level.
(c) Compute the value of t. What is your decision regarding the null hypothesis? Briefly summarize your results.

Exercises

15. Given the following hypothesis:

$$H_0: \mu \leq 10$$
$$H_1: \mu > 10$$

For a random sample of 10 observations, the sample mean was 12 and the sample standard deviation 3. Using the .05 significance level:
a. State the decision rule.
b. Compute the value of the test statistic.
c. What is your decision regarding the null hypothesis?

16. Given the following hypothesis:

$$H_0: \mu = 400$$
$$H_1: \mu \neq 400$$

For a random sample of 12 observations, the sample mean was 407 and the sample standard deviation 6. Using the .01 significance level:
a. State the decision rule.
b. Compute the value of the test statistic.
c. What is your decision regarding the null hypothesis?

17. The Rocky Mountain district sales manager of Rath Publishing, Inc., a college textbook publishing company, claims that the sales representatives make an average of 40 sales calls per week on professors. Several reps say that this estimate is too low. To investigate, a random sample of 28 sales representatives reveals that the mean number of calls made last week was 42. The standard deviation of the sample is 2.1 calls. Using the .05 significance level, can we conclude that the mean number of calls per salesperson per week is more than 40?

18. The management of White Industries is considering a new method of assembling its golf cart. The present method requires 42.3 minutes, on the average, to assemble a cart. The mean assembly time for a random sample of 24 carts, using the new method, was 40.6 minutes, and the standard deviation of the sample was 2.7 minutes. Using the .10 level of significance, can we conclude that the assembly time using the new method is faster?

19. The records of Yellowstone Trucks reveal that the mean life of a set of spark plugs is 22,100 miles. The distribution of the life of the plugs is approximately normal. A spark plug manufacturer claimed that its plugs have a mean life in excess of 22,100 miles. The fleet owner purchased a large number of sets. A sample of 18 sets revealed that the mean life was 23,400 miles and the standard deviation was 1,500 miles. Is there enough evidence to substantiate the manufacturer's claim at the .05 significance level?

20. Fast Service, a chain of automotive tune-up shops, advertises that its personnel can change the oil, replace the oil filter, and lubricate any standard automobile in 15 minutes, on the average. The National Business Bureau received complaints from customers that service takes considerably longer. To check the Fast Service claim, the Bureau had service done on 21 unmarked cars. The mean service time was 18 minutes, and the standard deviation of the sample was 1 minute. Use the .05 significance level to check the reasonableness of the Fast Service claim.

In the previous example the mean and the standard deviation were stated in the problem. The following example requires this information to be computed from the sample data.

EXAMPLE

The mean length of a small counterbalance bar is 43 millimeters. The production supervisor is concerned that the adjustments of the machine producing the bars have changed. He asks the Engineering Department to investigate. Engineering selects a random sample of 12 bars and measures each. The results are reported below in millimeters.

42	39	42	45	43	40	39	41	40	42	43	42

Is it reasonable to conclude that there has been a change in the mean length of the bars? Use the .02 significance level.

SOLUTION

We begin by stating the null hypothesis and the alternate hypothesis.

H_0: $\mu = 43$
H_1: $\mu \neq 43$

The alternate hypothesis does not state a direction. So this is a two-tailed test. There are 11 degrees of freedom, found by $n - 1 = 12 - 1 = 11$. The t value is 2.718, found by referring to Appendix F for a two-tailed test, using the .02 significance level, with 11 degrees of freedom. The decision rule is: Reject the null hypothesis if the computed t is to the left of -2.718 or to the right of 2.718. This information is summarized in Chart 9–8.

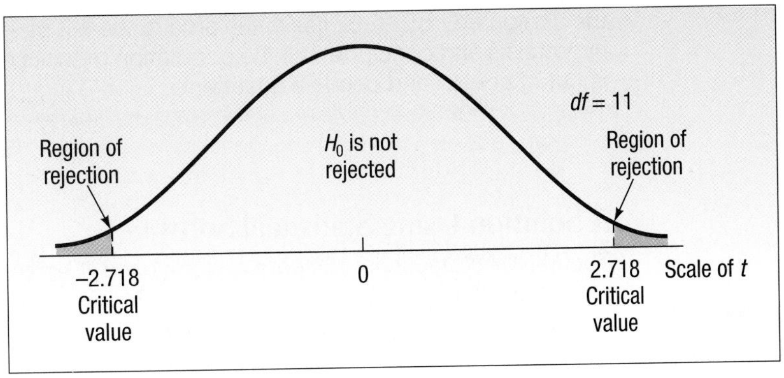

CHART 9–8 Regions of Rejection, Two-Tailed Test, Student's t Distribution, $\alpha = .02$

The standard deviation of the sample can be determined either by squaring the deviations from the mean or by an equivalent formula using the squares of the actual values. The two formulas from Chapter 3 are:

Using squared deviations from mean:

$$s = \sqrt{\frac{\Sigma(X - \overline{X})^2}{n - 1}}$$

Using squares of raw data:

$$s = \sqrt{\frac{\Sigma X^2 - \frac{(\Sigma X)^2}{n}}{n - 1}}$$

The necessary calculations for these two methods are shown in Table 9–2 below. The mean, $\overline{X}$, is 41.5 millimeters, and the standard deviation, s, is 1.78 millimeters.

TABLE 9–2 Calculations of the Sample Standard Deviation

X (mm)	$X - \overline{X}$	$(X - \overline{X})^2$	X^2
42	0.5	0.25	1,764
39	−2.5	6.25	1,521
42	0.5	0.25	1,764
45	3.5	12.25	2,025
43	1.5	2.25	1,849
40	−1.5	2.25	1,600
39	−2.5	6.25	1,521
41	−0.5	0.25	1,681
40	−1.5	2.25	1,600
42	0.5	0.25	1,764
43	1.5	2.25	1,849
42	0.5	0.25	1,764
498	0	35.00	20,702

$$\overline{X} = \frac{498}{12} = 41.5 \text{ mm}$$

Squared deviation method:

$$s = \sqrt{\frac{\Sigma(X - \overline{X})^2}{n - 1}} = \sqrt{\frac{35}{12 - 1}} = 1.78$$

Squaring raw data:

$$s = \sqrt{\frac{\Sigma X^2 - \frac{(\Sigma X)^2}{n}}{n - 1}} = \sqrt{\frac{20{,}702 - \frac{(498)^2}{12}}{12 - 1}}$$

$$= 1.78$$

Now we are ready to compute the value of t, using formula 9–5.

$$t = \frac{\overline{X} - \mu}{s/\sqrt{n}} = \frac{41.5 - 43.0}{1.78/\sqrt{12}} = -2.92$$

The null hypothesis that the population mean is 43 millimeters is rejected because the computed t of −2.92 lies in the area to the left of −2.718. We accept the alternate hypothesis and conclude that the population mean is not 43 millimeters. The machine is out of control and needs adjustment.

below the mean

A Solution Using Statistical Software

The MINITAB statistical software system, used in earlier chapters, provides an efficient way of conducting a one-sample test of hypothesis for a population mean. The steps to generate the following output are shown in the Computer Commands section at the end of the chapter. Note that the computed value of t (−2.91) is approximately the same as the value found using formula 9–5 (−2.92). The slight difference is due to rounding.

A random sample of five resulted in the following values: 18, 15, 12, 19, and 21. Using the .01 significance level, can we conclude the population mean is less than 20?

a. State the decision rule.
b. Compute the value of the test statistic.
c. What is your decision regarding the null hypothesis?
d. Estimate the *p*-value.

22. Given the following hypothesis:

$$H_0: \mu = 100$$
$$H_1: \mu \neq 100$$

A random sample of six resulted in the following values: 118, 105, 112, 119, 105, and 111. Using the .05 significance level, can we conclude the mean is different from 100?

a. State the decision rule.
b. Compute the value of the test statistic.
c. What is your decision regarding the null hypothesis?
d. Estimate the *p*-value.

23. Experience raising New Jersey Red chickens revealed the mean weight of the chickens at five months is 4.35 pounds. The weights follow the normal distribution. In an effort to increase their weight, a special additive is added to the chicken feed. The subsequent weights of a sample of five-month-old chickens were (in pounds):

4.41	4.37	4.33	4.35	4.30	4.39	4.36	4.38	4.40	4.39

At the .01 level, has the special additive increased the mean weight of the chickens? Estimate the *p*-value.

24. The liquid chlorine added to swimming pools to combat algae has a relatively short shelf life before it loses its effectiveness. Records indicate that the mean shelf life of a 5-gallon jug of chlorine is 2,160 hours (90 days). As an experiment, Holdlonger was added to the chlorine to find whether it would increase the shelf life. A sample of nine jugs of chlorine had these shelf lives (in hours):

2,159	2,170	2,180	2,179	2,160	2,167	2,171	2,181	2,185

At the .025 level, has Holdlonger increased the shelf life of the chlorine? Estimate the *p*-value.

25. Wyoming fisheries contend that the mean number of cutthroat trout caught during a full day of fly-fishing on the Snake, Buffalo, and other rivers and streams in the Jackson Hole area is 4.0. To make their yearly update, the fishery personnel asked a sample of fly-fishermen to keep a count of the number caught during the day. The numbers were: 4, 4, 3, 2, 6, 8, 7, 1, 9, 3, 1, and 6. At the .05 level, can we conclude that the mean number caught is greater than 4.0? Estimate the *p*-value.

26. Hugger Polls contends that an agent conducts a mean of 53 in-depth home surveys every week. A streamlined survey form has been introduced, and Hugger wants to evaluate its effectiveness. The number of in-depth surveys conducted during a week by a random sample of agents are:

53	57	50	55	58	54	60	52	59	62	60	60	51	59	56

At the .05 level of significance, can we conclude that the mean number of interviews conducted by the agents is more than 53 per week? Estimate the *p*-value.

Chapter Outline

I. The objective of hypothesis testing is to check the validity of a statement about a population parameter.

II. The steps in conducting a test of hypothesis are:

A. State the null hypothesis (H_0) and the alternate hypothesis (H_1).

B. Select the level of significance.

1. The level of significance is the likelihood of rejecting a true null hypothesis.

2. The most frequently used significance levels are .01, .05, and .10, but any value between 0 and 1.00 is possible.

C. Select the test statistic.

1. A test statistic is a value calculated from sample information used to determine whether to reject the null hypothesis.

2. Two test statistics were considered in this chapter.

a. The standard normal distribution is used when the population follows the normal distribution and the population standard deviation is known.

b. The standard normal distribution is used when the population standard deviation is unknown, but the sample contains at least 30 observations.

c. The *t* distribution is used when the population follows the normal distribution, the population standard deviation is unknown, and the sample contains fewer than 30 observations.

D. State the decision rule.

1. The decision rule indicates the condition or conditions when the null hypothesis is rejected.

2. In a two-tailed test, the rejection region is evenly split between the upper and lower tails.

3. In a one-sample test, all of the rejection region is in either the upper or the lower tail.

E. Select a sample, compute the value of the test statistic, make a decision regarding the null hypothesis, and interpret the results.

III. A *p*-value is the probability that the value of the test statistic is as extreme as the value computed, when the null hypothesis is true.

IV. Testing a hypothesis about a population mean.

A. If the population standard deviation, σ, is known, the test statistic is the standard normal distribution and is determined from:

$$z = \frac{\overline{X} - \mu}{\sigma/\sqrt{n}} \qquad \textbf{[9–1]}$$

B. If the population standard deviation is not known, but there are at least 30 observations in the sample, *s* is substituted for σ. The test statistic is the standard normal distribution, and its value is determined from:

$$z = \frac{\overline{X} - \mu}{s/\sqrt{n}} \qquad \textbf{[9–2]}$$

V. Testing about a population proportion.

A. Both $n\pi$ and $n(1 - \pi)$ must be at least 5.

B. The test statistic is

$$z = \frac{p - \pi}{\sqrt{\dfrac{\pi(1 - \pi)}{n}}} \qquad \textbf{[9–4]}$$

VI. In a test for means if the population standard deviation is not known, but there are fewer than 30 observations in the sample, *s* is substituted for σ.

A. The test statistic is the *t* distribution, and its value is determined from:

$$t = \frac{\overline{X} - \mu}{s/\sqrt{n}} \qquad \textbf{[9–5]}$$

B. The major characteristics of the *t* distribution are:
1. It is a continuous distribution.
2. It is mound-shaped and symmetrical.
3. It is flatter, or more spread out, than the standard normal distribution.
4. There is a family of *t* distributions, depending on the number of degrees of freedom.

Pronunciation Key

SYMBOL	MEANING	PRONUNCIATION
H_0	Null hypothesis	*H sub zero*
H_1	Alternate hypothesis	*H sub one*
$\alpha/2$	Two-tailed significance level	*Alpha over 2*

Chapter Exercises

27. A new weight-watching company, Weight Reducers International, advertises that those who join will lose, on the average, 10 pounds the first two weeks. A random sample of 50 people who joined the new weight reduction program revealed the mean loss to be 9 pounds with a standard deviation of 2.8 pounds. At the .05 level of significance, can we conclude that those joining Weight Reducers on average will lose less than 10 pounds? Determine the *p*-value.

28. Dole Pineapple, Inc. is concerned that the 16-ounce can of sliced pineapple is being overfilled. The quality-control department took a random sample of 50 cans and found that the arithmetic mean weight was 16.05 ounces, with a sample standard deviation of 0.03 ounces. At the 5 percent level of significance, can we conclude that the mean weight is greater than 16 ounces? Determine the *p*-value.

29. The Peoria Board of Education wants to consider a new academic program funded by the U.S. Department of Education. To be eligible for the federal grant, the arithmetic mean income per household must not be more than $15,000. The board hired a research firm to gather the required data. In its report the firm indicated that the arithmetic mean income in the district is $17,000. They further reported that 75 households were surveyed and that the standard deviation of the sample was $3,000. Can the board argue that the difference between the mean income resulting from the sample survey and the mean specified by the Department of Education is due to chance (sampling)? Use the .05 significance level.

30. A statewide real estate sales agency, Farm Associates, specializes in selling farm property in the state of Nebraska. Their records indicate that the mean selling time of farm property is 90 days. Because of recent drought conditions, they believe that the mean selling time is now greater than 90 days. A statewide survey of 100 farms sold recently revealed that the mean selling time was 94 days, with a standard deviation of 22 days. At the .10 significance level, has there been an increase in selling time?

31. According to the local union president, the mean gross income of plumbers in the Salt Lake City area is normally distributed, with a mean of $30,000 and a standard deviation of $3,000. A recent investigative reporter for KYAK TV found, for a sample of 120 plumbers, the mean gross income was $30,500. At the .10 significance level, is it reasonable to conclude that the mean income is not equal to $30,000? Determine the *p*-value.

32. A recent article in *Vitality* magazine reported that the mean amount of leisure time per week for American men is 40.0 hours. You believe this figure is too large and decide to conduct your own test. In a random sample of 60 men, you find that the mean is 37.8 hours of leisure per week and that the standard deviation of the sample is 12.2 hours. Can you conclude that the information in the article is untrue? Use the .05 significance level. Determine the *p*-value and explain its meaning.

33. NBC TV news, in a segment on the price of gasoline, reported last evening that the mean price nationwide is $1.50 per gallon for self-serve regular unleaded. A random sample of 35 stations in the Milwaukee, WI, area revealed that the mean price was $1.52 per gallon and that the standard deviation was $0.05 per gallon. At the .05 significance level, can we conclude that the price of gasoline is higher in the Milwaukee area? Determine the *p*-value.

34. The Rutter Nursery Company packages their pine bark mulch in 50-pound bags. From a long history, the production department reports that the distribution of the bag weights follows the normal distribution and the standard deviation of this process is 3 pounds per bag. At the end of each day, Jeff Rutter, the production manager, weighs 10 bags and computes the mean weight of the sample. Below are the weights of 10 bags from today's production.

45.6	47.7	47.6	46.3	46.2	47.4	49.2	55.8	47.5	48.5

a. Can Mr. Rutter conclude that the mean weight of the bags is less than 50 pounds? Use the .01 significance level.
b. In a brief report, tell why Mr. Rutter can use the *z* distribution as the test statistic.
c. Compute the *p*-value.

35. Tina Dennis is the comptroller for Meek Industries. She believes that the current cash-flow problem at Meek is due to the slow collection of accounts receivable. She believes that more than 60 percent of the accounts are in arrears more than three months. A random sample of 200 accounts showed that 140 were more than three months old. At the .01 significance level, can she conclude that more than 60 percent of the accounts are in arrears for more than three months?

36. The policy of the Suburban Transit Authority is to add a bus route if more than 55 percent of the potential commuters indicate they would use the particular route. A sample of 70 commuters revealed that 42 would use a proposed route from Bowman Park to the downtown area. Does the Bowman-to-downtown route meet the STA criterion? Use the .05 significance level.

37. Past experience at the Crowder Travel Agency indicated that 44 percent of those persons who wanted the agency to plan a vacation for them wanted to go to Europe. During the most recent busy season, a sampling of 1,000 plans was selected at random from the files. It was found that 480 persons wanted to go to Europe on vacation. Has there been a significant shift upward in the percentage of persons who want to go to Europe? Test at the .05 significance level.

38. From past experience a television manufacturer found that 10 percent or less of its sets needed any type of repair in the first two years of operation. In a sample of 50 sets manufactured two years ago, 9 needed repair. At the .05 significance level, has the percent of sets needing repair increased? Determine the *p*-value.

39. An urban planner claims that, nationally, 20 percent of all families renting condominiums move during a given year. A random sample of 200 families renting condominiums in Dallas revealed that 56 had moved during the past year. At the .01 significance level, does this evidence suggest that a larger proportion of condominium owners moved in the Dallas area? Determine the *p*-value.

40. The manufacturer of the Ososki motorcycle advertises that the cycle will average 87 miles per gallon of gasoline. A sample of eight bikes revealed the following mileage.

88	82	81	87	80	78	79	89

At the .05 level, is the mean mileage less than the advertised 87 miles per gallon?

41. The Myers Summer Casual Furniture Store tells customers that a special order will take six weeks (42 days). During recent months the owner has received several complaints that the special orders are taking longer than 42 days. A sample of 12 special orders delivered in the last month showed that the mean waiting time was 51 days, with a standard deviation of 8 days. At the .05 significance level, are customers waiting an average of more than 42 days? Estimate the *p*-value.

42. A recent article in the *Wall Street Journal* reported that the prime rate for large banks now exceeds 9 percent. A sample of eight small banks in the Midwest revealed the following prime rates (in percent):

10.1	9.3	9.2	10.2	9.3	9.6	9.4	8.8

At the .01 significance level, can we conclude that the prime rate for small banks also exceeds 9 percent? Estimate the p-value.

43. A typical college student drinks an average of 27 gallons of coffee each year, or 2.25 gallons per month. A sample of 12 students at Northwestern State University revealed the following amounts of coffee consumed last month.

1.75	1.96	1.57	1.82	1.85	1.82	2.43	2.65	2.60	2.24	1.69	2.66

At the .05 significance level, is there a significant difference between the average amount consumed at Northwestern State and the national average?

44. The postanesthesia care area (recovery room) at St. Luke's Hospital in Maumee, Ohio, was recently enlarged. The hope was that with the enlargement the mean number of patients per day would be more than 25. A random sample of 15 days revealed the following numbers of patients.

25	27	25	26	25	28	28	27	24	26	25	29	25	27	24

At the .01 significance level, can we conclude that the mean number of patients per day is more than 25? Estimate the p-value and interpret it.

45. *egolf.com* receives an average of 6.5 returns per day from online shoppers. For a sample of 12 days, they received the following number of returns.

0	4	3	4	9	4	5	9	1	6	7	10

At the .01 significance level, can we conclude the mean number of returns is less than 6.5?

46. During recent seasons, Major League Baseball has been criticized for the length of the games. A report indicated that the average game lasts 3 hours and 30 minutes. A sample of 17 games revealed the following times to completion. (Note that the minutes have been changed to fractions of hours, so that a game that lasted 2 hours and 24 minutes is reported at 2.40 hours.)

2.98	2.40	2.70	2.25	3.23	3.17	2.93	3.18	2.80
2.38	3.75	3.20	3.27	2.52	2.58	4.45	2.45	

Can we conclude that the mean time for a game is less than 3.50 hours? Use the .05 significance level.

47. The Watch Corporation of Switzerland claims that their watches on average will neither gain nor lose time during a week. A sample of 18 watches provided the following gains (+) or losses (−) in seconds per week.

−0.38	−0.20	−0.38	−0.32	+0.32	−0.23	+0.30	+0.25	−0.10
−0.37	−0.61	−0.48	−0.47	−0.64	−0.04	−0.20	−0.68	+0.05

Is it reasonable to conclude that the mean gain or loss in time for the watches is 0? Use the .05 significance level. Estimate the p-value.

48. Listed below is the rate of return for one year (reported in percent) for a sample of 12 mutual funds that are classified as taxable money market funds.

4.63	4.15	4.76	4.70	4.65	4.52	4.70	5.06	4.42	4.51	4.24	4.52

Using the .05 significance level is it reasonable to conclude that the mean rate of return is more than 4.50 percent?

49. A national grocer's magazine reports the typical shopper spends eight minutes in line waiting to check out. A sample of 24 shoppers at the local Farmer Jack's showed a mean of 7.5 minutes with a standard deviation of 3.2 minutes. Is the waiting time at the local Farmer Jack's less than that reported in the national magazine? Use the .05 significance level.

50. In the year 2002 the mean fare to fly from Charlotte, North Carolina, to Seattle, Washington, on a discount ticket was $267. A random sample of round-trip discount fares on this route last month gives:

$321	$286	$290	$330	$310	$250	$270	$280	$299	$265	$291	$275	$281

At the .01 significance level can we conclude that the mean fare has increased? What is the *p*-value?

51. The President's call for designing and building a missile defense system that ignores restrictions of the Anti-Ballistic Missile Defense System treaty (ABM) is supported by 483 of the respondents in a nationwide poll of 1,002 adults. Is it reasonable to conclude that the nation is evenly divided on the issue? Use the .05 significance level.

exercises.com

52. The *USA Today* (http://www.usatoday.com/sports/mtb.htm) and Major League Baseball (http://www.majorleaguebaseball.com) websites regularly report information on individual player salaries. Go to one of these sites and find the individual salaries for your favorite team. Compute the mean and the standard deviation. Is it reasonable to conclude that the mean salary on your favorite team is *different from* $2.0 million? If you are more of a football, basketball, or hockey enthusiast, information is also available on their salaries.

53. The Gallup Organization in Princeton, New Jersey, is one of the best-known polling organizations in the United States. They often combine with *USA Today* or CNN to conduct polls of current interest. They also maintain a website at: http://www.gallup.com. Consult this website to find the most recent polling results on Presidential approval ratings. You may need to click on Fast Facts. Test whether the majority (more than 50 percent) approve of the President's performance. If the article does not report the number of respondents included in the survey, assume that it is 1,000, a number that is typically used.

Computer Data Exercises

54. Refer to the Real Estate data, which reports information on the homes sold in Venice, Florida, last year.
   a. A recent article in the *Tampa Times* indicated that the mean selling price of the homes on the west coast of Florida is more than $220,000. Can we conclude that the mean selling price in the Venice area is more than $220,000? Use the .01 significance level. What is the *p*-value?
   b. The same article reported the mean size was more than 2,100 square feet. Can we conclude that the mean size of homes sold in the Venice area is more than 2,100 square feet? Use the .01 significance level. What is the *p*-value?
   c. Determine the proportion of homes that have an attached garage. At the .05 significance level can we conclude that more than 60 percent of the homes sold in the Venice area had an attached garage? What is the *p*-value?
   d. Determine the proportion of homes that have a pool. At the .05 significance level, can we conclude that more than 60 percent of the homes sold in the Venice area had a pool? What is the *p*-value?

55. Refer to the Baseball 2001 data, which reports information on the 30 Major League Baseball teams for the 2001 season.

a. Conduct a test of hypothesis to determine whether the mean salary of the teams was different from \$50.0 million. Use the .05 significance level.

b. Conduct a test of hypothesis to determine whether the mean attendance was more than 2,000,000 per team.

56. Refer to the wage data, which reports information on annual wages for a sample of 100 workers. Also included are variables relating to industry, years of education, and gender for each worker. Conduct a test of hypothesis to determine if the mean annual wage is greater than \$30,000. Determine the *p*-value.

57. Refer to the CIA data, which reports demographic and economic information on 46 countries.

a. Conduct a test of hypothesis to determine if the mean number of cell phones is greater than 4.0. Use the .05 significance level. What is the *p*-value?

b. Conduct a test of hypothesis to determine if the mean size of the labor force is below 50. Use the .01 significance level. What is the *p*-value?

Computer Commands

1. The MINITAB commands for the one-sample *t* test on page 309 are:
   - **a.** Enter the data into column C1 and name the variable *Length.*
   - **b.** From the menu bar select **Stat, Basic Statistics, 1-Sample t,** and then hit Enter. The following dialog box will appear.
   - **c.** Select *Length* as the variable, select **Test mean,** insert *43.* Click on **Options,** and select **Alternative** and the **not equal** option. Then click **OK** for both dialog boxes.

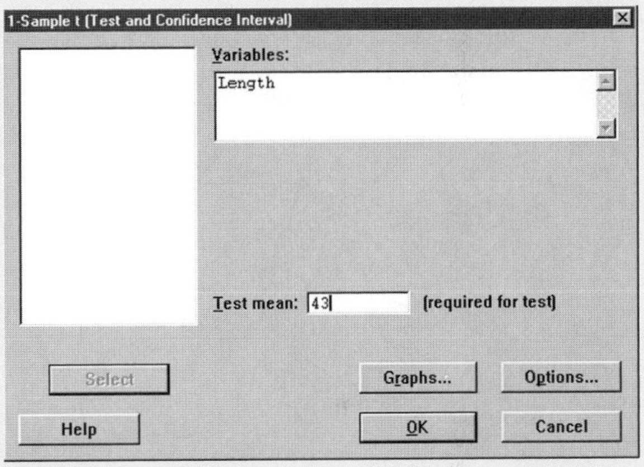

Chapter 9 Answers to Self-Review

9–1 **(a)** H_0: $\mu = 6.0$; H_1: $\mu \neq 6.0$

(b) .05

(c) $z = \dfrac{\overline{X} - \mu}{\sigma/\sqrt{n}}$

(d) Do not reject the null hypothesis if the computed z value falls between -1.96 and $+1.96$.

(e) Yes. Computed $z = -2.56$, found by:

$$z = \frac{5.84 - 6.0}{0.5/\sqrt{64}} = \frac{-0.16}{.0625} = -2.56$$

Reject H_0 at the .05 level. Accept H_1. The mean turnover rate is not equal to 6.0.

9–2 **(a)** H_0: $\mu \geq 6.0$

(b) H_1: $\mu < 6.0$

(c) Note that the inequality sign (<) in the alternate hypothesis points in the direction of the region of rejection. To determine the critical value: $.5000 - .05 = .4500$. z from Appendix D is about -1.65.

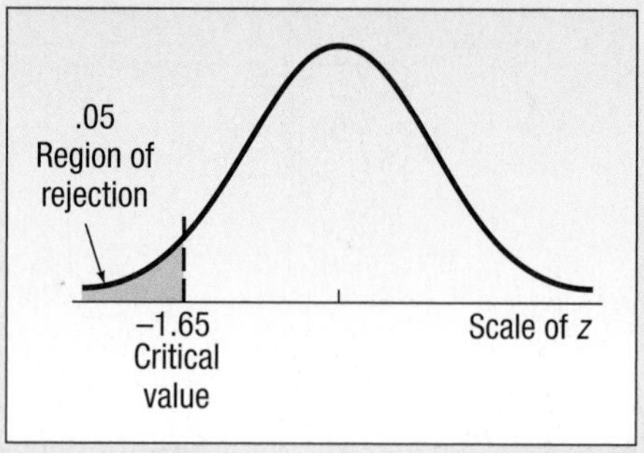

9–3 **(a)** Yes, because both $n\pi$ and $n(1 - \pi)$ exceed 5: $n\pi = 200(.40) = 80$, and $n(1 - \pi) = 200(.60) = 120$.

(b) H_0: $\pi \geq .40$
H_1: $\pi < .40$

(c)

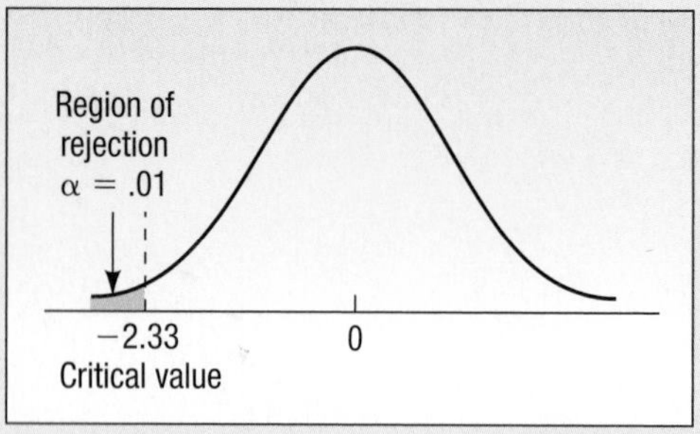

(d) $z = -0.87$, found by:

$$z = \frac{.37 - .40}{\sqrt{\dfrac{.40(1 - .40)}{200}}} = \frac{-.03}{\sqrt{.0012}} = -0.87$$

Do not reject H_0.

(e) The p-value is .1922, found by $.5000 - .3078$.

9–4 **(a)** H_0: $\mu \leq 305$, H_1: $\mu > 305$

(b) $df = n - 1 = 20 - 1 = 19$

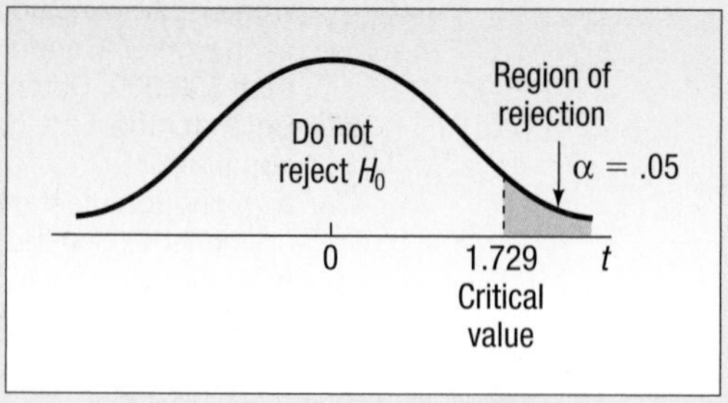

(c) $t = \dfrac{\overline{X} - \mu}{s/\sqrt{n}} = \dfrac{311 - 305}{12/\sqrt{20}} = 2.236$

Reject H_0 because $2.236 > 1.729$. The modification increased the mean battery life to more than 305 days.

9–5 **(a)** H_0: $\mu \geq 9.0$, H_1: $\mu < 9.0$.

(b) 7, found by $n - 1 = 8 - 1 = 7$.

(c) Reject H_0 if $t < -2.998$.

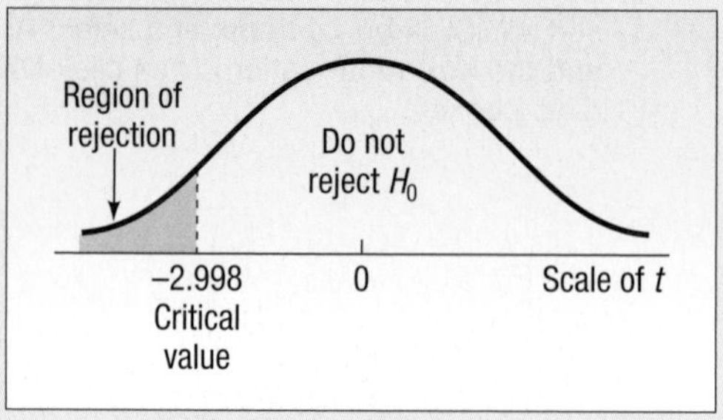

(d) $t = -2.494$, found by:

$$s = \sqrt{\frac{619.88 - \dfrac{(70.4)^2}{8}}{8 - 1}} = 0.2268$$

$$\overline{X} = \frac{70.4}{8} = 8.8$$

Then

$$t = \frac{8.8 - 9.0}{0.2268/\sqrt{8}} = -2.494$$

Since -2.494 lies to the right of -2.998, H_0 is not rejected. We have not shown that the mean is less than 9.0.

(e) The p-value is between .025 and .010.

10

Two-Sample Tests of Hypothesis

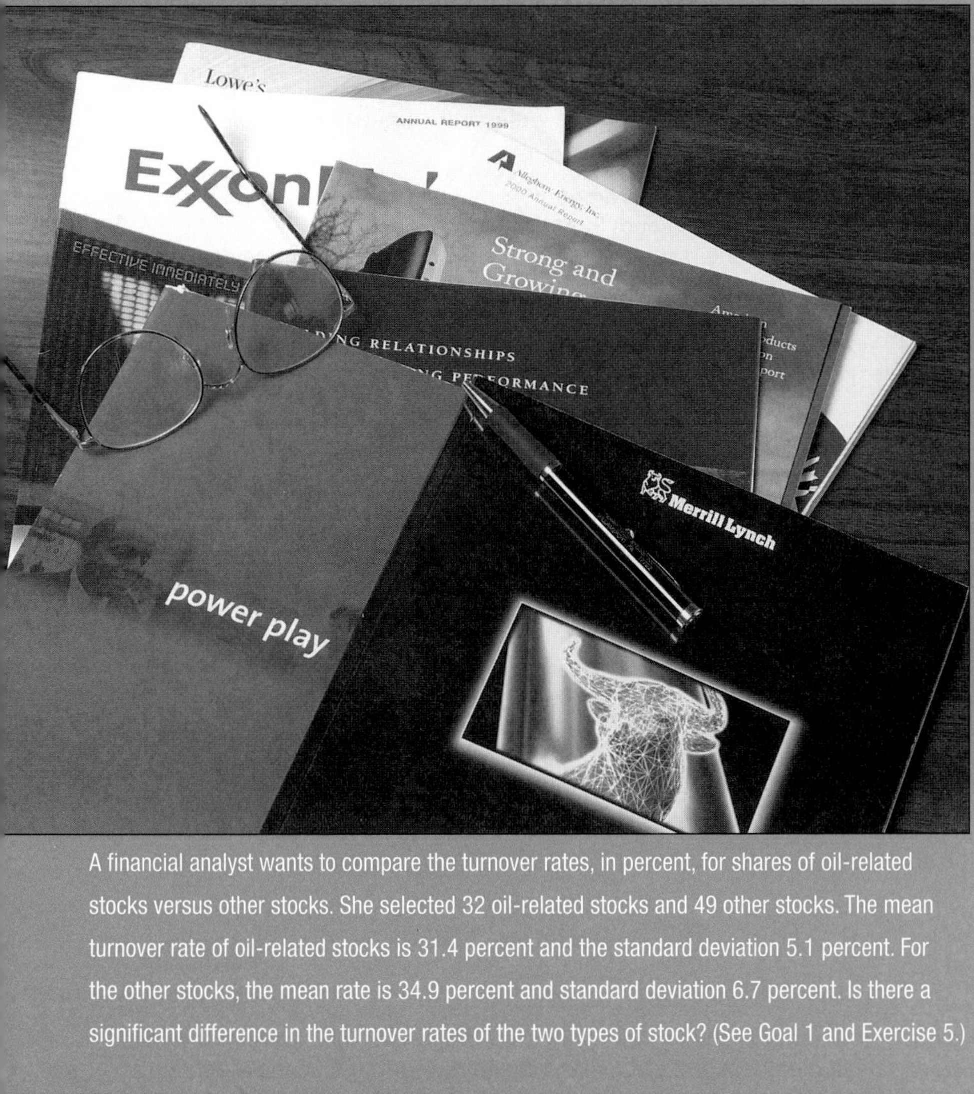

GOALS

When you have completed this chapter, you will be able to:

1 Conduct a test of a hypothesis about the difference between two independent population means.

2 Conduct a test of a hypothesis about the difference between two population proportions.

3 Conduct a test of a hypothesis about the mean difference between paired or dependent observations.

4 Understand the difference between dependent and independent samples.

A financial analyst wants to compare the turnover rates, in percent, for shares of oil-related stocks versus other stocks. She selected 32 oil-related stocks and 49 other stocks. The mean turnover rate of oil-related stocks is 31.4 percent and the standard deviation 5.1 percent. For the other stocks, the mean rate is 34.9 percent and standard deviation 6.7 percent. Is there a significant difference in the turnover rates of the two types of stock? (See Goal 1 and Exercise 5.)

Statistics in Action

The Election of 2000 turned out to be one of the closest in history. The news media were unable to project a winner, and the final decision, including recounts and court decisions, took more than five weeks. This was not the only election in which there was controversy. Shortly before the 1936 presidential election, the *New York Times* carried the headline: "*Digest* Poll Gives Landon 32 States: Landon Leads 4–3." However, Alfred Landon of Kansas was not elected President. In fact, Roosevelt won by more than 11 million votes and received 523 Electoral College votes. How could the headline have been so wrong?

The *Literary Digest* collected a sample of voters from lists of telephone numbers, automobile registrations, and *Digest* readers.

Introduction

Chapter 9 began our study of hypothesis testing. We described the nature of hypothesis testing and conducted tests of a hypothesis in which we compared the results of a single sample to a population value. That is, we selected a single random sample from a population and conducted a test of whether the proposed population value was reasonable. Recall, in Chapter 9 we selected a sample of the number of desks assembled per week at the Jamestown Steel Company to determine whether there was a change in the production rate. Similarly, we sampled voters in one area of a particular state to determine whether the population proportion that would support the governor for reelection was less than .80. In both of these cases, we compared the results of a *single* sample statistic to a population parameter.

In this chapter we expand the idea of hypothesis testing to two samples. That is, we select two random samples to determine whether the population means are equal. Some questions we might want to test are:

1. Is there a difference in the mean amount of residential real estate sold by male agents and female agents in south Florida?
2. Is there a difference in the mean number of defects produced on the day and the afternoon shifts at Kimble Products?
3. Is there a difference in the mean number of days absent between young workers (under 21 years of age) and older workers (more than 60 years of age) in the fast-food industry?

4. Is there is a difference in the proportion of Ohio State University graduates and University of Cincinnati graduates who pass the state Certified Public Accounting Examination on their first attempt?
5. Is there an increase in the production rate if music is piped into the production area?

We begin this chapter with the case in which we select random samples from two populations and wish to investigate whether these populations have the same mean.

Two-Sample Tests of Hypothesis: Independent Samples

A city planner in Florida wishes to know whether there is a difference in the mean hourly wage rate of plumbers and electricians in central Florida. A financial accountant wishes to know whether the mean rate of return for high yield mutual funds is different from the mean rate of return on global mutual funds. In each of these cases there are two independent populations. In the first case, the plumbers represent one population and the electricians the other. In the second case, high yield mutual funds are one population and global mutual funds the other.

In 1936 not many people could afford a telephone or an automobile. In addition those who read the *Digest* tended to be wealthier and vote Republican. Thus, the population that was sampled did not represent the population of voters. A second problem was with the nonresponses. More than 10 million people were sent surveys, and more than 2.3 million responded. However, no attempt was made to see whether those responding represented a cross-section of all the voters.

With modern computers and survey methods, samples are carefully selected and checked to ensure they are representative. What happened to the *Literary Digest?* It went out of business shortly after the 1936 election.

In each of these cases, to investigate the question, we would select a random sample from each population and compute the mean of the two samples. If the two populations are the same, that is, the mean hourly rate is the same for the plumbers and the electricians, we would expect the *difference* between the two sample means to be zero. But what if our sample results yield a difference other than zero? Is that difference due to chance or is it because there is a difference in the hourly earnings? A two-sample test of means will help to answer this question.

We do need to return to the results of Chapter 7. Recall that we showed that a distribution of sample means would tend to approximate the normal distribution when the sample size is at least 30. We need to again assume that a distribution of sample means will follow the normal distribution. It can be shown mathematically that the distribution of the differences between two normal distributions is also normal.

We can illustrate this theory in terms of the city planner in Florida. To begin, let's assume some information that is not usually available. Suppose that the population of plumbers has a mean of \$30.00 per hour and a standard deviation of \$5.00 per hour. The population of electricians has a mean of \$29.00 and a standard deviation of \$4.50. Now, from this information it is clear that the two population means are not the same. The plumbers actually earn \$1.00 per hour more than the electricians. But we cannot expect to uncover this difference each time we sample the two populations.

Suppose we select a random sample of 40 plumbers and a random sample of 35 electricians and compute the mean of each sample. Then, we determine the difference between the sample means. It is this difference between the sample means that holds our interest. If the populations have the same mean, then we would expect the difference between the two sample means to be zero. If there is a difference between the population means, then we expect to find a difference between the sample means.

To understand the theory, we need to take several pairs of samples, compute the mean of each, determine the difference between the sample means, and study the distribution of the differences in the sample means. Because of our study of the distribution of sample means in Chapter 7, we know that the distribution of the sample means follows the normal distribution (assume at least $n = 30$). If the two distributions of sample means follow the normal distribution, then we can reason that the distribution of their differences will also follow the normal distribution. This is the first hurdle.

The second hurdle refers to the mean of this distribution of differences. If we find the mean of this distribution is zero, that implies that there is no difference in the two populations. On the other hand, if the mean of the distribution of differences is equal to some value other than zero, either positive or negative, then we conclude that the two populations do not have the same mean.

To report some concrete results, let's return to the city planner in Florida. Table 10–1 shows the result of selecting 20 samples of 40 plumbers and 35 electricians, computing the mean of each sample, and finding the difference between the two sample means. In the first case the sample of 40 plumbers has a mean of \$29.80, and for the 35 electricians the mean is \$28.76. The difference between the sample means is \$1.04. This process was repeated 19 more times. Observe that in 17 of the 20 cases the mean of the plumbers is larger than the mean of the electricians.

Our final hurdle is that we need to know something about the *variability* of the distribution of differences. To put it another way, what is the standard deviation of this distribution of differences? Statistical theory shows that when we have independent populations, such as the case here, the distribution of the differences has a variance (standard deviation squared) equal to the sum of the two individual variances. This means that we can add the variances of the two sampling distributions.

TABLE 10–1 The Means of Random Samples of Plumbers and Electricians

Sample	Plumbers	Electricians	Difference
1	$29.80	$28.76	$ 1.04
2	30.32	29.40	0.92
3	30.57	29.94	0.63
4	30.04	28.93	1.11
5	30.09	29.78	0.31
6	30.02	28.66	1.36
7	29.60	29.13	0.47
8	29.63	29.42	0.21
9	30.17	29.29	0.88
10	30.81	29.75	1.06
11	30.09	28.05	2.04
12	29.35	29.07	0.28
13	29.42	28.79	0.63
14	29.78	29.54	0.24
15	29.60	29.60	0.00
16	30.60	30.19	0.41
17	30.79	28.65	2.14
18	29.14	29.95	−0.81
19	29.91	28.75	1.16
20	28.74	29.21	−0.47

VARIANCE OF THE DISTRIBUTION OF DIFFERENCES IN SAMPLE MEANS

$$s^2_{\bar{X}_1-\bar{X}_2} = \frac{s_1^2}{n_1} + \frac{s_2^2}{n_2} \qquad \textbf{[10–1]}$$

The term $s^2_{\bar{X}_1-\bar{X}_2}$ looks complex but need not be difficult to interpret. The s^2 portion reminds us that it is a sample variance, and the subscript $\bar{X}_1 - \bar{X}_2$ that it is a distribution of differences in the sample means.

We can put this equation in more usable form by taking the square root, so that we have the standard deviation of the distribution of the differences. Finally, we standardize the distribution of the differences. The result is the following equation.

TEST STATISTIC FOR THE DIFFERENCE BETWEEN TWO SAMPLE MEANS

$$z = \frac{\bar{X}_1 - \bar{X}_2}{\sqrt{\dfrac{s_1^2}{n_1} + \dfrac{s_2^2}{n_2}}} \qquad \textbf{[10–2]}$$

Assumptions for large sample test

Before we present an example, let's review the assumptions necessary for using formula 10–2.

1. The two samples must be unrelated, that is, independent.
2. The samples must be large enough that the distribution of the sample means follows the normal distribution. The usual practice is to require that both samples have at least 30 observations.

The following example shows the details of the two-sample test of hypothesis for means.

EXAMPLE

Each patient at Aloha Memorial Hospital is asked to evaluate the service at the time of release. Recently there have been complaints that resident physicians and nurses on the surgical wing respond too slowly to calls of senior citizens. In fact, it is claimed that the other patients receive faster service. Mr. Robert Armstrong, president of the hospital, asked the quality-assurance (QA) department to investigate. After studying the problem, the QA department collected the following sample information. At the .01 significance level, is it reasonable to conclude the mean response time is longer for the senior citizen cases? What is the *p*-value in this case?

Patient Type	Sample Mean	Sample Standard Deviation	Sample Size
Senior citizens	5.50 minutes	0.40 minutes	50
Other	5.30 minutes	0.30 minutes	100

SOLUTION

We use the five-step hypothesis testing procedure to investigate the question.

Step 1: State the null hypothesis and the alternate hypothesis. The null hypothesis is that there is no difference in the mean response times for the two groups. In other words, the difference of 0.20 minutes between the mean response time for the senior citizens and the mean response time for the other patients is due to chance. The alternate hypothesis is that the mean response time is longer for senior citizens. We will let μ_s refer to the mean response time for the population of senior citizens and μ_o the mean response time for the other patients. The null and alternative hypotheses are:

$$H_0: \mu_s \leq \mu_o$$
$$H_1: \mu_s > \mu_o$$

Step 2: Select the level of significance. The significance level is the probability that we reject the null hypothesis when it is actually true. This likelihood is determined prior to selecting the sample or performing any calculations. The .05 and .01 significance levels are the most common, but other values, such as .02 and .10, are also used. In theory, we may select any value between 0 and 1 for the significance level. In this case the QA department selected the .01 significance level.

Step 3: Determine the test statistic. In Chapter 9 we used the standard normal distribution (that is z) and t as test statistics. In this case, because the samples are large, we use the z distribution as the test statistic.

Step 4: Formulate a decision rule. The decision rule is based on the null and the alternate hypotheses (i.e., one-tailed or two-tailed test), the level of significance, and the test statistic used. We selected the .01 significance level, the z distribution as the test statistic, and we wish to determine whether the mean response time is longer for senior citizens. We set the alternate hypothesis to indicate that the mean response time is longer for the senior citizens than for the other group. Hence, the rejection region is in the upper tail of the standard normal distribution. To find the critical value, place .01 of the total area in the upper tail. This means that .4900 (.5000 − .0100) of the area is located between the z value of 0 and the critical value. Next, we search the body of Appendix D for a value located near .4900. It is 2.33, so our decision rule is to reject H_0 if the value computed from the test statistic exceeds 2.33. Chart 10–1 depicts the decision rule.

Statistics in Action

Do you live to work or work to live? A recent poll of 802 working Americans revealed that, among those who considered their work as a career, the mean number of hours worked per day was 8.7. Among those who considered their work a job, the mean number of hours worked per day was 7.6.

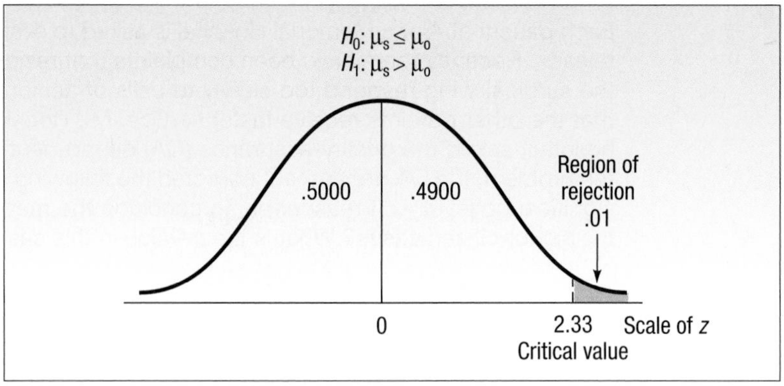

CHART 10–1 Decision Rule for One-Tailed Test at .01 Significance Level

Step 5: Make the decision regarding H_0 and interpret the result. We use formula 10–2 to compute the value of the test statistic.

$$z = \frac{\bar{X}_s - \bar{X}_o}{\sqrt{\frac{s_s^2}{n_s} + \frac{s_o^2}{n_o}}} = \frac{5.5 - 5.3}{\sqrt{\frac{0.40^2}{50} + \frac{0.30^2}{100}}} = \frac{0.2}{0.064} = 3.13$$

The computed value of 3.13 is larger than the critical value of 2.33. Our decision is to reject the null hypothesis and accept the alternate hypothesis. The difference of .20 minutes between the mean response time of the senior citizens and the other patients is too large to have occurred by chance. The QA department can report to President Armstrong that the mean response time is longer for senior citizens than for other patients.

What is the *p*-value for the test statistic? Recall that the *p*-value is the probability of finding a value of the test statistic this extreme when the null hypothesis is true. To calculate the *p*-value we need the probability of a *z* value larger than 3.13. From Appendix D we cannot find the probability associated with 3.13. The largest value available is 3.09. The area corresponding to 3.09 is .4990. In this case we can report that the *p*-value is less than .0010, found by .5000 − .4990. We conclude that there is very little likelihood that the null hypothesis is true!

In summary, the criteria for using the large sample test of means are:

1. *The samples are from independent populations*. This means, for example, that the sample response time for the senior citizens is unrelated to the response time for the other patients. If Mr. Smith is a senior citizen and his response time is sampled, that does not affect the response time for any other patient.
2. *Both samples are at least 30*. In the Aloha Hospital example, one sample was 50 and the other 100. Because both samples are considered large, we can substitute the sample standard deviations for the population standard deviations and use formula 10–2 to find the value of the test statistic.

Self-Review 10–1

Tom Sevits is the owner of the Appliance Patch. Recently Tom observed a difference in the dollar value of sales between the men and women he employs as sales associates. A sample of 40 days revealed the men sold a mean of \$1,400 worth of appliances per day with a standard deviation of \$200. For a sample of 50 days, the women sold a mean of \$1,500 worth of appliances per day with a standard deviation of \$250. At the .05 significance level can Mr. Sevits conclude that the mean amount sold per day is larger for the women?

(a) State the null hypothesis and the alternate hypothesis.
(b) What is the decision rule?
(c) What is the value of the test statistic?
(d) What is your decision regarding the null hypothesis?
(e) What is the *p*-value?
(f) Interpret the result.

Exercises

1. A sample of 40 observations is selected from one population. The sample mean is 102 and the sample standard deviation is 5. A sample of 50 observations is selected from a second population. The sample mean is 99 and the sample standard deviation is 6. Conduct the following test of hypothesis using the .04 significance level.

H_0: $\mu_1 = \mu_2$
H_1: $\mu_1 \neq \mu_2$

a. Is this a one-tailed or a two-tailed test?
b. State the decision rule.
c. Compute the value of the test statistic.
d. What is your decision regarding H_0?
e. What is the *p*-value?

2. A sample of 65 observations is selected from one population. The sample mean is 2.67 and the sample standard deviation is 0.75. A sample of 50 observations is selected from a second population. The sample mean is 2.59 and the sample standard deviation is 0.66. Conduct the following test of hypothesis using the .08 significance level.

H_0: $\mu_1 \leq \mu_2$
H_1: $\mu_1 > \mu_2$

a. Is this a one-tailed or a two-tailed test?
b. State the decision rule.
c. Compute the value of the test statistic.
d. What is your decision regarding H_0?
e. What is the *p*-value?

Note: Use the five-step hypothesis testing procedure to solve the following exercises.

3. The Gibbs Baby Food Company wishes to compare the weight gain of infants using their brand versus their competitor's. A sample of 40 babies using the Gibbs products revealed a mean weight gain of 7.6 pounds in the first three months after birth. The standard deviation of the sample was 2.3 pounds. A sample of 55 babies using the competitor's brand revealed a mean increase in weight of 8.1 pounds, with a standard deviation of 2.9 pounds. At the .05 significance level, can we conclude that babies using the Gibbs brand gained less weight? Compute the *p*-value and interpret it.

4. As part of a study of corporate employees, the Director of Human Resources for PNC, Inc. wants to compare the distance traveled to work by employees at their office in downtown Cincinnati with the distance for those in downtown Pittsburgh. A sample of 35 Cincinnati employees showed they travel a mean of 370 miles per month, with a standard deviation of 30 miles per month. A sample of 40 Pittsburgh employees showed they travel a mean of 380 miles per month, with a standard deviation of 26 miles per month. At the .05 significance level, is there a difference in the mean number of miles traveled per month between Cincinnati and Pittsburgh employees? Use the five-step hypothesis-testing procedure.

5. A financial analyst wants to compare the turnover rates, in percent, for shares of oil-related stocks versus other stocks, such as GE and IBM. She selected 32 oil-related stocks and 49 other stocks. The mean turnover rate of oil-related stocks is 31.4 percent and the standard deviation 5.1 percent. For the other stocks, the mean rate was computed to be 34.9 percent and the standard deviation 6.7 percent. Is there a significant difference in the turnover rates of the two types of stock? Use the .01 significance level.
6. Mary Jo Fitzpatrick is the Vice President for Nursing Services at St. Luke's Memorial Hospital. Recently she noticed in the job postings for nurses that those that are unionized seem to offer higher wages. She decided to investigate and gathered the following sample information.

Group	Mean Wage	Sample Standard Deviation	Sample Size
Union	\$20.75	\$2.25	40
Nonunion	\$19.80	\$1.90	45

Would it be reasonable for her to conclude that union nurses earn more? Use the .02 significance level. What is the *p*-value?

Two-Sample Tests about Proportions

In the previous section, we considered a test involving population means. However, we are often interested also in whether two sample proportions came from populations that are equal. Here are several examples.

- The Vice President of Human Resources wishes to know whether there is a difference in the proportion of hourly employees who miss more than 5 days of work per year at the Atlanta and the Houston plants.
- General Motors is considering a new design for the Pontiac Grand Am. The design is shown to a group of potential buyers under 30 years of age and another group over 60 years of age. Pontiac wishes to know whether there is a difference in the proportion of the two groups who like the new design.
- United Airlines is investigating the fear of flying among adults. Specifically, they wish to know whether there is a difference in the proportion of men versus women who are fearful of flying.

In the above cases each sampled item or individual can be classified as a "success" or a "failure." That is, in the Grand Am example each potential buyer is classified as "liking the new design" or "not liking the new design." We then compare the proportion in the under 30 group with the proportion in the over 60 group who indicated they liked the new design. Can we conclude that the differences are due to chance? In this study there is no measurement obtained, only classifying the individuals or objects. Then we assume the nominal scale of measurement.

To conduct the test, we assume each sample is large enough that the normal distribution will serve as a good approximation of the binomial distribution. The test statistic follows the standard normal distribution. We compute the value of z from the following formula:

TWO-SAMPLE TEST OF PROPORTIONS

$$z = \frac{p_1 - p_2}{\sqrt{\dfrac{p_c(1 - p_c)}{n_1} + \dfrac{p_c(1 - p_c)}{n_2}}} \qquad [10\text{–}3]$$

Formula 10–3 is formula 10–2 with the respective sample proportions replacing the sample means and $p_c(1 - p_c)$ replacing the two sample standard deviations. In addition:

n_1 is the number of observations in the first sample.
n_2 is the number of observations in the second sample.
p_1 is the proportion in the first sample possessing the trait.
p_2 is the proportion in the second sample possessing the trait.
p_c is the pooled proportion possessing the trait in the combined samples. It is called the pooled estimate of the population proportion and is computed from the following formula.

POOLED PROPORTION

$$p_c = \frac{X_1 + X_2}{n_1 + n_2} \qquad [10\text{–}4]$$

where:

X_1 is the number possessing the trait in the first sample.
X_2 is the number possessing the trait in the second sample.

The following example will illustrate the two-sample test of proportions.

EXAMPLE

The Manelli Perfume Company recently developed a new fragrance that they plan to market under the name "Heavenly." A number of market studies indicate that Heavenly has very good market potential. The Sales Department at Manelli is particularly interested in whether there is a difference in the proportions of younger and older women who would purchase Heavenly if it were marketed. There are two independent populations, a population consisting of the younger women and a population consisting of the older women. Each sampled woman will be asked to smell Heavenly and indicate whether she likes the fragrance well enough to purchase a bottle.

SOLUTION

We will use the usual five-step hypothesis-testing procedure.

Step 1: State H_0 and H_1. In this case the null hypothesis is: "There is no difference in the proportion of young women and older women who prefer Heavenly." We designate π_1 as the proportion of young women who would purchase Heavenly and π_2 as the proportion of older women who would purchase. The alternate hypothesis is that the two proportions are not equal.

$$H_0: \pi_1 = \pi_2$$
$$H_1: \pi_1 \neq \pi_2$$

Step 2: Select the level of significance. We use the .05 significance level in this example.

Step 3: Determine the test statistic. The test statistic follows the standard normal distribution. The value of the test statistic can be computed from formula 10–3.

Step 4: Formulate the decision rule. Recall that the alternate hypothesis from step 1 does not state a direction, so this is a two-tailed test. To determine the critical value, we divide the significance level in half and place this amount in each tail of the z distribution. Next, we subtract this amount from the total area to the right of zero. That is $.5000 - .0250 = .4750$. Finally, we search the body of the z table (Appendix D) for the closest value. It is 1.96. The critical values are -1.96 and $+1.96$. As before, if the computed z value falls in the region between $+1.96$ and -1.96, the null hypothesis is not rejected. If that does occur, it is assumed that any difference between the two sample proportions is due to chance variation. This information is summarized in Chart 10–2.

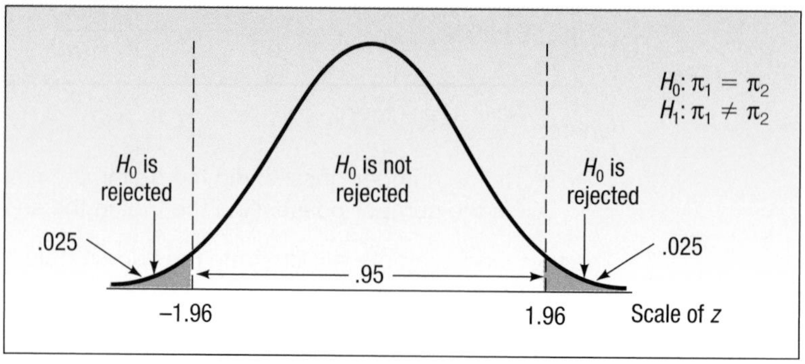

CHART 10–2 Decision Rules for Heavenly Fragrance Test, .05 Significance Level

Step 5: Select a sample and make a decision. A random sample of 100 young women revealed 20 liked the Heavenly fragrance well enough to purchase it. Similarly, a sample of 200 older women revealed 100 liked the fragrance well enough to make a purchase. We let p_1 refer to the young women and p_2 to the older women.

$$p_1 = \frac{X_1}{n_1} = \frac{20}{100} = .20 \qquad p_2 = \frac{X_2}{n_2} = \frac{100}{200} = .50$$

The research question is whether the difference of .30 in the two sample proportions is due to chance or whether there is a difference in the proportion of younger and older women who like the Heavenly fragrance.

Next, we combine or pool the sample proportions. We use formula 10–4.

$$p_c = \frac{X_1 + X_2}{n_1 + n_2} = \frac{20 + 100}{100 + 200} = .40$$

Note that the pooled proportion is closer to .50 than to .20 because more older women than younger women were sampled.

We use formula 10–3 to find the value of the test statistic.

$$z = \frac{p_1 - p_2}{\sqrt{\dfrac{p_c(1 - p_c)}{n_1} + \dfrac{p_c(1 - p_c)}{n_2}}} = \frac{.20 - .50}{\sqrt{\dfrac{.40(1 - .40)}{100} + \dfrac{.40(1 - .40)}{200}}} = -5.00$$

The computed value of −5.00 is in the area of rejection; that is, it is to the left of −1.96. Therefore, the null hypothesis is rejected at the .05 significance level. To put it another way, the null hypothesis that the proportion of young women who would purchase Heavenly is equal to the proportion of older women who would purchase Heavenly is rejected. It is unlikely that the difference between the two sample proportions is due to chance. To find the *p*-value we go to Appendix D and look for the likelihood of finding a *z* value less than −5.00 or greater than 5.00. The largest value of *z* reported is 3.09, with a corresponding probability of .4990. So the probability of finding a *z* value greater than 5.00 or less than −5.00 is virtually zero. So we report zero as the *p*-value. There is very little likelihood the null hypothesis is true. We conclude that there is a difference in the proportion of younger and older women who would purchase Heavenly.

Self-Review 10–2

Of 150 adults who tried a new peach-flavored peppermint patty, 87 rated it excellent. Of 200 children sampled, 123 rated it excellent. Using the .10 level of significance, can we conclude that there is a significant difference in the proportion of adults and the proportion of children who rate the new flavor excellent?

(a) State the null hypothesis and the alternate hypothesis.
(b) What is the probability of a Type I error?
(c) Is this a one-tailed or a two-tailed test?
(d) What is the decision rule?
(e) What is the value of the test statistic?
(f) What is your decision regarding the null hypothesis?
(g) What is the *p*-value? Explain what it means in terms of this problem.

Exercises

7. The null and alternate hypotheses are:

H_0: $\pi_1 \leq \pi_2$
H_1: $\pi_1 > \pi_2$

A sample of 100 observations from the first population indicated that X_1 is 70. A sample of 150 observations from the second population revealed X_2 to be 90. Use the .05 significance level to test the hypothesis.

a. State the decision rule.
b. Compute the pooled proportion.
c. Compute the value of the test statistic.
d. What is your decision regarding the null hypothesis?

8. The null and alternate hypotheses are:

H_0: $\pi_1 = \pi_2$
H_1: $\pi_1 \neq \pi_2$

A sample of 200 observations from the first population indicated that X_1 is 170. A sample of 150 observations from the second population revealed X_2 to be 110. Use the .05 significance level to test the hypothesis.

a. State the decision rule.
b. Compute the pooled proportion.
c. Compute the value of the test statistic.
d. What is your decision regarding the null hypothesis?

Note: Use the five-step hypothesis-testing procedure in solving the following exercises.

9. The Damon family owns a large grape vineyard in western New York along Lake Erie. The grapevines must be sprayed at the beginning of the growing season to protect against various insects and diseases. Two new insecticides have just been marketed: Pernod 5 and Action. To test their effectiveness, three long rows were selected and sprayed with Pernod 5, and three others were sprayed with Action. When the grapes ripened, 400 of the vines treated with Pernod 5 were checked for infestation. Likewise, a sample of 400 vines sprayed with Action were checked. The results are:

Insecticide	Number of Vines Checked (sample size)	Number of Infested Vines
Pernod 5	400	24
Action	400	40

At the .05 significance level, can we conclude that there is a difference in the proportion of vines infested using Pernod 5 as opposed to Action?

10. The Roper Organization conducted identical surveys in 1990 and 2000. One question asked women was, "Are most men basically kind, gentle, and thoughtful?" The 1990 survey revealed that, of the 3,000 women surveyed, 2,010 said that they were. In 2000, 1,530 of the 3,000 women surveyed thought that men were kind, gentle, and thoughtful. At the .05 level, can we conclude that women think men are less kind, gentle, and thoughtful in 2000 compared with 1990?

11. A nationwide sample of influential Republicans and Democrats was asked as a part of a comprehensive survey whether they favored lowering environmental standards so that high-sulfur coal could be burned in coal-fired power plants. The results were:

	Republicans	Democrats
Number sampled	1,000	800
Number in favor	200	168

At the .02 level of significance, can we conclude that there is a larger proportion of Democrats in favor of lowering the standards?

12. The research department at the home office of New Hampshire Insurance conducts ongoing research on the causes of automobile accidents, the characteristics of the drivers, and so on. A random sample of 400 policies written on single persons revealed 120 had at least one accident in the previous three-year period. Similarly, a sample of 600 policies written on married persons revealed that 150 had been in at least one accident. At the .05 significance level, is there a significant difference in the proportions of single and married persons having an accident during a three-year period?

Comparing Population Means with Small Samples

In an earlier section we assumed that the two population standard deviations were unknown but that we selected random samples containing 30 or more observations each. In this section we consider the case in which the population standard deviations are unknown and the number of observations in at least one of the samples is less than 30. We often refer to this as a "small sample test of means." The requirements for the small sample test are more stringent. The three required assumptions are:

Assumptions for small sample test of means

1. The sampled populations follow the normal distribution.
2. The two samples are from independent populations.
3 The standard deviations of the two populations are equal.

In this case, the t distribution is used to compare two population means. The formula for computing the test statistic t is similar to 10–2, but an additional calculation is necessary. The third assumption above indicates that the population standard deviations must be equal. The two sample variances are pooled to form a single estimate of the unknown population variance. In essence, we compute a weighted mean of the two sample standard deviations and use this as an estimate of the population standard deviation. The weights are the degrees of freedom that each sample provides. Why do we need to pool the standard deviations? In most cases when the samples each have fewer than 30 observations, the population standard deviations are not known. Thus, we calculate s, the sample standard deviation, and substitute it for σ, the population standard deviation. Because we assume that the two populations have equal standard deviations, the best estimate we can make of that value is to combine or pool all the information we have about the value of the population standard deviation.

The following formula is used to pool the sample variances. Notice that two factors are involved: the number of observations in each sample and the sample standard deviations themselves.

POOLED VARIANCE

$$s_p^2 = \frac{(n_1 - 1)s_1^2 + (n_2 - 1)s_2^2}{n_1 + n_2 - 2} \qquad [10\text{–}5]$$

where:

s_1^2 is the variance (standard deviation squared) of the first sample.
s_2^2 is the variance of the second sample.

The value of t is computed from the following equation.

TWO-SAMPLE TEST OF MEANS—SMALL SAMPLES

$$t = \frac{\overline{X}_1 - \overline{X}_2}{\sqrt{s_p^2\left(\frac{1}{n_1} + \frac{1}{n_2}\right)}} \qquad [10\text{–}6]$$

where:

$\overline{X}_1$ is the mean of the first sample.
$\overline{X}_2$ is the mean of the second sample.
n_1 is the number of observations in the first sample.
n_2 is the number of observations in the second sample.
s_p^2 is the pooled estimate of the population variance.

The number of degrees of freedom in the test is the total number of items sampled minus the total number of samples. Because there are two samples, there are $n_1 + n_2 - 2$ degrees of freedom.

EXAMPLE

Owens Lawn Care, Inc. manufactures and assembles lawnmowers that are shipped to dealers throughout the United States and Canada. Two different procedures have been proposed for mounting the engine on the frame of the lawnmower. The question is: Is there a difference in the mean time to mount the engines on the frames of the lawnmowers? The first procedure was developed by longtime Owens employee Herb Welles (designated as procedure 1), and the other procedure was developed by Owens Vice-President of Engineering William Atkins (designated as procedure 2). To evaluate the two methods, it was decided to conduct a time and motion study. A sample of five employees was timed using procedure 1 and six using procedure 2. The results, in minutes, are shown below. Is there a difference in the mean mounting times? Use the .10 significance level.

Procedure 1 (minutes)	Procedure 2 (minutes)
2	3
4	7
9	5
3	8
2	4
	3

SOLUTION

Following the five steps to test a hypothesis, the null hypothesis states that there is no difference in mean mounting times between the two procedures. The alternate hypothesis indicates that there is a difference.

H_0: $\mu_1 = \mu_2$
H_1: $\mu_1 \neq \mu_2$

The required assumptions are:

1. The observations in the Welles sample are *independent* of the observations in the Atkins sample and of each other.
2. The two populations follow the normal distribution.
3. The two populations have equal standard deviations.

Is there a difference between the mean assembly times using the Welles and the Atkins methods? The degrees of freedom are equal to the total number of items sampled minus the number of samples. In this case that is $n_1 + n_2 - 2$. Five assemblers used the Welles method and six the Atkins method. Thus, there are 9 degrees of freedom, found by $5 + 6 - 2$. The critical values of t, from Appendix F for $df = 9$, a two-tailed test, and the .10 significance level, are -1.833 and 1.833. The decision rule is portrayed graphically in Chart 10–3. We do not reject the null hypothesis if the computed value of t falls between -1.833 and 1.833.

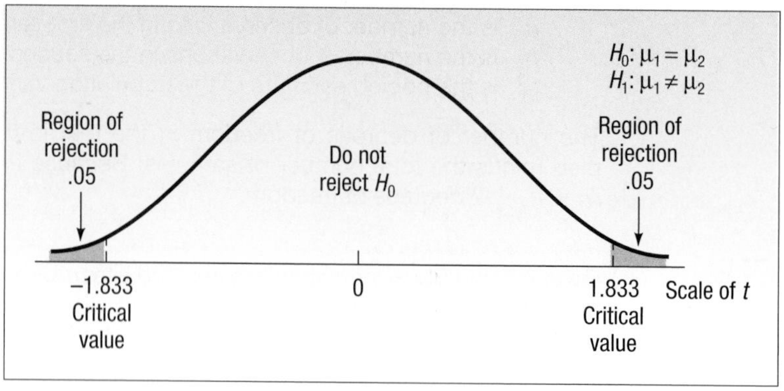

CHART 10–3 Regions of Rejection, Two-Tailed Test, $df = 9$, and .10 Significance Level

We use three steps to compute the value of t.

Step 1: Calculate the Sample Standard Deviations. See the details below.

Procedure 1		Procedure 2	
X_1	X_1^2	X_2	X_2^2
2	4	3	9
4	16	7	49
9	81	5	25
3	9	8	64
2	4	4	16
20	114	3	9
		30	172

$$s_1 = \sqrt{\frac{\Sigma X_1^2 - \frac{(\Sigma X_1)^2}{n_1}}{n_1 - 1}} \qquad s_2 = \sqrt{\frac{\Sigma X_2^2 - \frac{(\Sigma X_2)^2}{n_2}}{n_2 - 1}}$$

$$= \sqrt{\frac{114 - \frac{(20)^2}{5}}{5 - 1}} = 2.9155 \qquad = \sqrt{\frac{172 - \frac{(30)^2}{6}}{6 - 1}} = 2.0976$$

Step 2: Pool the Sample Variances. We use formula 10–5 to pool the sample variances (standard deviations squared).

$$s_p^2 = \frac{(n_1 - 1)s_1^2 + (n_2 - 1)s_2^2}{n_1 + n_2 - 2} = \frac{(5 - 1)(2.9155)^2 + (6 - 1)(2.0976)^2}{5 + 6 - 2} = 6.2222$$

Step 3: Determine the value of *t*. The mean mounting time for procedure 1 is 4.00 minutes, found by $\overline{X}_1 = 20/5$. The mean mounting time for procedure 2 is 5.00 minutes, found by $\overline{X}_2 = 30/6$. We use formula 10–6 to calculate the value of t.

$$t = \frac{\overline{X}_1 - \overline{X}_2}{\sqrt{s_p^2\left(\frac{1}{n_1} + \frac{1}{n_2}\right)}} = \frac{4.00 - 5.00}{\sqrt{6.2222\left(\frac{1}{5} + \frac{1}{6}\right)}} = -0.662$$

The decision is not to reject the null hypothesis, because -0.662 falls in the region between -1.833 and 1.833. We conclude that there is no difference in the mean times to mount the engine on the frame using the two methods.

We can also estimate the p-value using Appendix F. Locate the row with 9 degrees of freedom, and use the two-tailed test column. Find the t value, without regard to the sign, which is closest to our computed value of 0.662. It is 1.383, corresponding to a significance level of .20. Thus, even had we used the 20 percent significance level, we would not have rejected the null hypothesis of equal means. We can report that the p-value is greater than .20.

Excel has a procedure called "t-Test: Two Sample Assuming Equal Variances" that will perform the calculations of formulas 10–5 and 10–6 as well as find the sample means and sample variances. The data are input in the first two columns of the Excel

spreadsheet. They are labeled "One" and "Two." The output follows. The value of t, called the "t Stat," is -0.66205, and the two-tailed p-value is .52453. As we would expect, the p-value is larger than the significance level of .10. The conclusion is not to reject the null hypothesis.

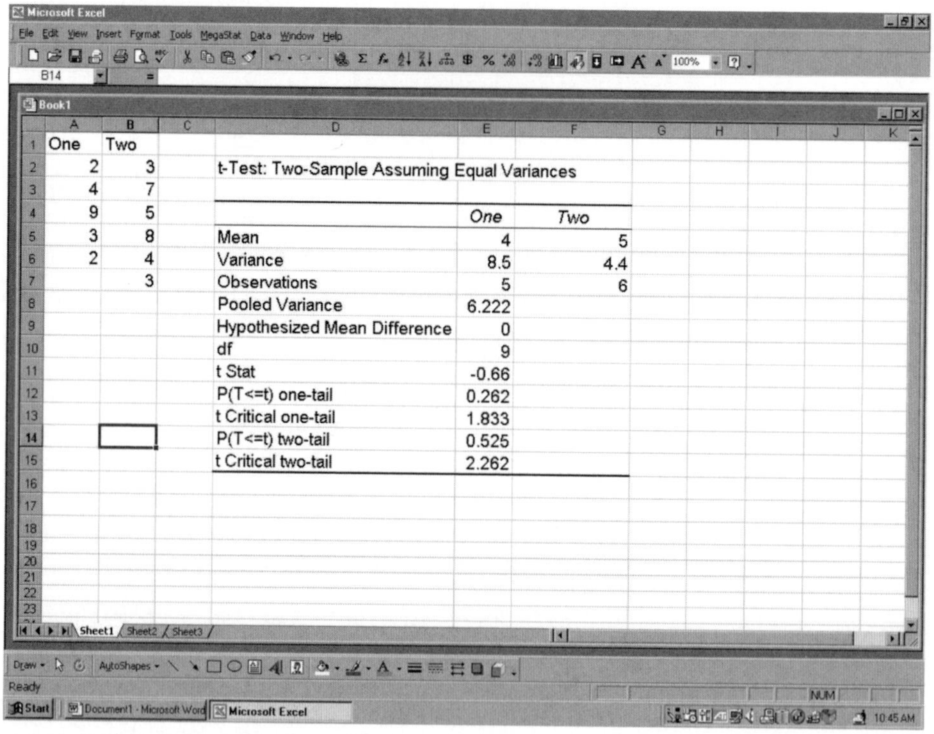

Self-Review 10–3

The production manager at Bellevue Steel, a manufacturer of wheelchairs, wants to compare the number of defective wheelchairs produced on the day shift with the number on the afternoon shift. A sample of the production from 6 day shifts and 8 afternoon shifts revealed the following number of defects.

Day	5	8	7	6	9	7		
Afternoon	8	10	7	11	9	12	14	9

At the .05 significance level, is there a difference in the mean number of defects per shift?

(a) State the null hypothesis and the alternate hypothesis.
(b) What is the decision rule?
(c) What is the value of the test statistic?
(d) What is your decision regarding the null hypothesis?
(e) What is the p-value?
(f) Interpret the result.

Exercises

For Exercises 13 and 14: (a) state the decision rule, (b) compute the pooled estimate of the population variance, (c) compute the test statistic, (d) state your decision about the null hypothesis, and (e) estimate the p-value.

13. The null and alternate hypotheses are:

H_0: $\mu_1 = \mu_2$
H_1: $\mu_1 \neq \mu_2$

A random sample of 10 observations from one population revealed a sample mean of 23 and a sample deviation of 4. A random sample of 8 observations from another population revealed a sample mean of 26 and a sample standard deviation of 5. At the .05 significance level, is there a difference between the population means?

14. The null and alternate hypotheses are:

H_0: $\mu_1 = \mu_2$
H_1: $\mu_1 \neq \mu_2$

A random sample of 15 observations from the first population revealed a sample mean of 350 and a sample standard deviation of 12. A random sample of 17 observations from the second population revealed a sample mean of 342 and a sample standard deviation of 15. At the .10 significance level, is there a difference in the population means?

Note: Use the five-step hypothesis testing procedure for the following exercises.

15. A sample of scores on an examination given in Statistics 201 are:

Men	72	69	98	66	85	76	79	80	77
Women	81	67	90	78	81	80	76		

At the .01 significance level, is the mean grade of the women higher than that of the men?

16. A recent study compared the time spent together by single- and dual-earner couples. According to the records kept by the wives during the study, the mean amount of time spent together watching television among the single-earner couples was 61 minutes per day, with a standard deviation of 15.5 minutes. For the dual-earner couples, the mean number of minutes spent watching television was 48.4 minutes, with a standard deviation of 18.1 minutes. At the .01 significance level, can we conclude that the single-earner couples on average spend more time watching television together? There were 15 single-earner and 12 dual-earner couples studied.

17. Ms. Lisa Monnin is the budget director for the New Process Company. She would like to compare the daily travel expenses for the sales staff and the audit staff. She collected the following sample information.

Sales ($)	131	135	146	165	136	142	
Audit ($)	130	102	129	143	149	120	139

At the .10 significance level, can she conclude that the mean daily expenses are greater for the sales staff than the audit staff? What is the *p*-value?

18. The Tampa Bay (Florida) Area Chamber of Commerce wanted to know whether the mean weekly salary of nurses was larger than that of school teachers. To investigate, they collected the following information on the amounts earned last week by a sample of school teachers and nurses.

School teachers ($)	845	826	827	875	784	809	802	820	829	830	842	832
Nurses ($)	841	890	821	771	850	859	825	829				

Is it reasonable to conclude that the mean weekly salary of nurses is higher? Use the .01 significance level. What is the *p*-value?

Two-Sample Tests of Hypothesis: Dependent Samples

On page 331, we tested the difference between the means from two independent samples. We compared the mean time required to mount an engine using the Welles method to the time to mount the engine using the Atkins method. The samples were *independent,* meaning that the sample of assembly times using the Welles method was in no way related to the sample of assembly times using the Atkins method.

There are situations, however, in which the samples are not independent. To put it another way, the samples are **dependent** or related. As an example, Nickel Savings and Loan employs two firms, Schadek Appraisals and Bowyer Real Estate, to appraise the value of the real estate properties on which they make loans. It is important that these two firms be similar in their appraisal values. To review the consistency of the two appraisal firms, Nickel Savings randomly selects 10 homes and has both Schadek Appraisals and Bowyer Real Estate appraise the value of the selected homes. For each home, there will be a pair of appraisal values. That is, for each home there will be an appraised value from both Schadek Appraisals and Bowyer Real Estate. The appraised values depend on, or are related to, the home selected. This is also referred to as a **paired sample.**

For hypothesis testing, we are interested in the distribution of the *differences* in the appraised value of each home. Hence, there is only one sample. To put it more formally, we are investigating whether the mean of the distribution of differences in the appraised values is 0. The sample is made up of the *differences* between the appraised values determined by Schadek Appraisals and the values from Bowyer Real Estate. If the two appraisal firms are reporting similar estimates, then sometimes Schadek Appraisals will be the higher value and sometimes Bowyer Real Estate will have the higher value. However, the mean of the distribution of differences will be 0. On the other hand, if one of the firms consistently reports the larger appraisal values, then the mean of the distribution of the differences will not be 0.

We will use the symbol μ_d to indicate the population mean of the distribution of differences. We assume the distribution of the population of differences follows the normal distribution. The test statistic follows the t distribution and we calculate its value from the following formula:

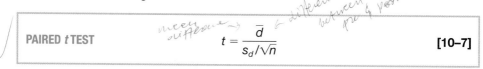

PAIRED *t* TEST

$$t = \frac{\bar{d}}{s_d/\sqrt{n}} \qquad \textbf{[10–7]}$$

There are $n - 1$ degrees of freedom and

- $\bar{d}$ is the mean of the difference between the paired or related observations.
- s_d is the standard deviation of the differences between the paired or related observations.
- n is the number of paired observations.

The standard deviation of the differences is computed using formula 3–12 except d is substituted for X. The formula is:

$$s_d = \sqrt{\frac{\Sigma d^2 - \frac{(\Sigma d)^2}{n}}{n - 1}}$$

The following example illustrates this test.

EXAMPLE

Recall that Nickel Savings and Loan wishes to compare the two companies they use to appraise the value of residential homes. Nickel Savings selected a sample of 10 residential properties and scheduled both firms for an appraisal. The results, reported in $000, are:

Home	Schadek	Bowyer
1	135	128
2	110	105
3	131	119
4	142	140
5	105	98
6	130	123
7	131	127
8	110	115
9	125	122
10	149	145

At the .05 significance level, can we conclude there is a difference in the mean appraised values of the homes?

SOLUTION

The first step is to state the null and the alternate hypotheses. In this case a two-tailed alternative is appropriate because we are interested in determining whether there is a *difference* in the appraised values. We are not interested in showing whether one particular firm appraises property at a higher value than the other. The question is whether the sample differences in the appraised values could have come from a population with a mean of 0. If the population mean of the differences is 0, then we conclude that there is no difference in the appraised values. The null and alternate hypotheses are:

H_0: $\mu_d = 0$
H_1: $\mu_d \neq 0$

There are 10 homes appraised by both firms, so $n = 10$, and $df = n - 1 = 10 - 1 = 9$. We have a two-tailed test, and the significance level is .05. To determine the critical value, go to Appendix F, move across the row with 9 degrees of freedom to the column for a two-tailed test and the .05 significance level. The value at the intersection is 2.262. This value appears in the box in Table 10–2 which is on the following page. The decision rule is to reject the null hypothesis if the computed value of t is less than -2.262 or greater than 2.262. Here are the computational details.

Home	Schadek	Bowyer	Difference, d	Difference Squared, d^2
1	135	128	7	49
2	110	105	5	25
3	131	119	12	144
4	142	140	2	4
5	105	98	7	49
6	130	123	7	49
7	131	127	4	16
8	110	115	−5	25
9	125	122	3	9
10	149	145	4	16
			46	386

$$\bar{d} = \frac{\Sigma d}{n} = \frac{46}{10} = 4.60$$

$$s_d = \sqrt{\frac{\Sigma d^2 - \frac{(\Sigma d)^2}{n}}{n - 1}} = \sqrt{\frac{386 - \frac{(46)^2}{10}}{10 - 1}} = 4.402$$

Using formula 10–7, the value of the test statistic is 3.305, found by

$$t = \frac{\bar{d}}{s_d/\sqrt{n}} = \frac{4.6}{4.402/\sqrt{10}} = 3.305$$

Because the computed t falls in the rejection region, the null hypothesis is rejected. The population distribution of differences does not have a mean of 0. We conclude that there is a difference in the mean appraised values of the homes. The largest difference of \$12,000 is for Home 3. Perhaps that would be an appropriate place to begin a more detailed review.

To find the p-value, we use Appendix F and the section for a two-tailed test. Move along the row with 9 degrees of freedom and find the values of t that are closest to our calculated value. For a .01 significance level, the value of t is 3.250. The computed value is larger than this value, but smaller than the value of 4.781 corresponding to the .001 significance level. Hence, the p-value is less than .01. This information is highlighted in Table 10–2 below.

TABLE 10–2 A Portion of the t Distribution from Appendix F

	Confidence Intervals					
	80%	90%	95%	98%	99%	99.9%
	Level of Significance for One-Tailed Test					
df	0.100	0.050	0.025	0.010	0.005	0.0005
	Level of Significance for Two-Tailed Test					
	0.20	0.10	0.05	0.02	0.01	0.001
1	3.078	6.314	12.706	31.821	63.657	636.619
2	1.886	2.920	4.303	6.965	9.925	31.599
3	1.638	2.353	3.182	4.541	5.841	12.924
4	1.533	2.132	2.776	3.747	4.604	8.610
5	1.476	2.015	2.571	3.365	4.032	6.869
6	1.440	1.943	2.447	3.143	3.707	5.959
7	1.415	1.895	2.365	2.998	3.499	5.408
8	1.397	1.860	2.306	2.896	3.355	5.041
9	1.383	1.833	2.262	2.821	3.250	4.781
10	1.372	1.812	2.228	2.764	3.169	4.587

Excel has a procedure called "t-Test: Paired Two-Sample for Means" that will perform the calculations of formula 10–7. The output from this procedure is given on the following page.

The computed value of t is 3.3045, and the two-tailed p-value is .00916. Because the p-value is less than .05, we reject the hypothesis that the mean of the distribution of the differences between the appraised values is zero. In fact, this p-value is less than 1.0 percent. There is very little likelihood that the null hypothesis is true.

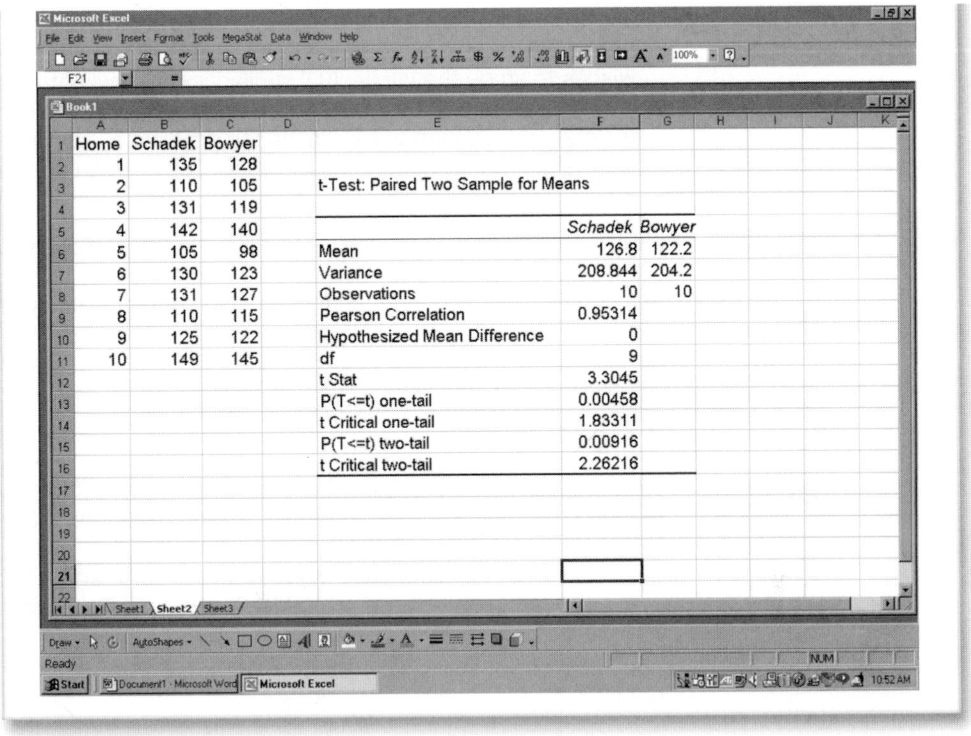

Home	Schadek	Bowyer
1	135	128
2	110	105
3	131	119
4	142	140
5	105	98
6	130	123
7	131	127
8	110	115
9	125	122
10	149	145

t-Test: Paired Two Sample for Means

	Schadek	Bowyer
Mean	126.8	122.2
Variance	208.844	204.2
Observations	10	10
Pearson Correlation	0.95314	
Hypothesized Mean Difference	0	
df	9	
t Stat	3.3045	
P(T<=t) one-tail	0.00458	
t Critical one-tail	1.83311	
P(T<=t) two-tail	0.00916	
t Critical two-tail	2.26216	

Comparing Dependent and Independent Samples

Beginning students are often confused by the difference between tests for independent samples (formula 10–6) and tests for dependent samples (formula 10–7). How do we tell the difference between dependent and independent samples? There are two types of dependent samples: (1) those characterized by a measurement, an intervention of some type, and then another measurement; and (2) a matching or pairing of the observations. To explain further:

1. The first type of dependent sample is characterized by a measurement followed by an intervention of some kind and then another measurement. This could be called a "before" and "after" study. Two examples will help to clarify. Suppose we want to show that, by placing speakers in the production area and playing soothing music, we are able to increase production. We begin by selecting a sample of workers and measuring their output under the current conditions. The speakers are then installed in the production area, and we again measure the output of the same workers. There are two measurements, before placing the speakers in the production area and after. The intervention is placing speakers in the production area.

   A second example involves an educational firm that offers courses designed to increase test scores and reading ability. Suppose the firm wants to offer a course that will help high school juniors increase their SAT scores. To begin, each student takes the SAT in the junior year in high school. During the summer between the junior and senior year, they participate in the course that gives them tips on taking tests. Finally, during the fall of their senior year in high school, they retake the SAT. Again, the procedure is characterized by a measurement (taking the SAT as a junior), an intervention (the summer workshops), and another measurement (taking the SAT during their senior year).
2. The second type of dependent sample is characterized by matching or pairing observations. Nickel Savings in the previous example is a dependent sample of

this type. They selected a property for appraisal and then had two appraisals on the same property. As a second example, suppose an industrial psychologist wishes to study the intellectual similarities of newly married couples. She selects a sample of newlyweds. Next, she administers a standard intelligence test to both the man and woman to determine the difference in the scores. Notice the matching that occurred: comparing the scores of the man and the woman.

Why do we prefer dependent samples to independent samples? By using dependent samples, we are able to reduce the variation in the sampling distribution. To illustrate, we will use the Nickel Savings and Loan example just completed. Suppose we assume that we have two independent samples of real estate property for appraisal and conduct the following test of hypothesis, using formula 10–6. The null and alternate hypotheses are:

H_0: $\mu_1 = \mu_2$
H_1: $\mu_1 \neq \mu_2$

There are now two independent samples of 10 each. So the number of degrees of freedom is 10 + 10 − 2 = 18. From Appendix D, using the .05 significance level, H_0 is rejected if t is less than −2.101 or greater than 2.101.

The mean of the appraised value of the 10 properties by Schadek is $126,800, and the standard deviation is $14,500. For Bowyer Real Estate the mean appraised value is $122,200, and the standard deviation is $14,300. To make the calculations easier, we use $000 instead of $. The value of the pooled estimate of the variance from formula 10–5 is

$$s_p^2 = \frac{(n_1 - 1)s_1^2 + (n_2 - 1)s_2^2}{n_1 + n_2 - 2} = \frac{(10 - 1)14.5^2 + (10 - 1)14.3^2}{10 + 10 - 2} = 207.37$$

Using formula 10–6, t is 0.714.

$$t = \frac{\overline{X}_1 - \overline{X}_2}{\sqrt{s_p^2\left(\frac{1}{n_1} + \frac{1}{n_2}\right)}} = \frac{126.8 - 122.2}{\sqrt{207.37\left(\frac{1}{10} + \frac{1}{10}\right)}} = \frac{4.6}{6.4403} = 0.714$$

The computed t (0.714) is less than 2.101, so the null hypothesis is not rejected. We cannot show that there is a difference in the mean appraisal value. That is not the same conclusion that we got before! Why does this happen? The numerator is the same in the paired observations test (4.6). However, the denominator is smaller. In the paired test the denominator is 1.3920 (see the calculations on page 338). In the case of the independent samples, the denominator is 6.4403. There is more variation or uncertainty. This accounts for the difference in the t values and the difference in the statistical decisions. The denominator measures the standard error of the statistic. When the samples are *not* paired, two kinds of variation are present: differences between the two appraisal firms and the difference in the value of the real estate. Properties numbered 4 and 10 have relatively high values, whereas number 5 is relatively low. These data show how different the values of the property are, but we are really interested in the difference between the two appraisal firms.

The trick is to pair the values to reduce the variation among the properties. The paired test uses only the difference between the two appraisal firms for the same property. Thus, the paired or dependent statistic focuses on the variation between Schadek Appraisals and Bowyer Real Estate. Thus, its standard error is always smaller. That, in turn, leads to a larger test statistic and a greater chance of rejecting the null hypothesis. So whenever possible you should pair the data.

There is a bit of bad news here. In the paired observations test, the degrees of freedom are half of what they are if the samples are not paired. For the real estate example, the degrees of freedom drop from 18 to 9 when the observations are paired. However, in most cases, this is a small price to pay for a better test.

Self-Review 10–4

Advertisements by Sylph Fitness Center claim that completing their course will result in losing weight. A random sample of eight recent participants showed the following weights before and after completing the course. At the .01 significance level, can we conclude the students lost weight?

Name	Before	After
Hunter	155	154
Cashman	228	207
Mervine	141	147
Massa	162	157
Creola	211	196
Perterson	164	150
Redding	184	170
Poust	172	165

(a) State the null hypothesis and the alternate hypothesis.
(b) What is the critical value of t?
(c) What is the computed value of t?
(d) Interpret the result. What is the p-value?

Exercises

19. The null and alternate hypotheses are:

H_0: $\mu_d \leq 0$
H_1: $\mu_d > 0$

The following sample information shows the number of defective units produced on the day shift and the afternoon shift for a sample of four days last month.

	Day			
	1	2	3	4
Day shift	10	12	15	19
Afternoon shift	8	9	12	15

At the .05 significance level, can we conclude there are more defects produced on the afternoon shift?

20. The null and alternate hypotheses are:

H_0: $\mu_d = 0$
H_1: $\mu_d \neq 0$

The following paired observations show the number of traffic citations given for speeding by Officer Dhondt and Officer Meredith of the South Carolina Highway Patrol for the last five months.

	Day				
	May	June	July	August	September
Officer Dhondt	30	22	25	19	26
Officer Meredith	26	19	20	15	19

At the .05 significance level, is there a difference in the mean number of citations given by the two officers?

Note: Use the five-step hypothesis testing procedure to solve the following exercises.

21. The management of Discount Furniture, a chain of discount furniture stores in the Northeast, designed an incentive plan for salespeople. To evaluate this innovative plan, 12 salespeople were selected at random, and their weekly incomes before and after the plan were recorded.

Salesperson	Before	After
Sid Mahone	$320	$340
Carol Quick	290	285
Tom Jackson	421	475
Andy Jones	510	510
Jean Sloan	210	210
Jack Walker	402	500
Peg Mancuso	625	631
Anita Loma	560	560
John Cuso	360	365
Carl Utz	431	431
A. S. Kushner	506	525
Fern Lawton	505	619

Was there a significant increase in the typical salesperson's weekly income due to the innovative incentive plan? Use the .05 significance level. Estimate the *p*-value, and interpret it.

22. The federal government recently granted funds for a special program designed to reduce crime in high-crime areas. A study of the results of the program in eight high-crime areas of Miami, FL, yielded the following results.

	Number of Crimes by Area							
	A	B	C	D	E	F	G	H
Before	14	7	4	5	17	12	8	9
After	2	7	3	6	8	13	3	5

Has there been a decrease in the number of crimes since the inauguration of the program? Use the .01 significance level. Estimate the *p*-value.

Chapter Outline

I. In comparing two population means we wish to know whether they could be equal.

A. We are investigating whether the distribution of the difference between the means could have a mean of 0.

B. The test statistic is the standard normal (z) if the samples both contain at least 30 observations and the population standard deviations are unknown.

1. No assumption about the shape of either population is required.
2. The samples are from independent populations.
3. The formula to compute the value of z is

$$z = \frac{\overline{X}_1 - \overline{X}_2}{\sqrt{\frac{s_1^2}{n_1} + \frac{s_2^2}{n_2}}} \quad \text{[10–2]}$$

II. We can also test whether two samples came from populations with an equal proportion of successes.

A. The two sample proportions are pooled using the following formula:

$$p_c = \frac{X_1 + X_2}{n_1 + n_2} \quad \textbf{[10–4]}$$

B. We compute the value of the test statistic from the following formula:

$$z = \frac{p_1 - p_2}{\sqrt{\frac{p_c(1-p_c)}{n_1} + \frac{p_c(1-p_c)}{n_2}}} \quad \textbf{[10–3]}$$

III. The test statistic to compare two means is the *t* distribution if one or both of the samples contain fewer than 30 observations.

A. Both populations must follow the normal distribution.

B. The populations must have equal standard deviations.

C. The samples are independent.

D. Finding the value of *t* requires two steps.

1. The first step is to pool the standard deviations according to the following formula:

$$s_p^2 = \frac{(n_1 - 1)s_1^2 + (n_2 - 1)s_2^2}{n_1 + n_2 - 2} \quad \textbf{[10–5]}$$

2. The value of *t* is computed from the following formula:

$$t = \frac{\overline{X}_1 - \overline{X}_2}{\sqrt{s_p^2\left(\frac{1}{n_1} + \frac{1}{n_2}\right)}} \quad \textbf{[10–6]}$$

IV. For dependent samples, we assume the distribution of the differences in the populations has a mean of 0.

A. We first compute the mean and the standard deviation of the sample differences.

B. The value of the test statistic is computed from the following formula:

$$t = \frac{\bar{d}}{s_d/\sqrt{n}} \quad \textbf{[10–7]}$$

Pronunciation Key

SYMBOL	MEANING	PRONUNCIATION
p_c	Pooled proportion	*p sub c*
s_p^2	Pooled sample variance	*s sub p squared*
$\overline{X}_1$	Mean of the first sample	*X bar sub 1*
$\overline{X}_2$	Mean of the second sample	*X bar sub 2*
$\bar{d}$	Mean of the difference between dependent observations	*d bar*
s_d	Standard deviation of the difference between dependent observations	*s sub d*

Chapter Exercises

23. An official of the Iowa Department of Highways wants to compare the useful life, in months, of two brands of paint used for striping roads. The mean number of months Cooper Paint lasted was 36.2, with a standard deviation of 1.14 months. The official reviewed 35 road stripes. For King Paint, the mean number of months was 37.0, with a standard deviation of 1.3 months. The official reviewed 40 road stripes. At the .01 significance level, is there a difference in the useful life of the two paints? Compute the p-value.

24. Clark Heter is an industrial engineer at Lyons Products. He would like to determine whether there are more units produced on the afternoon shift than on the day shift. A sample of 54 day-shift workers showed that the mean number of units produced was 345, with a standard deviation of 21. A sample of 60 afternoon-shift workers showed that the mean number of units produced was 351, with a standard deviation of 28 units. At the .05 significance level, is the number of units produced on the afternoon shift larger?

25. Fry Brothers Heating and Air Conditioning, Inc. employs Larry Clark and George Murnen to make service calls to repair furnaces and air conditioning units in homes. Tom Fry, the owner, would like to know whether there is a difference in the mean number of service calls they make per day. A random sample of 40 days last year showed that Larry Clark made an average of 4.77 calls per day, with a standard deviation of 1.05 calls per day. For a sample of 50 days George Murnen made an average of 5.02 calls per day, with a standard deviation of 1.23 calls per day. At the .05 significance level, is there a difference in the mean number of calls per day between the two employees? What is the p-value?

26. A coffee manufacturer is interested in whether the mean daily consumption of regular-coffee drinkers is less than that of decaffeinated-coffee drinkers. A random sample of 50 regular-coffee drinkers showed a mean of 4.35 cups per day, with a standard deviation of 1.20 cups per day. A sample of 40 decaffeinated-coffee drinkers showed a mean of 5.84 cups per day, with a standard deviation of 1.36 cups per day. Use the .01 significance level. Compute the p-value.

27. The manufacturer of Advil, a common headache remedy, recently developed a new formulation of the drug that is claimed to be more effective. To evaluate the new drug, a sample of 200 current users is asked to try it. After a one-month trial, 180 indicated the new drug was more effective in relieving a headache. At the same time a sample of 300 current Advil users is given the current drug but told it is the new formulation. From this group, 261 said it was an improvement. At the .05 significance level can we conclude that the new drug is more effective?

28. Each month the National Association of Purchasing Managers publishes the NAPM index. One of the questions asked on the survey to purchasing agents is: Do you think the economy is expanding? Last month, of the 300 responses 160 answered yes to the question. This month, 170 of the 290 responses indicated they felt the economy was expanding. At the .05 significance level, can we conclude that a larger proportion of the agents believe the economy is expanding this month?

29. As part of a recent survey among dual-wage-earner couples, an industrial psychologist found that 990 men out of the 1,500 surveyed believed the division of household duties was fair. A sample of 1,600 women found 970 believed the division of household duties was fair. At the .01 significance level, is it reasonable to conclude that the proportion of men who believe the division of household duties is fair is larger? What is the p-value?

30. There are two major Internet providers in the Colorado Springs, CO, area, one called HTC and the other Mountain. We want to investigate whether there is a difference in the proportion of times a customer is able to access the Internet. During a one-week period, 500 calls were placed at random times throughout the day and night to HTC. A connection was made to the Internet on 450 occasions. A similar one-week study with Mountain showed the Internet to be available on 352 of 400 trials. At the .01 significance level, is there a difference in the percent of time that access to the Internet is successful?

31. The owner of Bun 'N' Run Hamburger wishes to compare the sales per day at two locations. The mean number sold for 10 randomly selected days at the Northside site was 83.55, and the standard deviation was 10.50. For a random sample of 12 days at the Southside location, the mean number sold was 78.80 and the standard deviation was 14.25. At the .05 significance level, is there a difference in the mean number of hamburgers sold at the two locations? What is the p-value?

32. The Engineering Department at Sims Software, Inc., recently developed two chemical solutions designed to increase the usable life of computer disks. A sample of disks treated with the first solution lasted 86, 78, 66, 83, 84, 81, 84, 109, 65, and 102 hours. Those treated with the second solution lasted 91, 71, 75, 76, 87, 79, 73, 76, 79, 78, 87, 90, 76, and 72 hours. At the .10 significance level, can we conclude that there is a difference in the length of time the two types of treatment lasted?

33. The Willow Run Outlet Mall has two Haggar Outlet Stores, one located on Peach Street and the other on Plum Street. The two stores are laid out differently, but both store managers claim their layout maximizes the amounts customers will purchase on impulse. A sample of 10 customers at the Peach Street store revealed they spent the following amounts more than planned: \$17.58, \$19.73, \$12.61, \$17.79, \$16.22, \$15.82, \$15.40, \$15.86, \$11.82, and \$15.85. A sample of 14 customers at the Plum Street store revealed they spent the following amounts more than they planned: \$18.19, \$20.22, \$17.38, \$17.96, \$23.92, \$15.87, \$16.47, \$15.96, \$16.79, \$16.74, \$21.40, \$20.57, \$19.79, and \$14.83. At the .01 significance level, is there a difference in the mean amounts purchased on impulse at the two stores?

34. The Grand Strand Family Medical Center is specifically set up to treat minor medical emergencies for visitors to the Myrtle Beach area. There are two facilities, one in the Little River Area and the other in Murrells Inlet. The Quality Assurance Department wishes to compare the mean waiting time for patients at the two locations. Samples of the waiting times, reported in minutes, follow:

Location	Waiting Time											
Little River	31.73	28.77	29.53	22.08	29.47	18.60	32.94	25.18	29.82	26.49		
Murrells Inlet	22.93	23.92	26.92	27.20	26.44	25.62	30.61	29.44	23.09	23.10	26.69	22.31

At the .05 significance level, is there a difference in the mean waiting time?

35. The Commercial Bank and Trust Company is studying the use of its automatic teller machines (ATMs). Of particular interest is whether young adults (under 25 years) use the machines more than senior citizens. To investigate further, samples of customers under 25 years of age and customers over 60 years of age were selected. The number of ATM transactions last month was determined for each selected individual, and the results are shown below. At the .01 significance level, can bank management conclude that younger customers use the ATMs more?

Under 25	10	10	11	15	7	11	10	9			
Over 60	4	8	7	7	4	5	1	7	4	10	5

36. Two boats, the *Sea Hawk* and the *Sea Queen,* are competing for a spot in the upcoming *America's Cup* race. To decide which will represent the United States, they race over a part of the course several times. Below are the sample times in minutes. At the .05 significance level, can we conclude that there is a difference in their mean times?

Boat	Times (minutes)											
Sea Hawk	12.9	12.5	11.0	13.3	11.2	11.4	11.6	12.3	14.2	11.3		
Sea Queen	14.1	14.1	14.2	17.4	15.8	16.7	16.1	13.3	13.4	13.6	10.8	19.0

37. The manufacturer of a compact disc player wanted to know whether a 10 percent reduction in price is enough to increase the sales of their product. To investigate, the owner randomly selected eight outlets and sold the disc player at the reduced price. At seven randomly selected outlets, the disc player was sold at the regular price. Reported below is the number of units sold last month at the sampled outlets. At the .01 significance level, can the manufacturer conclude that the price reduction resulted in an increase in sales?

Regular price	138	121	88	115	141	125	96	
Reduced price	128	134	152	135	114	106	112	120

38. A number of minor automobile accidents occur at various high-risk intersections in Teton County despite traffic lights. The traffic department claims that a modification in the type of light will reduce these accidents. The county commissioners have agreed to a proposed experiment. Eight intersections were chosen at random, and the lights at those intersections were modified. The numbers of minor accidents during a six-month period before and after the modifications were:

	Number of Accidents							
	A	B	C	D	E	F	G	H
Before modification	5	7	6	4	8	9	8	10
After modification	3	7	7	0	4	6	8	2

At the .01 significance level is it reasonable to conclude that the modification reduced the number of traffic accidents?

39. Lester Hollar is Vice President for Human Resources for a large manufacturing company. In recent years he has noticed an increase in absenteeism that he thinks is related to the general health of the employees. Four years ago, in an attempt to improve the situation, he began a fitness program in which employees exercise during their lunch hour. To evaluate the program, he selected a random sample of eight participants and found the number of days each was absent in the six months before the exercise program began and in the last six months. Below are the results. At the .05 significance level, can he conclude that the number of absences has declined? Estimate the *p*-value.

Employee	Before	After
1	6	5
2	6	2
3	7	1
4	7	3
5	4	3
6	3	6
7	5	3
8	6	7

40. The president of the American Insurance Institute wants to compare the yearly costs of auto insurance offered by two leading companies. He selects a sample of 15 families, some with only a single insured driver, others with several teenage drivers, and pays each family a stipend to contact the two companies and ask for a price quote. To make the data comparable, certain features, such as the amount deductible and limits of liability, are standardized. The sample information is reported below. At the .10 significance level, can we conclude that there is a difference in the amounts quoted?

Family	American Car Insurance	St. Paul Mutual Insurance
Becker	$2,090	$1,610
Berry	1,683	1,247
Cobb	1,402	2,327
Debuck	1,830	1,367
DuBrul	930	1,461
Eckroate	697	1,789
German	1,741	1,621
Glasson	1,129	1,914
King	1,018	1,956
Kucic	1,881	1,772
Meredith	1,571	1,375
Obeid	874	1,527
Price	1,579	1,767
Phillips	1,577	1,636
Tresize	860	1,188

41. Fairfield Homes is developing two parcels near Pigeon Fork, Tennessee. In order to test different advertising approaches, they use different media to reach potential buyers. The mean annual family income for 75 people making inquiries at the first development is $150,000, with a standard deviation of $40,000. A corresponding sample of 120 people at the second development had a mean of $180,000, with a standard deviation of $30,000. At the .05 significance level, can Fairfield conclude that the population means are different?

42. The following data resulted from a taste test of two different chocolate bars. The first number is a rating of the taste, which could range from 0 to 5, with a 5 indicating the person liked the taste. The second number indicates whether a "secret ingredient" was present. If the ingredient was present a code of "1" was used and a "0" otherwise. At the .05 significance level, does this data show a difference in the taste ratings?

Rating	"With/ Without"	Rating	"With/ Without"
3	1	1	1
1	1	4	0
0	0	4	0
2	1	2	1
3	1	3	0
1	1	4	0

43. An investigation of the effectiveness of an antibacterial soap in reducing operating room contamination resulted in the accompanying table. The new soap was tested in a sample of eight operating rooms in the greater Seattle area during the last year.

	Operating Room							
	A	B	C	D	E	F	G	H
Before	6.6	6.5	9.0	10.3	11.2	8.1	6.3	11.6
After	6.8	2.4	7.4	8.5	8.1	6.1	3.4	2.0

At the 0.05 significance level, can we conclude the contamination measurements are lower after use of the new soap?

44. The following data on annual rates of return were collected from five stocks listed on the New York Stock Exchange ("the big board") and five stocks listed on NASDAQ. At the .10 significance level, can we conclude that the annual rates of return are higher on the big board?

NYSE	NASDAQ
17.16	15.80
17.08	16.28
15.51	16.21
8.43	17.97
25.15	7.77

exercises.com

45. Listed on the next page are several prominent companies and their stock prices in December 2001. Go to the Web and look up today's price. There are many sources to find stock prices, such as Yahoo and CNNFI. The Yahoo address is http://www.quote.yahoo.com. Enter the symbol identification to find the current price. At the .05 significance level, can we conclude that the prices have changed?

Company	Symbol	Price
Coca-Cola	KO	46.46
Walt Disney	DIS	20.98
Eastman Kodak	EK	30.57
Ford Motor Company	F	15.18
General Motors	GM	47.53
Goodyear Tire	GT	24.60
IBM	IBM	122.73
McDonald's	MCD	26.43
McGraw-Hill Publishing	MHP	59.16
Oracle	ORCL	15.10
Johnson and Johnson	JNJ	57.10
General Electric	GE	39.85
Home Depot	HD	50.93

46. The *USA Today* (http://www.usatoday.com/sports/mlb.htm) and Major League Baseball's Website (http://www.majorleaguebaseball.com) regularly report information on individual player salaries. Go to one of these sites and find the individual salaries for your favorite team. Compute the mean and the standard deviation. Is it reasonable to conclude that your favorite (or local) team has a mean player salary different from $1,500,000?

Computer Data Exercises

47. Refer to the Real Estate data, which reports information on the homes sold in Venice, Florida, last year.

- **a.** At the .05 significance level, can we conclude that there is a difference in the mean selling price of homes with a pool and homes without a pool?
- **b.** At the .05 significance level, can we conclude that there is a difference in the mean selling price of homes with an attached garage and homes without a garage?
- **c.** At the .05 significance level, can we conclude that there is a difference in the mean selling price of homes in Township 1 and Township 2?
- **d.** Find the median selling price of the homes. Divide the homes into two groups, those that sold for more than (or equal to) the median price and those that sold for less. Is there a difference in the proportion of homes with a pool for those that sold at or above the median price versus those that sold for less than the median price? Use the .05 significance level.

48. Refer to the Baseball 2001 data, which reports information on the 30 Major League Baseball teams for the 2001 season.

- **a.** At the .05 significance level, can we conclude that there is a difference in the mean salary of teams in the American League versus teams in the National League?
- **b.** At the .05 significance level, can we conclude that there is a difference in the mean home attendance of teams in the American League versus teams in the National League?
- **c.** At the .05 significance level, can we conclude that there is a difference in the mean number of wins for teams that have artificial turf home fields versus teams that have grass home fields?
- **d.** At the .05 significance level, can we conclude that there is a difference in the mean number of home runs for teams that have artificial turf home fields versus teams that have grass home fields?

49. Refer to the wage data, which reports information on annual wages for a sample of 100 workers. Also included are variables relating to industry, years of education, and gender for each worker.

- **a.** Conduct a test of hypothesis to determine if there is a difference in the mean annual wages of southern residents versus nonsouthern residents.

b. Conduct a test of hypothesis to determine if there is a difference in the mean annual wages of white and nonwhite wage earners.
c. Conduct a test of hypothesis to determine if there is a difference in the mean annual wages of Hispanic and non-Hispanic wage earners.
d. Conduct a test of hypothesis to determine if there is a difference in the mean annual wages of female and male wage earners.
e. Conduct a test of hypothesis to determine if there is a difference in the mean annual wages of married and nonmarried wage earners.

50. Refer to the CIA data, which reports demographic and economic information on 46 countries. Conduct a test of hypothesis to determine whether the mean percent of the population over 65 years of age in G20 countries is different from those that are not G20 members.

Computer Commands

1. The Excel commands for the two-sample *t*-test on page 334 are:
   a. Enter the data into columns A and B (or any other columns) in the spreadsheet. Use the first row of each column to enter the variable name.
   b. From the menu bar select **Tools** and **Data Analysis**. Select **t-Test**: **Two-Sample Assuming Equal Variances**, then click **OK**.
   c. In the dialog box indicate that the range of **Variable 1** is from *A1* to *A6* and **Variable 2** from *B1* to *B7*, the **Hypothesized Mean Difference** is 0, the **Labels** are in the first row, **Alpha** is *0.05*, and the **Output Range** is *D2*. Click **OK**.

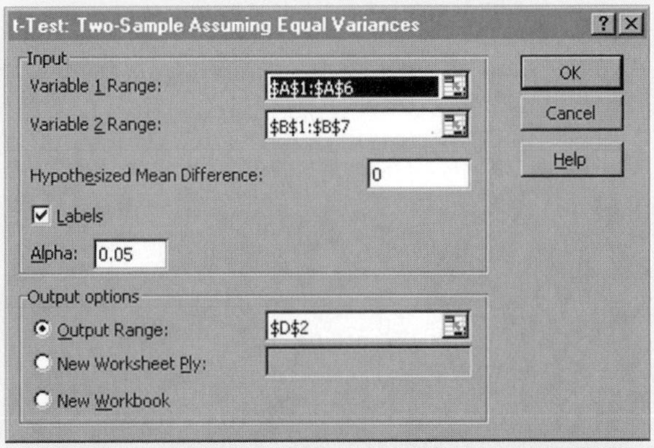

2. The Excel commands for the paired *t*-test on page 339 are:
   a. Enter the data into columns B and C (or any other two columns) in the spreadsheet, with the variable names in the first row.
   b. From the menu bar select **Tools** and **Data Analysis**. Select **t-Test**: **Paired Two Sample for Means**, then click **OK**.
   c. In the dialog box indicate that the range of **Variable 1** is from *B1* to *B11* and **Variable 2** from *C1* to *C11*, the **Hypothesized Mean Difference** is *0*, the **Labels** are in the first row, **Alpha** is *.05*, and the **Output Range** is *D2*. Click **OK**.

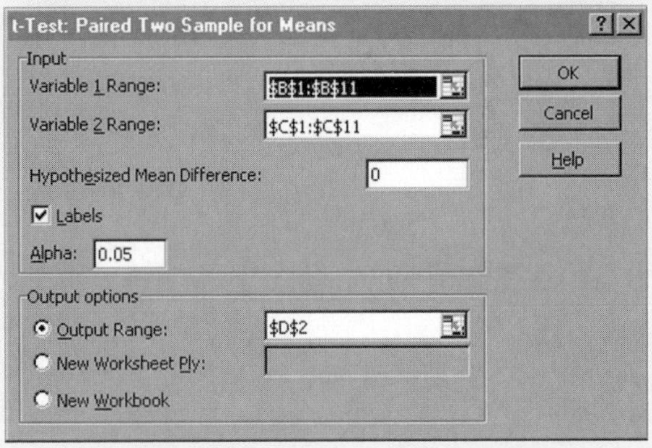

Chapter 10 Answers to Self-Review

10–1 **(a)** $H_0: \mu_W \leq \mu_M$
$H_1: \mu_W > \mu_M$
The subscript W refers to the women and M to the men.

(b) Reject H_0 if $z > 1.65$

(c) $$z = \frac{\$1{,}500 - \$1{,}400}{\sqrt{\frac{(\$250)^2}{50} + \frac{(\$200)^2}{40}}} = 2.11$$

(d) Reject the null hypothesis

(e) p-value = .5000 − .4826 = .0174

(f) The mean amount sold per day is larger for women.

10–2 **(a)** $H_0: \pi_1 = \pi_2$
$H_1: \pi_1 \neq \pi_2$

(b) .10

(c) Two-tailed

(d) Reject H_0 if z is less than −1.65 or greater than 1.65.

(e) $$p_c = \frac{87 + 123}{150 + 200} = \frac{210}{350} = .60$$

$$p_1 = \frac{87}{150} = .58 \qquad p_2 = \frac{123}{200} = .615$$

$$z = \frac{.58 - .615}{\sqrt{\frac{.60(.40)}{150} + \frac{.60(.40)}{200}}} = -\,0.66$$

(f) Do not reject H_0.

(g) p-value = 2(.5000 − .2454) = .5092
There is no difference in the proportion of adults and children that liked the proposed flavor.

10–3 **(a)** $H_0: \mu_d = \mu_a$
$H_1: \mu_d \neq \mu_a$

(b) $df = 6 + 8 - 2 = 12$
Reject H_0 if t is less than −2.179 or t is greater than 2.179.

(c) $$\bar{X}_1 = \frac{42}{6} = 7.00 \qquad s_1 = \sqrt{\frac{304 - \frac{42^2}{6}}{6 - 1}} = 1.4142$$

$$\bar{X}_2 = \frac{80}{8} = 10.00 \qquad s = \sqrt{\frac{836 - \frac{80^2}{8}}{8 - 1}} = 2.2678$$

$$s_p^2 = \frac{(6 - 1)(1.4142)^2 + (8 - 1)(2.2678)^2}{6 + 8 - 2}$$

$$= 3.8333$$

$$t = \frac{7.00 - 10.00}{\sqrt{3.8333\left(\frac{1}{6} + \frac{1}{8}\right)}} = -2.837$$

(d) Reject H_0 because −2.837 is less than the critical value.

(e) The p-value is less than .02.

(f) The mean number of defects is not the same on the two shifts.

10–4 **(a)** $H_0: \mu_d \leq 0$, $H_1: \mu_d > 0$.

(b) Reject H_0 if $t > 2.998$.

(c)

Name	Before	After	d	d^2
Hunter	155	154	1	1
Cashman	228	207	21	441
Mervine	141	147	−6	36
Massa	162	157	5	25
Creola	211	196	15	225
Peterson	164	150	14	196
Redding	184	170	14	196
Poust	172	165	7	49
			71	1,169

$$\bar{d} = \frac{71}{8} = 8.875$$

$$s_d = \sqrt{\frac{1{,}169 - \frac{(71)^2}{8}}{8 - 1}} = 8.774$$

$$t = \frac{8.875}{8.774/\sqrt{8}} = 2.861$$

(d) Do not reject H_0. We cannot conclude that the students lost weight. The p-value is less than .025 but larger than .01.

11

Analysis of Variance

Three assembly lines are used to produce a certain component for an airliner. To examine the production rate, a random sample of six hourly periods is chosen for each assembly line, recording the number of components produced during these periods. Use the data provided to complete an ANOVA table. (See Goal 4 and Exercise 32.)

GOALS

When you have completed this chapter, you will be able to:

1. **Discuss the general idea of analysis of variance.**
2. **List the characteristics of the *F* distribution.**
3. **Conduct a test of hypothesis to determine whether the variances of two populations are equal.**
4. **Organize data into a one-way ANOVA table.**
5. **Conduct a test of hypothesis among three or more treatment means.**
6. **Develop confidence intervals for the difference in treatment means.**

Introduction

In this chapter we continue our discussion of hypothesis testing. Recall that in Chapters 9 and 10 we examined the general theory of hypothesis testing. We described the case where a large sample was selected from the population. We used the z distribution (the standard normal distribution) to determine whether it was reasonable to conclude that the population mean was equal to a specified value. We tested whether two population means are the same. We also conducted both one- and two-sample tests for population proportions, again using the standard normal distribution as the distribution of the test statistic. We described methods for conducting tests of means where the populations were assumed normal but the samples were small (contained fewer than 30 observations). In that case the t distribution was used as the distribution of the test statistic. In this chapter we expand further our idea of hypothesis tests. We describe a test for variances and then a test that simultaneously compares several means to determine if they came from equal populations.

The *F* Distribution

The probability distribution used in this chapter is the F distribution. It was named to honor Sir Ronald Fisher, one of the founders of modern-day statistics. This probability distribution is used as the test statistic for several situations. It is used to test whether two samples are from populations having equal variances, and it is also applied when we want to compare several population means simultaneously. The simultaneous comparison of several population means is called **analysis of variance (ANOVA).** In general an F statistic is used to calculate the ratio of two variances. In both of these situations, the populations must be normal, and the data must be at least interval-scale.

What are the characteristics of the F distribution?

Characteristics of the *F* distribution

1. **There is a "family" of *F* distributions.** A particular member of the family is determined by two parameters: the degrees of freedom in the numerator and the degrees of freedom in the denominator. The shape of the distribution is illustrated by the following graph. There is one F distribution for the combination of 29 degrees of freedom in the numerator and 28 degrees of freedom in the denominator. There is another F distribution for 19 degrees in the numerator and 6 degrees of freedom in the denominator. Note that the shape of the curves changes as the degrees of freedom change.

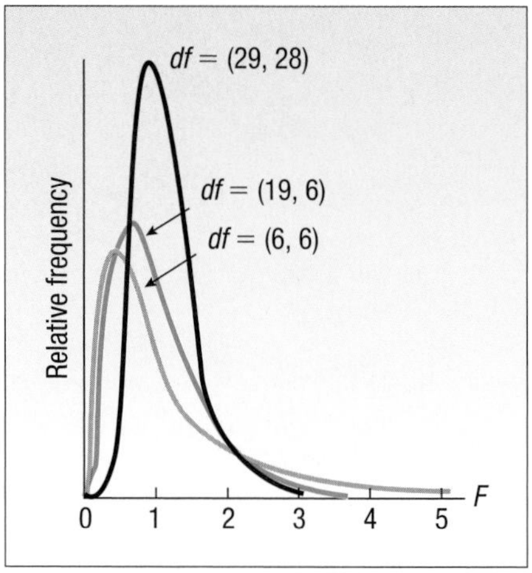

2. **The *F* distribution is continuous.** This means that it can assume an infinite number of values between 0 and plus infinity.
3. **The *F* distribution cannot be negative.** The smallest value *F* can assume is 0.
4. **It is positively skewed.** The long tail of the distribution is to the right-hand side. As the number of degrees of freedom increases in both the numerator and denominator the distribution approaches a normal distribution.
5. **It is asymptotic.** As the values of *X* increase, the *F* curve approaches the *X*-axis but never touches it. This is similar to the behavior of the normal distribution, described in Chapter 6.

Comparing Two Population Variances

The *F* distribution is used to test the hypothesis that the variance of one normal population equals the variance of another normal population. The following examples will show the use of the test:

- Two Barth shearing machines are set to produce steel bars of the same length. The bars, therefore, should have the same mean length. We want to ensure that in addition to having the same mean length they also have similar variation.

- The mean rate of return on two types of common stock may be the same, but there may be more variation in the rate of return in one than the other. A sample of 10 Internet stocks and 10 utility stocks shows the same mean rate of return, but there is likely more variation in the Internet stocks.
- A study by the marketing department for a large newspaper found that men and women spent about the same amount of time per day reading the paper. However, the same report indicated there was nearly twice as much variation among the men as the women.

The *F* distribution is also used to test assumptions for some statistical tests. Recall that in the previous chapter when small samples were assumed, we used the *t* test to investigate whether the means of two independent populations differed. To employ that test, we assume that the variances of two normal populations are the same. See this list of assumptions on page 330. The *F* distribution provides a way to conduct a test comparing the variances of two normal populations.

Regardless of whether we want to determine if one population has more variation than another population or validate an assumption for a statistical test, we first state the null hypothesis. The null hypothesis is that the variance of one normal population, σ_1^2, equals the variance of the other normal population, σ_2^2. The alternate hypothesis could be that the variances differ. In this instance the null hypothesis and the alternate hypothesis are:

$$H_0: \sigma_1^2 = \sigma_2^2$$
$$H_1: \sigma_1^2 \neq \sigma_2^2$$

To conduct the test, we select a random sample of n_1 observations from one population and a sample of n_2 observations from the second population. The test statistic is defined as follows.

TEST STATISTIC FOR COMPARING TWO VARIANCES	$F = \frac{s_1^2}{s_2^2}$	**[11–1]**

The terms s_1^2 and s_2^2 are the respective sample variances. If the null hypothesis is true, the test statistic follows the F distribution with $n_1 - 1$ degrees of freedom in the numerator and $n_2 - 1$ degrees of freedom in the denominator. In order to reduce the size of the table of critical values, the *larger* sample variance is placed in the numerator; hence, the tabled F ratio is always larger than 1.00. Thus, the right-tail critical value is the only one required. The critical value of F for a two-tailed test is found by dividing the significance level in half ($\alpha/2$) and then referring to the appropriate degrees of freedom in Appendix G. An example will illustrate.

EXAMPLE

Lammers Limos offers limousine service from the city hall in Toledo, Ohio, to Metro Airport in Detroit. Sean Lammers, president of the company, is considering two routes. One is via U.S. 25 and the other via I-75. He wants to study the time it takes to drive to the airport using each route and then compare the results. He collected the following sample data, which is reported in minutes. Using the .10 significance level, is there a difference in the variation in the driving times using the two routes?

U.S. Route 25	Interstate 75
52	59
67	60
56	61
45	51
70	56
54	63
64	57
	65

SOLUTION

The mean driving times along the two routes are nearly the same. The mean time is 58.29 minutes for the U.S. 25 route and 59.0 minutes along the I-75 route. However, in evaluating travel times, Mr. Lammers is also concerned about the variation in the travel times. The first step is to compute the two sample variances. We'll use formula 3–12 to compute the sample standard deviations. To obtain the sample variances, we can compute the variances directly or square the standard deviations.

U.S. Route 25

$$\overline{X} = \frac{\Sigma X}{n} = \frac{408}{7} = 58.29 \qquad s = \sqrt{\frac{\Sigma X^2 - \frac{(\Sigma X)^2}{n}}{n-1}} = \sqrt{\frac{24{,}266 - \frac{(408)^2}{7}}{7-1}} = 8.9947$$

Interstate 75

$$\overline{X} = \frac{\Sigma X}{n} = \frac{472}{8} = 59.00 \qquad s = \sqrt{\frac{\Sigma X^2 - \frac{(\Sigma X)^2}{n}}{n-1}} = \sqrt{\frac{27{,}982 - \frac{(472)^2}{8}}{8-1}} = 4.3753$$

There is more variation, as measured by the standard deviation, in the U.S. 25 route than in the I-75 route. This is somewhat consistent with his knowledge of the two routes; the U.S. 25 route contains more stoplights, whereas I-75 is a limited-access interstate highway. However, the I-75 route is several miles longer. It is important that the service offered be both timely and consistent, so he decides to conduct a statistical test to determine whether there really is a difference in the variation of the two routes.

The usual five-step hypothesis-testing procedure will be employed.

Step 1: We begin by stating the null hypothesis and the alternate hypothesis. The test is two-tailed because we are looking for a difference in the variation of the two routes. We are *not* trying to show that one route has more variation than the other.

$$H_0: \sigma_1^2 = \sigma_2^2$$
$$H_1: \sigma_1^2 \neq \sigma_2^2$$

Step 2: We selected the .10 significance level.

Step 3: The appropriate test statistic follows the *F* distribution.

Step 4: The critical value is obtained from Appendix G, a portion of which is reproduced as Table 11–1. Because we are conducting a two-tailed test, the tabled significance level is .05, found by $\alpha/2 = .10/2 = .05$. There are $n_1 - 1 = 7 - 1 = 6$ degrees of freedom in the numerator, and $n_2 - 1 = 8 - 1 = 7$ degrees of freedom in the denominator. To find the critical value, move horizontally across the top portion of the *F* table (Table 11–1 or Appendix G) for the .05 significance level to 6 degrees of freedom in the numerator. Then move down that column to the critical value opposite 7 degrees of freedom in the denominator. The critical value is 3.87. Thus, the decision rule is: Reject the null hypothesis if the ratio of the sample variances exceeds 3.87.

TABLE 11–1 Critical Values of the *F* Distribution, $\alpha = .05$

Degrees of Freedom for Denominator	Degrees of Freedom for Numerator 5	6	7	8
1	230	234	237	239
2	19.3	19.3	19.4	19.4
3	9.01	8.94	8.89	8.85
4	6.26	6.16	6.09	6.04
5	5.05	4.95	4.88	4.82
6	4.39	4.28	4.21	4.15
7	3.97	3.87	3.79	3.73
8	3.69	3.58	3.50	3.44
9	3.48	3.37	3.29	3.23
10	3.33	3.22	3.14	3.07

Step 5: The final step is to take the ratio of the two sample variances, determine the value of the test statistic, and make a decision regarding the null hypothesis. Note that formula 11–1 refers to the sample *variances* but we calculated the sample *standard deviations*. We need to square the standard deviations to determine the variances.

$$F = \frac{s_1^2}{s_2^2} = \frac{(8.9947)^2}{(4.3753)^2} = 4.23$$

The decision is to reject the null hypothesis, because the computed F value (4.23) is larger than the critical value (3.87). We conclude that there is a difference in the variation of the travel times along the two routes.

As noted, the usual practice is to determine the F ratio by putting the larger of the two sample variances in the numerator. This will force the F ratio to be at least 1.00. This allows us to always use the right tail of the F distribution, thus avoiding the need for more extensive F tables.

A logical question arises regarding one-tailed tests. For example, suppose in the previous example we suspected that the variance of the times using the U.S. 25 route is *larger* than the variance of the times along the I-75 route. We would state the null and the alternate hypothesis as

$$H_0: \sigma_1^2 \le \sigma_2^2$$
$$H_1: \sigma_1^2 > \sigma_2^2$$

The test statistic is computed as s_1^2/s_2^2. Notice that we labeled the population with the suspected larger variance as population 1. So s_1^2 appears in the numerator. The F ratio will be larger than 1.00, so we can use the upper tail of the F distribution. Under these conditions, it is not necessary to divide the significance level in half. Because Appendix G gives us only the .05 and .01 significance levels, we are restricted to these levels for one-tailed tests and .10 and .02 for two-tailed tests unless we consult a more complete table or use the distribution function on either MINITAB or Excel.

The Excel software system has a procedure to perform a test of variances. Below is the output. The computed value of F is the same as determined using formula 11–1.

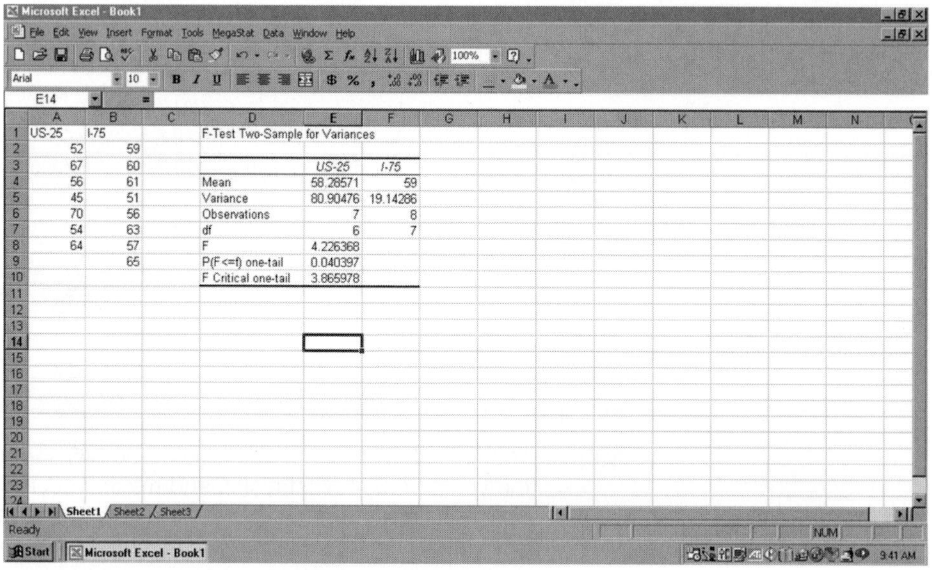

US-25	I-75		F-Test Two-Sample for Variances		
52	59				
67	60			US-25	I-75
56	61		Mean	58.28571	59
45	51		Variance	80.90476	19.14286
70	56		Observations	7	8
54	63		df	6	7
64	57		F	4.226368	
	65		P(F<=f) one-tail	0.040397	
			F Critical one-tail	3.865978	

Self-Review 11-1

Steele Electric Products, Inc. assembles electrical components for stereo equipment. For the last 10 days Mark Nagy has averaged 9 rejects, with a standard deviation of 2 rejects per day. Debbie Richmond averaged 8.5 rejects, with a standard deviation of 1.5 rejects, over the same period. At the .05 significance level, can we conclude that there is more variation in the number of rejects per day attributed to Mark?

Exercises

1. What is the critical F value for a sample of six observations in the numerator and four in the denominator? Use a two-tailed test and the .10 significance level.
2. What is the critical F value for a sample of four observations in the numerator and seven in the denominator? Use a one-tailed test and the .01 significance level.
3. The following hypotheses are given.

   H_0: $\sigma_1^2 = \sigma_2^2$
   H_1: $\sigma_1^2 \neq \sigma_2^2$

   A random sample of eight observations from the first population resulted in a standard deviation of 10. A random sample of six observations from the second population resulted in a standard deviation of 7. At the .02 significance level, is there a difference in the variation of the two populations?
4. The following hypotheses are given.

   H_0: $\sigma_1^2 \leq \sigma_2^2$
   H_1: $\sigma_1^2 > \sigma_2^2$

   A random sample of five observations from the first population resulted in a standard deviation of 12. A random sample of seven observations from the second population showed a standard deviation of 7. At the .01 significance level, is there more variation in the first population?
5. Stargell Research Associates conducted a study of the radio listening habits of men and women. One facet of the study involved the mean listening time. It was discovered that the mean listening time for men was 35 minutes per day. The standard deviation of the sample of the 10 men studied was 10 minutes per day. The mean listening time for the 12 women studied was also 35 minutes, but the standard deviation of the sample was 12 minutes. At the .10 significance level, can we conclude that there is a difference in the variation in the listening times for men and women?
6. A stockbroker at Critical Securities reported that the mean rate of return on a sample of 10 oil stocks was 12.6 percent with a standard deviation of 3.9 percent. The mean rate of return on a sample of 8 utility stocks was 10.9 percent with a standard deviation of 3.5 percent. At the .05 significance level, can we conclude that there is more variation in the oil stocks?

ANOVA Assumptions

Another use of the F distribution is the analysis of variance (ANOVA) technique in which we compare three or more population means to determine whether they could be equal. To use ANOVA, we assume the following:

1. The populations follow a normal distribution.
2. The populations have equal standard deviations (σ).
3. The populations are independent.

When these conditions are met, F is used as the distribution of the test statistic.

Why do we need to study ANOVA? Why can't we just use the test of differences in population means discussed in the previous chapter? We could compare the means two at a time. The major reason is the unsatisfactory buildup of Type I error. To explain further, suppose we have four different methods (A, B, C, and D) of training new recruits to be firefighters. We randomly assign each of the 40 recruits in this year's class to one of the four methods. At the end of the training program, we administer to the four groups a common test to measure understanding of firefighting techniques. The question to be explored is: Is there a difference in the mean test scores among the four groups? An answer to this question will allow us to compare the four training methods.

Using the *t* distribution leads to a buildup of Type I error.

Using the *t* distribution to compare the four population means, we would have to conduct six different *t* tests. That is, we would need to compare the mean scores for the four methods as follows: A versus B, A versus C, A versus D, B versus C, B versus D, and C versus D. If we set the significance level at .05, the probability of a single correct statistical decision is .95, found by 1 − .05. Because we conduct six separate tests the probability that we do *not* make an incorrect decision due to sampling in any of the six tests is:

$$P(\textit{All correct}) = (.95)(.95)(.95)(.95)(.95)(.95) = .735$$

To find the probability of a least one error due to sampling, we subtract this result from 1. Thus, the probability of at least one incorrect decision due to sampling is 1 − .735 = .265. To summarize, if we conduct six independent tests using the *t* distribution, the likelihood of at least one sampling error is increased from .05 to an unsatisfactory level of .265. It is obvious that we need a better method than conducting six *t* tests. ANOVA will allow us to compare the treatment means simultaneously and avoid the buildup of the Type I error.

ANOVA was developed for applications in agriculture, and many of the terms related to that context remain. In particular the term *treatment* is used to identify the different populations being examined. The following illustration will clarify the term *treatment* and demonstrate an application of ANOVA.

Joyce Kuhlman manages a regional financial center. She wishes to compare the productivity, as measured by the number of customers served, among three employees. Four days are randomly selected and the number of customers served by each employee is recorded. The results are:

Wolfe	White	Korosa
55	66	47
54	76	51
59	67	46
56	71	48

Is there a difference in the mean number of customers served? Chart 11–1 illustrates how the populations would appear if there was a difference in the treatment means. Note that the populations are approximately normal and the variation in each population is the same, but the means are *not* the same.

Suppose the populations are the same. That is, there is no difference in the (treatment) means. This is shown in Chart 11–2. This would indicate that the population

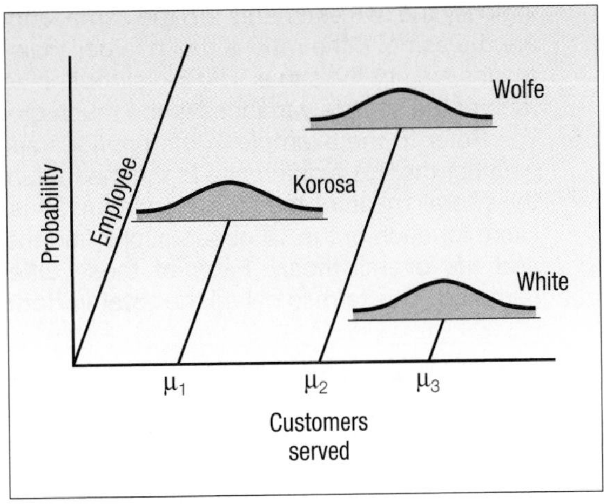

CHART 11–1 Case Where Treatment Means Are Different

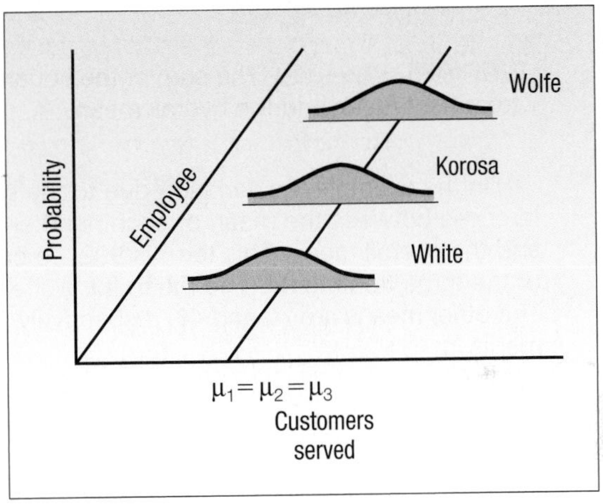

CHART 11–2 Case Where Treatment Means Are the Same

means are the same. Note again that the populations are approximately normal and the variation in each of the populations is the same.

The ANOVA Test

How does the ANOVA test work? Recall that we want to determine whether the various sample means came from a single population or populations with different means. We actually compare these sample means through their variances. To explain, recall that on page 357 we listed the assumptions required for ANOVA. One of those assumptions was that the standard deviations of the various normal populations had to be the same. We take advantage of this requirement in the ANOVA test. The underlying strategy is to estimate the population variance (standard deviation squared) two ways and then find the ratio of these two estimates. If this ratio is about 1, then logically the two estimates are the same, and we conclude that the population means are the same. If the ratio is much larger than 1, then we conclude that the population means are not the same. The *F* distribution serves as a referee by indicating when the ratio of the sample variances is too much greater than 1 to have occurred by chance.

Refer to the example in the previous section. The manager wants to determine whether there is a difference in the mean number of customers served. To begin, find the overall mean of the 12 observations. It is 58, found by $(55 + 54 + \cdots + 48)/12$. Next, for each of the 12 observations find the difference between the particular value and the overall mean. Each of these differences is squared and these squares summed. This term is called the **total variation.**

> **TOTAL VARIATION** The sum of the squared differences between each observation and the overall mean.

In our example the total variation is 1,082, found by $(55 - 58)^2 + (54 - 58)^2 + \cdots + (48 - 58)^2$.

Next, break this total variation into two components: that which is due to the **treatments** and that which is **random.** To find these two components, determine the mean of each of the treatments. The first source of variation is due to the treatments.

> **TREATMENT VARIATION** The sum of the squared differences between each treatment mean and the overall mean.

In the example the variation due to the treatments is the sum of the squared differences between the mean of each number of customers served by each employee and the overall mean. This term is 992. To calculate it we first find the mean of each of the three treatments. The mean for Wolfe is 56, found by $(55 + 54 + 59 + 56)/4$. The other means are 70 and 48, respectively. The sum of the squares due to the treatments is:

$$(56 - 58)^2 + (56 - 58)^2 + \cdots + (48 - 58)^2 = 4(56 - 58)^2 + 4(70 - 58)^2 + 4(48 - 58)^2$$
$$= 992$$

If there is considerable variation among the treatment means, it is logical that this term will be large. If the treatment means are similar, this term will be a small value. The smallest possible value would be zero. This would occur when all the treatment means are the same. This result would also indicate that each treatment mean is equal to the overall mean.

The other source of variation is referred to as the **random** component, or the error component.

> **RANDOM VARIATION** The sum of the squared differences between each observation and its treatment mean.

In the example this term is the sum of the squared differences between each value and the mean for that particular employee. The error variation is 90.

$$(55 - 56)^2 + (54 - 56)^2 + \cdots + (48 - 48)^2 = 90$$

We determine the test statistic, which is the ratio of the two estimates of the population variance, from the following equation.

$$F = \frac{\text{Estimate of the population variance based on the differences among the sample means}}{\text{Estimate of the population variance based on the variation within the samples}}$$

Our first estimate of the population variance is based on the treatment variation, that is, the difference *between* the means. It is 992/2. Why did we divide by 2? Recall from Chapter 3, to find a sample variance (see formula 3–10), we divide by the number of observations minus one. In this case there are three treatments, so we divide by 2. Our first estimate of the population variance is 992/2.

The variance estimate *within* the treatments is the random variation divided by the total number of observations less the number of treatments. That is 90/(12 − 3). Hence, our second estimate of the population variance is 90/9. This is actually a generalization of formula 10–5, where we pooled the sample variances from two populations.

The last step is to take the ratio of these two estimates.

$$F = \frac{992/2}{90/9} = 49.6$$

Because this ratio is quite different from 1, we can conclude that the treatment means are not the same. There is a difference in the mean number of customers served by the three employees.

The above conceptual view of ANOVA is fairly difficult to carry out. That is, the calculations can be quite tedious, particularly when the overall mean and the treatment means are not whole numbers. There are two alternatives to avoid the extensive calculations. In the following example we provide an efficient method that minimizes the calculations for solving the ANOVA problem. We could also use a spreadsheet or statistical software package. Later in the chapter we will provide such an example.

Here's another example, which shows some shortcut computational formulas and also deals with samples of different sizes.

EXAMPLE

Professor James Brunner had students in his marketing class rate his performance as Excellent, Good, Fair, or Poor. A graduate student collected the ratings and assured the students that Professor Brunner would not receive them until after course grades had been sent to the records office. The rating (i.e., the treatment) a student gave the professor was matched with his or her course grade, which could range from 0 to 100. The sample information is reported below. Is there a difference in the mean score of the students in each of the four rating categories? Use the .01 significance level.

Course Grades			
Excellent	**Good**	**Fair**	**Poor**
94	75	70	68
90	68	73	70
85	77	76	72
80	83	78	65
	88	80	74
		68	65
		65	

SOLUTION

We will follow the usual five-step hypothesis-testing procedure.

Step 1: State the null hypothesis and the alternate hypothesis. The null hypothesis is that the mean scores are the same for the four ratings. We can write this symbolically as:

$$H_0: \mu_1 = \mu_2 = \mu_3 = \mu_4$$

The alternate hypothesis is that the mean scores are not all the same for the four ratings.

H_1: The mean scores are not all equal.

We can also think of the alternate hypothesis as "at least two mean scores are not equal."

If the null hypothesis is not rejected, we conclude that there is no difference in the mean course grades based on the instructor ratings. If H_0 is rejected, we conclude that there is a difference in at least one pair of mean ratings, but at this point we do not know which pair or how many pairs differ.

Step 2: Select the level of significance. We selected the .01 significance level.

Step 3: Determine the test statistic. The test statistic follows the F distribution.

Step 4: Formulate the decision rule. To determine the decision rule, we need the critical value. The critical value for the F statistic is found in Appendix G. The critical values for the .05 significance level are found on the first page and the .01 significance level on the second page. To use this table we need to know the degrees of freedom in the numerator and the denominator. The degrees of freedom in the numerator equals the number of treatments, designated as k, minus 1. The degrees of freedom in the denominator is the total number of observations, n, minus the number of treatments. For this problem there are four treatments and a total of 22 observations.

Degrees of freedom in the numerator $= k - 1 = 4 - 1 = 3$
Degrees of freedom in the denominator $= n - k = 22 - 4 = 18$

Refer to Appendix G and the .01 significance level. Move horizontally across the top of the page to 3 degrees of freedom in the numerator. Then move down that column to the row with 18 degrees of freedom. The value at this intersection is 5.09. So the decision rule is to reject H_0 if the computed value of F exceeds 5.09.

Step 5: Select the sample, perform the calculations, and make a decision. It is convenient to summarize the calculations of the F statistic in an **ANOVA table.** The format for an ANOVA table is as follows. (This is also the format used in statistical software packages.)

ANOVA Table

Source of Variation	Sum of Squares	Degrees of Freedom	Mean Square	F
Treatments	SST	$k - 1$	$\text{SST}/(k - 1) = \text{MST}$	MST/MSE
Error	SSE	$n - k$	$\text{SSE}/(n - k) = \text{MSE}$	
Total	SS total	$n - 1$		

There are three values, the **sum of squares,** used to compute F. We can determine these values by finding SS total and SST, then finding SSE by subtraction. The SS total term is the total variation, SST is the variation due to the treatments, and SSE is the variation within the treatments.

To find the value of F, we work our way across the table. The degrees of freedom for the numerator and the denominator are the same as those for finding the critical values of F. The term **mean square** is another expression for an estimate of the variance. The mean square for the treatment is SST divided by its degrees of freedom. The result is the **mean square for treatments** and is written MST. We compute the **mean square error** (MSE) similarly. We divide the SSE term by its degrees of freedom. To complete the process and find F, we divide MST by MSE.

We usually start the process by finding SS total. This is the sum of the squared differences between each observation and the overall mean. The formula for finding SS total is

SUM OF SQUARES TOTAL

$$\text{SS total} = \Sigma X^2 - \frac{(\Sigma X)^2}{n} \qquad \textbf{[11–2]}$$

where:

ΣX^2 is the X values squared and then summed.
$(\Sigma X)^2$ is the X values summed and then squared.
n is the total number of observations.

Next we determine SST, the sum of squares due to the treatments. The formula for finding SST is

SUM OF SQUARES TREATMENT

$$\text{SST} = \Sigma\left(\frac{T_c^2}{n_c}\right) - \frac{(\Sigma X)^2}{n} \qquad \textbf{[11–3]}$$

where:

T_c is the column total for each treatment.
n_c is the number of observations (sample size) for each treatment.

Finally we determine SSE, the sum of squares error, by subtraction. The formula is

SUM OF SQUARES ERROR

$$\text{SSE} = \text{SS total} - \text{SST} \qquad \textbf{[11–4]}$$

The detailed calculations for this example are shown in Table 11–2.

TABLE 11–2 Calculations Necessary for Computing the Value of F

	Excellent		Good		Fair		Poor		Total
	X	X^2	X	X^2	X	X^2	X	X^2	
	94	8,836	75	5,625	70	4,900	68	4,624	
	90	8,100	68	4,624	73	5,329	70	4,900	
	85	7,225	77	5,929	76	5,776	72	5,184	
	80	6,400	83	6,889	78	6,084	65	4,225	
			88	7,744	80	6,400	74	5,476	
					68	4,624	65	4,225	
					65	4,225			
T_c	349		391		510		414		1,664
n_c	4		5		7		6		22
X^2		30,561		30,811		37,338		28,634	127,344

Statistics in Action

Have you ever waited in line for a telephone and it seemed like the person using the phone talked on and on? There is evidence that people actually talk longer on public telephones when someone is waiting. In a recent survey, researchers measured the length of time that 56 shoppers in a mall spent on the phone (1) when they were alone, (2) when a person was using the adjacent phone, and (3) when a person was using an adjacent phone and someone was waiting to use the phone. The study, using the one-way ANOVA technique, showed that the mean time using the telephone was significantly less when the person was alone.

The entries for the ANOVA table are computed as follows. First, using formula 11–2, we compute the total variation:

$$\text{SS total} = \Sigma X^2 - \frac{(\Sigma X)^2}{n} = 127{,}344 - \frac{1{,}664^2}{22} = 1{,}485.09$$

Next, using formula 11–3, we compute the treatment variation.

$$\text{SST} = \Sigma\left(\frac{T_c^2}{n_c}\right) - \frac{(\Sigma X)^2}{n} = \frac{349^2}{4} + \frac{391^2}{5} + \frac{510^2}{7} + \frac{414^2}{6} - \frac{1{,}664^2}{22} = 890.68$$

Finally, by subtraction, we determine the error variation.

$$\text{SSE} = \text{SS total} - \text{SST} = 1{,}485.09 - 890.68 = 594.41$$

Inserting these values into an ANOVA table and computing the value of F:

Source of Variation	Sum of Squares	Degrees of Freedom	Mean Square	F
Treatments	890.68	3	296.89	8.99
Error	594.41	18	33.02	
Total	1,485.09	21		

The computed value of F is 8.99, which is greater than the critical value of 5.09, so the null hypothesis is rejected. We conclude the population means are not all equal. The mean scores are not the same in each of the four ratings groups. It is likely that the grades students earned in the course are related to the opinion they have of the overall competency and classroom performance of the instructor. At this point we can only conclude there is a difference in the treatment means. We cannot determine which treatment groups differ or how many treatment groups differ.

As noted in the previous example, the calculations become very tedious if the number of observations in each treatment is large. There are many software packages that will output the results. Below is the Excel output in the form of an ANOVA table for the previous example involving student ratings in a marketing class.

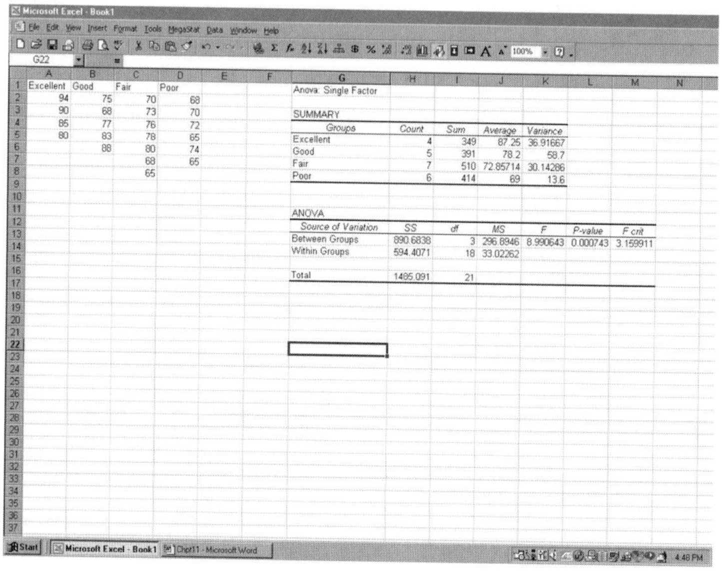

Notice Excel uses the term "Between Groups" for "Treatments" and "Within Groups" for "Error." However, they have the same meanings. The *p*-value is .000743. This is the probability of finding a value of the test statistic this large or larger when the null hypothesis is true. To put it another way, it is the likelihood of calculating an *F* value larger than 8.99 with 3 degrees of freedom in the numerator and 18 degrees of freedom in the denominator. So when we reject the null hypothesis in this instance there is a very small likelihood of committing a Type I error!

Following is the MINITAB output from the student ratings example, which is similar to the Excel output. The output is in the form of an ANOVA table. In addition, MINITAB provides information about the differences between means. This is discussed in the next section.

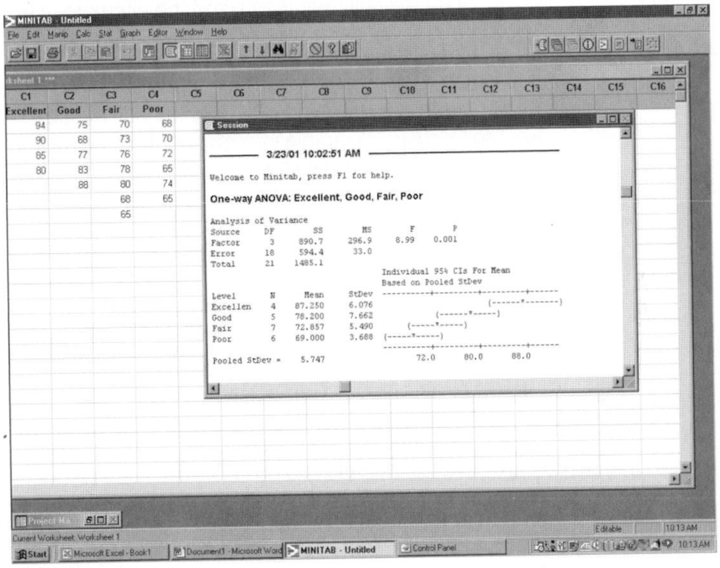

The MINITAB system uses the term *factor* instead of *treatment,* with the same intended meaning.

Self-Review 11-2

Clean All is a new all-purpose cleaner being test marketed by placing displays in three different locations within various supermarkets. The number of 12-ounce bottles sold from each location within the supermarket is reported below.

Near the bread	20	15	24	18
Near the beer	12	18	10	15
With other cleaners	25	28	30	32

At the .05 significance level, is there a difference in the mean number of bottles sold at the three locations?

(a) State the null hypothesis and the alternate hypothesis.
(b) What is the decision rule?
(c) Compute the values of SS total, SST, and SSE.
(d) Develop an ANOVA table.
(e) What is your decision regarding the null hypothesis?

Exercises

7. The following is sample information. Test the hypothesis that the treatment means are equal. Use the .05 significance level.

Treatment 1	Treatment 2	Treatment 3
8	3	3
6	2	4
10	4	5
9	3	4

a. State the null hypothesis and the alternate hypotheses.
b. What is the decision rule?
c. Compute SST, SSE, and SS total.
d. Complete an ANOVA table.
e. State your decision regarding the null hypothesis.

8. The following is sample information. Test the hypothesis at the .05 significance level that the treatment means are equal.

Treatment 1	Treatment 2	Treatment 3
9	13	10
7	20	9
11	14	15
9	13	14
12		15
10		

a. State the null hypothesis and the alternate hypotheses.
b. What is the decision rule?
c. Compute SST, SSE, and SS total.
d. Complete an ANOVA table.
e. State your decision regarding the null hypothesis.

9. A real estate developer is considering investing in a shopping mall on the outskirts of Atlanta, Georgia. Three parcels of land are being evaluated. Of particular importance is the income in the area surrounding the proposed mall. A random sample of four families is selected near each proposed mall. Following are the sample results. At the .05 significance level, can the developer conclude there is a difference in the mean income? Use the usual five-step hypothesis testing procedure.

Southwyck Area ($000)	Franklin Park ($000)	Old Orchard ($000)
64	74	75
68	71	80
70	69	76
60	70	78

10. The manager of a computer software company wishes to study the number of hours top executives spend at their computer terminals by type of industry. The manager selected a sample of five executives from each of three industries. At the .05 significance level, can she conclude there is a difference in the mean number of hours spent at a terminal per week by industry?

Banking	Retail	Insurance
12	8	10
10	8	8
10	6	6
12	8	8
10	10	10

Inferences about Pairs of Treatment Means

Suppose we carry out the ANOVA procedure and make the decision to reject the null hypothesis. This allows us to conclude that two or more treatment means are not the same. Sometimes we may be satisfied with this conclusion, but in other instances we may want to know which treatment means differ. This section provides the details for such a test.

Recall that in the example regarding student opinions and grades there was a difference in the treatment means. That is, the null hypothesis was rejected and the alternate hypothesis accepted. If the student opinions do differ, the question is: Between which groups do the treatment means differ?

Several procedures are available to answer this question. The simplest is through the use of confidence intervals, that is, formula 8–2. From the computer output of the previous example (see page 365), note that the sample mean score for those students rating the instruction Excellent is 87.250, and for those rating the instruction Poor it is 69.000. Thus, those students who rated the instruction Excellent seemingly earned higher grades than those who rated the instruction Poor. Is there enough disparity to justify the conclusion that there is a significant difference in the mean scores of the two groups?

The *t* distribution, described in Chapters 8, 9 and 10, is used as the basis for this test. Recall that one of the assumptions of ANOVA is that the population variances are the same for all treatments. This common population value is estimated by the **mean square error,** or MSE, and is determined by SSE/$(n - k)$. A confidence interval for the difference between two populations is found by:

CONFIDENCE INTERVAL FOR THE DIFFERENCE IN TREATMENT MEANS

$$(\overline{X}_1 - \overline{X}_2) \pm t\sqrt{\text{MSE}\left(\frac{1}{n_1} + \frac{1}{n_2}\right)} \qquad \textbf{[11–5]}$$

where:

- $\overline{X}_1$ is the mean of the first sample.
- $\overline{X}_2$ is the mean of the second sample.
- t is obtained from Appendix F. The degrees of freedom is equal to $n - k$.
- MSE is the mean square error term obtained from the ANOVA table [SSE/$(n - k)$].
- n_1 is the number of observations in the first sample.
- n_2 is the number of observations in the second sample.

How do we decide whether there is a difference in the treatment means? If the confidence interval includes zero, there is *not* a difference between the treatment means. For example, if the left endpoint of the confidence interval has a negative sign and the right endpoint has a positive sign, the two means do not differ. So if we develop a confidence interval from formula 11–5 and find the difference in the sample means was 5.00, that is, if $\overline{X}_1 - \overline{X}_2 = 5$ and $t\sqrt{\text{MSE}\left(\frac{1}{n_1} + \frac{1}{n_2}\right)} = 12$, the confidence interval would range from -7.00 up to 17.00. To put it in symbols:

$$(\overline{X}_1 - \overline{X}_2) \pm t\sqrt{\text{MSE}\left(\frac{1}{n_1} + \frac{1}{n_2}\right)} = 5.00 \pm 12.00 = -7.00 \text{ up to } 17.00$$

Note that zero is included in this interval. Therefore, we conclude that there is no significant difference in the selected treatment means.

On the other hand, if the endpoints of the confidence interval have the same sign, this indicates that the treatment means differ. For example, if $\overline{X}_1 - \overline{X}_2 = -0.35$ and

$t\sqrt{\text{MSE}\left(\frac{1}{n_1}+\frac{1}{n_2}\right)} = 0.25$, the confidence interval would range from -0.60 up to -0.10. Because -0.60 and -0.10 have the same sign, both negative, we conclude that these treatment means differ.

Using the previous student opinion example let us compute the confidence interval for the difference between the mean scores of all students who provide "Excellent" and "Poor" ratings. Assume the populations are labeled 1 and 4. With a 95 percent level of confidence, the endpoints of the confidence interval are 10.46 and 26.04.

$$(\overline{X}_1 - \overline{X}_4) \pm t\sqrt{\text{MSE}\left(\frac{1}{n_1}+\frac{1}{n_4}\right)} = (87.25 - 69.00) \pm 2.101\sqrt{33.0\left(\frac{1}{4}+\frac{1}{6}\right)}$$
$$= 18.25 \pm 7.79$$

where:

$\overline{X}_1$ is 87.25.
$\overline{X}_4$ is 69.00.
t is 2.101: from Appendix F with $(n - k) = 22 - 4 = 18$ degrees of freedom.
MSE is 33.0: from the ANOVA table with $\text{SSE}/(n - k) = 594.4/18$.
n_1 is 4.
n_4 is 6.

The 95 percent confidence interval ranges from 10.46 up to 26.04. Both endpoints are positive; hence, we can conclude these treatment means differ significantly and the difference is positive. That is, students who rated the instructor Excellent have significantly higher grades than those who rated the instructor as Poor.

Approximate results can also be obtained directly from the MINITAB output. Below is the lower portion of the output from page 365. On the left side is the number of observations, the mean, and the standard deviation for each treatment. Seven students, for example, rated the instructor as Fair. The mean course grade they earned is 72.857. The standard deviation of their scores is 5.490.

```
                                     Individual 95% CIs For Mean
                                     Based on Pooled StDev
Level       N     Mean     StDev   ----------+----------+----------+------
Excellen    4   87.250     6.076                              (------*------)
Good        5   78.200     7.662                  (------*------)
Fair        7   72.857     5.490         (------*------)
Poor        6   69.000     3.688   (------*------)
                                   ----------+----------+----------+------
Pooled StDev =    5.747                    72.0       80.0       88.0
```

On the right side of the printout is a graphical representation of a confidence interval for each treatment mean. The asterisk (*) indicates the location of the treatment mean and the open parenthesis and close parenthesis, the endpoints of the confidence interval. In those instances where there is overlap (common area), the treatment means may not differ. If there is no common area in the confidence intervals, that pair of means differ.

The endpoints of a 95 percent confidence interval for the scores of students rating the instructor Fair are about 69 and 77. For students rating the instructor Poor, the endpoints of the confidence interval are about 64 and 74. There is common area in this confidence interval, so we conclude that this pair of means does not differ. In other words, there is no significant difference between the scores of students rating the instructor Fair and those rating him Poor.

There are two pairs of means that differ. The scores of students who rated the instructor Excellent differ from the scores of the students who rated the instructor Fair and those who rated the instructor Poor. There is no common area between the two pairs of confidence intervals.

We should emphasize that this investigation is a step-by-step process. The initial step is to conduct the ANOVA test. Only if the null hypothesis that the treatment means are equal is rejected should any analysis of the individual treatment means be attempted.

Self-Review 11-3

The following data are the tuition charges ($000) for a sample of private colleges in various regions of the United States. At the .05 significance level, can we conclude there is a difference in the mean tuition rates for the various regions?

Northeast ($000)	Southeast ($000)	West ($000)
20	18	17
21	19	18
22	20	16
20	18	17
22		16

(a) State the null and the alternate hypotheses.
(b) What is the decision rule?
(c) Develop an ANOVA table. What is the value of the test statistic?
(d) What is your decision regarding the null hypothesis?
(e) Could there be a significant difference between the mean tuition in the Northeast and that of the West? If so, develop a 95 percent confidence interval for that difference.

Exercises

11. Given the following sample information, test the hypothesis that the treatment means are equal at the .05 significance level.

Treatment 1	Treatment 2	Treatment 3
8	3	3
11	2	4
10	1	5
	3	4
	2	

a. State the null hypothesis and the alternate hypothesis.
b. What is the decision rule?
c. Compute SST, SSE, and SS total.
d. Complete an ANOVA table.
e. State your decision regarding the null hypothesis.
f. If H_0 is rejected, can we conclude that treatment 1 and treatment 2 differ? Use the 95 percent level of confidence.

12. Given the following sample information, test the hypothesis that the treatment means are equal at the .05 significance level.

Treatment 1	Treatment 2	Treatment 3
3	9	6
2	6	3
5	5	5
1	6	5
3	8	5
1	5	4
	4	1
	7	5
	6	
	4	

a. State the null hypothesis and the alternate hypothesis.
b. What is the decision rule?
c. Compute SST, SSE, and SS total.
d. Complete an ANOVA table.
e. State your decision regarding the null hypothesis.
f. If H_0 is rejected, can we conclude that treatment 2 and treatment 3 differ? Use the 95 percent level of confidence.

13. A senior accounting major at Midsouth State University has job offers from four CPA firms. To explore the offers further, she asked a sample of recent trainees how many months each worked for the firm before receiving a raise in salary. The sample information is submitted to MINITAB with the following results:

```
Analysis of Variance
Source    DF      SS        MS       F        P
Factor     3   32.33     10.78    2.36    0.133
Error     10   45.67      4.57
Total     13   78.00
```

At the .05 level of significance, is there a difference in the mean number of months before a raise was granted among the four CPA firms?

14. A stock analyst wants to determine whether there is a difference in the mean rate of return for three types of stock: utility, retail, and banking stocks. The following output is obtained:

```
Analysis of Variance
Source     DF        SS        MS       F        P
Factor      2     86.49     43.25   13.09    0.001
Error      13     42.95      3.30
Total      15    129.44
                                   Individual 95% CIs For Mean
                                   Based on Pooled StDev
Level       N      Mean     StDev  ----------+----------+----------+------
Utility     5    17.400     1.916                      (------*------)
Retail      5    11.620     0.356   (------*------)
Banking     6    15.400     2.356                (------*------)
                                   ----------+----------+----------+------
Pooled StDev =   1.818                     12.0       15.0       18.0
```

a. Using the .05 level of significance, is there a difference in the mean rate of return among the three types of stock?
b. Suppose the null hypothesis is rejected. Can the analyst conclude there is a difference between the mean rates of return for the utility and the retail stocks? Explain.

Chapter Outline

I. The characteristics of the F distribution are:
- **A.** It is continuous.
- **B.** Its values cannot be negative.
- **C.** It is positively skewed.
- **D.** There is a family of F distributions. Each time the degrees of freedom in either the numerator or the denominator changes, a new distribution is created.

II. The F distribution is used to test whether two population variances are the same.
- **A.** The sampled populations must be normal.
- **B.** The larger of the two sample variances is placed in the numerator, forcing the ratio to be at least 1.00.
- **C.** The value of F is computed using the following equation:

$$F = \frac{s_1^2}{s_2^2} \qquad \textbf{[11–1]}$$

III. A one-way ANOVA is used to compare several treatment means.
- **A.** A treatment is a source of variation.
- **B.** The assumptions underlying ANOVA are:
  1. The samples are from populations which follow the normal distribution.
  2. The populations have equal standard deviations.
  3. The samples are from independent populations.
- **C.** The information for finding the value of F is summarized in an ANOVA table.
  1. The formula for SS total, the sum of squares total, is:

$$\text{SS total} = \Sigma X^2 - \frac{(\Sigma X)^2}{n} \qquad \textbf{[11–2]}$$

  2. The formula for the SST, the sum of squares treatment, is:

$$\text{SST} = \Sigma\left(\frac{T_c^2}{n_c}\right) - \frac{(\Sigma X)^2}{n} \qquad \textbf{[11–3]}$$

  3. The SSE, the sum of squares error, is found by subtraction.

$$\text{SSE} = \text{SS total} - \text{SST} \qquad \textbf{[11–4]}$$

  4. This information is summarized in the following table and the value of F determined.

Source of Variation	Sum of Squares	Degrees of Freedom	Mean Square	F
Treatments	SST	$k - 1$	SST/$(k - 1)$ = MST	MST/MSE
Error	SSE	$n - k$	SSE/$(n - k)$ = MSE	
Total	SS total	$n - 1$		

IV. If a null hypothesis of equal treatment means is rejected, we can identify the pairs that differ from the following confidence interval.

$$(\bar{X}_1 - \bar{X}_2) \pm t\sqrt{\text{MSE}\left(\frac{1}{n_1} + \frac{1}{n_2}\right)} \qquad \textbf{[11–5]}$$

source df F
Between SSB dfB 3.49
within SSW dfW
Total SST dfT

(2, 27) p<.05 = 3.39

Pronunciation Key

SYMBOL	MEANING	PRONUNCIATION
SS total	Sum of squares total	*S S total*
SST	Sum of squares treatment	*S S T*
SSE	Sum of squares error	*S S E*
T_c^2	Column totals squared	*T sub c squared*
n_c	Number of observations in each treatment	*n sub c*
MSE	Mean square error	*M S E*

Chapter Exercises

15. A real estate agent in the coastal area of the Carolinas wants to compare the variation in the selling price of homes on the oceanfront with those one to three blocks from the ocean. A sample of 21 oceanfront homes sold within the last year revealed the standard deviation of the selling prices was $45,600. A sample of 18 homes, also sold within the last year, that were one to three blocks from the ocean revealed that the standard deviation was $21,330. At the .01 significance level, can we conclude that there is more variation in the selling prices of the oceanfront homes?

16. A computer manufacturer is about to unveil a new, faster personal computer. The new machine clearly is faster, but initial tests indicate there is more variation in the processing time. The processing time depends on the particular program being run, the amount of input data, and the amount of output. A sample of 16 computer runs, covering a range of production jobs, showed that the standard deviation of the processing time was 22 (hundredths of a second) for the new machine and 12 (hundredths of a second) for the current machine. At the .05 significance level can we conclude that there is more variation in the processing time of the new machine?

17. There are two Chevrolet dealers in Jamestown, New York. The mean weekly sales at Sharkey Chevy and Dave White Chevrolet are about the same. However, Tom Sharkey, the owner of Sharkey Chevy, believes his sales are more consistent. Below is the number of new cars sold at Sharkey in the last seven months and for the last eight months at Dave White. Do you agree with Mr. Sharkey? Use the .01 significance level.

Sharkey	98	78	54	57	68	64	70	
Dave White	75	81	81	30	82	46	58	101

18. Random samples of five were selected from each of three populations. The sum of squares total was 100. The sum of squares due to the treatments was 40.
a. Set up the null hypothesis and the alternate hypothesis.
b. What is the decision rule? Use the .05 significance level.
c. Complete the ANOVA table. What is the value of *F*?
d. What is your decision regarding the null hypothesis?

19. In an ANOVA table MSE was equal to 10. Random samples of six were selected from each of four populations, where the sum of squares total was 250.
a. Set up the null hypothesis and the alternate hypothesis.
b. What is the decision rule? Use the .05 significance level.
c. Complete the ANOVA table. What is the value of *F*?
d. What is your decision regarding the null hypothesis?

20. The following is a partial ANOVA table.

Source	Sum of Squares	*df*	Mean Square	*F*
Treatment		2		
Error			20	
Total	500	11		

Complete the table and answer the following questions. Use the .05 significance level.

a. How many treatments are there?
b. What is the total sample size?
c. What is the critical value of *F*?
d. Write out the null and alternate hypotheses.
e. What is your conclusion regarding the null hypothesis?

21. A consumer organization wants to know whether there is a difference in the price of a particular toy at three different types of stores. The price of the toy was checked in a sample of five discount stores, five variety stores, and five department stores. The results are shown below. Use the .05 significance level.

Discount	Variety	Department
$12	$15	$19
13	17	17
14	14	16
12	18	20
15	17	19

22. A physician who specializes in weight control has three different diets she recommends. As an experiment, she randomly selected 15 patients and then assigned 5 to each diet. After three weeks the following weight losses, in pounds, were noted. At the .05 significance level, can she conclude that there is a difference in the mean amount of weight loss among the three diets?

Plan A	Plan B	Plan C
5	6	7
7	7	8
4	7	9
5	5	8
4	6	9

23. The City of Maumee comprises four districts. Chief of police Andy North wants to determine whether there is a difference in the mean number of crimes committed among the four districts. He recorded the number of crimes reported in each district for a sample of six days. At the .05 significance level, can the chief of police conclude there is a difference in the mean number of crimes?

Number of Crimes			
Rec Center	Key Street	Monclova	Whitehouse
13	21	12	16
15	13	14	17
14	18	15	18
15	19	13	15
14	18	12	20
15	19	15	18

24. The personnel director of Cander Machine Products is investigating "perfectionism" on the job. A test designed to measure perfectionism was administered to a random sample of 18 employees. The scores ranged from 20 to about 40. One of the facets of the study involved the early background of each employee. Did the employee come from a rural background, a small city, or a large city? The scores are:

Rural Area	Small Urban Area	Large Urban Area
35	28	24
30	24	28
36	25	26
38	30	30
29	32	34
34	28	
31		

a. At the .05 level, can it be concluded that there is a difference in the three mean scores?
b. If the null hypothesis is rejected, can you state that the mean score of those with a rural background is different from the score of those with a large-city background?

25. It can be shown that when only two treatments are involved, ANOVA and the Student *t* test (Chapter 9) result in the same conclusions. Also, $t^2 = F$. As an example, suppose that 14 randomly selected students were divided into two groups, one consisting of 6 students and the other of 8. One group was taught using a combination of lecture and programmed instruction, the other using a combination of lecture and television. At the end of the course, each group was given a 50-item test. The following is a list of the number correct for each of the two groups.

Lecture and Programmed Instruction	Lecture and Television
19	32
17	28
23	31
22	26
17	23
16	24
	27
	25

a. Using analysis of variance techniques, test H_0 that the two mean test scores are equal; $\alpha = .05$.
b. Using the *t* test from Chapter 9, compute *t*.
c. Interpret the results.

26. One reads that a business school graduate with an undergraduate degree earns more than a high school graduate with no additional education, and a person with a master's degree or a doctorate earns even more. To test this, a random sample of 25 executives from companies with assets over $1 million was selected. Their incomes, classified by highest level of education, follow.

Income ($ thousands)		
High School or Less	**Undergraduate Degree**	**Master's Degree or More**
45	49	51
47	57	73
53	85	82
62	73	59
39	81	94
43	84	89
54	89	89
	92	95
	62	73

Test at the .05 level of significance that there is no difference in the arithmetic mean salaries of the three groups. If the null hypothesis is rejected, conduct further tests to determine which groups differ.

27. There are four auto body shops in a community and all claim to promptly serve customers. To check if there is any difference in service, customers are randomly selected from each repair shop and their waiting times in days are recorded. The output from a statistical software package is:

Summary

Groups	Count	Sum	Average	Variance
Body Shop A	3	15.4	5.133333	0.323333
Body Shop B	4	32	8	1.433333
Body Shop C	5	25.2	5.04	0.748
Body Shop D	4	25.9	6.475	0.595833

ANOVA

Source of Variation	SS	*df*	MS	*F*	*p*-value
Between Groups	23.37321	3	7.791069	9.612506	0.001632
Within Groups	9.726167	12	0.810514		
Total	33.09938	15			

Is there evidence to suggest a difference in the mean waiting times at the four body shops? Use the .05 significance level.

28. The fuel efficiencies for a sample of 27 compact, midsize, and large cars are entered into a statistical software package. In order to test whether there is a difference among the mean gas mileages for the three car types, an analysis of variance is computed. What do you conclude? Use the .01 significance level.

Summary

Groups	Count	Sum	Average	Variance
Compact	12	268.3	22.35833	9.388106
Midsize	9	172.4	19.15556	7.315278
Large	6	100.5	16.75	7.303

ANOVA

Source of Variation	SS	*df*	MS	*F*	*p*-value
Between Groups	136.4803	2	68.24014	8.258752	0.001866
Within Groups	198.3064	24	8.262766		
Total	334.7867	26			

29. Three assembly lines are used to produce a certain component for an airliner. To examine the production rate, a random sample of six hourly periods is chosen for each assembly line and the number of components produced during these periods for each line is recorded. The output from a statistical software package is:

Summary

Groups	Count	Sum	Average	Variance
Line A	6	250	41.66667	0.266667
Line B	6	260	43.33333	0.666667
Line C	6	249	41.5	0.7

ANOVA					
Source of Variation	SS	*df*	MS	*F*	*p*-value
Between Groups	12.33333	2	6.166667	11.32653	0.001005
Within Groups	8.166667	15	0.544444		
Total	20.5	17			

a. Use a .01 level of significance to test if there is a difference in the mean production of the three assembly lines.

b. Develop a 99 percent confidence interval for the difference in the means between Line B and Line C.

30. A grocery store wants to monitor the amount of withdrawals that its customers make from automatic teller machines (ATMs) located within their stores. They sample 10 withdrawals from each location and the output from a statistical software package is:

Summary				
Groups	Count	Sum	Average	Variance
Location X	10	825	82.5	1,808.056
Location Y	10	540	54	921.1111
Location Z	10	382	38.2	1,703.733

ANOVA					
Source of Variation	SS	*df*	MS	*F*	*p*-value
Between Groups	1,0081.27	2	5,040.633	3.411288	0.047766
Within Groups	3,9896.1	27	1,477.633		
Total	4,9977.37	29			

a. Use a .01 level of significance to test if there is a difference in the mean amount of money withdrawn.

b. Develop a 90 percent confidence interval for the difference in the means between Location X and Location Z.

31. Listed below are the weights (in grams) of a sample of M&M's Plain candies, classified according to color. Use a statistical software system to determine whether there is a difference in the mean weights of candies of different colors. Use the .05 significance level.

Red	Orange	Yellow	Brown	Tan	Green
0.946	0.902	0.929	0.896	0.845	0.935
1.107	0.943	0.960	0.888	0.909	0.903
0.913	0.916	0.938	0.906	0.873	0.865
0.904	0.910	0.933	0.941	0.902	0.822
0.926	0.903	0.932	0.838	0.956	0.871
0.926	0.901	0.899	0.892	0.959	0.905
1.006	0.919	0.907	0.905	0.916	0.905
0.914	0.901	0.906	0.824	0.822	0.852
0.922	0.930	0.930	0.908		0.965
1.052	0.883	0.952	0.833		0.898
0.903		0.939			
0.895		0.940			
		0.882			
		0.906			

32. There are four radio stations in Midland. The stations have different formats (hard rock, classical, country/western, and easy listening), but each is concerned with the number of minutes of music played per hour. From a sample of 10 hours from each station, the following sample means were offered.

$\overline{X}_1 = 51.43 \quad \overline{X}_2 = 44.64 \quad \overline{X}_3 = 47.2 \quad \overline{X}_4 = 50.85$

SS total = 650.75

a. Determine SST.
b. Determine SSE.
c. Complete an ANOVA table.
d. At the .05 significance level, is there a difference in the treatment means?
e. Is there a difference in the mean amount of music time between station 1 and station 4? Use the .05 significance level.

exercises.com

33. Many real estate companies and rental agencies now publish their listings on the Web. One example is the Dunes Realty Company, located in Garden City Beach, South Carolina. Go to their website, http://www.dunes.com, select **Cottage Search,** then indicate 5 bedroom, accommodations for 14 people, second row (this means it is across the street from the beach), no pool or floating dock, select a period in July and August, indicate that you are willing to spend $5,000 per week, and then click on **Search the Cottages.** The output should include details on the cottages that met your criteria. At the .05 significance level, is there a difference in the mean rental prices for the different number of bedrooms? (You may want to combine some of the larger homes, such as 8 or more bedrooms.) Which pairs of means differ?

34. The percentages of quarterly changes in the gross domestic product for 20 countries are available at the following site: http://www.oecd.org/std/qnagdp/qnagdp.htm. Copy the data for Germany, Japan, and the United States into three columns in MINITAB or Excel. Perform an ANOVA to see whether there is a difference in the means. What can you conclude?

Computer Data Exercises

35. Refer to the Real Estate data, which reports information on the homes sold in the Venice, Florida, area last year.

a. At the .02 significance level, is there a difference in the variability of the selling prices of the homes that have a pool versus those that do not have a pool?
b. At the .02 significance level, is there a difference in the variability of the selling prices of the homes with an attached garage versus those that do not have an attached garage?
c. At the .05 significance level, is there a difference in the mean selling price of the homes among the five townships?

36. Refer to the Baseball 2001 data, which reports information on the 30 Major League Baseball teams for the 2001 season.

a. At the .10 significance level, is there a difference in the variation of the number of stolen bases among the teams that play their home games on natural grass versus on artificial turf?
b. Create a variable that classifies a team's total attendance into three groups: less than 2.0 (million), 2.0 up to 3.0, and 3.0 or more. At the .05 significance level, is there a difference in the mean number of games won among the three groups? Use the .01 significance level.
c. Using the same attendance variable developed in part (b), is there a difference in the mean team batting average? Use the .01 significance level.
d. Using the same attendance variable developed in part (b), is there a difference in the mean salary of the three groups? Use the .01 significance level.

37. Refer to the wage data, which reports information on annual wages for a sample of 100 workers. Also included are variables relating to industry, years of education, and gender for each worker.

a. Conduct a test of hypothesis to determine if there is a difference in the mean annual wages for workers in the three industries. If there is a difference in the means, which pair or pairs of means differ? Use the .05 significance level.
b. Conduct a test of hypothesis to determine if there is a difference in the mean annual wages for workers in the six different occupations. If there is a difference in the means, which pair or pairs of means differ? Use the .05 significance level.

c. Conduct a test of hypothesis to determine if there is a difference in the variation of the annual wages of union members and nonunion members. Use the .05 significance level.

38. Refer to the CIA data, which reports demographic and economic information on 46 countries.

a. At the .05 significance level, is there a difference in the mean percent of the population over 65 years of age by level of petroleum usage?

b. At the .05 significance level, is there a difference in the mean GDP per capita by level of petroleum usage?

Computer Commands

1. The Excel commands for the test of variances on page 356 are:
   a. Enter the data for U.S. 25 in column A and for I-75 in column B. Label the two columns.
   b. Click on **Tools**, **Data Analysis**, select **F-Test: Two-Sample for Variances,** and click **OK.**
   c. The range of the first variable is *A1:A8* and *B1:B9* for the second, click on **Labels,** select *D1* for the output range, and click **OK.**

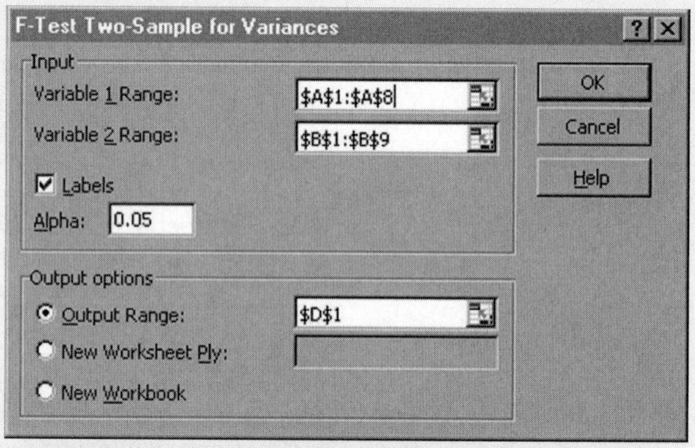

2. The Excel commands for the one-way ANOVA on page 364 are:
   a. Key in data into four columns labeled: Excellent, Good, Fair, and Poor.
   b. Click on **Tools** on the Excel Toolbar and select **Data Analysis.** In the dialog box select **ANOVA, Single Factor ANOVA,** and click **OK.**
   c. In the subsequent dialog box make the input range *A1:D8,* click on **Grouped by Columns,** click on **Labels in First Row,** the **Alpha** text box is .05, and finally select **Output range** as *G1* and click **OK.**

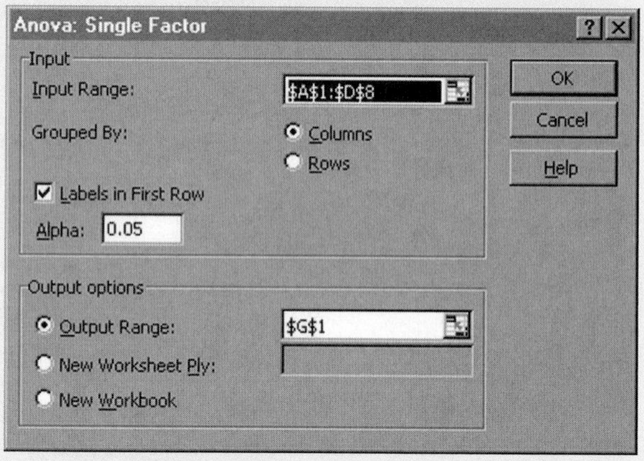

3. The MINITAB commands for the one-way ANOVA on page 365 are:
   a. Input the data into four columns and identify the columns as *Excellent, Good, Fair,* and *Poor.*
   b. Select **Stat**, **ANOVA**, and **Oneway (Unstacked)** and click **OK.**

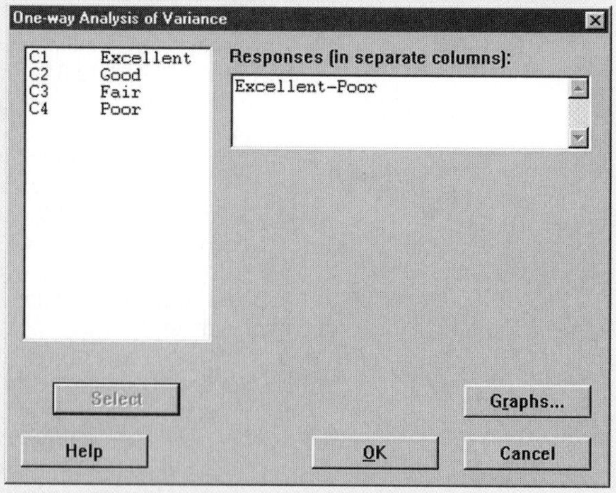

Chapter 11 Answers to Self-Review

11–1 Let Mark's assemblies be population 1, then H_0: $\sigma_1^2 \le \sigma_2^2$; H_1: $\sigma_1^2 > \sigma_2^2$; $df_1 = 10 - 1 = 9$; and df_2 also equals 9. H_0 is rejected if $F > 3.18$.

$$F = \frac{(2.0)^2}{(1.5)^2} = 1.78$$

H_0 is not rejected. The variation is the same for both employees.

11–2 **(a)** H_0: $\mu_1 = \mu_2 = \mu_3$
H_1: At least one treatment mean is different.

(b) Reject H_0 if $F > 4.26$.

(c) $$\text{SS total} = 5{,}651 - \frac{(247)^2}{12} = 566.92$$

$$\text{SST} = \frac{(77)^2}{4} + \frac{(55)^2}{4} + \frac{(115)^2}{4} - \frac{(247)^2}{12}$$
$$= 460.67$$
$$\text{SSE} = 566.92 - 460.67 = 106.25$$

(d)

Source	Sum of Squares	Degrees of Freedom	Mean Square	*F*
Treatment	460.67	2	230.335	19.510
Error	106.25	9	11.806	

(e) H_0 is rejected. There is a difference in the mean number of bottles sold at the various locations.

11–3 **(a)** H_0: $\mu_1 = \mu_2 = \mu_3$
H_1: Not all means are equal.

(b) H_0 is rejected if $F > 3.98$.

(c) $$\text{SS total} = 5{,}032 - \frac{(264)^2}{14} = 53.71$$

$$\text{SST} = \frac{(105)^2}{5} + \frac{(75)^2}{4} + \frac{(84)^2}{5} - \frac{(264)^2}{14} = 44.16$$

$$\text{SSE} = 53.71 - 44.16 = 9.55$$

Source	Sum of Squares	*df*	Mean Square	*F*
Treatment	44.16	2	22.08	25.43
Error	9.55	11	0.8682	
Total	53.71	13		

(d) H_0 is rejected. The treatment means differ.

(e) $(21.0 - 16.8) \pm 2.201\sqrt{0.8682(\frac{1}{5} + \frac{1}{5})} =$
$4.2 \pm 1.30 = 2.90$ and 5.50

These treatment means differ because both endpoints of the confidence interval are of the same sign—positive in this problem.

12

Linear Regression and Correlation

GOALS

When you have completed this chapter, you will be able to:

1. **Draw a scatter diagram.**

2. **Understand and interpret the terms *dependent variable* and *independent variable.***

3. **Calculate and interpret the coefficient of correlation, the coefficient of determination, and the standard error of estimate.**

4. **Conduct a test of hypothesis to determine whether the coefficient of correlation in the population is zero.**

5. **Calculate the least squares regression line.**

6. **Construct and interpret confidence intervals and prediction intervals for the dependent variable.**

7. **Set up and interpret an ANOVA table.**

The Bio-lo Appliance Store in the Northeast is having a sale on Saturday going through Sunday on digital cameras. The general sales manager plans to air a commercial on selected TV stations prior to the sale. She plans to get the information on Saturday–Sunday digital camera sales at the various outlets and pair them with the number of times the ad was shown on TV to find whether there's a correlation between the ad and digital camera sales. What is the dependent variable? (See Goal 2 and Exercise 3.)

Introduction

Chapters 2 and 3 dealt with *descriptive statistics.* We organized raw data into a frequency distribution and computed several measures of location and measures of dispersion to describe the major characteristics of the data. Chapter 4 started the study of *statistical inference.* The main emphasis was on inferring something about a population parameter, such as the population mean, based on a sample. We tested for the reasonableness of a population mean or a population proportion, the difference between two population means, or whether several population means were equal. All of these tests involved just *one* interval- or ratio-level variable, such as the weight of a plastic soft drink bottle, the income of bank presidents, or the number of patients admitted to a particular hospital.

We shift our emphasis in this chapter. Here we study the *relationship between two variables* and *develop an equation that allows us to estimate one variable based on another.* Is there a relationship between the amount Healthtex spends on advertising and its sales? Can we estimate the cost to heat a home in January in the upper Midwest based on the number of square feet in the home? Is there a relationship between the advertising rate per line in a newspaper and the circulation of the paper? Is there a relationship between the number of years a production worker has been on the job and the number of units produced? Note in each of these instances there are two variables—for example, the number of years on the job and the number of units produced.

We begin this chapter by examining the meaning and purpose of **correlation analysis.** Then we look at a chart designed to portray the relationship between two variables: a **scatter diagram.** We continue our study by developing a mathematical equation that will allow us to estimate the value of one variable based on the value of another. This is called **regression analysis.** We will (1) determine the equation of the line that best fits the data, (2) estimate the value of one variable based on another, (3) measure the error in our estimate, and (4) establish confidence and prediction intervals for our estimate.

What Is Correlation Analysis?

Correlation analysis is the study of the relationship between variables. To explain, suppose the sales manager of Copier Sales of America, which has a large sales force throughout the United States and Canada, wants to determine whether there is a relationship between the number of sales calls made in a month and the number of copiers sold that month. The manager selects a random sample of 10 representatives and determines the number of sales calls each representative made last month and the number of copiers sold. The sample information is shown in Table 12–1.

TABLE 12–1 Sales Calls and Copiers Sold for 10 Salespeople

Sales Representative	Number of Sales Calls	Number of Copiers Sold
Tom Keller	20	30
Jeff Hall	40	60
Brian Virost	20	40
Greg Fish	30	60
Susan Welch	10	30
Carlos Ramirez	10	40
Rich Niles	20	40
Mike Kiel	20	50
Mark Reynolds	20	30
Soni Jones	30	70

There does seem to be some relationship between the number of sales calls and the number of units sold. That is, the salespeople who made the most sales calls sold the most units. The relationship is not "perfect" or exact, however. For example, Soni Jones made fewer sales calls than Jeff Hall, but she sold more units.

Instead of talking in generalities, as we have been doing up to this point, we will develop some statistical measures to portray more precisely the relationship between the two variables, sales calls and copiers sold. This group of statistical techniques is called **correlation analysis.**

CORRELATION ANALYSIS A group of techniques to measure the strength of the association between two variables.

The basic idea of correlation analysis is to report the strength of the association between two variables. The usual first step is to plot the data in a **scatter diagram.**

SCATTER DIAGRAM A chart that portrays the relationship between two variables.

An example will show how a scatter diagram is used.

EXAMPLE

Copier Sales of America, Inc., sells copiers to businesses of all sizes throughout the United States and Canada. Ms. Marcy Bancer was recently promoted to the position of national sales manager. At the upcoming sales meeting, the sales representatives from all over the country will be in attendance. She would like to impress upon them the importance of making an extra sales call each day. She decides to gather some information on the relationship between the number of sales calls and the number of copiers sold. She selected a random sample of 10 sales representatives and determined the number of sales calls they made last month and the number of copiers they sold. The sample information is reported in Table 12–1. What observations can you make about the relationship between the number of sales calls and the number of copiers sold? Develop a scatter diagram to display the information.

SOLUTION

Based on the information in Table 12–1, Ms. Bancer suspects there is a relationship between the number of sales calls made in a month and the number of copiers sold. Soni Jones sold the most copiers last month, and she was one of three representatives making 30 or more sales calls. On the other hand, Susan Welch and Carlos Ramirez made only 10 sales calls last month. Ms. Welch had the lowest number of copiers sold among the sampled representatives.

The implication is that the number of copiers sold is related to the number of sales calls made. As the number of sales calls increases, the number of copiers sold also increases. We refer to number of sales calls as the *independent variable* and number of copiers sold as the *dependent variable.*

DEPENDENT VARIABLE The variable that is being predicted or estimated.

INDEPENDENT VARIABLE A variable that provides the basis for estimation. It is the predictor variable.

It is common practice to scale the dependent variable (copiers sold) on the vertical or Y-axis and the independent variable (number of sales calls) on the horizontal or X-axis. To develop the scatter diagram of the Copier Sales of America sales information, we begin with the first sales representative, Tom Keller. Tom made 20 sales calls last month and sold 30 copiers, so $X = 20$ and $Y = 30$. To plot this point, move along the horizontal axis to $X = 20$, then go vertically to $Y = 30$ and place a dot at the intersection. This process is continued until all the paired data are plotted, as shown in Chart 12–1.

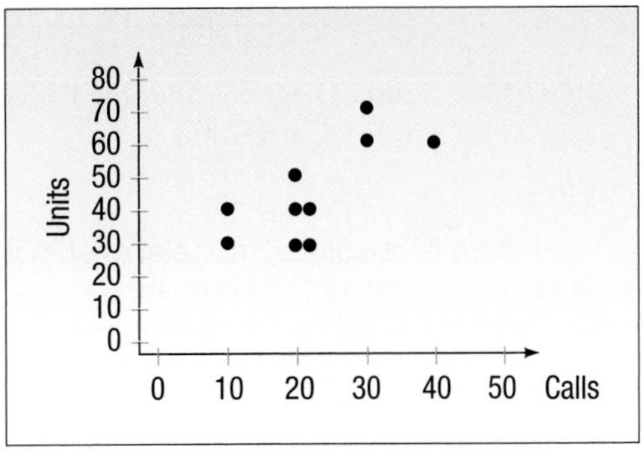

CHART 12–1 Scatter Diagram Showing Sales Calls and Copiers Sold

The scatter diagram shows graphically that the sales representatives who make more calls tend to sell more copiers. It is reasonable for Ms. Bancer, the national sales manager at Copier Sales of America, to tell her salespeople that the more sales calls they make the more copiers they can expect to sell. Note that while there appears to be a positive relationship between the two variables, all the points do not fall on a line. In the following section you will measure the strength and direction of this relationship between two variables by determining the coefficient of correlation.

The Coefficient of Correlation

Interval- or ratio-level data are required.

Characteristics of r

Originated by Karl Pearson about 1900, the **coefficient of correlation** describes the strength of the linear relationship between two sets of interval-scaled or ratio-scaled variables. Designated r, it is often referred to as *Pearson's r* and as the *Pearson product-moment correlation coefficient.* It can assume any value from -1.00 to $+1.00$ inclusive. A correlation coefficient of -1.00 or $+1.00$ indicates *perfect correlation.* For example, a correlation coefficient for the preceding example computed to be $+1.00$ would indicate that the number of sales calls and the number of copiers sold are perfectly related in a positive linear sense. A computed value of -1.00 reveals that sales calls and the number of copiers sold are perfectly related in a negative linear sense. How the scatter diagram would appear if the relationship between the two sets of data were linear and perfect is shown in Chart 12–2.

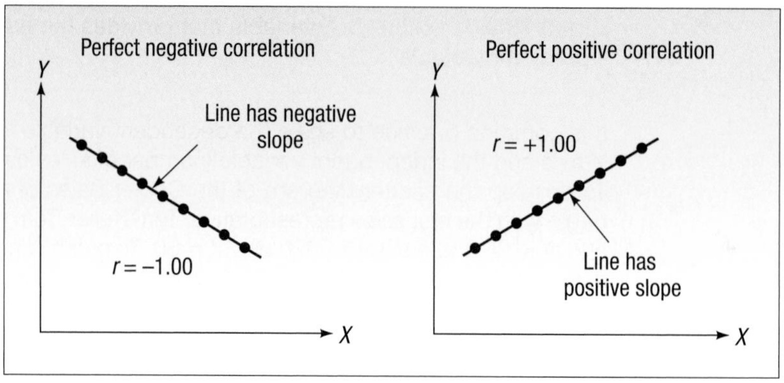

CHART 12–2 Scatter Diagrams Showing Perfect Negative Correlation and Perfect Positive Correlation

If there is absolutely no relationship between the two sets of variables, Pearson's r is zero. A coefficient of correlation r close to 0 (say, .08) shows that the relationship is quite weak. The same conclusion is drawn if $r = -.08$. Coefficients of $-.91$ and $+.91$ have equal strength; both indicate very strong correlation between the two variables. Thus, *the strength of the correlation does not depend on the direction (either − or +).*

Scatter diagrams for $r = 0$, a weak r (say, $-.23$), and a strong r (say, $+.87$) are shown in Chart 12–3. Note that if the correlation is weak, there is considerable scatter about a line drawn through the center of the data. For the scatter diagram representing a strong relationship, there is very little scatter about the line. This indicates, in the example shown on the chart, that high school GPA is a good predictor of performance in college.

Examples of degrees of correlation

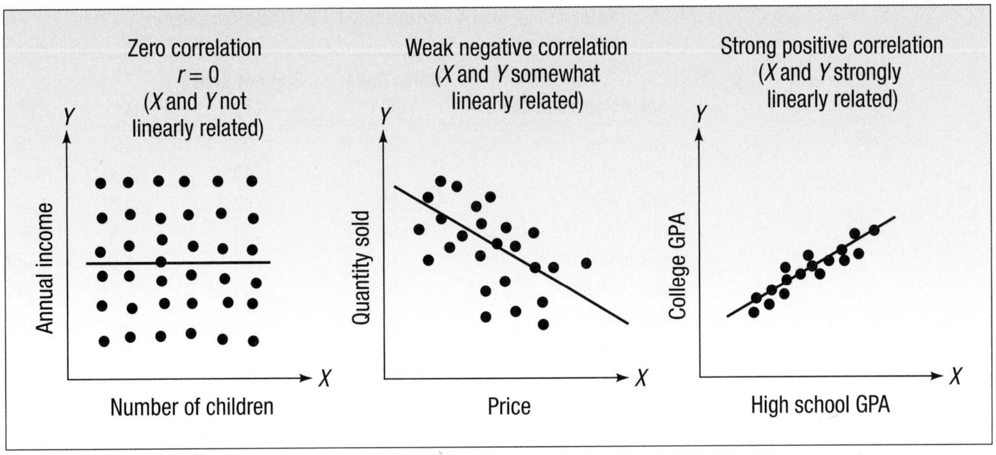

CHART 12–3 Scatter Diagrams Depicting Zero, Weak, and Strong Correlation

The following drawing summarizes the strength and direction of the coefficient of correlation.

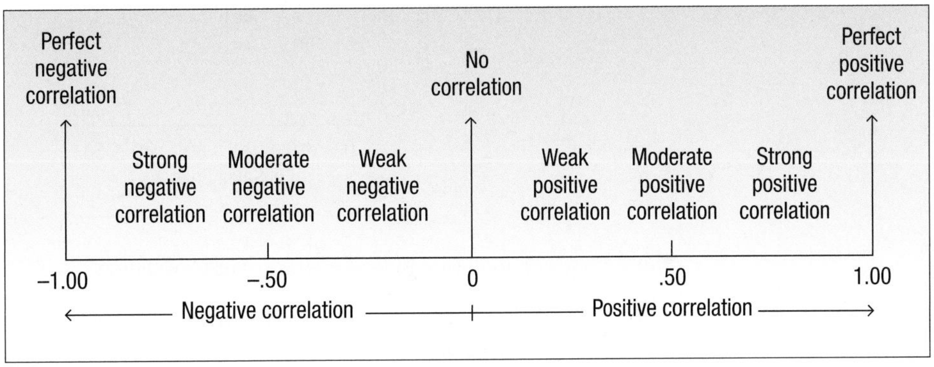

COEFFICIENT OF CORRELATION A measure of the strength of the linear relationship between two variables.

How is the value of the coefficient of correlation determined? We will use the Copier Sales of America data, which are reported in Table 12–2, as an example. We begin with a scatter diagram, similar to Chart 12–1. Draw a vertical line through the data values at the mean of the X-values and a horizontal line at the mean of the Y-values. In Chart 12–4 we've added a vertical line at 22.0 calls ($\overline{X} = \Sigma X/n = 220/10 = 22$) and a horizontal line at 45.0 copiers ($\overline{Y} = \Sigma Y/n = 450/10 = 45.0$). These lines pass through the "center" of the data and divide the scatter diagram into four quadrants. Think of moving the origin from (0,0) to (22,45).

If the two variables are positively related, when the number of copiers sold is above the mean the number of sales calls will also be above the mean. These points appear in the upper-right quadrant of Chart 12–4. Similarly, when the number of copiers sold is less than the mean, so is the number of sales calls; these points fall in the lower-left quadrant. For example, the last person on the list in Table 12–2, Soni

TABLE 12–2 Sales Calls and Copiers Sold for 10 Salespeople

Sales Representative	Sales Calls (X)	Copiers Sold (Y)	X^2	Y^2	XY
Tom Keller	20	30	400	900	600
Jeff Hall	40	60	1,600	3,600	2,400
Brian Virost	20	40	400	1,600	800
Greg Fish	30	60	900	3,600	1,800
Susan Welch	10	30	100	900	300
Carlos Ramirez	10	40	100	1,600	400
Rich Niles	20	40	400	1,600	800
Mike Kiel	20	50	400	2,500	1,000
Mark Reynolds	20	30	400	900	600
Soni Jones	30	70	900	4,900	2,100
Total	220	450	5,600	22,100	10,800

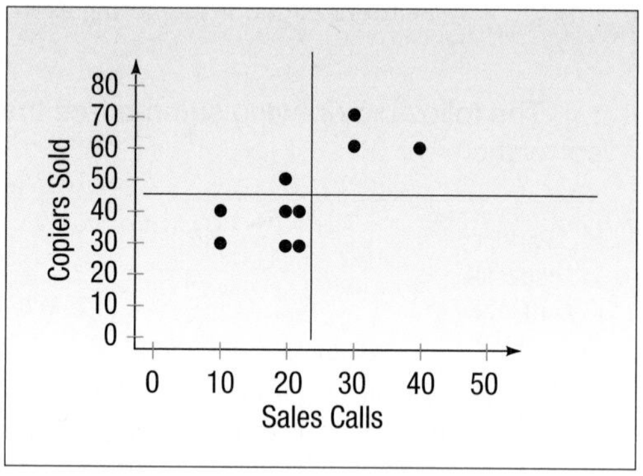

CHART 12–4 Computation of the Coefficient of Correlation

Jones, made 30 sales calls and sold 70 copiers. These values are above their respective means, so this point is located in the upper-right quadrant. She made 8 ($X - \bar{X} = 30 - 22$) more sales calls than the mean and sold 25 ($Y - \bar{Y} = 70 - 45$) more copiers than the mean. Tom Keller, the first name on the list in Table 12–2, made 20 sales calls and sold 30 copiers. Both of these values are less than their respective means; hence this point is in the lower-left quadrant. Tom made 2 less sales calls and sold 15 less copiers than the respective means. The deviations from the mean number of sales calls and for the mean number of copiers sold are summarized in Table 12–3 for the 10 sales representatives. The sum of the products of the deviations from the respective means is 900. That is, the term $\Sigma(X - \bar{X})(Y - \bar{Y}) = 900$.

In both the upper-right and the lower-left quadrants, the product of $(X - \bar{X})(Y - \bar{Y})$ is positive because both of the factors have the same sign. In our example this happens for all sales representatives except Mike Kiel. We can therefore expect the coefficient of correlation to have a positive value.

If the two variables are inversely related, one variable will be above its mean and the other below its mean. Most of the points in this case occur in the upper-left and lower-right quadrants. Now $(X - \bar{X})$ and $(Y - \bar{Y})$ will have opposite signs, so their product is negative. The resulting correlation coefficient is negative.

What happens if there is no linear relationship between the two variables? The points in the scatter diagram will appear in all four quadrants. The negative products of $(X - \bar{X})(Y - \bar{Y})$ offset the positive products, so the sum is near zero. This leads to a correlation coefficient near zero.

TABLE 12–3 Deviations from the Mean and Their Products

Sales Representative	Calls Y	Sales X	$X - \bar{X}$	$Y - \bar{Y}$	$(X - \bar{X})(Y - \bar{Y})$
Tom Keller	20	30	−2	−15	30
Jeff Hall	40	60	18	15	270
Brian Virost	20	40	−2	−5	10
Greg Fish	30	60	8	15	120
Susan Welch	10	30	−12	−15	180
Carlos Ramirez	10	40	−12	−5	60
Rich Niles	20	40	−2	−5	10
Mike Kiel	20	50	−2	5	−10
Mark Reynolds	20	30	−2	−15	30
Soni Jones	30	70	8	25	200
					900

Pearson also wanted the correlation coefficient to be unaffected by the measurement units of the two variables. For example, if we had used hundreds of copiers sold instead of the number sold, the coefficient of correlation would be the same. The coefficient of correlation is independent of the scale used if we divide the term $\Sigma(X - \bar{X})(Y - \bar{Y})$ by the sample standard deviations. It is also made independent of the sample size and bounded by the values +1.00 and −1.00 if we divide by $(n - 1)$.

This reasoning leads to the following formula:

CORRELATION COEFFICIENT—CONCEPTUAL FORM

$$r = \frac{\Sigma(X - \bar{X})(Y - \bar{Y})}{(n - 1)\, s_x\, s_y} \qquad \textbf{[12–1]}$$

To compute the coefficient of correlation, we use the standard deviations of the sample of 10 sales calls and 10 copiers sold. We could use formula 3–12 to calculate the sample standard deviations or we could use one of the software packages. The following is the Excel output. The standard deviation of the number of sales calls is 9.189 and of the number of copiers sold 14.337.

EXCEL

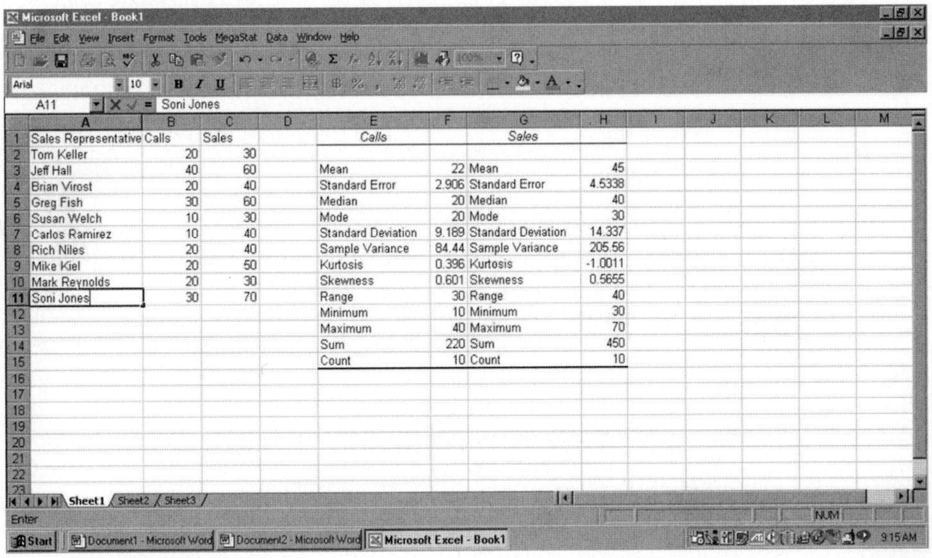

We now insert these values into formula 12–1 to determine the coefficient of correlation:

$$r = \frac{\Sigma(X - \bar{X})(Y - \bar{Y})}{(n - 1)\, s_x\, s_y} = \frac{900}{(10 - 1)(9.189)(14.337)} = 0.759$$

The coefficient of correlation can also be computed from a computational formula based on the actual values of X and Y. The formula is:

CORRELATION COEFFICIENT

$$r = \frac{n(\Sigma XY) - (\Sigma X)(\Sigma Y)}{\sqrt{[n(\Sigma X^2) - (\Sigma X)^2][n(\Sigma Y^2) - (\Sigma Y)^2]}} \qquad \textbf{[12–2]}$$

where:

- n is the number of paired observations.
- ΣX is the X variable summed.
- ΣY is the Y variable summed.
- (ΣX^2) is the X variable squared and the squares summed.
- $(\Sigma X)^2$ is the X variable summed and the sum squared.
- (ΣY^2) is the Y variable squared and the squares summed.
- $(\Sigma Y)^2$ is the Y variable summed and the sum squared.
- ΣXY is the sum of the products of X and Y.

EXAMPLE

Refer to the previous example where we developed a scatter diagram depicting the relationship between the number of sales calls and the number of copiers sold. Determine the coefficient of correlation and interpret its value.

SOLUTION

Table 12–2 repeats the information on the number of sales calls and the number of copiers sold. Also included are additional totals necessary to determine the coefficient of correlation.

The coefficient of correlation is 0.759, found by using formula 12–2.

$$r = \frac{n(\Sigma XY) - (\Sigma X)(\Sigma Y)}{\sqrt{[n(\Sigma X^2) - (\Sigma X)^2][n(\Sigma Y^2) - (\Sigma Y)^2]}}$$

$$= \frac{10(10{,}800) - (220)(450)}{\sqrt{[10(5{,}600) - (220)^2][10(22{,}100) - (450)^2]}}$$

$$= 0.759$$

How do we interpret a correlation of 0.759? First, it is positive, so we see there is a direct relationship between the number of sales calls and the number of copiers sold. This confirms our reasoning based on the scatter diagram, Chart 12–4. The value of 0.759 is fairly close to 1.00, so we conclude that the association is strong.

The Coefficient of Determination

In the previous Example regarding the relationship between the number of sales calls and the units sold, the coefficient of correlation, 0.759, was interpreted as being "strong." Terms such as *weak, moderate,* and *strong,* however, do not have precise meaning. A measure that has a more easily interpreted meaning is the **coefficient of determination.** It is computed by squaring the coefficient of correlation. In the example, the coefficient of determination, r^2, is 0.576, found by $(0.759)^2$. This is a proportion or a percent; we can say that 57.6 percent of the variation in the number of copiers sold is explained, or accounted for, by the variation in the number of sales calls.

COEFFICIENT OF DETERMINATION The proportion of the total variation in the dependent variable Y that is explained, or accounted for, by the variation in the independent variable X.

Further discussion of the coefficient of determination is found later in the chapter.

A Word of Caution

If there is a strong relationship (say, $r^2 = 0.91$) between two variables, we are tempted to assume that an increase or decrease in one variable *causes* a change in the other variable. For example, it can be shown that the consumption of Georgia peanuts and the consumption of aspirin have a strong correlation. However, this does not indicate that an increase in the consumption of peanuts *caused* the consumption of aspirin to increase. Likewise, the incomes of professors and the number of inmates in mental institutions have increased proportionately. Further, as the population of donkeys has decreased, there has been an increase in the number of doctoral degrees granted. Relationships such as these are called **spurious correlations.** What we can conclude when we find two variables with a strong correlation is that there is a relationship between the two variables, not that a change in one causes a change in the other.

Self-Review 12-1

Reliable Furniture is a family business that has been selling to retail customers in the Chicago area for many years. They advertise extensively on radio and TV, emphasizing their low prices and easy credit terms. The owner would like to review the relationship between sales and the amount spent on advertising. Below is information on sales and advertising expense for the last four months.

Month	Advertising Expense ($ million)	Sales Revenue ($ million)
July	2	7
August	1	3
September	3	8
October	4	10

(a) The owner wants to forecast sales based on advertising expense. Which variable is the dependent variable? Which variable is the independent variable?
(b) Draw a scatter diagram.
(c) Determine the coefficient of correlation.
(d) Interpret the strength of the correlation coefficient.
(e) Determine the coefficient of determination. Interpret.

Exercises

1. The following sample observations were randomly selected.

X:	4	5	3	6	10
Y:	4	6	5	7	7

Determine the coefficient of correlation and the coefficient of determination. Interpret.

2. The following sample observations were randomly selected.

X:	5	3	6	3	4	4	6	8
Y:	13	15	7	12	13	11	9	5

Determine the coefficient of correlation and the coefficient of determination. Interpret.

3. Bi-lo Appliance Stores has outlets in several large metropolitan areas in the Northeast. The general sales manager plans to air a commercial for a digital camera on selected local TV stations prior to a sale starting on Saturday and ending Sunday. She plans to get the information for Saturday–Sunday digital camera sales at the various outlets and pair them with the number of times the advertisement was shown on the local TV stations. The purpose is to find whether there is any relationship between the number of times the advertisement was aired and digital camera sales. The pairings are:

Location of TV Station	Number of Airings	Saturday–Sunday Sales ($ thousands)
Buffalo	4	15
Albany	2	8
Erie	5	21
Syracuse	6	24
Rochester	3	17

a. What is the dependent variable?
b. Draw a scatter diagram.
c. Determine the coefficient of correlation.
d. Determine the coefficient of determination.
e. Interpret these statistical measures.

4. The production department of NDB Electronics wants to explore the relationship between the number of employees who assemble a subassembly and the number produced. As an experiment, two employees were assigned to assemble the subassemblies. They produced 15 during a one-hour period. Then four employees assembled them. They produced 25 during a one-hour period. The complete set of paired observations follows.

Number of Assemblers	One-Hour Production (units)
2	15
4	25
1	10
5	40
3	30

The dependent variable is production; that is, it is assumed that the level of production depends upon the number of employees.

a. Draw a scatter diagram.
b. Based on the scatter diagram, does there appear to be any relationship between the number of assemblers and production? Explain.
c. Compute the coefficient of correlation.
d. Evaluate the strength of the relationship by computing the coefficient of determination.

5. The city council of Pine Bluffs is considering increasing the number of police in an effort to reduce crime. Before making a final decision, the council asks the Chief of Police to survey other cities of similar size to determine the relationship between the number of police and the number of crimes reported. The Chief gathered the following sample information.

City	Police	Number of Crimes	City	Police	Number of Crimes
Oxford	15	17	Holgate	17	7
Starksville	17	13	Carey	12	21
Danville	25	5	Whistler	11	19
Athens	27	7	Woodville	22	6

a. If we want to estimate crimes based on the number of police, which variable is the dependent variable and which is the independent variable?
b. Draw a scatter diagram.
c. Determine the coefficient of correlation.
d. Determine the coefficient of determination.
e. Interpret these statistical measures. Does it surprise you that the relationship is inverse?

6. The owner of Maumee Motors wants to study the relationship between the age of a car and its selling price. Listed below is a random sample of 12 used cars sold at Maumee Motors during the last year.

Car	Age (years)	Selling Price ($000)	Car	Age (years)	Selling Price ($000)
1	9	8.1	7	8	7.6
2	7	6.0	8	11	8.0
3	11	3.6	9	10	8.0
4	12	4.0	10	12	6.0
5	8	5.0	11	6	8.6
6	7	10.0	12	6	8.0

a. If we want to estimate selling price based on the age of the car, which variable is the dependent variable and which is the independent variable?
b. Draw a scatter diagram.
c. Determine the coefficient of correlation.
d. Determine the coefficient of determination.
e. Interpret these statistical measures. Does it surprise you that the relationship is inverse?

Testing the Significance of the Correlation Coefficient

Recall the sales manager of Copier Sales of America found the correlation between the number of sales calls and the number of copiers sold was 0.759. This indicated a strong association between the two variables. However, only 10 salespeople were sampled. Could it be that the correlation in the population is actually 0? This would mean the correlation of 0.759 was due to chance. The population in this example is all the salespeople employed by the firm.

Could the correlation in the population be zero?

Resolving this dilemma requires a test to answer the obvious question: Could there be zero correlation in the population from which the sample was selected? To put it another way, did the computed *r* come from a population of paired observations with zero correlation? To continue our convention of allowing Greek letters to represent a population parameter, we will let ρ represent the correlation in the population. It is pronounced "rho."

We will continue with the illustration involving sales calls and copiers sold. The null hypothesis and the alternate hypothesis are:

H_0: $\rho = 0$ (The correlation in the population is zero.)
H_1: $\rho \neq 0$ (The correlation in the population is different from zero.)

From the way H_1 is stated, we know that the test is two-tailed.

The formula for t is:

t TEST FOR THE COEFFICIENT OF CORRELATION

$$t = \frac{r\sqrt{n-2}}{\sqrt{1-r^2}} \quad \text{with } n - 2 \text{ degrees of freedom} \qquad \textbf{[12–3]}$$

Using the .05 level of significance, the decision rule states that if the computed t falls in the area between plus 2.306 and minus 2.306, the null hypothesis is not rejected. To locate the critical value of 2.306, refer to Appendix F for $df = n - 2 = 10 - 2 = 8$. See Chart 12–5.

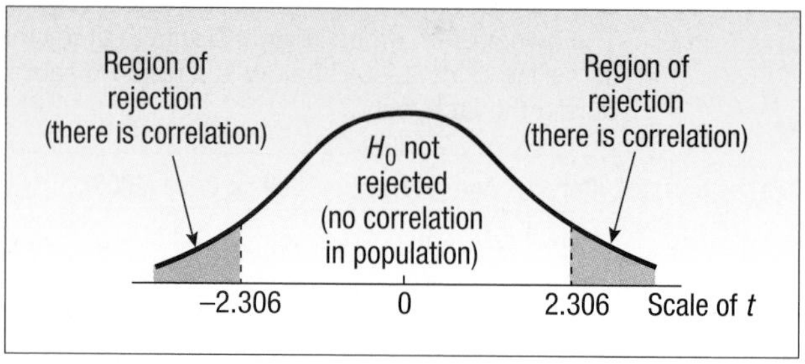

CHART 12–5 Decision Rule for Test of Hypothesis at .05 Significance Level and 8 *df*

Applying formula 12–3 to the example regarding the number of sales calls and units sold:

$$t = \frac{r\sqrt{n-2}}{\sqrt{1-r^2}} = \frac{.759\sqrt{10-2}}{\sqrt{1-.759^2}} = 3.297$$

The computed t is in the rejection region. Thus, H_0 is rejected at the .05 significance level. This means the correlation in the population is not zero. From a practical standpoint, it indicates to the sales manager that there is correlation in the population of salespeople with respect to the number of sales calls made and the number of copiers sold.

We can also interpret the test of hypothesis in terms of p-values. A p-value is the likelihood of finding a value of the test statistic more extreme than the one computed, when H_0 is true. To determine the p-value, go to the t distribution in Appendix F and find the row for 8 degrees of freedom. The value of the test statistic is 3.297, so in the row for 8 degrees of freedom and a two-tailed test, find the value closest to 3.297. For a two-tailed test at the .02 significance level, the critical value is 2.896, and the critical value at the .01 significance level is 3.355. Because 3.297 is between 2.896 and 3.355 we conclude that the p-value is less than .02.

Both MINITAB and Excel will report the correlation between two variables. In addition to the correlation, MINITAB reports the p-value for the test of hypothesis that the correlation in the population between the two variables is 0. The MINITAB output showing the results is below. They are the same as those calculated earlier.

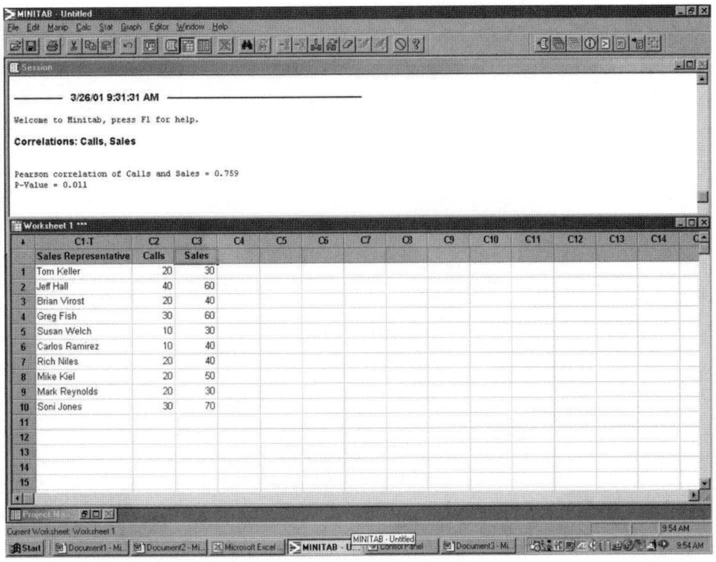
MINITAB - Untitled
File Edit Manip Calc Stat Graph Editor Window Help
Session
3/26/01 9:31:31 AM
Welcome to Minitab, press F1 for help.
Correlations: Calls, Sales
Pearson correlation of Calls and Sales = 0.759
P-Value = 0.011
Worksheet 1 ***
C1-T C2 C3 C4 C5 C6 C7 C8 C9 C10 C11 C12 C13 C14
Sales Representative Calls Sales
1 Tom Keller 20 30
2 Jeff Hall 40 60
3 Brian Virost 20 40
4 Greg Fish 30 60
5 Susan Welch 10 30
6 Carlos Ramirez 10 40
7 Rich Niles 20 40
8 Mike Kiel 20 50
9 Mark Reynolds 20 30
10 Soni Jones 30 70
Current Worksheet: Worksheet 1
9:54 AM
Start
MINITAB - Untitled

Self-Review 12-2

A sample of 25 mayoral campaigns in cities with populations larger than 50,000 showed that the correlation between the percent of the vote received and the amount spent on the campaign by the candidate was .43. At the .05 significance level, is there a positive association between the variables?

Exercises

7. The following hypotheses are given.

H_0: $\rho \leq 0$
H_1: $\rho > 0$

A random sample of 12 paired observations indicated a correlation of .32. Can we conclude that the correlation in the population is greater than zero? Use the .05 significance level.

8. The following hypotheses are given.

H_0: $\rho \geq 0$
H_1: $\rho < 0$

A random sample of 15 paired observations have a correlation of 2.46. Can we conclude that the correlation in the population is less than zero? Use the .05 significance level.

9. The Pennsylvania Refining Company is studying the relationship between the pump price of gasoline and the number of gallons sold. For a sample of 20 stations last Tuesday, the correlation was $-.78$. At the .01 significance level, is the correlation in the population less than zero?

10. A study of 20 worldwide financial institutions showed the correlation between their assets and pretax profit to be .86. At the .05 significance level, can we conclude that there is positive correlation in the population?

Regression Analysis

In the previous section we developed measures to express the strength and the direction of the relationship between two variables. In this section we wish to develop an equation to express the *linear* (straight line) relationship between two variables. In addition we want to estimate the value of the dependent variable *Y* based on a selected value of the independent variable *X*. The technique used to develop the equation and provide the estimates is called **regression analysis.**

In Table 12–1 we reported the number of sales calls and the number of units sold for a sample of 10 sales representatives employed by Copier Sales of America. Chart 12–1 portrayed this information in a scatter diagram. Now we want to develop a linear equation that expresses the relationship between the number of sales calls and the number of units sold. The equation for the line used to estimate *Y* based on *X* is referred to as the **regression equation.**

REGRESSION EQUATION An equation that defines the linear relationship between two variables.

The scatter diagram in Chart 12–1 is reproduced in Chart 12–6, with a line drawn with a ruler through the dots to illustrate that a straight line would probably fit the data. However, the line drawn using a straight edge has one disadvantage: Its position is based in part on the judgment of the person drawing the line. The hand-drawn lines in Chart 12–7 represent the judgments of four people. All the lines except line *A* seem to be reasonable. However, each would result in a different estimate of units sold for a particular number of sales calls.

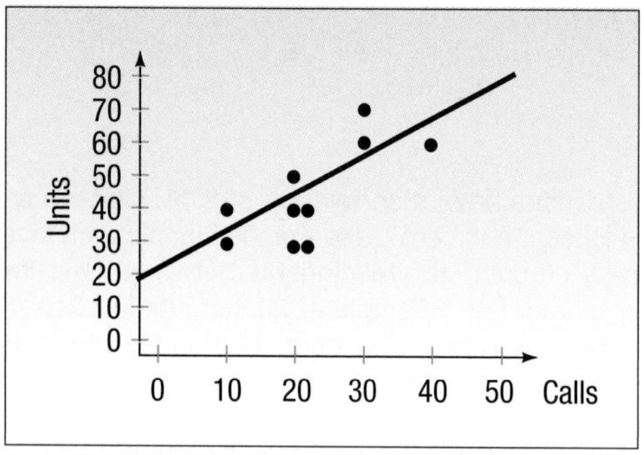

CHART 12–6 Sales Calls and Copiers Sold for 10 Sales Representatives

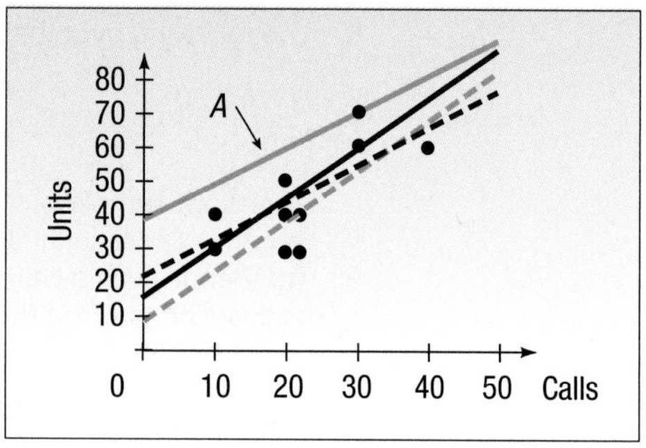

CHART 12–7 Four Lines Superimposed on the Scatter Diagram

Least Squares Principle

Least squares line gives "best" fit; subjective method is unreliable.

Judgment is eliminated by determining the regression line using a mathematical method called the **least squares principle.** This method gives what is commonly referred to as the "best-fitting" line.

> **LEAST SQUARES PRINCIPLE** Determining a regression equation by minimizing the sum of the squares of the vertical distances between the actual Y values and the predicted values of Y.

To illustrate this concept, suppose a company is interested in the relationship between an employee's years of service with the company and his or her achievement score. Three employees are selected. Their respective years of service (*X*) and performance rating (*Y*) are: (3, 8), (4, 18), and (5, 16). Chart 12–8 shows the plots of these observations and the regression line determined with the least squares method. It is called the best-fitting line because the sum of the squares of the vertical deviations about it is at a minimum. The first plot ($X = 3$, $Y = 8$) deviates by 2 from the line, found by $10 - 8$. The deviation squared is 4. The squared deviation for the plot $X = 4$, $Y = 18$ is 16. The squared deviation for the plot $X = 5$, $Y = 16$ is 4. The sum of the squared deviations is 24, found by $4 + 16 + 4$.

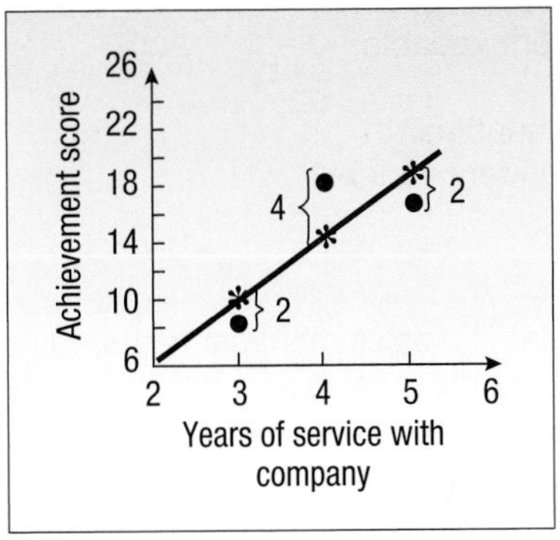

CHART 12–8 The Least Squares Line

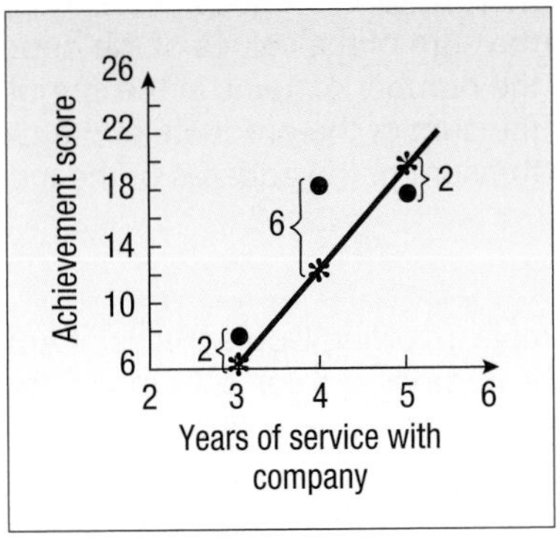

CHART 12–9 Line Drawn Using a Straight Edge

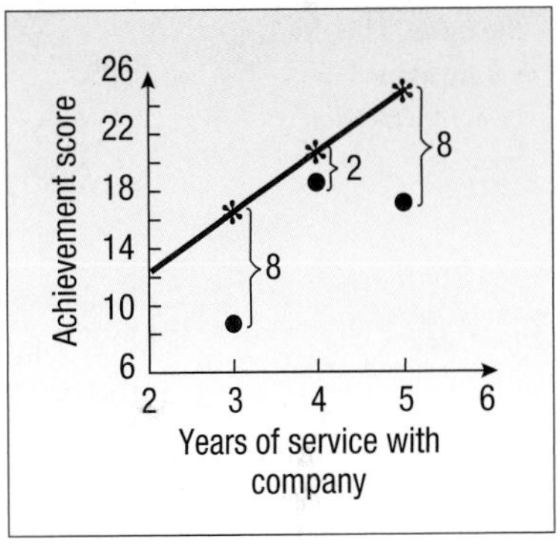

CHART 12–10 Line Drawn Using a Straight Edge

Assume that the lines in Charts 12-9 and 12–10 were drawn using a straight edge. The sum of the squared vertical deviations in Chart 12-9 is 44. For Chart 12–10 it is 132. Both sums are greater than the sum for the line in Chart 12–8, found using the least squares method.

The general form of the regression equation is:

GENERAL FORM OF LINEAR REGRESSION EQUATION	$Y' = a + bX$	**[12–4]**

where:

- Y' read *Y* prime, is the predicted value of the *Y* variable for a selected *X* value.
- a is the *Y*-intercept. It is the estimated value of *Y* when $X = 0$. Another way to put it is: *a* is the estimated value of *Y* where the regression line crosses the *Y*-axis when *X* is zero.

b is the slope of the line, or the average change in Y' for each change of one unit (either increase or decrease) in the independent variable X.
X is any value of the independent variable that is selected.

It should be noted that the linear regression equation for the sample of salespeople is just an estimate of the relationship between the two variables in the population. Thus, the values of a and b in the regression equation are usually referred to as the **estimated regression coefficients,** or simply the **regression coefficients.**

The formulas for b and a are:

SLOPE OF THE REGRESSION LINE $$b = \frac{n(\Sigma XY) - (\Sigma X)(\Sigma Y)}{n(\Sigma X^2) - (\Sigma X)^2} \qquad \textbf{[12–5]}$$

***Y*-INTERCEPT** $$a = \frac{\Sigma Y}{n} - b\frac{\Sigma X}{n} \qquad \textbf{[12–6]}$$

where:

ΣX is the sum of the values of the independent variable.
ΣY is the sum of the values of the dependent variable.
n is the number of items in the sample.
ΣXY is the sum of the products of the two variables.
ΣX^2 is the sum of the squares of the independent variable.

Statistics in Action

Sir Francis Galton compared the heights of parents with the heights of their children. He converted the heights of parents and their children to z-values and noted that the children's z-value deviated less from the mean than did the value for their parents. He called this "regression" toward the mean. This discovery formed the basis of regression analysis.

EXAMPLE

Recall the example involving Copier Sales of America. The sales manager gathered information on the number of sales calls made and the number of copiers sold for a random sample of 10 sales representatives. As a part of her presentation at the upcoming sales meeting, Ms. Bancer, the sales manager, would like to offer specific information about the relationship between the number of sales calls and the number of copiers sold. Use the least squares method to determine a linear equation to express the relationship between the two variables. What is the expected number of copiers sold by a representative who makes 20 calls?

SOLUTION

Table 12–4 repeats the sample information from Table 12–2. It also includes the sums needed in formulas (12–5) and (12–6) to calculate the regression equation.

The calculations necessary to determine the regression equation are as follows:

$$b = \frac{n(\Sigma XY) - \Sigma X \Sigma Y}{n\Sigma X^2 - (\Sigma X)^2} = \frac{10(10{,}800) - (220)(450)}{10(5{,}600) - (220)^2} = 1.1842$$

$$a = \frac{\Sigma Y}{n} - b\frac{\Sigma X}{n} = \frac{450}{10} - (1.1842)\frac{220}{10} = 18.9476$$

Thus, the regression equation is $Y' = 18.9476 + 1.1842X$. So if a salesperson makes 20 calls, they can expect to sell 42.6316 copiers, found by $Y' = 18.9476 + 1.1842X = 18.9476 + 1.1842(20)$. The b value of 1.1842 means that for each additional sales call made the sales representative can expect to increase the number of copiers sold by about 1.2. To put it another way, five additional sales calls in a month will result in about six more copiers being sold [1.1842(5) = 5.921].

TABLE 12–4 Calculations Needed for Determining the Least Squares Regression Equation

Sales Representative	Sales Calls (*X*)	Copiers Sold (*Y*)	X^2	Y^2	*XY*
Tom Keller	20	30	400	900	600
Jeff Hall	40	60	1,600	3,600	2,400
Brian Virost	20	40	400	1,600	800
Greg Fish	30	60	900	3,600	1,800
Susan Welch	10	30	100	900	300
Carlos Ramirez	10	40	100	1,600	400
Rich Niles	20	40	400	1,600	800
Mike Kiel	20	50	400	2,500	1,000
Mark Reynolds	20	30	400	900	600
Soni Jones	30	70	900	4,900	2,100
Total	220	450	5,600	22,100	10,800

The *a* value of 18.9476 is the point where the equation crosses the *Y*-axis. A literal translation is that if no sales calls are made, that is, $X = 0$, 18.9476 copiers will be sold. Note that $X = 0$ is outside the range of values included in the sample and, therefore, should not be used to estimate the number of copiers sold. The sales calls ranged from 10 to 40, so estimates should be made within that range.

Drawing the Line of Regression

The least squares equation, $Y' = 18.9476 + 1.1842X$, can be drawn on the scatter diagram. The first sales representative in the sample is Tom Keller. He made 20 calls. His estimated number of copiers sold is $Y' = 18.9476 + 1.1842(20) = 42.6316$. The plot $X = 20$ and $Y = 42.6316$ is located by moving to 20 on the *X*-axis and then going vertically to 42.6316. The other points on the regression equation can be determined by substituting the particular value of *X* into the regression equation.

Sales Representative	Sales Calls (*X*)	Estimated Sales (*Y'*)	Sales Representative	Sales Calls (*X*)	Estimated Sales (*Y'*)
Tom Keller	20	42.6316	Carlos Ramirez	10	30.7896
Jeff Hall	40	66.3156	Rich Niles	20	42.6316
Brian Virost	20	42.6316	Mike Kiel	20	42.6316
Greg Fish	30	54.4736	Mark Reynolds	20	42.6316
Susan Welch	10	30.7896	Soni Jones	30	54.4736

All the other points are connected to draw the line. See Chart 12–11.

This line has some interesting features. As we have discussed, there is no other line through the data for which the sum of the squared deviations is less. In addition, this line will pass through the points represented by the mean of the *X* values and the mean of the *Y* values, that is, $\bar{X}$ and $\bar{Y}$. In this example $\bar{X} = 22.0$ and $\bar{Y} = 45.0$.

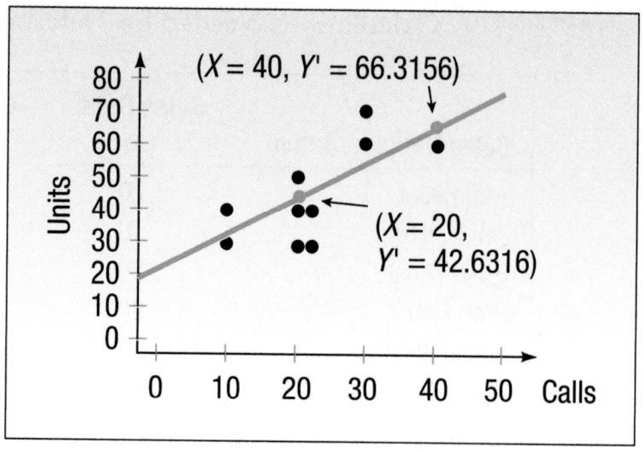

CHART 12–11 The Line of Regression Drawn on the Scatter Diagram

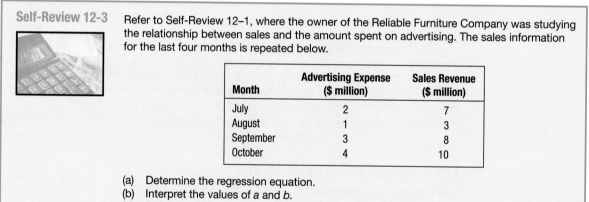

Self-Review 12-3

Refer to Self-Review 12–1, where the owner of the Reliable Furniture Company was studying the relationship between sales and the amount spent on advertising. The sales information for the last four months is repeated below.

Month	Advertising Expense ($ million)	Sales Revenue ($ million)
July	2	7
August	1	3
September	3	8
October	4	10

(a) Determine the regression equation.
(b) Interpret the values of *a* and *b*.
(c) Estimate sales when $3 million is spent on advertising.

Exercises

Note: It is suggested that you save your values for ΣX, ΣX^2, ΣXY, ΣY, and ΣY^2, as these exercises will be referred to later in the chapter.

11. The following sample observations were randomly selected.

X:	4	5	3	6	10
Y:	4	6	5	7	7

a. Determine the regression equation.
b. Determine the value of Y' when X is 7.

12. The following sample observations were randomly selected.

X:	5	3	6	3	4	4	6	8
Y:	13	15	7	12	13	11	9	5

a. Determine the regression equation.
b. Determine the value of Y' when X is 7.

13. The Bradford Electric Illuminating Company is studying the relationship between kilowatt-hours (thousands) used and the number of rooms in a private single-family residence. A random sample of 10 homes yielded the following.

Number of Rooms	Kilowatt-Hours (thousands)	Number of Rooms	Kilowatt-Hours (thousands)
12	9	8	6
9	7	10	8
14	10	10	10
6	5	5	4
10	8	7	7

a. Determine the regression equation.
b. Determine the number of kilowatt-hours, in thousands, for a six-room house.

14. Mr. James McWhinney, president of Daniel-James Financial Services, believes there is a relationship between the number of client contacts and the dollar amount of sales. To document this assertion, Mr. McWhinney gathered the following sample information. The X column indicates the number of client contacts last month, and the Y column shows the value of sales ($ thousands) last month for each client sampled.

Number of Contacts, X	Sales ($ thousands), Y	Number of Contacts, X	Sales ($ thousands), Y
14	24	23	30
12	14	48	90
20	28	50	85
16	30	55	120
46	80	50	110

a. Determine the regression equation.
b. Determine the estimated sales if 40 contacts are made.

15. A recent article in *Business Week* listed the "Best Small Companies." We are interested in the current results of the companies' sales and earnings. A random sample of 12 companies was selected and the sales and earnings, in millions of dollars, are reported below.

Company	Sales ($ millions)	Earnings ($ millions)	Company	Sales ($ millions)	Earnings ($ millions)
Papa John's International	$89.2	$4.9	Checkmate Electronics	$17.5	$ 2.6
Applied Innovation	18.6	4.4	Royal Grip	11.9	1.7
Integracare	18.2	1.3	M-Wave	19.6	3.5
Wall Data	71.7	8.0	Serving-N-Slide	51.2	8.2
Davidson Associates	58.6	6.6	Daig	28.6	6.0
Chico's Fas	46.8	4.1	Cobra Golf	69.2	12.8

Let sales be the independent variable and earnings be the dependent variable.
a. Draw a scatter diagram.
b. Compute the coefficient of correlation.
c. Compute the coefficient of determination.
d. Interpret your findings in parts b and c.
e. Determine the regression equation.
f. For a small company with $50.0 million in sales, estimate the earnings.

16. We are studying mutual bond funds for the purpose of investing in several funds. For this particular study, we want to focus on the assets of a fund and its five-year performance.

The question is: Can the five-year rate of return be estimated based on the assets of the fund? Nine mutual funds were selected at random, and their assets and rates of return are shown below.

Fund	Assets ($ millions)	Return (%)	Fund	Assets ($ millions)	Return (%)
AARP High Quality Bond	$622.2	10.8	MFS Bond A	$494.5	11.6
Babson Bond L	160.4	11.3	Nichols Income	158.3	9.5
Compass Capital Fixed Income	275.7	11.4	T. Raive Price Short-term	681.0	8.2
Galaxy Bond Retail	433.2	9.1	Thompson Income B	241.3	6.8
Keystone Custodian B-1	437.9	9.2			

a. Draw a scatter diagram.
b. Compute the coefficient of correlation.
c. Compute the coefficient of determination.
d. Write a brief report of your findings for parts b and c.
e. Determine the regression equation. Use assets as the independent variable.
f. For a fund with $400.0 million in sales, determine the five-year rate of return (in percent).

17. Refer to Exercise 5.
    a. Determine the regression equation.
    b. Estimate the number of crimes for a city with 20 police.
    c. Interpret the regression equation.
18. Refer to Exercise 6.
    a. Determine the regression equation.
    b. Estimate the selling price of a 10-year-old car.
    c. Interpret the regression equation.

The Standard Error of Estimate

Note in the preceding scatter diagram (Chart 12–11) that all of the points do not lie exactly on the regression line. If they all were on the line, and if the number of observations were sufficiently large, there would be no error in estimating the number of units sold. To put it another way, if all the points were on the regression line, units sold could be predicted with 100 percent accuracy. Thus, there would be no error in predicting the Y variable based on an X variable. This is true in the following hypothetical case (see Chart 12–12). Theoretically, if $X = 4$, then an exact Y of 100 could be predicted with 100

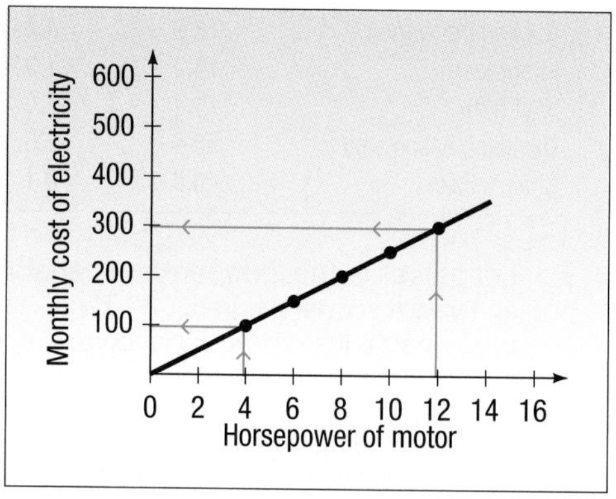

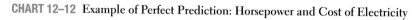

CHART 12–12 Example of Perfect Prediction: Horsepower and Cost of Electricity

percent confidence. Or if $X = 12$, then $Y = 300$. Because there is no difference between the observed values and the predicted values, there is no error in this estimate.

Perfect prediction unrealistic in business

Perfect prediction in economics and business is practically impossible. For example, the revenue for the year from gasoline sales (Y) based on the number of automobile registrations (X) as of a certain date could no doubt be approximated fairly closely, but the prediction would not be exact to the nearest dollar, or probably even to the nearest thousand dollars. Even predictions of tensile strength of steel wires based on the outside diameters of the wires are not always exact due to slight differences in the composition of the steel.

What is needed, then, is a measure that describes how precise the prediction of Y is based on X or, conversely, how inaccurate the estimate might be. This measure is called the **standard error of estimate.** The standard error of estimate, symbolized by $s_{y \cdot x}$, is the same concept as the standard deviation discussed in Chapter 3. The standard deviation measures the dispersion around the mean. The standard error of estimate measures the dispersion about the regression line.

STANDARD ERROR OF ESTIMATE A measure of the scatter, or dispersion, of the observed values around the line of regression.

The standard error of estimate is found by the following equation. Note that the equation is quite similar to the one for the standard deviation of a sample.

STANDARD ERROR OF ESTIMATE

$$s_{y \cdot x} = \sqrt{\frac{\Sigma(Y - Y')^2}{n - 2}} \quad \textbf{[12–7]}$$

The standard deviation is based on squared deviations from the mean, whereas the standard error of estimate is based on squared deviations from the regression line. If the squared deviations result in a small total, this means that the regression line is representative of the data. If the squared deviations are a large value, then the regression line may not represent the data.

EXAMPLE

Recall the example involving Copier Sales of America. The sales manager determined the least squares regression equation to be $Y' = 18.9476 + 1.1842X$, where Y refers to the number of copiers sold and X the number of sales calls made. Determine the standard error of estimate as a measure of how well the values fit the regression line.

SOLUTION

To find the standard error, we begin by finding the difference between the value, Y, and the value estimated from the regression equation, Y'. Next we square this difference, that is, $(Y - Y')^2$. We do this for each of the n observations and sum the results. That is, we compute $\Sigma(Y - Y')^2$, which is the numerator of formula 12–7. Finally, we divide by the number of observations minus 2. Why minus 2? We lose a degree of freedom each for estimating the intercept value, a, and the slope value, b. The details of the calculations are summarized in Table 12–5.

Statistics in Action

Studies indicate that for both men and women, those who are considered good looking earn higher wages than those who are not. In addition, for men there is a correlation between height and salary. For each additional inch of height, a man can expect to earn an additional \$250 per year. So a man 6'6"· tall receives a \$3,000 "stature" bonus over his 5'6" counterpart. Being overweight or underweight is also related to earnings, particularly among women. A study of young women showed the heaviest 10 percent earned about 6 percent less than their lighter counterparts.

TABLE 12–5 Computations Needed for the Standard Error of Estimate

Sales Representative	Actual Sales (Y)	Estimated Sales (Y')	Deviation ($Y - Y'$)	Deviation Squared ($(Y - Y')^2$)
Tom Keller	30	42.6316	−12.6316	159.557
Jeff Hall	60	66.3156	−6.3156	39.887
Brian Virost	40	42.6316	−2.6316	6.925
Greg Fish	60	54.4736	5.5264	30.541
Susan Welch	30	30.7896	−0.7896	0.623
Carlos Ramirez	40	30.7896	9.2104	84.831
Rich Niles	40	42.6316	−2.6316	6.925
Mike Kiel	50	42.6316	7.3684	54.293
Mark Reynolds	30	42.6316	−12.6316	159.557
Soni Jones	70	54.4736	15.5264	241.069
			0.0000	784.208

The standard error of estimate is 9.901, found by using formula 12–7.

$$s_{y \cdot x} = \sqrt{\frac{\Sigma(Y - Y')^2}{n - 2}} = \sqrt{\frac{784.208}{10 - 2}} = 9.901$$

The deviations $(Y - Y')$ are the vertical deviations from the regression line. To illustrate, the 10 deviations from Table 12–5 are shown in Chart 12–13. Note in Table 12–5 that the sum of the signed deviations is zero. This indicates that the positive deviations (above the regression line) are offset by the negative deviations (below the regression line).

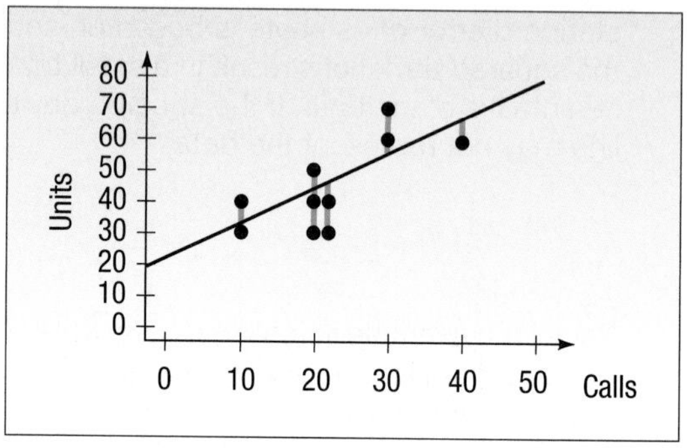

CHART 12–13 Sales Calls and Copiers Sold for 10 Salespeople

Formula 12–7 for the standard error of estimate was applied to show the similarity in concept and computation between the standard deviation and the standard error of estimate. Suppose a large number of observations are being studied, and the numbers are large. Computing each Y' point on the regression line and then squaring the differences—that is, $(Y - Y')^2$—would be rather tedious. The following formula is algebraically equivalent to formula 12–7 but is much easier to use.

COMPUTATION FORMULA FOR THE STANDARD ERROR OF ESTIMATE

$$s_{y \cdot x} = \sqrt{\frac{\Sigma Y^2 - a(\Sigma Y) - b(\Sigma XY)}{n - 2}} \quad \textbf{[12–8]}$$

The squares, sums, and other numbers for the Copier Sales of America example were calculated in Table 12–4. Inserting these values into the formula:

$$s_{y \cdot x} = \sqrt{\frac{22{,}100 - 18.9476(450) - 1.1842(10{,}800)}{10 - 2}}$$

$$= 9.901$$

This is the same standard error of estimate as computed previously. How do we interpret 9.901? Think of it as the typical vertical distance of the observation from the regression line.

Software eases computation when finding the least squares regression line, calculating fitted values, or finding the standard error. The Excel output from the Copier Sales of America example is included below. The slope and intercept are in the column "Coefficients" (cells F17 and F18). The fitted values for each sales representative are the column "Predicted Sales" (cells F23:F32). The "Residuals" or differences between the actual and the estimated values are in the next column (cells G23:G32). The standard error of estimate is in cell F7. All of these values are highlighted below.

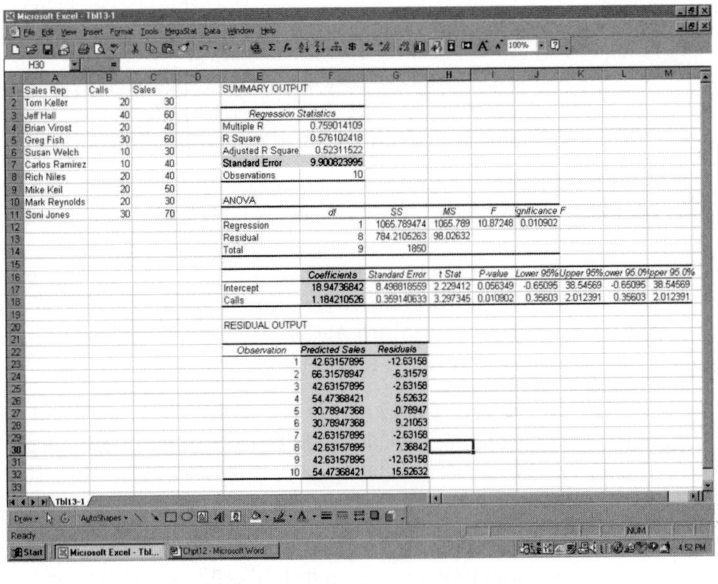

Sales Rep	Calls	Sales
Tom Keller	20	30
Jeff Hall	40	60
Brian Virost	20	40
Greg Fish	30	60
Susan Welch	10	30
Carlos Ramirez	10	40
Rich Niles	20	40
Mike Keil	20	50
Mark Reynolds	20	30
Soni Jones	30	70

SUMMARY OUTPUT

Regression Statistics	
Multiple R	0.759014109
R Square	0.576102418
Adjusted R Square	0.52311522
Standard Error	9.900823995
Observations	10

ANOVA

	df	SS	MS	F	ignificance F
Regression	1	1065.789474	1065.789	10.87248	0.010902
Residual	8	784.2105263	98.02632		
Total	9	1850			

	Coefficients	Standard Error	t Stat	P-value	Lower 95%	Upper 95%	ower 95.0%	pper 95.0%
Intercept	18.94736842	8.498818559	2.229412	0.056349	-0.65095	38.54569	-0.65095	38.54569
Calls	1.184210526	0.359140633	3.297345	0.010902	0.35603	2.012391	0.35603	2.012391

RESIDUAL OUTPUT

Observation	Predicted Sales	Residuals
1	42.63157895	-12.63158
2	66.31578947	-6.31579
3	42.63157895	-2.63158
4	54.47368421	5.52632
5	30.78947368	-0.78947
6	30.78947368	9.21053
7	42.63157895	-2.63158
8	42.63157895	7.36842
9	42.63157895	-12.63158
10	54.47368421	15.52632

Assumptions Underlying Linear Regression

To properly apply linear regression, several assumptions must be met. Chart 12–14 illustrates these assumptions.

1. For each value of X, there is a group of Y values. These Y values follow the normal distribution.
2. The means of these normal distributions lie on the regression line.
3. The standard deviations of these normal distributions are all the same. The best estimate we have of this common standard deviation is the standard error of estimate ($s_{y \cdot x}$).

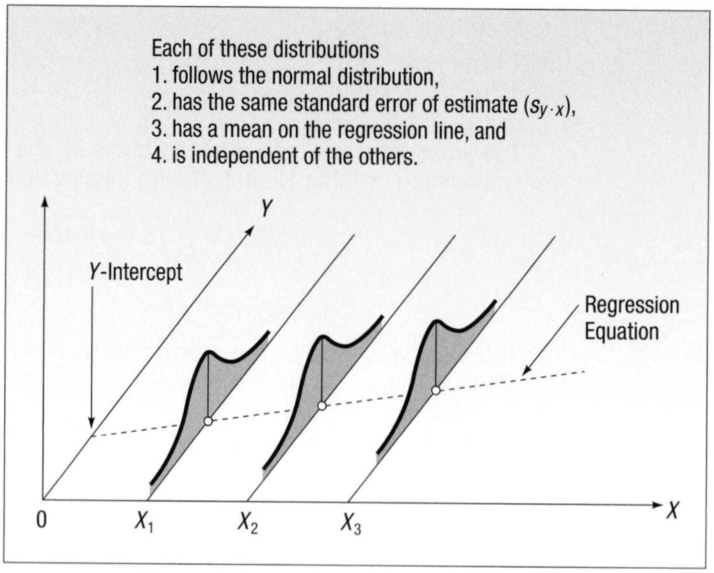
Each of these distributions
1. follows the normal distribution,
2. has the same standard error of estimate ($s_{y \cdot x}$),
3. has a mean on the regression line, and
4. is independent of the others.
Y
Y-Intercept
Regression Equation
0
X_1
X_2
X_3
X

CHART 12–14 Regression Assumptions Shown Graphically

4. The *Y* values are statistically independent. This means that in selecting a sample a particular *X* does not depend on any other value of *X*. This assumption is particularly important when data are collected over a period of time. In such situations, the errors for a particular time period are often correlated with those of other time periods.

Recall from Chapter 6 that if the values follow a normal distribution, then the mean plus or minus one standard deviation will encompass 68 percent of the observations, the mean plus or minus two standard deviations will encompass 95 percent of the observations, and the mean plus or minus three standard deviations will encompass virtually all of the observations. The same relationship exists between the predicted values Y' and the standard error of estimate ($s_{y \cdot x}$).

1. $Y' \pm s_{y \cdot x}$ will include the middle 68 percent of the observations.
2. $Y' \pm 2s_{y \cdot x}$ will include the middle 95 percent of the observations.
3. $Y' \pm 3s_{y \cdot x}$ will include virtually all the observations.

We can now relate these assumptions to Copier Sales of America, where we studied the relationship between the number of sales calls and the number of copiers sold. Assume that we took a much larger sample than $n = 10$, but that the standard error of estimate was still 9.901. If we drew a parallel line 9.901 units above the regression line and another 9.901 units below the regression line, about 68 percent of the points would fall between the two lines. Similarly, a line 19.862 [$2s_{y \cdot x} = 2(9.901)$] units above the regression line and another 19.802 units below the regression line should include about 95 percent of the data values.

As a rough check, refer to the second column from the right in Table 12–5 on page 402, i.e., the column headed "Deviation." Three of the 10 deviations exceed one standard error of estimate. That is, the deviation of −12.6316 for Tom Keller, −12.6316 for Mark Reynolds, and +15.5264 for Soni Jones all exceed the value of 9.901, which is one standard error from the regression line. All of the values are within 19.802 units of the regression line. To put it another way, 7 of the 10 deviations in the sample are within one standard error of the regression line and all are within two—a good result for a relatively small sample.

Self-Review 12–4

Refer to Self-Reviews 12–1 and 12–3, where the owner of Reliable Furniture was studying the relationship between sales and the amount spent on advertising. Determine the standard error of estimate.

Exercises

19. Refer to Exercise 11.
   a. Determine the standard error of estimate.
   b. Suppose a large sample is selected (instead of just five). About 68 percent of the predictions would be between what two values?

20. Refer to Exercise 12.
   a. Determine the standard error of estimate.
   b. Suppose a large sample is selected (instead of just eight). About 95 percent of the predictions would be between what two values?

21. Refer to Exercise 13.
   a. Determine the standard error of estimate.
   b. Suppose a large sample is selected (instead of just 10). About 95 percent of the predictions regarding kilowatt-hours would occur between what two values?

22. Refer to Exercise 14.
   a. Determine the standard error of estimate.
   b. Suppose a large sample is selected (instead of just 10). About 95 percent of the predictions regarding sales would occur between what two values?

23. Refer to Exercise 5. Determine the standard error of estimate.

24. Refer to Exercise 6. Determine the standard error of estimate.

Confidence Intervals and Prediction Intervals

The standard error of estimate is also used to establish confidence intervals when the sample size is large and the scatter around the regression line approximates the normal distribution. In our example involving the number of sales calls and the number of copiers sold, the sample size is small; hence, we need a correction factor to account for the size of the sample. In addition, when we move away from the mean of the independent variable, our estimates are subject to more variation, and we also need to adjust for this.

We are interested in providing interval estimates of two types. The first, which is called a **confidence interval,** reports the *mean* value of Y for a given X. The second type of estimate is called a **prediction interval,** and it reports the *range of values* of Y for a *particular* value of X. To explain further, suppose we estimate the salary of executives in the retail industry based on their years of experience. If we want an interval estimate of the mean salary of *all* retail executives with 20 years of experience, we calculate a confidence interval. If we want an estimate of the salary of Curtis Bender, a particular retail executive with 20 years of experience, we calculate a prediction interval.

To determine the confidence interval for the mean value of Y for a given X, the formula is:

CONFIDENCE INTERVAL FOR THE MEAN OF *Y*, GIVEN *X*.

$$Y' \pm t(s_{y \cdot x})\sqrt{\frac{1}{n} + \frac{(X - \bar{X})^2}{\Sigma X^2 - \frac{(\Sigma X)^2}{n}}} \qquad \textbf{[12–9]}$$

where:

Y' is the predicted value for any selected X value.
X is any selected value of X.
$\overline{X}$ is the mean of the Xs, found by $\Sigma X/n$.
n is the number of observations.
$s_{y \cdot x}$ is the standard error of estimate.
t is the value of t from Appendix F with $n - 2$ degrees of freedom.

It is sufficient to again note that the concept of t was developed by William Gossett in the early 1900s. He noticed that $\overline{X} \pm z(s)$ was not precisely correct for small samples. He observed, for example, for samples of size 120, that 95 percent of the items fell within $\overline{X} \pm 1.98s$ instead of $\overline{X} \pm 1.96s$. This difference is not too critical, but note what happens as the sample size becomes smaller:

df	*t*
120	1.980
60	2.000
21	2.080
10	2.228
3	3.182

This is logical. The smaller the sample, the larger the possible error. The increase in the t value compensates for this possibility.

EXAMPLE

We return to the Copier Sales of America illustration. Determine a 95 percent confidence interval for all sales representatives who make 25 calls and for Sheila Baker, a West Coast sales representative who made 25 calls.

SOLUTION

We use formula 12–9 to determine a confidence interval. Table 12–6 includes the necessary totals and a repeat of the information of Table 12–2 on page 386.

TABLE 12–6 Calculations Needed for Determining the Confidence Interval and Prediction Interval

Sales Representative	Sales Calls (X)	Copiers Sold (Y)	X^2	Y^2	XY
Tom Keller	20	30	400	900	600
Jeff Hall	40	60	1,600	3,600	2,400
Brian Virost	20	40	400	1,600	800
Greg Fish	30	60	900	3,600	1,800
Susan Welch	10	30	100	900	300
Carlos Ramirez	10	40	100	1,600	400
Rich Niles	20	40	400	1,600	800
Mike Kiel	20	50	400	2,500	1,000
Mark Reynolds	20	30	400	900	600
Soni Jones	30	70	900	4,900	2,100
Total	220	450	5,600	22,100	10,800

The first step is to determine the number of copiers we expect a sales representative to sell if he or she makes 25 calls. It is 48.5526, found by $Y' = 18.9476 + 1.1842X = 18.9476 + 1.1842(25)$.

To find the t value, we need to first know the number of degrees of freedom. In this case the degrees of freedom is $n - 2 = 10 - 2 = 8$. We set the confidence level at 95 percent. To find the value of t, move down the left-hand column to 8 degrees of freedom, then move across to the column with the 95 percent level of confidence. The value of t is 2.306.

In the previous section we calculated the standard error of estimate to be 9.901, $X = 25$, and from Table 12–6 $\Sigma X = 220$ and $\Sigma X^2 = 5{,}600$. In addition $\bar{X} = \Sigma X/n = 220/10 = 22$. Inserting these values in formula 12–9, we can determine the confidence interval.

$$\text{Confidence interval} = Y' \pm t(s_{y \cdot x})\sqrt{\frac{1}{n} + \frac{(X - \bar{X})^2}{\Sigma X^2 - \frac{(\Sigma X)^2}{n}}}$$

$$= 48.5526 \pm 2.306(9.901)\sqrt{\frac{1}{10} + \frac{(25 - 22)^2}{5{,}600 - \frac{(220)^2}{10}}}$$

$$= 48.5526 \pm 7.6356$$

Thus, the 95 percent confidence interval of copiers sold for all sales representatives who make 25 calls is from 40.9170 up to 56.1882. To interpret, let's round the values. If a sales representative makes 25 calls, he or she can expect to sell 48.6 copiers. It is likely that copiers sold will range from 40.9 to 56.2 copiers.

To determine the prediction interval for a particular value of Y for a given X, formula 12–9 is modified slightly: A "1" is added under the radical. The formula becomes:

PREDICTION INTERVAL FOR *Y*, GIVEN *X*

$$Y' \pm t(s_{y \cdot x})\sqrt{1 + \frac{1}{n} + \frac{(X - \bar{X})^2}{\Sigma X^2 - \frac{(\Sigma X)^2}{n}}} \quad \textbf{[12–10]}$$

Suppose we want to estimate the number of copiers sold by Sheila Baker, who made 25 sales calls. The 95 percent prediction interval is determined as follows:

$$\text{Prediction Interval} = Y' \pm t(s_{y \cdot x})\sqrt{1 + \frac{1}{n} + \frac{(X - \bar{X})^2}{\Sigma X^2 - \frac{(\Sigma X)^2}{n}}}$$

$$= 48.5526 \pm 2.306(9.901)\sqrt{1 + \frac{1}{10} + \frac{(25 - 22)^2}{5{,}600 - \frac{(220)^2}{10}}}$$

$$= 48.5526 \pm 24.0746$$

Thus, the interval is from 24.478 up to 72.627 copiers. We conclude that the number of copiers sold will be between about 24 and 73 for a particular sales representative. This interval is quite large. It is much larger than the confidence interval for the mean of all sales representatives who made 25 calls. It is logical, however, that there should be more variation in the sales estimate for an individual than for the mean of a group.

The following MINITAB graph shows the relationship between the regression line, the confidence interval, and the prediction interval. The bands for the prediction interval are always further from the regression line than for the confidence interval. Also, as the values of X move away from the mean number of calls (22) in either the positive or the negative direction the confidence interval and prediction interval bands widen. This is caused by the numerator of the right-hand term under the radical in formulas 12–9 and 12–10. That is, as the term $(X - \bar{X})^2$ increases, the widths of the confidence interval and the prediction interval also increase. To put it another way, there is less precision in our estimates as we move away, in either direction, from the mean of the independent variable.

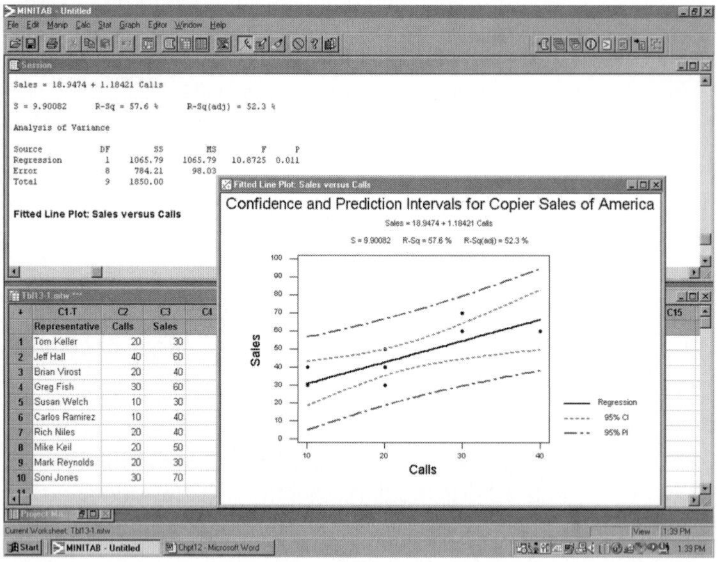

We wish to emphasize again the distinction between a confidence interval and a prediction interval. A confidence interval refers to the mean of all observations for a given value of X and is computed using formula 12–9. A prediction interval refers to a particular observation for a given value of X and is computed using formula 12–10. The prediction interval will always be wider because of the extra "1" under the radical in the second equation.

Self-Review 12-5

Refer to the sample data in Self-Reviews 12–1, 12–3, and 12–4, where the owner of Reliable Furniture was studying the relationship between sales and the amount spent on advertising. The sales information for the last four months is repeated below.

Month	Advertising Expense ($ millions)	Sales Revenue ($ millions)
July	2	7
August	1	3
September	3	8
October	4	10

The regression equation was computed to be $Y' = 1.5 + 2.2X$, and the standard error is 0.9487. Both variables are reported in millions of dollars. Determine the 90 percent confidence interval for the typical month in which $3 million was spent on advertising.

Exercises

25. Refer to Exercise 11.
  a. Determine the .95 confidence interval for the mean predicted when $X = 7$.
  b. Determine the .95 prediction interval for an individual predicted when $X = 7$.

26. Refer to Exercise 12.
  a. Determine the .95 confidence interval for the mean predicted when $X = 7$.
  b. Determine the .95 prediction interval for an individual predicted when $X = 7$.

27. Refer to Exercise 13.
  a. Determine the .95 confidence interval, in thousands of kilowatt-hours, for the mean of all six-room homes.
  b. Determine the .95 prediction interval, in thousands of kilowatt-hours, for a particular six-room home.

28. Refer to Exercise 14.
  a. Determine the .95 confidence interval, in thousands of dollars, for the mean of all sales personnel who make 40 contacts.
  b. Determine the .95 prediction interval, in thousands of dollars, for a particular salesperson who makes 40 contacts.

More on the Coefficient of Determination

Formula 12–2 is a convenient computational formula to determine the coefficient of correlation, r. The coefficient of determination is found by squaring the coefficient of correlation.

To further examine the basic concept of the coefficient of determination, suppose there is interest in the relationship between years on the job, X, and weekly production, Y. Sample data revealed:

Employee	Years on Job, X	Weekly Production, Y
Gordon	14	6
James	7	5
Ford	3	3
Salter	15	9
Artes	11	7

The sample data were plotted in a scatter diagram. Since the relationship between X and Y appears to be linear, a line was drawn through the plots (see Chart 12–15). The equation is $Y' = 2 + 0.4X$.

Note in Chart 12–15 that if we were to use that line to predict weekly production for an employee, in no case would our prediction be exact. That is, there would be some error in each of our predictions. As an example, for Gordon, who has been with the company 14 years, we would predict weekly production to be 7.6 units; however, he produces only 6 units.

To measure the overall error in our prediction, every deviation from the line is squared and the squares summed. The predicted point on the line is designated Y', read Y prime, and the observed point is designated Y. For Gordon, $(Y - Y')^2 = (6 - 7.6)^2 = (-1.6)^2 = 2.56$. Logically, this variation cannot be explained by the independent variable, so it is referred to as the *unexplained variation.* Specifically, we cannot explain why Gordon's production of 6 units is 1.6 units below his predicted production of 7.6 units, based on the number of years he has been on the job.

Unexplained variation

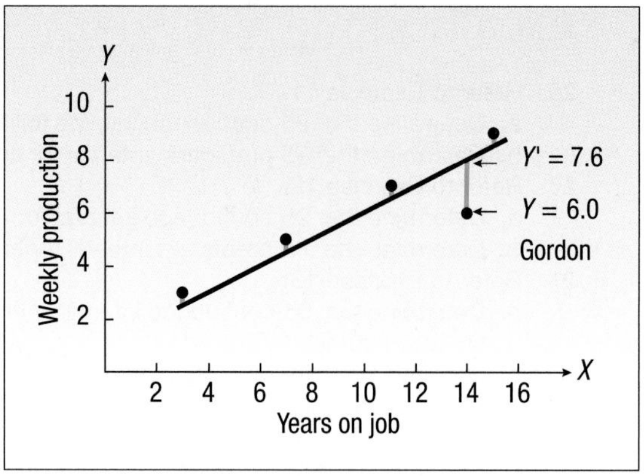

CHART 12–15 Observed Data and the Least Squares Line

The sum of the squared deviations, $\Sigma(Y - Y')^2$, is 4.00. (See Table 12–7.) The term $\Sigma(Y - Y')^2 = 4.00$ is the variation in Y (production) that cannot be predicted from X. It is the "unexplained" variation in Y.

TABLE 12–7 Computations Needed for the Unexplained Variation

	X	Y	Y'	$Y - Y'$	$(Y - Y')^2$
Gordon	14	6	7.6	−1.6	2.56
James	7	5	4.8	0.2	0.04
Ford	3	3	3.2	−0.2	0.04
Salter	15	9	8.0	1.0	1.00
Artes	11	7	6.4	0.6	0.36
Total	50	30		0.0*	4.00

*Must be 0.

Now suppose *only* the Y values (weekly production, in this problem) are known and we want to predict production for every employee. The actual production figures for the employees are 6, 5, 3, 9, and 7 (from Table 12–7). To make these predictions, we could assign the mean weekly production (6 units, found by $\Sigma Y/n = 30/5 = 6$) to each employee. This would keep the sum of the squared prediction errors at a minimum. (Recall from Chapter 3 that the sum of the squared deviations from the arithmetic mean for a set of numbers is smaller than the sum of the squared deviations from any other value, such as the median.) Table 12–8 shows the necessary calculations. The sum of the squared deviations is 20, as shown in Table 12–8. The value 20 is referred to as the *total variation in* Y. What we did to arrive at the total variation in Y is shown diagrammatically in Chart 12–16.

Total variation in Y

Logically, the total variation in Y can be subdivided into unexplained variation and explained variation. To arrive at the explained variation, since we know the total variation and unexplained variation, we simply subtract: Explained variation = Total variation − Unexplained variation. Dividing the explained variation by the total variation gives the coefficient of determination, r^2, which is a proportion. In terms of a formula:

COEFFICIENT OF DETERMINATION

$$r^2 = \frac{\text{Total variation} - \text{Unexplained variation}}{\text{Total variation}} = \frac{\Sigma(Y - \bar{Y})^2 - \Sigma(Y - Y')^2}{\Sigma(Y - \bar{Y})^2} \quad \textbf{[12–11]}$$

In this problem:

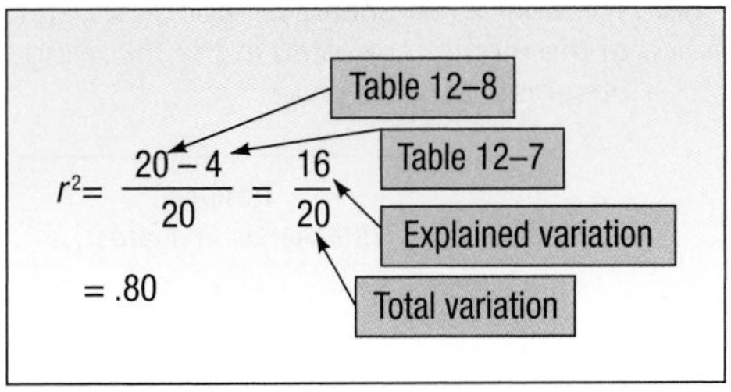

As mentioned, .80 is a proportion. We say that 80 percent of the variation in weekly production, *Y*, is determined, or accounted for, by its linear relationship with *X* (years on the job).

TABLE 12–8 Calculations Needed for the Total Variation in Y

Name	Weekly Production, Y	Mean Weekly Production, $\bar{Y}$	$Y - \bar{Y}$	$(Y - \bar{Y})^2$
Gordon	6	6	0	0
James	5	6	−1	1
Ford	3	6	−3	9
Salter	9	6	3	9
Artes	7	6	1	1
Total			0*	20

*Must be 0.

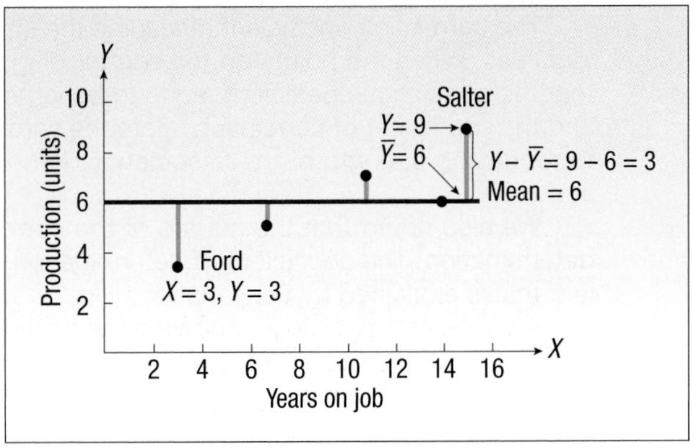

CHART 12–16 Plots Showing Deviations from the Mean of Y

As a check, the computational formula (12–1) for the coefficient of correlation could be used. Squaring r gives the coefficient of determination. Exercise 29 offers a check on the preceding problem.

Exercises

29. Using the preceding problem, involving years on the job and weekly production, verify that the coefficient of determination is in fact .80.

30. The number of shares of Icom, Inc., turned over during a month, and the price at the end of the month, are listed in the following table. Also, the Y' plots on the line going through observed data are given.

Turnover (thousands of shares), X	Actual Price, Y	Estimated Price, Y'
4	\$2	\$2.7
1	1	0.6
5	4	3.4
3	2	2.0
2	1	1.3

a. Draw a scatter diagram. Plot a line through the dots.
b. Compute the coefficient of determination using formula 12–11.
c. As a check, use the computational formula 12–2 for r.
d. Interpret the coefficient of determination.

The Relationships among the Coefficient of Correlation, the Coefficient of Determination, and the Standard Error of Estimate

In an earlier section, we discussed the standard error of estimate, which measures how close the actual values are to the regression line. When the standard error is small, it indicates that the two variables are closely related. In the calculation of the standard error, the key term is $\Sigma(Y - Y')^2$. If the value of this term is small, then the standard error will also be small.

The correlation coefficient measures the strength of the association between two variables. When the points on the scatter diagram appear close to the line, we note that the correlation coefficient tends to be large. Thus, the standard error of estimate and the coefficient of correlation relate the same information but use a different scale to report the strength of the association. However, both measures involve the term $\Sigma(Y - Y')^2$.

We also noted that the square of the correlation coefficient is the coefficient of determination. The coefficient of determination measures the percent of the variation in Y that is explained by the variation in X.

A convenient vehicle for showing the relationship among these three measures is an ANOVA table. This table is similar to the analysis of variance table developed in Chapter 11. In that chapter, the total variation was divided into two components: that due to the *treatments* and that due to *random error.* The concept is similar in regression analysis. The total variation, $\Sigma(Y - \overline{Y})^2$, is divided into two components: (1) that explained by the *regression* (explained by the independent variable) and (2) the *error,* or unexplained variation. These two categories are identified in the first column of the ANOVA table that follows. The column headed "*df*" refers to the degrees of freedom associated with each category. The total number of degrees of freedom is $n - 1$. The number of degrees of freedom in the regression is 1, since there is only one independent variable. The number of degrees of freedom associated with the error term is $n - 2$. The term "SS" located in the middle of the ANOVA table refers to the sum of squares—the variation. The terms are computed as follows:

$$\text{Regression} = \text{SSR} = \Sigma(Y' - \overline{Y})^2$$

$$\text{Error variation} = \text{SSE} = \Sigma(Y - Y')^2$$

$$\text{Total variation} = \text{SS total} = \Sigma(Y - \overline{Y})^2$$

The format for the ANOVA table is:

Source	*df*	SS	MS
Regression	1	SSR	SSR/1
Error	$n - 2$	SSE	SSE/($n - 2$)
Total	$n - 1$	SS total*	

*SS total = SSR + SSE.

The coefficient of determination, r^2, can be obtained directly from the ANOVA table by:

COEFFICIENT OF DETERMINATION

$$r^2 = \frac{\text{SSR}}{\text{SS total}} = 1 - \frac{\text{SSE}}{\text{SS total}} \qquad \textbf{[12–12]}$$

The term "SSR/SS total" is the proportion of the variation in *Y explained* by the independent variable, *X*. Note the effect of the SSE term on r^2. As SSE decreases, r^2 will increase. Conversely, as the standard error decreases, the r^2 term increases.

The standard error of estimate can also be obtained from the ANOVA table using the following equation:

STANDARD ERROR OF ESTIMATE

$$s_{y \cdot x} = \sqrt{\frac{\text{SSE}}{n - 2}} \qquad \textbf{[12–13]}$$

The Copier Sales of America example is used to illustrate the computations of the coefficient of determination and the standard error of estimate from an ANOVA table.

EXAMPLE

In the Copier Sales of America example we studied the relationship between the number of sales calls made and the number of copiers sold. Use a computer software package to determine the least squares regression equation and the ANOVA table. Identify the regression equation, the standard error of estimate, and the coefficient of determination on the computer output. From the ANOVA table on the computer output, determine the coefficient of determination and the standard error of estimate using formulas 12–12 and 12–13.

SOLUTION

Following is the output from Excel.

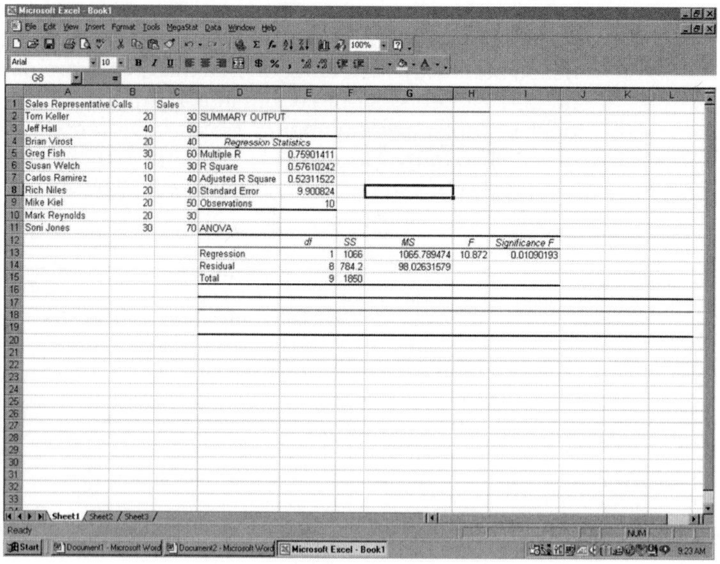

Using formula 12–12 the coefficient of determination is .576, found by

$$r^2 = \frac{\text{SSR}}{\text{SS total}} = \frac{1066}{1850} = .576$$

This is the same value we computed earlier in the chapter, when we found the coefficient of determination by squaring the coefficient of correlation. Again, the interpretation is that the independent variable, *Calls,* explains 57.6 percent of the variation in the number of copiers sold. If we needed the coefficient of correlation, we could find it by taking the square root of the coefficient of determination:

$$r = \sqrt{r^2} = \sqrt{.576} = .759$$

A problem does remain, and that involves the sign for the coefficient of correlation. Recall that the square root of a value could have either a positive or a negative sign. The sign of the coefficient of correlation will always be the same as that of the slope. That is, b and r will always have the same sign. In this case the sign is positive, so the coefficient of correlation is .759.

To find the standard error of estimate, we use formula 12–13:

$$s_{y \cdot x} = \sqrt{\frac{\text{SSE}}{n-2}} = \sqrt{\frac{784.2}{10-2}} = 9.901$$

Again, this is the same value calculated earlier in the chapter. These values are identified on the Excel computer output.

Exercises

31. Given the following ANOVA table:

SOURCE	DF	SS	MS	F
Regression	1	1000.0	1000.00	26.00
Error	13	500.0	38.46	
Total	14	1500.0		

a. Determine the coefficient of determination.
b. Assuming a direct relationship between the variables, what is the coefficient of correlation?
c. Determine the standard error of estimate.

32. On the first statistics exam the coefficient of determination between the hours studied and the grade earned was 80 percent. The standard error of estimate was 10. There were 20 students in the class. Develop an ANOVA table.

Chapter Outline

I. A scatter diagram is a graphic tool to portray the relationship between two variables.
  A. The dependent variable is scaled on the Y-axis and is the variable being estimated.
  B. The independent variable is scaled on the X-axis and is the variable used as the estimator.

II. The coefficient of correlation measures the strength of the association between two variables.
  A. Both variables must be at least the interval scale of measurement.
  B. The coefficient of correlation can range from -1.00 up to 1.00.
  C. If the correlation between two variables is 0, there is no association between them.
  D. A value of 1.00 indicates perfect positive correlation, and -1.00 perfect negative correlation.
  E. A positive sign means there is a direct relationship between the variables, and a negative sign means there is an inverse relationship.
  F. It is designated by the letter r and found by the following equations:

$$r = \frac{\Sigma(X - \bar{X})(Y - \bar{Y})}{(n - 1)\, s_x\, s_y} = \frac{n(\Sigma XY) - (\Sigma X)(\Sigma Y)}{\sqrt{[n(\Sigma X^2) - (\Sigma X)^2]\,[n(\Sigma Y^2) - (\Sigma Y)^2]}} \qquad \textbf{[12–1, 12–2]}$$

  G. The following equation is used to determine whether the correlation in the population is different from 0.

$$t = \frac{r\sqrt{n - 2}}{\sqrt{1 - r^2}} \qquad \textbf{[12–3]}$$

III. The coefficient of determination is the fraction of the variation in one variable that is explained by the variation in the other variable.
  A. It ranges from 0 to 1.0.
  B. It is the square of the coefficient of correlation.

IV. In regression analysis we estimate one variable based on another variable.
  A. The variable being estimated is the dependent variable.
  B. The variable used to make the estimate is the independent variable.
    1. The relationship between the variables must be linear.
    2. Both the independent and the dependent variable must be interval or ratio scale.
    3. The least squares criterion is used to determine the regression equation.

V. The least squares regression line is of the form $Y' = a + bX$.
  A. Y' is the estimated value of Y for a selected value of X.
  B. b is the slope of the line.
    1. It shows the amount of change in Y' for a change of 1 in X.
    2. A positive value for b indicates a direct relationship between the two variables, and a negative value an inverse relationship.
    3. The sign of b and the sign of r, the coefficient of correlation, are always the same.
    4. b is computed using the following equation.

$$b = \frac{n(\Sigma XY) - (\Sigma X)(\Sigma Y)}{n(\Sigma X^2) - (\Sigma X)^2} \qquad \textbf{[12–5]}$$

  C. a is the constant or intercept.
    1. It is the value of Y' when $X = 0$.

2. a is computed using the following equation.

$$a = \frac{\Sigma Y}{n} - b\frac{\Sigma X}{n} \qquad \textbf{[12–6]}$$

D. X is the value of the independent variable.

VI. The standard error of estimate measures the variation around the regression line.
   A. It is in the same units as the dependent variable.
   B. It is based on squared deviations from the regression line.
   C. Small values indicate that the points cluster closely about the regression line.
   D. It is computed using the following formula.

$$s_{y \cdot x} = \sqrt{\frac{\Sigma(Y - Y')^2}{n-2}} = \sqrt{\frac{\Sigma Y^2 - a(\Sigma Y) - b(\Sigma XY)}{n-2}} \qquad \textbf{[12–7, 12–8]}$$

VII. Inference about linear regression is based on the following assumptions.
   A. For a given value of X, the values of Y are normally distributed about the line of regression.
   B. The standard deviation of each of the normal distributions is the same for all values of X and is estimated by the standard error of estimate.
   C. The deviations from the regression line are independent, with no pattern to the size or direction.

VIII. There are two types of interval estimates.
   A. In a confidence interval the mean value of Y is estimated for a given value of X.
      1. It is computed from the following formula.

$$Y' \pm t(s_{y \cdot x})\sqrt{\frac{1}{n} + \frac{(X - \bar{X})^2}{\Sigma X^2 - \frac{(\Sigma X)^2}{n}}} \qquad \textbf{[12–9]}$$

      2. The width of the interval is affected by the level of confidence, the size of the standard error of estimate, and the size of the sample, as well as the value of the independent variable.
   B. In a prediction interval the individual value of Y is estimated for a given value of X.
      1. It is computed from the following formula.

$$Y' \pm t(s_{y \cdot x})\sqrt{1 + \frac{1}{n} + \frac{(X - \bar{X})^2}{\Sigma X^2 - \frac{(\Sigma X)^2}{n}}} \qquad \textbf{[12–10]}$$

      2. The difference between formulas 12–9 and 12–10 is the 1 under the radical.
         a. The prediction interval will be wider than the confidence interval.
         b. The prediction interval is also based on the level of confidence, the size of the standard error of estimate, the size of the sample, and the value of the independent variable.

Pronunciation Key

SYMBOL	MEANING	PRONUNCIATION
ΣXY	Sum of the products of X and Y	*Sum X Y*
ρ	Coefficient of correlation in the population	*Rho*
Y'	Estimated value of Y	*Y prime*
$s_{y \cdot x}$	Standard error of estimate	*s sub y dot x*
r^2	Coefficient of determination	*r square*

Chapter Exercises

33. A major airline selected a random sample of 25 flights and found that the correlation between the number of passengers and the total weight, in pounds, of luggage stored in the luggage compartment is 0.94. Using the .05 significance level, can we conclude that there is a positive association between the two variables?

34. A sociologist claims that the success of students in college (measured by their GPA) is related to their family's income. For a sample of 20 students, the coefficient of correlation is 0.40. Using the 0.01 significance level, can we conclude that there is a positive correlation between the variables?

35. An Environmental Protection Agency study of 12 automobiles revealed a correlation of 0.47 between the engine size and performance. At the .01 significance level, can we conclude that there is a positive association between these variables? What is the *p*-value? Interpret.

36. A study of college soccer games revealed the correlation between the number of shots attempted and the number of goals scored to be 0.21 for a sample of 20 games. Is it reasonable to conclude that there is a positive correlation between the two variables? Use the .05 significance level. Determine the *p*-value.

37. A sample of 30 used cars sold by Northcut Motors in 2002 revealed that the correlation between the selling price and the number of miles driven was −.45. At the .05 significance level, can we conclude that there is a negative association in the population between the two variables?

38. For a sample of 32 large U.S. cities, the correlation between the mean number of square feet per office worker and the mean monthly rental rate in the central business district is −.363. At the .05 significance level, can we conclude that there is a negative association in the population between the two variables?

39. What is the relationship between the amount spent per week on food and the size of the family? Do larger families spend more on food? A sample of 10 families in the Chicago area revealed the following figures for family size and the amount spent on food per week.

Family Size	Amount Spent on Food	Family Size	Amount Spent on Food
3	$ 99	3	$111
6	104	4	74
5	151	4	91
6	129	5	119
6	142	3	91

a. Compute the coefficient of correlation.
b. Determine the coefficient of determination.
c. Can we conclude that there is a positive association between the amount spent on food and the family size? Use the .05 significance level.

40. A sample of 12 homes sold last week in St. Paul, Minnesota, is selected. Can we conclude that as the size of the home (reported below in thousands of square feet) increases, the selling price (reported in $ thousands) also increases?

Home Size (thousands of square feet)	Selling Price ($ thousands)	Home Size (thousands of square feet)	Selling Price ($ thousands)
1.4	100	1.3	110
1.3	110	0.8	85
1.2	105	1.2	105
1.1	120	0.9	75
1.4	80	1.1	70
1.0	105	1.1	95

a. Compute the coefficient of correlation.
b. Determine the coefficient of determination.
c. Can we conclude that there is a positive association between the size of the home and the selling price? Use the .05 significance level.

41. The manufacturer of Cardio Glide exercise equipment wants to study the relationship between the number of months since the glide was purchased and the length of time the equipment was used last week.

Person	Months Owned	Hours Exercised	Person	Months Owned	Hours Exercised
Rupple	12	4	Massa	2	8
Hall	2	10	Sass	8	3
Bennett	6	8	Karl	4	8
Longnecker	9	5	Malrooney	10	2
Phillips	7	5	Veights	5	5

a. Plot the information on a scatter diagram. Let hours of exercise be the dependent variable. Comment on the graph.
b. Determine the coefficient of correlation. Interpret.
c. At the .01 significance level, can we conclude that there is a negative association between the variables?

42. The following regression equation was computed from a sample of 20 observations:

$$Y' = 15 - 5X$$

SSE was found to be 100 and SS total 400.
a. Determine the standard error of estimate.
b. Determine the coefficient of determination.
c. Determine the coefficient of correlation. (Caution: Watch the sign!)

43. An ANOVA table is:

SOURCE	DF	SS	MS	F
Regression	1	50		
Error				
Total	24	500		

a. Complete the ANOVA table.
b. How large was the sample?
c. Determine the standard error of estimate.
d. Determine the coefficient of determination.

44. Following is a regression equation.

$$Y' = 17.08 + 0.16X$$

This information is also available: $s_{y \cdot x} = 4.05$, $\Sigma X = 210$, $\Sigma X^2 = 9{,}850$, and $n = 5$.
a. Estimate the value of Y' when $X = 50$.
b. Develop a 95 percent prediction interval for an individual value of Y for $X = 50$.

45. The National Highway Association is studying the relationship between the number of bidders on a highway project and the winning (lowest) bid for the project. Of particular interest is whether the number of bidders increases or decreases the amount of the winning bid.

Project	Number of Bidders, X	Winning Bid ($ millions), Y	Project	Number of Bidders, X	Winning Bid ($ millions), Y
1	9	5.1	9	6	10.3
2	9	8.0	10	6	8.0
3	3	9.7	11	4	8.8
4	10	7.8	12	7	9.4
5	5	7.7	13	7	8.6
6	10	5.5	14	7	8.1
7	7	8.3	15	6	7.8
8	11	5.5			

a. Determine the regression equation. Interpret the equation. Do more bidders tend to increase or decrease the amount of the winning bid?
b. Estimate the amount of the winning bid if there were seven bidders.
c. A new entrance is to be constructed on the Ohio Turnpike. There are seven bidders on the project. Develop a 95 percent prediction interval for the winning bid.
d. Determine the coefficient of determination. Interpret its value.

46. Mr. William Profit is studying companies going public for the first time. He is particularly interested in the relationship between the size of the offering and the price per share. A sample of 15 companies that recently went public revealed the following information.

Company	Size ($ millions), *X*	Price per Share, *Y*	Company	Size ($ millions), *X*	Price per Share, *Y*
1	9.0	10.8	9	160.7	11.3
2	94.4	11.3	10	96.5	10.6
3	27.3	11.2	11	83.0	10.5
4	179.2	11.1	12	23.5	10.3
5	71.9	11.1	13	58.7	10.7
6	97.9	11.2	14	93.8	11.0
7	93.5	11.0	15	34.4	10.8
8	70.0	10.7			

a. Determine the regression equation.
b. Determine the coefficient of determination. Do you think Mr. Profit should be satisfied with using the size of the offering as the independent variable?

47. Below is information on the price per share and the dividend for a sample of 30 companies.

Company	Price per Share	Dividend	Company	Price per Share	Dividend
1	$20.00	$ 3.14	16	$57.06	$ 9.53
2	22.01	3.36	17	57.40	12.60
3	31.39	0.46	18	58.30	10.43
4	33.57	7.99	19	59.51	7.97
5	35.86	0.77	20	60.60	9.19
6	36.12	8.46	21	64.01	16.50
7	36.16	7.62	22	64.66	16.10
8	37.99	8.03	23	64.74	13.76
9	38.85	6.33	24	64.95	10.54
10	39.65	7.96	25	66.43	21.15
11	43.44	8.95	26	68.18	14.30
12	49.08	9.61	27	69.56	24.42
13	53.73	11.11	28	74.90	11.54
14	54.41	13.28	29	77.91	17.65
15	55.10	10.22	30	80.00	17.36

a. Calculate the regression equation using selling price based on the annual dividend. Interpret the slope value.
b. Determine the coefficient of determination. Interpret its value.
c. Determine the coefficient of correlation. Can you conclude that it is greater than 0 using the .05 significance level?

48. A highway employee performed a regression analysis of the relationship between the number of construction work-zone fatalities and the number of unemployed people in a state. The regression equation is Fatalities = 12.7 +0.000114 (Unemp) and some more of the output is:

Predictor	Coef	SE Coef	T	P
Constant	12.726	8.115	1.57	0.134
Unemp	0.00011386	0.00002896	3.93	0.001

Analysis of Variance

Source	DF	SS	MS	F	P
Regression	1	10354	10354	15.46	0.001
Residual Error	18	12054	670		
Total	19	22408			

a. How many states were in the sample?
b. Determine the standard error of estimate.
c. Determine the coefficient of determination.
d. Determine the coefficient of correlation.
e. At the .05 significance level does the evidence suggest there is a positive association between fatalities and the number unemployed?

49. Regression analysis relating the current market value in dollars to the size in square feet of homes in Greene County has been developed. The computer output follows. The regression equation is: Value = – 3,7186 + 65.0 Size.

Predictor	Coef	SE Coef	T	P
Constant	-37186	4629	-8.03	0.000
Size	64.993	3.047	21.33	0.000

Analysis of Variance

Source	DF	SS	MS	F	P
Regression	1	13548662082	13548662082	454.98	0.000
Residual Error	33	982687392	29778406		
Total	34	14531349474			

a. How many homes were in the sample?
b. Compute the standard error of estimate.
c. Compute the coefficient of determination.
d. Compute the coefficient of correlation.
e. At the .05 significance level does the evidence suggest a positive association between the market value of homes and the size of the home in square feet?

exercises.com

WWW

50. Suppose you want to study the association between the literacy rate in a country, the population, and the country's gross domestic product (GDP). Go to the website of *Information Please Almanac* (http://www.infoplease.com). Select the category **World,** and then select **Countries.** A list of 195 countries starting with Afghanistan and ending with Zimbabwe will appear. Randomly select a sample of about 20 countries. It may be convenient to use a systematic sample. In other words, randomly select 1 of the first 10 countries and then select every tenth country thereafter. Click on each country name and scan the information to find the literacy rate, the population, and the GDP. Compute the correlation among the variables. In other words, find the correlation between: literacy and population, literacy and GDP, and population and GDP. *Warning:* Be careful of the units. Sometimes population is reported in millions, other times in thousands. At the .05 significance level, can we conclude that the correlation is different from 0?

51. Many real estate companies and rental agencies now publish their listings on the Web. One example is the Dunes Realty Company, located in Garden City and Surfside Beaches in South Carolina. Go to the website http://www.dunes.com and select **Cottage Search.** Then indicate 5 bedroom, accommodations for 14 people, second row (this means it is across the street from the beach), and no pool or floating dock; select a period in July or August; indicate that you are willing to spend $5,000 per week; and then click on **Search the Cottages.** The output should include details on the cottages that met your criteria.

a. Determine the correlation between the number of baths in each cottage and the weekly rental price. Can you conclude that the correlation is greater than zero at the .05 significance level? Determine the coefficient of determination.
b. Determine the regression equation using the number of bathrooms as the independent variable and the price per week as the dependent variable. Interpret the regression equation.
c. Calculate the correlation between the number of people the cottage will accommodate and the weekly rental price. At the .05 significance level can you conclude that it is different from zero?

Computer Data Exercises

52. Refer to the Real Estate data, which reports information on homes sold in Venice, Florida, last year.
a. Let selling price be the dependent variable and size of the home the independent variable. Determine the regression equation. Estimate the selling price for a home with an area of 2,200 square feet. Determine the 95 percent confidence interval and the 95 percent prediction interval for the selling price of a home with 2,200 square feet.
b. Let selling price be the dependent variable and distance from the center of the city the independent variable. Determine the regression equation. Estimate the selling price of a home 20 miles from the center of the city. Determine the 95 percent confidence interval and the 95 percent prediction interval for homes 20 miles from the center of the city.
c. Can you conclude that the independent variables "distance from the center of the city" and "selling price" are negatively correlated and that the area of the home and the selling price are positively correlated? Use the .05 significance level. Report the *p*-value of the test.

53. Refer to the Baseball 2001 data, which reports information on the 2001 Major League Baseball season.
a. Let the games won be the dependent variable and total team salary, in millions of dollars, be the independent variable. Can you conclude that there is a positive association between the two variables? Determine the regression equation. Interpret the slope, that is the value of *b*. How many additional wins will an additional $5 million in salary bring?
b. Determine the correlation between games won and ERA and between games won and team batting average. Which has the stronger correlation? Can we conclude that there is, a positive correlation between wins and team batting and a negative correlation between wins and ERA? Use the .05 significance level.
c. Assume the number of games won is the dependent variable and attendance the independent variable. Can we conclude that the correlation between these two variables is greater than 0? Use the .05 significance level.

54. Refer to the wage data, which reports information on annual wages for a sample of 100 workers. Also included are variables relating to industry, years of education, and gender for each worker.
a. Determine the correlation between the annual wage and the years of education. At the .05 significance level can we conclude there is a positive correlation between the two variables?
b. Determine the correlation between the annual wage and the years of work experience. At the .05 significance level can we conclude there is a positive correlation between the two variables?

55. Refer to the CIA data, which reports demographic and economic information on 46 countries.
a. You wish to use the Labor force variable as the independent variable to predict the unemployment rate. Interpret the slope value. Use the appropriate linear regression equation to predict unemployment in the United Arab Emirates.
b. Find the correlation coefficient between the levels of exports and imports. Use the .05 significance level to test whether there is a positive correlation between these two variables.
c. Does there appear to be a relationship between the percentage of the population over 65 and the literacy percentage? Support your answer with statistical evidence. Conduct an appropriate test of hypothesis and interpret the result.

Computer Commands

1. The MINITAB commands for the output showing the coefficient of correlation on page 393 are:
   a. Enter the data in columns C1 and C2. Use the **Name** command to identify the variables. We've used the names *Calls* and *Sales.*
   b. Select **Stat, Basic Statistics,** and **Correlation.**
   c. Select *Calls* and *Sales* as the variables, click on **Display *p*-values,** and then click **OK.**

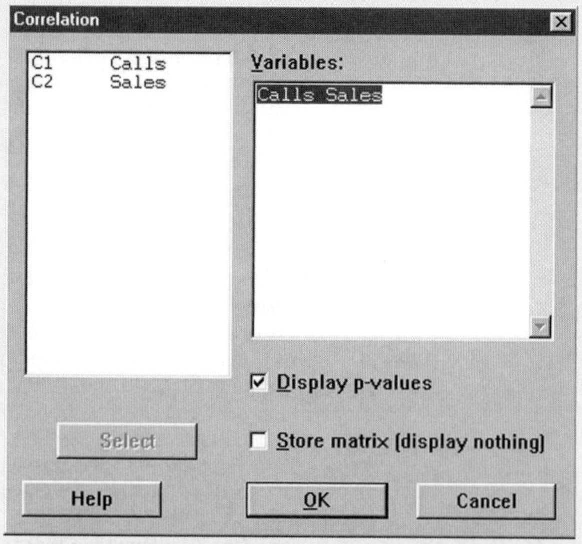

2. The computer commands for the Excel output on page 403 are:
   a. Enter the variable names in row 1 of columns A and B. Enter the data in rows 2 through 11 in the same columns.
   b. Select **Tools, Data Analysis,** and then select **Regression.**
   c. For our spreadsheet we have *Calls* in column B and *Sales* in column C. The **Input Y-Range** is *C1:C11* and the **Input X-Range** is *B1:B11,* click on **Labels,** select *D2* as the **Output Range,** and click **OK.**

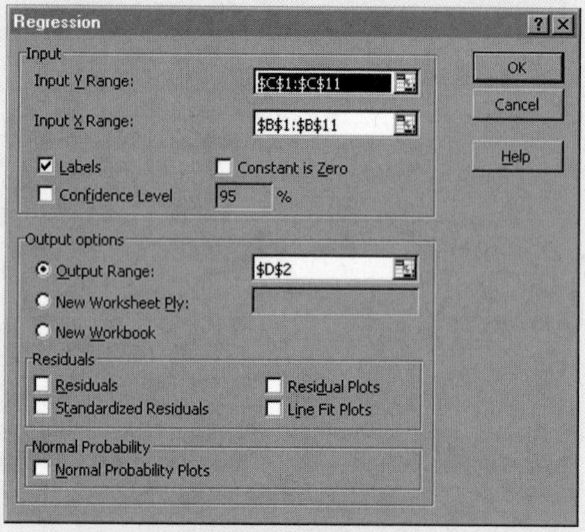

3. The Minitab commands to the confidence intervals and prediction intervals on page 408 are:
   a. Select **Stat, Regression,** and **Fitted line plot.**
   b. In the next dialog box the **Response (Y)** is Sales and **Predictor (X)** is Calls. Select **Linear** for the type of regression model and then click on **Options.**
   c. In the Options dialog box click on **Display confidence and prediction bands,** use the **95.0 for confidence level,** and then in the **Title** box type an appropriate heading, then click **OK** and then **OK** again.

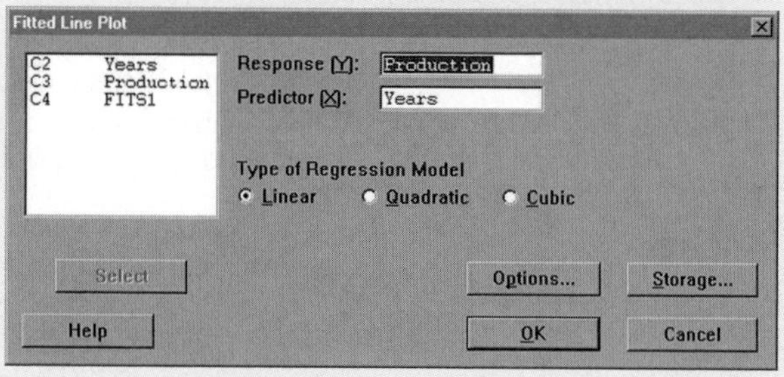

Chapter 12 Answers to Self-Review

12–1 (a) Advertising expense is the independent variable and sales revenue is the dependent variable.

(b)

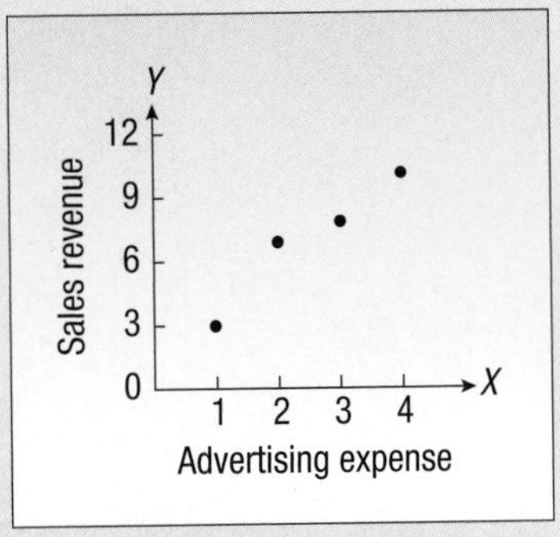

(c)

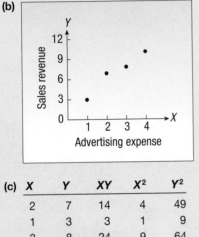

X	Y	XY	X^2	Y^2
2	7	14	4	49
1	3	3	1	9
3	8	24	9	64
4	10	40	16	100
10	28	81	30	222

$r = .96$, found by

$$r = \frac{4(81) - (10)(28)}{\sqrt{[4(30) - (10)^2][4(222) - (28)^2]}}$$

$$= \frac{44}{\sqrt{2{,}080}} = \frac{44}{45.607017} = .9648$$

(d) There is a strong correlation between the advertising expense and sales.

(e) $r^2 = .93$, 93% of the variation in sales is "explained" by variation in advertising.

12–2 H_0: $\rho \leq 0$, H_1: $\rho > 0$. H_0 is rejected if $t > 1.714$.

$$t = \frac{.43\sqrt{25 - 2}}{\sqrt{1 - (.43)^2}} = 2.284$$

H_0 is rejected. There is a positive correlation between the percent of the vote received and the amount spent on the campaign.

12–3 (a) See the calculations in Self-Review 12–1, part (c).

$$b = \frac{4(81) - (10)(28)}{4(30) - (10)^2}$$

$$= \frac{324 - 280}{120 - 100} = 2.2$$

$$a = \frac{28}{4} - 2.2\left(\frac{10}{4}\right)$$

$$= 7 - 5.5 = 1.5$$

(b) The slope is 2.2. This indicates that an increase of \$1 million in advertising will result in an increase of \$2.2 million in sales. The intercept is 1.5. If there was no expenditure for advertising, sales would be \$1.5 million.

(c) $Y' = 1.5 + 2.2(3) = 8.1$

12–4 0.9487, found by:

$$s_{y \cdot x} = \sqrt{\frac{\Sigma Y^2 - a(\Sigma Y) - b(\Sigma XY)}{n - 2}}$$

$$= \sqrt{\frac{222 - 1.5(28) - 2.2(81)}{4 - 2}}$$

$$= \sqrt{\frac{1.8}{2}} = 0.9487$$

12–5 6.58 and 9.62, since Y' for an X of 3 is 8.1, found by $Y' = 1.5 + 2.2(3) = 8.1$, then $\bar{X} = 2.5$ and $\Sigma X^2 = 30$ and $\Sigma X = 10$.

t from Appendix F for $4 - 2 = 2$ degrees of freedom at the .10 level is 2.920.

$$Y' \pm t(s_{y \cdot x})\sqrt{\frac{1}{n} + \frac{(X - \bar{X})^2}{\Sigma X^2 - \frac{(\Sigma X)^2}{n}}}$$

$$= 8.1 \pm 2.920(0.9487)\sqrt{\frac{1}{4} + \frac{(3 - 2.5)^2}{30 - \frac{(10)^2}{4}}}$$

$$= 8.1 \pm 2.920(0.9487)(0.5477)$$

$$= 6.58 \text{ and } 9.62 \text{ (in \$ millions)}$$

13

Multiple Regression and Correlation Analysis

GOALS

When you have completed this chapter, you will be able to:

1 Describe the relationship between several independent variables and a dependent variable using a multiple regression equation.

2 Compute and interpret the multiple standard error of estimate and the coefficient of determination.

3 Interpret a correlation matrix.

4 Set up and interpret an ANOVA table.

5 Conduct a test of hypothesis to determine whether regression coefficients differ from zero.

6 Conduct a test of hypothesis on each of the regression coefficients.

The district manager of Jason's, a large discount retail chain, is investigating why certain stores in her region are performing better than others. She believes that three factors are related to total sales: the number of competitors in the region, the population in the surrounding area, and the amount spent on advertising. From her district, consisting of several hundred stores, she selects a random sample of 30 stores. From the data provided in the exercise, compute the multiple standard error of estimate. (See Goal 2 and Exercise 13.)

B. The alternate hypothesis is: At least one regression coefficient is not zero.
C. The test statistic is the F distribution with k (the number of independent variables) degrees of freedom in the numerator and $n - (k + 1)$ degrees of freedom in the denominator, where n is the sample size.
D. The formula to calculate the value of the test statistic for the global test is:

$$F = \frac{\text{SSR}/k}{\text{SSE}/[n - (k + 1)]} \qquad \textbf{[13–6]}$$

VII. The test for individual variables determines which independent variables have nonzero regression coefficients.
A. The variables that have zero regression coefficients are usually dropped from the analysis.
B. The test statistic is the t distribution with $n - (k + 1)$ degrees of freedom.
C. The formula to calculate the value of the test statistic for the individual test is:

$$t = \frac{b_i - 0}{s_{b_i}} \qquad \textbf{[13–7]}$$

VIII. Dummy variables are used to represent qualitative variables and can assume only one of two possible conditions.
IX. A residual is the difference between the actual value of Y and the predicted value of Y.
A. Residuals should be approximately normally distributed. Histograms and stem-and-leaf charts are useful in checking this requirement.
B. A plot of the residuals and their corresponding Y' values is useful for showing that there are no trends or patterns in the residuals.

Pronunciation Key

SYMBOL	MEANING	PRONUNCIATION
b_1	Regression coefficient for the first independent variable	*b sub 1*
b_k	Regression coefficient for any independent variable	*b sub k*
$s_{y \cdot 12 \cdots k}$	Multiple standard error of estimate	*s sub y dot 1, 2 . . . k*

Chapter Exercises

9. A multiple regression equation yields the following partial results.

Source	Sum of Squares	*df*
Regression	750	4
Error	500	35

a. What is the total sample size?
b. How many independent variables are being considered?
c. Compute the coefficient of determination.
d. Compute the standard error of estimate.
e. Test the hypothesis that none of the regression coefficients is equal to zero. Let $\alpha = .05$.

10. In a multiple regression equation two independent variables are considered, and the sample size is 25. The regression coefficients and the standard errors are as follows.

$b_1 = 2.676$ $\qquad s_{b_1} = 0.56$

$b_2 = -0.880$ $\qquad s_{b_2} = 0.71$

Conduct a test of hypothesis to determine whether either independent variable has a coefficient equal to zero. Would you consider deleting either variable from the regression equation? Use the .05 significance level.

11. The following output was obtained.

Analysis of variance

SOURCE	DF	SS	MS
Regression	5	100	20
Error	20	40	2
Total	25	140	

Predictor	Coef	StDev	t-ratio
Constant	3.00	1.50	2.00
X_1	4.00	3.00	1.33
X_2	3.00	0.20	15.00
X_3	0.20	0.05	4.00
X_4	−2.50	1.00	−2.50
X_5	3.00	4.00	0.75

a. What is the sample size?
b. Compute the value of R^2.
c. Compute the multiple standard error of estimate.
d. Conduct a global test of hypothesis to determine whether any of the regression coefficients are significant. Use the .05 significance level.
e. Test the regression coefficients individually. Would you consider omitting any variable(s)? If so, which one(s)? Use the .05 significance level.

12. In a multiple regression equation $k = 5$ and $n = 20$, the MSE value is 5.10, and SS total is 519.68. At the .05 significance level, can we conclude that any of the regression coefficients are not equal to 0?

13. The district manager of Jasons, a large discount retail chain, is investigating why certain stores in her region are performing better than others. She believes that three factors are related to total sales: the number of competitors in the region, the population in the surrounding area, and the amount spent on advertising. From her district, consisting of several hundred stores, she selects a random sample of 30 stores. For each store she gathered the following information.

Y = total sales last year (in $ thousands).
X_1 = number of competitors in the region.
X_2 = population of the region (in millions).
X_3 = advertising expense (in $ thousands).

The sample data were run on MINITAB, with the following results.

Analysis of variance

SOURCE	DF	SS	MS
Regression	3	3050.00	1016.67
Error	26	2200.00	84.62
Total	29	5250.00	

Predictor	Coef	StDev	t-ratio
Constant	14.00	7.00	2.00
X_1	−1.00	0.70	−1.43
X_2	30.00	5.20	5.77
X_3	0.20	0.08	2.50

a. What are the estimated sales for the Bryne Store, which has four competitors, a regional population of 0.4 (400,000), and advertising expense of 30 ($30,000)?
b. Compute the R^2 value.
c. Compute the multiple standard error of estimate.
d. Conduct a global test of hypothesis to determine whether any of the regression coefficients are not equal to zero. Use the .05 level of significance.
e. Conduct tests of hypotheses to determine which of the independent variables have significant regression coefficients. Which variables would you consider eliminating? Use the .05 significance level.

2. The Excel commands to produce the multiple regression output on page 428 are:
   a. Import the data from the CD. The file name is **Tbl13–1.**
   b. Select **Tools,** the **Data Analysis,** highlight **Regression,** and click **OK.**
   c. Make the **Input Y Range** *A1:A21,* the **Input X Range** *B1:D21,* check the **Labels** box, the **Output Range** is *F1,* click **OK.**

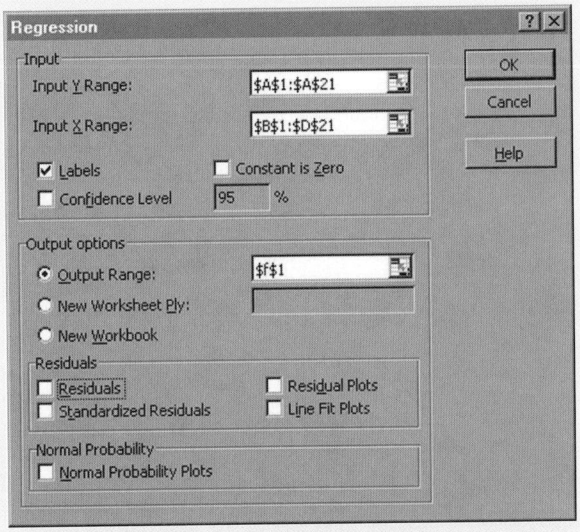

3. The Excel commands to develop the correlation matrix on page 437 are:
   a. Import the data from the CD. The file name is Tbl13–1.
   b. Select **Tools, Data Analysis,** then hit **Enter.** Select the command **Correlation** and then hit **OK.**
   c. The **Input Range** is *A1:D21,* grouped by **Columns,** check the **Labels** box, select the **Output Range** as *G1,* and click **OK.**

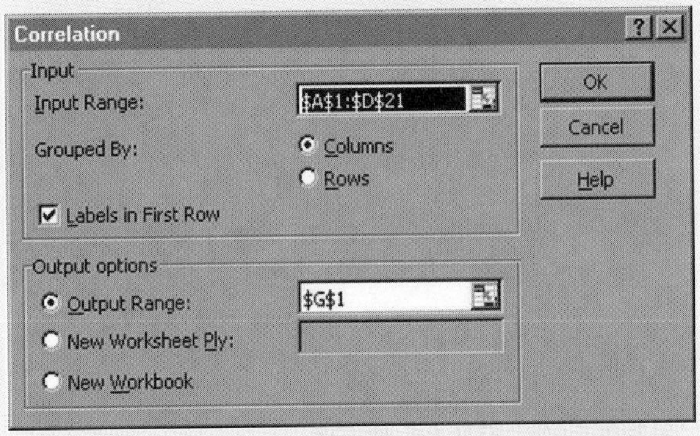

4. The MINITAB commands for the multiple regression output on page 447 are:
   a. Import the data from the CD. The file name is Tbl13–1.
   b. Select **Stat**, **Regression,** and then click on **Regression**.
   c. Select *Cost* as the **Response** variable, and *Temp, Insulation,* and *Age* as the **Predictors**, then click on **OK.**
   d. Click on **Storage,** then check **Residuals** and **Fits,** and click **OK** in both dialog boxes.

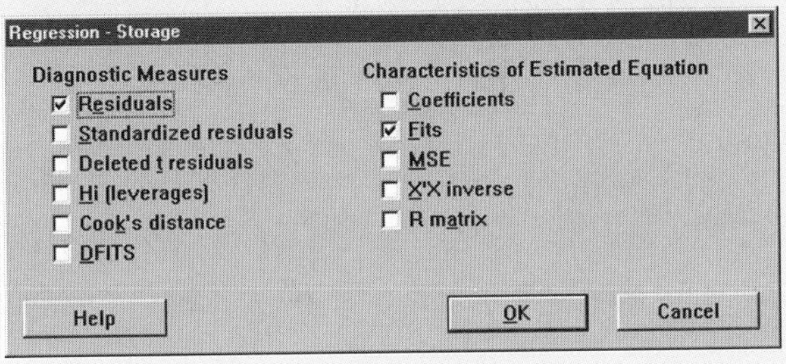

Chapter 13 Answers to Self-Review

13–1 **(a)** 12.9 psi, found by $Y' = -0.5 + 20(.35) + 1(6.4)$.

(b) The b_1 of 20 indicates that the tensile strength of the wire will increase 20 psi for each increase of 1 mm in outside diameter, with the amount of molybdenum held constant. That is, tensile strength will increase 20 psi if there is no change in the amount of molybdenum in the wire.

13–2 **(a)** $n = 25$

(b) 4

(c) $R^2 = \frac{10}{15} = 0.667$

(d) $s_{y \cdot 1234} = \sqrt{\frac{5}{20}} = 0.50$

13–3 **(a)** $Y' = 490 - 5.15X_1 - 14.7X_2$

(b) .776. A total of 77.6% of the variation in heating cost is explained by temperature and insulation.

(c) The results of the global test indicate that at least one of the regression coefficients is not zero. To arrive at that conclusion, we first stated the null hypothesis as H_0: $\beta_1 = \beta_2 = 0$. The critical value of F is 3.59, and the computed value 29.4, found by 82,597/2,807. Since 29.4 lies in the region of rejection beyond 3.59, we reject H_0.

(d) The p-value is .008. The probability of a t-value less than -2.98 or greater than 2.98, with 17 degrees of freedom, is .008.

14

Chi-Square Applications for Nominal Data

GOALS

When you have completed this chapter, you will be able to:

1. List the characteristics of the chi-square distribution.
2. Conduct a test of hypothesis comparing an observed set of frequencies to an expected distribution.
3. Conduct a test of hypothesis to determine whether two classification criteria are related.

There are four entrances to the Government Center Building in downtown Philadelphia. To investigate if the entrances are equally utilized, 400 people were observed entering the building. At the .01 significance level, is there a difference in the use of the four entrances based on the data provided? (See Goal 2 and Exercise 20.)

Introduction

Chapters 8 through 11 deal with data of at least interval scale, such as weights, incomes, and ages. We conduct tests of hypothesis about a single population mean, two population means, and three or more population means. For these tests we assume the populations follow the normal distribution. However, there are tests available in which no assumption regarding the shape of the population is necessary. There are also tests exclusively for data of nominal scale of measurement. Recall from Chapter 1 that nominal data is the "lowest" or most primitive. For this type of measurement, data are classified into categories where there is no natural order. Examples include gender, state of birth, or brand of peanut butter purchased. In this chapter we introduce a new test statistic, the chi-square statistic. We can use it for data of the nominal scale.

Goodness-of-Fit Test: Equal Expected Frequencies

The goodness-of-fit test is one of the most commonly used tests. The first illustration of this test involves the case in which the expected cell frequencies are equal.

As the full name implies, the purpose of the goodness-of-fit test is to compare an observed distribution to an expected distribution. An example will describe the hypothesis-testing situation.

EXAMPLE

Ms. Jan Kilpatrick is the marketing manager for a manufacturer of sports cards. She plans to begin a series of cards with pictures and playing statistics of former Major League Baseball players. One of the problems is the selection of the former players. At the baseball card show at the Southwyck Mall last weekend, she set up a booth and offered cards of the following six Hall of Fame baseball players: Tom Seaver, Nolan Ryan, Ty Cobb, George Brett, Hank Aaron, and Johnny Bench. At the end of the day she sold a total of 120 cards. The number of cards sold for each old-time player is shown in Table 14–1. Can she conclude the sales are not the same for each player?

TABLE 14–1 Number of Cards Sold for Each Player

Player	Cards Sold
Tom Seaver	13
Nolan Ryan	33
Ty Cobb	14
George Brett	7
Hank Aaron	36
Johnny Bench	17
Total	120

If there is no significant difference in the popularity of the players, we would expect that the observed frequencies (f_o) would be equal—or nearly equal. That is, we would expect to sell as many cards for Tom Seaver as for Nolan Ryan. Thus, any discrepancy in the observed and expected frequencies could be attributed to sampling (chance).

What about the level of measurement in this problem? Notice when a card is sold, the "measurement" of the card is based on the player's name. There is no natural order to the players. No one player is better than another. Therefore, a nominal scale is used to evaluate each observation.

Because there are 120 cards in the sample, we expect that 20 (f_e) cards will fall in each of the six categories. These categories are called **cells.** An examination of the set of observed frequencies in Table 14–1 indicates that the card for George Brett is sold rather infrequently, whereas the cards for Hank Aaron and Nolan Ryan are sold more often. Is the difference in sales due to chance, or can we conclude that there is a preference for the cards of certain players?

TABLE 14–2 Observed and Expected Frequencies for the 120 Cards Sold

Player	Cards Sold, f_o	Expected Number Sold, f_e
Tom Seaver	13	20
Nolan Ryan	33	20
Ty Cobb	14	20
George Brett	7	20
Hank Aaron	36	20
Johnny Bench	17	20
Total	120	120

SOLUTION

We will use the same systematic five-step hypothesis-testing procedure followed in previous chapters.

Step 1: State the null hypothesis and the alternate hypothesis. The null hypothesis, H_0, is that there is no difference between the set of observed frequencies and the set of expected frequencies; that is, any difference between the two sets of frequencies can be attributed to sampling (chance). The alternate hypothesis, H_1, is that there is a difference between the observed and expected sets of frequencies. If H_0 is rejected and H_1 is accepted, it means that sales are not equally distributed among the six categories (cells).

Step 2: Select the level of significance. We selected the .05 level, which is the same as the Type I error probability. Thus, the probability is .05 that a true null hypothesis will be rejected.

Step 3: Select the test statistic. It is the chi-square distribution, designated as χ^2:

CHI-SQUARE TEST STATISTIC

$$\chi^2 = \Sigma\left[\frac{(f_o - f_e)^2}{f_e}\right] \quad \textbf{[14–1]}$$

with $k - 1$ degrees of freedom, where:

k is the number of categories.
f_o is an observed frequency in a particular category.
f_e is an expected frequency in a particular category.

We will examine the characteristics of the chi-square distribution in more detail shortly.

Step 4: Formulate the decision rule. Recall the decision rule in hypothesis testing requires finding a number that separates the region where we do not reject H_0 from the region of rejection. This number is called the *critical value.* As we will soon see, the chi-square distribution is really a family of distributions. Each distribution has a slightly different shape, depending on the number of degrees of freedom. The number of degrees of freedom in this type of problem is found by $k - 1$, where k is the number of categories. In this particular problem there are six. Since there are six categories, there are $k - 1 = 6 - 1 = 5$ degrees of freedom. As noted, a category is called a *cell,* so there are six cells. The critical value for 5 degrees of freedom and the .05 level of significance is found in Appendix B. A portion of that table is shown in Table 14–3. The critical value is 11.070, found by locating 5 degrees of freedom in the left margin and then moving horizontally (to the right) and reading the critical value in the .05 column.

TABLE 14–3 A Portion of the Chi-Square Table

Degrees of Freedom	Right-Tail Area			
df	.10	.05	.02	.01
1	2.706	3.841	5.412	6.635
2	4.605	5.991	7.824	9.210
3	6.251	7.815	9.837	11.345
4	7.779	9.488	11.668	13.277
5	9.236	11.070	13.388	15.086

The decision rule is to reject H_0 if the computed value of chi-square is greater than 11.070. If it is less than or equal to 11.070, do not reject H_0. Chart 14–1 shows the decision rule.

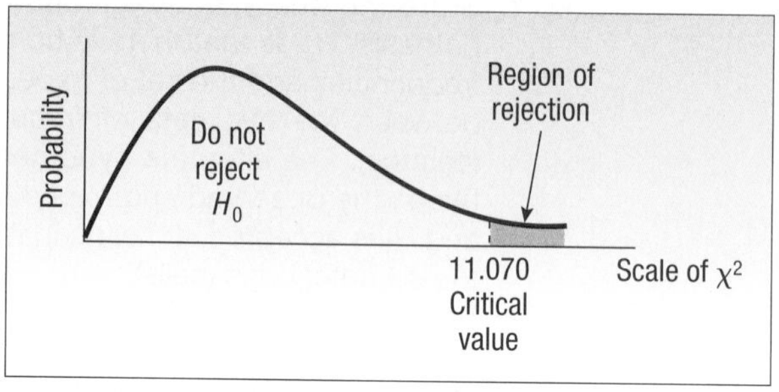

CHART 14–1 Chi-Square Probability Distribution for 5 Degrees of Freedom, Showing the Region of Rejection, .05 Level of Significance

The decision rule indicates that if there are large differences between the observed and expected frequencies, resulting in a computed χ^2 of more than 11.070, the null hypothesis should be rejected. However, if the differences between f_o and f_e are small, the computed χ^2 value will be 11.070 or less, and the null hypothesis should not be rejected. The reasoning is that such small differences between the observed and expected frequencies are probably due to chance. Remember, the 120 observations are a sample of the population.

Step 5: Compute the value of chi-square and make a decision. Of the 120 cards sold in the sample, we counted the number of times Tom Seaver and Nolan Ryan, and each of the others were sold. The counts were reported in Table 14–1. The calculations for chi-square follow. (Note again that the expected frequencies are the same for each cell.)

Column 1: Determine the differences between each f_o and f_e. That is, $(f_o - f_e)$. The sum of these differences is zero.

Column 2: Square the difference between each observed and expected frequency. That is, $(f_o - f_e)^2$.

Column 3: Divide the result for each observation by the expected frequency. That is, $\frac{(f_o - f_e)^2}{f_e}$. Finally, sum these values.

The result is the value of χ^2, which is 34.40.

Baseball Player	f_o	f_e	(1) $(f_o - f_e)$	(2) $(f_o - f_e)^2$	(3) $\frac{(f_o - f_e)^2}{f_e}$
Tom Seaver	13	20	−7	49	49/20 = 2.45
Nolan Ryan	33	20	13	169	169/20 = 8.45
Ty Cobb	14	20	−6	36	36/20 = 1.80
George Brett	7	20	−13	169	169/20 = 8.45
Hank Aaron	36	20	16	256	256/20 = 12.80
Johnny Bench	17	20	−3	9	9/20 = 0.45
			0 ← Must be		34.40 ← χ^2

The computed χ^2 of 34.40 is in the rejection region beyond the critical value of 11.070. The decision, therefore, is to reject H_0 at the .05 level and to accept H_1. The difference between the observed and the expected frequencies is not due to chance. Rather, the differences between f_o and f_e are large enough to be considered significant. The chance of these differences being due to sampling is very small. So we conclude that it is unlikely that card sales are the same among the six players.

We can use software to compute the value of chi-square. The output of MegaStat follows. The steps are shown in the Computer Commands section at the end of the chapter. The computed value of chi-square is 34.40, the same value obtained in our earlier calculations.

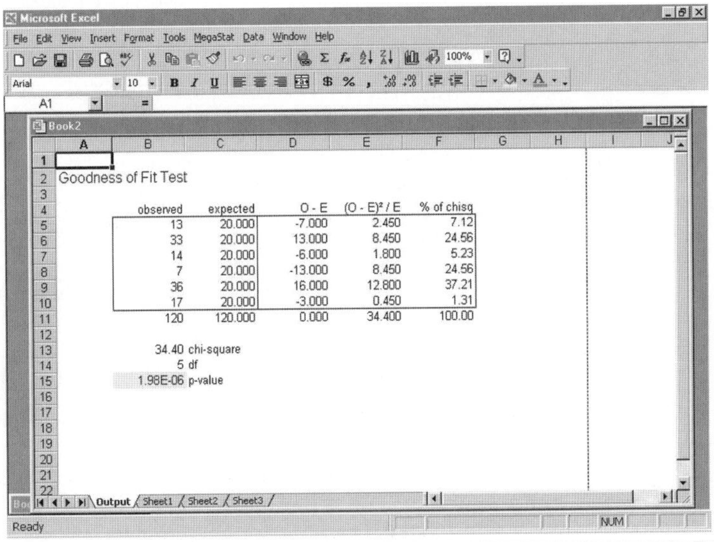

The chi-square distribution, which is used as the test statistic in this chapter, has the following characteristics.

1. **Chi-square is never negative.** This is because the difference between f_o and f_e is squared, that is, $(f_o - f_e)^2$.
2. **There is a family of chi-square distributions.** There is a chi-square distribution for 1 degree of freedom, another for 2 degrees of freedom, another for 3 degrees of freedom, and so on. In this type of problem the number of degrees of freedom is determined by $k - 1$, where k is the number of categories. Therefore, the shape of the chi-square distribution does *not* depend on the size of the sample, but on the number of categories used. For example, if 200 employees of an airline were classified into one of three categories—flight personnel, ground support, and administrative personnel—there would be $k - 1 = 3 - 1 = 2$ degrees of freedom.
3. **The chi-square distribution is positively skewed.** However, as the number of degrees of freedom increases, the distribution begins to approximate the normal distribution. Chart 14–2 shows the distributions for selected degrees of freedom. Notice that for 10 degrees of freedom the curve is approaching a normal distribution.

Shape of χ^2 distribution approaches normal distribution as *df* becomes larger

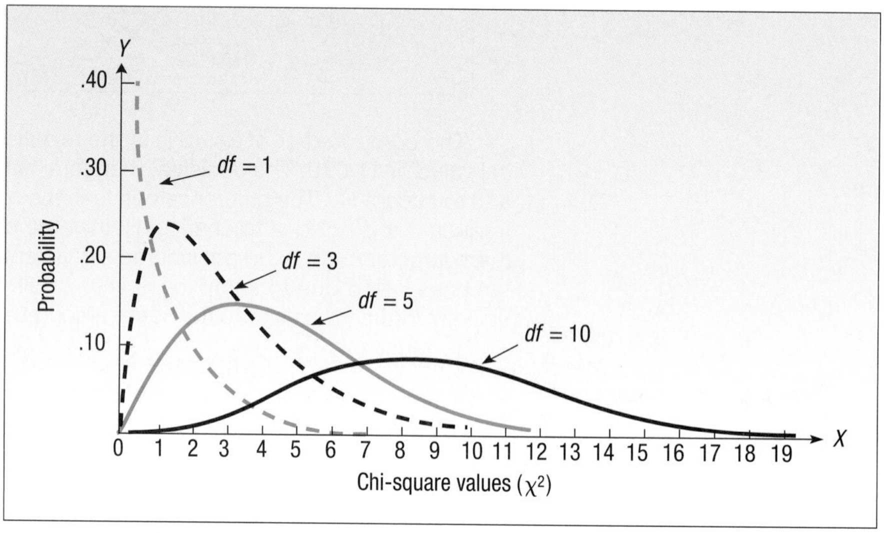

CHART 14–2 Chi-Square Distributions for Selected Degrees of Freedom

Self-Review 14-1

The human resources director at Georgetown Paper, Inc. is concerned about absenteeism among hourly workers. She decides to sample the records to determine whether absenteeism is distributed evenly throughout the six-day workweek. The null hypothesis to be tested is: Absenteeism is distributed evenly throughout the week. The .01 level is to be used. The sample results are:

	Number Absent		Number Absent
Monday	12	Thursday	10
Tuesday	9	Friday	9
Wednesday	11	Saturday	9

(a) What are the numbers 12, 9, 11, 10, 9, and 9 called?
(b) How many categories (cells) are there?
(c) What is the *expected* frequency for each day?
(d) How many degrees of freedom are there?
(e) What is the chi-square critical value at the 1 percent significance level?
(f) Compute the χ^2 test statistic.
(g) What is the decision regarding the null hypothesis?
(h) Specifically, what does this indicate to the human resources director?

Exercises

1. In a particular chi-square goodness-of-fit test there are four categories and 200 observations. Use the .05 significance level.
a. How many degrees of freedom are there?
b. What is the critical value of chi-square?

2. In a particular chi-square goodness-of-fit test there are six categories and 500 observations. Use the .01 significance level.
a. How many degrees of freedom are there?
b. What is the critical value of chi-square?

3. The null hypothesis and the alternate are:

H_0: The cell categories are equal.
H_1: The cell categories are not equal.

Category	f_o
A	10
B	20
C	30

a. State the decision rule, using the .05 significance level.
b. Compute the value of chi-square.
c. What is your decision regarding H_0?

4. The null hypothesis and the alternate are:

H_0: The cell categories are equal.
H_1: The cell categories are not equal.

Category	f_o
A	10
B	20
C	30
D	20

a. State the decision rule, using the .05 significance level.
b. Compute the value of chi-square.
c. What is your decision regarding H_0?

5. A six-sided die is rolled 30 times and the numbers 1 through 6 appear as shown in the following frequency distribution. At the .10 significance level, can we conclude that the die is fair?

Outcome	Frequency	Outcome	Frequency
1	3	4	3
2	6	5	9
3	2	6	7

6. The Director of Golf for the Links Group wishes to study the number of rounds of golf played by members on weekdays. He gathered the following sample information for 520 rounds.

Day	Rounds
Monday	124
Tuesday	74
Wednesday	104
Thursday	98
Friday	120

At the .05 significance level, is there a difference in the number of rounds played by day of the week?

7. A group of department store buyers viewed a new line of dresses and gave their opinions of them. The results were:

Opinion	Number of Buyers	Opinion	Number of Buyers
Outstanding	47	Good	39
Excellent	45	Fair	35
Very good	40	Undesirable	34

Because the largest number (47) indicated the new line is outstanding, the head designer thinks that this is a mandate to go into mass production of the dresses. The head sweeper (who somehow became involved in this) believes that there is not a clear mandate and claims that the opinions are evenly distributed among the six categories. He further states that the slight differences among the various counts are probably due to chance. Test the null hypothesis that there is no significant difference among the opinions of the buyers. Test at the .01 level of risk. Follow a formal approach; that is, state the null hypothesis, the alternate hypothesis, and so on.

8. The safety director of Honda USA took samples at random from the file of minor work-related accidents and classified them according to the time the accident took place.

Time	Number of Accidents	Time	Number of Accidents
8 up to 9 A.M.	6	1 up to 2 P.M.	7
9 up to 10 A.M.	6	2 up to 3 P.M.	8
10 up to 11 A.M.	20	3 up to 4 P.M.	19
11 up to 12 P.M.	8	4 up to 5 P.M.	6

Using the goodness-of-fit test and the .01 level of significance, determine whether the accidents are evenly distributed throughout the day. Write a brief explanation of your conclusion.

Goodness-of-Fit Test: Unequal Expected Frequencies

The expected frequencies (f_e) in the previous distribution involving baseball cards were all equal (20). According to the null hypothesis, it was expected that a picture of Tom Seaver would appear 20 times at random, a picture of Johnny Bench would appear 20 times out of 120 trials, and so on. The chi-square test can also be used if the expected frequencies are not equal.

Expected frequencies not equal in this problem

The following example illustrates the case of unequal frequencies and also gives a practical use of chi-square—namely, to find whether a local experience differs from the national experience.

EXAMPLE

The American Hospital Administrators Association (AHAA) reports the following information concerning the number of times senior citizens are admitted to a hospital during a one-year period. Forty percent are not admitted; 30 percent are admitted once; 20 percent are admitted twice, and the remaining 10 percent are admitted three or more times.

A survey of 150 residents of Bartow Estates, a community devoted to active seniors located in Central Florida, revealed 55 residents were not admitted during the last year, 50 were admitted to a hospital once, 32 were admitted twice, and the rest of those in the survey were admitted three or more times. Can we conclude the survey at Bartow Estates is consistent with the information suggested by the AHAA? Use the .05 significance level.

SOLUTION

We begin by organizing the above information into Table 14–4. Clearly, we cannot compare percentages given in the study by the Hospital Administrators to the frequencies reported for the Bartow Estates. However, these percentages can be converted to expected frequencies, f_e. According to the Hospital Administrators, 40 percent of the Bartow residents in the survey did not require hospitalization. Thus, if there is no difference between the national experience and those of Bartow Estates, then 40 percent of the 150 seniors surveyed (60 residents) would not have been hospitalized. Further, 30 percent of those surveyed were admitted once (45 residents) would have been admitted once, and so on. The observed frequencies for Bartow residents and the expected frequencies based on the percents in the national study are given in Table 14–4.

TABLE 14–4 Summary of Study by AHAA and a Survey of Bartow Estates Residents

Number of Times Admitted	AHAA Percent of Total	Number of Bartow Residents (f_o)	Expected Number of Residents (f_e)
0	40	55	60
1	30	50	45
2	20	32	30
3 or more	10	13	15
Total	100	150	150

The null hypothesis and the alternate hypotheses are:

H_0: There is no difference between local and national experience for hospital admissions.

H_1: There is a difference between local and national experience for hospital admissions.

To find the decision rule we use Appendix B. There are four admitting categories, so the degrees of freedom are $df = 4 - 1 = 3$. The critical value is 7.815. Therefore, the decision rule is to reject the null hypothesis if $\chi^2 > 7.815$. The decision rule is portrayed in Chart 14–3.

Now to compute the chi-square test statistic:

Number of Times Admitted	(f_o)	(f_e)	$f_o - f_e$	$(f_o - f_e)^2/f_e$
0	55	60	−5	0.4167
1	50	45	5	0.5556
2	32	30	2	0.1333
3 or more	13	15	−2	0.2667
Total	150	150	0	1.3723

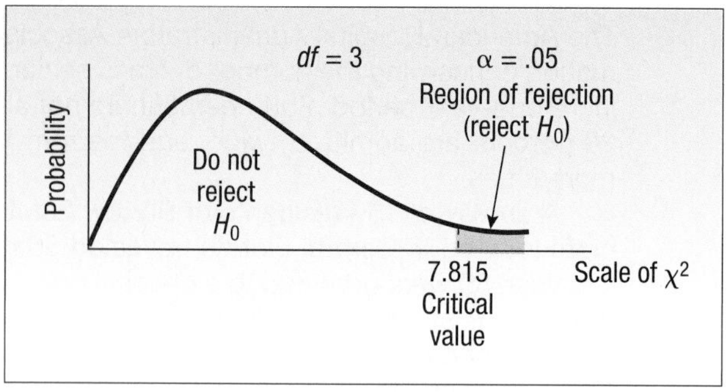

CHART 14–3 Decision Criteria for the Bartow Estates Research Study

The computed values of χ^2 (1.3723) lies to the left of 7.815. Thus, we cannot reject the null hypothesis. We conclude that there is no difference between local and national experience for hospital admissions.

Limitations of Chi-Square

Be careful in applying χ^2 to some problems

If there is an unusually small expected frequency in a cell, chi-square (if applied) might result in an erroneous conclusion. This can happen because f_e appears in the denominator, and dividing by a very small number makes the quotient quite large! Two generally accepted rules regarding small cell frequencies are:

1. If there are only two cells, the *expected* frequency in each cell should be 5 or more. The computation of chi-square would be permissible in the following problem, involving a minimum f_e of 6.

Individual	f_o	f_e
Literate	643	642
Illiterate	7	6

2. For more than two cells, chi-square should *not* be used if more than 20 percent of the f_e cells have expected frequencies less than 5. According to this rule, it would not be appropriate to use the goodness-of-fit test on the following data. Three of the seven cells, or 43 percent, contain less than five observations.

Level of Management	f_o	f_e
Foreman	30	32
Supervisor	110	113
Manager	86	87
Middle management	23	24
Assistant vice president	5	2
Vice president	5	4
Senior vice president	4	1
Total	263	263

To show the reason for the 20 percent policy, we conducted the goodness-of-fit test on the above data on the levels of management. The MegaStat output follows.

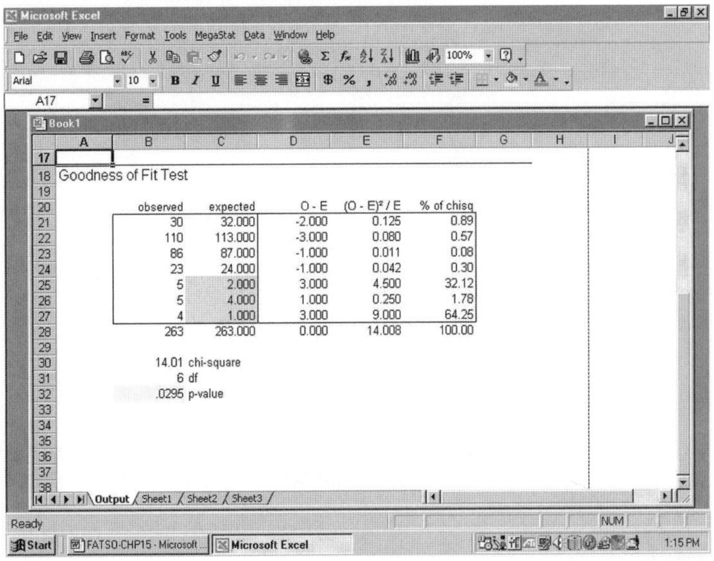

Goodness of Fit Test

observed	expected	O - E	(O - E)² / E	% of chisq
30	32.000	-2.000	0.125	0.89
110	113.000	-3.000	0.080	0.57
86	87.000	-1.000	0.011	0.08
23	24.000	-1.000	0.042	0.30
5	2.000	3.000	4.500	32.12
5	4.000	1.000	0.250	1.78
4	1.000	3.000	9.000	64.25
263	263.000	0.000	14.008	100.00

14.01 chi-square
6 df
.0295 p-value

For this test at the .05 significance level, H_0 is rejected if the computed value of chi-square is greater than 12.592. The computed value is 14.01, so we reject the null hypothesis that the observed frequencies represent a random sample from the population of the expected values. Examine the MegaStat output. More than 98 percent of the computed chi-square value is accounted for by the three vice president categories ([4.500 + .250 + 9.000]/14.008 = 0.9815). Logically, too much weight is being given to these categories.

The dilemma can be resolved by combining categories if it is logical to do so. In the above example we combine the three vice-presidential categories, which satisfies the 20 percent rule.

Level of Management	f_o	f_e
Foreman	30	32
Supervisor	110	113
Manager	86	87
Middle management	23	24
Vice president	14	7
Total	263	263

The computed value of chi-square with the revised categories is 7.26. See the following output. This value is less than the critical value of 9.488 for the .05 significance level. The null hypothesis is, therefore, not rejected at the .05 significance level. This indicates there is no significant difference between the observed distribution and the expected distribution.

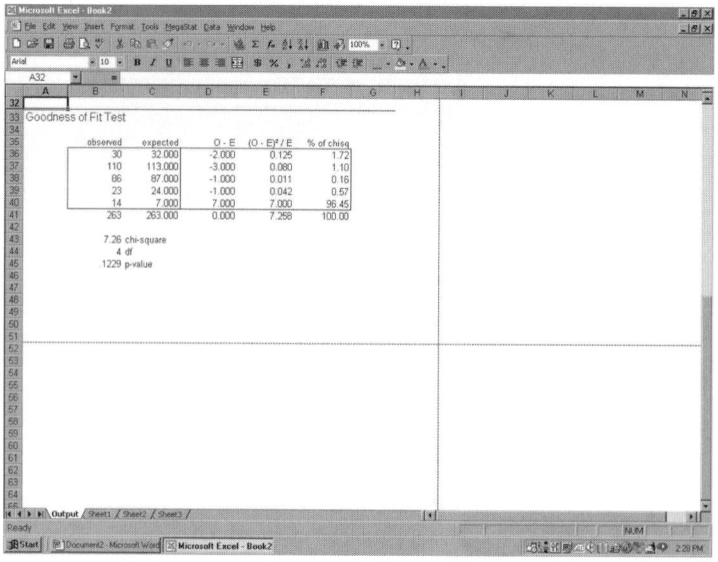

Goodness of Fit Test

observed	expected	O - E	$(O - E)^2 / E$	% of chisq
30	32.000	-2.000	0.125	1.72
110	113.000	-3.000	0.080	1.10
86	87.000	-1.000	0.011	0.16
23	24.000	-1.000	0.042	0.57
14	7.000	7.000	7.000	96.45
263	263.000	0.000	7.258	100.00

7.26 chi-square
4 df
.1229 p-value

Self-Review 14-2

The American Accounting Association classifies accounts receivable as "current," "late," and "not collectible." Industry figures show that 60 percent of accounts receivable are current, 30 percent are late, and 10 percent are not collectible. Massa and Barr, attorneys in Greenville, Ohio, has 500 accounts receivable: 320 are current, 120 are late, and 60 are not collectible. Are these numbers in agreement with the industry distribution? Use the .05 significance level.

Exercises

9. The following hypotheses are given:

H_0: Forty percent of the observations are in category A, 40 percent are in B, and 20 percent are in C.
H_1: The observations are not as described in H_0.

We took a sample of 60, with the following results.

Category	f_o
A	30
B	20
C	10

a. State the decision rule using the .01 significance level.
b. Compute the value of chi-square.
c. What is your decision regarding H_0?

10. The chief of security for the Mall of the Dakotas was directed to study the problem of missing goods. He selected a sample of 100 boxes that had been tampered with and ascertained that for 60 of the boxes, the missing pants, shoes, and so on were attributed to shoplifting. For 30 other boxes employees had stolen the goods, and for the remaining 10 boxes he blamed poor inventory control. In his report to the mall management, can he say that shoplifting is *twice* as likely to be the cause of the loss as compared with either employee theft or poor inventory control and that employee theft and poor inventory control are equally likely? Use the .02 level.

11. The bank credit card department of Carolina Bank knows from experience that 5 percent of the card holders have had some high school, 15 percent have completed high school, 25 percent have had some college, and 55 percent have completed college. Of the 500 card holders whose cards have been called in for failure to pay their charges this month, 50 had some high school, 100 had completed high school, 190 had some college, and 160 had completed college. Can we conclude that the distribution of card holders who do not pay their charges is different from all others? Use the .01 significance level.

12. For many years TV executives used the guideline that 30 percent of the audience were watching each of the prime-time networks and 10 percent cable stations on a weekday night. A random sample of 500 viewers in the Tampa–St. Petersburg, Florida, area last Monday night showed that 165 homes were tuned in to the ABC affiliate, 140 to the CBS affiliate, 125 to the NBC affiliate, and the remainder were viewing a cable station. At the .05 significance level, can we conclude that the guideline is still reasonable?

Contingency Table Analysis

The goodness-of-fit tests applied in the previous sections were concerned with only a single variable. The chi-square test can also be used for a research project involving the relationship between *two* nominal variables. As examples:

- The quality control manager of a company that operates three shifts (24 hours a day) wishes to know if there is a difference in quality on the three shifts. To investigate he selects a sample of 500 parts from yesterday's production. Each part is classified according to two criteria: whether the part is acceptable or not and on which of the shifts it was manufactured.
- Does a male released from federal prison make a different adjustment to civilian life if he returns to his hometown or if he goes elsewhere to live? The two variables are adjustment to civilian life and place of residence. Note that both variables are measured on the nominal scale.

EXAMPLE

The Federal Correction Agency is investigating the last question cited above: Does a male released from federal prison make a different adjustment to civilian life if he returns to his hometown or if he goes elsewhere to live? To put it another way, is there a relationship between adjustment to civilian life and place of residence after release from prison?

SOLUTION

As before, the first step in hypothesis testing is to state the null and alternate hypotheses.

H_0: There is no relationship between adjustment to civilian life and where the individual lives after being released from prison.

H_1: There is a relationship between adjustment to civilian life and where the individual lives after being released from prison.

The .01 level of significance will be used to test the hypothesis.

The agency's psychologists interviewed 200 randomly selected former prisoners. Using a series of questions, the psychologists classified the adjustment of each individual to civilian life as outstanding, good, fair, or unsatisfactory. The classifications for the 200 former prisoners were tallied as follows. Joseph Camden, for example, returned to his hometown and has shown outstanding adjustment to civilian life. His case is one of the 27 tallies in the upper left box.

Residence after Release from Prison	Adjustment to Civilian Life			
	Outstanding	Good	Fair	Unsatisfactory
Hometown	卌 卌 卌 卌 卌 ||	卌 卌 卌 卌 卌 卌 卌	卌 卌 卌 卌 卌 卌 |||	卌 卌 卌 卌 卌
Not hometown	卌 卌 |||	卌 卌 卌	卌 卌 卌 卌 卌 ||	卌 卌 卌 卌 卌

Contingency table consists of count data

The tallies in each box, or *cell,* were counted. The counts are given in the following **contingency table.** (See Table 14–5.) In this case, the Federal Correction Agency wondered whether adjustment to civilian life is *contingent on* where the prisoner goes after release from prison.

TABLE 14–5 Adjustment to Civilian Life and Place of Residence

Residence after Release from Prison	Adjustment to Civilian Life				
	Outstanding	Good	Fair	Unsatisfactory	Total
Hometown	27	35	33	25	120
Not hometown	13	15	27	25	80
Total	40	50	60	50	200

Once we know how many rows (2) and columns (4) there are in the contingency table, we can determine the critical value and the decision rule. For a chi-square test of significance where two traits are classified in a contingency table, the degrees of freedom are found by:

$$df = (\text{number of rows} - 1)(\text{number of columns} - 1) = (r - 1)(c - 1)$$

In this problem:

$$df = (r - 1)(c - 1) = (2 - 1)(4 - 1) = 3$$

To find the critical value for 3 degrees of freedom and the .01 level (selected earlier), refer to Appendix B. It is 11.345. The decision rule is to reject the null hypothesis if the computed value of χ^2 is greater than 11.345. The decision rule is portrayed graphically in Chart 14–4.

Now to find the computed value of χ^2: The observed frequencies, f_o, are shown in Table 14–5. How are the corresponding expected frequencies, f_e, determined? Note in the "Total" column of Table 14–5 that 120 of the 200 former prisoners (60 percent) returned to their hometowns. *If there were no relationship* between adjustment and residency after release from prison, we would expect 60 percent of the 40 ex-prisoners who made outstanding adjustment to civilian life to reside in their hometowns. Thus,

Statistics in Action

A study of 1,000 Americans over the age of 24 showed that 28 percent never married. Of those, 22 percent completed college. Twenty-three percent of the 1,000 married and completed college. Can we conclude for the information given that being married is related to completing college? The study indicated that the two variables were related, that the computed value of the chi-square statistic was 11,525, and the *p*-value was less than .0001. Can you duplicate these results?

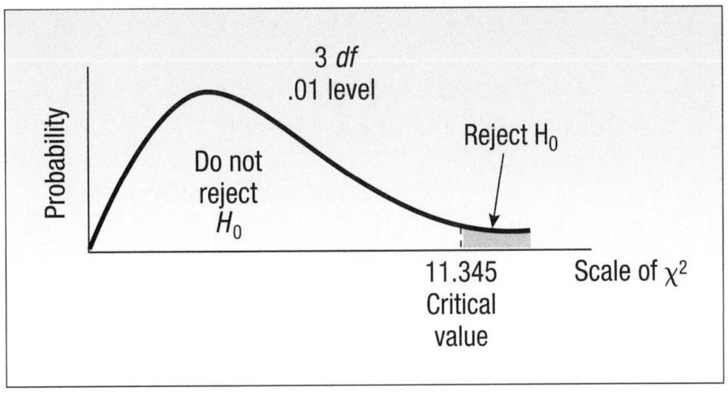

CHART 14–4 Chi-Square Distribution for 3 Degrees of Freedom

the expected frequency f_e for the upper left cell is $.60 \times 40 = 24$. Likewise, if there were no relationship between adjustment and present residence, we would expect 60 percent of the 50 ex-prisoners (30) who had "good" adjustment to civilian life to reside in their hometowns.

Further, notice that 80 of the 200 ex-prisoners studied (40 percent) did not return to their hometowns to live. Thus, of the 60 considered by the psychologists to have made "fair" adjustment to civilian life, $.40 \times 60$, or 24, would be expected not to return to their hometowns.

The expected frequency for any cell can be determined by

EXPECTED FREQUENCY

$$f_e = \frac{(\text{Row total})(\text{Column total})}{\text{Grand total}} \quad \textbf{[14–2]}$$

Using this formula, the expected frequency for the upper left cell in Table 14–5 is:

$$\text{Expected frequency} = \frac{(\text{Row total})(\text{Column total})}{\text{Grand total}} = \frac{(120)(40)}{200} = 24$$

The observed frequencies, f_o, and the expected frequencies, f_e, for all of the cells in the contingency table are listed in Table 14–6.

TABLE 14–6 Observed and Expected Frequencies

Residence after Release from Prison	Adjustment to Civilian Life								Total	
	Outstanding		Good		Fair		Unsatisfactory			
	f_o	f_e	f_o	f_e	f_o	f_e	f_o	f_e	f_o	f_e
Hometown	27	24	35	30	33	36	25	30	120	120
Not hometown	13	16	15	20	27	24	25	20	80	80
Total	40	40	50	50	60	60	50	50	200	200

Must be equal (Outstanding total f_o and f_e)

$\frac{(80)(50)}{200}$ (Not hometown, Good, f_e)

Must be equal (Total f_o and f_e)

Recall that the computed value of chi-square using formula (14–1) is found by:

$$\chi^2 = \Sigma\left[\frac{(f_o - f_e)^2}{f_e}\right]$$

Starting with the upper left cell:

$$\chi^2 = \frac{(27-24)^2}{24} + \frac{(35-30)^2}{30} + \frac{(33-36)^2}{36} + \frac{(25-30)^2}{30}$$

$$+ \frac{(13-16)^2}{16} + \frac{(15-20)^2}{20} + \frac{(27-24)^2}{24} + \frac{(25-20)^2}{20}$$

$$= 0.375 + 0.833 + 0.250 + 0.833 + 0.563 + 1.250 + 0.375 + 1.250$$

$$= 5.729$$

Because the computed value of chi-square (5.729) lies in the region to the left of 11.345, the null hypothesis is not rejected at the .01 level. We conclude there is no relationship between adjustment to civilian life and where the prisoner resides after being released from prison. For the Federal Correction Agency's advisement program, adjustment to civilian life is not related to where the ex-prisoner lives.

The following output is from the MINITAB system.

MINITAB

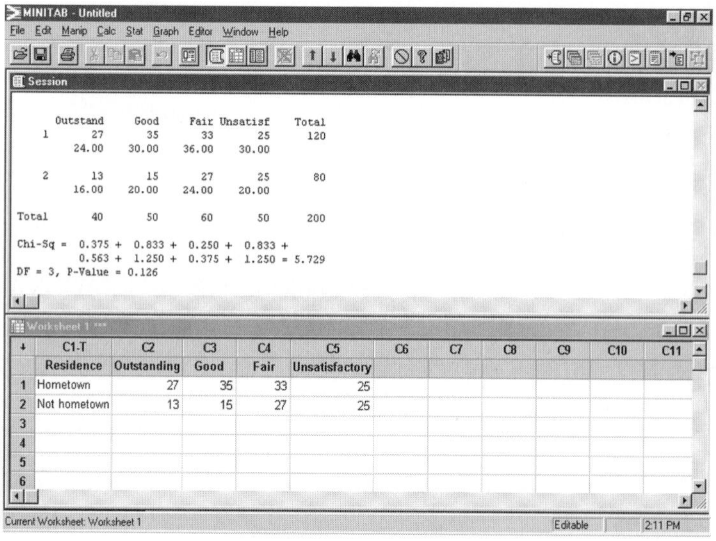
MINITAB - Untitled
File Edit Manip Calc Stat Graph Editor Window Help
Session
Outstand Good Fair Unsatisf Total
1 27 35 33 25 120
24.00 30.00 36.00 30.00
2 13 15 27 25 80
16.00 20.00 24.00 20.00
Total 40 50 60 50 200
Chi-Sq = 0.375 + 0.833 + 0.250 + 0.833 +
0.563 + 1.250 + 0.375 + 1.250 = 5.729
DF = 3, P-Value = 0.126
Worksheet 1 ***
C1-T C2 C3 C4 C5 C6 C7 C8 C9 C10 C11
Residence Outstanding Good Fair Unsatisfactory
1 Hometown 27 35 33 25
2 Not hometown 13 15 27 25
3
4
5
6
Current Worksheet: Worksheet 1
Editable
2:11 PM

Observe that the value of chi-square is the same as that computed earlier. In addition, the p-value is reported, .126. So the probability of finding a value of the test statistic as large or larger is .126 when the null hypothesis is true.

Self-Review 14-3

Current projections suggest, with the current strong economy, the federal government will be generating budget surpluses for the next 10 years. How to spend this money is an issue being debated. The major options are reduce taxes, pay down the debt, or improve Social Security benefits. A sample of 135 voters was classified according to political affiliation and which of the major options should be paid first. The results follow. Use the .05 significance level.

Budget Surplus Option	Democrat	Republican	Independent	Total
Reduce taxes	18	12	10	40
Pay down debt	17	15	13	45
Improve social security	9	9	22	40
Total	44	36	45	125

(a) What is this table called?
(b) State the null hypothesis.
(c) Determine the value of chi-square. What is your decision regarding the null hypothesis?
(d) Interpret the results.

Exercises

13. The director of advertising for the *Carolina Sun Times,* the largest newspaper in the Carolinas, is studying the relationship between the type of community in which a subscriber resides and the portion of the newspaper he or she reads first. For a sample of readers, she collected the following sample information.

	National News	Sports	Comics
City	170	124	90
Suburb	120	112	100
Rural	130	90	88

At the .05 significance level, can we conclude there is a relationship between the type of community where the person resides and the portion of the paper read first?

14. Four brands of light bulbs are being considered for use in a large manufacturing plant. The director of purchasing asked for samples of 100 from each manufacturer. The numbers of acceptable and unacceptable bulbs from each manufacturer are shown below. At the .05 significance level, is there a difference in the quality of the bulbs?

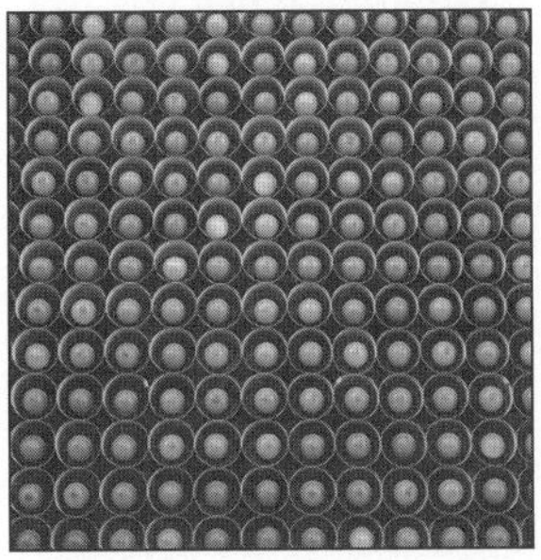

	Manufacturer			
	A	B	C	D
Unacceptable	12	8	5	11
Acceptable	88	92	95	89
Total	100	100	100	100

15. The Quality Control Department at Food Town, Inc., a grocery chain in upstate New York, conducts a monthly check on the comparison of scanned prices to posted prices. The chart below summarizes the results of a sample of 500 items last month. Company management would like to know whether there is any relationship between error rates on regular priced items and specially priced items. Use the .01 significance level.

	Regular Price	Advertised Special Price
Undercharge	20	10
Overcharge	15	30
Correct price	200	225

16. The use of cellular phones in automobiles has increased dramatically in the last few years. Of concern to traffic experts, as well as manufacturers of cellular phones, is the effect on accident rates. Is someone who is using a cellular phone more likely to be involved in a traffic accident? What is your conclusion from the following sample information? Use the .05 significance level.

	Had Accident in the Last Year	Did Not Have an Accident in the Last Year
Cellular phone in use	25	300
Cellular phone not in use	50	400

Chapter Outline

I. The characteristics of the chi-square distribution are:
- **A.** The value of chi-square is never negative.
- **B.** The chi-square distribution is positively skewed.
- **C.** There is a family of chi-square distributions.
  - **1.** Each time the degrees of freedom change, a new distribution is formed.
  - **2.** As the degrees of freedom increase, the distribution approaches a normal distribution.

II. A goodness-of-fit test will show whether an observed set of frequencies could have come from a hypothesized population distribution.
- **A.** The degrees of freedom are $k - 1$, where k is the number of categories.
- **B.** The formula for computing the value of chi-square is

$$\chi^2 = \Sigma\left[\frac{(f_o - f_e)^2}{f_e}\right] \quad \textbf{[14–1]}$$

III. A contingency table is used to test whether two traits or characteristics are related.
- **A.** Each observation is classified according to two traits.
- **B.** The expected frequency is determined as follows:

$$f_e = \frac{\text{(Row total)(Column total)}}{\text{(Grand total)}} \quad \textbf{[14–2]}$$

- **C.** The degrees of freedom are found by:

$$df = (\text{Rows} - 1)(\text{Columns} - 1)$$

- **D.** The usual hypothesis testing procedure is used.

Pronunciation Key

SYMBOL	MEANING	PRONUNCIATION
χ^2	Probability distribution	*ki square*
f_o	Observed frequency	*f sub oh*
f_e	Expected frequency	*f sub e*

Chapter Exercises

17. Vehicles heading west on Front Street may turn right, left, or go straight ahead at Elm Street. The city traffic engineer believes that half of the vehicles will continue straight through the intersection. Of the remaining half, equal proportions will turn right and left. Two hundred vehicles were observed, with the following results. Use the .10 significance level. Can we conclude that the traffic engineer is correct?

	Straight	Right Turn	Left Turn
Frequency	112	48	40

18. The publisher of a sports magazine plans to offer new subscribers one of three gifts: a sweatshirt with the logo of their favorite team, a coffee cup with the logo of their favorite team, or a pair of earrings also with the logo of their favorite team. In a sample of 500 new subscribers, the number selecting each gift is reported below. At the .05 significance level, is there a preference for the gifts or should we conclude that the gifts are equally well liked?

Gift	Frequency
Sweatshirt	183
Coffee cup	175
Earrings	142

19. In a particular market there are three commercial television stations, each with its own evening news program from 6:00 to 6:30 P.M. According to a report in this morning's local newspaper, a random sample of 150 viewers last night revealed 53 watched the news on WNAE (channel 5), 64 watched on WRRN (channel 11), and 33 on WSPD (channel 13). At the .05 significance level, is there a difference in the proportion of viewers watching the three channels?

20. There are four entrances to the Government Center Building in downtown Philadelphia. The building maintenance supervisor would like to know if the entrances are equally utilized. To investigate, 400 people were observed entering the building. The number using each entrance is reported below. At the .01 significance level, is there a difference in the use of the four entrances?

Entrance	Frequency
Main Street	140
Broad Street	120
Cherry Street	90
Walnut Street	50
Total	400

21. The owner of a mail-order catalog would like to compare her sales with the geographic distribution of the population. According to the United States Bureau of the Census, 21 percent of the population lives in the Northeast, 24 percent in the Midwest, 35 percent in the South, and 20 percent in the West. Listed below is a breakdown of a sample of 400 orders randomly selected from those shipped last month.

At the .01 significance level, does the distribution of the orders reflect the population?

Region	Frequency
Northeast	68
Midwest	104
South	155
West	73
Total	400

22. The Banner Mattress and Furniture Company wishes to study the number of credit applications received per day for the last 300 days. The information is reported on the next page.

Number of Credit Applications	Frequency (Number of Days)
0	50
1	77
2	81
3	48
4	31
5 or more	13

To interpret, there were 50 days on which no credit applications were received, 77 days on which only one application was received, and so on. Would it be reasonable to conclude that the population distribution is Poisson with a mean of 2.0? Use the .05 significance level. *Hint:* To find the expected frequencies use the Poisson distribution with a mean of 2.0. Find the probability of exactly one success given a Poisson distribution with a mean of 2.0. Multiply this probability by 300 to find the expected frequency for the number of days in which there was exactly one application. Determine the expected frequency for the other days in a similar manner.

23. In the 1990s the Deep Down Mining Company implemented new safety guidelines. Prior to these new guidelines, management expected there to be no accidents in 40 percent of the months, one accident in 30 percent of the months, two accidents in 20 percent of the months, and three accidents in 10 percent of the months. Over the last 10 years, or 120 months, there have been 46 months in which there were no accidents, 40 months in which there was one accident, 22 months in which there were two accidents, and 12 months in which there were 3 accidents. At the .05 significance level can the management at Deep Down conclude that there has been a change in the monthly accident distribution?

24. A recent study by a large retailer designed to determine whether there was a relationship between the importance a store manager placed on advertising and the size of the store revealed the following sample information:

	Important	Not Important
Small	40	52
Medium	106	47
Large	67	32

What is your conclusion? Use the .05 significance level.

25. Two hundred managers from various levels were randomly selected and interviewed regarding their concern about environmental issues. The response of each person was tallied into one of three categories: no concern, some concern, and great concern. The results were:

Level of Management	No Concern	Some Concern	Great Concern
Top management	15	13	12
Middle management	20	19	21
Supervisor	7	7	6
Group leader	28	21	31

Use the .01 significance level to determine whether there is a relationship between management level and environmental concern.

26. A study regarding the relationship between age and the amount of pressure sales personnel feel in relation to their jobs revealed the following sample information. At the .01 significance level, is there a relationship between job pressure and age?

	Degree of Job Pressure		
Age (years)	**Low**	**Medium**	**High**
Less than 25	20	18	22
25 up to 40	50	46	44
40 up to 60	58	63	59
60 and older	34	43	43

27. The claims department at the Wise Insurance Company believes that younger drivers have more accidents and, therefore, should be charged higher insurance rates. Investigating a sample of 1,200 Wise policyholders revealed the following breakdown on whether a claim had been filed in the last three years and the age of the policyholder. Is it reasonable to conclude that there is a relationship between the age of the policyholder and whether or not the person filed a claim? Use the .05 significance level.

Age Group	No Claim	Claim
16 up to 25	170	74
25 up to 40	240	58
40 up to 55	400	44
55 or older	190	24
Total	1,000	200

28. A sample of employees at a large chemical plant was asked to indicate a preference for one of three pension plans. The results are given in the following table. Does it seem that there is a relationship between the pension plan selected and the job classification of the employees? Use the .01 significance level.

	Pension Plan		
Job Class	**Plan A**	**Plan B**	**Plan C**
Supervisor	10	13	29
Clerical	19	80	19
Labor	81	57	22

exercises.com

WWW

29. Did you ever purchase a bag of M&M candies and wonder about the distribution of colors? You can go to the website www.baking.m-ms.com and click on **About M&Ms,** then click on **History, Products,** and **Peanut** and find the percentage breakdown according to the manufacturer, as well as a brief history of the product. Did you know in the beginning they were all brown? For M&M peanuts 20 percent are blue, 20 percent brown, 20 percent yellow, 20 percent red, 10 percent green, and 10 percent orange. A 6 oz. bag purchased at the Book Store at Coastal Carolina University on November 26, 2001 had 13 blue, 17 brown, 20 yellow, 7 red, 9 orange, and 6 green. Is it reasonable to conclude that actual distribution agrees with the expected distribution? Use the .05 significance level. Conduct your own trial. Be sure to share with your instructor.

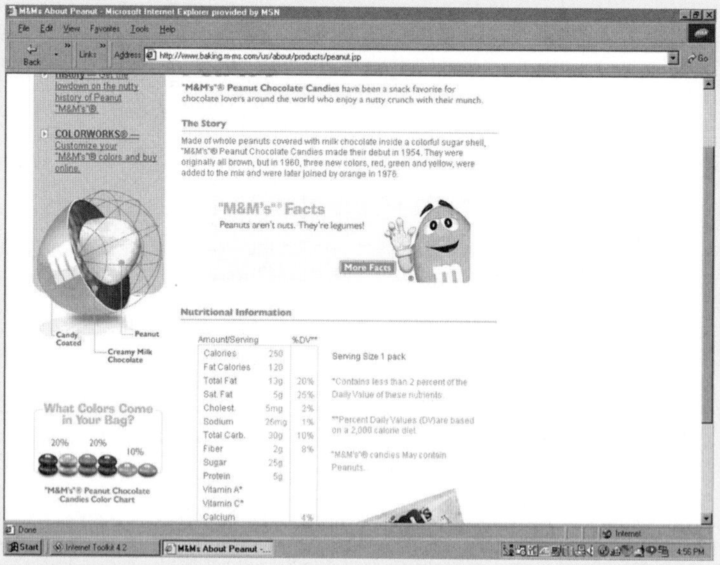

30. As described in earlier chapters, many real estate companies and rental agencies now publish their listings on the World Wide Web. One example is the Dunes Realty Company, located in Garden City and Surfside Beaches in South Carolina. Go to the website www.dunes.com, select **Cottage Search,** then indicate 5 bedroom, accommodations for 14 people, oceanfront, and no pool or floating dock; select a period in July and August; indicate that you are willing to spend $5,000 per week; and then click on **Search the Cottages.** The output should include details on the cottages that met your criteria. Organize the rental rates into a frequency distribution. Is it reasonable to conclude that the distribution is normal with a population mean of $3,000 and standard deviation of $900?

Computer Data Exercises

31. Refer to the Real Estate data, which reports information on homes sold in the Venice, Florida, area last year.

   a. Develop a contingency table that shows whether a home has a pool and the township in which the house is located. Is there an association between the variables "pool" and "township"? Use the .05 significance level.

   b. Develop a contingency table that shows whether a home has an attached garage and the township in which the home is located. Is there an association between the variables "attached garage" and "township"? Use the .05 significance level.

32. Refer to the Baseball 2001 data, which reports information on the 30 Major League Baseball teams for the 2001 season. Set up a variable that divides the teams into two groups, those that had a winning season and those that did not. There are 162 games in the season, so define a winning season as having won 81 or more games. Next, divide the teams into two salary groups. Let the 15 teams with the largest salaries be in one group and the 15 teams with the smallest salaries in the other. At the .05 significance level is there a relationship between salaries and winning?

33. Refer to the wage data, which reports information on annual wages for a sample of 100 workers. Also included are variables relating to industry, years of education, and gender for each worker. Develop a table showing the industry of employment by gender. At the .05 significance level is it reasonable to conclude that industry of employment and gender are related?

34. Refer to the CIA data, which reports demographic and economic information on 46 countries.

   a. Develop a contingency table that shows G-20 membership versus level of petroleum activity. Is there a significant association at the .05 level of significance between these variables?

b. Group the countries into "young" (percent of population over 65 is less than 10) and "old" (percent of population over 65 is more than 10). Then develop a contingency table between this "age" variable and the level of petroleum activity. At the .05 level of significance can we conclude these variables are related?

Computer Commands

1. The MegaStat commands to create the chi-square goodness-of-fit test on page 465 are:
   a. Enter the information from Table 14–1 into a worksheet as shown.
   b. Select **MegaStat, Chi-Square/Crosstabs,** and **Goodness-of-fit** and hit **Enter.**
   c. In the dialog box select *B2:B7* as the **Observed values,** *C2:C7* as the **Expected values,** and enter *0* as the **Number of parameters estimated from the data.** Click on **OK.**

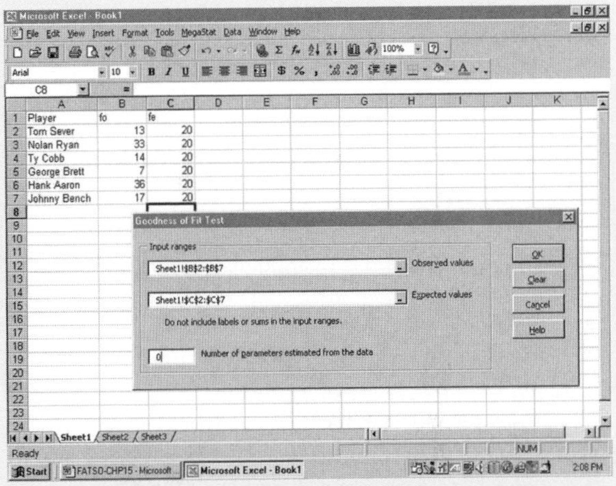

2. The MegaStat commands to create the chi-square goodness-of-fit tests on pages 471 and 472 are the same except for the number of items in the observed and expected frequency columns. Only one dialog box is shown.
   a. Enter the Levels of Management information shown on page 470.
   b. Select **MegaStat, Chi-Square/Crosstabs,** and **Goodness-of-fit** and hit **Enter.**
   c. In the dialog box select *B2:B8* as the **Observed values,** *C2:C8* as the **Expected values,** and enter *0* as the **Number of parameters estimated from the data.** Click on **OK.**

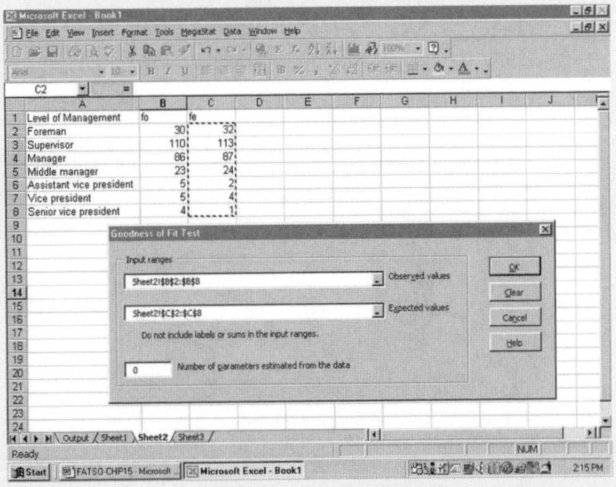

3. The MINITAB commands for the chi-square analysis on page 476 are:
   a. Enter the names of the variables in the first row and the data in the next two rows.
   b. Select **Stat, Table,** and then click on **Chi-square test** and hit **Enter.**
   c. In the dialog box select the columns labeled *Outstanding* to *Unsatisfactory* and click **OK.**

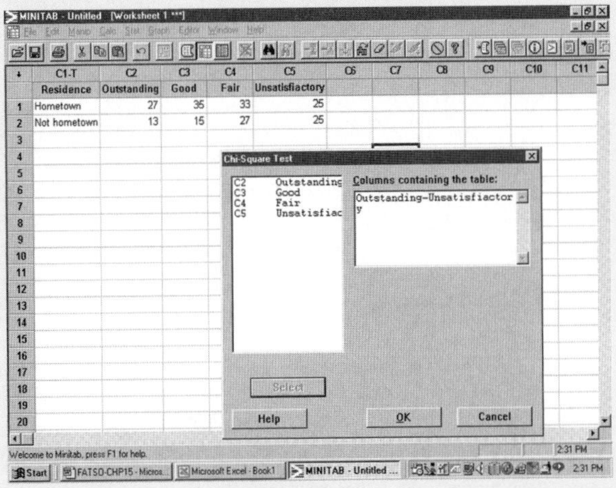

Chapter 14 Answers to Self-Review

14–1 **(a)** Observed frequencies.

(b) Six (six days of the week).

(c) 10. Total observed frequencies ÷ 6 = 60/6 = 10.

(d) 5; $k - 1 = 6 - 1 = 5$.

(e) 15.086 (from the chi-square table in Appendix B).

(f)

$$\chi^2 = \Sigma\left[\frac{(f_o - f_e)^2}{f_e}\right] = \frac{(12 - 10)^2}{10} + \cdots + \frac{(9 - 10)^2}{10} = 0.8$$

(g) No. We do not reject H_0.

(h) Absenteeism is distributed evenly throughout the week. The observed differences are due to sampling variation.

14–2 H_0: $P_C = .60$, $P_L = .30$, and $P_U = .10$.

H_1: Distribution is not as above.

Reject H_0 if $\chi^2 > 5.991$.

Category	f_o	f_e	$\frac{(f_o - f_e)^2}{f_e}$
Current	320	300	1.33
Late	120	150	6.00
Uncollectible	60	50	2.00
	500	500	9.33

Reject H_0. The accounts receivable data does not reflect the national average.

14–3 **(a)** Contingency table

(b) There is no relationship between political affiliation and budget surplus option.

(c) The value of chi-square is computed from the following table.

	Democrat		Republican		Independent		
Option	f_o	f_e	f_o	f_e	f_o	f_e	Total
Reduce taxes	18	14.08	12	11.52	10	14.40	40
Pay down debt	17	15.84	15	12.96	13	16.20	45
Improve Social Security	9	14.08	9	11.52	22	14.40	40
	44	44.00	36	36.00	45	45.00	125

$$\chi^2 = \frac{(18 - 14.08)^2}{14.08} + \frac{(12 - 11.52)^2}{11.52} + \cdots + \frac{(22 - 14.40)^2}{14.40}$$

$$= 9.889$$

The critical value of chi-square is 9.488, so H_0 is rejected.

(d) There is a relationship between the political affiliation and the preferred option.

Appendixes

TABLES AND DATA SETS

Appendix A

Binomial Probability Distribution

n = 1

Probability

x	0.05	0.10	0.20	0.30	0.40	0.50	0.60	0.70	0.80	0.90	0.95
0	0.950	0.900	0.800	0.700	0.600	0.500	0.400	0.300	0.200	0.100	0.050
1	0.050	0.100	0.200	0.300	0.400	0.500	0.600	0.700	0.800	0.900	0.950

n = 2

Probability

x	0.05	0.10	0.20	0.30	0.40	0.50	0.60	0.70	0.80	0.90	0.95
0	0.903	0.810	0.640	0.490	0.360	0.250	0.160	0.090	0.040	0.010	0.003
1	0.095	0.180	0.320	0.420	0.480	0.500	0.480	0.420	0.320	0.180	0.095
2	0.003	0.010	0.040	0.090	0.160	0.250	0.360	0.490	0.640	0.810	0.903

n = 3

Probability

x	0.05	0.10	0.20	0.30	0.40	0.50	0.60	0.70	0.80	0.90	0.95
0	0.857	0.729	0.512	0.343	0.216	0.125	0.064	0.027	0.008	0.001	0.000
1	0.135	0.243	0.384	0.441	0.432	0.375	0.288	0.189	0.096	0.027	0.007
2	0.007	0.027	0.096	0.189	0.288	0.375	0.432	0.441	0.384	0.243	0.135
3	0.000	0.001	0.008	0.027	0.064	0.125	0.216	0.343	0.512	0.729	0.857

n = 4

Probability

x	0.05	0.10	0.20	0.30	0.40	0.50	0.60	0.70	0.80	0.90	0.95
0	0.815	0.656	0.410	0.240	0.130	0.063	0.026	0.008	0.002	0.000	0.000
1	0.171	0.292	0.410	0.412	0.346	0.250	0.154	0.076	0.026	0.004	0.000
2	0.014	0.049	0.154	0.265	0.346	0.375	0.346	0.265	0.154	0.049	0.014
3	0.000	0.004	0.026	0.076	0.154	0.250	0.346	0.412	0.410	0.292	0.171
4	0.000	0.000	0.002	0.008	0.026	0.063	0.130	0.240	0.410	0.656	0.815

n = 5

Probability

x	0.05	0.10	0.20	0.30	0.40	0.50	0.60	0.70	0.80	0.90	0.95
0	0.774	0.590	0.328	0.168	0.078	0.031	0.010	0.002	0.000	0.000	0.000
1	0.204	0.328	0.410	0.360	0.259	0.156	0.077	0.028	0.006	0.000	0.000
2	0.021	0.073	0.205	0.309	0.346	0.313	0.230	0.132	0.051	0.008	0.001
3	0.001	0.008	0.051	0.132	0.230	0.313	0.346	0.309	0.205	0.073	0.021
4	0.000	0.000	0.006	0.028	0.077	0.156	0.259	0.360	0.410	0.328	0.204
5	0.000	0.000	0.000	0.002	0.010	0.031	0.078	0.168	0.328	0.590	0.774

Binomial Probability Distribution *(continued)*

$n = 6$

Probability

x	0.05	0.10	0.20	0.30	0.40	0.50	0.60	0.70	0.80	0.90	0.95
0	0.735	0.531	0.262	0.118	0.047	0.016	0.004	0.001	0.000	0.000	0.000
1	0.232	0.354	0.393	0.303	0.187	0.094	0.037	0.010	0.002	0.000	0.000
2	0.031	0.098	0.246	0.324	0.311	0.234	0.138	0.060	0.015	0.001	0.000
3	0.002	0.015	0.082	0.185	0.276	0.313	0.276	0.185	0.082	0.015	0.002
4	0.000	0.001	0.015	0.060	0.138	0.234	0.311	0.324	0.246	0.098	0.031
5	0.000	0.000	0.002	0.010	0.037	0.094	0.187	0.303	0.393	0.354	0.232
6	0.000	0.000	0.000	0.001	0.004	0.016	0.047	0.118	0.262	0.531	0.735

$n = 7$

Probability

x	0.05	0.10	0.20	0.30	0.40	0.50	0.60	0.70	0.80	0.90	0.95
0	0.698	0.478	0.210	0.082	0.028	0.008	0.002	0.000	0.000	0.000	0.000
1	0.257	0.372	0.367	0.247	0.131	0.055	0.017	0.004	0.000	0.000	0.000
2	0.041	0.124	0.275	0.318	0.261	0.164	0.077	0.025	0.004	0.000	0.000
3	0.004	0.023	0.115	0.227	0.290	0.273	0.194	0.097	0.029	0.003	0.000
4	0.000	0.003	0.029	0.097	0.194	0.273	0.290	0.227	0.115	0.023	0.004
5	0.000	0.000	0.004	0.025	0.077	0.164	0.261	0.318	0.275	0.124	0.041
6	0.000	0.000	0.000	0.004	0.017	0.055	0.131	0.247	0.367	0.372	0.257
7	0.000	0.000	0.000	0.000	0.002	0.008	0.028	0.082	0.210	0.478	0.698

$n = 8$

Probability

x	0.05	0.10	0.20	0.30	0.40	0.50	0.60	0.70	0.80	0.90	0.95
0	0.663	0.430	0.168	0.058	0.017	0.004	0.001	0.000	0.000	0.000	0.000
1	0.279	0.383	0.336	0.198	0.090	0.031	0.008	0.001	0.000	0.000	0.000
2	0.051	0.149	0.294	0.296	0.209	0.109	0.041	0.010	0.001	0.000	0.000
3	0.005	0.033	0.147	0.254	0.279	0.219	0.124	0.047	0.009	0.000	0.000
4	0.000	0.005	0.046	0.136	0.232	0.273	0.232	0.136	0.046	0.005	0.000
5	0.000	0.000	0.009	0.047	0.124	0.219	0.279	0.254	0.147	0.033	0.005
6	0.000	0.000	0.001	0.010	0.041	0.109	0.209	0.296	0.294	0.149	0.051
7	0.000	0.000	0.000	0.001	0.008	0.031	0.090	0.198	0.336	0.383	0.279
8	0.000	0.000	0.000	0.000	0.001	0.004	0.017	0.058	0.168	0.430	0.663

Appendix A

Binomial Probability Distribution *(continued)*

$n = 9$

Probability

x	0.05	0.10	0.20	0.30	0.40	0.50	0.60	0.70	0.80	0.90	0.95
0	0.630	0.387	0.134	0.040	0.010	0.002	0.000	0.000	0.000	0.000	0.000
1	0.299	0.387	0.302	0.156	0.060	0.018	0.004	0.000	0.000	0.000	0.000
2	0.063	0.172	0.302	0.267	0.161	0.070	0.021	0.004	0.000	0.000	0.000
3	0.008	0.045	0.176	0.267	0.251	0.164	0.074	0.021	0.003	0.000	0.000
4	0.001	0.007	0.066	0.172	0.251	0.246	0.167	0.074	0.017	0.001	0.000
5	0.000	0.001	0.017	0.074	0.167	0.246	0.251	0.172	0.066	0.007	0.001
6	0.000	0.000	0.003	0.021	0.074	0.164	0.251	0.267	0.176	0.045	0.008
7	0.000	0.000	0.000	0.004	0.021	0.070	0.161	0.267	0.302	0.172	0.063
8	0.000	0.000	0.000	0.000	0.004	0.018	0.060	0.156	0.302	0.387	0.299
9	0.000	0.000	0.000	0.000	0.000	0.002	0.010	0.040	0.134	0.387	0.630

$n = 10$

Probability

x	0.05	0.10	0.20	0.30	0.40	0.50	0.60	0.70	0.80	0.90	0.95
0	0.599	0.349	0.107	0.028	0.006	0.001	0.000	0.000	0.000	0.000	0.000
1	0.315	0.387	0.268	0.121	0.040	0.010	0.002	0.000	0.000	0.000	0.000
2	0.075	0.194	0.302	0.233	0.121	0.044	0.011	0.001	0.000	0.000	0.000
3	0.010	0.057	0.201	0.267	0.215	0.117	0.042	0.009	0.001	0.000	0.000
4	0.001	0.011	0.088	0.200	0.251	0.205	0.111	0.037	0.006	0.000	0.000
5	0.000	0.001	0.026	0.103	0.201	0.246	0.201	0.103	0.026	0.001	0.000
6	0.000	0.000	0.006	0.037	0.111	0.205	0.251	0.200	0.088	0.011	0.001
7	0.000	0.000	0.001	0.009	0.042	0.117	0.215	0.267	0.201	0.057	0.010
8	0.000	0.000	0.000	0.001	0.011	0.044	0.121	0.233	0.302	0.194	0.075
9	0.000	0.000	0.000	0.000	0.002	0.010	0.040	0.121	0.268	0.387	0.315
10	0.000	0.000	0.000	0.000	0.000	0.001	0.006	0.028	0.107	0.349	0.599

$n = 11$

Probability

x	0.05	0.10	0.20	0.30	0.40	0.50	0.60	0.70	0.80	0.90	0.95
0	0.569	0.314	0.086	0.020	0.004	0.000	0.000	0.000	0.000	0.000	0.000
1	0.329	0.384	0.236	0.093	0.027	0.005	0.001	0.000	0.000	0.000	0.000
2	0.087	0.213	0.295	0.200	0.089	0.027	0.005	0.001	0.000	0.000	0.000
3	0.014	0.071	0.221	0.257	0.177	0.081	0.023	0.004	0.000	0.000	0.000
4	0.001	0.016	0.111	0.220	0.236	0.161	0.070	0.017	0.002	0.000	0.000
5	0.000	0.002	0.039	0.132	0.221	0.226	0.147	0.057	0.010	0.000	0.000
6	0.000	0.000	0.010	0.057	0.147	0.226	0.221	0.132	0.039	0.002	0.000
7	0.000	0.000	0.002	0.017	0.070	0.161	0.236	0.220	0.111	0.016	0.001
8	0.000	0.000	0.000	0.004	0.023	0.081	0.177	0.257	0.221	0.071	0.014
9	0.000	0.000	0.000	0.001	0.005	0.027	0.089	0.200	0.295	0.213	0.087
10	0.000	0.000	0.000	0.000	0.001	0.005	0.027	0.093	0.236	0.384	0.329
11	0.000	0.000	0.000	0.000	0.000	0.000	0.004	0.020	0.086	0.314	0.569

$n = 12$

Probability

x	0.05	0.10	0.20	0.30	0.40	0.50	0.60	0.70	0.80	0.90	0.95
0	0.540	0.282	0.069	0.014	0.002	0.000	0.000	0.000	0.000	0.000	0.000
1	0.341	0.377	0.206	0.071	0.017	0.003	0.000	0.000	0.000	0.000	0.000
2	0.099	0.230	0.283	0.168	0.064	0.016	0.002	0.000	0.000	0.000	0.000
3	0.017	0.085	0.236	0.240	0.142	0.054	0.012	0.001	0.000	0.000	0.000
4	0.002	0.021	0.133	0.231	0.213	0.121	0.042	0.008	0.001	0.000	0.000
5	0.000	0.004	0.053	0.158	0.227	0.193	0.101	0.029	0.003	0.000	0.000
6	0.000	0.000	0.016	0.079	0.177	0.226	0.177	0.079	0.016	0.000	0.000
7	0.000	0.000	0.003	0.029	0.101	0.193	0.227	0.158	0.053	0.004	0.000
8	0.000	0.000	0.001	0.008	0.042	0.121	0.213	0.231	0.133	0.021	0.002
9	0.000	0.000	0.000	0.001	0.012	0.054	0.142	0.240	0.236	0.085	0.017
10	0.000	0.000	0.000	0.000	0.002	0.016	0.064	0.168	0.283	0.230	0.099
11	0.000	0.000	0.000	0.000	0.000	0.003	0.017	0.071	0.206	0.377	0.341
12	0.000	0.000	0.000	0.000	0.000	0.000	0.002	0.014	0.069	0.282	0.540

$n = 13$

Probability

x	0.05	0.10	0.20	0.30	0.40	0.50	0.60	0.70	0.80	0.90	0.95
0	0.513	0.254	0.055	0.010	0.001	0.000	0.000	0.000	0.000	0.000	0.000
1	0.351	0.367	0.179	0.054	0.011	0.002	0.000	0.000	0.000	0.000	0.000
2	0.111	0.245	0.268	0.139	0.045	0.010	0.001	0.000	0.000	0.000	0.000
3	0.021	0.100	0.246	0.218	0.111	0.035	0.006	0.001	0.000	0.000	0.000
4	0.003	0.028	0.154	0.234	0.184	0.087	0.024	0.003	0.000	0.000	0.000
5	0.000	0.006	0.069	0.180	0.221	0.157	0.066	0.014	0.001	0.000	0.000
6	0.000	0.001	0.023	0.103	0.197	0.209	0.131	0.044	0.006	0.000	0.000
7	0.000	0.000	0.006	0.044	0.131	0.209	0.197	0.103	0.023	0.001	0.000
8	0.000	0.000	0.001	0.014	0.066	0.157	0.221	0.180	0.069	0.006	0.000
9	0.000	0.000	0.000	0.003	0.024	0.087	0.184	0.234	0.154	0.028	0.003
10	0.000	0.000	0.000	0.001	0.006	0.035	0.111	0.218	0.246	0.100	0.021
11	0.000	0.000	0.000	0.000	0.001	0.010	0.045	0.139	0.268	0.245	0.111
12	0.000	0.000	0.000	0.000	0.000	0.002	0.011	0.054	0.179	0.367	0.351
13	0.000	0.000	0.000	0.000	0.000	0.000	0.001	0.010	0.055	0.254	0.513

Appendix A

Binomial Probability Distribution *(continued)*

n = 14

Probability

x	0.05	0.10	0.20	0.30	0.40	0.50	0.60	0.70	0.80	0.90	0.95
0	0.488	0.229	0.044	0.007	0.001	0.000	0.000	0.000	0.000	0.000	0.000
1	0.359	0.356	0.154	0.041	0.007	0.001	0.000	0.000	0.000	0.000	0.000
2	0.123	0.257	0.250	0.113	0.032	0.006	0.001	0.000	0.000	0.000	0.000
3	0.026	0.114	0.250	0.194	0.085	0.022	0.003	0.000	0.000	0.000	0.000
4	0.004	0.035	0.172	0.229	0.155	0.061	0.014	0.001	0.000	0.000	0.000
5	0.000	0.008	0.086	0.196	0.207	0.122	0.041	0.007	0.000	0.000	0.000
6	0.000	0.001	0.032	0.126	0.207	0.183	0.092	0.023	0.002	0.000	0.000
7	0.000	0.000	0.009	0.062	0.157	0.209	0.157	0.062	0.009	0.000	0.000
8	0.000	0.000	0.002	0.023	0.092	0.183	0.207	0.126	0.032	0.001	0.000
9	0.000	0.000	0.000	0.007	0.041	0.122	0.207	0.196	0.086	0.008	0.000
10	0.000	0.000	0.000	0.001	0.014	0.061	0.155	0.229	0.172	0.035	0.004
11	0.000	0.000	0.000	0.000	0.003	0.022	0.085	0.194	0.250	0.114	0.026
12	0.000	0.000	0.000	0.000	0.001	0.006	0.032	0.113	0.250	0.257	0.123
13	0.000	0.000	0.000	0.000	0.000	0.001	0.007	0.041	0.154	0.356	0.359
14	0.000	0.000	0.000	0.000	0.000	0.000	0.001	0.007	0.044	0.229	0.488

n = 15

Probability

x	0.05	0.10	0.20	0.30	0.40	0.50	0.60	0.70	0.80	0.90	0.95
0	0.463	0.206	0.035	0.005	0.000	0.000	0.000	0.000	0.000	0.000	0.000
1	0.366	0.343	0.132	0.031	0.005	0.000	0.000	0.000	0.000	0.000	0.000
2	0.135	0.267	0.231	0.092	0.022	0.003	0.000	0.000	0.000	0.000	0.000
3	0.031	0.129	0.250	0.170	0.063	0.014	0.002	0.000	0.000	0.000	0.000
4	0.005	0.043	0.188	0.219	0.127	0.042	0.007	0.001	0.000	0.000	0.000
5	0.001	0.010	0.103	0.206	0.186	0.092	0.024	0.003	0.000	0.000	0.000
6	0.000	0.002	0.043	0.147	0.207	0.153	0.061	0.012	0.001	0.000	0.000
7	0.000	0.000	0.014	0.081	0.177	0.196	0.118	0.035	0.003	0.000	0.000
8	0.000	0.000	0.003	0.035	0.118	0.196	0.177	0.081	0.014	0.000	0.000
9	0.000	0.000	0.001	0.012	0.061	0.153	0.207	0.147	0.043	0.002	0.000
10	0.000	0.000	0.000	0.003	0.024	0.092	0.186	0.206	0.103	0.010	0.001
11	0.000	0.000	0.000	0.001	0.007	0.042	0.127	0.219	0.188	0.043	0.005
12	0.000	0.000	0.000	0.000	0.002	0.014	0.063	0.170	0.250	0.129	0.031
13	0.000	0.000	0.000	0.000	0.000	0.003	0.022	0.092	0.231	0.267	0.135
14	0.000	0.000	0.000	0.000	0.000	0.000	0.005	0.031	0.132	0.343	0.366
15	0.000	0.000	0.000	0.000	0.000	0.000	0.000	0.005	0.035	0.206	0.463

Binomial Probability Distribution *(continued)*

$n = 16$

Probability

x	0.05	0.10	0.20	0.30	0.40	0.50	0.60	0.70	0.80	0.90	0.95
0	0.440	0.185	0.028	0.003	0.000	0.000	0.000	0.000	0.000	0.000	0.000
1	0.371	0.329	0.113	0.023	0.003	0.000	0.000	0.000	0.000	0.000	0.000
2	0.146	0.275	0.211	0.073	0.015	0.002	0.000	0.000	0.000	0.000	0.000
3	0.036	0.142	0.246	0.146	0.047	0.009	0.001	0.000	0.000	0.000	0.000
4	0.006	0.051	0.200	0.204	0.101	0.028	0.004	0.000	0.000	0.000	0.000
5	0.001	0.014	0.120	0.210	0.162	0.067	0.014	0.001	0.000	0.000	0.000
6	0.000	0.003	0.055	0.165	0.198	0.122	0.039	0.006	0.000	0.000	0.000
7	0.000	0.000	0.020	0.101	0.189	0.175	0.084	0.019	0.001	0.000	0.000
8	0.000	0.000	0.006	0.049	0.142	0.196	0.142	0.049	0.006	0.000	0.000
9	0.000	0.000	0.001	0.019	0.084	0.175	0.189	0.101	0.020	0.000	0.000
10	0.000	0.000	0.000	0.006	0.039	0.122	0.198	0.165	0.055	0.003	0.000
11	0.000	0.000	0.000	0.001	0.014	0.067	0.162	0.210	0.120	0.014	0.001
12	0.000	0.000	0.000	0.000	0.004	0.028	0.101	0.204	0.200	0.051	0.006
13	0.000	0.000	0.000	0.000	0.001	0.009	0.047	0.146	0.246	0.142	0.036
14	0.000	0.000	0.000	0.000	0.000	0.002	0.015	0.073	0.211	0.275	0.146
15	0.000	0.000	0.000	0.000	0.000	0.000	0.003	0.023	0.113	0.329	0.371
16	0.000	0.000	0.000	0.000	0.000	0.000	0.000	0.003	0.028	0.185	0.440

$n = 17$

Probability

x	0.05	0.10	0.20	0.30	0.40	0.50	0.60	0.70	0.80	0.90	0.95
0	0.418	0.167	0.023	0.002	0.000	0.000	0.000	0.000	0.000	0.000	0.000
1	0.374	0.315	0.096	0.017	0.002	0.000	0.000	0.000	0.000	0.000	0.000
2	0.158	0.280	0.191	0.058	0.010	0.001	0.000	0.000	0.000	0.000	0.000
3	0.041	0.156	0.239	0.125	0.034	0.005	0.000	0.000	0.000	0.000	0.000
4	0.008	0.060	0.209	0.187	0.080	0.018	0.002	0.000	0.000	0.000	0.000
5	0.001	0.017	0.136	0.208	0.138	0.047	0.008	0.001	0.000	0.000	0.000
6	0.000	0.004	0.068	0.178	0.184	0.094	0.024	0.003	0.000	0.000	0.000
7	0.000	0.001	0.027	0.120	0.193	0.148	0.057	0.009	0.000	0.000	0.000
8	0.000	0.000	0.008	0.064	0.161	0.185	0.107	0.028	0.002	0.000	0.000
9	0.000	0.000	0.002	0.028	0.107	0.185	0.161	0.064	0.008	0.000	0.000
10	0.000	0.000	0.000	0.009	0.057	0.148	0.193	0.120	0.027	0.001	0.000
11	0.000	0.000	0.000	0.003	0.024	0.094	0.184	0.178	0.068	0.004	0.000
12	0.000	0.000	0.000	0.001	0.008	0.047	0.138	0.208	0.136	0.017	0.001
13	0.000	0.000	0.000	0.000	0.002	0.018	0.080	0.187	0.209	0.060	0.008
14	0.000	0.000	0.000	0.000	0.000	0.005	0.034	0.125	0.239	0.156	0.041
15	0.000	0.000	0.000	0.000	0.000	0.001	0.010	0.058	0.191	0.280	0.158
16	0.000	0.000	0.000	0.000	0.000	0.000	0.002	0.017	0.096	0.315	0.374
17	0.000	0.000	0.000	0.000	0.000	0.000	0.000	0.002	0.023	0.167	0.418

Appendix A

Binomial Probability Distribution *(continued)*

n = 18

	Probability										
x	0.05	0.10	0.20	0.30	0.40	0.50	0.60	0.70	0.80	0.90	0.95
0	0.397	0.150	0.018	0.002	0.000	0.000	0.000	0.000	0.000	0.000	0.000
1	0.376	0.300	0.081	0.013	0.001	0.000	0.000	0.000	0.000	0.000	0.000
2	0.168	0.284	0.172	0.046	0.007	0.001	0.000	0.000	0.000	0.000	0.000
3	0.047	0.168	0.230	0.105	0.025	0.003	0.000	0.000	0.000	0.000	0.000
4	0.009	0.070	0.215	0.168	0.061	0.012	0.001	0.000	0.000	0.000	0.000
5	0.001	0.022	0.151	0.202	0.115	0.033	0.004	0.000	0.000	0.000	0.000
6	0.000	0.005	0.082	0.187	0.166	0.071	0.015	0.001	0.000	0.000	0.000
7	0.000	0.001	0.035	0.138	0.189	0.121	0.037	0.005	0.000	0.000	0.000
8	0.000	0.000	0.012	0.081	0.173	0.167	0.077	0.015	0.001	0.000	0.000
9	0.000	0.000	0.003	0.039	0.128	0.185	0.128	0.039	0.003	0.000	0.000
10	0.000	0.000	0.001	0.015	0.077	0.167	0.173	0.081	0.012	0.000	0.000
11	0.000	0.000	0.000	0.005	0.037	0.121	0.189	0.138	0.035	0.001	0.000
12	0.000	0.000	0.000	0.001	0.015	0.071	0.166	0.187	0.082	0.005	0.000
13	0.000	0.000	0.000	0.000	0.004	0.033	0.115	0.202	0.151	0.022	0.001
14	0.000	0.000	0.000	0.000	0.001	0.012	0.061	0.168	0.215	0.070	0.009
15	0.000	0.000	0.000	0.000	0.000	0.003	0.025	0.105	0.230	0.168	0.047
16	0.000	0.000	0.000	0.000	0.000	0.001	0.007	0.046	0.172	0.284	0.168
17	0.000	0.000	0.000	0.000	0.000	0.000	0.001	0.013	0.081	0.300	0.376
18	0.000	0.000	0.000	0.000	0.000	0.000	0.000	0.002	0.018	0.150	0.397

n = 19

	Probability										
x	0.05	0.10	0.20	0.30	0.40	0.50	0.60	0.70	0.80	0.90	0.95
0	0.377	0.135	0.014	0.001	0.000	0.000	0.000	0.000	0.000	0.000	0.000
1	0.377	0.285	0.068	0.009	0.001	0.000	0.000	0.000	0.000	0.000	0.000
2	0.179	0.285	0.154	0.036	0.005	0.000	0.000	0.000	0.000	0.000	0.000
3	0.053	0.180	0.218	0.087	0.017	0.002	0.000	0.000	0.000	0.000	0.000
4	0.011	0.080	0.218	0.149	0.047	0.007	0.001	0.000	0.000	0.000	0.000
5	0.002	0.027	0.164	0.192	0.093	0.022	0.002	0.000	0.000	0.000	0.000
6	0.000	0.007	0.095	0.192	0.145	0.052	0.008	0.001	0.000	0.000	0.000
7	0.000	0.001	0.044	0.153	0.180	0.096	0.024	0.002	0.000	0.000	0.000
8	0.000	0.000	0.017	0.098	0.180	0.144	0.053	0.008	0.000	0.000	0.000
9	0.000	0.000	0.005	0.051	0.146	0.176	0.098	0.022	0.001	0.000	0.000
10	0.000	0.000	0.001	0.022	0.098	0.176	0.146	0.051	0.005	0.000	0.000
11	0.000	0.000	0.000	0.008	0.053	0.144	0.180	0.098	0.017	0.000	0.000
12	0.000	0.000	0.000	0.002	0.024	0.096	0.180	0.153	0.044	0.001	0.000
13	0.000	0.000	0.000	0.001	0.008	0.052	0.145	0.192	0.095	0.007	0.000
14	0.000	0.000	0.000	0.000	0.002	0.022	0.093	0.192	0.164	0.027	0.002
15	0.000	0.000	0.000	0.000	0.001	0.007	0.047	0.149	0.218	0.080	0.011
16	0.000	0.000	0.000	0.000	0.000	0.002	0.017	0.087	0.218	0.180	0.053
17	0.000	0.000	0.000	0.000	0.000	0.000	0.005	0.036	0.154	0.285	0.179
18	0.000	0.000	0.000	0.000	0.000	0.000	0.001	0.009	0.068	0.285	0.377
19	0.000	0.000	0.000	0.000	0.000	0.000	0.000	0.001	0.014	0.135	0.377

Appendix A

Binomial Probability Distribution *(continued)*

n = 20

Probability

x	0.05	0.10	0.20	0.30	0.40	0.50	0.60	0.70	0.80	0.90	0.95
0	0.358	0.122	0.012	0.001	0.000	0.000	0.000	0.000	0.000	0.000	0.000
1	0.377	0.270	0.058	0.007	0.000	0.000	0.000	0.000	0.000	0.000	0.000
2	0.189	0.285	0.137	0.028	0.003	0.000	0.000	0.000	0.000	0.000	0.000
3	0.060	0.190	0.205	0.072	0.012	0.001	0.000	0.000	0.000	0.000	0.000
4	0.013	0.090	0.218	0.130	0.035	0.005	0.000	0.000	0.000	0.000	0.000
5	0.002	0.032	0.175	0.179	0.075	0.015	0.001	0.000	0.000	0.000	0.000
6	0.000	0.009	0.109	0.192	0.124	0.037	0.005	0.000	0.000	0.000	0.000
7	0.000	0.002	0.055	0.164	0.166	0.074	0.015	0.001	0.000	0.000	0.000
8	0.000	0.000	0.022	0.114	0.180	0.120	0.035	0.004	0.000	0.000	0.000
9	0.000	0.000	0.007	0.065	0.160	0.160	0.071	0.012	0.000	0.000	0.000
10	0.000	0.000	0.002	0.031	0.117	0.176	0.117	0.031	0.002	0.000	0.000
11	0.000	0.000	0.000	0.012	0.071	0.160	0.160	0.065	0.007	0.000	0.000
12	0.000	0.000	0.000	0.004	0.035	0.120	0.180	0.114	0.022	0.000	0.000
13	0.000	0.000	0.000	0.001	0.015	0.074	0.166	0.164	0.055	0.002	0.000
14	0.000	0.000	0.000	0.000	0.005	0.037	0.124	0.192	0.109	0.009	0.000
15	0.000	0.000	0.000	0.000	0.001	0.015	0.075	0.179	0.175	0.032	0.002
16	0.000	0.000	0.000	0.000	0.000	0.005	0.035	0.130	0.218	0.090	0.013
17	0.000	0.000	0.000	0.000	0.000	0.001	0.012	0.072	0.205	0.190	0.060
18	0.000	0.000	0.000	0.000	0.000	0.000	0.003	0.028	0.137	0.285	0.189
19	0.000	0.000	0.000	0.000	0.000	0.000	0.000	0.007	0.058	0.270	0.377
20	0.000	0.000	0.000	0.000	0.000	0.000	0.000	0.001	0.012	0.122	0.358

Appendix A

Binomial Probability Distribution *(concluded)*

n = 25

Probability

x	0.05	0.10	0.20	0.30	0.40	0.50	0.60	0.70	0.80	0.90	0.95
0	0.277	0.072	0.004	0.000	0.000	0.000	0.000	0.000	0.000	0.000	0.000
1	0.365	0.199	0.024	0.001	0.000	0.000	0.000	0.000	0.000	0.000	0.000
2	0.231	0.266	0.071	0.007	0.000	0.000	0.000	0.000	0.000	0.000	0.000
3	0.093	0.226	0.136	0.024	0.002	0.000	0.000	0.000	0.000	0.000	0.000
4	0.027	0.138	0.187	0.057	0.007	0.000	0.000	0.000	0.000	0.000	0.000
5	0.006	0.065	0.196	0.103	0.020	0.002	0.000	0.000	0.000	0.000	0.000
6	0.001	0.024	0.163	0.147	0.044	0.005	0.000	0.000	0.000	0.000	0.000
7	0.000	0.007	0.111	0.171	0.080	0.014	0.001	0.000	0.000	0.000	0.000
8	0.000	0.002	0.062	0.165	0.120	0.032	0.003	0.000	0.000	0.000	0.000
9	0.000	0.000	0.029	0.134	0.151	0.061	0.009	0.000	0.000	0.000	0.000
10	0.000	0.000	0.012	0.092	0.161	0.097	0.021	0.001	0.000	0.000	0.000
11	0.000	0.000	0.004	0.054	0.147	0.133	0.043	0.004	0.000	0.000	0.000
12	0.000	0.000	0.001	0.027	0.114	0.155	0.076	0.011	0.000	0.000	0.000
13	0.000	0.000	0.000	0.011	0.076	0.155	0.114	0.027	0.001	0.000	0.000
14	0.000	0.000	0.000	0.004	0.043	0.133	0.147	0.054	0.004	0.000	0.000
15	0.000	0.000	0.000	0.001	0.021	0.097	0.161	0.092	0.012	0.000	0.000
16	0.000	0.000	0.000	0.000	0.009	0.061	0.151	0.134	0.029	0.000	0.000
17	0.000	0.000	0.000	0.000	0.003	0.032	0.120	0.165	0.062	0.002	0.000
18	0.000	0.000	0.000	0.000	0.001	0.014	0.080	0.171	0.111	0.007	0.000
19	0.000	0.000	0.000	0.000	0.000	0.005	0.044	0.147	0.163	0.024	0.001
20	0.000	0.000	0.000	0.000	0.000	0.002	0.020	0.103	0.196	0.065	0.006
21	0.000	0.000	0.000	0.000	0.000	0.000	0.007	0.057	0.187	0.138	0.027
22	0.000	0.000	0.000	0.000	0.000	0.000	0.002	0.024	0.136	0.226	0.093
23	0.000	0.000	0.000	0.000	0.000	0.000	0.000	0.007	0.071	0.266	0.231
24	0.000	0.000	0.000	0.000	0.000	0.000	0.000	0.001	0.024	0.199	0.365
25	0.000	0.000	0.000	0.000	0.000	0.000	0.000	0.000	0.004	0.072	0.277

Appendix B

Critical Values of Chi-Square

This table contains the values of χ^2 that correspond to a specific right-tail area and specific number of degrees of freedom.

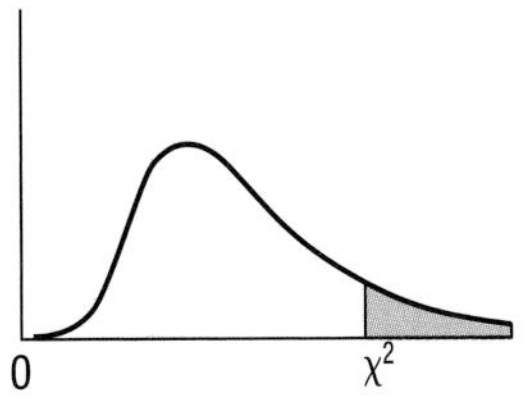

Example: With 17 *df* and a .02 area in the upper tail, χ^2=30.995

Degrees of Freedom, *df*	Right-Tail Area			
	0.10	**0.05**	**0.02**	**0.01**
1	2.706	3.841	5.412	6.635
2	4.605	5.991	7.824	9.210
3	6.251	7.815	9.837	11.345
4	7.779	9.488	11.668	13.277
5	9.236	11.070	13.388	15.086
6	10.645	12.592	15.033	16.812
7	12.017	14.067	16.622	18.475
8	13.362	15.507	18.168	20.090
9	14.684	16.919	19.679	21.666
10	15.987	18.307	21.161	23.209
11	17.275	19.675	22.618	24.725
12	18.549	21.026	24.054	26.217
13	19.812	22.362	25.472	27.688
14	21.064	23.685	26.873	29.141
15	22.307	24.996	28.259	30.578
16	23.542	26.296	29.633	32.000
17	24.769	27.587	30.995	33.409
18	25.989	28.869	32.346	34.805
19	27.204	30.144	33.687	36.191
20	28.412	31.410	35.020	37.566
21	29.615	32.671	36.343	38.932
22	30.813	33.924	37.659	40.289
23	32.007	35.172	38.968	41.638
24	33.196	36.415	40.270	42.980
25	34.382	37.652	41.566	44.314
26	35.563	38.885	42.856	45.642
27	36.741	40.113	44.140	46.963
28	37.916	41.337	45.419	48.278
29	39.087	42.557	46.693	49.588
30	40.256	43.773	47.962	50.892

Appendix C

Poisson Distribution

	μ								
x	**0.1**	**0.2**	**0.3**	**0.4**	**0.5**	**0.6**	**0.7**	**0.8**	**0.9**
0	0.9048	0.8187	0.7408	0.6703	0.6065	0.5488	0.4966	0.4493	0.4066
1	0.0905	0.1637	0.2222	0.2681	0.3033	0.3293	0.3476	0.3595	0.3659
2	0.0045	0.0164	0.0333	0.0536	0.0758	0.0988	0.1217	0.1438	0.1647
3	0.0002	0.0011	0.0033	0.0072	0.0126	0.0198	0.0284	0.0383	0.0494
4	0.0000	0.0001	0.0003	0.0007	0.0016	0.0030	0.0050	0.0077	0.0111
5	0.0000	0.0000	0.0000	0.0001	0.0002	0.0004	0.0007	0.0012	0.0020
6	0.0000	0.0000	0.0000	0.0000	0.0000	0.0000	0.0001	0.0002	0.0003
7	0.0000	0.0000	0.0000	0.0000	0.0000	0.0000	0.0000	0.0000	0.0000

	μ								
x	**1.0**	**2.0**	**3.0**	**4.0**	**5.0**	**6.0**	**7.0**	**8.0**	**9.0**
0	0.3679	0.1353	0.0498	0.0183	0.0067	0.0025	0.0009	0.0003	0.0001
1	0.3679	0.2707	0.1494	0.0733	0.0337	0.0149	0.0064	0.0027	0.0011
2	0.1839	0.2707	0.2240	0.1465	0.0842	0.0446	0.0223	0.0107	0.0050
3	0.0613	0.1804	0.2240	0.1954	0.1404	0.0892	0.0521	0.0286	0.0150
4	0.0153	0.0902	0.1680	0.1954	0.1755	0.1339	0.0912	0.0573	0.0337
5	0.0031	0.0361	0.1008	0.1563	0.1755	0.1606	0.1277	0.0916	0.0607
6	0.0005	0.0120	0.0504	0.1042	0.1462	0.1606	0.1490	0.1221	0.0911
7	0.0001	0.0034	0.0216	0.0595	0.1044	0.1377	0.1490	0.1396	0.1171
8	0.0000	0.0009	0.0081	0.0298	0.0653	0.1033	0.1304	0.1396	0.1318
9	0.0000	0.0002	0.0027	0.0132	0.0363	0.0688	0.1014	0.1241	0.1318
10	0.0000	0.0000	0.0008	0.0053	0.0181	0.0413	0.0710	0.0993	0.1186
11	0.0000	0.0000	0.0002	0.0019	0.0082	0.0225	0.0452	0.0722	0.0970
12	0.0000	0.0000	0.0001	0.0006	0.0034	0.0113	0.0263	0.0481	0.0728
13	0.0000	0.0000	0.0000	0.0002	0.0013	0.0052	0.0142	0.0296	0.0504
14	0.0000	0.0000	0.0000	0.0001	0.0005	0.0022	0.0071	0.0169	0.0324
15	0.0000	0.0000	0.0000	0.0000	0.0002	0.0009	0.0033	0.0090	0.0194
16	0.0000	0.0000	0.0000	0.0000	0.0000	0.0003	0.0014	0.0045	0.0109
17	0.0000	0.0000	0.0000	0.0000	0.0000	0.0001	0.0006	0.0021	0.0058
18	0.0000	0.0000	0.0000	0.0000	0.0000	0.0000	0.0002	0.0009	0.0029
19	0.0000	0.0000	0.0000	0.0000	0.0000	0.0000	0.0001	0.0004	0.0014
20	0.0000	0.0000	0.0000	0.0000	0.0000	0.0000	0.0000	0.0002	0.0006
21	0.0000	0.0000	0.0000	0.0000	0.0000	0.0000	0.0000	0.0001	0.0003
22	0.0000	0.0000	0.0000	0.0000	0.0000	0.0000	0.0000	0.0000	0.0001

Appendix D

Areas under the Normal Curve

Example:
If $z = 1.96$, then
$P(0 \text{ to } z) = 0.4750$

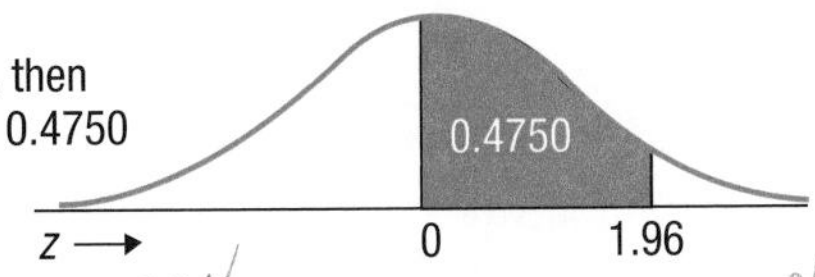

z	0.00	0.01	0.02	0.03	0.04	0.05	0.06	0.07	0.08	0.09
0.0	0.0000	0.0040	0.0080	0.0120	0.0160	0.0199	0.0239	0.0279	0.0319	0.0359
0.1	0.0398	0.0438	0.0478	0.0517	0.0557	0.0596	0.0636	0.0675	0.0714	0.0753
0.2	0.0793	0.0832	0.0871	0.0910	0.0948	0.0987	0.1026	0.1064	0.1103	0.1141
0.3	0.1179	0.1217	0.1255	0.1293	0.1331	0.1368	0.1406	0.1443	0.1480	0.1517
0.4	0.1554	0.1591	0.1628	0.1664	0.1700	0.1736	0.1772	0.1808	0.1844	0.1879
0.5	0.1915	0.1950	0.1985	0.2019	0.2054	0.2088	0.2123	0.2157	0.2190	0.2224
0.6	0.2257	0.2291	0.2324	0.2357	0.2389	0.2422	0.2454	0.2486	0.2517	0.2549
0.7	0.2580	0.2611	0.2642	0.2673	0.2704	0.2734	0.2764	0.2794	0.2823	0.2852
0.8	0.2881	0.2910	0.2939	0.2967	0.2995	0.3023	0.3051	0.3078	0.3106	0.3133
0.9	0.3159	0.3186	0.3212	0.3238	0.3264	0.3289	0.3315	0.3340	0.3365	0.3389
1.0	0.3413	0.3438	0.3461	0.3485	0.3508	0.3531	0.3554	0.3577	0.3599	0.3621
1.1	0.3643	0.3665	0.3686	0.3708	0.3729	0.3749	0.3770	0.3790	0.3810	0.3830
1.2	0.3849	0.3869	0.3888	0.3907	0.3925	0.3944	0.3962	0.3980	0.3997	0.4015
1.3	0.4032	0.4049	0.4066	0.4082	0.4099	0.4115	0.4131	0.4147	0.4162	0.4177
1.4	0.4192	0.4207	0.4222	0.4236	0.4251	0.4265	0.4279	0.4292	0.4306	0.4319
1.5	0.4332	0.4345	0.4357	0.4370	0.4382	0.4394	0.4406	0.4418	0.4429	0.4441
1.6	0.4452	0.4463	0.4474	0.4484	0.4495	0.4505	0.4515	0.4525	0.4535	0.4545
1.7	0.4554	0.4564	0.4573	0.4582	0.4591	0.4599	0.4608	0.4616	0.4625	0.4633
1.8	0.4641	0.4649	0.4656	0.4664	0.4671	0.4678	0.4686	0.4693	0.4699	0.4706
1.9	0.4713	0.4719	0.4726	0.4732	0.4738	0.4744	0.4750	0.4756	0.4761	0.4767
2.0	0.4772	0.4778	0.4783	0.4788	0.4793	0.4798	0.4803	0.4808	0.4812	0.4817
2.1	0.4821	0.4826	0.4830	0.4834	0.4838	0.4842	0.4846	0.4850	0.4854	0.4857
2.2	0.4861	0.4864	0.4868	0.4871	0.4875	0.4878	0.4881	0.4884	0.4887	0.4890
2.3	0.4893	0.4896	0.4898	0.4901	0.4904	0.4906	0.4909	0.4911	0.4913	0.4916
2.4	0.4918	0.4920	0.4922	0.4925	0.4927	0.4929	0.4931	0.4932	0.4934	0.4936
2.5	0.4938	0.4940	0.4941	0.4943	0.4945	0.4946	0.4948	0.4949	0.4951	0.4952
2.6	0.4953	0.4955	0.4956	0.4957	0.4959	0.4960	0.4961	0.4962	0.4963	0.4964
2.7	0.4965	0.4966	0.4967	0.4968	0.4969	0.4970	0.4971	0.4972	0.4973	0.4974
2.8	0.4974	0.4975	0.4976	0.4977	0.4977	0.4978	0.4979	0.4979	0.4980	0.4981
2.9	0.4981	0.4982	0.4982	0.4983	0.4984	0.4984	0.4985	0.4985	0.4986	0.4986
3.0	0.4987	0.4987	0.4987	0.4988	0.4988	0.4989	0.4989	0.4989	0.4990	0.4990

Appendix E

Table of Random Numbers

02711	08182	75997	79866	58095	83319	80295	79741	74599	84379
94873	90935	31684	63952	09865	14491	99518	93394	34691	14985
54921	78680	06635	98689	17306	25170	65928	87709	30533	89736
77640	97636	37397	93379	56454	59818	45827	74164	71666	46977
61545	00835	93251	87203	36759	49197	85967	01704	19634	21898
17147	19519	22497	16857	42426	84822	92598	49186	88247	39967
13748	04742	92460	85801	53444	65626	58710	55406	17173	69776
87455	14813	50373	28037	91182	32786	65261	11173	34376	36408
08999	57409	91185	10200	61411	23392	47797	56377	71635	08601
78804	81333	53809	32471	46034	36306	22498	19239	85428	55721
82173	26921	28472	98958	07960	66124	89731	95069	18625	92405
97594	25168	89178	68190	05043	17407	48201	83917	11413	72920
73881	67176	93504	42636	38233	16154	96451	57925	29667	30859
46071	22912	90326	42453	88108	72064	58601	32357	90610	32921
44492	19686	12495	93135	95185	77799	52441	88272	22024	80631
31864	72170	37722	55794	14636	05148	54505	50113	21119	25228
51574	90692	43339	65689	76539	27909	05467	21727	51141	72949
35350	76132	92925	92124	92634	35681	43690	89136	35599	84138
46943	36502	01172	46045	46991	33804	80006	35542	61056	75666
22665	87226	33304	57975	03985	21566	65796	72915	81466	89205
39437	97957	11838	10433	21564	51570	73558	27495	34533	57808
77082	47784	40098	97962	89845	28392	78187	06112	08169	11261
24544	25649	43370	28007	06779	72402	62632	53956	24709	06978
27503	15558	37738	24849	70722	71859	83736	06016	94397	12529
24590	24545	06435	52758	45685	90151	46516	49644	92686	84870
48155	86226	40359	28723	15364	69125	12609	57171	86857	31702
20226	53752	90648	24362	83314	00014	19207	69413	97016	86290
70178	73444	38790	53626	93780	18629	68766	24371	74639	30782
10169	41465	51935	05711	09799	79077	88159	33437	68519	03040
81084	03701	28598	70013	63794	53169	97054	60303	23259	96196
69202	20777	21727	81511	51887	16175	53746	46516	70339	62727
80561	95787	89426	93325	86412	57479	54194	52153	19197	81877
08199	26703	95128	48599	09333	12584	24374	31232	61782	44032
98883	28220	39358	53720	80161	83371	15181	11131	12219	55920
84568	69286	76054	21615	80883	36797	82845	39139	90900	18172
04269	35173	95745	53893	86022	77722	52498	84193	22448	22571
10538	13124	36099	13140	37706	44562	57179	44693	67877	01549
77843	24955	25900	63843	95029	93859	93634	20205	66294	41218
12034	94636	49455	76362	83532	31062	69903	91186	65768	55949
10524	72829	47641	93315	80875	28090	97728	52560	34937	79548
68935	76632	46984	61772	92786	22651	07086	89754	44143	97687
89450	65665	29190	43709	11172	34481	95977	47535	25658	73898
90696	20451	24211	97310	60446	73530	62865	96574	13829	72226
49006	32047	93086	00112	20470	17136	28255	86328	07293	38809
74591	87025	52368	59416	34417	70557	86746	55809	53628	12000
06315	17012	77103	00968	07235	10728	42189	33292	51487	64443
62386	09184	62092	46617	99419	64230	95034	85481	07857	42510
86848	82122	04028	36959	87827	12813	08627	80699	13345	51695
65643	69480	46598	04501	40403	91408	32343	48130	49303	90689
11084	46534	78957	77353	39578	77868	22970	84349	09184	70603

Student's *t* Distribution

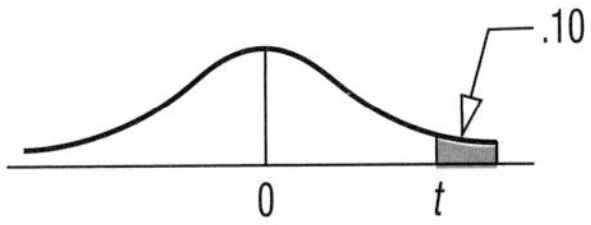

Example: With $df = 9$ and .10 area in the upper tail, $t = 1.383$

	Confidence Intervals					
	80%	90%	95%	98%	99%	99.9%
	Level of Significance for One-Tailed Test					
df	0.100	0.050	0.025	0.010	0.005	0.0005
	Level of Significance for Two-Tailed Test					
	0.20	0.10	0.05	0.02	0.01	0.001
1	3.078	6.314	12.706	31.821	63.657	636.619
2	1.886	2.920	4.303	6.965	9.925	31.599
3	1.638	2.353	3.182	4.541	5.841	12.924
4	1.533	2.132	2.776	3.747	4.604	8.610
5	1.476	2.015	2.571	3.365	4.032	6.869
6	1.440	1.943	2.447	3.143	3.707	5.959
7	1.415	1.895	2.365	2.998	3.499	5.408
8	1.397	1.860	2.306	2.896	3.355	5.041
9	1.383	1.833	2.262	2.821	3.250	4.781
10	1.372	1.812	2.228	2.764	3.169	4.587
11	1.363	1.796	2.201	2.718	3.106	4.437
12	1.356	1.782	2.179	2.681	3.055	4.318
13	1.350	1.771	2.160	2.650	3.012	4.221
14	1.345	1.761	2.145	2.624	2.977	4.140
15	1.341	1.753	2.131	2.602	2.947	4.073
16	1.337	1.746	2.120	2.583	2.921	4.015
17	1.333	1.740	2.110	2.567	2.898	3.965
18	1.330	1.734	2.101	2.552	2.878	3.922
19	1.328	1.729	2.093	2.539	2.861	3.883
20	1.325	1.725	2.086	2.528	2.845	3.850
21	1.323	1.721	2.080	2.518	2.831	3.819
22	1.321	1.717	2.074	2.508	2.819	3.792
23	1.319	1.714	2.069	2.500	2.807	3.768
24	1.318	1.711	2.064	2.492	2.797	3.745
25	1.316	1.708	2.060	2.485	2.787	3.725
26	1.315	1.706	2.056	2.479	2.779	3.707
27	1.314	1.703	2.052	2.473	2.771	3.690
28	1.313	1.701	2.048	2.467	2.763	3.674
29	1.311	1.699	2.045	2.462	2.756	3.659
30	1.310	1.697	2.042	2.457	2.750	3.646
40	1.303	1.684	2.021	2.423	2.704	3.551
60	1.296	1.671	2.000	2.390	2.660	3.460
120	1.289	1.658	1.980	2.358	2.617	3.373
∞	1.282	1.645	1.960	2.326	2.576	3.291

Appendix G

Critical Values of the F Distribution at a 5 Percent Level of Significance

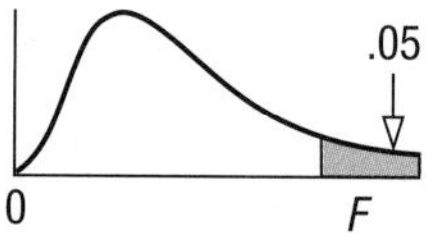

Degrees of Freedom for the Denominator	Degrees of Freedom for the Numerator															
	1	2	3	4	5	6	7	8	9	10	12	15	20	24	30	40
1	161	200	216	225	230	234	237	239	241	242	244	246	248	249	250	251
2	18.5	19.0	19.2	19.2	19.3	19.3	19.4	19.4	19.4	19.4	19.4	19.4	19.4	19.5	19.5	19.5
3	10.1	9.55	9.28	9.12	9.01	8.94	8.89	8.85	8.81	8.79	8.74	8.70	8.66	8.64	8.62	8.59
4	7.71	6.94	6.59	6.39	6.26	6.16	6.09	6.04	6.00	5.96	5.91	5.86	5.80	5.77	5.75	5.72
5	6.61	5.79	5.41	5.19	5.05	4.95	4.88	4.82	4.77	4.74	4.68	4.62	4.56	4.53	4.50	4.46
6	5.99	5.14	4.76	4.53	4.39	4.28	4.21	4.15	4.10	4.06	4.00	3.94	3.87	3.84	3.81	3.77
7	5.59	4.74	4.35	4.12	3.97	3.87	3.79	3.73	3.68	3.64	3.57	3.51	3.44	3.41	3.38	3.34
8	5.32	4.46	4.07	3.84	3.69	3.58	3.50	3.44	3.39	3.35	3.28	3.22	3.15	3.12	3.08	3.04
9	5.12	4.26	3.86	3.63	3.48	3.37	3.29	3.23	3.18	3.14	3.07	3.01	2.94	2.90	2.86	2.83
10	4.96	4.10	3.71	3.48	3.33	3.22	3.14	3.07	3.02	2.98	2.91	2.85	2.77	2.74	2.70	2.66
11	4.84	3.98	3.59	3.36	3.20	3.09	3.01	2.95	2.90	2.85	2.79	2.72	2.65	2.61	2.57	2.53
12	4.75	3.89	3.49	3.26	3.11	3.00	2.91	2.85	2.80	2.75	2.69	2.62	2.54	2.51	2.47	2.43
13	4.67	3.81	3.41	3.18	3.03	2.92	2.83	2.77	2.71	2.67	2.60	2.53	2.46	2.42	2.38	2.34
14	4.60	3.74	3.34	3.11	2.96	2.85	2.76	2.70	2.65	2.60	2.53	2.46	2.39	2.35	2.31	2.27
15	4.54	3.68	3.29	3.06	2.90	2.79	2.71	2.64	2.59	2.54	2.48	2.40	2.33	2.29	2.25	2.20
16	4.49	3.63	3.24	3.01	2.85	2.74	2.66	2.59	2.54	2.49	2.42	2.35	2.28	2.24	2.19	2.15
17	4.45	3.59	3.20	2.96	2.81	2.70	2.61	2.55	2.49	2.45	2.38	2.31	2.23	2.19	2.15	2.10
18	4.41	3.55	3.16	2.93	2.77	2.66	2.58	2.51	2.46	2.41	2.34	2.27	2.19	2.15	2.11	2.06
19	4.38	3.52	3.13	2.90	2.74	2.63	2.54	2.48	2.42	2.38	2.31	2.23	2.16	2.11	2.07	2.03
20	4.35	3.49	3.10	2.87	2.71	2.60	2.51	2.45	2.39	2.35	2.28	2.20	2.12	2.08	2.04	1.99
21	4.32	3.47	3.07	2.84	2.68	2.57	2.49	2.42	2.37	2.32	2.25	2.18	2.10	2.05	2.01	1.96
22	4.30	3.44	3.05	2.82	2.66	2.55	2.46	2.40	2.34	2.30	2.23	2.15	2.07	2.03	1.98	1.94
23	4.28	3.42	3.03	2.80	2.64	2.53	2.44	2.37	2.32	2.27	2.20	2.13	2.05	2.01	1.96	1.91
24	4.26	3.40	3.01	2.78	2.62	2.51	2.42	2.36	2.30	2.25	2.18	2.11	2.03	1.98	1.94	1.89
25	4.24	3.39	2.99	2.76	2.60	2.49	2.40	2.34	2.28	2.24	2.16	2.09	2.01	1.96	1.92	1.87
30	4.17	3.32	2.92	2.69	2.53	2.42	2.33	2.27	2.21	2.16	2.09	2.01	1.93	1.89	1.84	1.79
40	4.08	3.23	2.84	2.61	2.45	2.34	2.25	2.18	2.12	2.08	2.00	1.92	1.84	1.79	1.74	1.69
60	4.00	3.15	2.76	2.53	2.37	2.25	2.17	2.10	2.04	1.99	1.92	1.84	1.75	1.70	1.65	1.59
120	3.92	3.07	2.68	2.45	2.29	2.18	2.09	2.02	1.96	1.91	1.83	1.75	1.66	1.61	1.55	1.50
∞	3.84	3.00	2.60	2.37	2.21	2.10	2.01	1.94	1.88	1.83	1.75	1.67	1.57	1.52	1.46	1.39

Appendix G

Critical Values of the *F* Distribution at a 1 Percent Level of Significance

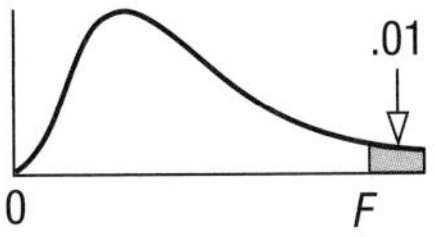

Degrees of Freedom for the Denominator	Degrees of Freedom for the Numerator															
	1	2	3	4	5	6	7	8	9	10	12	15	20	24	30	40
1	4052	5000	5403	5625	5764	5859	5928	5981	6022	6056	6106	6157	6209	6235	6261	6287
2	98.5	99.0	99.2	99.2	99.3	99.3	99.4	99.4	99.4	99.4	99.4	99.4	99.4	99.5	99.5	99.5
3	34.1	30.8	29.5	28.7	28.2	27.9	27.7	27.5	27.3	27.2	27.1	26.9	26.7	26.6	26.5	26.4
4	21.2	18.0	16.7	16.0	15.5	15.2	15.0	14.8	14.7	14.5	14.4	14.2	14.0	13.9	13.8	13.7
5	16.3	13.3	12.1	11.4	11.0	10.7	10.5	10.3	10.2	10.1	9.89	9.72	9.55	9.47	9.38	9.29
6	13.7	10.9	9.78	9.15	8.75	8.47	8.26	8.10	7.98	7.87	7.72	7.56	7.40	7.31	7.23	7.14
7	12.2	9.55	8.45	7.85	7.46	7.19	6.99	6.84	6.72	6.62	6.47	6.31	6.16	6.07	5.99	5.91
8	11.3	8.65	7.59	7.01	6.63	6.37	6.18	6.03	5.91	5.81	5.67	5.52	5.36	5.28	5.20	5.12
9	10.6	8.02	6.99	6.42	6.06	5.80	5.61	5.47	5.35	5.26	5.11	4.96	4.81	4.73	4.65	4.57
10	10.0	7.56	6.55	5.99	5.64	5.39	5.20	5.06	4.94	4.85	4.71	4.56	4.41	4.33	4.25	4.17
11	9.65	7.21	6.22	5.67	5.32	5.07	4.89	4.74	4.63	4.54	4.40	4.25	4.10	4.02	3.94	3.86
12	9.33	6.93	5.95	5.41	5.06	4.82	4.64	4.50	4.39	4.30	4.16	4.01	3.86	3.78	3.70	3.62
13	9.07	6.70	5.74	5.21	4.86	4.62	4.44	4.30	4.19	4.10	3.96	3.82	3.66	3.59	3.51	3.43
14	8.86	6.51	5.56	5.04	4.69	4.46	4.28	4.14	4.03	3.94	3.80	3.66	3.51	3.43	3.35	3.27
15	8.68	6.36	5.42	4.89	4.56	4.32	4.14	4.00	3.89	3.80	3.67	3.52	3.37	3.29	3.21	3.13
16	8.53	6.23	5.29	4.77	4.44	4.20	4.03	3.89	3.78	3.69	3.55	3.41	3.26	3.18	3.10	3.02
17	8.40	6.11	5.18	4.67	4.34	4.10	3.93	3.79	3.68	3.59	3.46	3.31	3.16	3.08	3.00	2.92
18	8.29	6.01	5.09	4.58	4.25	4.01	3.84	3.71	3.60	3.51	3.37	3.23	3.08	3.00	2.92	2.84
19	8.18	5.93	5.01	4.50	4.17	3.94	3.77	3.63	3.52	3.43	3.30	3.15	3.00	2.92	2.84	2.76
20	8.10	5.85	4.94	4.43	4.10	3.87	3.70	3.56	3.46	3.37	3.23	3.09	2.94	2.86	2.78	2.69
21	8.02	5.78	4.87	4.37	4.04	3.81	3.64	3.51	3.40	3.31	3.17	3.03	2.88	2.80	2.72	2.64
22	7.95	5.72	4.82	4.31	3.99	3.76	3.59	3.45	3.35	3.26	3.12	2.98	2.83	2.75	2.67	2.58
23	7.88	5.66	4.76	4.26	3.94	3.71	3.54	3.41	3.30	3.21	3.07	2.93	2.78	2.70	2.62	2.54
24	7.82	5.61	4.72	4.22	3.90	3.67	3.50	3.36	3.26	3.17	3.03	2.89	2.74	2.66	2.58	2.49
25	7.77	5.57	4.68	4.18	3.85	3.63	3.46	3.32	3.22	3.13	2.99	2.85	2.70	2.62	2.54	2.45
30	7.56	5.39	4.51	4.02	3.70	3.47	3.30	3.17	3.07	2.98	2.84	2.70	2.55	2.47	2.39	2.30
40	7.31	5.18	4.31	3.83	3.51	3.29	3.12	2.99	2.89	2.80	2.66	2.52	2.37	2.29	2.20	2.11
60	7.08	4.98	4.13	3.65	3.34	3.12	2.95	2.82	2.72	2.63	2.50	2.35	2.20	2.12	2.03	1.94
120	6.85	4.79	3.95	3.48	3.17	2.96	2.79	2.66	2.56	2.47	2.34	2.19	2.03	1.95	1.86	1.76
∞	6.63	4.61	3.78	3.32	3.02	2.80	2.64	2.51	2.41	2.32	2.18	2.04	1.88	1.79	1.70	1.59

Appendix H

Data Set 1—Real Estate

x_1 = Selling price in \$000
x_2 = Number of bedrooms
x_3 = Size of the home in square feet
x_4 = Pool (1 = yes, 0 = no)
x_5 = Distance from the center of the city
x_6 = Township
x_7 = Garage attached (1 = yes, 0 = no)
x_8 = Number of bathrooms

x_1	x_2	x_3	x_4	x_5	x_6	x_7	x_8
263.1	4	2,300	0	17	5	1	2
182.4	4	2,100	1	19	4	0	2
242.1	3	2,300	1	12	3	0	2
213.6	2	2,200	1	16	2	0	2.5
139.9	2	2,100	1	28	1	0	1.5
245.4	2	2,100	0	12	1	1	2
327.2	6	2,500	1	15	3	1	2
271.8	2	2,100	1	9	2	1	2.5
221.1	3	2,300	0	18	1	0	1.5
266.6	4	2,400	1	13	4	1	2
292.4	4	2,100	1	14	3	1	2
209	2	1,700	1	8	4	1	1.5
270.8	6	2,500	1	7	4	1	2
246.1	4	2,100	1	18	3	1	2
194.4	2	2,300	1	11	3	0	2
281.3	3	2,100	1	16	2	1	2
172.7	4	2,200	0	16	3	0	2
207.5	5	2,300	0	21	4	0	2.5
198.9	3	2,200	0	10	4	1	2
209.3	6	1,900	0	15	4	1	2
252.3	4	2,600	1	8	4	1	2
192.9	4	1,900	0	14	2	1	2.5
209.3	5	2,100	1	20	5	0	1.5
345.3	8	2,600	1	9	4	1	2
326.3	6	2,100	1	11	5	1	3
173.1	2	2,200	0	21	5	1	1.5
187	2	1,900	1	26	4	0	2
257.2	2	2,100	1	9	4	1	2
233	3	2,200	1	14	3	1	1.5
180.4	2	2,000	1	11	5	0	2
234	2	1,700	1	19	3	1	2
207.1	2	2,000	1	11	5	1	2
247.7	5	2,400	1	16	2	1	2
166.2	3	2,000	0	16	2	1	2
177.1	2	1,900	1	10	5	1	2

Data Set 1—Real Estate *(continued)*

X_1	X_2	X_3	X_4	X_5	X_6	X_7	X_8
182.7	4	2,000	0	14	4	0	2.5
216	4	2,300	1	19	2	0	2
312.1	6	2,600	1	7	5	1	2.5
199.8	3	2,100	1	19	3	1	2
273.2	5	2,200	1	16	2	1	3
206	3	2,100	0	9	3	0	1.5
232.2	3	1,900	0	16	1	1	1.5
198.3	4	2,100	0	19	1	1	1.5
205.1	3	2,000	0	20	4	0	2
175.6	4	2,300	0	24	4	1	2
307.8	3	2,400	0	21	2	1	3
269.2	5	2,200	1	8	5	1	3
224.8	3	2,200	1	17	1	1	2.5
171.6	3	2,000	0	16	4	0	2
216.8	3	2,200	1	15	1	1	2
192.6	6	2,200	0	14	1	0	2
236.4	5	2,200	1	20	3	1	2
172.4	3	2,200	1	23	3	0	2
251.4	3	1,900	1	12	2	1	2
246	6	2,300	1	7	3	1	3
147.4	6	1,700	0	12	1	0	2
176	4	2,200	1	15	1	1	2
228.4	3	2,300	1	17	5	1	1.5
166.5	3	1,600	0	19	3	0	2.5
189.4	4	2,200	1	24	1	1	2
312.1	7	2,400	1	13	3	1	3
289.8	6	2,000	1	21	3	1	3
269.9	5	2,200	0	11	4	1	2.5
154.3	2	2,000	1	13	2	0	2
222.1	2	2,100	1	9	5	1	2
209.7	5	2,200	0	13	2	1	2
190.9	3	2,200	0	18	3	1	2
254.3	4	2,500	0	15	3	1	2
207.5	3	2,100	0	10	2	0	2
209.7	4	2,200	0	19	2	1	2
294	2	2,100	1	13	2	1	2.5
176.3	2	2,000	0	17	3	0	2
294.3	7	2,400	1	8	4	1	2
224	3	1,900	0	6	1	1	2
125	2	1,900	1	18	4	0	1.5
236.8	4	2,600	0	17	5	1	2
164.1	4	2,300	1	19	4	0	2
217.8	3	2,500	1	12	3	0	2
192.2	2	2,400	1	16	2	0	2.5
125.9	2	2,400	1	28	1	0	1.5

Appendix H

Data Set 1—Real Estate *(concluded)*

x_1	x_2	x_3	x_4	x_5	x_6	x_7	x_8
220.9	2	2,300	0	12	1	1	2
294.5	6	2,700	1	15	3	1	2
244.6	2	2,300	1	9	2	1	2.5
199	3	2,500	0	18	1	0	1.5
240	4	2,600	1	13	4	1	2
263.2	4	2,300	1	14	3	1	2
188.1	2	1,900	1	8	4	1	1.5
243.7	6	2,700	1	7	4	1	2
221.5	4	2,300	1	18	3	1	2
175	2	2,500	1	11	3	0	2
253.2	3	2,300	1	16	2	1	2
155.4	4	2,400	0	16	3	0	2
186.7	5	2,500	0	21	4	0	2.5
179	3	2,400	0	10	4	1	2
188.3	6	2,100	0	15	4	1	2
227.1	4	2,900	1	8	4	1	2
173.6	4	2,100	0	14	2	1	2.5
188.3	5	2,300	1	20	5	0	1.5
310.8	8	2,900	1	9	4	1	2
293.7	6	2,400	1	11	5	1	3
179	3	2,400	1	8	4	1	2
188.3	6	2,100	0	14	2	1	2.5
227.1	4	2,900	1	20	5	0	1.5
173.6	4	2,100	1	9	4	1	2
188.3	5	2,300	1	11	5	1	3

Appendix I

Data Set 2—Major League Baseball

x_1 = Team
x_2 = League (American = 1, National = 0)
x_3 = Built (Year Stadium Was Built)
x_4 = Size (Stadium Capacity)
x_5 = Salary (Total 2001 Team Salary $ Mil)
x_6 = Attendance (Total 2001 Team Attendance)
x_7 = Wins (Number of Wins in 2001)
x_8 = ERA (Earned Run Average)
x_9 = Batting (Team Batting Average)
x_{10} = HR (Number of Home Runs for the Team)
x_{11} = Surface (Natural = 0, Artificial = 1)
x_{12} = Stolen (Stolen Bases)
x_{13} = Errors (Team Errors)
x_{14} = Year
x_{15} = Average (Average Player Salary)
x_{16} = Median (Median Player Salary)

Team x_1	League x_2	Built x_3	Size x_4	Salary x_5	Attendance x_6	Wins x_7
Boston	1	1912	33871	110	2625333	82
New York Yankees	1	1923	57746	112.3	3264777	95
Oakland	1	1966	43662	33.8	2133277	102
Baltimore	1	1992	48262	74.3	3094841	63
Anaheim	1	1966	45050	47.7	2000919	75
Cleveland	1	1994	43368	93.4	3175523	91
Chicago	1	1991	44321	65.6	1766142	83
Toronto	1	1989	50516	76.9	1915438	80
Minnesota	1	1982	48678	24.1	1782926	85
Tampa Bay	1	1990	44027	57	1298365	62
Texas	1	1994	52000	88.6	2831111	73
Detroit	1	2000	40000	49.5	1921305	66
Seattle	1	1999	45611	74.7	3507507	116
Kansas City	1	1973	40529	35.4	1536371	65
Atlanta	0	1993	50062	91.9	2823494	88
Arizona	0	1998	49075	85.5	2744433	92
Houston	0	2000	42000	60.9	2904280	93
Cincinnati	0	1970	52953	49	1879872	66
New York Mets	0	1964	55775	93.7	2658279	82
Pittsburgh	0	2001	38127	57.8	2436290	62
Los Angeles	0	1962	56000	109.1	3017502	86
San Diego	0	1967	53166	38.9	2378116	79
Montreal	0	1976	46500	35.2	619451	68
San Francisco	0	2000	40800	63.3	3307686	90
St. Louis	0	1966	49625	78.5	3113091	93
Florida	0	1987	42531	35.8	1261220	76
Philadelphia	0	1971	62411	41.7	1782054	86
Milwaukee	0	2001	42400	43.9	2811041	68
Chicago Cubs	0	1914	38957	64.7	2779454	88
Colorado	0	1995	50381	71.5	3140416	73

Appendix I

Data Set 2—Major League Baseball *(concluded)*

Team x_1	Wins x_7	ERA x_8	Batting x_9	HR x_{10}	Surface x_{11}	Stolen x_{12}	Errors x_{13}
Boston	82	4.15	266	198	0	46	113
New York Yankees	95	4.02	267	203	0	161	109
Oakland	102	3.59	264	199	0	68	125
Baltimore	63	4.67	248	136	0	133	125
Anaheim	75	4.2	261	158	0	116	103
Cleveland	91	4.64	278	212	0	79	107
Chicago	83	4.55	268	214	0	123	118
Toronto	80	4.28	263	195	1	156	97
Minnesota	85	4.51	272	164	1	146	108
Tampa Bay	62	4.94	258	121	1	115	139
Texas	73	5.71	275	246	0	97	114
Detroit	66	5.01	260	139	0	133	131
Seattle	116	3.54	288	169	0	100	83
Kansas City	65	4.87	266	152	0	174	117
Atlanta	88	3.59	260	174	0	85	103
Arizona	92	3.87	267	208	0	71	84
Houston	93	4.37	271	208	0	64	110
Cincinnati	66	4.77	262	176	0	103	138
New York Mets	82	4.07	249	147	0	66	101
Pittsburgh	62	5.05	247	161	0	93	113
Los Angeles	86	4.25	255	206	0	89	116
San Diego	79	4.52	252	161	0	129	145
Montreal	68	4.68	253	131	1	101	108
San Francisco	90	4.18	266	235	0	57	118
St. Louis	93	3.93	270	199	0	91	110
Florida	76	4.32	264	166	0	89	103
Philadelphia	86	4.15	260	164	1	153	91
Milwaukee	68	4.64	251	209	0	66	103
Chicago Cubs	88	4.03	261	194	0	67	109
Colorado	73	5.29	292	213	0	132	96

Year x_{14}	Average x_{15}	Median x_{16}
1976	52300	
1977	74000	
1978	97800	
1979	121900	
1980	146500	
1981	196500	
1982	245000	
1983	289000	207500
1984	325900	229750
1985	368998	265833
1986	410517	275000
1987	402579	235000
1988	430688	235000
1989	489539	280000
1990	589483	350000
1991	845383	412000
1992	1012424	392500
1993	1062780	371500
1994	1154486	450000
1995	1094440	275000
1996	1101455	300000
1997	1314420	400000
1998	1384530	427500
1999	1567873	495000
2000	1983849	700000
2001	2138896	975000

Appendix J

Data Set 3—Wages and Wage Earners

x_1 = Annual wage in dollars
x_2 = Industry (1=Manufacturing, 2=Construction, 0=Other)
x_3 = Occupation (1=Mgmt., 2=Sales, 3=Clerical, 4=Service, 5=Prof., 0=Other)
x_4 = Years of education
x_5 = Southern resident (1=Yes, 0=No)
x_6 = Non-white (1=Yes, 0=No)
x_7 = Hispanic (1=Yes, 0=No)
x_8 = Female (1=Yes, 0=No)
x_9 = Years of Work Experience
x_{10} = Married (1=Yes, 0=No)
x_{11} = Age in years
x_{12} = Union member (1=Yes, 0=No)

Row	Wage x_1	Industry x_2	Occupation x_3	Education x_4	South x_5	Non-white x_6	Hispanic x_7
1	19388	1	0	6	1	0	0
2	49898	2	0	12	0	0	0
3	28219	0	3	12	1	0	0
4	83601	0	5	17	0	0	1
5	29736	0	4	8	0	0	1
6	50235	1	0	16	0	0	0
7	45976	0	2	12	0	0	0
8	33411	1	2	12	1	0	0
9	21716	0	5	12	0	0	0
10	37664	0	5	18	0	0	0
11	26820	0	5	18	0	0	0
12	29977	0	4	16	0	1	0
13	33959	0	5	17	0	0	0
14	11780	0	2	11	0	0	0
15	10997	0	4	14	0	1	0
16	17626	0	3	12	0	0	0
17	22133	0	5	16	0	0	0
18	21994	0	1	12	0	0	0
19	29390	0	0	13	0	0	0
20	32138	0	4	14	0	0	0
21	30006	1	3	16	0	0	0
22	68573	0	5	16	1	0	0
23	17694	0	4	8	0	0	0
24	26795	0	0	7	1	0	0
25	19981	0	4	4	0	0	0
26	14476	0	5	12	0	0	0
27	19452	0	4	13	0	1	0
28	28168	1	0	13	0	0	0
29	19306	0	5	9	1	1	0
30	13318	1	0	11	1	0	0

Appendix J

Data Set 3—Wages and Wage Earners *(continued)*

Row	Wage x_1	Industry x_2	Occupation x_3	Education x_4	South x_5	Nonwhite x_6	Hispanic x_7
31	25166	0	4	12	0	0	0
32	18121	1	3	12	0	0	0
33	13162	1	0	12	0	1	0
34	32094	0	3	12	1	0	0
35	16667	0	3	12	1	0	0
36	50171	0	5	12	0	0	0
37	31691	1	0	12	0	0	0
38	36178	0	3	12	0	0	0
39	15234	0	1	12	1	0	1
40	16817	0	3	12	1	0	0
41	22485	0	3	12	0	0	0
42	30308	0	4	12	0	0	0
43	11702	0	2	14	1	0	0
44	11186	0	0	12	0	0	0
45	12285	0	1	12	0	0	0
46	19284	1	4	16	0	0	0
47	11451	1	0	12	0	0	0
48	57623	0	1	15	0	0	0
49	25670	0	3	13	0	0	0
50	83443	0	5	17	0	0	0
51	49974	1	1	16	0	1	0
52	46646	2	0	5	1	0	0
53	31702	0	3	12	1	0	0
54	13312	0	4	12	1	0	0
55	44543	0	2	18	0	0	0
56	15013	0	4	16	0	0	0
57	33389	0	1	14	0	1	0
58	60626	0	5	18	0	0	0
59	24509	0	5	14	0	0	1
60	20852	1	0	12	0	0	0
61	30133	2	0	10	0	0	0
62	31799	0	3	12	0	0	0
63	16796	0	4	12	0	0	0
64	20793	0	0	12	1	0	0
65	29407	0	4	10	1	0	0
66	29191	0	0	12	0	0	0
67	15957	0	2	12	1	0	0
68	34484	0	3	13	1	0	0
69	35185	1	3	14	0	0	0
70	26614	1	0	12	0	0	0
71	41780	0	0	12	1	0	0
72	55777	0	1	14	1	0	0
73	15160	0	4	8	1	0	0
74	66738	0	0	9	1	0	0
75	33351	0	5	16	1	0	0

Data Set 3—Wages and Wage Earners *(continued)*

Row	Wage x_1	Industry x_2	Occupation x_3	Education x_4	South x_5	Nonwhite x_6	Hispanic x_7
76	33498	0	1	10	0	0	0
77	29809	0	4	8	0	1	0
78	15193	1	0	12	0	0	0
79	23027	0	4	14	0	1	0
80	75165	0	1	15	0	0	0
81	18752	0	4	11	0	0	0
82	83569	0	1	18	0	0	0
83	32235	0	3	12	0	0	0
84	20852	0	0	12	1	0	0
85	13787	0	4	11	0	0	0
86	34746	0	3	14	1	0	0
87	17690	0	1	12	1	1	0
88	52762	0	5	18	0	0	0
89	60152	0	5	16	1	0	0
90	33461	0	1	16	0	0	1
91	13481	0	4	12	1	0	1
92	9879	0	3	12	1	0	0
93	16789	0	3	13	1	0	0
94	31304	0	1	16	0	0	0
95	37771	0	5	15	0	0	0
96	50187	0	3	12	0	0	0
97	39888	0	3	12	1	0	0
98	19227	0	3	12	0	0	0
99	32786	1	0	11	1	0	0
100	28440	0	4	12	0	0	0

Appendix J

Data Set 3—Wages and Wage Earners *(continued)*

Row	Female x_8	Experience x_9	Married x_{10}	Age x_{11}	Union x_{12}
1	0	45	1	57	0
2	0	33	1	51	1
3	0	12	1	30	0
4	0	18	1	41	0
5	0	47	1	61	1
6	0	12	1	34	0
7	0	43	1	61	1
8	0	20	1	38	0
9	1	11	0	29	0
10	0	19	1	43	0
11	0	33	0	57	1
12	1	6	1	28	0
13	1	26	1	49	1
14	1	33	1	50	0
15	0	0	0	20	0
16	1	45	1	63	0
17	1	10	0	32	1
18	1	24	1	42	0
19	0	18	1	37	0
20	0	22	1	42	1
21	1	27	1	49	0
22	0	14	1	36	1
23	1	38	1	52	0
24	0	44	1	57	0
25	0	54	1	64	0
26	1	3	1	21	0
27	0	3	0	22	0
28	0	17	0	36	0
29	1	34	1	49	1
30	1	25	1	42	1
31	1	10	0	28	0
32	1	18	1	36	0
33	0	6	0	24	1
34	1	14	1	32	0
35	0	4	0	22	0
36	0	39	1	57	1
37	0	13	0	31	0
38	1	40	1	58	0
39	1	4	0	22	0
40	1	26	0	44	0
41	0	22	0	40	0
42	0	10	1	28	0
43	1	6	1	26	0
44	0	0	0	18	0
45	1	42	1	60	0
46	0	3	0	25	0
47	1	8	1	26	0
48	0	31	1	52	0
49	1	8	0	27	1
50	1	5	0	28	0

Row	Female x_8	Experience x_9	Married x_{10}	Age x_{11}	Union x_{12}
51	0	26	1	48	1
52	0	44	1	55	0
53	1	39	1	57	0
54	1	9	1	27	0
55	0	10	1	34	0
56	0	21	1	43	0
57	0	22	0	42	0
58	0	7	1	31	0
59	1	15	0	35	0
60	1	38	1	56	0
61	0	27	1	43	0
62	1	25	0	43	0
63	1	14	1	32	0
64	1	6	0	24	0
65	0	19	0	35	0
66	0	9	0	27	0
67	1	10	0	28	0
68	1	28	0	47	0
69	1	12	1	32	0
70	1	19	1	37	0
71	0	9	1	27	0
72	0	21	1	41	0
73	1	45	0	59	0
74	0	29	1	44	0
75	1	4	1	26	0
76	0	20	1	36	0
77	1	29	0	43	0
78	1	15	0	33	0
79	0	34	1	54	1
80	0	12	1	33	0
81	1	45	0	62	1
82	0	29	1	53	0
83	1	38	1	56	0
84	0	1	0	19	0
85	0	4	1	21	0
86	1	15	1	35	0
87	0	14	1	32	0
88	0	7	1	31	0
89	0	38	1	60	0
90	0	7	1	29	1
91	0	7	0	25	0
92	1	28	1	46	0
93	1	6	1	25	0
94	1	26	1	48	0
95	0	5	0	26	0
96	1	24	1	42	0
97	0	5	0	23	0
98	1	15	1	33	0
99	0	37	1	54	1
100	1	24	1	42	0

Appendix K

Data Set 4—CIA International Economic and Demographic Data

x_1 = Country name
x_2 = Total area (square kilometers)
x_3 = Member of the G-20, group of industrial nations to promote international financial stability (0 = nonmember, 1 = member)
x_4 = Country has petroleum as a natural resource [(0 = no, 1 = petroleum is a natural resource, 2 = country is a member of OPEC (Organization of Petroleum Exporting Countries)]
x_5 = Population (expressed in thousands)
x_6 = Percent of population aged 65 years and over
x_7 = Life expectancy at birth
x_8 = Literacy: percent of population age 15 or more that can read and write
x_9 = Gross Domestic Product per capita expressed in thousands
x_{10} = Labor force (expressed in millions)
x_{11} = Percent unemployment
x_{12} = Exports expressed in billions of dollars
x_{13} = Imports expressed in billions of dollars
x_{14} = Number of mobile or cellular phones expressed in millions

Country x_1	Area (km) x_2	G-20 x_3	Petroleum x_4	Pop (1000s) x_5	65 & over x_6	Life Expectancy x_7
Algeria	2,381,740	0	2	31,736	4.07	69.95
Argentina	2,766,890	1	1	37,385	10.42	75.26
Australia	7,686,850	1	1	19,357	12.5	79.87
Austria	83,858	0	0	8,150	15.38	77.84
Belgium	30,510	0	0	10,259	16.95	77.96
Brazil	8,511,965	1	1	174,469	5.45	63.24
Canada	9,976,140	1	1	31,592	12.77	79.56
China	9,596,960	1	1	1,273,111	7.11	71.62
Czech Republic	79	0	0	10,264	13.92	74.73
Denmark	43,094	0	1	5,352	14.85	76.72
Finland	337,030	0	0	5,175	15.03	77.58
France	547,030	1	0	59,551	16.13	78.9
Germany	357,021	1	0	83,029	16.61	77.61
Greece	131,940	0	1	10,623	17.72	78.59
Hungary	93,030	0	0	10,106	14.71	71.63
Iceland	103,000	0	0	278	11.81	79.52
India	3,287,590	1	1	1,029,991	4.68	62.68
Indonesia	1,919,440	1	2	228,437	4.63	68.27
Iran	1,648,000	0	2	66,129	4.65	69.95
Iraq	437,072	0	2	23,332	3.08	66.95
Ireland	70,280	0	0	3,840	11.35	76.99
Italy	301,230	1	0	57,680	18.35	79.14
Japan	377,835	1	0	126,771	17.35	80.8
Kuwait	17,820	0	2	2,041	2.42	76.27
Libya	1,759,540	0	2	5,240	3.95	75.65

Appendix K

Data Set 4—CIA International Economic and Demographic Data *(continued)*

Country X_1	Area (km) X_2	G-20 X_3	Petroleum X_4	Pop (1000s) X_5	65 & over X_6	Life Expectancy X_7
Luxembourg	2,586	0	0	443	14.06	77.3
Mexico	1,972,550	1	1	101,879	4.4	71.76
Netherlands	41,526	0	1	15,981	13.72	78.43
New Zealand	286,680	0	0	3,864	11.53	77.99
Nigeria	923,768	0	2	126,635	2.82	51.07
Norway	324,220	0	1	4,503	15.1	78.79
Poland	312,685	0	0	38,634	12.44	73.42
Portugal	92,391	0	0	10,066	15.62	75.94
Qatar	11,437	0	2	769	2.48	72.62
Russia	17,075,200	1	1	145,470	12.81	67.34
Saudi Arabia	1,960,582	1	2	22,757	2.68	68.09
South Africa	1,219,912	1	0	43,586	4.88	48.09
South Korea	98,480	1	0	47,904	7.27	74.65
Spain	504,782	0	0	40,038	17.18	78.93
Sweden	449,964	0	0	8,875	17.28	79.71
Switzerland	41,290	0	0	7,283	15.3	79.73
Turkey	780,580	1	0	66,494	6.13	71.24
United Arab Emirates	82,880	0	2	2,407	2.4	74.29
United Kingdom	244,820	1	1	59,648	15.7	77.82
United States	9,629,091	1	1	278,059	12.61	77.26
Venezuela	912,050	0	2	23,917	4.72	73.31

Appendix K

Data Set 4—CIA International Economic and Demographic Data *(concluded)*

Country x_1	Literacy % x_8	GDP/cap x_9	Labor force x_{10}	Unemployment x_{11}	Exports x_{12}	Imports x_{13}	Cell phones x_{14}
Algeria	61.6	5.5	9.1	30	19.6	9.2	0.034
Argentina	96.2	12.9	15	15	26.5	25.2	3
Australia	100	23.2	9.5	6.4	69	77	6.4
Austria	98	25	3.7	5.4	63.2	65.6	4.5
Belgium	98	25.3	4.34	8.4	181.4	166	1
Brazil	83.3	6.5	79	7.1	55.1	55.8	4.4
Canada	97	24.8	16.1	6.8	272.3	238.2	4.2
China	81.5	3.6	700	10	232	197	65
Czech Republic	99.9	12.9	5.2	8.7	28.3	31.4	4.3
Denmark	100	25.5	2.9	5.3	50.8	43.6	1.4
Finland	100	22.9	2.6	9.8	44.4	32.7	2.2
France	99	24.4	25	9.7	325	320	11.1
Germany	99	23.4	40.5	9.9	578	505	15.3
Greece	95	17.2	4.32	11.3	15.8	33.9	0.937
Hungary	99	11.2	4.2	9.4	25.2	27.6	1.3
Iceland	100	24.8	0.16	2.7	2	2.2	0.066
India	52	2.2	*	*	43.1	60.8	2.93
Indonesia	83.8	2.9	99	17.5	64.7	40.4	1
Iran	72.1	6.3	17.3	14	25	15	0.265
Iraq	58	2.5	4.4	*	21.8	13.8	0
Ireland	98	21.6	1.82	4.1	73.5	45.7	2
Italy	98	22.1	23.4	10.4	241.1	231.4	20.5
Japan	99	24.9	67.7	4.7	450	355	63.9
Kuwait	78.6	15	1.3	1.8	23.2	7.6	0.21
Libya	76.2	8.9	1.5	30	13.9	7.6	0
Luxembourg	100	36.4	0.248	2.7	7.6	10	0.215
Mexico	89.6	9.1	39.8	2.2	168	176	2
Netherlands	99	24.4	7.2	2.6	210.3	201.2	4.1
New Zealand	99	17.7	1.88	6.3	14.6	14.3	0.6
Nigeria	57.1	0.95	66	28	22.2	10.7	0.027
Norway	100	27.7	2.4	3	59.2	35.2	2
Poland	99	8.5	17.2	12	28.4	42.7	1.8
Portugal	87.4	15.8	5	4.3	26.1	41	3
Qatar	79	20.3	0.233	*	9.8	3.8	0.043
Russia	98	7.7	66	10.5	105.1	44.2	2.5
Saudi Arabia	62.8	10.5	7	*	81.2	30.1	1
South Africa	81.1	8.5	17	30	30.8	27.6	2
South Korea	98	16.1	22	4.1	172.6	160.5	27
Spain	97	18	17	14	120.5	153.9	8.4
Sweden	99	22.2	4.4	6	95.5	80	3.8
Switzerland	99	28.6	3.9	1.9	91.3	91.6	2
Turkey	85	6.8	23	5.6	26.9	55.7	12.1
United Arab Emirates	79.2	22.8	1.4	*	46	34	1
United Kingdom	99	22.8	29.2	5.5	282	324	13
United States	97	36.2	140.9	4	776	1223	69
Venezuela	91.1	6.2	9.9	14	32.8	14.7	2

Appendix L

MegaStat Quick Reference Guide

What Is MegaStat?

MegaStat is an Excel add-in that performs statistical analysis within an Excel workbook. After it is installed it appears on the Excel menu and works like **Edit, View,** or any of the other Excel options. MegaStat contains options to perform most of the calculations described in an introductory business statistics course.

When you click on **MegaStat** its main menu appears. Most of the options contain submenus. If the menu item is followed by the periods, i.e., ". . . ," clicking on that item will display a dialog box. If the menu item contains the symbol "▶" additional submenu items are available. Below is the screen if you select **MegaStat** and then **Frequency Distributions.**

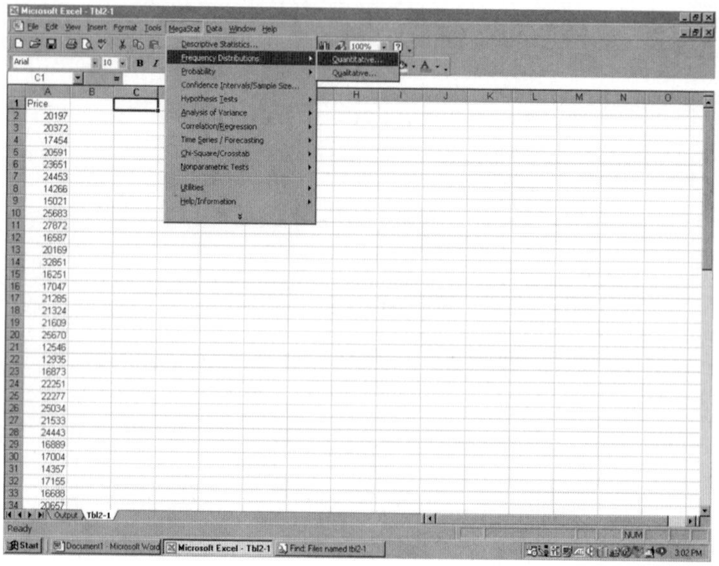

How MegaStat Works

Most MegaStat input is from dialog boxes. For example, if you selected **MegaStat, Frequency Distributions,** and **Quantitative** you will see the following dialog box. The dialog boxes allow you to specify the data cells for the procedure and to specify options. All dialog boxes have a **Help** button that will provide more information about the procedure. When the required information has been provided, click **OK** to perform the procedure.

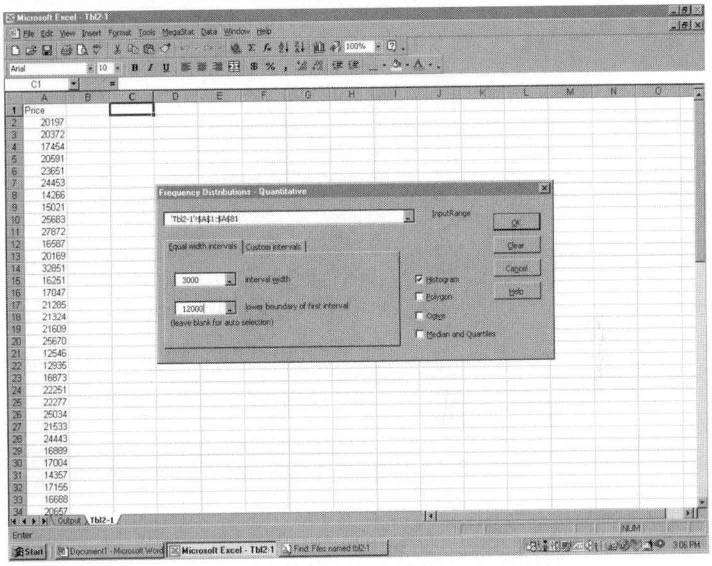

Most dialog boxes require you to specify the data for the procedure. This can be done in one of several ways:

1. Pointing and dragging with the mouse. This is the easiest and most common method.
2. Typing the name of the named data range.
3. Typing the range address.
4. Using **Ctrl, Shift,** and **Arrow** keystroke combinations.

For most procedures the first cell in each input range is the label. If the first cell in a range is text, it is considered a label; if it is a numeric value, it is considered data.

MegaStat Output

MegaStat output is placed in a worksheet titled "Output." If there is an existing Output sheet, the new output is placed at the end. The MegaStat output is in the standard Excel format, so you may insert, modify, or delete any cells. You can copy all or part of the output to another worksheet or to a word processing application.

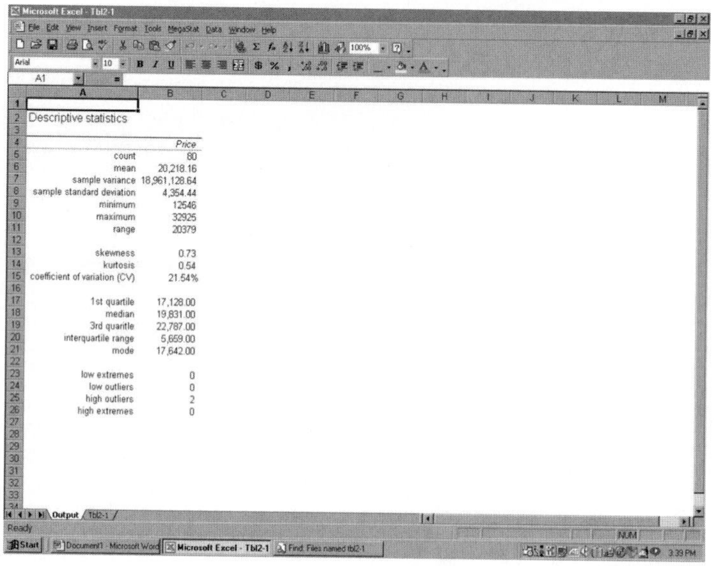

Help Is Always Available

Most of the dialog boxes are self-explanatory, but if you need more information, click on **Help** and browse the Help contents.

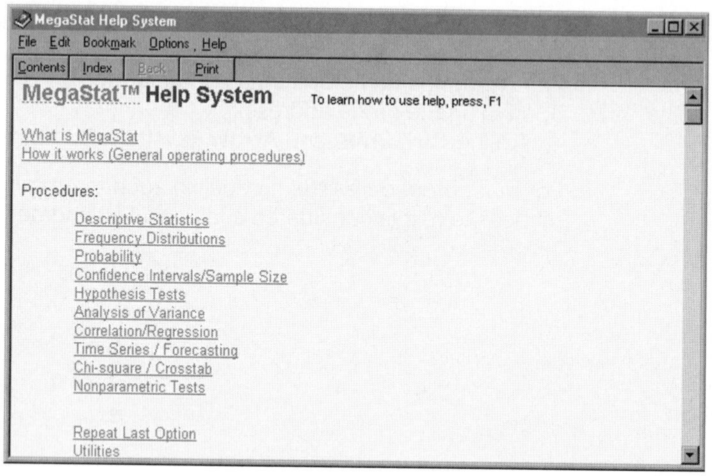

Answers

to Odd-Numbered Chapter Exercises

Chapter 1

1. a. Interval
   b. Ratio
   c. Interval
   d. Nominal
   e. Ordinal
   f. Ratio
3. Answers will vary.
5. Qualitative data is not numerical, whereas quantitative data is numerical. Examples will vary by student.
7. Nominal, ordinal, interval, and ratio. Examples will vary.
9. A classification is exhaustive if every object appears in some category.
11. Based on these sample findings, we can infer that 270/300, or 90 percent, of the executives would move.
13. Discrete variables can assume only certain values, but continuous variables can assume any values within some range. Examples will vary.
15. Answers will vary.
17. a. Grass or artificial turf field is a qualitative variable, the others are quantitative.
    b. Grass or artificial turf field is a nominal level variable, the others are ratio level variables.
19. a. All variables are qualitative except G-20 and Petroleum.
    b. All variables are ratio except G-20 and Petroleum.

Chapter 2

1. $2^5 = 32$, $2^6 = 64$ Therefore, 6 classes.
3. $2^7 = 128$, $2^8 = 256$ Suggests 8 classes.

   $i \geq \frac{567 - 235}{8} = 41$ Use interval of 45.
5. a. $2^4 = 16$ Suggests 5 classes.
   b. $i \geq \frac{31 - 25}{5} = 1.10$ Use interval of 1.5.
   c. 24
   d.

Patients	f	Relative frequency
24.0 up to 25.5	2	0.125
25.5 up to 27.0	4	0.250
27.0 up to 28.5	8	0.500
28.5 up to 30.0	0	0.000
30.0 up to 31.5	2	0.125
Total	16	1.000

   e. The largest concentration is in the 27 up to 28.5 class (8).
7. a.

Number of Shoppers	f
0 up to 3	9
3 up to 6	21
6 up to 9	13
9 up to 12	4
12 up to 15	3
15 up to 18	1
Total	51

   b. The largest group of shoppers (21) shop at Food Queen 3, 4, or 5 times during a month. Some customers visit the store only 1 time during the month, but others shop as many as 15 times.
   c.

Number of Visits	Percent of Total
0 up to 3	17.65
3 up to 6	41.18
6 up to 9	25.49
9 up to 12	7.84
12 up to 15	5.88
15 up to 18	1.96
Total	100.00

9. a. Histogram
   b. 100
   c. 5
   d. 28
   e. 0.28
   f. 12.5
   g. 13
11. a. 50
    b. 1.5 thousand miles, or 1,500 miles.
    c. Using lower limits on the X-axis:

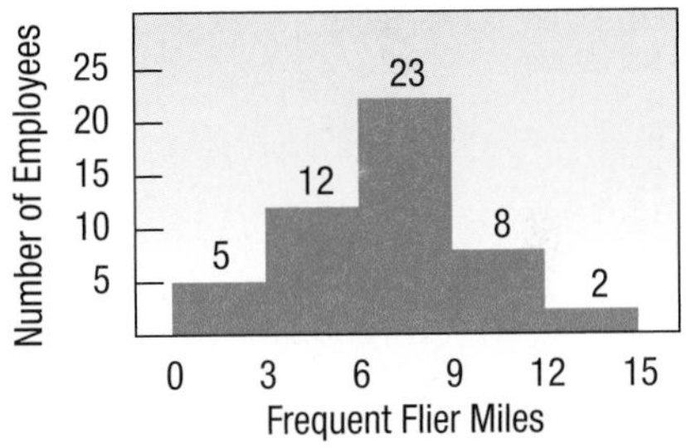

    d. $X = 1.5$, $Y = 5$
    e.

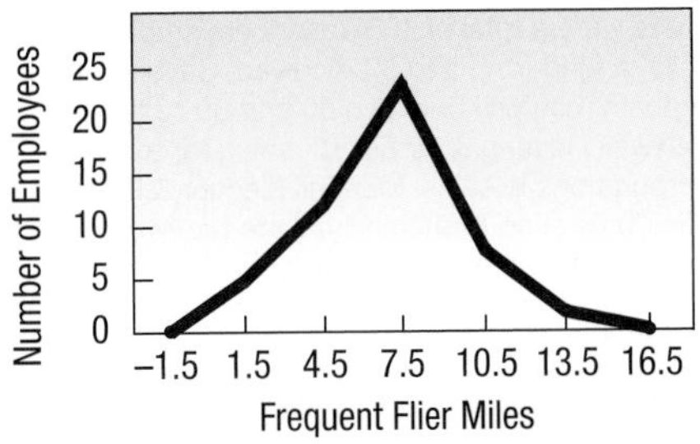

    f. For the 50 employees about half traveled between 6,000 and 9,000 miles. Five employees traveled less than 3,000 miles, and 2 traveled more than 12,000 miles.
13. a. 40
    b. 5
    c. 11 or 12

d. About \$18/hr
e. About \$9/hr
f. About 75%

15. a. 5
b.

Frequent Flier Miles	f	CF
0 up to 3	5	5
3 up to 6	12	17
6 up to 9	23	40
9 up to 12	8	48
12 up to 15	2	50

c.

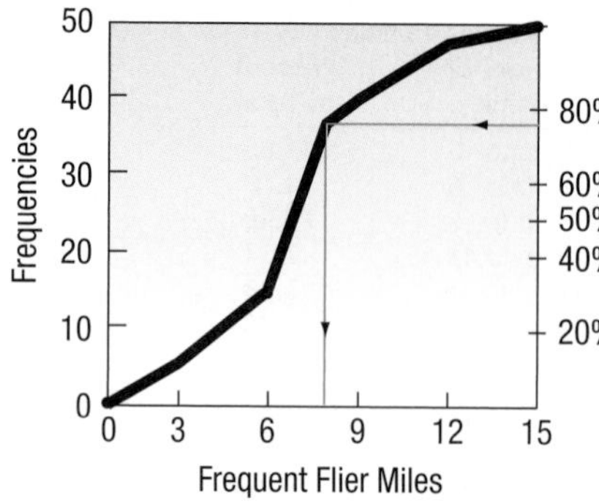

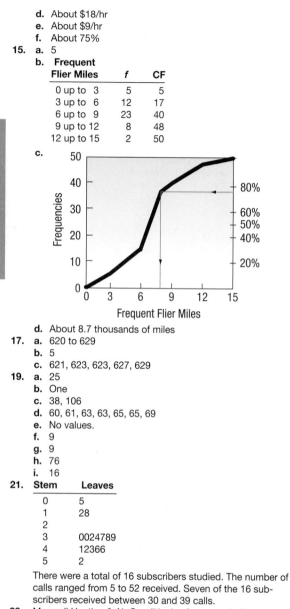

d. About 8.7 thousands of miles

17. a. 620 to 629
b. 5
c. 621, 623, 623, 627, 629

19. a. 25
b. One
c. 38, 106
d. 60, 61, 63, 63, 65, 65, 69
e. No values.
f. 9
g. 9
h. 76
i. 16

21.

Stem	Leaves
0	5
1	28
2	
3	0024789
4	12366
5	2

There were a total of 16 subscribers studied. The number of calls ranged from 5 to 52 received. Seven of the 16 subscribers received between 30 and 39 calls.

23. Maxwell Heating & Air Conditioning far exceeds the other corporations in sales. Mancell Electric & Plumbing and Mizelle Roofing & Sheet Metal are the two corporations with the least amount of fourth quarter sales.

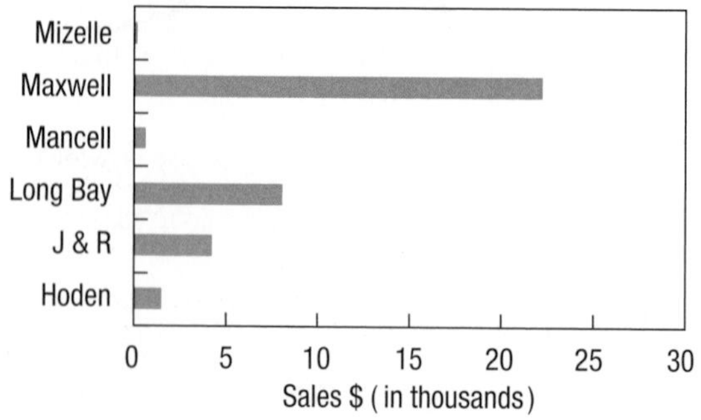

25. Homicides reached the highest number in 1993. They decreased steadily since 1993.

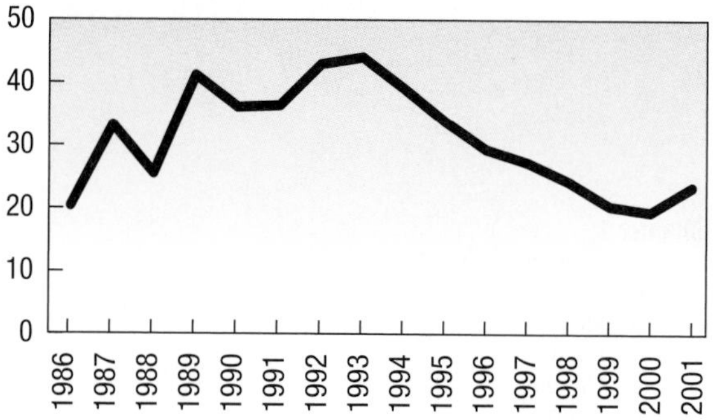

27. **Population Growth in the United States**
Population in the United States has increased steadily since 1950.

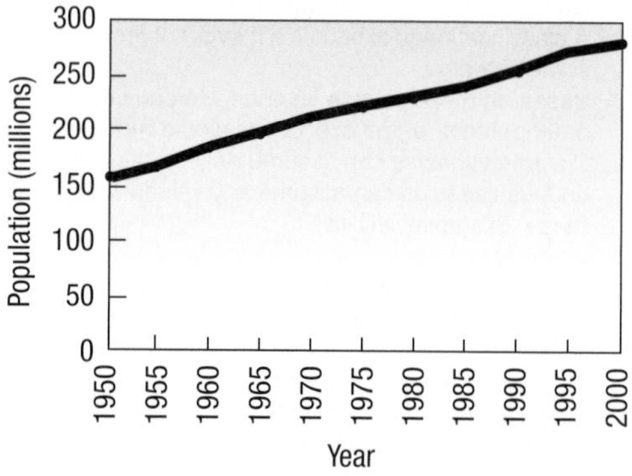

29. $2^6 = 64$ and $2^7 = 128$. Suggest 7 classes.

31. a. 5, because $2^4 = 16 < 25$ and $2^5 = 32 > 25$.
b. $i \geq \frac{48 - 16}{5} = 6.4$ Use interval of 7.
c. 15
d.

Class	Frequency	
15 up to 22	|||	3
22 up to 29	~~||||~~ |||	8
29 up to 36	~~||||~~ ||	7
36 up to 43	~~||||~~	5
43 up to 50	||	2
		25

e. It is fairly symmetric, with most of the values between 22 and 36.

33. a. 70
b. one
c. 0, 145
d. 30, 30, 32, 39
e. 24
f. 21
g. 77.5
h. 25

35. a. 56
b. 10 (found by 60 − 50)
c. 55
d. 17

37. a. \$36.60, found by (\$265 − \$82)/5.
b. \$40.

c.

\$ 80 up to \$120	8
120 up to 160	19
160 up to 200	10
200 up to 240	6
240 up to 280	1
Total	44

d. The purchases ranged from a low of about \$80 to a high of about \$280. The concentration is in the \$120 up to \$160 class.

39.

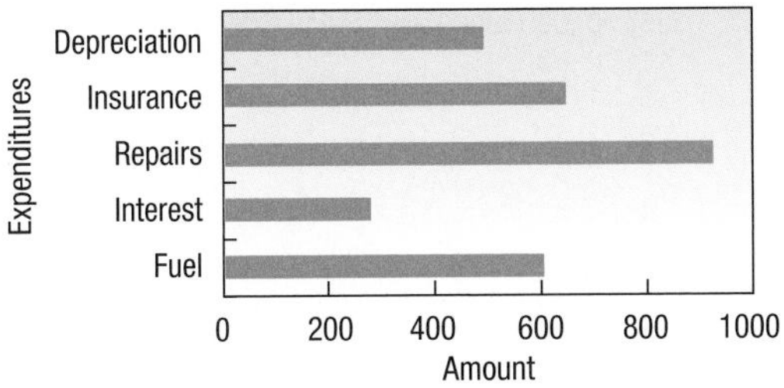

41. Unit = 0.10

3	76	149
3	77	
4	78	1
(2)	79	77
6	80	14
4	81	04
2	82	77

The lowest percent of on time is 76.1%, the largest is 82.7%. The typical airline is on time 79.9% of the time.

43. a. Since $2^6 = 64 < 70 < 128 = 2^7$, 7 classes are recommended. The interval should be at least (1,002.2 − 3.3)/7 = 142.7. Use 150 as a convenient value.

b.

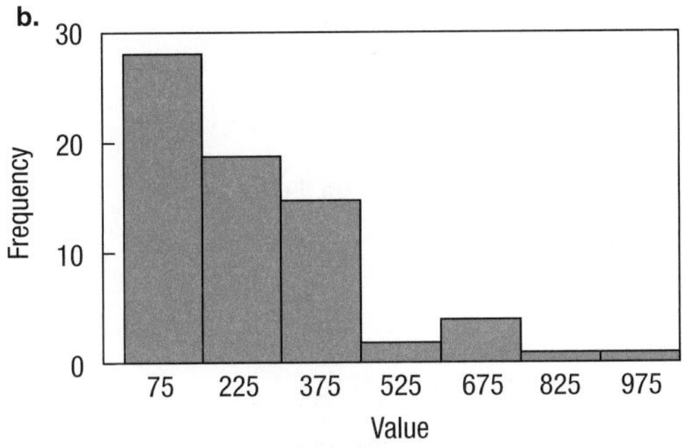

45.

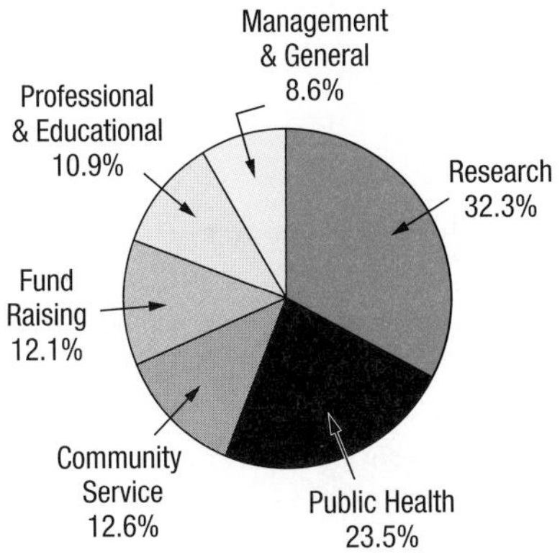

More than half of the expenses are concentrated in the categories Research and Public Health Education.

47.

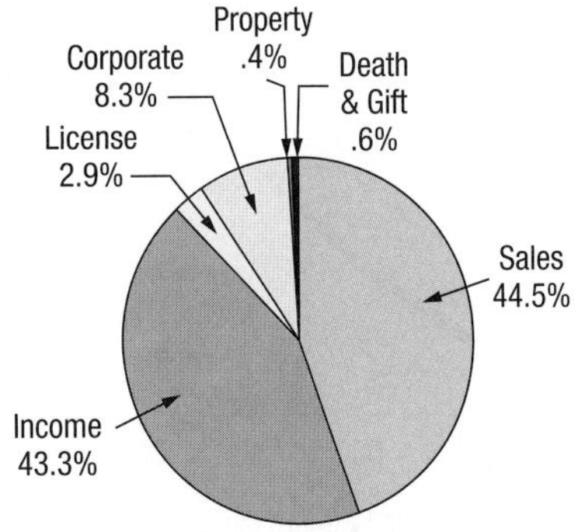

Sales tax and income tax dominate the total revenues for the state of Georgia.

49. There are 50 observations, so the recommended number of classes is 6. However, there are several states that have many more farms than the others, so it may be useful to have an open-ended class. One possible frequency distribution is:

Farms in USA	Frequency
0 up to 20	16
20 up to 40	13
40 up to 60	8
60 up to 80	6
80 up to 100	4
100 or more	3
Total	50

Twenty-nine of the 50 states, or 58 percent, have fewer than 40,000 farms. There are three states that have more than 100,000 farms.

51. In 1993 the price for a Toyota Camry and a Ford Taurus was about the same, a little more than \$11,000 each. Since that time the price of both cars has increased, but the rate of increase of the Camry has been larger than the Taurus. The difference in the selling price between the two cars was the largest in 1999, about \$6,500. From 1999 to 2000 the selling price of the Camry decreased about \$500, the only price decrease for either car during the 9-year period.

53. Answers will vary depending on when you collect the data.

55. a. Since $2^4 = 16 < 30 < 32 = 2^5$, use 5 classes. The interval should be (112.3 − 24.1)/5 = 17.64. Use 20. The resulting frequency distribution is:

Salary, mil \$	*f*
20 up to 40	6
40 up to 60	7
60 up to 80	9
80 up to 100	5
100 up to 120	3
	30

1. The typical team salary is about \$70.0 (\$70,000,000). The salaries range from about \$20.0 (\$20,000,000) to \$120.0 (\$120,000,000). The frequency distribution is used to find the estimates.
2. The distribution is positively skewed. The New York Yankees, Boston Red Sox, and Los Angeles

Dodgers all have a team salary greater than $100,000,000.

b. The cumulative frequency polygon follows.

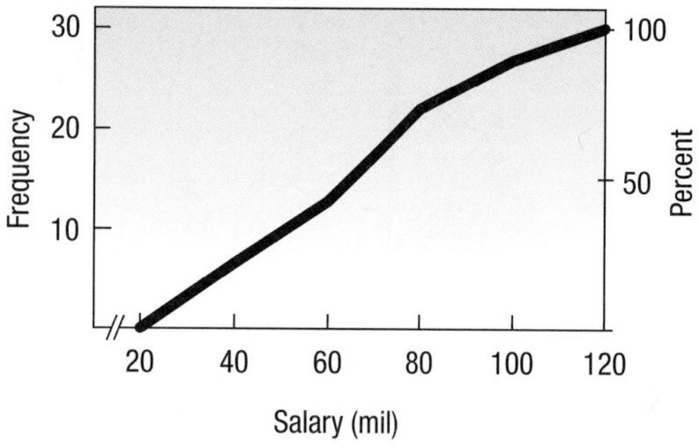

1. Forty percent of the teams have a total salary less than about $57,000,000.
2. Eleven teams have a salary less than $50,000,000.
3. Five teams have total salaries less than $36,000,000.

c. Use 5 classes. The interval should be at least (62,411 − 33,871)/5 = 5,708. Use 6,000 for convenience. The frequency distribution is:

Stadium size	f
33,000 up to 39,000	3
39,000 up to 45,000	10
45,000 up to 51,000	10
51,000 up to 57,000	5
57,000 up to 63,000	2
	30

1. A typical stadium seats about 46,000. Twenty of the stadiums seat between 39,000 and 51,000.
2. The distribution is well balanced. No stadium is out of line with the others.

d. Use 5 classes. The interval should be at least 17.8, found by (2,001 − 1,912)/5 = 17.8. Use 25 years to include extreme values. The resulting frequency distribution follows.

Year	f
1900 up to 1925	3
1925 up to 1950	0
1950 up to 1975	9
1975 up to 2000	13
2000 up to 2025	5
	30

1. There are three "old" stadiums, Yankees, Red Sox, and Cubs, built prior to 1925. There are five new stadiums built after the turn of the century.
2. The distribution is negatively skewed.

57. a. Use 5 classes. The interval should be at least (36.4 − 0.95)/5 = 7.09. Use an interval of 8.

GDP/cap	f
0 up to 8	11
8 up to 16	10
16 up to 24	13
24 up to 32	10
32 up to 40	2
	46

Nearly half (21/46) of the countries have a GDP/cap less than 20.0. Only two have a rate larger than 32.0.

b. The stem-and-leaf display follows. Note the distribution is positively skewed. Three countries have more than 60.0 million cell phones.

Stem-and-Leaf Display: Cell phones

Stem-and-leaf of Cell pho N = 46
Leaf Unit = 1.0

(35)	0	00000000000111111122222222233344444
11	0	68
9	1	123
6	1	5
5	2	0
4	2	7
3	3	
3	3	
3	4	
3	4	
3	5	
3	5	
3	6	3
2	6	59

Chapter 3

1. $\mu = 5.4$, found by 27/5.

3. a. $\bar{X} = 7.0$, found by 28/4.
b. $(5 - 7) + (9 - 7) + (4 - 7) + (10 - 7) = 0$

5. $\bar{X} = 14.58$, found by 43.74/3.

7. a. 15.4, found by 154/10.
b. Population parameter, since it includes all the salespersons at Midtown Ford.

9. a. $54.55, found by $1,091/20.
b. A sample statistic—assuming that the power company serves more than 20 customers.

11. $22.91, found by $\dfrac{300(\$20) + 400(\$25) + 400(\$23)}{300 + 400 + 400}$.

13. $11.50, found by ($400 + $500 + $1,400)/200.

15. a. No mode
b. The given value would be the mode.
c. 3 and 4 bimodal.

17. Median = 5, Mode = 5

19. a. Median = 2.9
b. 2.9

21. 12.8 percentage increase, found by $\sqrt[5]{(1.08)(1.12)(1.14)(1.26)(1.05)} = 1.128$.

23. 12.28 percentage increase, found by $\sqrt[5]{(1.094)(1.138)(1.117)(1.119)(1.147)} = 1.1228$.

25. 10.33%, found by $\sqrt[13]{\dfrac{14.0}{3.9}} - 1$.

27. 10.76%, found by $\sqrt[5]{\dfrac{70}{42}} - 1$.

29. a. 7, found by 10 − 3.
b. 6, found by 30/5.
c. 2.4, found by 12/5.
d. The difference between the highest number sold (10) and the smallest number sold (3) is 7. On average, the number of service reps on duty deviates by 2.4 from the mean of 6.

31. a. 30, found by 54 − 24.
b. 38, found by 380/10.
c. 7.2, found by 72/10.

d. The difference of 54 and 24 is 30. On average, the number of minutes required to install a door deviates 7.2 minutes from the mean of 38 minutes.

33. **a.** 15, found by 41 − 26.
b. 33.9, found by 339/10.
c. 4.12, found by 41.2/10.
d. The ratings deviate 4.12 from the mean of 33.9 on average.

35. **a.** 5
b. 4.4, found by

$$\frac{(8-5)^2+(3-5)^2+(7-5)^2+(3-5)^2+(4-5)^2}{5}.$$

37. **a.** \$2.77
b. 1.26, found by

$$\frac{(2.68-2.77)^2+(1.03-2.77)^2+(2.26-2.77)^2+(4.30-2.77)^2+(3.58-2.77)^2}{5}.$$

39. **a.** Range: 7.3, found by 11.6 − 4.3. Arithmetic mean: 6.94, found by 34.7/5. Variance: 6.5944, found by 32.972/5. Standard deviation: 2.568, found by $\sqrt{6.5944}$.
b. Dennis has a higher mean return (11.76 > 6.94). However, Dennis has greater spread in their returns on equity (16.89 > 6.59).

41. **a.** $\bar{X} = 4$

$$s^2 = \frac{(7-4)^2+\cdots+(3-4)^2}{5-1} = 5.5$$

b. $$s^2 = \frac{102 - \frac{(20)^2}{5}}{5-1} = 5.50$$

c. $s = 2.3452$

43. **a.** $\bar{X} = 38$

$$s^2 = \frac{(28-38)^2+\cdots+(42-38)^2}{10-1} = 82.6667$$

b. $$s^2 = \frac{15{,}184 - \frac{(380)^2}{10}}{10-1} = 82.6667$$

c. $s = 9.0921$

45. **a.** $\bar{X} = 124$

$$s^2 = \frac{(124-124)^2+\cdots+(121-124)^2}{10-1} = 4.6667$$

b. $$s^2 = \frac{153{,}802 - \frac{(1240)^2}{10}}{10-1} = 4.6667$$

c. $s = \sqrt{4.6667} = 2.1602$

47. About 69%, found by $1 - 1/(1.8)^2$.

49. **a.** About 95%.
b. 47.5%, 2.5%.

51. 8.06%, found by (.25/3.10)(100).

53. **a.** Because the two series are in different units of measurement.
b. P.E. ratio is 16.51%. ROI 20.8%. Less spread in the P.E. ratios.

55. **a.** The mean is 30.8, found by 154/5. The median is 31.0, and the standard deviation is 3.96, found by

$$\sqrt{\frac{4{,}806 - \frac{154^2}{5}}{4}}.$$

b. −0.15, foun

c. **Salary**

36
26
33
28
31

0.125, found by [5/(4 × 3)]

57. **a.** The mean is 21.93, found by 328.9/15. The median is 15.8, and the standard deviation is 21.18,

$$\sqrt{\frac{13{,}494.67 - \frac{328.9^2}{15}}{14}}.$$

b. 0.868, found by [3(21.93 − 15.8)]/21.18.
c. 2.444, found by [15/(14 × 13)] × 29.658.

59. Median = 53, found by $(11+1)(\frac{1}{2})$ ∴ 6 value in from lowest.
$Q_1 = 49$, found by $(11+1)(\frac{1}{4})$ ∴ 3 value in from lowest.
$Q_3 = 55$, found by $(11+1)(\frac{3}{4})$ ∴ 9 value in from lowest.

61. **a.** $Q_1 = 33.25$, $Q_3 = 50.25$
b. $D_2 = 27.8$, $D_8 = 52.6$
c. $P_{67} = 47$

63. **a.** 350
b. $Q_1 = 175$, $Q_3 = 930$
c. 930 − 175 = 755
d. Less than 0, or more than about 2060.
e. There are no outliers.
f. The distribution is positively skewed.

65.

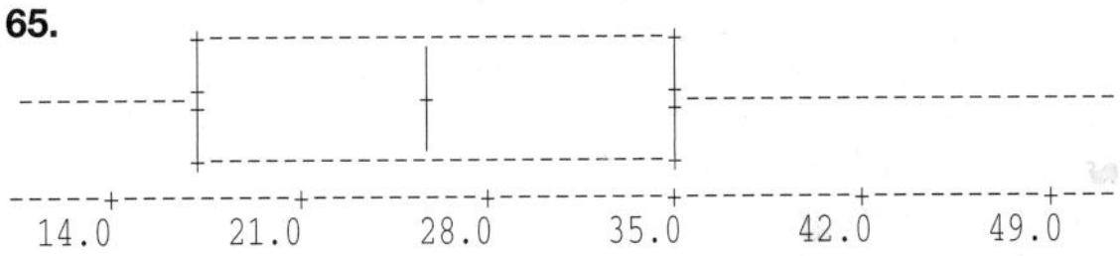

The distribution is somewhat positively skewed. Note that the dashed line above 35 is longer than below 18.

67. Because the exact values in a frequency distribution are not known, the midpoint is used for every member of that class.

69.

Class	*f*	*M*	*fM*	*fM*²
20 up to 30	7	25	175	4,375
30 up to 40	12	35	420	14,700
40 up to 50	21	45	945	42,525
50 up to 60	18	55	990	54,450
60 up to 70	12	65	780	50,700
	70		3,310	166,750

$$\bar{X} = \frac{3{,}310}{70} = 47.2857$$

$$s = \sqrt{\frac{166{,}750 - \frac{(3310)^2}{70}}{70-1}} = 12.18$$

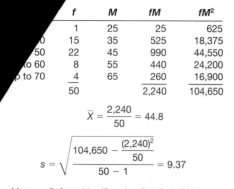

	f	M	fM	fM²
	1	25	25	625
0	15	35	525	18,375
50	22	45	990	44,550
o 60	8	55	440	24,200
p to 70	4	65	260	16,900
	50		2,240	104,650

$$\bar{X} = \frac{2{,}240}{50} = 44.8$$

$$s = \sqrt{\frac{104{,}650 - \frac{(2{,}240)^2}{50}}{50 - 1}} = 9.37$$

73. **a.** Mean = 5, found by (6 + 4 + 3 + 7 + 5)/5. Median is 5, found by rearranging the values and selecting the middle value.
b. Population, because all partners were included.
c. $\Sigma(X - \mu) = (6 - 5) + (4 - 5) + (3 - 5) + (7 - 5) + (5 - 5) = 0$.

75. $\bar{X} = \frac{545}{16} = 34.06$
Median = 37.50

77. 370.08, found by 18,504/50.

79. $\bar{X}_W = \frac{\$5.00(270) + \$6.50(300) + \$8.00(100)}{270 + 300 + 100} = \$6.12$

81. $\bar{X}_w = \frac{[15{,}300(4.5) + 10{,}400(3.0) + 150{,}600(10.2)]}{176{,}300}$
$= 9.28$

83. $\text{GM} = \sqrt[21]{\frac{6{,}286{,}800}{5{,}164{,}900}} - 1 = 1.0094 - 1.0 = .0094$

85. **a.** 55, found by 72 − 17.
b. 14.4, found by 144/10, where $\bar{X} = 43.2$.
c. 17.6245.

87. **a.** Population.
b. 183.47.
c. 94.92%.

89.

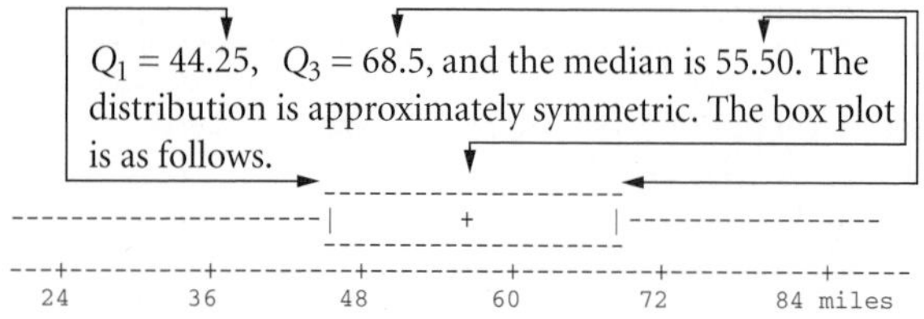

The above results are found using MINITAB.

91. The distribution is positively skewed. The first quartile is approx. \$20 and the third quartile is approx. \$90. There is one outlier located at \$255. The median is about \$50.

93. **a.** $\bar{X} = \frac{857.90}{50} = 17.158$, median = 16.35

b. $s = \sqrt{\frac{20{,}206.73 - \frac{(857.90)^2}{50}}{50 - 1}} = 10.58$

c. 17.158 ± (1.5)(10.58) = 1.288 up to 33.028
d. 17.158 ± (2)(10.58) = −4.002, 38.318

e. $\text{CV} = \frac{10.58}{17.158}(100) = 61.66\%$

f. $sk = \frac{3(17.158 - 16.35)}{10.58} = 0.23$

g. $L_{25} = (50 + 1)\frac{25}{100} = 12.75 \qquad Q_1 = 7.825$

$L_{75} = (50 + 1)\frac{75}{100} = 38.25 \qquad Q_3 = 27.400$

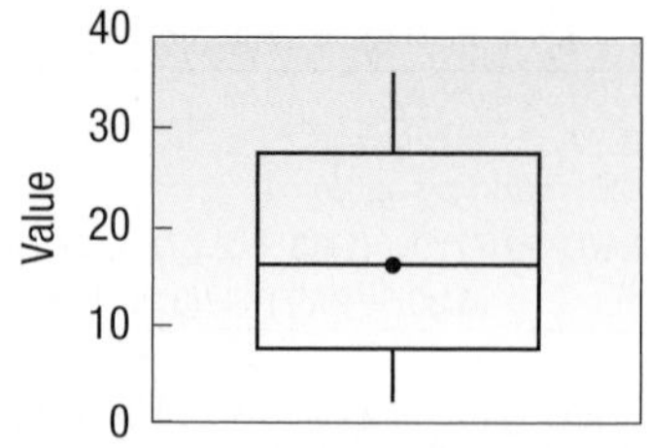

h. The distribution is nearly symmetrical. The mean is 17.158, the median is 16.35, and the standard deviation is 10.58. About 75 percent of the companies have a value less than 27.4, and 25 percent have a value less than 7.825.

95. **a.** The mean is 173.77 hours, found by 2,259/13. The median is 195 hours.

$s = 105.61$ hours, found by $\sqrt{\frac{526{,}391 - \frac{2{,}259^2}{13}}{12}}$.

b. CV = 60.78%, found by $\frac{105.61}{173.77}(100)$.
Coefficient of skewness is − 0.697.

c. $L_{45} = 14 \times .45 = 6.3$. So the 45th percentile is 192 + 0.3(195 − 192) = 192.9.
$L_{82} = 14 \times .82 = 11.48$. So the 82nd percentile is 260 + 0.48(295 − 260) = 276.8.

d.

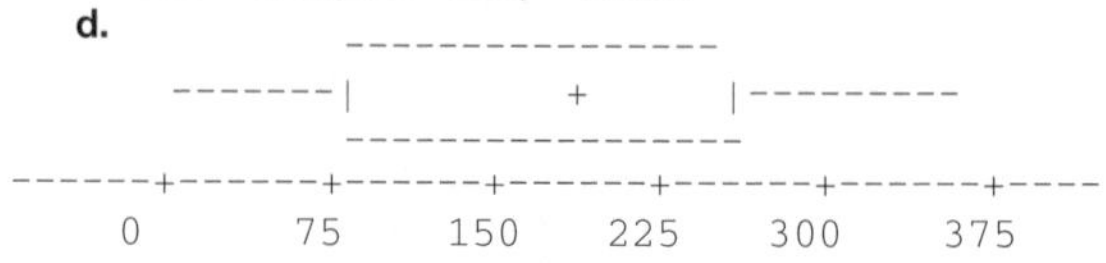

There is a slight negative skewness visible, but no outliers.

97. Mean is 13, found by 910/70.

$$s = \sqrt{\frac{13{,}637.50 - \frac{(910)^2}{70}}{69}} = 5.118$$

99. Answers will vary.

101. **a.** **1.** A software package gave the output:

Descriptive Statistics: Price

Variable	N	Mean	Median	TrMean	StDev	SE Mean
Price	105	221.10	213.60	220.00	47.11	4.60

Variable	Minimum	Maximum	Q1	Q3
Price	125.00	345.30	186.85	251.85

2. The coefficient of skewness is 0.474, which indicates a small positive tail.

3.

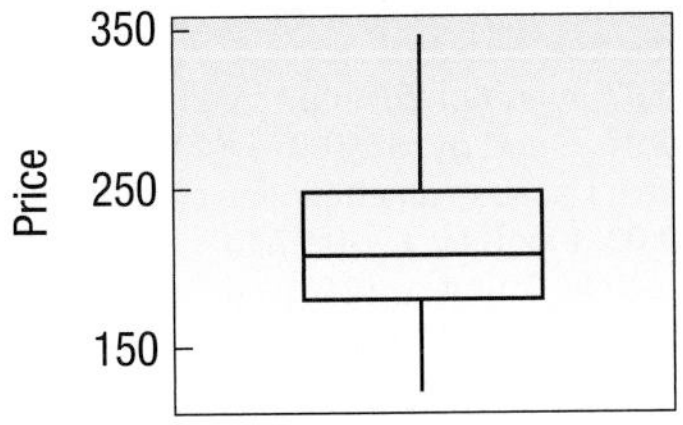

There are no outliers. The first quartile is near 190; the third, about 250.

4. The distribution is symmetric about $220,000 with most of the prices less than $30,000 away from the center.

b. 1. A software package gave the output:

Descriptive Statistics: Size

Variable	N	Mean	Median	TrMean	StDev	SE Mean
Size	105	2223.8	2200.0	2218.9	248.7	24.3

Variable	Minimum	Maximum	Q1	Q3
Size	1600.0	2900.0	2100.0	2400.0

2. The coefficient of skewness is 0.323, which indicates a small positive tail.

3.

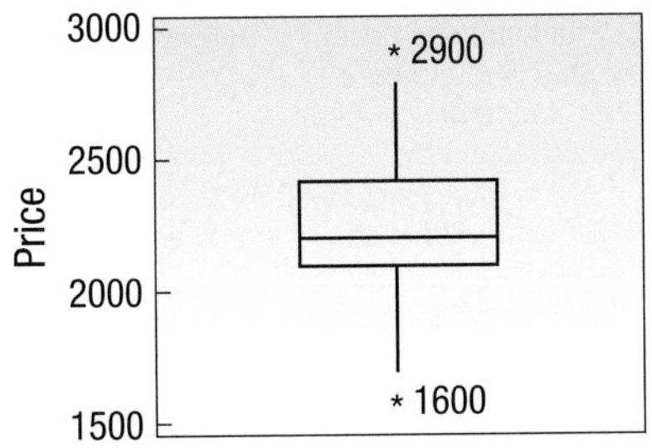

There are outliers at both ends of the distribution. One house at 1600 square feet is unusually small and three houses at 2900 square feet are unusually large. The first quartile is near 2100; the third, about 2400.

4. The distribution is symmetric about 2200 square feet with most of the sizes less than 200 square feet away from the center.

103. a. 1. A software system gave the output:

Descriptive Statistics: Life Expectancy

Variable	N	Mean	Median	TrMean	StDev	SE Mean
Life Exp	46	73.81	76.10	74.65	6.90	1.02

Variable	Minimum	Maximum	Q1	Q3
Life Exp	48.09	80.80	71.53	78.47

2. $sk = -2.10$, which indicates negative skewness

3. **Boxplot**

```
                                  +------------+
 0   0          ------------------I     I      I----
                                  +------------+
+---------+---------+---------+---------+---------+---Life Exp
48.0     54.0      60.0      66.0      72.0      78.0
```

There are two outliers at 48 and 51 years. $Q_1 = 71.53$ and $Q_3 = 78.47$

4. The distribution is negatively skewed, with two outliers. The mean life expectancy is 73.81 years and the median is 76.10 years.

b. 1. A software system gave the following output:

Descriptive Statistics: GDP/cap

Variable	N	Mean	Median	TrMean	StDev	SE Mean
GDP/cap	46	16.58	17.45	16.36	9.27	1.37

Variable	Minimum	Maximum	Q1	Q3
GDP/cap	0.95	36.40	8.30	24.40

2. $sk = .057$, so the distribution is nearly symmetric.

3. **Boxplot**

```
              +-----------------------+
   -----------I          I            I-----------------
              +-----------------------+
+---------+---------+---------+---------+---------+---GDP/cap
0.0      7.0       14.0      21.0      28.0      35.0
```

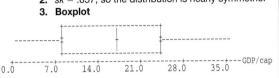

There are no outliers. $Q_1 = 8.30$ and $Q_3 = 24.40$

4. The distribution is nearly symmetric. The mean is 16.58 and the median 17.45.

Chapter 4

1.

Outcome	Person 1	Person 2
1	A	A
2	A	F
3	F	A
4	F	F

3. **a.** .176, found by $\frac{6}{34}$.
   b. Empirical.

5. **a.** Empirical.
   b. Classical.
   c. Classical.
   d. Empirical, based on seismological data.

7. **a.** The survey of 40 people about environmental issues.
   b. 26 or more respond yes, for example.
   c. 10/40 = .25
   d. Empirical.
   e. The events are not equally likely, but they are mutually exclusive.

9. **a.** Answers will vary. Here are some possibilities: 123, 124, 125, 999.
   b. $(1/10)^3$
   c. Classical.

11. $P(A \text{ or } B) = P(A) + P(B) = .30 + .20 = .50$
    $P(\text{neither}) = 1 - .50 = .50.$

13. **a.** 102/200 = .51
    b. .49, found by 61/200 + 37/200 = .305 + .185. Special rule of addition.

15. $P(\text{above } C) = .25 + .50 = .75$

17. $P(A \text{ or } B) = P(A) + P(B) - P(A \text{ and } B)$
    $= .20 + .30 - .15 = .35$

19. When two events are mutually exclusive, it means that if one occurs the other event cannot occur. Therefore, the probability of their joint occurrence is zero.

21. **a.** .65, found by .35 + .40 − .10.
    b. A joint probability.
    c. No, an executive might read more than one magazine.

23. $P(A \text{ and } B) = P(A) \times P(B|A) = .40 \times .30 = .12$

25. .90, found by (.80 + .60) − .5.
    .10, found by (1 − .90).

27. **a.** $P(A_1) = 3/10 = .30$
b. $P(B_1|A_2) = 1/3 = .33$
c. $P(B_2 \text{ and } A_3) = 1/10 = .10$

29. **a.** A contingency table.
b. .27, found by 300/500 × 135/300.
c. The tree diagram would appear as:

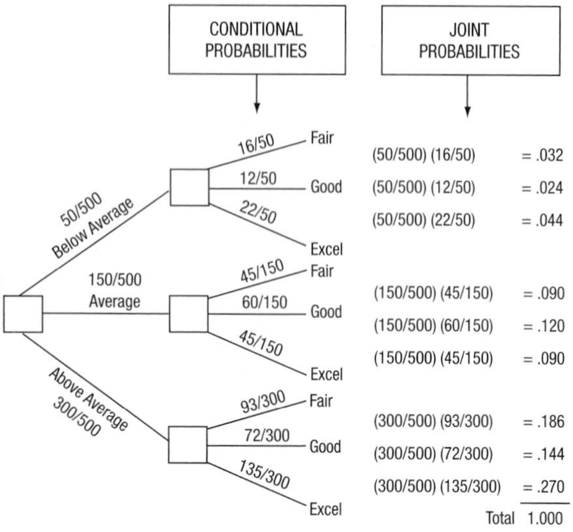

31. Probability the first presentation wins = 3/5 = .60.
Probability the second presentation wins = 2/5 (3/4) = .30.
Probability the third presentation wins = (2/5)(1/4)(3/3) = .10.

33. **a.** 78,960,960
b. 840, found by (7)(6)(5)(4). That is 7!/3!.
c. 10, found by 5!/3!2!.

35. 210, found by (10)(9)(8)(7)/(4)(3)(2).

37. 120, found by 5!.

39. 10,897,286,400, found by
$_{15}P_{10}$ = (15)(14)(13)(12) (11)(10)(9)(8)(7)(6).

41. **a.** Asking teenagers to compare their reactions to a newly developed soft drink.
b. Answers will vary. One possibility is more than half of the respondents like it.

43. Subjective.

45. **a.** The likelihood an event will occur, assuming that another event has already occurred.
b. The collection of one or more outcomes of an experiment.
c. A measure of the likelihood that two or more events will happen concurrently.

47. **a.** .8145, found by $(.95)^4$.
b. Special rule of multiplication.
c. $P(A \text{ and } B \text{ and } C \text{ and } D) = P(A) \times P(B) \times P(C) \times P(D)$.

49. **a.** .08, found by .80 × .10.
b.

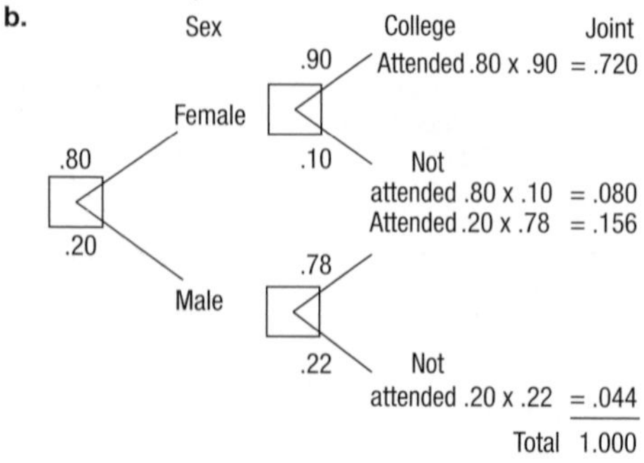

c. Yes, because all the possible outcomes are shown on the tree diagram.

51. **a.** 0.57, found by 57/100.
b. 0.97, found by (57/100) + (40/100).
c. Yes, because an employee cannot be both.
d. 0.03, found by 1 − 0.97.

53. **a.** 0.4096, found by $(0.8)^4$.
b. 0.0016, found by $(0.2)^4$.
c. 0.9984, found by 1 − 0.0016.

55. **a.** 0.9039, found by $(0.98)^5$.
b. 0.0961, found by 1 − 0.9039.

57. **a.** 0.0333, found by (4/10)(3/9)(2/8).
b. 0.1667, found by (6/10)(5/9)(4/8).
c. 0.8333, found by 1 − 0.1667.
d. Dependent

59. **a.** 0.3818, found by (9/12)(8/11)(7/10).
b. 0.6182, found by 1 − 0.3818.

61. **a.** 0.5467, found by 82/150.
b. 0.76, found by (39/150) + (75/150).
c. 0.6267, found by 82/150 + 39/150 − 27/150. General rule of addition.
d. 0.3293, found by 27/82.
e. 0.2972, found by (82/150)(81/149).

63. **a.** $P(\text{P or D}) = (1/50)(9/10) + (49/50)(1/10) = 0.116$
b. $P(\text{No}) = (49/50)(9/10) = 0.882$
c. $P(\text{No on 3}) = (0.882)^3 = 0.686$
d. $P(\text{at least one prize}) = 1 - 0.686 = 0.314$

65. Yes. 256 is found by 2^8.

67. .9744, found by $1 - (.40)^4$.

69. **a.** .185, found by (.15)(.95) + (.05)(.85).
b. .0075, found by (.15)(.05).

71. **a.** $P(\text{F and} > 60) = .25$, found by solving with the general rule of multiplication:
$P(F) \cdot P(>60|F) = (.5)(.5)$
b. 0
c. .3333, found by 1/3.

73. $26^4 = 456{,}976$

75. 1/3,628,800

77. Answer depends on the game show host.

79. **a.**

Winning Season	Low Attendance	Moderate Attendance	High Attendance	Total
No	7	5	2	14
Yes	3	7	6	16
	10	12	8	30

1. $P(\text{win}) = 16/30 = .533$
2. $P(\text{win or} > 3{,}000{,}000) = 16/30 + 8/30 - 6/30 = .60$
3. $P(\text{win}/> 3{,}000{,}000) = 6/8 = 0.75$
4. $P(\text{Lose and} < 2{,}000{,}000) = 7/30 = .233$

b.

Winning Season	Grass	Artificial	Total
No	11	3	14
Yes	14	2	16
	25	5	30

1. $P(\text{grass}) = 25/30 = .833$
2. $P(\text{win/grass}) = 14/25 = .56$, $P(\text{win/artificial}) = 2/5 = .40$
3. $P(\text{win or artificial}) = 16/30 + 5/30 - 2/30 = 19/30 = .633$

Chapter 5

1. $\mu = 1.3$, $\sigma^2 = .81$, found by:
$\mu = 0(.20) + 1(.40) + 2(.30) + 3(.10) = 1.3$
$\sigma^2 = (0 - 1.3)^2\,(.2) + (1 - 1.3)^2\,(.4)$
$+ (2 - 1.3)^2\,(.3) + (3 - 1.3)^2\,(.1)$
$= .81$

3. $\mu = 0(.3) + 1(.4) + 2(.2) + 3(.1) = 1.1$
$\sigma^2 = (0 - 1.1)^2(.3) + (1 - 1.1)^2(.4)$
$+ (2 - 1.1)^2(.2) + (3 - 1.1)^2(.1) = 0.89$
$\sigma = .943.$

5. **a.** .20
b. .55
c. .95
d. $\mu = 0(.45) + 10(.30) + 100(.20) + 500(.05) = 48.0$
$\sigma^2 = (0 - 48)^2(.45) + (10 - 48)^2(.3)$
$+ (100 - 48)^2(.2) + (500 - 48)^2(.05) = 12{,}226$
$\sigma = 110.57$, found by $\sqrt{12{,}226}$

7. **a.** $P(2) = \frac{4!}{2!(4-2)!}(.25)^2(.75)^{4-2} = .2109$
b. $P(3) = \frac{4!}{3!(4-3)!}(.25)^3(.75)^{4-3} = .0469$

9. **a.**

X	$P(X)$
0	.064
1	.288
2	.432
3	.216

b. $\mu = 1.8$
$\sigma^2 = 0.72$
$\sigma = \sqrt{0.72} = .8485$

11. **a.** .2668, found by $P(2) = \frac{9!}{(9-2)!2!}(.3)^2(.7)^7$.
b. .1715, found by $P(4) = \frac{9!}{(9-4)!4!}(.3)^4(.7)^5$.
c. .0404, found by $P(0) = \frac{9!}{(9-0)!0!}(.3)^0(.7)^9$.

13. **a.** .2824, found by $P(0) = \frac{12!}{(12-0)!0!}(.10)^0(.9)^{12}$.
b. .3765, found by $P(1) = \frac{12!}{(12-1)!1!}(.10)^1(.9)^{11}$.
c. .2301, found by $P(2) = \frac{12!}{(12-2)!2!}(.10)^2(.9)^{10}$.
d. $\mu = 1.2$, found by 12(.10).
$\sigma = 1.0392$, found by $\sqrt{1.08}$.

15. **a.** 0.1858, found by $\frac{15!}{2!13!}(0.23)^2(0.77)^{13}$.
b. 0.1416, found by $\frac{15!}{5!10!}(0.23)^5(0.77)^{10}$.
c. 3.45, found by (0.23)(15).

17. **a.** 0.296, found by using Appendix A with n of 8, π of 0.30, and x of 2.
b. $P(x \le 2) = 0.058 + 0.198 + 0.296 = 0.552$
c. 0.448, found by $P(x \ge 3) = 1 - P(x \le 2) = 1 - 0.552$.

19. **a.** 0.387, found from Appendix A with n of 9, π of 0.90, and x of 9.
b. $P(x < 5) = 0.001$
c. 0.992, found by 1 − 0.008.
d. 0.947, found by 1 − 0.053.

21. **a.** $\mu = 10.5$, found by 15(0.7) and $\sigma = \sqrt{15(0.7)(0.3)} = 1.7748$.
b. 0.2061, found by $\frac{15!}{10!5!}(0.7)^{10}(0.3)^5$.
c. 0.4247, found by 0.2061 + 0.2186.
d. 0.5154, found by 0.2186 + 0.1700 + 0.0916 + 0.0305 + 0.0047.

23. $P(2) = \frac{[{}_6C_2][{}_4C_1]}{{}_{10}C_3} = \frac{15(4)}{120} = .50$

25. $P(0) = \frac{[{}_7C_2][{}_3C_0]}{[{}_{10}C_2]} = \frac{21(1)}{45} = .4667$

27. $P(2) = \frac{[{}_9C_3][{}_6C_2]}{[{}_{15}C_5]} = \frac{84(15)}{3003} = .4196$

29. **a.** .6703
b. .3297

31. **a.** .0613
b. .0803

33. $\mu = 6$
$P(X \ge 5) = .7149 = 1 - (.0025 + .0149 + .0446 + .0892 + .1339)$

35. A random variable is a quantitative or qualitative outcome that results from a chance experiment. A probability distribution also includes the likelihood of each possible outcome.

37. The binomial distribution is a discrete probability distribution for which there are only two possible outcomes. A second important part is that data collected are a result of counts. Additionally, one trial is independent from the next, and the chance for success remains the same from one trial to the next.

39. $\mu = 0(.1) + 1(.2) + 2(.3) + 3(.4) = 2.00$
$\sigma^2 = (0 - 2)^2(.1) + \cdots + (3 - 2)^2(.40) = 1.0$
$\sigma = 1$

41. $\mu = 0(.4) + 1(.2) + 2(.2) + 3(.1) + 4(.1) = 1.3$
$\sigma^2 = (0 - 1.30)^2(.4) + \cdots + (4 - 1.30)^2(.1) = 1.81$
$\sigma = 1.3454$

43. **a.** 6, found by 0.4×15.
b. 0.0245, found by $\frac{15!}{10!5!}(0.4)^{10}(0.6)^5$
c. 0.0338, found by 0.0245 + 0.0074 + 0.0016 + 0.0003 + 0.0000.
d. 0.0093, found by 0.0338 − 0.0245.

45. **a.** $\mu = 20(0.075) = 1.5$
$\sigma = \sqrt{20(0.075)(0.925)} = 1.1779$
b. 0.2103, found by $\frac{20!}{0!20!}(0.075)^0(0.925)^{20}$.
c. 0.7897, found by 1 − 0.2103.

47. **a.** 0.1311, found by $\frac{16!}{4!12!}(0.15)^4(0.85)^{12}$.
b. 2.4, found by (0.15)(16).
c. 0.2100, found by 1 − 0.0743 − 0.2097 − 0.2775 − 0.2285.

49. $P(2) = \frac{[{}_6C_2][{}_4C_2]}{[{}_{10}C_4]} = \frac{(15)(6)}{210} = 0.4286$

51. **a.**

0	0.0002
1	0.0019
2	0.0116
3	0.0418
4	0.1020
5	0.1768
6	0.2234
7	0.2075
8	0.1405
9	0.0676
10	0.0220
11	0.0043
12	0.0004

b. $\mu = 12(0.52) = 6.24$
$\sigma = \sqrt{12(0.52)(0.48)} = 1.7307$
c. 0.1768
d. 0.3343, found by 0.0002 + 0.0019 + 0.0116 + 0.0418 + 0.1020 + 0.1768.

53. $P(X = 0) = \frac{[{}_8C_4][{}_4C_0]}{[{}_{12}C_4]} = \frac{70}{495} = .141$

55. $\mu = 4.0$, from Appendix C.
a. .0183
b. .1954
c. .6289
d. .5665

57. **a.** 0.1733, found by $\frac{(3.1)^4 e^{-3.1}}{4!}$.
b. 0.0450, found by $\frac{(3.1)^0 e^{-3.1}}{0!}$.
c. 0.9550, found by 1 − 0.0450.

59. For NASA, $\mu = n\pi = 25(1/60{,}000) = 0.0004$

$$P(0) = \frac{0.0004^0 e^{-0.0004}}{0!} = 0.9996$$

$P(X \geq 1) = 1 - 0.9996 = 0.0004$
For Air Force, $\mu = 25(1/35) = .7143$

$$P(0) = \frac{0.7143^0 e^{-0.7143}}{0!} = 0.4895$$

$P(X \geq 1) = 1 - .4895 = 0.5105$
Summarizing, Air Force estimate is .5105 and NASA estimate is 0.0004.

61. Let $\mu = n\pi = 155(1/3709) = 0.042$

$$P(5) = \frac{0.042^5 e^{-0.042}}{5!} = 0.000000001$$

Very unlikely!

63. $P(2) = \frac{({}_5C_2)({}_{25}C_3)}{{}_{30}C_5} = \frac{10(2300)}{142{,}506} = .1614$

Chapter 6

1. The actual shape of a normal distribution depends on its mean and standard deviation. Thus, there is a normal distribution, and an accompanying normal curve, for a mean of 7 and a standard deviation of 2. There is another normal curve for a mean of $25,000 and a standard deviation of $1,742, and so on.

3. **a.** 490 and 510, found by 500 ± 1(10).
b. 480 and 520, found by 500 ± 2(10).
c. 470 and 530, found by 500 ± 3(10).

5. $$Z_{Rob} = \frac{\$50{,}000 - \$60{,}000}{\$5000} = -2.00$$

$$Z_{Rachel} = \frac{\$50{,}000 - \$35{,}000}{\$8000} = 1.875$$

Adjusting for their industries, Rob is well below average and Rachel well above.

7. **a.** 1.25, found by $z = \frac{25 - 20}{4.0} = 1.25$.
b. 0.3944, found in Appendix D.
c. 0.3085, found by $z = \frac{18 - 20}{2.5} = -0.5$.
Find 0.1915 in Appendix D for $z = -0.5$. Then 0.5000 − 0.1915 = 0.3085.

9. **a.** 0.3413, found by $z = \frac{\$20 - \$16.50}{\$3.50} = 1.00$. Then find 0.3413 in Appendix D for $z = 1$.
b. 0.1587, found by 0.5000 − 0.3413 = 0.1587.
c. 0.3336, found by $z = \frac{\$15.00 - \$16.50}{\$3.50} = -0.43$.
Find 0.1664 in Appendix D, for $z = -0.43$, then 0.5000 − 0.1664 = 0.3336.

11. **a.** 0.8276: First find $z = -1.5$, found by (44 − 50)/4 and $z = 1.25 = (55 - 50)/4$. The area between −1.5 and 0 is 0.4332 and the area between 0 and 1.25 is 0.3944, both from Appendix D. Then adding the two areas we find that 0.4332 + 0.3944 = 0.8276.
b. 0.1056, found by 0.5000 − 0.3994, where $z = 1.25$.
c. 0.2029: Recall that the area for $z = 1.25$ is 0.3944, and the area for $z = 0.5$, found by (52 − 50)/4, is 0.1915. Then subtract 0.3944 − 0.1915 and find 0.2029.

13. **a.** 0.1525, found by subtracting 0.4938 − 0.3413, which are the areas associated with z values of 2.5 and 1.00, respectively.
b. 0.0062, found by 0.5000 − 0.4938.
c. 0.9710, found by recalling that the area of the z value of 2.5 is 0.4938. Then find $z = -2.00$, found by (6.8 − 7.0)/0.1. Thus, 0.4938 + 0.4772 = 0.9710.

15. **a.** 0.0764, found by $z = (20 - 15)/3.5 = 1.43$, then 0.5000 − 0.4236 = 0.0764.
b. 0.9236, found by 0.5000 + 0.4236, where $z = 1.43$.
c. 0.1185, found by $z = (12 - 15)/3.5 = -0.86$.
The area under the curve is 0.3051, then $z = (10 - 15)/3.5) = -1.43$. The area is 0.4236.
Finally, 0.4236 − 0.3051 = 0.1185.

17. $X = 56.60$, found by adding 0.5000 (the area left of the mean) and then finding a z value that forces 45 percent of the data to fall inside the curve. Solving for X: 1.65 = $(X - 50)/4 = 56.60$.

19. 7.233: Find a z value where 0.4900 of area is between 0 and z. That value is $z = 2.33$. Then solve for X: $(X - 7)/0.1$, so $X = 7.233$.

21. $1,630, found by $2,100 − 1.88($250).

23. **a.** $\mu = n\pi = 50(0.25) = 12.5$
$\sigma^2 = n\pi(1 - \pi) = 12.5(1 - 0.25) = 9.375$
$\sigma = \sqrt{9.375} = 3.0619$
b. 0.2578, found by (14.5 − 12.5)/3.0619 = 0.65.
The area is 0.2422. Then 0.5000 − 0.2422 = 0.2578.
c. 0.2578, found by (10.5 − 12.5)/3.0619 = − 0.65.
The area is 0.2422. Then 0.5000 − 0.2422 = 0.2578.

25. **a.** 0.0192, found by 0.500 − 0.4808.
b. 0.0694, found by 0.500 − 0.4306.
c. 0.0502, found by 0.0694 − 0.0192.

27. **a.** Yes. (1) There are two mutually exclusive outcomes: overweight and not overweight. (2) It is the result of counting the number of successes (overweight members). (3) Each trial is independent. (4) The probability of 0.30 remains the same for each trial.
b. 0.0084, found by
$\mu = 500(0.30) = 150$
$\sigma^2 = 500(.30)(.70) = 105$
$\sigma = \sqrt{105} = 10.24695$

$$z = \frac{X - \mu}{\sigma} = \frac{174.5 - 150}{10.24695} = 2.39$$

The area under the curve for 2.39 is 0.4916. Then 0.5000 − 0.4916 = 0.0084.
c. 0.8461, found by $z = \frac{139.5 - 150}{10.24695} = -1.02$
The area between 139.5 and 150 is 0.3461. Adding 0.3461 + 0.5000 = 0.8461.

29. **a.** −0.4 for net sales, found by (170 − 180)/25. 2.92 for employees, found by (1,850 − 1,500)/120.
b. Net sales are 0.4 standard deviations below the mean. Employees is 2.92 standard deviations above the mean.
c. 65.54 percent of the aluminum fabricators have greater net sales compared with Clarion, found by 0.1554 + 0.5000. Only 0.18 percent have more employees than Clarion, found by 0.5000 − 0.4982.

31. a. 0.5000, because $z = \frac{30 - 490}{90} = -5.11$.
b. 0.2514, found by 0.5000 − 0.2486.
c. 0.6374, found by 0.2486 + 0.3888.
d. 0.3450, found by 0.3888 − 0.0438.

33. a. 0.3015, found by 0.5000 − 0.1985.
b. 0.2579, found by 0.4564 − 0.1985.
c. 0.0011, found by 0.5000 − 0.4989.
d. 1,818, found by 1,280 + 1.28(420).

35. a. 0.0026, found by 0.5000 − 0.4974.
b. 0.1129, found by 0.4772 − 0.3643.
c. 0.8617, found by 0.4974 + 0.3643.

37. About 4,099 units, found by solving for X.
$1.65 = (X - 4000)/60$

39. a. 15.39%, found by $(8 - 10.3)/2.25 = -1.02$, then 0.5000 − 0.3461 = 0.1539.
b. 17.31%, found by:
$z = (12 - 10.3)/2.25 = 0.76$. Area is 0.2764.
$z = (14 - 10.3)/2.25 = 1.64$. Area is 0.4495.
The area between 12 and 14 is 0.1731, found by 0.4495 − 0.2764.
c. Yes, but it is rather remote. Reasoning: On 99.73 percent of the days, returns are between 3.55 and 17.03, found by $10.3 \pm 3(2.25)$. Thus, the chance of less than 3.55 returns is rather remote.

41. a. 0.9678, found by:
$\mu = 60(0.64) = 38.4$.
$\sigma^2 = 60(0.64)(0.36) = 13.824$
$\sigma = \sqrt{13.824} = 3.72$
Then $(31.5 - 38.4)/3.72 = -1.85$, for which the area is 0.4678.
Then 0.5000 + 0.4678 = 0.9678.
b. 0.0853, found by $(43.5 - 38.4)/3.72 = 1.37$, for which the area is 0.4147. Then 0.5000 − 0.4147 = .0853.
c. 0.8084, found by 0.4441 + 0.3643.
d. 0.0348, found by 0.4495 − 0.4147.

43. 0.0968, found by:
$\mu = 50(0.40) = 20$
$\sigma^2 = 50(0.40)(0.60) = 12$
$\sigma = \sqrt{12} = 3.4641$
$z = (24.5 - 20)/3.4641 = 1.30$.
The area is 0.4032. Then, for 25 or more, 0.5000 − 0.4032 = 0.0968.

45. a. $1.65 = (45 - \mu)/5$ $\quad \mu = 36.75$
b. $1.65 = (45 - \mu)/10$ $\quad \mu = 28.5$
c. $z = (30 - 28.5)/10 = 0.15$, then 0.5000 + 0.0596 = 0.5596.

47. a. $\frac{2 - 3.1}{0.3} = -3.67 \qquad \frac{3 - 3.1}{0.3} = -0.33$
0.3707, found by 0.5000 − 0.1293.
b. None.
c. 0.0228, found by 0.5000 − 0.4772; leads to 228 students, found by 10,000(.0228).
d. 3.484, found by 3.1 + 1.28(0.3).

49. a. 21.19 percent found by $z = (9.00 - 9.20)/0.25 = -0.80$; so 0.5000 − 0.2881 = 0.2119.
b. Increase the mean. $z = (9.00 - 9.25)/0.25 = -1.00$; $P = 0.5000 - 0.3413 = 0.1587$.
Reduce the standard deviation. $z = (9.00 - 9.20)/0.15 = -1.33$; $P = 0.500 - 0.4082 = 0.0918$.
Reducing the standard deviation is better because a smaller percent of the hams will be below the limit.

51. a. $z = (52 - 60)/5 = 1.60$, so 0.5000 − 0.4452 = 0.0548.
b. Let $z = 0.67$, so $0.67 = (X - 52)/5$ and $X = 55.35$. Set mileage at 55,350.
c. $z = (45 - 52)/5 = -1.40$, so 0.5000 − 0.4192 = 0.0808.

53. $\frac{470 - \mu}{\sigma} = 0.25 \qquad \frac{500 - \mu}{\sigma} = 1.28$
$\sigma = 29.126$ and $\mu = 462.719$

55. $\mu = 150(0.15) = 22.5 \quad \sigma = \sqrt{150(0.15)(0.85)} = 4.3732$
$z = (30.5 - 22.5)/4.3732 = 1.83$
$P(z > 1.83) = 0.5000 - 0.4664 = 0.0336$

57. a. 0.0668, found by 0.5000 − 0.4332; leads to 2 teams, found by 30 (0.0668). One team (Seattle) actually had attendance of more than 3.5 million. So the estimate is fairly accurate.
b. 0.7324, found by 0.5000 + 0.2324; leads to 22 teams, found by 30(0.7324). 19 teams actually had salaries of more than $50 million. So there are 3 fewer than expected.

Chapter 7

1. a. 303 Louisiana, 5155 S. Main, 3501 Monroe, 2652 W. Central
b. Answers will vary.
c. 630 Dixie Hwy, 835 S. McCord Rd, 4624 Woodville Rd
d. Answers will vary.

3. a. Bob Schmidt Chevrolet
Great Lakes Ford Nissan
Grogan Towne Chrysler
Southside Lincoln Mercury
Rouen Chrysler Jeep Eagle
b. Answers will vary.
c. York Automotive
Thayer Chevrolet Geo Toyota
Franklin Park Lincoln Mercury
Mathews Ford Oregon Inc
Valiton Chrysler

5. a.

Sample	Values	Sum	Mean
1	12, 12	24	12
2	12, 14	26	13
3	12, 16	28	14
4	12, 14	26	13
5	12, 16	28	14
6	14, 16	30	15

b. $\mu_{\bar{X}} = (12 + 13 + 14 + 13 + 14 + 15)/6 = 13.5$
$\mu = (12 + 12 + 14 + 16)/4 = 13.5$
c. More dispersion with population data compared to the sample means. The sample means vary from 12 to 15, whereas the population varies from 12 to 16.

7. a.

Sample	Values	Sum	Mean
1	12, 12, 14	38	12.66
2	12, 12, 15	39	13.00
3	12, 12, 20	44	14.66
4	14, 15, 20	49	16.33
5	12, 14, 15	41	13.66
6	12, 14, 15	41	13.66
7	12, 15, 20	47	15.66
8	12, 15, 20	47	15.66
9	12, 14, 20	46	15.33
10	12, 14, 20	46	15.33

b. $\mu_{\bar{X}} = \frac{(12.66 + \cdots + 15.33 + 15.33)}{10} = 14.6$
$\mu = (12 + 12 + 14 + 15 + 20)/5 = 14.6$
c. The dispersion of the population is greater than that of the sample means. The sample means vary from 12.66 to 16.33, whereas the population varies from 12 to 20.

9. a. 20, found by ${}_6C_3$

b.

Sample	Cases	Sum	Mean
Ruud, Austin, Sass	3, 6, 3	12	4.00
Ruud, Sass, Palmer	3, 3, 3	9	3.00
⋮	⋮	⋮	⋮
Sass, Palmer, Schueller	3, 3, 1	7	2.33

c. $\mu_{\bar{X}} = 2.66$, found by $\frac{52.33}{20}$.

$\mu = 2.66$, found by $(3 + 6 + 3 + 3 + 0 + 1)/6$.
They are equal.

d.

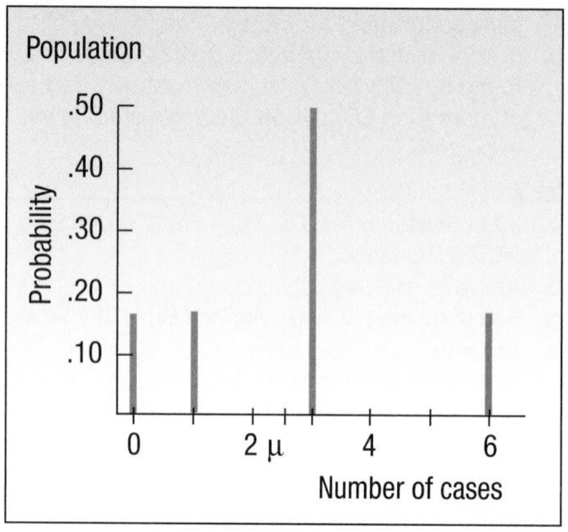

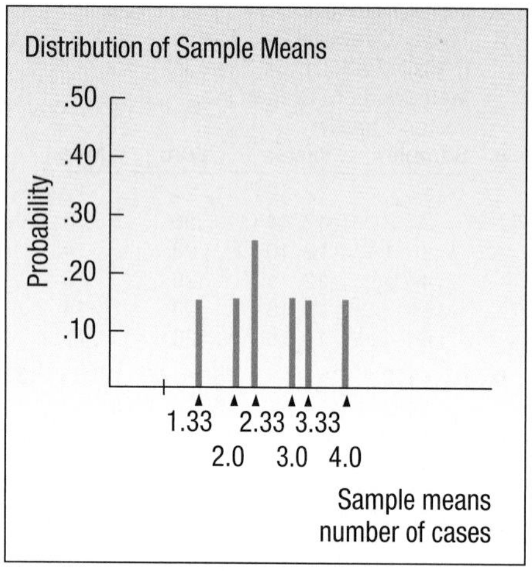

Sample Mean	Number of Means	Probability
1.33	3	.1500
2.00	3	.1500
2.33	5	.2500
3.00	3	.1500
3.33	3	.1500
4.00	3	.1500
	20	1.0000

The population has more dispersion than the sample means. The sample means vary from 1.33 to 4.0. The population varies from 0 to 6.

11. a.

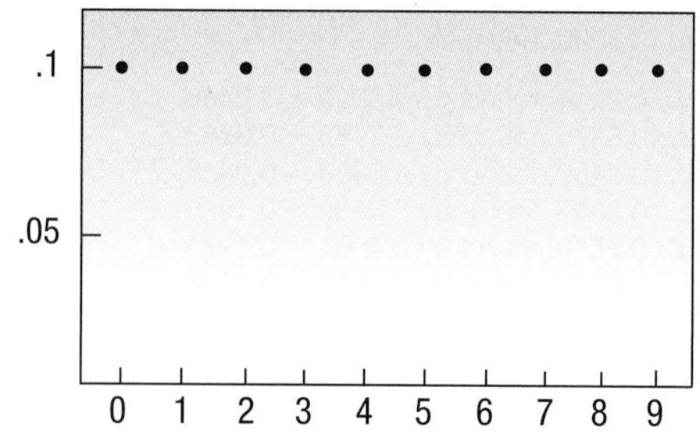

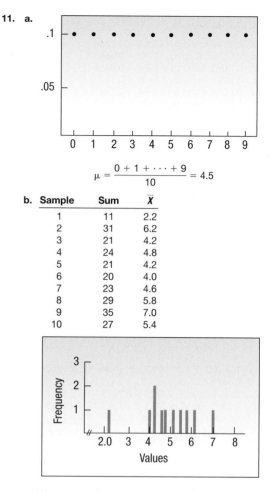

$$\mu = \frac{0 + 1 + \cdots + 9}{10} = 4.5$$

b.

Sample	Sum	$\bar{X}$
1	11	2.2
2	31	6.2
3	21	4.2
4	24	4.8
5	21	4.2
6	20	4.0
7	23	4.6
8	29	5.8
9	35	7.0
10	27	5.4

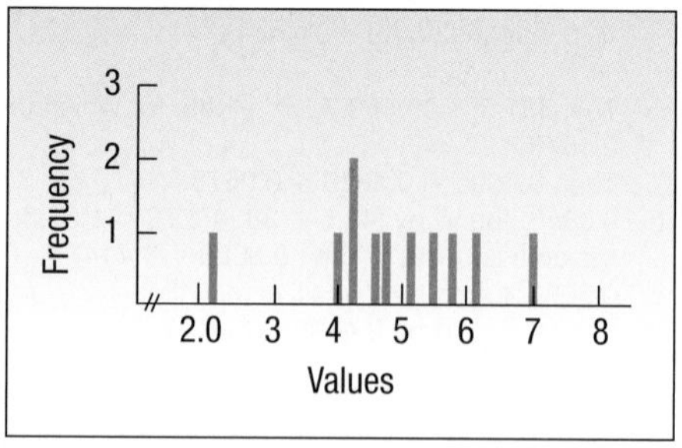

The mean of the 10 sample means is 4.84, which is close to the population mean of 4.5. The sample means range from 2.2 to 7.0, whereas the population values range from 0 to 9. From the above graph, the sample means tend to cluster between 4 and 5.

13. a. $z = \frac{63 - 60}{12/\sqrt{9}} = 0.75$

$P = .2266$, found by $.5000 - .2734$.

b. $z = \frac{56 - 60}{12/\sqrt{9}} = -1.00$

$P = .1587$, found by $.5000 - .3413$.

c. $P = .6147$, found by $.0.3413 + 0.2734$.

15. $z = \frac{950 - 1200}{250/\sqrt{50}} = -7.07$ $P = 1$, or virtually certain.

17. a. Formal Man, Summit Stationers, Bootleggers, Leather Ltd, Petries.

b. Answers may vary.

c. Elder-Beerman, Frederick's of Hollywood, Summit Stationers, Lion Store, Leather Ltd., Things Remembered, County Seat, Coach House Gifts, Regis Hairstylists

19. The difference between a sample statistic and the population parameter. Yes, the difference could be zero. The sample mean and the population parameter are equal.

21. Use of either a proportional or nonproportional stratified random sample would be appropriate. For example, suppose the number of banks in the Southwest were as follows:

Assets	Number	Percent of Total
$500 million and more	20	2.0
$100–$499 million	324	32.4
Less than $100 million	656	65.6
	1,000	100.0

For a proportional stratified sample, if the sample size is 100, then two banks with assets of $500 million would be selected, 32 medium-size banks, and 66 small banks. For a nonproportional sample, 10 or even all 20 large banks could be selected and fewer medium- and small-size banks and the sample results weighted by the appropriate percents of the total.

23. a. We selected 60, 104, 75, 72, and 48. Answers will vary.
  b. We selected the third observation. So the sample consists of 75, 72, 68, 82, 48. Answers will vary.
  c. Number the first 20 motels from 00 to 19. Randomly select three numbers. Then number the last five numbers 20 to 24. Randomly select two numbers from that group.

25. a. 15, found by ${}_6C_2$.
  b.

Sample	Value	Sum	Mean
1	79, 64	143	71.5
2	79, 84	163	81.5
.	.	.	.
.	.	.	.
.	.	.	.
15	92, 77	169	84.5
			1,195.0

  c. $\mu_{\bar{X}} = 79.67$, found by 1,195/15.
  $\mu = 79.67$, found by 478/6.
  They are equal.
  d. No. The student is not graded on all available information. He/she is as likely to get a lower grade based on the sample as a higher grade.

27. a. 10, found by ${}_5C_2$.
  b.

Number of Shutdowns	Mean	Number of Shutdowns	Mean
4, 3	3.5	3, 3	3.0
4, 5	4.5	3, 2	2.5
4, 3	3.5	5, 3	4.0
4, 2	3.0	5, 2	3.5
3, 5	4.0	3, 2	2.5

Sample Mean	Frequency	Probability
2.5	2	.20
3.0	2	.20
3.5	3	.30
4.0	2	.20
4.5	1	.10
	10	1.00

  c. $\mu_{\bar{X}} = (3.5 + 4.5 + \cdots + 2.5)/10 = 3.4$
  $\mu = (4 + 3 + 5 + 3 + 2)/5 = 3.4$
  The two means are equal.
  d. The population values are relatively uniform in shape. The distribution of sample means tends toward normality.

29. a. The sampling distribution will be normal.
  b. $\sigma_{\bar{X}} = \dfrac{5.5}{\sqrt{25}} = 1.1$
  c. $z = \dfrac{36 - 35}{5.5/\sqrt{25}} = 0.91$
  $P = 0.1814$, found by $0.5000 - 0.3186$.
  d. $z = \dfrac{34.5 - 35}{5.5/\sqrt{25}} = -0.45$
  $P = 0.6736$, found by $0.5000 + 0.1736$.
  e. 0.4922, found by $0.3186 + 0.1736$.

31. $z = \dfrac{\$335 - \$350}{\$45/\sqrt{40}} = -2.11$
  $P = 0.9826$, found by $0.5000 + 0.4826$.

33. $z = \dfrac{25.1 - 24.8}{2.5/\sqrt{60}} = 0.93$
  $P = 0.8238$, found by $0.5000 + 0.3238$.

35. Between 5,954 and 6,046, found by $6{,}000 \pm 1.96(150/\sqrt{40})$.

37. $z = \dfrac{900 - 947}{205/\sqrt{60}} = -1.78$
  $P = 0.0375$, found by $0.5000 - 0.4625$.

39. a. Alaska, Ohio, New Jersey, Texas, Utah, Florida Vermont, and Connecticut.
  b. Maine, Maryland, Michigan, Missouri, Florida, South Carolina, Oklahoma, Wyoming, Washington
  c. Answers will vary.

41. Answers will vary.

43. Answers will vary.

Chapter 8

1. 51.314 and 58.686, found by $55 \pm 2.58(10/\sqrt{49})$.

3. a. 1.581, found by $\sigma_{\bar{X}} = 5/\sqrt{10}$.
  b. The population is normally distributed and the population variance is known.
  c. 16.901 and 23.099, found by 20 ± 3.099.

5. a. $20. It is our best estimate of the population mean.
  b. $18.60 and $21.40, found by $\$20 \pm 1.96(\$5/\sqrt{49})$. About 95 percent of the intervals similarly constructed will include the population mean.

7. a. 8.60 gallons.
  b. 7.83 and 9.37, found by $8.60 \pm 2.58(2.30/\sqrt{60})$.
  c. If 100 such intervals were determined, the population mean would be included in about 99 intervals.

9. a. 2.201
  b. 1.729
  c. 3.499

11. a. The population mean is unknown, but the best estimate is 20, the sample mean.
  b. Use the *t* distribution as the standard deviation is unknown and the sample size is small. However, assume the population is normally distributed.
  c. 2.093
  d. Between 19.06 and 20.94, found by $20 \pm 2.093(2/\sqrt{20})$.
  e. Neither value is reasonable, because they are not inside the interval.

13. Between 95.39 and 101.81, found by $98.6 \pm 1.833(5.54/\sqrt{10})$.

15. a. 0.8, found by 80/100.
  b. 0.04, found by $\sqrt{\dfrac{0.8(1 - 0.8)}{100}}$.
  c. Between 0.72 and 0.88, found by
  $0.8 \pm 1.96\left(\sqrt{\dfrac{0.8(1 - 0.8)}{100}}\right)$.

d. We are reasonably sure the population proportion is between 72 and 88 percent.

17. a. 0.625, found by 250/400.
b. 0.0242, found by $\sqrt{\frac{0.625(1-0.625)}{400}}$.
c. Between 0.563 and 0.687, found by $0.625 \pm 2.58\left(\sqrt{\frac{0.625(1-0.625)}{400}}\right)$.
d. We are reasonably sure the population proportion is between 56 and 69 percent.

19. 33.465 and 36.535, found by $35 \pm 1.96\left(\frac{5}{\sqrt{36}}\right)\sqrt{\frac{300-36}{300-1}}$.

21. 1.689 up to 2.031, found by $1.86 \pm 2.58\left(\frac{0.50}{\sqrt{50}}\right)\sqrt{\frac{400-50}{400-1}}$.

23. 97, found by $n = \left[\frac{1.96 \times 10}{2}\right]^2 = 96.04$.

25. 196, found by $n = 0.15(0.85)\left(\frac{1.96}{0.05}\right)^2 = 195.9216$.

27. 554, found by $n = \left(\frac{1.96 \times 3}{0.25}\right)^2 = 553.19$.

29. a. 577, found by $n = 0.60(0.40)\left(\frac{1.96}{0.04}\right)^2 = 576.24$.
b. 601, found by $n = 0.50(0.50)\left(\frac{1.96}{0.04}\right)^2 = 600.25$.

31. 6.14 years to 6.86 years, found by $6.5 \pm 1.96(1.7/\sqrt{85})$.

33. a. Between $1.168 and 1.190, found by $1.179 \pm 2.68\left(\frac{0.03}{\sqrt{50}}\right)$.
b. $1.20 is not reasonable, because it is outside of the confidence interval. A z value of 2.58 leads to the same answer.

35. a. Between 7.22 and 8.78, found by $8 \pm 1.68(3/\sqrt{40})$.
b. 9 is not reasonable because it is outside of the confidence interval. A z value of 1.65 leads to the same answer.

37. a. 65.61 up to 71.59 hours, found by $68.6 \pm 2.58(8.2/\sqrt{50})$.
b. The value suggested by the NCAA is included in the confidence interval. Therefore, it is reasonable.
c. Changing the confidence level to 95 would reduce the width of the interval. The value of 2.58 would change to 1.96.

39. 61, found by $1.96(16/\sqrt{n}) = 4$.

41. Between $13,734 up to $15,028, found by $14,381 ± 1.711($1,892/$\sqrt{25}$). 15,000 is reasonable because it is inside of the confidence interval.

43. a. $62.583, found by $751/12.
b. Between $60.54 and $64.63, found by $62.583 \pm 1.796(3.94/\sqrt{12})$.
c. $60 is not reasonable, because it is outside of the confidence interval.

45. a. 89.4667, found by 1,342/15.
b. Between 84.99 and 93.94, found by $89.4667 \pm 2.145(8.08/\sqrt{15})$.
c. Yes, because even the lower limit of the confidence interval is above 80.

47. Between .647 and 0.753, found by $.7 \pm 2.58\left(\sqrt{\frac{0.7(1-0.7)}{500}}\right)$.
Yes, because even the lower limit of the confidence interval is above 0.500.

49. $52.56 and $55.44, found by $54.00 ± 1.96 $\frac{\$4.50}{\sqrt{35}}\sqrt{\frac{(500-35)}{500-1}}$.

51. 369, found by $n = 0.60(1-0.60)[1.96/0.05]^2$.

53. 97, found by $[(1.96 \times 500)/100]^2$.

55. a. 708.13, rounded up to 709, found by $0.21(1-0.21)[1.96/0.03]^2$.
b. 1,068, found by $0.50(0.50)(1.96/0.03)^2$.

57. Between 0.573 and 0.653, found by $.613 \pm 2.58\left(\sqrt{\frac{0.613(1-0.613)}{1{,}000}}\right)$.
Yes, because even the lower limit of the confidence interval is above 0.500.

59. Between 12.69 and 14.11, found by $13.4 \pm 1.96(6.8/\sqrt{352})$.

61. Answers will vary.

63. a. For selling price: 212.09 up to 230.11, found by $221.1 \pm (1.96)(47.11/\sqrt{105}) = 221.1 \pm 9.01$.
b. For distance: 13.697 up to 15.561, found by $14.629 \pm (1.96)(4.874/\sqrt{105}) = 14.629 \pm 0.932$.
c. For garage: 0.5867 up to 0.7657, found by $0.6762 \pm (1.96)\sqrt{\frac{0.6762(1-0.6762)}{105}} = 0.6762 \pm 0.0895$.

65. a. $\$30{,}833 \pm 1.96\frac{\$16{,}947}{\sqrt{100}} = \$30{,}833 \pm \$3322$, so the limits are $27,511 and $34,155. It is not reasonable because the population mean is $35,000.
b. $12.73 \pm 1.96\frac{\$2.792}{\sqrt{100}} = 12.73 \pm 0.55$, so the limits are 12.18 and 13.28. The population mean could be 13 years.
c. $39.11 \pm 1.96\frac{12.57}{\sqrt{100}} = 39.11 \pm 2.46$, so the limits are 36.65 and 41.57. The mean age of the workers could be 40 years.

Chapter 9

1. a. Two-tailed.
b. Reject H_0 and accept H_1 when z does not fall in the region from −1.96 and 1.96.
c. −1.2, found by $z = (49-50)/(5/\sqrt{36}) = -1.2$
d. Fail to reject H_0.
e. $p = .2302$, found by 2(.5000 − .3849). A 23.02 percent chance of finding a z value this large when H_0 is true.

3. a. One-tailed.
b. Reject H_0 and accept H_1 when $z > 1.65$.
c. 1.2, found by $z = (21-20)/(5/\sqrt{36}) = 1.2$
d. Fail to reject H_0 at the .05 significance level.
e. $p = .1151$, found by .5000 − .3849. An 11.51 percent chance of finding a z-value this large or larger.

5. a. H_0: $\mu = 60{,}000$ H_1: $\mu \neq 60{,}000$
b. Reject H_0 if $z < -1.96$ or $z > 1.96$.
c. −0.69, found by:
$$z = \frac{59{,}500 - 60{,}000}{(5{,}000/\sqrt{48})} = -0.69$$
d. Do not reject H_0.
e. $p = .4902$, found by 2(.5000 − .2549). Crosset's experience is not different from that claimed by the manufacturer. If H_0 is true, the probability of finding a value more extreme than this is .4902.

7. a. H_0: $\mu \geq 6.8$ H_1: $\mu < 6.8$
b. Reject H_0 if $z < -1.65$
c. $z = \frac{6.2 - 6.8}{0.5/\sqrt{36}} = -7.2$
d. H_0 is rejected.
e. $p = 0$. The mean number of videos watched is less than 6.8 per month. If H_0 is true, there is virtually no chance of getting a statistic this small.

9. a. H_0 is rejected if $z > 1.65$.
b. 1.09, found by $z = (0.75 - 0.70)/\sqrt{(0.70) \times 0.30)/100}$.
c. H_0 is not rejected.

11. a. H_0: $\pi \leq 0.52$ H_1: $\pi > 0.52$
b. H_0 is rejected if $z > 2.33$.
c. 1.62, found by $z = (.5667 - .52)/\sqrt{(0.52 \times 0.48)/300}$.
d. H_0 is not rejected. We cannot conclude that the proportion of men driving on the Ohio Turnpike is larger than 0.52.

13. a. H_0: $\pi \geq 0.90$ H_1: $\pi < 0.90$
b. H_0 is rejected if $z < -1.28$.
c. −2.67, found by $z = (0.82 - 0.90)/\sqrt{(0.90 \times 0.10)/100}$
d. H_0 is rejected. Fewer than 90 percent of the customers receive their orders in less than 10 minutes.

15. a. Reject H_0 when $t > 1.833$.
b. $t = \frac{12 - 10}{(3/\sqrt{10})} = 2.108$
c. Reject H_0. The mean is greater than 10.

17. H_0: $\mu \leq 40$ H_1: $\mu > 40$
Reject H_0 if $t > 1.703$.

$$t = \frac{42 - 40}{(2.1/\sqrt{28})} = 5.040$$

Reject H_0 and conclude that the mean number of calls is greater than 40 per week.

19. H_0: $\mu = 22{,}100$ H_1: $\mu > 22{,}100$
Reject H_0 if $t > 1.740$.

$$t = \frac{23{,}400 - 22{,}100}{(1{,}500/\sqrt{18})} = 3.680$$

Reject H_0 and conclude that the mean life of the spark plugs is greater than 22,100 miles.

21. a. Reject H_0 if $t < -3.747$.
b. $\overline{X} = 17$ and $s = \sqrt{\frac{1495 - (85)^2/5}{5 - 1}} = 3.536$

$$t = \frac{17 - 20}{(3.536/\sqrt{5})} = -1.90$$

c. Do not reject H_0. We cannot conclude the population mean is less than 20.
d. Between .05 and .10, about .065.

23. H_0: $\mu \leq 4.35$ H_1: $\mu > 4.35$
Reject H_0 if $t > 2.821$.

$$t = \frac{4.368 - 4.35}{(0.0339/\sqrt{10})} = 1.68$$

Do not reject H_0. The additive did not increase the mean weight of the chickens. The p-value is between 0.10 and 0.05.

25. H_0: $\mu \leq 4.0$ H_1: $\mu > 4.0$
Reject H_0 if $t > 1.796$.

$$t = \frac{4.50 - 4.0}{(2.68/\sqrt{12})} = 0.65$$

Do not reject H_0. The mean number of fish caught has not been shown to be greater than 4.0. The p-value is greater than 0.10.

27. H_0: $\mu \geq 10$ H_1: $\mu < 10$
Reject H_0 if $z < -1.65$.

$$z = \frac{9.0 - 10.0}{2.8/\sqrt{50}} = -2.53$$

Reject H_0. The mean weight loss is less than 10 pounds. p-value = 0.5000 − 0.4943 = 0.0057

29. H_0: $\mu \leq \$15{,}000$ H_1: $\mu > \$15{,}000$
Reject H_0 if $z > 1.65$.

$$z = \frac{\$17{,}000 - \$15{,}000}{\$3000/\sqrt{75}} = 5.77$$

Reject H_0. At the 0.05 level we can conclude that the mean household income is greater than $15,000.

31. H_0: $\mu = \$30{,}000$ H_1: $\mu \neq \$30{,}000$
Reject H_0 if $z < 1.65$ or $z > 1.65$.

$$z = \frac{\$30{,}500 - \$30{,}000}{3000/\sqrt{120}} = 1.83$$

Reject H_0. We can conclude that the mean salary is not $30,000. p-value = 0.0672, found by 2(0.5000 − 0.4664).

33. H_0: $\mu \leq 1.50$ H_1: $\mu > 1.50$
Reject H_0 if $z > 1.65$.

$$z = \frac{\$1.52 - \$1.50}{\$0.05/\sqrt{35}} = 2.37$$

Reject H_0. The mean price of gasoline is greater than $1.50. The p-value = 0.5000 − 0.4911 = 0.0089.

35. H_0: $\pi \leq 0.60$ H_1: $\pi > 0.60$
H_0 is rejected if $z > 2.33$.

$$z = \frac{0.70 - 0.60}{\sqrt{(0.60 \times 0.40)/200}} = 2.89$$

H_0 is rejected. Ms. Dennis is correct. More than 60 percent of the accounts are more than 3 months old.

37. H_0: $\pi \leq 0.44$ H_1: $\pi > 0.44$
H_0 is rejected if $z > 1.65$.

$$z = \frac{0.48 - 0.44}{\sqrt{(0.44 \times 0.56)/1{,}000}} = 2.55$$

H_0 is rejected. We conclude that there has been an increase in the proportion of people wanting to go to Europe.

39. H_0: $\pi \leq 0.20$ H_1: $\pi > 0.20$
H_0 is rejected if $z > 2.33$.

$$z = \frac{(56/200) - 0.20}{\sqrt{(0.20 \times 0.80)/200}} = 2.83$$

H_0 is rejected. More than 20 percent of the owners move during a particular year. p-value = 0.5000 − 0.4977 = 0.0023.

41. H_0: $\mu \leq 42$ H_1: $\mu > 42$
Reject H_0 if $t > 1.796$.

$$t = \frac{51 - 42}{8/\sqrt{12}} = 3.90$$

Reject H_0. The mean time for delivery is more than 42 days. The p-value is less than 0.005.

43. H_0: $\mu = 2.25$ H_1: $\mu \neq 2.25$
Reject H_0 if $t < -2.201$ or $t > 2.201$.
$\overline{X} = 2.087$ $s_s = 0.4048$

$$t = \frac{2.087 - 2.25}{0.4048/\sqrt{12}} = -1.395$$

Do not reject H_0. There is not a difference in the mean amount of coffee consumed by students at Northwestern State and other college students.

45. $H_0: \mu \geq 6.5$ $H_1: \mu < 6.5$
Reject H_0 if $t < -2.178$.
$\bar{X} = 5.1667$ $s = 3.1575$

$$t = \frac{5.1667 - 6.5}{3.1575/\sqrt{12}} = -1.463$$

Do not reject H_0. The p-value is greater than 0.05.

47. $H_0: \mu = 0$ $H_1: \mu \neq 0$
Reject H_0 if $t < -2.110$ or $t > 2.110$.
$\bar{X} = -0.2322$ $s = 0.3120$

$$t = \frac{-0.2322 - 0}{0.3120/\sqrt{18}} = -3.158$$

Reject H_0. The mean gain or loss does not equal 0. The p-value is less than 0.01, but greater than 0.001.

49. $H_0: \mu \geq 8$ $H_1: \mu < 8$
Reject H_0 if $t < -1.714$.

$$t = \frac{7.5 - 8}{3.2/\sqrt{24}} = -0.77$$

Do not reject the null hypothesis. The time is not less.

51. $H_0: \pi = 0.50$ $H_1: \pi \neq 0.50$
Reject H_0 if z is not between −1.96 and 1.96.

$$z = \frac{0.482 - 0.500}{\sqrt{(0.5)(0.5)/1{,}002}} = -1.14$$

Do not reject the null. The nation may be evenly divided.

53. Answers will vary.

55. **a.** $H_0: \mu = 50$ $H_1: \mu \neq 50$
Reject H_0 if t is not between −2.045 and 2.045.

$$t = \frac{65.49 - 50}{24.87/\sqrt{30}} = 3.411$$

Reject H_0. The mean team salary is not 50.0 ($mil).

b. $H_0: \mu \leq 2{,}000{,}000$ $H_1: \mu > 2{,}000{,}000$
Reject H_0 if t is > 1.699.

$$t = \frac{2{,}417{,}017 - 2{,}000{,}000}{720{,}109/\sqrt{30}} = 3.172$$

Reject H_0. The mean attendance is more than 2,000,000.

57. **a.** $H_0: \mu \leq 4.0$ $H_1: \mu > 4.0$
Reject H_0 if $z > 1.65$

$$z = \frac{8.12 - 4.0}{16.43/\sqrt{46}} = 1.70$$

Reject H_0. The mean number of cell phones is greater than 4.0. p-value = .5000 − .4554 = .0446

b. $H_0: \mu \geq 50$ $H_1: \mu < 50$
Reject H_0 if $z < -1.65$. Note there is one missing value, so $n = 45$.

$$z = \frac{36.0 - 50.0}{105.5/\sqrt{45}} = -0.89$$

Do not reject H_0. The mean size of the labor force is not less than 50. The p-value is 5000 − .3159 = .1841.

Chapter 10

1. **a.** Two-tailed test.
b. Reject H_0 if $z < -2.05$ or $z > 2.05$.
c.
$$z = \frac{102 - 99}{\sqrt{\frac{5^2}{40} + \frac{6^2}{50}}} = 2.59$$
d. Reject H_0 and accept H_1.
e. p-value = .0096, found by 2(.5000 − .4952).

3. **Step 1** $H_0: \mu_1 \geq \mu_2$ $H_1: \mu_1 < \mu_2$
Step 2 The .05 significance level was chosen.
Step 3 Reject H_0 and accept H_1 if $z < -1.65$.
Step 4 −0.94, found by:

$$z = \frac{7.6 - 8.1}{\sqrt{\frac{(2.3)^2}{40} + \frac{(2.9)^2}{55}}} = -0.94$$

Step 5 Fail to reject H_0. Babies using the Gibbs brand did not gain less weight. p-value = .1736, found by .5000 − .3264.

5. Two-tailed test, because we are trying to show that a difference exists between the two means.
Reject H_0 if $z < -2.58$ or $z > 2.58$.

$$z = \frac{31.4 - 34.9}{\sqrt{\frac{(5.1)^2}{32} + \frac{(6.7)^2}{49}}} = -2.66$$

Reject H_0 at the .01 level. There is a difference in the mean turnover rate. p-value = 2(.5000 − .4961) = .0078

7. **a.** H_0 is rejected if $z > 1.65$.
b. 0.64, found by $p_c = \frac{70 + 90}{100 + 150}$.
c. 1.61, found by

$$z = \frac{0.70 - 0.60}{\sqrt{(0.64 \times 0.36)/100] + [(0.64 \times 0.36)/150]}}.$$

d. H_0 is not rejected.

9. **a.** $H_0: \pi_1 = \pi_2$ $H_1: \pi_1 \neq \pi_2$
b. H_0 is rejected if $z < -1.96$ or $z > 1.96$.
c. $p_c = \frac{24 + 40}{400 + 400} = 0.08$
d. −2.09, found by

$$z = \frac{0.06 - 0.10}{\sqrt{[(0.08 \times 0.92)/400] + [(0.08 \times 0.92)/400]}}.$$

e. H_0 is rejected. The proportion infested is not the same in the two fields.

11. $H_0: \pi_d \leq \pi_r$ $H_1: \pi_d > \pi_r$
H_0 is rejected if $z > 2.05$.

$$p_c = \frac{168 + 200}{800 + 1000} = 0.2044$$

$$z = \frac{0.21 - 0.20}{\sqrt{\frac{(0.2044)(0.7956)}{800} + \frac{(0.2044)(0.7956)}{1000}}} = 0.52$$

H_0 is not rejected. There is no difference in the proportion of Democrats and Republicans who favor lowering the standards.

13. **a.** Reject H_0 if $t > 2.120$ or $t < -2.120$.
$df = 10 + 8 - 2 = 16$
b. $s_p^2 = \frac{(10 - 1)(4)^2 + (8 - 1)(5)^2}{10 + 8 - 2} = 19.9375$
c. $t = \frac{23 - 26}{\sqrt{19.9375\left(\frac{1}{10} + \frac{1}{8}\right)}} = -1.416$
d. Do not reject H_0.
e. p-value is greater than 0.10 and less than 0.20.

15. $H_0: \mu_f \leq \mu_m$ $H_1: \mu_f > \mu_m$
$df = 9 + 7 - 2 = 14$
Reject H_0 if $t > 2.624$.

$$s_p^2 = \frac{(7 - 1)(6.88)^2 + (9 - 1)(9.49)^2}{7 + 9 - 2} = 71.749$$

$$t = \frac{79 - 78}{\sqrt{71.749\left(\frac{1}{7} + \frac{1}{9}\right)}} = 0.234$$

Do not reject H_0. There is no difference in the mean grades.

17. H_0: $\mu_s \leq \mu_a$ H_1: $\mu_s > \mu_a$
$df = 6 + 7 - 2 = 11$
Reject H_0 if $t > 1.363$.

$$s_p^2 = \frac{(6 - 1)(12.2)^2 + (7 - 1)(15.8)^2}{6 + 7 - 2} = 203.82$$

$$t = \frac{142.5 - 130.3}{\sqrt{203.82\left(\frac{1}{6} + \frac{1}{7}\right)}} = 1.536$$

Reject H_0. The mean daily expenses are greater for the sales staff. The p-value is between 0.05 and 0.10.

19. **a.** Reject H_0 if $t > 2.353$.

b. $\bar{d} = \frac{12}{4} = 3.00$ $\quad s_d = \sqrt{\frac{38 - 12^2/4}{3}} = 0.816$

c. $t = \frac{3.00}{0.816/\sqrt{4}} = 7.35$

d. Reject H_0. There are more defective parts produced on the day shift.

e. p-value is less than 0.005, but greater than 0.0005.

21. H_0: $\mu_d \leq 0$ H_d: $\mu_d > 0$
$\bar{d} = 25.917$
$s_d = 40.791$
Reject H_0 if $t > 1.796$

$$t = \frac{25.917}{40.791/\sqrt{12}} = 2.20$$

Reject H_0. The incentive plan resulted in an increase in daily income. The p-value is about .025.

23. H_0: $\mu_1 = \mu_2$ H_1: $\mu_1 \neq \mu_2$
Reject H_0 if $z < -2.58$ or $z > 2.58$.

$$z = \frac{36.2 - 37.0}{\sqrt{\frac{(1.14)^2}{35} + \frac{(1.30)^2}{40}}} = -2.84$$

Reject H_0. There is a difference in the useful life of the two brands of paint. The p-value is 0.0046, found by 2(0.5000 − 0.4977).

25. H_0: $\mu_1 = \mu_2$ H_1: $\mu_1 \neq \mu_2$
Reject H_0 if $z < -1.96$ or $z > 1.96$.

$$z = \frac{4.77 - 5.02}{\sqrt{\frac{(1.05)^2}{40} + \frac{(1.23)^2}{50}}} = -1.04$$

H_0 is not rejected. There is no difference in the mean number of calls. p-value = 2(0.5000 − 0.3508) = 0.2984.

27. H_0: $\pi_1 \leq \pi_2$ H_1: $\pi_1 > \pi_2$
Reject H_0 if $z > 1.65$.

$$p_c = \frac{180 + 261}{200 + 300} = 0.882$$

$$z = \frac{0.90 - 0.87}{\sqrt{\frac{0.882(0.118)}{200} + \frac{0.882(0.118)}{300}}} = 1.019$$

H_0 is not rejected. There is no difference in the proportions that found relief with the new and the old drugs.

29. H_0: $\pi_1 \leq \pi_2$ H_1: $\pi_1 > \pi_2$
If $z > 2.33$, reject H_0.

$$p_c = \frac{990 + 970}{1{,}500 + 1{,}600} = 0.63$$

$$z = \frac{.6600 - .60625}{\sqrt{\frac{.63(.37)}{1{,}500} + \frac{.63(.37)}{1{,}600}}} = 3.10$$

Reject the null hypothesis. We can conclude the proportion of men who believe the division is fair is greater.

31. H_0: $\mu_n = \mu_s$ H_1: $\mu_n \neq \mu_s$
Reject H_0 if $t < -2.086$ or $t > 2.086$.

$$s_p^2 = \frac{(10 - 1)(10.5)^2 + (12 - 1)(14.25)^2}{10 + 12 - 2} = 161.2969$$

$$t = \frac{83.55 - 78.8}{\sqrt{161.2969\left(\frac{1}{10} + \frac{1}{12}\right)}} = 0.874$$

Do not reject H_0. There is no difference in the mean number of hamburgers sold at the two locations.

33. H_0: $\mu_1 = \mu_2$ H_1: $\mu_1 \neq \mu_2$
Reject H_0 if $t > 2.819$ or $t < -2.819$.

$$s_p^2 = \frac{(10 - 1)(2.33)^2 + (14 - 1)(2.55)^2}{10 + 14 - 2} = 6.06$$

$$t = \frac{15.87 - 18.29}{\sqrt{6.06\left(\frac{1}{10} + \frac{1}{14}\right)}} = -2.374$$

Do not reject H_0. There is no difference in the mean amount purchased.

35. H_0: $\mu_1 \leq \mu_2$ H_1: $\mu_1 > \mu_2$
Reject H_0 if $t > 2.567$.

$$s_p^2 = \frac{(8 - 1)(2.2638)^2 + (11 - 1)(2.4606)^2}{8 + 11 - 2} = 5.672$$

$$t = \frac{10.375 - 5.636}{\sqrt{5.672\left(\frac{1}{8} + \frac{1}{11}\right)}} = 4.28$$

Reject H_0. The mean number of transactions by the young adults is more than for the senior citizens.

37. H_0: $\mu_1 \leq \mu_2$ H_1: $\mu_1 > \mu_2$
Reject H_0 if $t > 2.650$.
$\bar{X}_1 = 125.125$ $\quad s_1 = 15.094$
$\bar{X}_2 = 117.714$ $\quad s_2 = 19.914$

$$s_p^2 = \frac{(8 - 1)(15.094)^2 + (7 - 1)(19.914)^2}{8 + 7 - 2} = 305.708$$

$$t = \frac{125.125 - 117.714}{\sqrt{305.708\left(\frac{1}{8} + \frac{1}{7}\right)}} = 0.819$$

H_0 is not rejected. There is no difference in the mean number sold at the regular price and the mean number sold at reduced price.

39. H_0: $\mu_d \leq 0$ H_1: $\mu_d > 0$
Reject H_0 if $t > 1.895$.
$\bar{d} = 1.75$ $\quad s_d = 2.9155$

$$t = \frac{1.75}{2.9155/\sqrt{8}} = 1.698$$

Do not reject H_0. There is no difference in the mean number of absences. The p-value is greater than 0.05 but less than .10.

41. H_0: $\mu_1 = \mu_2$ H_1: $\mu_1 \neq \mu_2$
If z is not between -1.96 and 1.96, reject H_0.

$$z = \frac{150 - 180}{\sqrt{\frac{(40)^2}{75} + \frac{(30)^2}{120}}} = -5.59$$

Reject the null hypothesis. The population means are different.

43. H_0: $\mu_d \leq 0$ H_1: $\mu_d > 0$
Reject H_0 if $t > 1.895$.
$\bar{d} = 3.11$ $s_d = 2.91$

$$t = \frac{3.11}{2.91/\sqrt{8}} = 3.02$$

Reject H_0. The mean is lower.

45. Answers will vary.

47. **a.** μ_1 = without pool μ_2 = with pool
H_0: $\mu_1 = \mu_2$ H_1: $\mu_1 \neq \mu_2$
Reject H_0 if $t > 2.000$ or $t < -2.000$.
$\bar{X}_1 = 202.8$ $s_1 = 33.7$ $n_1 = 38$
$\bar{X}_2 = 231.5$ $s_2 = 50.6$ $n_2 = 67$

$$s_p^2 = \frac{(38 - 1)(33.7)^2 + (67 - 1)(50.6)^2}{38 + 67 - 2} = 2{,}048.6$$

$$t = \frac{202.8 - 231.5}{\sqrt{2048.6\left(\frac{1}{38} + \frac{1}{67}\right)}} = -3.12$$

Reject H_0. There is a difference in mean selling price for homes with and without a pool.

b. μ_1 = without garage μ_2 = with garage
H_0: $\mu_1 = \mu_2$ H_1: $\mu_1 \neq \mu_2$
Reject H_0 if $t > 2.000$ or $t < -2.000$.
$\alpha = 0.05$ $df = 34 + 71 - 2 = 103$
$\bar{X}_1 = 185.44$ $s_1 = 28.01$
$\bar{X}_2 = 238.18$ $s_2 = 44.88$

$$s_p^2 = \frac{(34 - 1)(28.01)^2 + (71 - 1)(44.88)^2}{103} = 1{,}620.25$$

$$t = \frac{185.44 - 238.18}{\sqrt{1{,}620.25\left(\frac{1}{34} + \frac{1}{71}\right)}} = -6.28$$

Reject H_0. There is a difference in mean selling price for homes with and without a garage.

c. H_0: $\mu_1 = \mu_2$ H_1: $\mu_1 \neq \mu_2$
Reject H_0 if $t > 2.036$ or $t < -2.036$.
$\bar{X}_1 = 196.91$ $s_1 = 35.78$ $n_1 = 15$
$\bar{X}_2 = 227.45$ $s_2 = 44.19$ $n_2 = 20$

$$s_p^2 = \frac{(15 - 1)(35.78)^2 + (20 - 1)(44.19)^2}{15 + 20 - 2} = 1{,}667.43$$

$$t = \frac{196.91 - 227.45}{\sqrt{1{,}667.43\left(\frac{1}{15} + \frac{1}{20}\right)}} = -2.19$$

Reject H_0. There is a difference in mean selling price for homes in Township 1 and Township 2.

d. H_0: $\pi_1 = \pi_2$ H_1: $\pi_1 \neq \pi_2$
If z is not between -1.96 and 1.96, reject H_0.

$$p_c = \frac{24 + 43}{52 + 53} = 0.64$$

$$z = \frac{0.462 - 0.811}{\sqrt{0.64 \times 0.36/52 + 0.64 \times 0.36/53}} = -3.73$$

Reject the null hypothesis. There is a difference.

49. **a.** H_0: $\mu_s = \mu_{ns}$ H_1: $\mu_s \neq \mu_{ns}$
Reject H_0 if $z < -1.96$ or $z > 1.96$

$$z = \frac{\$31{,}798 - \$28{,}876}{\sqrt{\frac{(17{,}403)^2}{67} + \frac{(16{,}062)^2}{33}}} = 0.83$$

Do not reject H_0. No difference in the mean wages.

b. H_0: $\mu_w = \mu_n$ H_1: $\mu_w \neq \mu_{nw}$
Note, because one sample is less than 30, use t and pool variances. Also answer reported in \$000.

$$s_p^2 = \frac{(90 - 1)(17.358)^2 + (10 - 1)(11.536)^2}{90 + 10 - 2} = 285.85$$

$$t = \frac{31.517 - 24.678}{\sqrt{285.85\left(\frac{1}{90} + \frac{1}{10}\right)}} = 1.214$$

Reject H_0 if $t < -1.99$ or $t > 1.99$.
Do not reject H_0. No difference in the mean wages

c. H_0: $\mu_h = \mu_{nh}$ H_1: $\mu_h \neq \mu_{nh}$
Reject H_0 if $t < -1.99$ or $t > 1.99$.
Because one sample is less than 30, use t. Answer reported in \$000

$$s_p^2 = \frac{(94 - 1)(16.413)^2 + (6 - 1)(25.843)^2}{94 + 6 - 2} = 289.72$$

$$t = \frac{30.674 - 33.337}{\sqrt{289.72\left(\frac{1}{96} + \frac{1}{6}\right)}} = -0.37$$

Do not reject H_0. No difference in the mean wages

d. H_0: $\mu_m = \mu_f$ H_1: $\mu_m \neq \mu_f$
Reject H_0 if $z < -1.96$ or $z > 1.96$

$$z = \frac{\$36{,}493 - \$24{,}452}{\sqrt{\frac{(18{,}448)^2}{53} + \frac{(12{,}446)^2}{47}}} = 3.86$$

Reject H_0. There is a difference in the mean wages for men and women.

e. H_0: $\mu_m = \mu_{nm}$ H_1: $\mu_m \neq \mu_{nm}$
Reject H_0 if $z < -1.96$ or $z > 1.96$

$$z = \frac{\$24{,}864 - \$33{,}773}{\sqrt{\frac{(13{,}055)^2}{33} + \frac{(17{,}933)^2}{67}}} = -2.822$$

Reject H_0. There is a difference in the mean salaries wages of the two groups.

Chapter 11

1. 9.01, from Appendix G.

3. Reject H_0 if $F > 10.5$, where degrees of freedom in the numerator are 7 and 5 in the denominator. Computed $F = 2.04$, found by:

$$F = \frac{s_1^2}{s_2^2} = \frac{(10)^2}{(7)^2} = 2.04$$

Do not reject H_0. There is no difference in the variations of the two populations.

5. H_0: $\sigma_1^2 = \sigma_2^2$ H_1: $\sigma_1^2 \neq \sigma_2^2$
Reject H_0 when $F > 3.10$. (3.10 is about halfway between 3.14 and 3.07.) Computed $F = 1.44$, found by:

$$F = \frac{(12)^2}{(10)^2} = 1.44$$

Do not reject H_0. There is no difference in the variations of the two populations.

7. a. H_0: $\mu_1 = \mu_2 = \mu_3$; H_1: Treatment means are not all the same.
b. Reject H_0 if $F > 4.26$.
c. & d.

Source	SS	df	MS	F
Treatment	62.17	2	31.08	21.94
Error	12.75	9	1.42	
Total	74.92	11		

e. Reject H_0. The treatment means are not all the same.

9. H_0: $\mu_1 = \mu_2 = \mu_3$; H_1: Treatment means are not all the same. Reject H_0 if $F > 4.26$.

Source	SS	df	MS	F
Treatment	276.50	2	138.25	14.18
Error	87.75	9	9.75	

Reject H_0. The treatment means are not all the same.

11. a. H_0: $\mu_1 = \mu_2 = \mu_3$; H_1: Not all means are the same.
b. Reject H_0 if $F > 4.26$.
c. SST = 107.20, SSE = 9.47, SS total = 116.67.
d.

Source	SS	df	MS	F
Treatment	107.20	2	53.600	50.96
Error	9.47	9	1.052	
Total	116.67	11		

e. Since $50.96 > 4.26$, H_0 is rejected. At least one of the means differs.
f. $(\bar{X}_1 - \bar{X}_2) \pm t\sqrt{MSE(1/n_1 + 1/n_2)}$
$= (9.667 - 2.20) \pm 2.262\sqrt{1.052(1/3 + 1/5)}$
$= 7.467 \pm 1.69$
$= [5.777, 9.157]$
Yes, we can conclude that treatments 1 and 2 have different means.

13. H_0: $\mu_1 = \mu_2 = \mu_3 = \mu_4$; H_1: Not all means are equal. H_0 is rejected if $F > 3.71$. Because 2.36 is less than 3.71, H_0 is not rejected. There is no difference in the mean number of weeks.

15. H_0: $\sigma_1^2 \le \sigma_2^2$; H_1: $\sigma_1^2 > \sigma_2^2$. $df_1 = 21 - 1 = 20$; $df_2 = 18 - 1 = 17$. H_0 is rejected if $F > 3.16$.

$$F = \frac{(45{,}600)^2}{(21{,}330)^2} = 4.57$$

Reject H_0. There is more variation in the selling price of oceanfront homes.

17. Sharkey: $n = 7$ $s_s = 14.79$
White: $n = 8$ $s_w = 22.95$
H_0: $\sigma_w^2 \le \sigma_s^2$; H_1: $\sigma_w^2 > \sigma_s^2$. $df_s = 7 - 1 = 6$; $df_w = 8 - 1 = 7$. Reject H_0 if $F > 8.26$.

$$F = \frac{(22.95)^2}{(14.79)^2} = 2.41$$

Cannot reject H_0. There is no difference in the variation of the weekly sales.

19. a. H_0: $\mu_1 = \mu_2 = \mu_3 = \mu_4$
H_1: Treatment means are not all equal.
b. $\alpha = .05$ Reject H_0 if $F > 3.10$.
c.

Source	SS	df	MS	F
Treatment	50	4 − 1 = 3	50/3	$\frac{50/3}{10} = 1.67$
Error	200	24 − 4 = 20	10	
Total	250	24 − 1 = 23		

d. Do not reject H_0.

21. H_0: $\mu_1 = \mu_2 = \mu_3$; H_1: Not all treatment means are equal. H_0 is rejected if $F > 3.89$.

Source	df	SS	MS	F
Treatment	2	63.33	31.667	13.38
Error	12	28.40	2.367	
Total	14	91.73		

H_0 is rejected. There is a difference in the treatment means.

23. H_0: $\mu_1 = \mu_2 = \mu_3 = \mu_4$; H_1: Not all means are equal. H_0 is rejected if $F > 3.10$

Source	df	SS	MS	F
Factor	3	87.79	29.26	9.12
Error	20	64.17	3.21	
Total	23	151.96		

Because computed F of $9.12 > 3.10$, the null hypothesis of no difference is rejected at the .05 level.

25. a. H_0: $\mu_1 = \mu_2$; H_1: $\mu_1 \ne \mu_2$. Critical value of $F = 4.75$.

Source	SS	df	MS	F
Treatment	219.43	1	219.43	23.10
Error	114.00	12	9.5	
Total	333.43	13		

b. $$t = \frac{19 - 27}{\sqrt{9.5\left(\frac{1}{6} + \frac{1}{8}\right)}} = -4.81$$

Then $t^2 = F$. That is $(-4.81)^2 \simeq 23.10$ (actually 23.14. Difference due to rounding)
c. H_0 is rejected. There is a difference in the mean scores.

27. H_0: $\mu_A = \mu_B = \mu_C = \mu_D$; H_1: Treatment means are not equal. Reject H_0 if $F > 3.49$. The computed value of F is 9.61. Reject H_0 and conclude the treatment means differ.

29. a. H_0: $\mu_A = \mu_B = \mu_C$; H_1: Treatment means are not equal. Reject H_0 if $F > 6.36$. The computed value of F is 11.33, so H_0 is rejected. There is a difference in the mean production of the three lines.
b. Line B vs Line C

$$(43.333 - 41.500) \pm 2.947\sqrt{.544\left(\frac{1}{6} + \frac{1}{6}\right)}$$

1.833 ± 1.255 This pair differs.

31. a. H_0: $\mu_1 = \mu_2 = \mu_3 = \mu_4 = \mu_5 = \mu_6$; H_1: The treatment means are not equal. Reject H_0 if $F > 2.37$.

Source	df	SS	MS	F
Treatment	5	0.03478	0.00696	3.86
Error	58	0.10439	0.0018	
Total	63	0.13917		

H_0 is rejected. There is a difference in the mean weight of the colors.

33. Answers will vary.

35. a. H_0: $\sigma_P^2 = \sigma_{NP}^2$; H_1: $\sigma_P^2 \ne \sigma_{NP}^2$. Reject H_0 if $F > 2.05$ (estimated).
$df_1 = 67 - 1 = 66$; $df_2 = 38 - 1 = 37$.

$$F = \frac{(50.57)^2}{(33.71)^2} = 2.25$$

Reject H_0. There is a difference in the variance of the two selling prices.

b. $H_0: \sigma_g^2 = \sigma_{ng}^2$; $H_1: \sigma_g^2 \neq \sigma_{ng}^2$. Reject H_0 if $F > 2.11$ (estimated).

$$F = \frac{(44.88)^2}{(28.00)^2} = 2.57$$

Reject H_0. There is a difference in the variance of the two selling prices.

c. $H_0: \mu_1 = \mu_2 = \mu_3 = \mu_4 = \mu_5$; H_1: Not all treatment means are equal. Reject H_0 if $F > 2.46$.

Source	SS	*df*	MS	*F*
Township	13,263	4	3,316	1.52
Error	217,505	100	2,175	
Total	230,768	104		

Do not reject H_0. There is no difference in the mean selling prices in the five townships.

37. a. $H_0: \mu_0 = \mu_1 = \mu_2$; H_1: Treatment means are not equal. Reject H_0 if $F > 3.09$. The computed value of F is 1.30. We conclude there is no difference among the industries.

b. $H_0: \mu_0 = \mu_1 = \mu_2 = \mu_3 = \mu_4 = \mu_5$; H_1: Treatment means are not equal.
Reject H_0 if $F > 2.31$. The computed value of F is 4.85. The treatment means differ. The MINITAB output follows.

```
Level      N      Mean     StDev
0         22     28921     14517
1         13     40074     22733
2          6     27228     16101
3         21     27619      9821
4         21     21510      6946
5         17     43002     22062

Pooled St Dev =  15507

Individual 95% CIs for Mean
Based on Pooled StDev
------+---------+---------+---------+
        (------*-----)
                     (------*-----)
     (---------*--------)
         (------*-----)
   (------*-----)
                        (------*-----)
------+---------+---------+---------+
  20000     30000     40000     50000
```

From the above graph the following means differ: 0 and 5, 1 and 4, 3 and 5, and 4 and 5.

c. $H_0: \sigma_u^2 = \sigma_{nu}^2$; $H_1: \sigma_u^2 \neq \sigma_{nu}^2$ Reject H_0 if $F > 2.03$. Computed F is 1.36, found by $(17{,}413)^2/(14{,}940)^2$. There is no difference in the variation of union and nonunion members.

Chapter 12

1. $\Sigma X = 28$, $\Sigma Y = 29$, $\Sigma X^2 = 186$, $\Sigma XY = 173$, $\Sigma Y^2 = 175$

$$r = \frac{5(173) - (28)(29)}{\sqrt{[5(186) - (28)^2][5(175) - (29)^2]}} = 0.75$$

The 0.75 coefficient indicates a rather strong positive correlation between X and Y. The coefficient of determination is 0.5625, found by $(0.75)^2$. More than 56 percent of the variation in Y is accounted for by X.

3. a. Sales.

b.

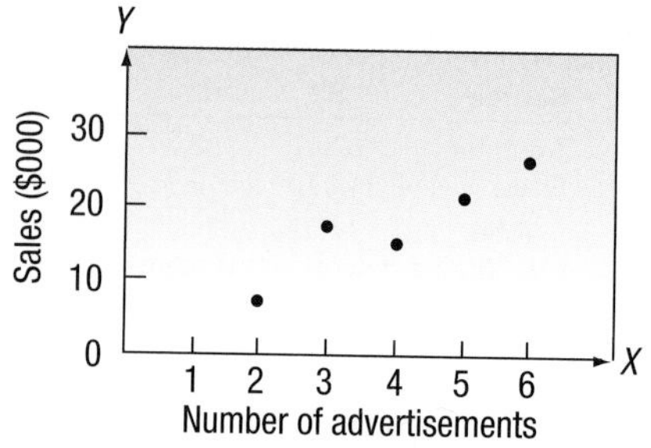

c. $n = 5$, $\Sigma X = 20$, $\Sigma X^2 = 90$, $\Sigma Y = 85$, $\Sigma Y^2 = 1595$, and $\Sigma XY = 376$, so:

$$r = \frac{5(376) - (20)(85)}{\sqrt{[5(90) - (20)^2][5(1595) - (85)^2]}} = 0.93$$

d. The coefficient of determination is 0.8649, found by $(0.93)^2$.

e. There is a strong positive association between the variables. About 86 percent of the variation in sales is explained by the number of airings.

5. a. Police is the independent variable, and crime is the dependent variable.

b.

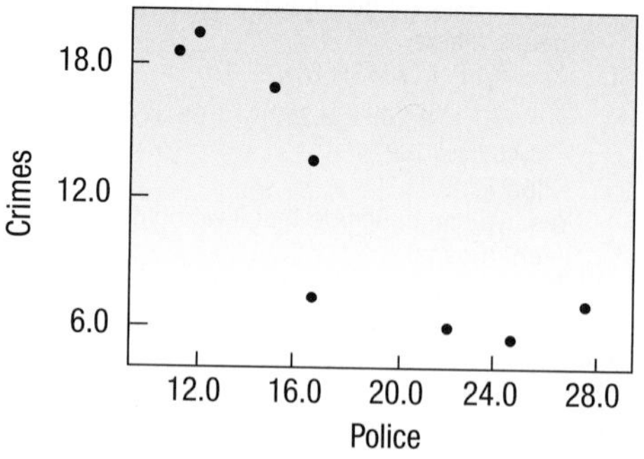

c. $n = 8$, $\Sigma X = 146$, $\Sigma X^2 = 2906$, $\Sigma Y = 95$, $\Sigma Y^2 = 1{,}419$, and $\Sigma XY = 1{,}502$

$$r = \frac{8(1{,}502) - 146(95)}{\sqrt{[8(2{,}906) - (146)^2][8(1{,}419) - (95)^2]}}$$
$$= -.874$$

d. 0.76, found by $(-.874)^2$

e. Strong inverse relationship. As the number of police increases, the crime decreases.

7. Reject H_0 if $t > 1.812$.

$$t = \frac{.82\sqrt{12 - 2}}{\sqrt{1 - (.32)^2}} = 1.07$$

Do not reject H_0.

9. $H_0: \rho \geq 0$; $H_1: \rho < 0$. Reject H_0 if $t < -2.552$. $df = 18$.

$$t = \frac{-.78\sqrt{20 - 2}}{\sqrt{1 - (-.78)^2}} = -5.288$$

Reject H_0. There is a negative correlation between gallons sold and the pump price.

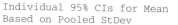

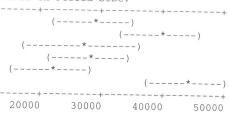

11. **a.** $Y' = 3.7671 + .3630X$

$$b = \frac{5(173) - (28)(29)}{5(186) - (28)^2} = 0.3630$$

$$a = \frac{29}{5} - (0.363)\frac{28}{5} = 3.7671$$

b. 6.3081, found by $Y' = 3.7671 + 0.3630(7)$

13. **a.** $b = \frac{10(718) - (91)(74)}{10(895) - (91)^2} = 0.667$

$$a = \frac{74}{10} - .667\left(\frac{91}{10}\right) = 1.333$$

b. $Y' = 1.333 + .667(6) = 5.335$

15. **a.**

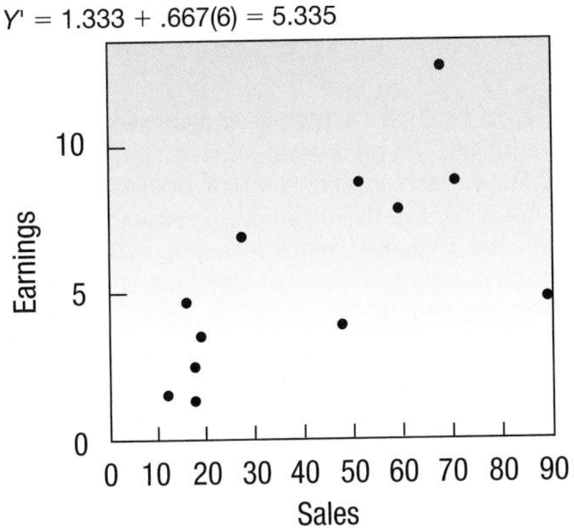

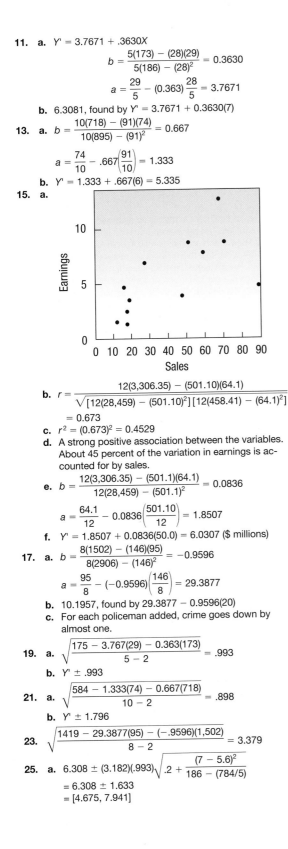

b. $r = \frac{12(3,306.35) - (501.10)(64.1)}{\sqrt{[12(28,459) - (501.10)^2][12(458.41) - (64.1)^2]}}$

$= 0.673$

c. $r^2 = (0.673)^2 = 0.4529$

d. A strong positive association between the variables. About 45 percent of the variation in earnings is accounted for by sales.

e. $b = \frac{12(3,306.35) - (501.1)(64.1)}{12(28,459) - (501.1)^2} = 0.0836$

$$a = \frac{64.1}{12} - 0.0836\left(\frac{501.10}{12}\right) = 1.8507$$

f. $Y' = 1.8507 + 0.0836(50.0) = 6.0307$ ($ millions)

17. **a.** $b = \frac{8(1502) - (146)(95)}{8(2906) - (146)^2} = -0.9596$

$$a = \frac{95}{8} - (-0.9596)\left(\frac{146}{8}\right) = 29.3877$$

b. 10.1957, found by $29.3877 - 0.9596(20)$

c. For each policeman added, crime goes down by almost one.

19. **a.** $\sqrt{\frac{175 - 3.767(29) - 0.363(173)}{5 - 2}} = .993$

b. $Y' \pm .993$

21. **a.** $\sqrt{\frac{584 - 1.333(74) - 0.667(718)}{10 - 2}} = .898$

b. $Y' \pm 1.796$

23. $\sqrt{\frac{1419 - 29.3877(95) - (-.9596)(1,502)}{8 - 2}} = 3.379$

25. **a.** $6.308 \pm (3.182)(.993)\sqrt{.2 + \frac{(7 - 5.6)^2}{186 - (784/5)}}$

$= 6.308 \pm 1.633$

$= [4.675, 7.941]$

b. $6.308 \pm (3.182)(.993)\sqrt{1 + 1/5 + .0671}$

$= [2.751, 9.865]$

27. **a.** [4.2939, 6.3721]

b. [2.9854, 7.6806]

29. $r = \frac{(5)(340) - (50)(30)}{\sqrt{[(5)(600) - (50)^2][(5)(200) - (30)^2]}} = .8944$

Then, $(.8944)^2 = .80$, the coefficient of determination.

31. **a.** $r^2 = 1000/1500 = .667$

b. .82, found by $\sqrt{.667}$

c. 6.20, found by $s_{y \cdot x} = \sqrt{\frac{500}{15 - 2}}$

33. $H_0: \rho \le 0$; $H_1: \rho > 0$. Reject H_0 if $t > 1.714$.

$$t = \frac{.94\sqrt{25 - 2}}{\sqrt{1 - (.94)^2}} = 13.213$$

Reject H_0. We have failed to show a positive correlation between passengers and weight of luggage.

35. $H_0: \rho \le 0$; $H_1: \rho > 0$. Reject H_0 if $t > 2.764$.

$$t = \frac{.47\sqrt{12 - 2}}{\sqrt{1 - (.47)^2}} = 1.684$$

Do not reject H_0. There is not a positive correlation between engine size and performance. p-value is greater than .05, but less than .10.

37. $H_0: \rho \ge 0$; $H_1: \rho < 0$. Reject H_0 if $t < -1.701$, $df = 28$.

$$t = \frac{-.45\sqrt{30 - 2}}{\sqrt{1 - .2025}} = -2.67$$

Reject H_0. There is a negative correlation between the selling price and the number of miles driven.

39. **a.** $r = 0.589$

b. $r^2 = (0.589)^2 = 0.3469$

c. $H_0: \rho \le 0$; $H_1: \rho > 0$. Reject H_0 if $t > 1.860$.

$$t = \frac{0.589\sqrt{10 - 2}}{\sqrt{1 - (.589)^2}} = 2.062$$

H_0 is rejected. There is a positive association between family size and the amount spent on food.

41. **a.**

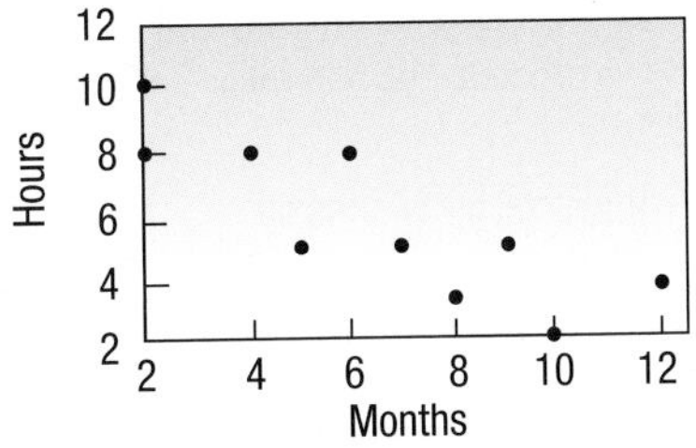

There is an inverse relationship between the variables. As the months owned increase, the number of hours exercised decreases.

b. $r = \frac{10(313) - (65)(58)}{\sqrt{[10(523) - (65)^2][10(396) - (58)^2]}}$

$= -0.827$

c. $H_0: \rho \ge 0$; $H_1: \rho < 0$. Reject H_0 if $t < -2.896$.

$$t = \frac{-0.827\sqrt{10 - 2}}{\sqrt{1 - (-0.827)^2}} = -4.16$$

Reject H_0. There is a negative association between months owned and hours exercised.

43. **a.**

Source	SS	df	MS	F
Regression	50	1	50	2.5556
Error	450	23	19.5652	
Total	500	24		

b. $n = 25$

c. $s_{y \cdot x} = \sqrt{19.5652} = 4.4233$

d. $r^2 = \frac{50}{500} = 0.10$

45. **a.** $n = 15$, $\Sigma X = 107$, $\Sigma X^2 = 837$, $\Sigma Y = 118.6$, $\Sigma Y^2 = 969.92$, $\Sigma XY = 811.60$, $s_{y \cdot x} = 1.114$

$$b = \frac{15(811.60) - (107)(118.6)}{15(837.0) - (107)^2} = -0.4667$$

$$a = \frac{118.6}{15} - (-0.4667)\left(\frac{107}{15}\right) = 11.2358$$

b. $Y' = 11.2358 - 0.4667(7.0) = 7.9689$

c. $7.9689 \pm (2.160)(1.114)\sqrt{1 + \frac{1}{15} + \frac{(7 - 7.1333)^2}{837 - \frac{(107)^2}{15}}}$

$= 7.9689 \pm 2.4854$
$= [5.4835, 10.4543]$

d. $r^2 = 0.499$. Nearly 50 percent of the variation in the amount of the bid is explained by the number of bidders.

47. **a.** $b = \frac{30(18{,}924) - (320.33)(1575.6)}{30(4292.5) - (320.33)^2} = 2.41$

$$a = \frac{1575.6}{30} - 2.41\left(\frac{320.33}{30}\right) = 26.8$$

The regression equation is: Price = 26.8 + 2.41 × dividend. For each additional dollar of dividend, the price increases by \$2.41.

b. $r^2 = \frac{5057.6}{7682.7} = 0.658$ Thus, 65.8 percent of the variation in price is explained by the dividend.

c. $r = \sqrt{.658} = 0.811$ $H_0: \rho \le 0$ $H_1: \rho > 0$

At the 5 percent level, reject H_0 when $t > 1.701$.

$$t = \frac{0.811\sqrt{30 - 2}}{\sqrt{1 - (0.811)^2}} = 7.34$$

Thus H_0 is rejected. The population correlation is positive.

49. **a.** 35

b. $s_{y \cdot x} = \sqrt{29{,}778{,}406} = 5456.96$

c. $r^2 = \frac{13{,}548{,}662{,}082}{14{,}531{,}349{,}474} = 0.932$

d. $r = \sqrt{0.932} = 0.966$

e. $H_0: \rho \le 0$, $H_1: \rho > 0$. Reject H_0 if $t > 1.697$

$$t = \frac{.966\sqrt{35 - 2}}{\sqrt{1 - (.966)^2}} = 21.46$$

Reject H_0. There is a positive association between market value and size of the home.

51. **a.** Answers will vary as the number of cottages available and their prices change. At this time there are 14 cottages that meet the criteria. The correlation between the number of baths and rental price is 0.668.
$H_0: \rho \le 0$, $H_1: \rho > 0$. Reject H_0 if $t > 1.782$.

$$t = \frac{0.668\sqrt{14 - 2}}{\sqrt{1 - (0.668)^2}} = 3.11$$

Reject H_0. There is a positive correlation between baths and cottage price.

b. The regression equation is $Y' = 758 + 347X$. The weekly price increases almost \$350 for each bathroom.

c. $H_0: \rho \le 0$, $H_1: \rho > 0$. Reject H_0 if $t > 1.782$.

$$t = \frac{0.085\sqrt{14 - 2}}{\sqrt{1 - (0.085)^2}} = .296$$

Do not reject H_0. We cannot conclude that there is an association between people and price.

53. **a.** The correlation between wins and salary is 0.313.
$H_0: \rho \le 0$, $H_1: \rho > 0$. Reject H_0 if $t > 1.701$.

$$t = \frac{0.313\sqrt{30 - 2}}{\sqrt{1 - (.313)^2}} = 1.744$$

Reject H_0. There is a positive association between the variables. The regression equation is $Y' = 70.2 + 0.164X$. Each additional million dollars of salary is .164 wins, five million in salary is about .82 wins, found by .164 (5). Note that r^2 is less than 10%, so salary does not explain much of the variation in wins.

b. Wins vs Batting

$r = 0.492$, critical value is 1.701.

$$t = \frac{.492\sqrt{30 - 2}}{\sqrt{1 - (.492)^2}} = 2.990$$

Wins vs ERA

$r = -0.766$, critical value is -1.701.

$$t = \frac{-0.766\sqrt{30 - 2}}{\sqrt{1 - (-0.766)^2}} = -6.305$$

Conclude there is positive association between wins and batting and negative association between wins and ERA. The stronger association is between wins and ERA.

c. $H_0: \rho \le 0$, $H_1: \rho > 0$. Reject H_0 if $t > 1.701$.
The correlation between wins and attendance is 0.499

$$t = \frac{0.499\sqrt{30 - 2}}{\sqrt{1 - (0.499)^2}} = 3.047$$

Reject H_0. There is a positive association between wins and attendance.

55. **a.** $Y' = 9.56 + 0.002X$. An increase of 1 in the labor force increase unemployment by .002. For United Arab Emirates, $Y' = 9.56 + .002\,(1.4) = 9.5628$. Use this equation with caution because r^2 is nearly 0. That is, there is almost no relationship between the variables.

b. The correlation between exports and imports is 0.948, very strong.
$H_0: \rho \le 0$, $H_1: \rho > 0$. Reject H_0 if $t > 1.684$.

$$t = \frac{.948\sqrt{46 - 2}}{\sqrt{1 - (.948)^2}} = 19.76$$

Reject H_0. Conclude a positive association between the variables.

c. The correlation between percent of the population over 65 and the literacy rate is 0.794.
$H_0: \rho \le 0$, $H_1: \rho > 0$. Reject H_0 if $t > 1.684$.

$$t = \frac{.794\sqrt{46 - 2}}{\sqrt{1 - (.794)^2}} = 8.664$$

Reject H_0. There is a positive correlation between the variables.

Chapter 13

1. a. Multiple regression equation.
   b. The Y-intercept.
   c. $Y' = 64{,}100 + 0.394(796{,}000) + 9.6(6{,}940) - 11{,}600(6.0) = \$374{,}748$
3. a. 497.736, found by
   $Y' = 16.24 + 0.017(18) + 0.0028(26{,}500) + 42(3) + 0.0012(156{,}000) + 0.19(141) + 26.8(2.5)$
   b. Two more social activities. Income added only 28 to the index; social activities added 53.6.
5. a. 19
   b. 3
   c. .318, found by 21/66.
   d. 1.732, found by $\sqrt{\frac{45}{[19 - (3 + 1)]}}$.
7. a.

Source	SS	df	MS	F
Regression	7,500.0	3	2,500	18
Error	2,500.0	18	138.89	
Total	10,000.0	21		

   b. H_0: $\beta_1 = \beta_2 = \beta_3 = 0$; H_1: Not all βs are 0. Reject H_0 if $F > 3.16$.
   Reject H_0. Not all net regression coefficients equal zero.
   c.

For X_1:	For X_2:	For X_3:
H_0: $\beta_1 = 0$	H_0: $\beta_2 = 0$	H_0: $\beta_3 = 0$
H_1: $\beta_1 \neq 0$	H_1: $\beta_2 \neq 0$	H_1: $\beta_3 \neq 0$
$t = -4.00$	$t = 1.50$	$t = -3.00$

   Reject H_0 if $t > 2.101$ or $t < -2.101$.
   Delete variable 2, keep 1 and 3.
9. a. $n = 40$
   b. 4
   c. $R^2 = \frac{750}{1250} = .60$
   d. $s_{y \cdot 1234} = \sqrt{500/35} = 3.7796$
   e. H_0: $\beta_1 = \beta_2 = \beta_3 = \beta_4 = 0$
   H_1: Not all the βs equal zero.
   H_0 is rejected if $F > 2.65$.
   $$F = \frac{750/4}{500/35} = 13.125$$
   H_0 is rejected. At least one β_i does not equal zero.
11. a. $n = 26$.
   b. $R^2 = 100/140 = .7143$
   c. 1.4142, found by $\sqrt{2}$.
   d. H_0: $\beta_1 = \beta_2 = \beta_3 = \beta_4 = \beta_5 = 0$
   H_1: Not all the βs are 0.
   H_0 is rejected if $F > 2.71$.
   Computed $F = 10.0$. Reject H_0. At least one regression coefficient is not zero.
   e. H_0 is rejected in each case if $t < -2.086$ or $t > 2.086$.
   X_1 and X_5 should be dropped.
13. a. \$28,000
   b. $R^2 = \frac{SSR}{SStotal} = \frac{3{,}050}{5{,}250} = .5809$
   c. 9.199, found by $\sqrt{84.62}$.
   d. H_0 is rejected if $F > 2.975$.
   $$\text{Computed } F = \frac{1016.67}{84.62} = 12.01$$
   H_0 is rejected. At least one regression coefficient is not zero.
   e. If computed t is to the left of -2.056 or to the right of 2.056, the null hypothesis in each of these cases is rejected. Computed t for X_2 and X_3 exceed the critical value. Thus, "population" and "advertising expenses" should be retained and "number of competitors," X_1, dropped.
15. a. The correlation matrix is:

	cars	*adv*	*sales*
adv	0.808		
sales	0.872	0.537	
city	0.639	0.713	0.389

   Size of sales force (0.872) has the strongest correlation with cars sold. Fairly strong relationship between location of dealership and advertising (0.713). Could be a problem.
   b. The regression equation is:
   $Y' = 31.1328 + 2.1516adv + 5.0140sales + 5.6651city$
   $Y' = 31.1328 + 2.1516(15) + 5.0140(20) + 5.6651(1) = 169.352$.
   c. H_0: $\beta_1 = \beta_2 = \beta_3 = 0$; H_1: Not all βs are 0. Reject H_0 if computed $F > 4.07$.

Analysis of Variance

Source	SS	df	MS
Regression	5504.4	3	1834.8
Error	420.2	8	52.5
Total	5924.7	11	

   $F = 1{,}834.8/52.5 = 34.95$.
   Reject H_0. At least one regression coefficient is not 0.
   d. H_0 is rejected in all cases if $t < -2.306$ or if $t > 2.306$. Advertising and sales force should be retained, city dropped. (Note that dropping city removes the problem with multicollinearity.)

Predictor	Coef	StDev	*t*-ratio	P
Constant	31.13	13.40	2.32	0.049
adv	2.1516	0.8049	2.67	0.028
sales	5.0140	0.9105	5.51	0.000
city	5.665	6.332	0.89	0.397

   e. The new output is
   $Y' = 2.30 + 2.6187adv + 5.0233sales$

Predictor	Coef	StDev	*t*-ratio
Constant	25.30	11.57	2.19
adv	2.6187	0.6057	4.32
sales	5.0233	0.9003	5.58

Analysis of Variance

Source	SS	df	MS
Regression	5462.4	2	2731.2
Error	462.3	9	51.4
Total	5924.7	11	

f. Stem-and-leaf
Leaf unit = 1.0

1	−1	6
1	−1	
2	−0	5
5	−0	110
(5)	0	01224
2	0	58

The normality assumption is reasonable.

g.

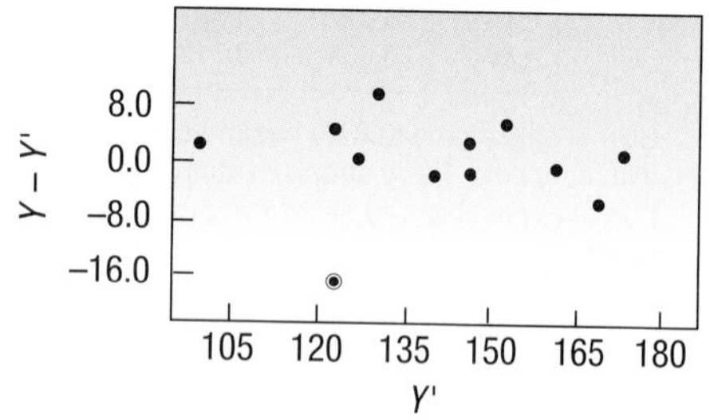

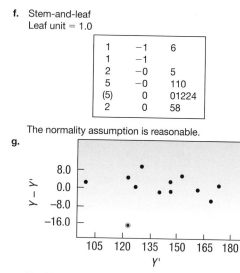

For this small sample the residual plot is acceptable.

17. a. The regression equation is:
$Y' = 965.3 + 2.865X_1 + 6.75X_2 + 0.2873X_3$
$Y' = \$2{,}458{,}780$

b.

Analysis of Variance

Source	SS	*df*	MS
Regression	45,510,092	3	15,170,032
Error	12,215,892	12	1,017,991
Total	57,725,984	15	

$$F = \frac{15{,}170{,}032}{1{,}017{,}991} = 14.902$$

H_0 is rejected because computed F of 14.902 is greater than the critical value of 3.49. At least one of the regression coefficients is not zero.

c. $H_0: \beta_1 = 0$ $H_0: \beta_2 = 0$ $H_0: \beta_3 = 0$
$H_1: \beta_1 \neq 0$ $H_1: \beta_2 \neq 0$ $H_1: \beta_3 \neq 0$
The H_0s are rejected if $t < -2.179$ or $t > 2.179$. Both workers and dividends are not significant variables. Inventory is significant. Delete dividends and return analysis.

d. The regression equation (if we used X_1 and X_3)
$Y' = 1134.8 + 3.258X_1 + 0.3099X_3$

Predictor	Coef	StDev	*t*-ratio
Constant	1134.8	418.6	2.71
Workers	3.258	1.434	2.27
Inv	0.3099	0.1033	3.00

Analysis of Variance

Source	SS	*df*	MS	*F*
Regression	45,070,624	2	22,535,312	23.15
Error	12,655,356	13	973,489	
Total	57,725,968	15		

e.

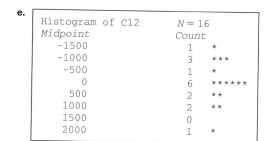

```
Histogram of C12        N = 16
Midpoint                Count
  -1500                   1   *
  -1000                   3   ***
   -500                   1   *
      0                   6   ******
    500                   2   **
   1000                   2   **
   1500                   0
   2000                   1   *
```

The normality assumption is reasonable.

f.

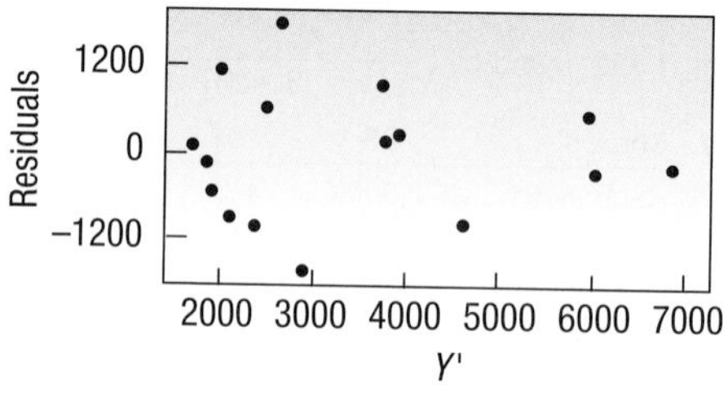

19. The computer output is:

```
Predictor      Coef    Stdev   t-ratio       p
Constant      651.9    345.3      1.89   0.071
Service      13.422    5.125      2.62   0.015
Age          -6.710    6.349     -1.06   0.301
Gender       205.65    90.27      2.28   0.032
Job          -33.45    89.55     -0.37   0.712
Analysis of Variance
SOURCE        DF       SS        MS       F       p
Regression     4  1066830    266708    4.77   0.005
Error         25  1398651     55946
Total         29  2465481
```

a. $Y' = 651.9 + 13.422X_1 - 6.710X_2 + 205.65X_3 - 33.45X_4$

b. $R^2 = .433$, which is somewhat low for this type of study.

c. $H_0: \beta_1 = \beta_2 = \beta_3 = \beta_4 = 0$; H_1: not all βs equal zero.
Reject H_0 if $F > 2.76$.

$$F = \frac{1{,}066{,}830/4}{1{,}398{,}651/25} = 4.77$$

H_0 is rejected. Not all the β_is equal 0.

d. Using the .05 significance level, reject the hypothesis that the regression coefficient is 0 if $t < -2.060$ or $t > 2.060$. Service and gender should remain in the analyses, age and job should be dropped.

e. Following is the computer output using the independent variables service and gender.

```
Predictor      Coef    Stdev   t-ratio       p
Constant      784.2    316.8      2.48   0.020
Service       9.021    3.106      2.90   0.007
Gender       224.41    87.35      2.57   0.016
Analysis of Variance
SOURCE        DF       SS        MS       F       p
Regression     2   998779    499389    9.19   0.001
Error         27  1466703     54322
Total         29  2465481
```

A man earns $224 more per month than a woman. The difference between technical and clerical jobs is not significant.

21. Answers will vary as the rental prices change.

23. The computer output is as follows:

```
Predictor        Coef    SE Coef       T       P
Constant        38.71      39.02    0.99   0.324
Bedrooms        7.118      2.551    2.79   0.006
Size          0.03800    0.01468    2.59   0.011
Pool           18.321      6.999    2.62   0.010
Distance      -0.9295     0.7279   -1.28   0.205
Garage         35.810      7.638    4.69   0.000
Baths          23.315      9.025    2.58   0.011

S = 33.21   R-Sq = 53.2%   R-Sq (adj) = 50.3%

Analysis of Variance
SOURCE            DF      SS     MS      F      P
Regression         6  122676  20446  18.54  0.000
Residual Error    98  108092   1103
Total            104  230768
```

a. Each additional bedroom adds about $7,000 to the selling price, a pool adds $18,300, an attached garage $35,800, and each mile the home is from the center of the city reduces the selling price by $929.

b. The *R*-square value is 0.532.

c. The correlation matrix is as follows:

	Price	Bedrooms	Size	Pool	Distance	Garage
Bedrooms	0.467					
Size	0.371	0.383				
Pool	0.294	0.005	0.201			
Distance	−0.347	−0.153	−0.117	−0.139		
Garage	0.526	0.234	0.083	0.114	−0.359	
Baths	0.382	0.329	0.024	0.055	−0.195	0.221

The independent variable *garage* has the strongest correlation with price. Distance is inversely related, as expected, and there does not seem to be a problem with correlation among the independent variables.

d. The results of the global test suggest that some of the independent variables have net regression coefficients different from zero.

e. We can delete *distance*.

f. The new regression output follows.

```
Predictor        Coef    SE Coef       T       P
Constant        17.01      35.24    0.48   0.630
Bedrooms        7.169      2.559    2.80   0.006
Size          0.03919    0.01470    2.67   0.009
Pool           19.110      6.994    2.73   0.007
Garage         38.847      7.281    5.34   0.000
Baths          24.624      8.995    2.74   0.007

S = 33.32   R-Sq = 52.4%   R-Sq (adj) = 50.0%

Analysis of Variance
SOURCE            DF      SS     MS      F      P
Regression         5  120877  24175  21.78  0.000
Residual Error    99  109890   1110
Total            104  230768
```

In reviewing the *p*-values for the various regression coefficients, all are less than .05. We leave all the independent variables.

g. & h. Analysis of the residuals, not shown, indicates the normality assumption is reasonable. In addition, there is no pattern to the plots of the residuals and the fitted values of *Y*.

25. a. $Y' = -14{,}174 + 3{,}325X_1 - 11{,}675X_2 + 448X_3 - 5{,}355X_4$
Note age is dropped because of association with other variables. Women earn $11,675 less than men, and union members 5,355 less than nonunion workers. Wages increase $3,325 for each year of education and $448 for each year of experience.

b. $R^2 = .366$, which is not too good.

c. Education and gender have the strongest association with wages; age and experience have a nearly perfect association. Drop age.

d. The computed value of *F* is 13.69, so we conclude some of the regression coefficients are not equal to zero.

e. Drop the union variable, $t = -1.40$.

f. Deleting union decreases R^2 to .352.

g & h. Analysis of the residuals, not shown, indicates the normality assumption is reasonable. In addition, there is no pattern to the plots of the residuals and the fitted values of *Y*.

Chapter 14

1. a. 3

b. 7.815

3. a. Reject H_0 if $\chi^2 > 5.991$.

b. $$\chi^2 = \frac{(10-20)^2}{20} + \frac{(20-20)^2}{20} + \frac{(30-20)^2}{20} = 10.0$$

c. Reject H_0. The proportions are not equal.

5. H_0: The outcomes are the same; H_1: The outcomes are not the same. Reject H_0 if $\chi^2 > 9.236$

$$\chi^2 = \frac{(3-5)^2}{5} + \cdots + \frac{(7-5)^2}{5} = 7.60$$

Do not reject H_0. Cannot reject H_0 that outcomes are the same.

7. H_0: There is no difference in the proportions.
H_1: There is a difference in the proportions.
Reject H_0 if $\chi^2 > 15.086$.

$$\chi^2 = \frac{(47-40)^2}{40} + \cdots + \frac{(34-40)^2}{40} = 3.400$$

Do not reject H_0. There is no difference in the proportions.

9. a. Reject H_0 if $\chi^2 > 9.210$.

b. $$\chi^2 = \frac{(30-24)^2}{24} + \frac{(20-24)^2}{24} + \frac{(10-12)^2}{12} = 2.50$$

c. Do not reject H_0.

11. H_0: Proportions are as stated; H_1: Proportions are not as stated. Reject H_0 if $\chi^2 > 11.345$.

$$\chi^2 = \frac{(50-25)^2}{25} + \cdots + \frac{(160-275)^2}{275} = 115.22$$

Reject H_0. The proportions are not as stated.

13. H_0: There is no relationship between community size and section read. H_1: There is a relationship. Reject H_0 if $\chi^2 > 9.488$.

$$\chi^2 = \frac{(170-157.50)^2}{157.50} + \cdots + \frac{(88-83.62)^2}{83.62} = 7.340$$

Do not reject H_0. There is no relationship between community size and section read.

15. H_0: No relationship between error rates and item type. H_1: There is a relationship between error rates and item type. Reject H_0 if $\chi^2 > 9.21$.

$$\chi^2 = \frac{(20 - 14.1)^2}{14.1} + \cdots + \frac{(225 - 225.25)^2}{225.25} = 8.033$$

Do not reject H_0. There is not a relationship between error rates and item type.

17. H_0: $\pi_s = 0.50$, $\pi_r = \pi_e = 0.25$
H_1: Distribution is not as given above.
$df = 2$. Reject H_0 if $\chi^2 > 4.605$.

Turn	f_o	f_e	$f_o - f_e$	$(f_o - f_e)^2/f_e$
Straight	112	100	12	1.44
Right	48	50	−2	0.08
Left	40	50	−10	2.00
Total	200	200		3.52

H_0 is not rejected. The proportions are as given in the null hypothesis.

19. H_0: There is no preference with respect to TV stations.
H_1: There is a preference with respect to TV stations.
$df = 3 - 1 = 2$. H_0 is rejected if $\chi^2 > 5.991$.

TV Station	f_o	f_e	$f_o - f_e$	$(f_o - f_e)^2$	$(f_o - f_e)^2/f_e$
WNAE	53	50	3	9	0.18
WRRN	64	50	14	196	3.92
WSPD	33	50	−17	289	5.78
	150	150	0		9.88

H_0 is rejected. There is a preference for TV stations.

21. H_0: $\pi_n = 0.21$, $\pi_m = 0.24$, $\pi_s = 0.35$, $\pi_w = 0.20$.
H_1: The distribution is not as given.
Reject H_0 if $\chi^2 > 11.345$.

Region	f_o	f_e	$f_o - f_e$	$(f_o - f_e)^2/f_e$
Northeast	68	84	−16	3.0476
Midwest	104	96	8	0.6667
South	155	140	15	1.6071
West	73	80	−7	0.6125
Total	400	400	0	5.9339

H_0 is not rejected. The distribution of order destinations reflects the population.

23. H_0: $\pi_0 = 0.40$, $\pi_1 = 0.30$, $\pi_2 = 0.20$, $\pi_3 = 0.1$
H_1: The proportions are not as given. Reject H_0 if $\chi^2 > 7.815$.

Accidents	f_o	f_e	$(f_o - f_e)^2/f_e$
0	46	48	0.083
1	40	36	0.444
2	22	24	0.167
3	12	12	0.000
Total	120		0.694

Do not reject H_0. Evidence does not show a change in the accident distribution.

25. H_0: Levels of management and concern regarding the environment are not related. H_1: Levels of management and concern regarding the environment are related. Reject H_0 if $\chi^2 > 16.812$.

$$\chi^2 = \frac{(15 - 14)^2}{14} + \cdots + \frac{(31 - 28)^2}{28} = 1.550$$

Do not reject H_0. Levels of management and environmental concern are not related.

27. H_0: Whether a claim is filed and age are not related.
H_1: Whether a claim is filed and age are related.
Reject H_0 if $\chi^2 > 7.815$.

$$\chi^2 = \frac{(170 - 203.33)^2}{203.33} + \cdots + \frac{(24 - 35.67)^2}{35.67} = 53.639$$

Reject H_0. Age is related to whether a claim is filed.

29. H_0: $\pi_{BL} = \pi_{BR} = \pi_Y = \pi_R = 0.2$, $\pi_G = \pi_O = 0.1$ H_1: The proportions are not as given. Reject H_0 if $\chi^2 > 11.070$.

Color	f_o	f_e	$(f_o - f_e)^2/f_e$
Blue	13	14.4	0.136
Brown	17	14.4	0.469
Yellow	20	14.4	2.178
Red	7	14.4	3.803
Green	9	7.2	0.450
Orange	6	7.2	0.200
Total	72		7.236

Do not reject H_0. The color distribution agrees with the manufacturer's information.

31. **a.** H_0: There is no relationship between pool and township.
H_1: There is a relationship between pool and township.
Reject H_0 if $\chi^2 > 9.488$.

	Township					
Pool	1	2	3	4	5	Total
No	9	8	7	11	3	38
Yes	6	12	18	18	13	67
Total	15	20	25	29	16	105

$$\chi^2 = \frac{(9 - 5.43)^2}{5.43} + \cdots + \frac{(13 - 10.21)^2}{10.21} = 6.680$$

Do not reject H_0. There is no relationship between pool and township.

b. H_0: There is no relationship between attached garage and township. H_1: There is a relationship between attached garage and township. Reject H_0 if $\chi^2 > 9.488$.

	Township					
Garage	1	2	3	4	5	Total
No	6	5	10	9	4	34
Yes	9	15	15	20	12	71
Total	15	20	25	29	16	105

$$\chi^2 = \frac{(6 - 4.86)^2}{4.86} + \cdots + \frac{(12 - 10.82)^2}{10.82} = 1.980$$

Do not reject H_0. There is no relationship between attached garage and township.

33. H_0: Industry and gender are not related.
H_1: Industry and gender are related.
Note: There are only 3 observations in the industry coded 2; hence 1 and 2 are combined. There is one degree of freedom, so H_0 is rejected if $\chi^2 > 3.841$.

$$\chi^2 = \frac{(41 - 42.40)^2}{42.40} + \cdots + \frac{(8 - 9.40)^2}{9.40} = 0.492$$

Do not reject H_0. We cannot conclude gender and industry are related.

Photo Credits

Chapter 1
p. 1: Jose Carillo/PhotoEdit; **p. 2:** Felicia Martinez/PhotoEdit; **p. 3:**Terry Wild Studio, Inc.; **p. 5:** Photo courtesy of Hewlett-Packard Company; **p. 10:** © elektra Vision AG/Picture Quest

Chapter 2
p. 21: Courtesy of Merrill Lynch; **p. 22:** Corbis; **p. 36:** PhotoDisc

Chapter 3
p. 62: Rachel Epstein/PhotoEdit; **p. 63:** Myrleen Ferguson Cate/PhotoEdit; **p. 71:** © Image Ideas, Inc./PictureQuest; **p. 80:** © RubberBall Productions/RubberBall Productions/Picture Quest; **p. 90:** Science Photo Library/Photo Researchers, Inc.

Chapter 4
p. 122: PhotoDisc; **p. 123:** Mitch Kezar/Tony Stone Images; **p. 131:** Courtesy Dean Foods; **p. 134:** © 2001 Busch Entertainment Corporation. All rights reserved

Chapter 5
p. **159:** Photo courtesy of Hewlett/Packard Company; **p. 164:** Corbis; **p. 167:** © Corbis Images/Picture Quest

Chapter 6
p. 191: Courtesy ALCOA; **p. 192:** Mitch Kezar/Tony Stone Images; **p. 205:** Image Bank/Getty Images

Chapter 7
p. 218: © Digital Vision/Picture Quest; **p. 220:** © PhotoLink/PhotoDisc/Picture Quest; **p. 239:** Terry Wild Studio

Chapter 8
p. 251: © Steve Chenn/CORBIS; **p. 253:** PhotoDisc; **p. 264:** PhotoDisc; **p. 267:** Corbis

Chapter 9
p. 283: PhotoDisc; **p. 284:** © Russell Illig/PhotoDisc/Picture Quest; **p. 287:** PhotoDisc; **p. 298:** PhotoDisc

Chapter 10
p. 319: Terry Wild Studio; **p. 320:** Corbis; **p. 327:** © Corbis Images/Picture Quest; **p. 336:** GettyImages/Photodisc #AA029911

Chapter 11
p. 351: Corbis Images/Picture Quest; **p. 353:** PhotoDisc; **p. 358:** GettyImages/Photodisc #AA036046

Chapter 12
p. 380: Bill Aron/PhotoEdit; **p. 381:** Courtesy VF Playwear, Healthtex Brand; **p. 394:** PhotoDisc

Chapter 13
p. 424: © Jim Craigmyle/CORBIS; **p. 427:** PhotoDisc; **p. 433:** PhotoDisc

Chapter 14
p. 461: Solum/PhotoLink/PhotoDisc/Picture Quest; **p. 462:** Sharon Hoogstraten; **p. 473:** Pepsi Company; **p. 477:** © Image Ideas, Inc./Picture Quest

Index